The Graphic Designer's Digital Toolkit

ALLAN B. WOOD

DELMAR
CENGAGE Learning™

Australia • Brazil • Japan • Korea • Mexico • Singapore • Spain • United Kingdom • United States

DELMAR
CENGAGE Learning

The Graphic Designer's Digital Toolkit, 5th Edition
Allan B. Wood

Vice President, Career and Professional Editorial: Dave Garza

Director of Learning Solutions: Sandy Clark

Senior Acquisitions Editor: Jim Gish

Managing Editor: Larry Main

Associate Product Manager: Meaghan O'Brien

Editorial Assistant: Sarah L. Timm

Vice President, Career and Professional Marketing: Jennifer Baker

Marketing Director: Deborah S. Yarnell

Marketing Manager: Erin Brennan

Marketing Coordinator: Erin Deangelo

Production Director: Wendy Troeger

Senior Content Project Manager: Glenn Castle

Senior Art Director: Joy Kocsis

Technology Product Manager: Christopher Catalina

Cover design: Steven Brower and Lisa Marie Pompilio

Cover Illustration: Stephanie Dalton

Printed in China
3 4 5 6 7 15 14 13 12

For product information and technology assistance, contact us at
Professional Group Cengage Learning Customer & Sales Support, 1-800-354-9706
For permission to use material from this text or product, submit all requests online at **cengage.com/permissions.**
Further permissions questions can be e-mailed to
permissionrequest@cengage.com.

Adobe® Photoshop®, Adobe® InDesign®, Adobe® Illustrator® are trademarks or registered trademarks of Adobe Systems, Inc. in the United States and/or other countries. Third party products, services, company names, logos, design, titles, words, or phrases within these materials may be trademarks of their respective owners.

Library of Congress Control Number: 2010926956

ISBN-13: 978-1-111-13801-1

ISBN-10: 1-111-13801-X

Delmar
5 Maxwell Drive
Clifton Park, NY 12065-2919
USA

Cengage Learning is a leading provider of customized learning solutions with office locations around the globe, including Singapore, the United Kingdom, Australia, Mexico, Brazil and Japan. Locate your local office at: **international.cengage.com/region**

Cengage Learning products are represented in Canada by Nelson Education, Ltd.

For your lifelong learning solutions, visit **delmar.cengage.com**

To learn more about Delmar, visit **www.cengage.com/delmar**

Purchase any of our products at your local college store or at our preferred online store **www.CengageBrain.com**

Notice to the Reader
Publisher does not warrant or guarantee any of the products described herein or perform any independent analysis in connection with any of the product information contained herein. Publisher does not assume, and expressly disclaims, any obligation to obtain and include information other than that provided to it by the manufacturer. The reader is expressly warned to consider and adopt all safety precautions that might be indicated by the activities described herein and to avoid all potential hazards. By following the instructions contained herein, the reader willingly assumes all risks in connection with such instructions. The publisher makes no representations or warranties of any kind, including but not limited to, the warranties of fitness for particular purpose or merchantability, nor are any such representations implied with respect to the material set forth herein, and the publisher takes no responsibility with respect to such material. The publisher shall not be liable for any special, consequential, or exemplary damages resulting, in whole or part, from the readers' use of, or reliance upon, this material.

TABLE OF CONTENTS

ANYONE WILL FIND THIS BOOK HELPFUL

Welcome to the *Graphic Designer's Digital Toolkit!* Here you will learn the essential skills and design techniques to get you comfortable using the newest versions of the premier graphics programs in the industry today: Photoshop, Illustrator, and InDesign. This book is set up as a challenging hands-on, project-based classroom book with which students will complete useful, real-world projects that a designer would normally create for a client. This book also contains terminology or language used in the graphics today to give the learner an understanding of terms and techniques. It is created for college students who are taking introductory classes in computer graphics applications, digital media, or graphic design or as a supplementary text providing projects for courses in Photoshop, Illustrator, and InDesign. It can also be used for a half-year course in digital media for college-bound upper classmen at the high school level. *All of the chapter assignments and most of the Toolkit Extra exercises can be completed using older versions of the software; most explanations are included for use with the newest version and older versions.*

For the professional who may need a refresher course in one or more of the applications, or for the individual looking for an edge in making a career change into the graphics industry, this book can be used as a self-paced study. It also makes a great reference text for professionals already in the field. The business owner who wants to create his or her own logo, business cards, promotional pieces, advertisements, newsletters, brochures, or to adjust and retouch a photograph can also use this book.

EMERGING TRENDS

With new versions of applications coming out constantly, most individuals do not need to learn every function and command, but they can learn the most essential of these to be productive in creating most types of projects. This is the focus of the book: to make the reader comfortable in each graphic application to be able to create the projects that a designer might be asked to produce, and to speak the language of the terminology used in the graphics industry today.

BACKGROUND OF THIS TEXT

After spending many years as an instructor and Program Chair at the college and evaluating books to be used by faculty, I was disappointed by the lack of depth in many of the project-based learning books. I also could not find a suitable book that was an introduction to the major graphic applications used in the industry today—Photoshop, Illustrator, and InDesign—and how they are used individually and together in creating quality projects. I wanted to design a book that not only addresses the essential skills a designer would need in each application without having to be bombarded with countless commands and functions that may never be used, but a book that also shows the design process involved in creating a project from start to finish, and the language of the graphics industry. Each hands-on project in this book builds upon the functions of select tools and commands with basic, similar concepts to show the reader what happens in the real world of graphics. This book assumes the reader knows the basics of working with computers.

TEXTBOOK ORGANIZATION

Welcome to a project-oriented, real-world approach to learning the three categories of graphics applications used in the industry today. Specifically, this book focuses on Adobe Photoshop for digital image editing, Adobe Illustrator for digital illustration, and Adobe InDesign for digital desktop publishing as the standards in their respective fields. Before introducing these applications, the book provides a foundation of Macintosh OS X Leopard and Windows 7 computer operations, terminology, and design elements, principles, typography, imagery, and color concepts, along with an understanding of the process of design from concept to completion in the first two chapters Each chapter provides insight on the design fundamentals, terminology, and technical aspects that a designer needs to know for each application. Although the book uses the newest versions of each program, older versions are also explained in many cases. The projects and information given for each application provide the essential skills a designer needs to feel comfortable using that application, no matter what version they are working with. This book can be used with either Macintosh or Windows computers.

The book is divided into four units, and each unit is divided into chapters with projects or assignments a designer could actually create for a client. Each chapter builds upon skills learned from the previous chapter to enhance the learning process. You will walk through and create a project from each chapter assignment using the necessary files in the accompanying CD, learning the process from concept to completion of the project, including design suggestions, special tips, and help on what to do if you run into a specific problem.

The first unit, Getting Ready for Production, focuses on getting comfortable using both Macintosh and Windows computers and understanding the design principles and elements that go into the creation of a good design. The other three units are set for each of the three graphic applications: Photoshop, Illustrator, and InDesign. In each chapter, there is also an advanced section to further challenge the student and a Digital Toolkit Extra section for a mini project to demonstrate an additional concept or technique. At the end of each chapter are review questions that could also serve as a chapter quiz to test the reader's knowledge of the material. Each unit contains a Unit Review Project Challenge that ties together all the chapters within the unit and provides a few additional functions or techniques to explore.

In the first unit, Getting Ready for Production, you will not only become familiar with both Macintosh OS X and Windows 7 environments, managing files and folders, creating shortcuts, learning keyboard shortcuts, creating electronic slide shows, using widgets (Mac) and gadgets (Windows 7), fun tools and techniques for organizing your desktop, and burning data, music, and photo CDs, you will also be exposed to design elements and principles, typography basics, imagery basics, and understanding color and how to use color to create posters.

In the second unit on Photoshop CS5, assignments involve adjusting poorly exposed or badly colored graphics, using Adobe Bridge and the new Mini Bridge to locate and manage files, completely changing the color of a sports car image for a realistic effect, creating a well-toned black and white image from a color image, creating a black and white and color composite image, combining images into one suitable image, digitally restoring an old image, creating photo business cards, creating a multicolor product ad from a single product, and combing images and special techniques to create a realistic front and back cover for a music CD. You will also learn about working with camera raw files as the new digital negative from professional level digital cameras.

In the Illustrator CS5 unit, you will create an electronic game board, a 3-D wine bottle with a perfectly fit label, special design symbols, a logo, playing cards, company business cards with logo, a clock face, a map, radio station web banners that combine both Photoshop and Illustrator images, and a promotional label on a 3-D mug. You will learn to use multiple artboards for various projects using the same logo. You will also learn to use the Live Trace and Live Paint features, and creating multiple artboards using one logo for various media.

The fourth and final unit demonstrates how to use InDesign CS5 as a desktop publishing tool. It provides assignments in creating a direct mail coupon ad, a photo or art desktop calendar, a four-page newsletter, an interactive PDF document, and a tri-fold brochure to get you right into the most familiar projects a designer might find, along with an understanding the process from preflighting or checking documents and graphics to packaging your project for the service provider.

You will find many of these same projects coming up in your design career. Enjoy the ride!

A CD is provided inside the back cover for all image and text files used in all the assignments and projects. You will find some extra goodies like additional information, more projects (yes, more!), and resource information that may be useful, too in the "Goodies" folder of your text CD. What, you want more? There is also a website I created at *www.digitoolkit.com* that not only provides an electronic view and info about the projects you'll be creating in the book, but there are more tutorials and resources you can use to expand your knowledge.

FEATURES

The following list provides some of the salient features of the text:

• Over 40 projects and tutorials in the text, more additional projects, tutorials, and info in the CD's Goodies folder.

• Objectives clearly state the learning goals of each chapter.

• Files needed for projects are included on the CD.

• Client Assignments involve multiple tools and techniques and resemble those that a designer might encounter on the job to complete a useful project.

• Toolkit Tips in each chapter explain tools and techniques and additional info.

• Design Tips in each chapter show how to master design fundamentals with each software application.

• Digital Toolkit Extra and Advanced Users sections at the end of each chapter provide added challenges and additional tools, techniques, and mini projects.

• Review questions reinforce material presented in the each chapter.

- Unit Review Project Challenges tie together all the chapters within the unit and provide a few additional functions or techniques to explore.

- All kinds of terms used in the graphics industry today so you can understand the designer's lingo

NEW TO EDITION

- Text provides a comprehensive overview of new functions, tools, and panels used in Adobe Illustrator CS5, Adobe InDesign CS5, and Adobe Photoshop CS5. Adobe CS5 Suite functions like the new Application bar for tabbed documents, community online help and support center, and using smart guides for increasing productivity are explored, along with improvements in Adobe Bridge and Camera RAW.

- All figure artwork is updated with the new Adobe CS5 format.

- Navigating Macintosh OS X Leopard desktop and having fun organizing and playing on your desktop using Widgets, Stacks, Spaces, and Dashboard programs. Electronic slide shows using Quick Look and Preview.

- Updated end-of-chapter projects will help reinforce tools and techniques taught throughout each chapter.

- Navigating through the new Windows 7 desktop with the new Pin function, using gadgets, and fun desktop organization features using Snap, Peek, and Shake. Electronic slide shows using Pictures Library, Windows Photo Viewer, and Windows Media Center.

- Text covers new Photoshop CS5 Mini Bridge, Content-Aware Fill and Scale functions, Scrubby Zoom, and new masking techniques and selection technologies with the Refine Edge function, along with various color and black and white resets and enhancements. Additional tutorials include use of the Curve function, selecting and replacing color on a sports car, and adjustments and enhancements to the multicolor product ad project.

- New projects using Illustrator creating custom shapes to create playing cards using new Shape Builder tool. New features are explored like new Drawing Modes, particularly Draw Behind mode, Shape builder tool, new Artboards panel and enhancements with using multiple artboards, Bristle Brush libraries and enhanced brishes features, revamped Stroke panel with variable widths, and other functions.

- InDesign CS5 contains many new features that help in production workflow. Exploring the new enhanced Layers panel, new Gap tool, pop-up Swatches panel, document installed fonts feature for Packaging, enhancements in paragraphs spanning columns, improved exporting to PDF features, and new presentation mode for full screen viewing.

- Additional tutorials and handouts are also offered in the Goodies folder that comes with the accompanying text CD.

- Accompanying website offers additional projects, expanded tutorials, and other valuable learning tools.

- See all completed projects and tutorials from each chapter together for quick refrence in Appendix A.

HOW TO USE THIS TEXT

OBJECTIVES

Learning Objectives start off each chapter. They describe the competencies readers should achieve once they understand the chapter material.

DESIGN AND TOOLKIT TIPS

These tips are located throughout the text. Design Tips show readers how to master design techniques, and Toolkit Tips demonstrate how to work more efficiently and effectively within each software application.

CLIENT ASSIGNMENTS

These projects involve multiple tools and techniques and resemble assignments that a designer might encounter on the job.

REVIEW QUESTIONS

Review Questions are located at the end of each chapter and allow readers to assess their understanding of the material.

ADVANCED USERS AND DIGITAL TOOLKIT EXTRA SECTIONS

These tutorials are located at the end of each chapter and provide added challenges using additional tools and techniques.

UNIT REVIEW PROJECTS

These projects link together all chapters within a unit and utilize a few additional functions or techniques.

THE LEARNING PACKAGE

E-RESOURCE

The instructor's CD was developed to assist instructors in planning and implementing their instructional programs. It includes all the files needed for the projects and assignments, PowerPoint presentations, and some extra projects and information in a "Goodies" folder. The CD also includes exams, review questions and answers from each chapter, syllabi, web references, additional assignments, and concept information.

THE GRAPHIC DESIGNER'S DIGITAL TOOLKIT

WHO IS THE AUTHOR?

Allan B. Wood served 12 years as an Associate Professor and Program Chair of the Graphic Design and Professional Photography degree programs at McIntosh College in New Hampshire. In 2006 he was awarded a second place standing for Educator of the Year in the Computer Design: Graphics and Photography category among 80 colleges participating. He has over 22 years of teaching experience and 15 years working in graphic design and photography environments, including five years as full-time portrait photographer and graphics lab business owner. During his years at McIntosh College, Allan created the professional project-based curriculum for college level courses in Photoshop, Illustrator, Web Page Fundamentals, and Desktop Publishing. He developed the curriculum for all courses in the Professional Photography program, including the computer graphics applications Photoshop, Illustrator, and InDesign used in this book. Allan also has a Master's degree in Instructional Design and Online learning.

As a member of the New Hampshire Professional Photographer's Association, in addition to being a portrait photographer, Allan is a New England lighthouse enthusiast and has had a 16-month lighthouse calendar published. He has also published two front-cover magazine photos. He has won various photography awards, including Best Professional in a state professional photo exhibition, and his images have appeared in national greeting cards, a calendar, and catalogs.

Recently, Allan left McIntosh College to pursue more independent work teaching digital media and photography courses, workshops, and seminars in local colleges. His future plans also include assisting other institutions in helping their faculty to develop quality online curriculum when needed in their computer graphics, design, and photography courses while maintaining the importance of integrating traditional design concepts and techniques. He has just completed an extensive (300 page) New England tourism web site at *www.nelights.com* using the nearly 160 lighthouses as guides for exploring local attractions. Future tourism books are in the works.

ACKNOWLEDGEMENTS

I'd like to thank the great folks at Delmar-Cengage for their patience and inspiration: James Gish, acquisitions editor, for his positive attitude, sincerity, and willingness to take a chance on this book in breaking some new ground; and to Meaghan O'Brien, my supreme coordinator and rudder for all her help and encouragement with the book, Tara Botelho for her keen eyes in reviewing the book, Sarah Timm, Glenn Castle, Joy Kocsis, and the crew in the art and production departments, the folks at Integra, and everyone else who helped me out on this project. You are all awesome!

Thanks also to some folks at McIntosh College for your support and sense of humor:

Travis Galzier for images used in the design chapter; Trey Aven for the dolphin illustration for the logo project; Michael Magoon for lending his 1964 Rambler for the CD cover project; and Phil Spates, for letting me use his "boys" image for the Photoshop retouching project. Thanks also to Greg Tenhover for helping out with layout for the newsletter and tri-fold brochure projects, and to Shelly Britton, who wrote and photographed what it's like to be on a lobster boat for the newsletter project. Check out a little slice of life in New England!

I also need to thank the most important people in my life for their support, especially my wife Chris, for supporting me while I spent countless hours, weekdays, and weekends on the book. It's been an interesting balancing act. Thanks to my two sons, Bryan and Steven, for dragging me away once in a while to play, and to Ma and Pa Wood (Kay and Larry) for giving me the positive attitude over the years to achieve anything I put my mind to.

The book and lighthouse images are also dedicated to the memory of my buddy Lisa Johnson.

Allan Wood, 2010

QUESTIONS AND FEEDBACK

Delmar Cengage Learning and the author welcome your questions and feedback. If you have suggestions that you think others would benefit from, please let us know, and we will try to include them in the next edition.

To send us your questions and/or feedback, you can contact the publisher at:

Delmar Cengage Learning
Executive Woods
5 Maxwell Drive
Clifton Park, NY 12065
Attn: Graphic Communications Team
800-998-7498

Or contact the author at:

alwood@nelights.com
www.digitoolkit.com

UNIT

1

1

Welcome to the Land of OS

CHAPTER OBJECTIVES: To understand how to be productive in a graphics environment, in this chapter you will:

▷ Learn the basics of the new Mac OS X Leopard and Windows 7 operating systems and techniques that allow Mac OS X and Windows 7 to work together.

▷ Use basic file management techniques to help organize workflow.

▷ Learn keystroke combinations to increase productivity.

▷ Use new fun applications and techniques to keep your desktop from becoming too cluttered.

▷ ADVANCED USERS: Create electronic slide shows of images using special applications within Macintosh OS X and Windows 7 operating systems.

▷ DIGITAL TOOLKIT EXTRA: Burn music, photo, and data CDs on Mac OS X and Windows 7 platforms using free programs within each.

Before we get into the various graphics applications, we will start by getting comfortable with Macintosh and Windows operating systems. An **operating system**—sometimes referred to as an *OS*—makes sure hardware and software work together nicely. **Applications** are software programs for a particular use, such as Photoshop, which is an application used for digital image editing. For instance, if you want to print an image created in Photoshop, you click on the command to print, and the operating system sets up the communications between the application and the printer to print the document accurately. This chapter will familiarize you with the basics of the **Macintosh OS X,** or *Mac OS X*, and **Windows 7** operating systems, some of their included special applications, along with tips on using both systems together to manage your files and set up the text CD for the chapter exercises, which will help you develop skills to improve your productivity as a designer or photographer.

Need additional fun computer graphics tutorials and info, and an additional look at the projects you'll be creating in this book? Check out my Artist's Digital Toolkit website at: **http://www.digitoolkit.com**

THE MAC OS X ENVIRONMENT

Welcome to the operating system of the graphics industry: Mac OS X. You will notice similarities between the Mac OS X **desktop**—the screen displayed when the system has loaded—and the Windows 7 desktop. Mac OS X displays your drives, portable media devices, and most frequently used applications, files, and folders on your computer screen as small picture representations, called **icons** (see Figure 1-1). When you double-click on an icon, it opens up that file, folder, or application; it is actually a link, or shortcut, that you can create as an **alias** on your desktop.

At the bottom of the desktop—or sometimes to the left or right side, depending on your System Preferences settings—is the **Dock**, which is used to display applications, files, and folders. The **Trash** icon is used to remove and restore files. The **Finder** menu (sometimes referred to as the desktop menu) at the top of the screen lets you navigate the computer; it also appears as a square, smiling face on the Dock. Each application has its own menu bar and commands to perform tasks. You can also transfer and store folders or aliases and their contents on the desktop for quick access, or you can click on the icon in the Dock.

▷ FIGURE 1-1

**The Macintosh OS X
Leopard desktop.**

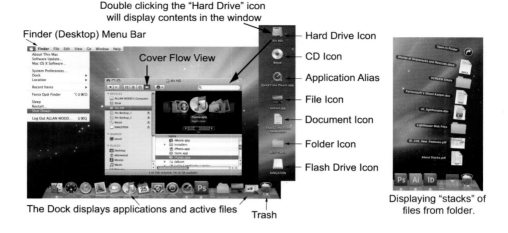

Double clicking the "Hard Drive" icon
will display contents in the window

Finder (Desktop) Menu Bar

Cover Flow View

Hard Drive Icon

CD Icon

Application Alias

File Icon

Document Icon

Folder Icon

Flash Drive Icon

The Dock displays applications and active files

Trash

Displaying "stacks" of
files from folder.

THE DOCK

The Dock can be set to reside at the bottom, side, or even out of view off the edge of your screen (see Figure 1-2). It can contain images, minimized windows, folders, applications, documents, and even links to websites. Each item stored on the Dock has its own icon. Click on the icon and the Dock restores the window in your workspace or launches the application. When you open an application, that application's icon appears on the Dock. In the current Leopard version, a white dot displays underneath when an application is active. You can create a copy or "alias" of an application on the Dock, so that when you quit the application, the icon remains on your Dock until you take it off. You will also see the Trash icon on the right side or bottom of the dock. Besides using it to remove and restore files, it can be used to eject drives, portable media devices, and CDs. On the left side or on top of the Dock is the smiling Finder interface; its desktop menu commands are also at the top of the screen. You will find that most standard Mac OS X application icons except for the Trash icon—will be displayed on the left side or top of the Dock, and minimized files will appear to the right. The current Leopard Mac OS X version displays a "Documents" folder for your most recent documents to retrieve, or you can simply create your own folder. Any folder placed on the Dock's right side can be used as part of a feature called "**stacks**". When you click a stack, it springs from the Dock to display the folder contents. To open a file in a stack, just click on it. To remove it, just drag it into the Trash.

TOOLKIT TIP To remove an application that is currently running from the Dock, click the application icon and hold it until a pop-up menu appears; when the menu bar displays that application, select Remove from Dock. If a shortcut or alias is created, it will have a broken arrow under the icon and can simply be dragged off the Dock; the icons are just links and do not affect the original application, which can be found in the applications folder.

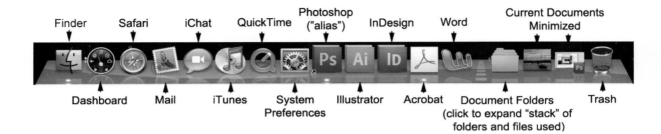

Finder   Safari   iChat   QuickTime   Photoshop ("alias")   InDesign   Word   Current Documents Minimized

Dashboard   Mail   iTunes   System Preferences   Illustrator   Acrobat   Document Folders (click to expand "stack" of folders and files used)   Trash

▷ FIGURE 1-2

The Dock displays applications, folders, files, and functions. Icons on the leftmost side are standard applications in Mac OS X, and those on the right are launched applications or minimized documents.

MAC OS X WINDOWS

In Mac OS X, windows that are opened to locate contents in folders or drives display a weblike page (default view), where you can use back and forward arrow buttons to move between windows and previous documents (see Figure 1-3). You can also select one of four View buttons to choose how you want the content displayed. These functions appear on the window **toolbar**, which shows special commands and functions for each application. In the top right corner is a button that acts as a toggle to hide and restore the toolbar.

All windows have a **title bar** that contains the file or function name and three colored buttons on the left side that control how the window displays. The red button closes the window, the yellow button minimizes the window to an icon on the Dock, and the green button increases the window to its full size or restores it to its original state. To resize the window, click and drag the gray lines in the lower right corner. Sometimes when you select a command or function, indicated by a gearlike icon called the Action button, a **dialog box** appears to provide more commands or functions.

▷ FIGURE 1-3

Mac windows used to locate and modify files and folders.

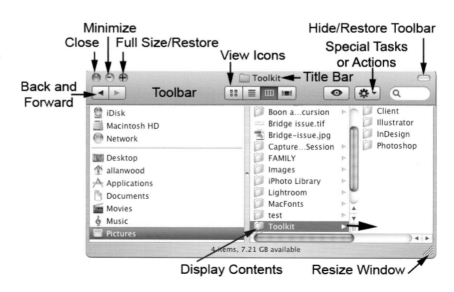

Minimize
Close | Full Size/Restore
View Icons
Hide/Restore Toolbar
Special Tasks or Actions
Back and Forward
Toolbar
Title Bar
Display Contents
Resize Window

THE HARD DRIVE

To display the contents of your hard drive, double-click on the Macintosh HD or hard drive icon on the desktop. On the toolbar, you will notice the View button, which lets you choose between displaying in Icon View, List View, Column View, and Cover Flow View. Column View makes it easy to navigate between drives, folders, and files; the contents of whatever is highlighted are displayed in the next column to the right (see Figure 1-4). When you select a folder, you will notice its contents are displayed. Cover Flow View shows graphic thumbnail representations of your files and documents.

The left side column of the window displays storage media—such as your hard drive and network connections—and organizes specific links to your desktop, your "Home'" space for your personal files on the computer, and available applications, including those that were included with Mac OS X, which are found in the System folder. There are specific media categories for your files and folders, such as Movies, Music, and Pictures to maintain peak computer performance. You can also search for previously used documents and applications.

TOOLKIT TIP If you are not sure what some of the icons mean on the toolbar, press the CTRL key, then click to display a menu, then choose "Icon and Text" to display both. You can click on the desktop to return to the Finder toolbar; select the Go menu to access the Computer, Home, Network, iDisk, Applications, Utilities, and Recent Folders to quickly locate contents. You can also select the View menu to arrange icons neatly in specific categories.

Now, we will learn to navigate around the Macintosh HD or hard drive icon.

1. Double-click on the Macintosh HD or hard drive icon on your desktop.
2. Select the Home icon (next to your username) link for your personal settings, files, and so on; locate a folder and display its contents, then use the back and forward arrow buttons to move around.
3. Select the Desktop and Applications buttons to display their contents.
4. Select the Applications button and select the View button on the toolbar to observe the four different views if you have the Leopard Mac OS X version.
5. Navigate around a little, then close the window.

▷ FIGURE 1-4

Options to view, locate, edit, and organize files and folders of various media on your hard drive or device.

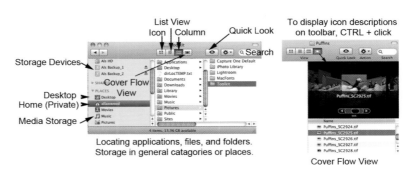

Locating applications, files, and folders. Storage in general catagories or places.

Cover Flow View

MAC OS X FINDER DESKTOP MENUS

The Mac OS X Finder interface on the desktop works much the same way as the Start menu does in Windows. It provides access to particular functions for applications, files, folders, and computer using a **Menu bar,** which contains commands from various menus specific to the Finder desktop interface shown here (see Figure 1-5) or for any other application, such as Photoshop. The menu descriptions below are found in the Mac OS X Leopard version.

The Apple Menu

The **Apple menu** is where you can find information about your Mac system (> About this Mac) and files, which includes a listing of the most recently opened applications and files; you can also set global, System Preferences here and check for software updates. To avoid damaging data and software by turning off the power to your Mac, use the Restart or Shut Down commands under this menu to power down your Mac safely.

The Finder Menu

The Finder menu lets you organize how icons are displayed and set desktop preferences. This is where you find the Empty Trash command to permanently remove files dragged into the Trash (for a shortcut, click and hold the Trash icon and select Empty Trash from the pop-up menu).

▷ FIGURE 1-5

Apple, Finder, and File menus with Finder desktop menu bar.

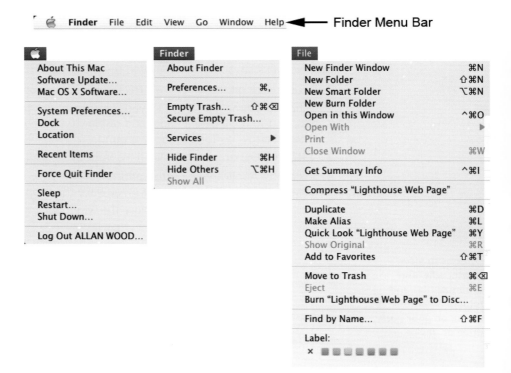

The File Menu

The **File menu** allows you to create new folders, search for and get info about folders and files, duplicate items, and create links or shortcuts to files and folders, called *aliases*. In this menu, you can eject discs, burn CDs, and move files to the Trash.

Some of the special commands in the File menu are described below.

- **Get Summary Info** gives details, such as date and size, about a selected icon.
- **Make Alias** makes an alias, shortcut, or *link* to a file, document, or folder, which can be dragged onto the desktop.
- **New Smart Folder** helps you to organize files by what they have in common based on criteria you set.
- **New Burn Folder** allows you to create a collection of files to be burned or written onto a CD or DVD multiple times.
- **Add to Favorites** allows you to add files to the Favorites submenu under the Go menu. This is similar to adding favorites on the Internet Explorer web browser.
- **Move to Trash** moves selected files and folders to the Trash icon on the Dock.
- **Find** locates files and folders through specific criteria in Home though category links.
- **Label** helps to organize groups of files by assigning color labels.

The Edit Menu

The **Edit menu** allows you to work with text and graphics, which includes selecting all components in a document (see Figure 1-6). It allows you to undo, copy, cut and paste, and see what is copied on the clipboard. The **clipboard** is a temporary memory site for storing text and graphics that have been cut or copied before pasting them into another document or to another location. Since the clipboard only "remembers" one thing at a time, anytime you cut or copy something else, the content of the clipboard is replaced by the new data.

The View Menu

The **View menu** on the desktop displays files and folders on various drives and discs. It lets you customize the toolbar and change the way files look and are

▷ FIGURE 1-6

Edit, View, and Window menus.

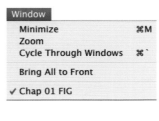

arranged on your system. Folders and files can be displayed as icons, either listed by name with additional data or arranged in columns to display contents inside folders and drives. The Leopard Mac OS X version offers a fourth Cover Flow View, also used in iPods.

The Window Menu

The **Window menu** allows you to minimize any open window and place it in the Dock. Anything minimized in the menu will show a black triangle beneath the icon on the Dock. To restore the window to the Desktop at its original size, click the icon on the Dock.

The Go Menu

The **Go** menu lets you view your favorite places and folders and connect to a server to share information with other computers (see Figure 1-7). You can jump to any location on your computer, the Internet, or on your network. The Go menu also lists recently used folders.

▷ FIGURE 1-7

The Go menu helps to navigate around the computer.

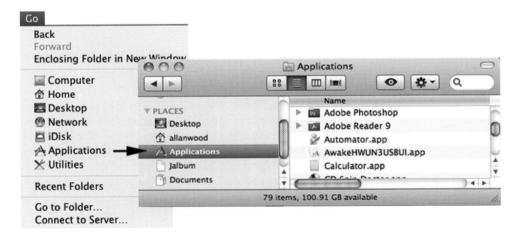

Some of the Go commands follow:

- **Computer** opens a window to display all the items on your desktop.
- **Home** displays contents of your personal Home folder.
- **Applications** displays all programs in the Applications folder
- **Recent Folders** shows a list of recently used folders.
- **Go to Folder** allows you to go to a particular folder.
- **Connect to Server** allows you to connect to a local or remote server

Get Mac Help

Mac Help in Mac OS X provides answers to questions and also gives instructions on how to perform various functions by clicking underlined links; it also lets you type a question, phrase, or term to display a list of topics to look for further information (see Figure 1-8). You can also use the help of an alphabetical index to narrow your search. You can get help from information stored on the hard drive,

▷ FIGURE 1-8

Mac Help provides you with information for your computer or application.

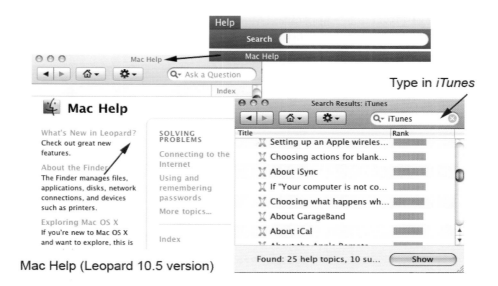

Mac Help (Leopard 10.5 version)

particularly all the Mac functions, or you can get help from the Apple website with an Internet connection. All applications have a Help command on their menu bars to bring up topics that pertain directly to that application. More recent versions of Mac OS X have a Help viewer menu bar to aid in searching for information.

Use Mac OS X Help tutorials to help you familiarize yourself with Mac OS X. In this exercise, you will learn about iTunes, an application that allows you to copy, play, and create your own music CDs.

1. Select Help > Mac Help (under the search bar) from your Finder desktop menu.

2. First, select the "Exploring Mac OS X" or "Learn the basics about your Mac" links to get familiar with your Mac OS X operating system and check out some cool features. In Leopard, you can check out built-in applications like Stacks, Spaces, Time Machine, Front Row, Synchronize X!, and others.

3. Type "iTunes" in the upper right blank box and press the Return key; a list of related topics appears. Also type in "Widgets," "iCal," and "Safari" for some other useful features included in Mac OS X.

4. Click on links that interest you, or try other variations or phrases, and print the pages on these topics (File > Print). You will be learning more about this at the end of this chapter.

5. Hit the red Close button to close the window when you are finished.

A Program's Application Menu

When you are working with a particular application, such as Photoshop, its menu bar contains various menus and commands for functions specific to Photoshop. Each program has a special Application menu in Mac OS X to the right of the Apple icon in its menu bar (see Figure 1-9). This **Application menu** contains commands for information about the application, changing settings, preferences, and quitting the application.

▷ FIGURE 1-9

The Application menu on the menu bar contains commands for that particular application.

The System Preferences program in the Apple menu on the far left allows you to make modifications within your computer, like adding hardware, adding and removing programs, updating applications, and modifying system functions and monitor displays (see Figure 1-10). Here is where you can change Internet options, adjust Accessibility options, and set network connections.

SYSTEM PREFERENCES IN THE APPLE MENU

The **System Preferences** program in the Apple menu on the far left allows you to make modifications within your computer, like adding hardware, adding and removing programs, updating applications, and modifying system functions and monitor displays (see Figure 1-10). Here is where you can change Internet options, adjust Accessibility options, and set network connections.

▷ FIGURE 1-10

System Preferences in the Mac allows you to make changes and adjustments within your computer.

THE WINDOWS 7 ENVIRONMENT

DESIGN TIP

To resize a window proportionately, hold down the Shift key while dragging from a window's corner point.

The Windows 7 desktop functions much like the Mac desktop; it has icons for files, applications, and special functions (see Figure 1-11). One of the special functions, the **Recycle Bin**, stores and restores deleted files much like the Mac's Trash icon. Windows uses what is called the **taskbar** to display minimized active files and applications, which is similar to the Dock on the Mac. To restore the application or file to original size, click on its minimized taskbar button. In Windows 7, the task-bar allows you to preview "**Jump Lists**" to navigate around recent files, images, or tasks. Another feature called **pinning** allows you to pin your favorite programs or files to the taskbar.

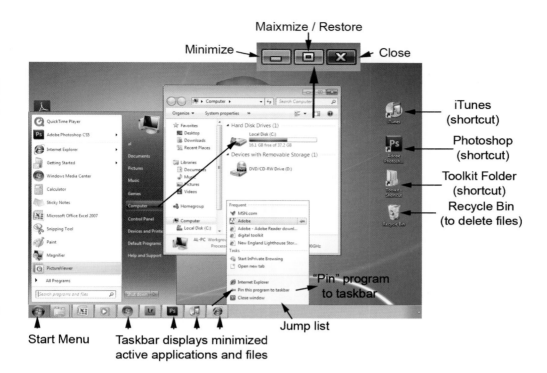

Minimize

Maixmize / Restore

Close

iTunes
(shortcut)

Photoshop
(shortcut)

Toolkit Folder
(shortcut)

Recycle Bin
(to delete files)

"Pin" program
to taskbar

Jump list

Start Menu   Taskbar displays minimized
                     active applications and files

▷ FIGURE 1-11

Windows desktop displays icons for shortcuts to common applications and special functions, the taskbar, and the Start menu, which is the control center for Windows.

All computers that use the Windows operating system are called **PCs**. Windows on a PC are adjusted much the same way as windows on the Mac, but with the sizing buttons on the top right side of the title bar instead of on the left. The dash button minimizes the window to the taskbar, the center button maximizes and restores the window, and the red X button closes the window. You can resize a window by clicking and dragging on the window's edge or corner. Sometimes when you select a command or function, a dialog box appears to provide more commands or functions. The Start menu is used in the same way as the Finder interface on the Mac; in Windows, the Start button is the control center.

THE START MENU, WINDOWS EXPLORER, AND THE COMPUTER FUNCTION

As the control center for Windows, when you click on the **Start menu** you can select from the most recently used applications, documents, stored images, and music; you can select and launch any programs on your computer, connect to the Internet, access e-mail, or use the Search command to locate files and folders and look for help. In Windows 7, you can select the All Programs link in the Start Menu display window to display the application programs on your hard drive. You can also locate and find information about outside hardware, such as portable drives, printers, and digital cameras; these devices are called **peripherals**.

The Start menu in Windows 7 also contains the Shut Down command to perform a proper shut down operation on your PC. Within the Start menu options, the

▷   FIGURE 1-12

The Start menu is the control center for Windows operations. Selecting the Computer option, or the Windows Explorer icon, helps you locate files and folders in drives, special links, and libraries.

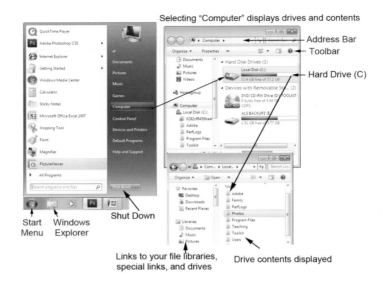

Selecting "Computer" displays drives and contents

Address Bar
Toolbar
Hard Drive (C)

Start   Windows   Shut Down
Menu   Explorer

Links to your file libraries,   Drive contents displayed
special links, and drives

Computer function provides access to information about disk drives, files, and folders, and it also provides special commands so you can choose what to do with those files (see Figure 1-12). You can use the forward and back arrow buttons in the toolbar to navigate between windows and previous documents in the same way you would navigate between web pages on the Internet. When a window is selected, its file or function name is displayed on the window's title bar.

Windows 7 uses the Window Explorer icon on the taskbar to locate files and folders in specialized **libraries**. These libraries can be used to gather content for special folders from various locations to be placed in certain categories of files. Lists of recent documents and applications can also be found using Windows Explorer.

TOOLKIT TIP You can create a shortcut to place the Computer link on the desktop by selecting the Start menu then the Computer link; right-click with your mouse to select Show on Desktop. This way, with the shortcut on the desktop, you can simply double-click on it to open the Computer dialog box.

Next, we will navigate around the Start Menu and use the Computer function to locate files.

1. From the desktop on your Windows computer, select the Start Menu (Windows icon).

2. Select Computer to display the drives (see Figure 1-12). Select the Local Disk (C:) to show folders, files, and applications on your hard drive, and use the back and forward arrow buttons to move between previous windows. Play with this feature until you are comfortable looking for files.

3. With folders displayed, select the View tab to display choices of various layouts, then select the view most comfortable for you.

▷ FIGURE 1-13

You can select from categories of file libraries on the right side to locate personal files; click the down arrow to return to a previous location.

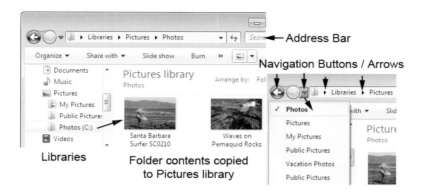

▷ FIGURE 1-13

You can select from categories of file libraries on the right side to locate personal files; click the down arrow to return to a previous location.

4. You will see various links to libraries and locations on the left side of the display window; feel free click on these links. If you are not sure where you are, click on the down arrows in the address bar or on the navigation arrows up top to display previous locations to go back to (see Figure 1-13).

5. Select Start > All Programs to display applications on your computer.

6. To restart the computer, select Start and click the right arrow icon next to the Shut Down icon (shown in Figure 1-12); then select Restart to restart the computer.

7. To shut down completely by powering off, select Start, then select Shut Down. *Always shut down your computer in this manner*; never try to power off by removing the plug, or shutting off the power, because this may damage data on your PC.

8. Click on the Windows Explorer icon on the taskbar and navigate around the libraries and folders within to see the ease of this function. The Pictures library, for example, is where you would locate and organize folders of images.

WINDOWS 7 HELP AND SUPPORT, AND CONTROL PANEL

The **Help and Support** center in the Start menu is where you will also find all kinds of tutorials, troubleshooting, and maintenance information to help keep your computer performing optimally and to customize your settings; a box area also allows you to search for information (see Figure 1-14). The **Control Panel** lets you make modifications within your computer, like adding and removing programs, updating applications, and modifying system functions and monitor displays. Here is where you add fonts, change Internet options, adjust Accessibility options, and set network connections.

Next, we will review your skills with the Windows 7 tutorials and get information about Windows Media Player for the Toolkit Extra section at the end of this chapter.

1. From the Start menu, select the Help and Support link; feel free to click on the Windows Basics link (see Figure 1-14) and browse through the tutorials.

2. After you feel comfortable working in Windows basics, in the Help and Support section, select the What's New link to get a peek at the new Windows 7 experience. Check out Using Windows Flip 3D, Side Bar, Aero Peek, and Using Gadgets; these programs make life more interesting and spice up your desktop. You can also type keywords in the Search box. Enoy!

▷ FIGURE 1-14

The Help and Support Center helps you to troubleshoot or fine-tune your computer and search for information. The Control Panel allows you to make changes within your computer.

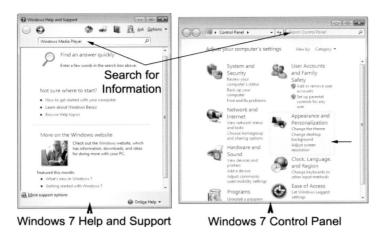

Windows 7 Help and Support   Windows 7 Control Panel

3. Back in Help and Support, type "Windows Media Center" in the Search box, then press Enter.

4. Look through the topics and navigate using the back and forward buttons to read about copying music from CDs and creating your own CDs.

5. Print out pages on these topics and on how to use Windows Media Player to play music, Internet radio, and videos by clicking in the print icon in the Navigation bar on top. Close the window when you have finished.

6. To check out your computer's display settings, select Start > Control Panel > Appearance and Personalization; observe your current settings. Note: If you are on a secure network you probably will not be able to access Control Panel for security reasons.

7. Close the window when you have finished.

MACS AND WINDOWS WORKING TOGETHER

You will find that functionally both Mac OS X and Windows 7 are very similar and can work together with a few helpful tips to keep documents consistent and universally acceptable to both systems.

SAVING AND READING MAC OS X AND WINDOWS FILES

Since you will be designing in the graphics industry, you will be working mostly in a Mac environment. This is because Macs can read most files created in Windows, but Windows may not be able to read certain Mac files, although the gap is getting narrower. All files within Windows need an extension to identify what kind of file it is and the application that created it. Mac files do not need extensions, but if they do not have them, then Windows cannot read the files. In Mac OS X, file extensions are automatically added in most new applications. Microsoft's new Office suites for both Mac and Windows systems allow Office users to read each

▷ FIGURE 1-15

Directory structure displayed in Windows Address Bar and Mac OS X Column View of files in Chapter 4 folder.

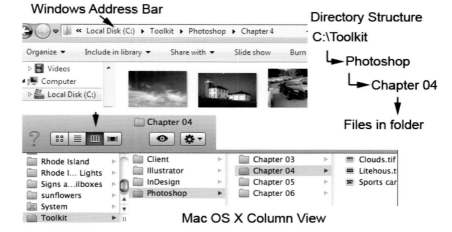

Mac OS X Column View

DESIGN TIP

If you have difficulty reading another computer's graphic images on either Mac or Windows platforms, you can have the file saved with more universal or cross-platform extensions, such as .JPG, .TIF, .EPS, .GIF, or PDF, depending on the type of file you are using. Graphic extensions all have specific purposes, which we will discuss in the following chapters.

other's documents regardless of what type of computer created the file. Files can be saved with universal graphic and text file extensions so that they may be read by either Macs or PCs. Files or applications that can be read by different operating systems are called **cross platform** files.

The **Save** command saves the file as the same name, with the same extension, and to the same location. The **Save As** command allows the designer or photographer to save files with different names and extensions for various purposes, to save them to different locations, and to create different file names for the same file. When using the Save As command in Mac OS X, the dialog box displays columns as a directory of files within folders to navigate, reading from left to right (see Figure 1-16). Creating folders and saving files within those folders creates an organized path, or directory structure, like having file cabinets with drawers where you organize your files and folders (see Figure 1-15). When saving files in Windows 7, icons on the toolbar are used to help navigate the directories in a vertical format.

▷ FIGURE 1-16

Save As dialog boxes within Mac OS X and Windows 7 from the Photoshop application.

Mac OS X Save As

Windows 7 Save As

TOOLKIT TIP When naming and saving a file in Windows to be opened on an earlier version of Mac OS X, keep the file name to a minimum of eight alphanumeric characters. Avoid naming files using the following characters: / \ : " ? * < >

SAME FUNCTION, DIFFERENT NAME

You will find there is really little difference between using a Mac or Windows operating system, especially when working within applications that can be used by both systems, like the ones we will present in this book. Photoshop, Illustrator, and InDesign, are the graphic standards in their respective industries today.

• The Macintosh HD or hard drive icon on the Mac desktop functions much the same as the Computer command or Windows Explorer function in Windows 7 for locating contents of drives and folders.

• Aliases, which create links for applications and files on the Mac, are called *shortcut icons* in Windows.

• The Trash function on the Mac is used the same way as the Recycle Bin in Windows to remove deleted files. The Trash icon also serves as an eject button for CD/DVD drives, external hard drives, memory cards, and flash drives.

• The Find command in the desktop Finder application (File > Find) locates files and folders, as does the Search command in Windows 7.

• The Dock in Mac OS X functions about the same as the taskbar in Windows 7. They display multiple applications that are running and store minimized documents or files. To work with a running application or active file, just click the icon on the Dock or the tab button on the taskbar.

• The System Preferences application allows you to change settings on your Mac the same way as the Control Panel in Windows.

MAC AND PC KEYSTROKES

You will find that many basic keystrokes are close to or the same for both Mac and PC platforms. These keys are mainly used with other keys for certain commands. The key name may be different, but the function is the same. Here are the main ones.

• The Option key on the Mac functions like the Alt key on the Windows keyboard. It can be used to copy files, folders, or object selections.

• The Command key (marked with the beside a loop-cornered square) on the Mac selects multiple nonadjacent items the same as the Ctrl (Control) key in Windows 7.

• The Shift key on both the Mac and PC keyboards selects a range of the same adjacent items within a group. It is also used to resize graphics proportionately.

• The Return key on the Mac functions the same as the Enter key on the PC; it accepts a command or operation.

• To display pop-up menus that list commands depending on where you click, the Control key on the Mac can be used in conjunction with the mouse. The Windows mouse uses a right-button click to display pop-up menus.

KEYSTROKES TO INCREASE PRODUCTIVITY

Mac and Windows computers use specific keys that perform the same functions or commands. Some of these commands are used universally with Mac and PC platforms. Others are specific to one or the other. Special keyboard shortcuts are also used for special functions within an application. To perform a particular function, hold down the first key mentioned—the *function* key—and then press the *secondary* key. The table below shows the universal keyboard shortcuts that can be used with any application.

TO DO THIS	MACINTOSH	WINDOWS
Create a new document	Command + N	CTRL + N
Save a file	Command + S	CTRL + S
Find	Command + F	CTRL + F
Select everything in document	Command + A	CTRL + A
Cut	Command + X	CTRL + X
Copy	Command + C	CTRL + C
Paste	Command + V	CTRL + V
Print a selected document	Command + P	CTRL + P
Bold text	Command + B	CTRL + B
Italicize text	Command + I	CTRL + I
Quit	Command + Q	CTRL + Q
Undo previous action	Command + Z	CTRL + Z
Redo action	Command + Y	SHIFT + Y
Move between menus	(F9 shows all open windows to choose from)	ALT, Arrow keys
Create alias or shortcut to link file or application	Command + L	Right-click mouse to create shortcut

OPTIONS FOR VIEWING AND TRANSPORTING PORTABLE MEDIA

Removable media are CDs, DVDs, memory cards, or portable external hard drives and USB flash drives that can be transported to other computers. Most Mac and Windows computers today have USB and Firewire connections that allow hardware portable drives to plug into any computer to transfer data.

• When you place a CD, DVD, flash or USB drive, or memory card from your digital device—like your camera—into a PC with Windows, a dialog box displays that allows you to choose what you would like to do with the drive; this feature lets you choose whether to copy images to a folder, view the images as electronic slides, view the drive contents, or burn a blank CD or DVD, depending on the type of files you have and the media used.

• Windows: To eject DVD or CD drives, press button beneath the drive tray.

• Macs: When you place a disc or CD, DVD, flash or USB Drive, or memory card from your digital device into a Mac, an icon displays on the desktop. You can double-click the icon to display the contents.

• Macs: When using a Mac to eject portable drives, such as USB flash drives, memory cards, CDs, and DVDs, the selected icons must be dragged to the trash icon first, otherwise your data may become corrupted or not open properly. Afterwards, you can then remove or physically eject the device.

• Macs: You can open and close the CD or DVD tray on the Mac by pressing the **Media Eject key**, which looks like a triangle with a line under it; this key is located on the upper right corner of the Mac keyboard (see Figure 1-17).

• On a Mac, you can also use the File Menu (File > Eject) to eject selected discs and drives. The Trash icon located on the Dock is also used for ejecting by dragging the drive icon into the Trash icon (see Figure 1-17).

• Both PCs and Macs provide different ways to view files and folders. In both, you can choose between viewing as lists with details or small icons, or as various sizes of icons. On a Mac you can use the Cover Flow View, which allows you to flip through your files, folders, and images for quick reference.

TOOLKIT TIP On the Mac, when removing USB drives, memory cards, or portable hard drives, do not remove them physically until they have been dragged into the Trash to be ejected and the icon does not display on the screen, otherwise the data on the drive could get corrupted. You can also click the "up" arrow next to the icon at the left of any open window, where the graphics for drives and folders are, or select the icon on the desktop and use the eject button.

Here, you will learn to insert and then eject the text CD from the book on either the Mac or PC. Leave the CD in whichever computer you are using for the upcoming exercises.

1. Mac users: Press the Media Eject key on the keyboard to open the CD tray (Figure 1-17). If your Mac has a Superdrive, you do not have to press the eject key: simply insert the disc in the drive.

2. On the Mac with a standard CD drive, place the text CD from the back of the book in the drive and press the Media Eject key again or lightly push the CD

Media Eject Key (Mac)

Trash Icon to eject media on Macs

Windows 7 provides a "What to do" display when removeable media are inserted in the computer.

Options using digital media with Finder's desktop menu on Mac

▷ FIGURE 1-17

Options for digital media and ejecting disks on Mac and Windows computers.

tray to close it. Notice a CD icon displays on the desktop. The text CD may have a special program that will automatically load the CD and display a menu of choices. You can still see the CD icon on the desktop.

3. Double-click the CD icon to view the contents. Select the various view options on the toolbar, from lists to icons to Cover View, which allows you to move graphic thumbnails across the screen (see Figure 1-18).

4. On the Mac, close the window, then select the CD icon on the desktop and drag it to the Trash icon on the Dock to open the tray again.

5. For Macs with a standard CD drive, press the Media Eject key again to close the CD tray.

6. Windows (PC) users, press the button under the CD drive to open the tray and place the text CD in the drive; then press the button again to close the tray.

7. Windows users, when the dialog box displays, choose "Open folder to view files". Take a look at the contents, select the Views tab to see what options suit your tastes, whether to view as icons, as a list, or showing details. and then close the window display when you have finished (see Figure 1-18).

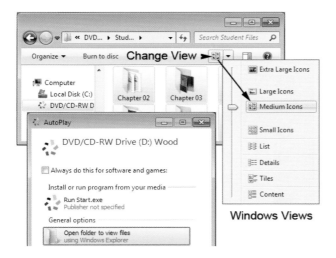

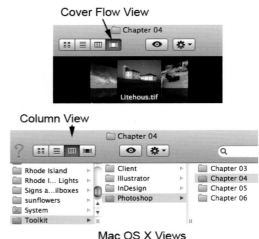

▷ FIGURE 1-18

**Options for
Windows and Mac
OS X to view files,
thumbnails, and
folders.**

CLIENT ASSIGNMENT

In each chapter, this is where you will be given an assignment from a potential client in which the thought process is discussed along with a list of action items for you to follow throughout the chapter. In this first chapter, you are the designer, and your assignment is to create specific folders on your hard drive that will be used to copy text assignment files from the CD. You will be able to retrieve, edit, and save files in these special folders.

Designers need to keep organized by managing files and folders to maintain productivity. These folders will help you manage files within these folders to keep you organized as you proceed through the chapters. You will be given the basics in both Mac OS X and Windows 7 platforms to familiarize you with their similarities and differences. You will also be shown various fun applications and techniques that both operating systems use to keep your desktop from being too cluttered with files and open windows. At the end of the chapter, in the Advanced Users section, you will create electronic slide shows of chosen images. In the Digital Toolkit Extra section, you will learn to burn music, photo, and data CDs using special applications in both Mac OS X and Windows 7.

PROJECT: TEST DRIVE MAC OS X AND WINDOWS 7

ACTION ITEMS

Each chapter will provide a bulleted list of "Action Items" that will give you an insight as to what main exercises you will be completing throughout the chapter, including an Advanced User section you can try at the end.

• Create an initial folder called *Toolkit* on your hard drive or portable drive.

• Inside the *Toolkit* folder, create *Client, InDesign, Photoshop,* and *Illustrator* folders for the book exercises.

• Create a shortcut (Windows) or an alias (Mac) on the desktop to the *Toolkit* folder for quick access.

• Copy chapters from the text CD to the folders you created.

• Create shortcuts or aliases on your desktop and search for files.

• Keep your desktop from getting too cluttered using special fun applications and techniques.

• Advanced User: Create an electronic slide shows of your images.

MANAGING FILES AND FOLDERS

One of the most important things a designer or photographer can do to be productive is to get organized. Creating folders and placing files within those folders saves time spent searching later on. You can also create shortcuts or aliases (Mac) for files and applications on the desktop, which also provides quick access to current files But be careful; having too many can create quite a mess on your desktop.

You can use the Dock on your Mac or the taskbar in Windows for shortcuts or aliases to software applications. Using commands to locate files eliminates the guesswork of having to manually look around. Understanding how to move and copy files to another location helps you build a logical directory of files and folders. Learning the basics of both Mac and PC operations will help familiarize you with their similarities and differences.

ORGANIZING TEXT CHAPTERS ON YOUR COMPUTER

All the files you will need for the assignments and exercises in the book are on the text CD. Before bringing in files and folders from the text CD to complete your assignments, it is important to create an organized group of folders on your hard drive, assigned network drive, or flash drive to place these files in as a work area. In either environment, you will create the main folder, called Toolkit, where all your work exercises from the text will be stored: This will act as a file cabinet. You will then create folders for the text units inside the *Toolkit* folder similar to drawers in a file cabinet; this directory of folders will help you keep track of the files used in the exercises. Chapter folders from the text CD will be placed inside the unit folders.

TOOLKIT TIP You can use the files for these exercises on your computer's hard drive, network drive, or on removable portable media like USB drives. If you are planning to use a USB flash drive for both Mac and PC drives for the text exercises, you may want to complete the PC portion first, since Macs can read PC files easier than PCs can read Mac files. If you are on a network drive at a school, ask your instructor about setting up your space on the network, where you may need to create a folder to store your work.

MAC OS X: CREATING A FOLDER DIRECTORY

Using the Finder menu on the Mac is one of the easier ways to create and manage folders on drives (see Figure 1-19). To navigate files and folders, you can set the View, from the Finder toolbar, to Columns; when you are opening or looking for a file on your Mac, you will find in Column View a blue horizontal scroll bar that displays the directory structure from left to right. You can also use the new Cover Flow View to quickly flip through images or documents.

▷ FIGURE 1-19

Creating a directory of folders for text exercises.

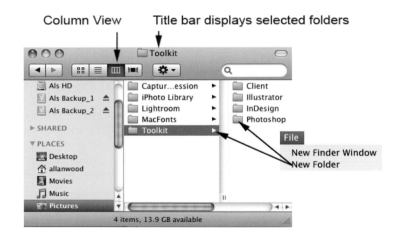

Using Mac OS X, you will create the main *Toolkit* folder and then add four unit folders within the *Toolkit* folder on either your hard drive, network drive, portable hard drive, or USB flash drive.

1. Option A: On your Mac desktop, double-click on the Macintosh HD or hard drive icon to open the display window. This will display all folders on the drive, and "Macintosh HD" or a hard drive name will be displayed in the title bar.

2. Option B: If you are using a USB flash drive, place it in the USB slot. When it displays on the desktop, double-click it to display contents.

3. Option C: If you are using a network drive, you will have a different name for the server drive. See the network administrator to determine the drive letter or name and to determine how to set up your folder on the drive or network server.

4. In the window display, make sure the View is set to Column View (Figure 1-19).

5. If you are using a hard drive from a local or home computer, make sure the Macintosh HD hard drive icon is selected in the leftmost column. Select the Pictures or Documents category link to create a folder for your work, because you will be using image and text files (Figure 1-19), or find a location determined by your instructor.

6. If you are using a USB flash drive, portable hard drive, or network drive, the right column will display the current files or folders on that drive.

7. In the window display, click on the white background to make sure no folders are selected.

8. To create a folder, select File > New Folder from the desktop Finder menu. You will see a highlighted "untitled" folder on the hard drive.

9. With the word "untitled" highlighted, type "Toolkit" over it, then press the return key or click outside the text area to save the folder name. If it becomes deselected, press the return key to make the folder name editable. To change a name, you can also click and drag the mouse over the text and type in the new name.

10. Double-click on the *Toolkit* folder icon to display an empty window with the name *Toolkit* in the title bar. This is where you will create your unit folders and store all the files you will be working on in the book.

11. Select File > New Folder from the desktop Finder menu and create four more folders: *Client, Photoshop, Illustrator,* and *InDesign.* Make sure the *Toolkit* folder is selected and displayed in the title bar (see Figure 1-19). If you are having a problem with the placement of these folders, just select them, drag them to the Trash icon, and try again.

12. With the four folders displayed inside the *Toolkit* folder window, leave the window display open for the next exercise (see Figure 1-20).

TOOLKIT TIP Another method of creating and organizing folders is on the desktop itself. When you select CTRL + click on the desktop (or right-clicking if you are using a two-button mouse), a content dialog box displays. Select New Folder to create the folder. Double-click the folder to open it, and create other folders inside as described in Step 11 of the previous exercise. You can either leave the folder on the desktop, or open the Hard Drive icon and drag the folder contents from the desktop to one of the Places icons (Document or Pictures) on the hard drive's sidebar, or onto the drive list itself. Be wary that if you are on a network such as a school network, if you need to restart the computer, the security setting may wipe out anything left on the desktop. This is a safer method on a home or local computer.

▷ FIGURE 1-20

With both windows open, drag folders and files between windows. You can also drag folders and files to the desktop.

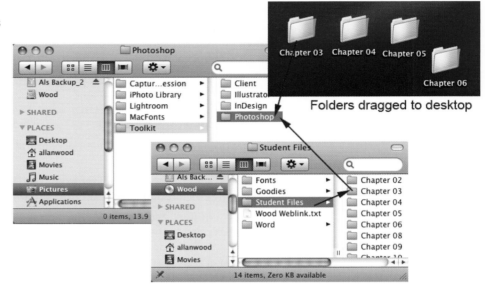

Folders dragged to desktop

Copying (dragging) folders from book CD

MAC OS X: COPYING FILES AND FOLDERS FROM THE TEXT CD

The CD that comes in the back of your text contains all the files you will need to create and complete the real-life projects and assignments in this book. These files and images are placed into each chapter folder. Since files cannot be saved to this CD, you will need to copy them to the folders you created on your drive by selecting and dragging each chapter folder. This way you can open, edit, and safely save files to your drive.

Setting the View on the Finder toolbar to Columns helps display files and folders for copying. Next, you will select and drag chapter folders that contain the exercise files from the text CD to the unit folders you created inside the main *Toolkit* folder on your drive. On the Mac, you can drag folders and files right onto the desktop as a temporary holding place, and then drag it into a folder on your drive; or you can drag them right to the folder.

TOOLKIT TIP Since the CD permanently stores the nonwritable text files, you can simply select and drag files to your hard drive window without affecting the originals. To move a file or folder to another location on any writable drive, select it and drag it to its new destination. You can also copy files from one location on any writable drive to another by dragging over the files, because they automatically copy over; or if you are copying to create a duplicate of a folder or file, you can create duplicates by holding down the Option/Alt key and dragging between windows on either platform. Copying leaves the original in its original location.

Here you will drag the chapter folders from the CD to the window of unit folders you created, or you can drag them to the desktop and then into the unit folders.

1. Press the Media Eject key on your keyboard, and place the text CD in the CD drive. Press again to close. You will notice that the CD icon will display on the desktop. The text CD may have a special program that will automatically load the CD and display a menu of choices, just close the window. You can still see the CD icon on the desktop.

2. On the desktop, double-click the hard drive, network drive, or flash drive icon you are going to use to display the contents in the window.

3. If you have closed the window display, locate the *Toolkit* folder you created and double-click to open it and display the four unit folders: *Client, Photoshop, Illustrator,* and *InDesign;* or if the display is open showing folders from the previous exercise, continue to the next step. If using the local hard drive, select the Pictures category, if you put the *Toolkit* folder there (Figure 1-20).

4. Make sure you are in Column View on the toolbar and resize the window display to about half the size of your computer screen by dragging the bottom right corner of your window. Click on the top title bar of the open window, and drag the window to the left side. This will be the "copy to" window.

5. Double-click the text CD drive icon (it may be labeled "Wood"), then double-click the Student Files folder to display the folders of the Chapters and Unit Reviews to display the chapters; resize the window by dragging the bottom right corner. Click and drag the title bar to place the Student Files window to the right of the *Toolkit* window. This will become the "copy from" window.

6. To place the chapters inside the unit folders, click and drag each chapter folder from the CD window to each unit folder in the *Toolkit* window described below. When it is highlighted, you can release the mouse to place the contents into the designated unit folder. You can also drag each chapter onto the desktop from the CD first, then drag it onto the *Toolkit* window.

7. Drag Chapter 2 to the *Client* folder, Chapters 3 through 6 to the *Photoshop* folder, Chapters 7 through 10 to the *Illustrator* folder, and Chapters 11 and 12 to the *InDesign* folder. Release the mouse to drop the file in. Note: There are no files needed in Chapter 7. If a Chapter 7 folder is missing from the text CD, feel free to create one to save your files in later.

8. When you have completed dragging the text CD chapter folders into the unit folders, you'll also notice four Unit Review folders displayed on your text CD. Each folder contains files for a special unit review project that encompasses what you have learned from each unit. Drag each Unit Review folder (Unit 1 Review through Unit 4 Review) so it will be located inside the *Toolkit* folder with the unit folders.

9. To see how the Mac's new "stacks" function works, drag the *Toolkit* folder to the right side of the Dock next to the Trash icon. Click on the folder to expand the *Toolkit* folder contents, and click on any unit folder and its file contents that you may be interested in.

10. When you're done, close the window; if you are using a flash drive, remember to drag the drive's icon into the trash to eject it, or you will receive an error message.

PROBLEM If you place a file or folder in the wrong place, you can try to drag it out and over to the correct folder, or simply delete it and try again.

 TOOLKIT TIP On the Mac, when you drag and hold the file icon over the folder to place the file, the folder will open to display the contents.

 TOOLKIT TIP When you select your drive from your home Mac computer, you'll notice a sidebar on the left with an area designated as Places. This contains icons for folders that you can access as the most frequently used, or wish to store as works in progress, and a search area for recently used files. To make it easier to locate your *Toolkit* folder, you can simply drag (or hold down the Option key to copy) your *Toolkit* folder with its contents and store it inside either the Documents icon as there are image and text files, or within the Pictures icon. Neither choice will harm your computer. To remove, just drag outside the Places onto the desktop or another location. If you are on a secure network this option may not be allowed. There is also nothing wrong with leaving the *Toolkit* folder inside your designated user folder for easier access, what is just mentioned is another method of storing and organizing your folders and files. This is your decision.

WINDOWS 7: CREATING A FOLDER DIRECTORY

Windows 7 uses the Computer function command, or Windows Explorer, to display drives, folders, and files. On the left side window display is a list of media libraries or options to locate your files, as in Mac OS X systems. Windows 7 uses libraries to store different types of media. These libraries can be used as another method to organize and gather content for special folders from various locations. You can create various folders in each library. You can use the Views tab to choose the best method of display to copy the text CD files (see Figure 1-21).

▷ FIGURE 1-21

To create new folders, select New Folder from the Tools menu, then highlight and name the folder, or right-click, then select New, then select Folder.

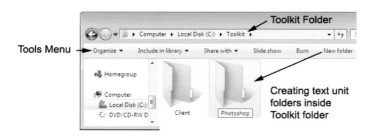

Toolkit Folder

Tools Menu

Creating text unit folders inside Toolkit folder

In Windows, you will create the main *Toolkit* folder and then add unit folders within the *Toolkit* folder.

1. Select the Start menu icon and then select the Computer function command to display various drives and contents.

2. Option A: If you are setting up to do your work directly on a local or home computer's hard drive, double-click on the C:\Local Disk icon to open the display window. This will display all folders that are on the drive; "C:\" designates the hard drive. You will also see the specific libraries on the left. You can either create a folder directly within the drive letter list, or create a folder inside one of the libraries.

3. Option B: If you are using a USB flash drive, place it in the USB slot and it will display with its own drive letter; when the dialog box opens to display what to do with contents, select "Open folder to view files", or click on the "x" in the display box and double-click the drive icon to display contents.

4. Option C: If you are using a network drive, you will have a different letter for that drive. See your instructor to determine the drive letter where you should set up your folder on the network drive.

5. In the window display, click on the Views tab to display options to choose the best method. List, Tiles, or Medium Icon View (Figure 1-21) work well.

6. For Option A, if you are using a local hard drive, or home computer, select the Documents library to create a folder for your work, because you will be using image and text files (Figure 1-21).

7. If you are using a USB flash drive or a network drive, the right column will display the current files or folders on that drive.

8. In the window display, click on the white background to make sure no folders are selected.

9. To create a folder, on any drive, with the contents of the drive displayed (or within the Documents library on your home computer) select New Folder from the Tools menu window display, or if it not displayed, you can right-click to find a display box then select New, then select Folder from the content menu. You will see a highlighted "untitled" folder on the hard drive.

10. Click and drag the mouse over the text and name your folder *Toolkit*, then press the Enter key or click outside the text area to save the folder name.

11. Double-click on the *Toolkit* folder icon to display an empty window with the name *Toolkit* in the Title bar. This is where you will create your unit folders and store all the files you will be working on in the book.

12. Select New Folder from the Tools menu window display or if it not displayed in the Tools menu, you can right-click to find a display box then select New, then select Folder from the content menu and create four more folders: *Client, Photoshop, Illustrator,* and *InDesign.* Make sure the *Toolkit* folder is selected and displayed in the title bar (Figure 1-21). If you are having a problem with placement of the folders, just highlight and press the delete key on your keyboard and try again.

13. With the four folders displayed inside the *Toolkit* folder window, select Organize > Close, or click on the X in the corner to close the window display.

14. Next, you will copy the contents of each chapter from the CD into these folders.

15. Leave everything open on your screen for the next exercise.

TOOLKIT TIP In Windows, if you saved one of the folders incorrectly, drag the folder to the desktop; select the back button on the window display to locate the *Toolkit* folder, then drag the folder back inside the *Toolkit* folder. Another method of creating and organizing folders is on the desktop itself by right-clicking on the desktop. When the content dialog box displays, select New, then Folder. You can then drag the folder and its contents from the desktop to one of the Library icons (Desktop or Pictures) on the hard drive's sidebar, or onto the drive list itself. Be wary that if you are on a network such as a school network, if you need to restart the computer, the security setting may wipe out anything left on the desktop. This is a safe method on a home or local computer.

WINDOWS 7: COPYING FILES AND FOLDERS FROM THE TEXT CD

▷ FIGURE 1-22

The easiest way to copy folders from one place to another is between open windows of each.

The CD that comes in the back of your text contains all the files you will need to complete the real-life projects and assignments in this book. In this exercise, you will copy those files over to the unit folders you created on your drive by selecting and dragging each chapter folder into the appropriate unit folders (see Figure 1-22). This way, you can open, edit, and save files to your drive. Use the Views tab to display the folders.

There are many ways to create and store folders with files. Here you will drag the chapter folders from the CD to the windows of unit folders you created, or you can drag them to the desktop then into the unit folders.

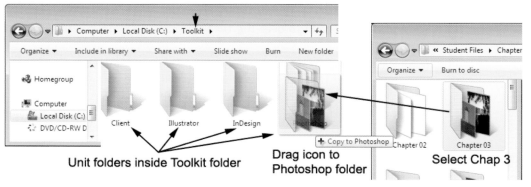

Unit folders inside Toolkit folder

Drag icon to Photoshop folder

Select Chap 3

Chapter contents from text CD

1. Press the button under the CD drive to open the CD tray and place the text CD in the CD drive. Press again to close. You will notice the CD icon will display on the desktop.

2. If the application program within the text CD opens up with choices, for this exercise, click on the red "x" up top to close the window. Note: For more advanced users, you can drag the contents from the text CD application window, but you may have to create each chapter folder first. On the desktop, double-click the hard drive, network drive, or flash drive icon to display the contents in the window.

3. If you have closed the window display, locate the *Toolkit* folder you created and double-click to open the folder to display the four unit folders: *Client, Photoshop, Illustrator,* and *InDesign.* Or if the display is showing the four unit folders from previous the exercise, continue to the next step.

4. Select the Views tab and make sure you are in List, Tiles, or Medium Icon View on the toolbar, and resize the window display to about half the size of your computer screen (drag the bottom right corner of the window to resize). Click on the top title bar of the window display and drag the window to the left side. This will be the "copy to" window.

5. Double-click the text CD drive icon (it may be labeled "Wood") then double-click the Student Files folder to display the chapters; resize the window by dragging the bottom right corner. Click and drag the title bar to place the Student CD window next to the *Toolkit* window. This will become the "copy from" window.

6. To place the chapters inside the unit folders, click and drag each chapter folder from the CD window to each unit folder in the *Toolkit* window described below. When it is highlighted, you can release the mouse to place the contents into the designated unit folder. You can also drag each chapter onto the desktop from the CD first, and then drag it into the *Toolkit* window.

7. Drag Chapter 2 to the *Client folder,* Chapters 3 through 6 to the *Photoshop* folder, Chapters 7 through 10 to the *Illustrator* folder, and Chapters 11 and 12 to the *InDesign* folder (Figure 1-22). Release the mouse to drop the file in. Note: There are no files needed in Chapter 7. If a Chapter 7 folder is missing from the text CD, feel free to create one to save your files in for later use.

8. If you have problems or are not sure where you are, or if you are curious and want to look at the files dragged over, you can click on the back or forward arrows to view previous actions, or click on the down arrows in the address bar to display folder contents (Figure 1-23).

9. When you have completed dragging the text CD chapter folders into the unit folders, you'll also notice four Unit Review folders displayed on your text CD. Each folder contains files for a special unit review project that encompasses what you have learned from each unit. Drag each Unit Review folder (Unit 1 Review through Unit 4 Review) so it will be located inside the *Toolkit* folder within the unit folders. When you're done, close the window. Eject the CD by pressing the button again to open the tray.

▷   FIGURE 1-23

The arrow pointing downward next to the back and forward arrow buttons displays a history of visited locations. To display a folders contents, click on the downward arrow next to the folder (highlighted) in the Address bar.

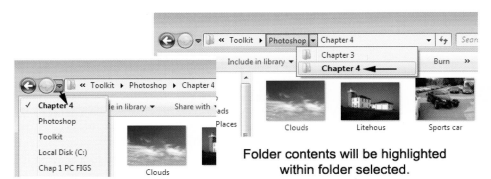

Select the downward arrow to display previous locations visited.

Folder contents will be highlighted within folder selected.

TOOLKIT TIP In Windows, as with Macs, you can create or drag folders and files right onto the desktop as a temporary holding place, and then drag them onto a folder on your drive. If you are using your own home computer, another method of storing and organizing your folders and files allows you to copy the folder and its contents into one of the categories of libraries located on the left sidebar. To copy the contents of the *Toolkit* folder you created into the Documents library, since your folders contain images and text (although if copied into the Pictures library, they will also work fine), right-click the *Toolkit* folder, then select Include in library > Documents. You'll see the *Toolkit* folder with its contents inside the chosen library. In Windows 7, to quickly view and access libraries and their contents, you can click on the Windows Explorer icon on the Taskbar to grab the files you need for your exercises. You can also choose to keep the folder just on your local drive. Your choice.

TOOLKIT TIP In either platform, click once with the mouse to select an item, and double-click to open it. When opening a Windows file on the Mac, you can double-click the files to open them, or launch the application first, and then select File > Open to display the file instead of double-clicking on the file icon.

SEARCHING FOR FILES

Both Mac OS X and Windows provide commands to locate folders and files (see Figure 1-24). Mac users select the File > Find command in the desktop's Finder menu to locate files and folders on a computer or network. You can also locate the contents of these files by searching for words or phrases. Windows 7 uses a Search command in the Start menu to focus your searches with an advanced search feature that can be used by typing in specific criteria.

Mac OS X: Use desktop Finder toolbar (File > Find >Search In)

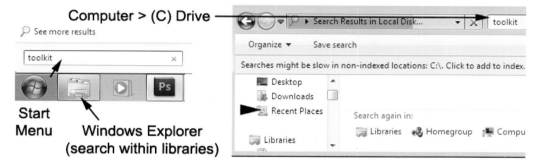

Search options in Windows 7

▷ FIGURE 1-24

Use the File > Find command in the desktop Finder menu of Mac OS X, or search box to search for files. Use the Start menu search box, Windows Explorer, or use the Computer link in Windows 7 to locate files and folders.

Here you will look for the *Toolkit* folder you just created on the hard drive and for the *Goodies* folder on the Student CD that comes with your text; it contains additional assignments and information for you to practice with. Check it out!

Macintosh OS X

1. Press the Media Eject key on your keyboard and insert the text CD.

2. Select File > Find from the Finder toolbar on the desktop.

3. Select Search In and type "Toolkit" in the Search box. You will come up with a list display indicating where the *Toolkit* folder is located. Close the Search when done.

4. Locate the *Goodies* folder on your text CD. Take a look at some of the additional projects and assignments in the various chapter folders. Close the window when finished.

Windows 7

1. Click Start button, then type "Toolkit" in the Start Search box. The matching folder will display as a list. Close the Search when done.

2. In the Start menu display, you can also select Recent Items (located above the Computer button) to view a list of the last files you worked on. You can use it to locate the *Toolkit* folder you just created. When the folder is displayed, you can double-click the folder to view the contents.

3. Insert the text CD and find the *Goodies* folder. Take a look at some of the additional projects and assignments in the various chapter folders. Try using Advanced Search in the Search window display for specific criteria, or click on Windows Explorer icon on the taskbar to locate the Goodies folder, or your *Toolkit* folder. Close the window when finished.

TOOLKIT TIP For Mac searches, you can also use the Go > Computer command on the desktop Finder toolbar, and type the file name in the Search box. For more advanced users, Mac OS X also has a sidebar that contains a Search For function to locate recently used files, movies, and images. This section also contains icons for creating "Smart Folders" that can collect files, folders, and applications that meet a specific criteria for fast access. For a Windows 7 search, you could also select the Computer function command, or click on the Windows Explorer icon in the taskbar. For advanced users, you can also search on the left sidebar under Favorites for Recent Places to find previously created documents and files to search all drives.

CREATING AN ALIAS OR SHORTCUT

You can create a link on your desktop called an *alias* (for Mac users) or a *shortcut* (for PC users) that links to an application, folder, or file that you plan to use frequently (see Figure 1-25). An alias or a shortcut is usually designated by a bent arrow on the icon. You can rename it, duplicate it, or remove it, and it will not harm the original; it is only a link. Mac users can also place documents or files into the original folder by dragging the items on top of the alias of that folder. Right-clicking with the mouse in Windows displays a menu of commands depending on where you click, including shortcuts of selected files and folders. This can also be done with Macs by holding down the Control key and clicking with the mouse.

▷ FIGURE 1-25

Creating a link to the *Toolkit* folder on your desktop.

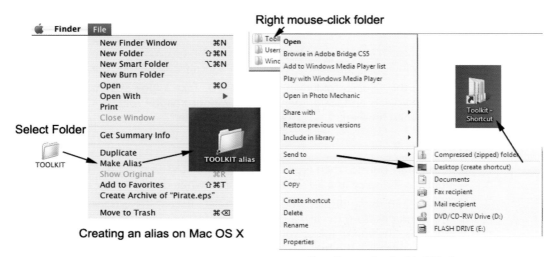

Creating an alias on Mac OS X

Creating a shortcut in Windows

Here you will create a link to the *Toolkit* folder to work on the exercises in this book.

Macintosh OS X

1. If you placed the *Toolkit* folder on your drive, double-click the Macintosh HD icon on the desktop, then locate and select the *Toolkit* folder you created. If you used a flash drive or network drive for your files, locate and select the *Toolkit* folder.

2. With the *Toolkit* folder selected, select File > Make Alias in the Finder menu bar. A copy with the label *Toolkit alias* will display in the window. You can also CTRL + click the folder and choose the Make Alias link.

3. Drag the Toolkit icon to the desktop: now you have a link to that folder. If you change the desktop location to the Dock, you can simply drag the folder/icon to the dock and it creates an alias automatically.

4. Double-click the alias on the desktop, and the *Toolkit* folder will open, displaying all the folders you created to work on.

TOOLKIT TIP For Mac OS X users, if you need to locate the original folder, you can select the alias by clicking once to highlight it; then select File > **Show Original** from the Finder menu.

 Need additional fun computer graphics tutorials and info, and an additional look at the projects you'll be creating in this book? Check out my Artist's Digital Toolkit website at: http://www.digitoolkit.com

Windows 7

1. Select Start > Computer and locate the *Toolkit* folder from the Local Disk (C:) hard drive icon. If you used a flash drive or network drive, locate and select the *Toolkit* folder you created.

2. Select the *Toolkit* folder and right-click to get a shortcut display box.

3. Select Send To > Desktop to create a shortcut; this will automatically put it on the desktop as a link. To remove shortcuts, files, and folders, right-click the selected icon and then select Delete, and they will be sent to the Recycle Bin.

4. Double-click the Toolkit shortcut on the desktop to display all the folders you created to work on.

MAC OS X AND WINDOWS 7: ORGANIZING YOUR DESKTOP

Sometimes your desktop becomes cluttered with windows of open applications and files that you are working on. Both Mac OS X and Windows 7 provide applications and functions to help keep you organized and productive, and still have fun. Each platform also contains additional mini programs to help with everyday tasks, as either gadgets (Windows) or widgets (Mac OS X).

Mac OS X Desktop

To organize your folders, Max OS X has a stacks feature mentioned earlier in the chapter, that allow you to create folders of documents, applications, images, or anything you use frequently so that when you click a stack, it springs open in an arc or a grid, depending on the number of items. To organize your windows into groups MAC OS X uses a function called **Spaces**. It defaults to four windows where you can organize your work in groups according to projects, applications used, or whatever by dragging the documents, or images between windows. To place the icon on the Dock, you can access it through System Preferences in the Finder desktop menu. **Exposé** is another mini application that helps you move or copy items between different windows in an application and from one application to another using combinations of keys. It is also used in combination with the Spaces. Even if you have many overlapping windows, Exposé lets you view large thumbnail versions of all of them so you can find the one you need. For instance, to use Exposé to copy text or graphics between windows within the same application, start dragging the selected item, and then press the F10 key to show all the application's windows. Drag the item over the window where you want to drop it, and press F10 again to make that the active window. Release the item you're dragging to add it to the document. To view all open windows (for laptops press the FN key on the left side of the keyboard, first then the appropriate F key), press the F9 key, to view all open windows within an application, press the F10 key, to hide all windows to see only the desktop, press the F11 key.

Dashboard is a feature of Mac OS X that contains small programs called **widgets** that have a wide variety of uses for everyday tasks such as checking stock prices, finding weather information, links with larger applications, etc. With the Address Book widget, for example, you can search for a name and address without opening the full Address Book application. Other widgets, such as Weather, provide web-based information without opening a web browser. To see Dashboard and the widgets, press the F12 key (FN + F12 with laptops). Press it again to hide Dashboard. To look for widgets at the apple website at www.apple.com, just type in widgets in the search box.

▷ FIGURE 1-26

MAC OS X provides features for organizing your desktop. Stacks is used for folders of frequently used programs and files, spaces for organizing active windows, and the Dashboard for using widgets.

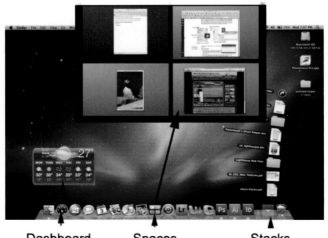

Dashboard   Spaces   Stacks
(contains Widgets)

To give you an idea of the power of these features, you'll open up multiple windows and use Expose and Spaces to organize, and then observe stacks from a folder of documents. You'll check the weather on your weather widget. Be wary that if you are on a network, secure settings may not allow you to perform this exercise.

1. With MAC OS X turned on, open a set of documents from your word processing program, or create some test documents. If you have a flash drive or have access to images, double-click on them to open them up in the default application on your computer.

2. First, to see how Exposé works, select the F10 key (FN + F10 on laptops) to see all the open windows as large thumbnails, press again to resume.

3. Select the F11 key (FN + F11 on laptops) to hide all the windows and show just the desktop, press again to toggle back the open windows.

4. To check out Spaces, click the icon on the dock, or select F8 (FN + F8 on laptops). When the four default windows open, drag your open document windows into the various squares as a special set of groups. Press F8 (FN + F8 on laptops) to close or click the icon on the Dock.

5. To understand the Stacks feature, create a junk folder on the desktop and save documents or copy files or into the folder. Drag the folder next to the Trash icon, and then click the folder to view the contents. Then you just click on the file you want to open. Drag off the folder onto the desktop when you are finished, then drag into the Trash.

6. To check out the Dashboard with its widgets, click on the Dashboard icon on the Dock, or Press F12 (FN + F12 on laptops) to see what widgets are displayed. If there is a weather widget, set up for your area or check out the weather in another city. Press F12 (or FN + F12) again to hide the Dashboard.

7. To get an idea of the wide variety of widgets available, go to the apple web site at www.apple.com and type in widgets in the search box to see this large list. Try to pick and download one to see how it works, be careful this can be addicting!

8. Close down your computer when finished.

Windows 7 Desktop

To organize open windows, Windows 7 provides features called Snap, Peek, and Shake. The **Snap** feature allows you to resize open windows, simply by dragging them to the edges of your screen. You can make your windows expand vertically, take up the entire screen, or appear side-by-side with another window. The **Peek** (show desktop) function gives you the opportunity to watch open windows instantly disappear to display only the Windows 7 desktop. On the far right edge of the taskbar you'll find a small rectangle, just click to show the desktop, and click again to toggle back to your open windows. If you just want to focus on one open window, use the **Shake** function by clicking the window you want to focus on and give your mouse a shake. All other open windows will disappear except for your chosen window. Go ahead and open a bunch of windows and try these features out!

For quick access to most used applications and files Windows 7 has created a **Pin** function to pin programs to the taskbar and the ability to pin files with a matching application as part of that application's jump list. A **jump list** allows you to navigate around recent files, images, tasks in an application, and even web sites. To pin an application, right click on its icon either in the Start menu and select Pin to Taskbar, or, just drag the program's icon if it is on the desktop to the taskbar and select to Pin to Taskbar. You can then just click on the icon much like the dock to open the application, and then click on the icon again to close. The pinned icons stay on the desktop until you unpin them. You can view the jump list to a program by right clicking on its icon in the taskbar, or by dragging the con to the desktop. To pin files to applications simply create an icon on the desktop and drag to the program's icon or the taskbar, which may select the appropriate program. Then select to pin to the application. That's it! From the jump list created for a particular application, you only need to click on the link to access the file. To view thumbnails of your active files in an application or just visited websites, just hover your mouse over the program's icon in the taskbar to see thumbnail previews of any open windows within that application.

▷ FIGURE 1-27

Windows 7 features for desktop organization include pinning applications to taskbar, jump lists of recent documents, or websites, peek function to toggle desktop view, and gadgets for fun and productivity.

Windows 7 contains mini-programs called gadgets, which offer information at a glance and provide easy access to frequently used tools. For example, you can use gadgets to display a picture slide show or view continuously updated headlines (See FIG 1-27). To see what gadgets you have, just right-click the desktop and select the Gadgets link to see what gadgets you have already, or select Desktop Gadget Gallery from the Start Menu. Double-click the gadget icon to open and drag anywhere on your desktop. You can also download gadgets from the Microsoft site and search for "Personalization Gallery" or just type in "gadgets". Go ahead and play!

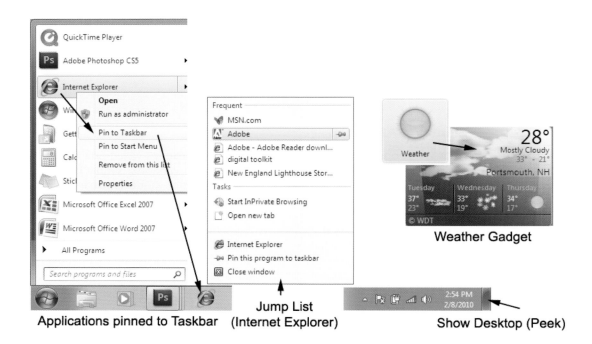

Applications pinned to Taskbar   Jump List (Internet Explorer)   Show Desktop (Peek)

Here you will pin the Internet Explorer program and another to the taskbar. Then locate gadgets on your computer. Be wary that if you are on a network, secure settings may not allow you to perform this exercise.

1. With Windows 7 on, click on the Start Menu button, and then right-click on the Internet Explorer icon (FIG 1-27).

2. Click on the Pin to Taskbar link and you'll see the icon displayed on the taskbar.

3. Go ahead onto the Internet, type www.microsoft.com to access the Microsoft site.

4. In the search box, type in "Personalization Gallery" then locate gadgets, or type in "gadgets" to find some information on these free programs you can download onto your computer. Try to download one and open it up by double-clicking on it on your computer.

5. Go to a few other sites and then hover your mouse over the Explorer icon in the taskbar to see a list or thumbnail previews of the sites you just visited.

6. If you drag the Internet Explorer icon to the desktop you may find a jump list of frequent sites and tasks.

7. Click the Start Menu button and click the All Programs link on the bottom to find Microsoft Word, or any application you would like to pin to the taskbar.

8. Right-click on the icon and select to Pin to Taskbar as was done with Internet Explorer. You'll see again the icon is now on the taskbar for quick access. You can then create a document and save to the desktop, then drag to the icon to pin to the application.

9. To see the gadgets on your desktop, right-click on the desktop and select the gadgets link.

10. From the list of choices, locate the weather gadget and set up for a city near you or pick another city.

11. Play around with this unique feature then shut down the computer when you are finished.

ADVANCED USER: Creating Electronic Slide Shows of Images

A designer or photographer may need to send their images to a potential client electronically. Both Mac OS X and Windows 7 operating systems provide additional applications that allow the designer or photographer to work with different media. In Mac OS X they are Quick Look, Preview, and in older versions iPhoto is included (it can be purchased separately if you have the newer Leopard version); and in Windows you can select between the Pictures category or link, Windows Photo Viewer, or Windows Media Center. Both Mac OS X and Windows have a storage folder on the computer's hard drive that you can access through the Pictures link. Windows 7 allows you to create an instant slide show from this link. In this exercise, you will learn to create slide shows of selected images using Quick Look and Preview applications on the Mac and on Windows 7 using the Pictures link, Windows Photo Viewer, and Windows Media Center.

TOOLKIT TIP When downloading images from the Internet, usually the image that you see is full size. Make sure you have an image large enough so that it will display adequately on your screen. Be aware also that when you create a full screen slide show the application may create larger images than the original, which may cause the original sharp image to have a soft or blurry look.

RETRIEVING IMAGES OFF THE INTERNET

Here you learn the most common method of saving images from the Internet to your computer drive (see Figure 1-28), but be wary of copyright laws when copying photos. In this case, you may download images for fair use for educational purposes, but not for marketing or for sale, unless you have direct permission from the originator on a release form. Make sure any images you download appear large enough on the screen you are downloading from.

▷ FIGURE 1-28

Saving images from the Internet on your drive.

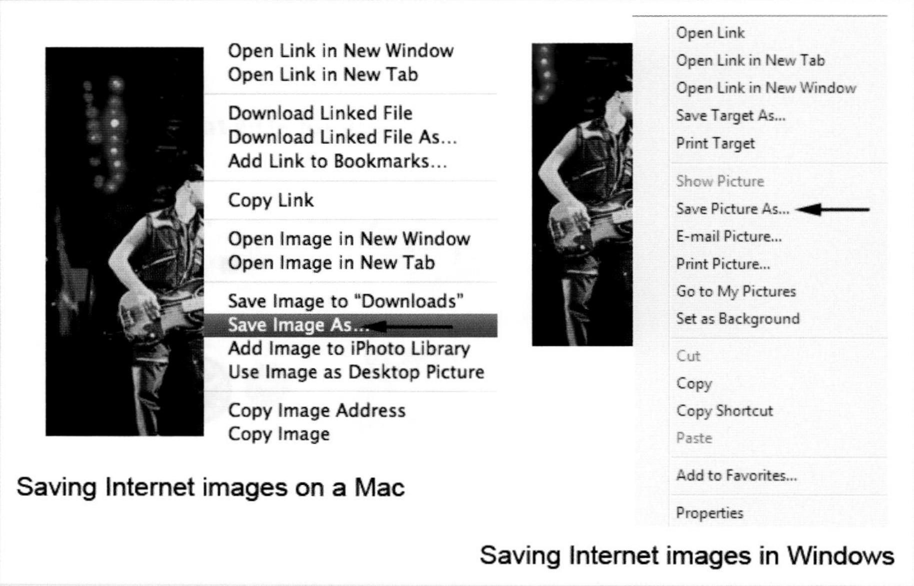

Saving Internet images on a Mac

Saving Internet images in Windows

Macintosh OS X

1. If you are using the computer hard drive, double-click the hard drive icon, then select the Pictures icon in the Places area and create a folder called *Images* to store your images in. If you are using a portable flash drive, double-click on the icon to open it and create a folder called *Images*. If you are using the Safari browser on your Mac, when saving an image from the Internet, you FIRST have to set up your download location in Preferences (Safari > Preferences). For this exercise, you can also just create a folder on the desktop and name it *Images*.

2. Connect to the Internet and find websites that contain images you would like to use for this exercise.

3. Using the Mac, press the Control key and then click the image to get the menu; when a display menu comes up, select the option Save Image As (earlier versions use Download Image to Disc). Another option you may find useful is to select Save image to Images and it will automatically perform the operation. If, when you CTRL + click on the image, the menu is not displayed, it is specially protected and cannot be copied. Find another set of images.

4. Locate the *Images* folder you created to store the images, and select Save. Your image will download to that folder.

5. Repeat until you have enough images to use in your electronic slide show. Try to keep your images the same size, it makes a better slide presentation.

Windows 7

1. If you are using the computer hard drive, select Start > Pictures, and create a folder called *Images* (New Folder). If you are using a portable drive or network drive, just create a folder called *Images*. For this exercise, you can also just create a folder on the desktop and name it *Images*.

2. Connect to the Internet and select websites that contain images you would like to use for this exercise.

3. Using Windows, right-click the image you have selected, and select Save Picture As. If, when you right-click on the image, the menu is not displayed, it is specially protected and cannot be copied. Find another set of images.

4. Locate the *Images* folder you created within the Pictures location, and select Save. Your image will download to that folder.

5. Repeat until you have enough images to use in your electronic slide show. Try to keep your images the same size, it makes a better slide presentation.

GATHERING FILE INFO AND PREVIEWING IMAGES

Once images are stored, it is a good idea to preview them before adding them to your slide show. Previewing helps you see if the image is too small, because they usually display at full size. It also helps to know what type of file you are using. It is important whenever working with electronic files to keep the file size as small as possible, while still maintaining image quality. Photographic files for electronic media should contain a universal extension, like .JPG, which indicates a compressed file format to keep the file size small. Or they may be saved with a .GIF extension for graphics. We will cover these aspects more in depth in later chapters.

• To see information about a file on the Mac, locate the photos in your *Images* folder, then click the image and select File > Get Info.

• To see what file extension is used in Windows, right-click on the image, then select Properties. Select the Details tab to see the file data.

• Most of the time, images will be either a JPEG of GIF file, such as photoname.jpg, which is fine for this exercise. Make sure your images have JPEG extensions for our purposes here. Other types will be discussed later. Also look for images with a range of a width of between 200 and 400 pixels for your slide show.

• To quickly view your images in Mac OS X, use Cover Flow View.

• To quickly view your images in Windows, use the Computer function to select the folder, and change the view to Extra Large icons to view good sized thumbnails.

• Note: If you double-click on an image and it opens up an application like Photoshop as the default application, check to see if the image is displayed at 100% in the toolbar. That way, you will know it will display on screen full size at 72 DPI, as if it were going to be used for the web. If not, use the View menu and select other options. More on that in Chapter 3.

MAC OS X: CREATING A SLIDE SHOW USING QUICK LOOK

The Mac OS X Leopard version has a Quick Look function that looks like an eye icon to create quick slide shows. This program works great when you need a simple slideshow of selected files that can even be displayed full screen.

Check out your images using Quick Look.

1. Locate your folder Images you just created.

2. Select the images you want to have in the slideshow, make sure you select the image files, not just the folder (Figure 1-29).

3. Click the Quick Look (eye) button on the Tools menu bar, or press the Space bar.

▷ FIGURE 1-29

The Quick Look function is a fast, easy way to view your images, and play a slideshow.

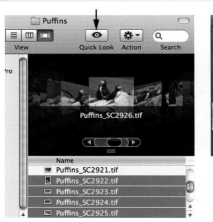

Play Slideshow   Index View   Full Screen

Select files for slideshow, then click Quick Look eye icon

4. A Quick Look window opens with the first selected image displayed.

5. Use the buttons along the bottom to move from slide to slide or switch to full screen view, or click on the index view to see thumbnails of your selected images.

6. To play the slideshow, just click on the large Play icon.

7. Select ESC key when done. Quick Look can also be used for all kinds of documents and files as well.

MAC OS X: CREATING A SLIDE SHOW USING PREVIEW

The Preview application is used not only for slideshows; you can also perform basic editing operations where you can resize and make adjustments to images and you can view all kinds of documents, as well as images. You can display a slideshow of all the images in a window, even at full screen, and controls at the bottom of the screen let you move from image to image or end the slideshow. You can also make annotated notes on files with Preview.

▷ FIGURE 1-30

Preview not only provides full screen slideshows, but also allows you to resize images, view all kinds of electronic documents, and make annotated comments.

In this exercise, you will use the Preview application to view a full screen slideshow of your *Images* folder.

1. Select Go > Applications > Preview and launch the Preview application.

2. Select File > Open and locate your *Images* folder you created.

3. You do not have to select the individual images, just the folder and all images will display in the Preview display.

4. Notice you have various options for what you can do with your images, including what view they can be displayed.

5. To view a full screen slide show, select View > Slideshow.

6. Press the ESC key when you have finished.

There are other applications that come with MAC OS X that, among other media uses, will also play image slideshows. Apple's free QuickTime application is one, which plays one image at a time, while predominantly playing downloaded movies from the Internet. Although beyond the scope of this book, Front Row in Mac OS X is a media center program that allows you to connect to the TV from your computer if it includes Apple Remote. Then you can view not only slide shows, but also TV shows, movies, music, and podcasts from another iTunes library on your network.

Earlier versions of Mac OS X included iPhoto. In the Leopard Mac OS X version iPhoto is part of the iLife suite that is purchased separately and is inexpensive. This is a great application for graphic designers to organize and display graphic work and photos. You'll find a tutorial on using iPhoto in the Goodies > Chap 1 folder on your text CD.

WINDOWS 7: CREATING AN ELECTRONIC SLIDE SHOW FROM THE PICTURES LIBRARY

Storing your images in the Pictures library section on your computer's hard drive allows quick access to folders of images when you select the Pictures link. By creating a folder of your images in Pictures, it allows you to make choices about what you want to do with the images, including displaying a slide show of a folder's contents (see Figure 1-31). Windows 7 users will find that the operating system prefers the user to place images in its Pictures library, which allows you to use the applications discussed here. If you have folders of images in the Pictures library, you can also use Windows Media Player, which not only is used for playing music but can also play slideshows of images, and burn CDs of your work. You can also select image files, create tags, and rate each image. Note: If you are on a secure network, you may not be able to perform this exercise.

1. If you are using a flash drive, you can use the Computer function to locate the Images folder you created, then select to "Include in library" and copy the folder into the Pictures library. If you are using your computer's hard drive, select Start > Pictures, or locate the Pictures library with the Windows Explorer icon, and locate the folder *Images* you created.

2. On the left sidebar, you will find libraries, including Pictures. Select the folder *Images* you created, and click on the *Slide Show* tab button below the Tools menu bar (you will notice there are other choices besides the slide show). View your images.

3. Press the ESC key on your keyboard to stop the slide show.

4. Other selections allow you to e-mail, print, or publish your images to a website. You can also burn a CD of your images from here.

▷ FIGURE 1-31

From the Windows Pictures library, select folder of images, then click the Slide Show button. Windows Media Player can also create professional slide shows.

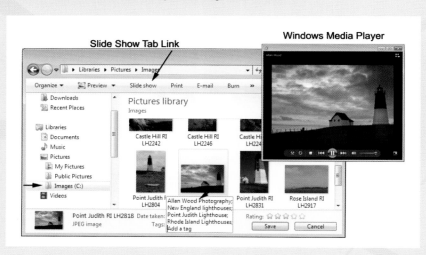

5. If you have folders of images in the Pictures library, you can also use Windows Media Player. Select Start > Windows Media Player or select the icon if it is pinned to the taskbar.

6. Select the *Images* folder to open, and select the Play button to play a professional looking slide show. Press ESC when finished.

7. EXTRA: To rate images and create captions, select the *Images* folder you created earlier inside the Pictures library. then select individual images and rate them using stars by selecting the number of stars for each image on the right side. You can also create tags or captions by typing in your tag and selecting Add Caption (Figure 1-31).

WINDOWS 7: CREATING AN ELECTRONIC SLIDE SHOW USING WINDOWS PHOTO VIEWER

The Windows Photo Viewer allows quick access to view, organize, edit, and print digital pictures (see Figure 1-32). When you plug a memory card from your digital camera or images from your flash drive into your computer, a dialog box opens to provide choices to transfer your images to the Pictures library, which is located on your hard drive. You can choose what you want to do with the images, including importing them or displaying a slide show of a folder's contents. You need to add images to the viewer first before you choose to edit or make changes. If you want to display images in a folder you already have created, select the folder, then right-click the first image and select to Open With > Windows Photo Viewer.

1. Locate the *Images* folder you created and double-click the folder to open it displaying the image files.

2. Right-click on the first image and when the dialog box displays, select Open With > Windows Photo Viewer. Note: Usually you can also double-click the image itself and it may default to open in Windows Photo Viewer.

3. When Windows Photo Viewer opens view your images as a full screen slide show by selecting the Slide Show button at the bottom middle of the display.

4. Press the ESC key on your keyboard to stop the show.

5. Extra: Other selections on the toolbar allow you to print, e-mail, or publish your images to a website. You can also burn a CD of your images from here.

▷ FIGURE 1-32

In Windows Photo Viewer, press the Slide Show button to view images in folder.

Slide Show

WINDOWS 7: DISPLAYING AN ELECTRONIC SLIDE SHOW USING WINDOWS MEDIA CENTER

The Windows Media Center allows you to view photos, movies, and all kinds of visual media full-screen on your computer or on your TV (see Figure 1-33). Photos display a very nice professional zoom technique to wow your audience. Simply import images first to the Pictures library on your hard drive, or create a folder to import your images in, right-click on the folder and select Include in library, then select Picture Library; locate the folder you want to display in Windows Media Center, and simply select Play Slide Show.

1. Select Start > All Programs > Windows Media Center.

2. When the program opens, select the Picture Library option from Pictures and Videos.

3. Option A: In the Picture Library, locate the folder *Images* you created (Computer > C:\ or Network drive, then locate your folder).

4. Option B: Previously, if you were using a media card from a digital camera, card reader, or flash drive, when you inserted the media, the dialog box would have displayed to allow you to Import images; select this option first to place images in the Pictures section. When images are imported, they are usually sorted automatically by date created; then, you can create folders to drag or copy the files into.

5. To enlarge images a little to see details before playing the slide show, let the mouse hover over the image and it will expand.

6. Select Play Slide Show to view your images. It will display images using appealing zoom techniques. Very cool!

7. To stop the show, select the Start Menu Windows icon (top left) to go back, or select the X (top right) to close the application.

▷ FIGURE 1-33

Using Windows Media Center to display slide shows, videos, and play music.

Windows Media Center

Windows Media Center is also used for not only photos and music, but also for recording live TV and free Internet TV. Another application that can be used for looking at your images is Picture Viewer, which is a component of the Quicktime movie application that also allows you to watch videos off the Internet.

DIGITAL TOOLKIT EXTRA: Burning Music, Photo, and Data CDs

Both Mac OS X and Windows 7 allow you to write or burn documents, images, video, and music onto recordable CDs or DVDs as long as you have a CD or DVD recorder drive. It is a good habit to backup important files and folders to a recordable medium, such as CDs, DVDs, USB flash drives, and portable pocket drives. Here you will learn how to burn the *Toolkit* folder on a backup CD and how to burn your favorite music CDs on either platform. You will find there are different applications for burning CDs.

MAC OS X: CREATING A DATA OR PHOTO CD

When you place a blank recordable CD in your Mac, a dialog box pops up asking what action you want to take. To burn data CDs of your important folders and files, and of your favorite images and music, you can use the Finder application (see Figure 1-34). Select the files you want to copy, hold down the Option key, and drag them onto the CD icon on the desktop. Then drag the CD icon into the Trash to burn the CD. Mac OS X burns discs that can also be used on Windows computers and other types of computers. You can also burn discs using applications such as Disk Utility, iTunes, iPhoto, or iDVD. If you frequently burn the same items to disc, create a burn folder by choosing File > New Burn Folder, and copy those items to it. Then, to create a disc with those items, open the burn folder and click Burn. If you want to burn items to a disc in more than one session until the disc is full, open Disk Utility in Applications/Utilities from the Finder desktop and follow the help instructions.

Here you will learn how to create a CD backup of your *Toolkit* folder from your hard drive.

1. Place a blank recordable CD in the CD recordable drive.

2. Choose Open Finder to use the Finder application from the dialog box menu; click OK and name the disk *Toolkit* (the iTunes application choice is best to burn audio files).

▷ FIGURE 1-34

Select the Finder application to copy data files and folders to a blank CD or DVD. Drag the files onto the CD or DVD icon on the desktop, then use the Trash icon to burn the CD or DVD; or create a burn folder to drag files into, then select File > Burn Disc.

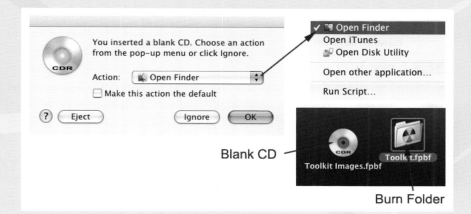

3. Double-click the hard drive icon and locate the *Toolkit* folder you created.

4. Select the *Toolkit* folder and hold down the Option key as you drag it to the CD disc icon on the desktop. Feel free to drag other files and folders onto the blank CD from a USB flash drive or other source.

5. When you have all the files you want to copy, drag the CD disc icon into the Trash icon on the Dock: It acts as a CD burning application.

6. Extra: In Mac OS X versions 10.2 and higher (see > About this Mac) if you are thinking about making multiple copies of the same contents, you can create a Burn Folder, like a suitcase to put your files in. To create a burn folder, select File > New Burn Folder from the Finder menu, then simply drag files and folders to the burn folder; it creates aliases temporarily until you are ready to copy or burn the original contents onto the blank CD. Then it locates the files chosen and helps to burn them onto a CD. When you are ready to burn the folder's contents to a disc, double-click it and then click Burn.

7. It will ask you to insert a blank disc: just follow the instructions.

Ⓧ PROBLEM If the Finder cannot find the original file for an alias shortcut while burning, it asks whether to cancel burning or to continue without that item. If you cancel, the disc remains empty. Another popular application you can purchase for easy disc burning is Toast, for Mac computers.

MAC OS X AND WINDOWS 7: CREATING MUSIC CDS USING ITUNES

The application iTunes lets you create your own personal digital music library, tune into Internet radio stations, download movies, download podcasts for an iPod, watch television shows, and burn your own audio CDs (see Figure 1-35). Before copying music tracks onto a blank CD, it is a good idea to import selected tracks from your music CD onto the iTunes music library first, or download paid songs from the iTunes music site. It converts them into compressed MP3 files to save space on your hard drive. Then create a Playlist and drag the music files you want to burn from your Library. Select your new Playlist, and burn the music CD using the Burn button at the bottom right of the iTunes window. This feature is also available for Windows platforms.

 TOOLKIT TIP You can also automatically add music files to the iTunes Library by creating a folder of songs on the desktop and selecting File > Add to Library. The newer versons of iTunes allow you to have playlists created for you using the Genius feature. The iTunes DJ will shuffle your songs for variety in playback.

Here you will learn how to import music files into the Library, how to create a Playlist, and how to burn your Playlist onto a blank CD.

1. Insert your music CD in computer, then select to import your CD tracks into the iTunes library.

2. When the iTunes window opens up with the list of your tracks, check only the ones you want to burn.

3. If songs do not start to import, click the Import button (or File > Import) to add the selected songs to the library. Once imported into the Library, they are compressed into MP3 files and are stored in the Music folder on the hard drive.

4. To create a Playlist of the files you want to link to on your hard drive, select File > New Playlist.

5. Type a name for the Playlist, then drag the songs you want into the Playlist you created. This would also be the same procedure if you wanted to burn songs downloaded from the iTunes store.

 FIGURE 1-35

The Macintosh iTunes program (also on Windows) allows you to create MP3 CDs of your favorite songs to be played on any computer or most stereo systems that will play MP3 compressed files.

Select tracks, import to Library, then create Playlist.
You can then drag selected songs to your playlist.

Import CD

Playlist name

Burn CD

To create MP3 music CD, insert blank CD, select favorite playlists to burn, then select Burn Disc button

6. To eject the music CD, select File > Eject, or, press the Media Eject key.

7. You can create regular audio CDs that can be played on any stereo or create compressed MP3 CDs that can be played on any computer or most CD players.

8. Insert a blank recordable CD, select iTunes as the application, select the Playlist or group of playlists you want to burn to the CD, and then click the Burn Disc button.

9. Have Fun!

TOOLKIT TIP If you are importing music copies and they appear as "track numbers", you can rename your files by selecting File > Get Info. When the song dialog box opens up, select Info and put in the song title, artist, and any other info. Select OK when done and the new title will be displayed in the music Library. Mac OS X also has the iPhoto application, which is in earlier MAC OS X versions, and is now part of the inexpensive iLIfe suite of fun applications. IPhoto allows you to create photo CDs of your images where the process is basically the same as in iTunes, in which chosen photos are stored in the Library. You create an album from the Library, and then you are ready to burn your images.

WINDOWS 7: CREATING DATA AND PHOTO CDS

When you need to create data CDs, photo CDs, or backup applications, Windows 7 allows you to copy files and folders onto a recordable (blank) CD or DVD, as long as you have a CD or DVD recorder drive.

Here you will learn how to create a copy of the *Toolkit* folder you just created. You can also use this technique to backup your important documents or your favorite digital images.

1. Insert a blank, writable CD or DVD in your CD or DVD drive recorder on your computer.

2. When the Blank CD options dialog box displays, click on the Burn files to disc link. The drive will then format or set up the CD or DVD to be able to burn files and folders (Figure 1-36). You'll be given a choice in the display "Like a USB flash" device, which allows you to delete files later as you would a regular flash drive, or the option "With a CD/DVD player", which allows you to burn a large collection of files. For this exercise select the CD/DVD option and label it *Toolkit*.

3. Locate the *Toolkit* folder you created on your hard drive, or locate files you want to burn.

4. With a window open displaying files you want to drag and burn, and the CD window of files and folders you want to drag contents to also open, resize both window displays and click and drag files and folders into the CD window. You will notice a copy files window to burn the selected contents onto your formatted CD or DVD (Figure 1-36).

5. Select the *Toolkit* folder, then select the Burn button in the Toolbar. Leave the default settings as the CD is being burnt.

6. To view the contents of your new CD, insert the CD or DVD; when the dialog window displays, select "Open folder to view files".

To burn data files or graphics files, select Burn files to disc, then choose how the new disc is to be used.

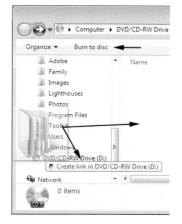

With CD/DVD drive highlighted,
Drag Toolkit folder to CD/DVD drive
or to the display box to the right side,
then select Burn to disc

▷ FIGURE 1-36
Once a blank CD/
DVD is formatted,
just select files and
folders and drag
them onto a CD/
DVD to copy con-
tents; the disc will
be burned for use
on any computer.

WINDOWS 7: CREATING MUSIC CDS USING WINDOWS MEDIA PLAYER

Windows has an application called **Windows Media Player**, which lets you create or burn your own audio and video CDs from files that you can drag over from folders on the computer or in the library of the Media Player itself.

Before copying music tracks to be burned on a recordable CD, they need to be placed in either a folder on the computer or in the Music library. Here you will copy or **rip** audio tracks from a music CD to the Music library, then copy the selected tracks from a Playlist to a blank recordable CD. **Ripping** involves converting audio music from store bought CDs (or those that have not been compressed or converted to MP3 format) to be used on the computer as MP3 compressed format (see Figure 1-37). If you are copying music that has simply been downloaded or already in MP3 compressed format, you won't need to rip your selected tracks. Skip those beginning steps.

TOOLKIT TIP When a music CD is inserted, it may default to play on Windows Media Center, depending on the computer's settings. Although ripping and burning music CDs is best served when using iTunes or Windows Media Player, you can also rip music to the Music library using Windows Media Center, then open up Windows Media Player to create playlists to burn new music CDs. To rip music to the Music library, insert a store bought (not MP3) music CD, then open Windows Media Center and select Rip CD from a tiny CD icon in the upper right of the window. Add your music to the library by checking those tracks you want to include, agree to understanding copyright when asked, and when the song is ripped, you'll find a check mark next to it. Then complete the playlist (Steps 4-9) using Windows Media Player.

This CD is from iTunes, and will not copy names

To Rip tracks to MP3 format, Select tracks, then select Rip. When finished, select Create playlist, and name the new playlist.

Ripping Using Windows Media Player

With original music CDs, names are also transferred.

With a playlist created, drag tracks to playlist window to add, then save.

Ripping Using Windows Media Center

▷ FIGURE 1-37

To copy music CDs, use Windows Media Player or Windows Media Center to convert, or rip, music tracks to the library; then create a Playlist using Windows Media Player by dragging selected tracks.

1. Insert a music CD into the CD drive; it will usually default to open Windows Media Player, and a Now Playing tab will be selected. If you insert a music CD and the CD dialog window displays, select Play Audio CD. You can also open the Media Player by choosing Start > Windows Media Player.

2. To prepare to burn to a blank CD, when Windows Media Player opens up, select the Rip tab, and set the Format to MP3. Set any other preferences and leave only the tracks you want to copy checked, and uncheck the rest.

3. With the tracks selected, click on the Start Rip button on the bottom of the window. Each track will be copied to the library, which will hold all your music (Figure 1-34).

4. Select the Library tab menu to display the tracks added to the library; select Create Playlist, then name the Playlist (Figure 1-34).

5. Drag the selected tracks from the Recently Added section on the left or from your CD tracks to your new Playlist on the right side. It will display how much is left: usually 10 megabytes (MB) equals one minute of audio play.

6. To burn the selected tracks from the Playlist to a recordable CD, select the Burn tab; click the Burn tab again for the menu and select Audio CD to Burn (see Figure 1-35).

7. Remove the music CD and insert a blank recordable disc; select Erase to format the disc.

8. Select whatever Playlist you want copied, and click check boxes for tracks that you want to copy. To add additional albums or tracks from the library, drag from the Details Pane display on the left side to the List Pane with the CD icon on the right. You can also right-click the album icon of tracks in the library, and select Add to Burn List.

9. With enough tracks in the Playlist, drag the tracks around for a specific order, then select Start Burn. The rest of the process is automatic, and the CD will eject when the CD copying is completed. That's it!

TOOLKIT TIP Do not copy more files than the CD can handle (650 to 800 MB depending on the CD) or you will receive a *What to do?* display or a *Will not fit* warning. You cannot burn additional tracks to the CD after copying is completed. If your computer has the capability to write to a DVD, then you have at least 4 gigabytes (GB) to play with.

▷ FIGURE 1-38

With a Playlist created, a blank CD can be turned into a music CD.

Select Burn tab, insert blank CD, drag selected tracks, and select Start burn to create music CD.

CHAPTER SUMMARY

As a designer or photographer, it is important to have a basic understanding of both Windows 7 and Mac OS X operating systems when working with files from various clients. In this chapter, you were able to learn the basics of Windows 7 and Mac OS X operating systems, their similarities and differences, and how to use files on both systems when possible. You also had an opportunity to navigate around each system. You got a taste of similarities in terms of various functions and keystrokes with different names applied. Folders were created to copy the text exercise files and create a manageable work environment. You played with various techniques and functions to keep your desktop organized, and to find your recently used applications and files quickly. In the Advanced Users section you created electronic slide shows using various applications that come with Mac OS X and Windows operating systems. In the Digital Toolkit Extra section, you learned to burn music, photo, and data CDs.

REVIEW QUESTIONS

1. Explain why Macintosh computers are preferred over Windows in most graphic environments.

2. Explain eight different functions and keys that have the same result on either system.

3. Why do PCs need to have files saved with extensions?

4. What is the purpose of file management to the designer or photographer?

5. Name some of the applications used within Mac OS X and Windows 7 operating systems to create slide shows and burn music and photo CDs.

▷ FIGURE 1-39

CHAPTER 1

File management projects and desktop fun using Macintosh OS X (top) or Windows 7 (bottom) operating systems.

Macintosh OS X Leopard Desktop

Windows 7 Desktop

▷ FIGURE 1-40

CHAPTER 1: ADVANCED

Applications included in Mac OS X and Windows 7 used in creating electronic slide shows.

Mac OS X Quick Look

Mac OS X Preview

Slide Show Tab Link

Windows Media Player

Windows 7 Pictures Library Toolbar

Windows 7 Photo Viewer

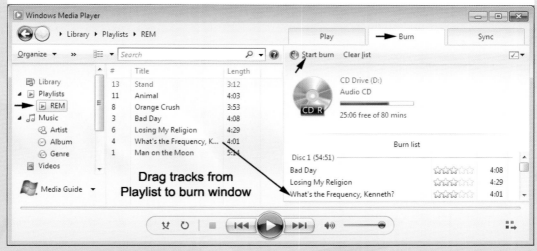

▷ FIGURE 1-41

CHAPTER 1: EXTRA

Creating music Playlists in libraries to burn music CDs using iTunes (top) and Windows Media Player (bottom).

2

Designing for the Client

CHAPTER OBJECTIVES: To understand the importance of design in creating the appropriate message for the intended audience, in this chapter you will:

▷ Learn the elements and principles of design.

▷ Learn the importance of using visual imagery, color, and typography to convey a message.

▷ Learn the design process, from working with a client to developing a concept to creating final proofs.

▷ Install fonts for the text exercises on Mac OS platform.

▷ Create thumbnail sketches and a final rough for client approval.

▷ ADVANCED USERS: Identify design elements and principles used in various ads.

▷ DIGITAL TOOLKIT EXTRA: Use Internet resources to research tutorials and locate application information.

It is great to have talent, because this will get you in the door to meet with a potential client. However, discipline and responsibility go a long way toward developing a profitable and rewarding career in graphics. Issues such as keeping deadlines, being a good communicator with a client, and establishing good relations will help ensure continued success and provide a network for new clientele. Always remember: you are not creating for your enjoyment; you are creating for your clients. In the final analysis, they determine what they like, whether you agree or not. This chapter will take you through the basic design principles and elements, the importance of typography and visual imagery, and the design processes involving the client.

 Need additional fun computer graphics tutorials and info, and an additional look at the projects you'll be creating in this book? Check out my Artist's Digital Toolkit website at: **http://www.digitoolkit.com**

ELEMENTS OF DESIGN

The placement of elements within a design, page, or website will have much influence on what kind of message is perceived by what kind of market. Formal design elements that are the basic building blocks of design are *line, shape, color, texture, value,* and *format.* Designers also use illusions of depth and motion to help create a 3-D effect on a 2-D surface. For every design, you are trying to communicate something. These physical elements of design are your communication tools; knowing when and how to use these elements is essential to building a successful design. All these formal elements are interdependent, and they interact to complement one another and function as a team.

LINES AND SHAPES

The way a line moves determines the type of line it is. **Lines** can be straight, angular, or curved, and they may be drawn in horizontal, vertical, or diagonal directions. A line's visual quality is determined by how the line is drawn, whether thick or thin, broken or smooth. **Shapes** are usually considered closed forms or outlines. How a shape is drawn, like a curved shape or an angular shape, gives it a specific quality. A designer uses lines as outlines or edges to create shapes, like a pyramid or a circle (Figure 2-1). Color can also define a shape without lines. If the color creates an edge, it also defines the shape.

| Strength | Peaceful | Graceful | Shape (defined by lines) | Shape (defined by color) |

▷ FIGURE 2-1

The manner in which lines and shapes are drawn defines various forms within a design.

TEXTURE

Texture describes surface quality, like rust, velvet, or sandpaper. The two categories of texture in the artistic sense are *tactile* and *visual*. **Tactile texture** involves the actual feeling of a surface texture like a sculpture. Designers and artists use **visual texture** to create the illusion of texture in artwork, using varying line qualities, patterns, or adjusting the value and colors of an element. Computers can create digital textures through various filters and effects within software programs (Figure 2-2).

▷ FIGURE 2-2

Value and texture help to determine the viewer's emotional response.

Logos displaying value and texture

High contrast images evoke a different response than low contrast images

VALUE

Value determines depth and dimension by the range of lightness or darkness of an element. Value is the shading, tonality, and tint of a color (light blue and dark blue). The use of shading can help provide a three-dimensional value to an image. Value creates a focal point or center of attention. **Value contrast** is the relationship between black and white or lightness and darkness of an image, and it is a result of the relationship between different elements; it produces both visual and emotional effects. As the viewer observes an image and interprets its value, the eye is drawn to light areas first, which the designer or artist can use to provide contrast and balance in an image.

Values in color and contrast can provoke a variety of emotional responses. Low contrast or closely related values can evoke a sense of calmness or tranquility, while high-contrast images or sharp-value images can create a sense of excitement, drama, or conflict between elements. An overall darker image can promote a sense of mystery or even sadness, while an overall lighter image invites the viewer with an uplifting tone or feeling of relaxation.

DEPTH PERCEPTION

In the two-dimensional world of drawings, photographs, paintings, and prints, designers often need to convey a feeling of space or depth perception. Some of the elements that convey these characteristics are the sizes of objects and their relationship to one another, the overall blending of colors and shapes by adjusting tonal values, and the point of view or depth perspective. By varying the size of similar shapes—for example, rectangles—the illusion is more pronounced than with differing shapes. Spatial depth is more pronounced if shapes become smaller as they overlap, creating the illusion of objects receding (Figure 2-3). This is a form of **spatial recession**. By combining elements and blending the tonal values to match the background, the illusion of receding into the background creates an even more pronounced sense of depth. **Tonal value** involves the lightness and darkness of an image by varying its tone or value to the surrounding background. In landscape, objects are placed in the foreground to give a feeling of depth; or **framing techniques** are employed in which another subject surrounds the main subject for emphasis. Using tree branches in the foreground, for instance, provides emphasis to a distant subject.

▷ FIGURE 2-3

One way of creating the illusion of special depth is to make similar shapes smaller, so they appear to recede into the background.

PERSPECTIVE AND ANGLE OF VIEW

Artists and photographers create images that show a higher or lower point of view that can enhance the feeling of depth in an image. One technique involves the use of **linear perspective**. This is where a horizon line is placed to approximate the eye level of the artist. From this line, invisible lines or edges—called *vanishing points*—are directed to lead the viewer into the image. **One-point perspective** involves using converging lines to lead the eye to a subject or point along a horizontal line to provide depth in perspective within the image. **Two-point perspective** involves a more natural approach, similar to how we view the world around us, at an angle with two edge points along the horizon line. In this view, vanishing points recede at either end of a horizontal line. Vertical lines would be parallel to the edges of the picture. An example would be if the viewer were standing on a city street corner, taking a photo of the buildings; there would be little or no vertical convergence, but rather parallel alignment of the sides of the buildings. It is not as dramatic an approach as using converging lines, and it permits the viewer to scan an image from one edge to the other.

Artists can also use fences, roads, stairways, and other techniques in compositions involving **leading lines** to create the effect of depth perception. **Aerial perspective** uses the lighter background contrast of the atmosphere with darker subjects that are closer to the viewer in landscapes to show a sense of depth. The background recedes to the lighter contrast from the darker foreground subject. To add drama to an image, artists and photographers constantly create images from lower and higher angles than a viewer's normal eye level (Figure 2-4).

▷ FIGURE 2-4

Linear perspective uses vanishing points along a horizontal plane. Changing the angle of view (above or below the subject) can add drama to images.

USING MOTION

Creating the illusion of motion can suggest an anticipation of movement either in slow motion or in what is termed as **stop action** (Figure 2-5). Artists use these techniques to trigger memories or record events, or with special effects like blurring water to give an image an ethereal quality. The feeling of movement can also be heightened by contrast, showing activity. Repeating figures or multi-exposed images have also been used to create the illusion of motion.

▷ FIGURE 2-5
Using images that employ a sense of motion is a technique that enhances anticipation.

COLOR

Color is one of the most powerful design elements. A designer needs to understand which colors are appropriate to complement the message. Color is based on wavelengths of light and contains a wide range of visual differences and contrasts. Color is divided into three categories: *hue, value,* and *saturation.* **Hue** is the name of the color (red, green, and blue). **Value** is the shading, tonality, or tint of a color (light and dark blue). **Saturation** is the intensity of color (bright red or dull red).

In design, a color wheel that displays basic colors and their **complementary colors**, or opposite colors, is used as a guideline. Most color wheels use 12 color hues as the basis for all color mixtures. With pigment colors that are used for painting or traditional artwork, the **traditional primary colors** are *red, yellow,* and *blue.* These are the main colors that create all others. For instance, combining red and yellow creates orange. The **secondary colors** are *orange, green,* and *purple,* and they can be further mixed for many color variations. The six **tertiary colors** are created by mixing one primary and one secondary color. They consist of *yellow orange, red orange, red violet, blue violet, blue green,* and *yellow green* (Figure 2-6).

Color intensity or saturation is the brightness of a color. To lower a color's intensity without changing its value, a designer can add gray or combine the color with its complementary color, which is the color across from it on the color wheel. When complementary colors are placed next to each other, their brightness is intensified. For example, the opposite of orange is blue; a designer might package oranges using blue lettering to highlight the fruit, thus making it look fresher. When various colors are coordinated together in the color scheme of an image, warm colors like reds, yellows, and oranges generally seem to come forward, while cool colors like blues, greens, and purples appear to fade to the back. High-contrast colors appear to come forward visually, while low-contrast colors appear to recede. Low-intensity versions of a color are generally considered the *tones* of a color. Colors mixed with neutral grays can result in different **tones** of color.

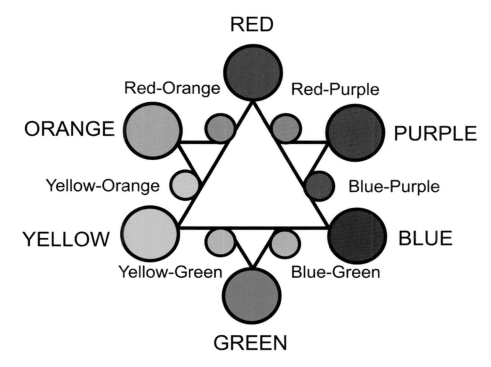

DESIGN TIP

Theoretically, the three primary colors used for printing (CMY) would combine to produce black; however, this may result in a more muddy color due to impurities in the ink pigments. Black ink is added as a fourth color to create true black and add contrast to images.

Colors created on the computer are made by adding the primary colors of light, *red, green,* and *blue* (*RGB*), which act differently than pigment but are fine for electronic document design such as web pages. The colors *cyan, magenta, yellow,* and *black* (*CMYK*) are used for commercial printing. Color plates used in commercial printing use the colors *cyan, magenta,* and *yellow* (*CMY*) as the basis for creating all other colors for print. *Black* (*K*) is then added for purity and contrast.

FORMAT, GUIDELINES, AND GRIDS

Brochures, CD covers, business cards, and posters are some of the **formats** designers use for their clients. The project the client brings to you will determine the format. Your design should work well within the given format. Formats have advantages and limitations that need to be considered in creating a particular design. For instance, will the final layout be a vertical or **portrait orientation**, or a horizontal display of elements, called a **landscape orientation**? What size paper and shape will it be? How will it be used, and where will it be seen? These are all considerations as you work with a particular format.

Most graphic computer applications have a set of rulers, or ruler guides, displayed along the top and left side of the document that a designer can use for measuring. A designer can click and drag from one of the ruler guides onto the document, creating what are called **guidelines**. These nonprintable guidelines are used for exact placement of specific sized text and graphics boxes on brochures, flyers, web pages, and so on. They also can be used to create **margin guides,** usually purple or blue in color, for outer margins and for spacing between text and graphic boxes for folding procedures and alignment (Figure 2-7).

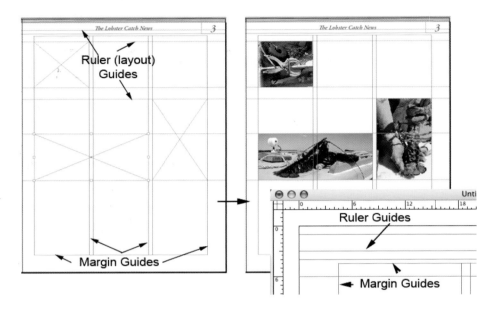

Grids are developed from a network of intersecting horizontal and vertical guidelines. Designers use grids for consistent placement and spacing of text and graphic elements within a unified theme on successive pages to create catalogs, books, newsletters, pamphlets, magazines, and so forth.

DESIGN PRINCIPLES

A designer must be careful to understand the client's needs. By researching what the client wants to convey to the target market, the designer will be able to create the appropriate message. Principles in design are followed to combine individual elements into one harmonious piece. This involves taking various elements and providing proper balance, adding selective emphasis to create a focal point, using rhythm to set the mood, and establishing unity.

BALANCE

The concept of balance is to arrange elements within an area so that these elements promote a harmonious response. Visual balance is determined by the weight, position, and arrangement of elements (Figure 2-8). Balance can be formal, informal, or radial. **Formal balance**, also referred to as **symmetrical balance**, places elements with equal distribution to convey trustworthiness and integrity, as used by

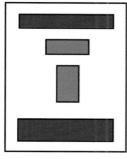
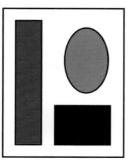
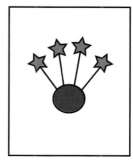

▷ FIGURE 2-8

Balance is the arrangement of various elements and their visual weights within the composition.

Formal Balance
(centered)

Informal Balance
(off-centered)

Radial Balance
(equal value)

financial institutions or insurance companies. **Informal balance**, also referred to as *asymmetrical balance,* uses elements that counterbalance one another instead to create a harmonious composition. This type of balance gives the appearance of being casual, energetic, or trendy. **Radial balance** arranges elements around a central point and is used to promote unity or teamwork.

USE OF NEGATIVE AND POSITIVE SPACE

Using empty or **negative space**, absent of visual elements, is a visual element in itself that actually does more to promote luxury or elegance, and sometimes a sense of mystery, than most other effects. This may utilize the "less is more" concept in design. **Positive space** uses content to fill up space to identify or explain something in a particular page. In an ad using empty space, a line of black type on a white background, or a line of white type on a black background, can change perception of the content of the page (Figure 2-9). Reversing colors sometimes makes an ad stand out in a crowd of ads. Care needs to be taken in the use of empty space over positive space, including type size in relation to the graphic.

▷ FIGURE 2-9

Positive space fills the frame with descriptive imagery and text. Negative space promotes elegance or mystery. Which message caught your eye first?

Create projects designers may encounter using Photoshop, Illustrator, and InDesign.

Learn what you need to know.

Come play...

digitoolkit.com

digitoolkit.com

EMPHASIS

Emphasis provides direction to various elements in a given design, promoting the concept that some things are more important than others. To find and decide what is most important, the reader searches for a focal point in a design. A primary focal point can be established with accents that lead the viewer to it. A **focal point** can be determined by an element's size, shape, color, texture, or position in the layout. Emphasis can be created by contrast, where one element differs from the surrounding elements, and by isolation, where an element is removed or isolated from the surrounding elements. Use of color or an element that is lighter than its surroundings draws attention to that subject.

Placement is another useful technique to emphasize the subject. In many cases, an artist may visibly divide an image into thirds for placement of elements within the composition. This technique is called the **Rule of Thirds** (Figure 2-10). Placing the subject in a noncentered position or off balance draws attention and keeps the elements of the composition from appearing static.

▷ FIGURE 2-10

Emphasis provides direction and focal point for elements in a composition.

RHYTHM

Rhythm is a visual pattern of repeating elements that creates a sense of movement (Figure 2-11). It is constantly used in printed media as well as in architecture. Variation in rhythm can be adjusted by changing the shape, size, color, spacing,

▷ FIGURE 2-11

Rhythm is a visual pattern leading the viewer through certain elements before others.

and position of elements in a design. This change in arrangement helps to promote the mood of the design. The viewer looks at certain elements before others.
Those elements that are larger, darker, or have a more unusual shape than their
surrounding counterparts are used to draw the viewer's eyes into the composition.

UNITY

Unity is the organization of elements in a design as though they belong together
(Figure 2-12). It allows the designer to view individual components as one integrated whole. Unity establishes continuity with a variety of elements and promotes
consistency within the piece, and it combines balance, rhythm, type, imagery,
and tone to evoke a particular emotion from the viewer.

▷ FIGURE 2-12

**Unity is the organi-
zation of visual ele-
ments as part of an
integrated whole.**

DESIGN STAGES: FROM CONCEPT TO COMPLETION

A design solution's "personality" is created when the formal elements of color,
line, shape, texture, format, and value are put together using the principles of
graphic design in spacial relationships, balance, rythm, emphasis, and unity. These
elements collaborate to elicit the kind of audience reaction the client desires.

WORKING WITH THE CLIENT

The whole idea behind designing is being able to solve problems visually that help
the client best communicate his or her message. Before you start designing, talk to
your client and listen; then keep your client involved in the process (Figure 2-13).

• Listen to the client to understand the design challenge. Make the client feel
involved. Try to assist gently when suggesting changes you feel would create a
better product, but do not make the client feel incompetent. You need to fully
understand the client's project in order to help.

• You need to know the market the design is intended for and what the client's design
specifications are. Is this design going to be used for print and electronic media?

Listen to the client's needs and keep them involved in the design process.

If so, then understanding different ways images and text are going to be presented for each medium is crucial to the success of the project.

• What materials are needed for the project, and what is your experience with these materials? What software or hardware are you comfortable with, and which ones will require that you rely on others for expertise?

• Know your budget and guidelines. Complete as much research as possible so you will be able to stay within your estimate. Set a time frame for completion of various components of the project.

THE DESIGNING PROCESS

Graphic design begins with a visual concept—the main idea behind creating the design piece. Before coming up with a concept, you need to plan a strategy and set design objectives that meet your client's needs. Then research information, material, and visuals about your subject, and start writing down your ideas. Make changes and decisions on those ideas with the client, and then generate final comps for the intended media.

Thumbnails

▷   FIGURE 2-14

Thumbnails are sketched variations of an idea.

Thumbnails are sketched variations of an idea (Figure 2-14). Once you have your design idea, thumbnails help create different possibilities for that idea. Create a dozen or more thumbnails, and then narrow them down to about six to ten per concept to show the client. For consistency, make thumbnails the same proportion as the final piece.

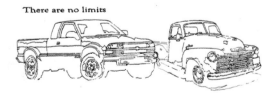

Roughs

Roughs are created as a result of combining specific elements from each thumbnail, or they may be the result of one good thumbnail (Figure 2-15). A rough is a full-size rendition of your design, including the layout of images and text and overall compositional elements that you show to the client. This version can be created while still at the drawing stage, or it can be done on the computer. The final rough usually must be created on the computer. Generating three to six roughs gives the client a good idea of what the final design will look like.

▷ FIGURE 2-15

Roughs are full-size representations created from elements in various thumbnails.

Comps

Comps show exactly what the final design will look like when printed. The designer must take painstaking efforts to make sure everything is exactly what the client had agreed to in the final rough. This is where all text, color, imagery, and compositional elements need to come together for the final client approval before going to press, electronic media, or both (Figure 2-16).

▷ FIGURE 2-16

Comps show the client exactly what the final design will look like when printed. In this case, the client wanted a painted effect for the final printed design.

Final Proofs for Press

The client should have the proof that provides instructions for the pressman and finishing operator. The **print proof** should show indications for folding, cutting, bleeding, trapping, registration, and any special requirements (this will be covered in depth in future chapters). Keep in mind that most ink-jet proofs will not show exact color but may be close enough for client approval, as long as the client understands before going to press that there may be a slight difference in some colors in the final product. Another final proof will be generated at the print site, provided for and to be approved by the client, so he or she knows precisely what all the elements will look like. The designer should also furnish a disc to the client with fonts and images used, along with any other specific information needed.

Final Electronic Proofs for Electronic Media

For website designers or multimedia designers, the **electronic media proof** should show indications for pixel dimensions, software used, resolution requirements, text and image locations, and information, if needed, for publishing to the web, along with any special requirements. A *final printed proof* is also needed for checking layout of type, imagery, and all elements used, along with the final layout supplied on disc to the client. The client should have the disc contents checked on a calibrated monitor to see as closely as possible what the web page or site will look like. When working with a limited color palette for web design, the client needs to check carefully to make sure that the colors are as accurate as possible to be displayed on the web. It must also be noted that colors on a Mac and colors on a PC vary slightly in their display.

TYPOGRAPHY

Typography is the study and use of text in a document. A designer uses type in titles or headlines and in the body of the document to enhance an ad; it helps to establish a mood or theme in the design or document (Figure 2-17). A **type family**, sometimes referred to as a **typeface**, is a group of fonts that share a basic character construction, like the Arial family, which includes Arial Black, Arial Narrow, Arial Alternative, and so on, similar to having your family of uncles, aunts, cousins, and grandparents. A **font** is a set of characters such as Arial, Times New Roman, Verdana, or Wingdings by themselves, like your immediate family. A **font size** is measured in **points** instead of inches (1 point = 1/72 inch). When you open a document, the default size is usually 12 points. When you need to bold, underline, or italicize type, you are creating a change to that type by applying a **font style**.

CHARACTER AND LINE SPACING

The spacing between characters and lines of text also determines how that type looks on your document. **Tracking** adjusts the spacing between characters and words. Adjusting the tracking of words too tightly in a paragraph can make it difficult to read, whereas adjusting too loosely can create "rivers" of white spacing in a paragraph, especially when type is either left or right justified. Sometimes a designer will create a loose tracking effect on a single word, or a few words, in the title of an ad or magazine cover as an attention getter. **Kerning** is a technique used for pairs of characters in titles or headlines that may need to be

DESIGN TIP

Typography should enhance a message, not detract from it, by using typefaces that are appropriate to the message. Color of type should also play a vital role in enhancing the visual expression but should not hinder readability. Because our eyes tend to read the largest elements first, such as headlines or titles, create a visual hierarchy for your text.

brought closer together for a more consistent look. **Leading** refers to the spacing between lines of text. Usually the default leading is 120 percent of the letter size for most documents.

This is a 12 point "Arial Regular" Font
This is a 12 point "Arial Regular" font with an Italicized style.
This is a 12 point "Arial Black" font in the Arial family
This is an18 point size "Arial Regular" Font

In long articles or newsletters, less space between lines of text tends to darken the document, whereas more space will lighten it up. The message or mood you want to convey will determine how you will set up your text and what fonts you will need. The style or arrangement of setting type is called **type alignment**. Left aligned flushes the type to the left and is easy to read; we associate right aligned with professional return addresses on letters. Centered lines of type are used in some headlines or titles, while **justified alignment** places text equally on left and right sides in a column (Figure 2-18).

▷ FIGURE 2-17
Typography consists of typeface families, measured in points, with some special styles applied.

DESIGN TIP
Word and line spacing creates the specific rhythm or pace at which the viewer reads the message. Alignment or arrangement of type should enahnce readbility.

▷ FIGURE 2-18
Character and line spacing, along with the alignment of type, help set a particular mood or send a message.

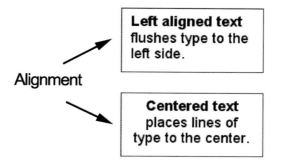

LOOSE TRACKING
TIGHT TRACKING
Leading
Kerning → AW AW

Alignment

Left aligned text flushes type to the left side.

Right-aligned text flushes lines of type to the right.

Centered text places lines of type to the center.

Justified text aligns type equally on both sides of a column.

CATEGORIES OF TYPE

Two main categories of type are *serif type* and *sans-serif type.* **Serif type** characters contain what look like "feet," or extended strokes, on the tops and bottoms; these are used to convey a conservative look and make it easier to read long articles or bodies of text. **Sans-serif type** has characters without these strokes, and it is more legible for labeling illustrations, headlines, and titles. **ASCII type** is the American standard of type: it is plain text and unformatted and can be read by any application or computer. It uses the extension .TXT. Other type categories include script type, decorative type, and symbol type (Figure 2-19). **Script fonts** are typically used in announcements or invitations and convey the appearance of being created with a pen or brush. **Decorative type** is sometimes used in headlines to create a specific meaning, and **symbol type** is a collection of related symbols, often called *dingbats,* that can be used for bullets, map symbols, or logos. The type you select should be appropriate and must complement your design.

▷ FIGURE 2-19

The five main categories of type are *serif, sans serif, script, decorative,* **and** *symbol type.*

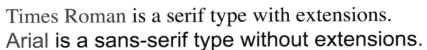

Times Roman is a serif type with extensions.
Arial is a sans-serif type without extensions.
Brush Script MT is a script type used in invitations.
Papyrus is used as a decorative type.
● ⓘ ✹ ▶▶ 🚲 ✔ Symbol type (Webdings) for bullets, logos, etc.

USING TYPE IN PRINT MEDIA

Here are a few design guidelines for starters when creating text documents to be printed:

• Use the same fonts and sizes for various headings in the same document. If you have to use different fonts, stick with the same type family for consistency.

• Use 10- or 12-point size serif type minimum for the body of text for easier reading on printed material.

• Use italics sparingly and infrequently, for emphasis only.

• When using text type, do not use type in all upper case and do not allow too much or too little spacing between lines of type. Use the default leading on your word processor as a guide.

DESIGN TIP

A designer needs to be very careful when combining different fonts together; look at whether they enhance the message appropriately; use contrast and weight, and provide a visual hierarchy. Fonts need to be similar to carry a consistent message, so try using fonts within the same type family.

TOOLKIT TIP To create universal text document files that can be read by older Mac and Windows systems, save with .RTF extensions for text that contains formatting commands like bold or italic, or use .TXT extensions for plain text. If you do not have Microsoft Word applications, both operating systems have basic ASCII word processors. You can open Wordpad in Windows (Start > All Programs > Accessories > Wordpad), or use TextEdit in Macintosh OS X (Go > Applications > TextEdit). Microsoft Office Word now works well between Macs and PCs.

USING TYPE FOR ELECTRONIC MEDIA

Here are a few design guidelines when creating electronic documents:

DESIGN TIP

On older computers, to create universal text document files that can be read by both Mac and PC, save with .RTF extensions for text that contains formatting commands like bold or italic, or use .TXT extensions for plain text. Plain text is used in HTML programming for web Pages. Microsoft Word can be used on both platforms.

• Try using sans-serif fonts especially for light-colored text against a dark or black background for easier reading. Bolder fonts also work better when reversing type out of a solid or textured background.

• Use a minimum 12-point size for body text, because text is displayed electronically and can be tiring on the eyes over periods of time.

• Use color for emphasis of graphic statements. Electronic media is a great means for entertaining visual stimulation.

• Usually it helps to keep sentences short and use small paragraphs to hold the reader's interest.

INSTALLING FONTS FOR TEXT ASSIGNMENTS (OPTIONAL)

Whether you are designing ads or creating multipage newsletters, text is one of the most important elements of any design. The CD for this book contains fonts that can be used on Macs. They are in a Fonts folder on the CD, because fonts in Windows may not exactly match the same fonts in Mac OS X. You will copy the fonts from the CD to the *Fonts* folder on the Mac hard drive (Figure 2-20). For any of the exercises you may always use your own standard fonts, although you may find issues in terms of spacing with those documents that use a lot of text. There is no Fonts folder for PCs on the text CD, but you can either download fonts from the Microsoft site or Google for "type foundry" sites and download to your flash drive. These exercises installing fonts are best for a home computer without network security.

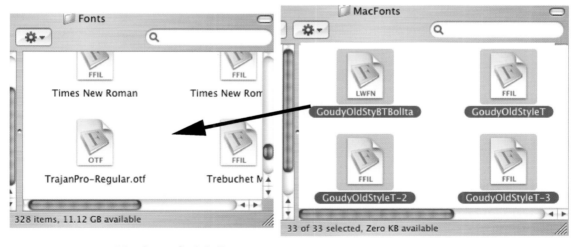

▷ FIGURE 2-20

To install the CD text fonts from the Mac *Fonts* **folder on your CD, select and drag them into the Fonts window inside the** *Library* **folder on your Mac.**

Macintosh OS X

On your Mac, the *Fonts* folder is located inside the *Library* folder within the *System* folder on the computer's hard drive. To install, just drag the fonts from the CD window into the Mac window. If you are using a computer on a very secure network, you may not have access to the system folder; in that case, you will have to use the font folder in your user library.

1. To locate the *Library* folder on your hard drive, double-click the hard drive icon on your desktop, then select Library > (double-click) Fonts to locate the fonts already installed on the computer, or select Go > Home > Library > Fonts.

2. Double-click the *Fonts* folder to open the window to display the current font files. Resize the window to fit the left half of your computer screen.

3. Insert the text CD. When the CD icon appears on the desktop, double-click the CD and double-click again to open the CD's *Fonts* folder.

4. Double-click the *Mac Fonts* folder to open the window with all the fonts.

5. Resize and position both windows next to one another, then click and drag the fonts from the CD *Fonts* folder into the *Fonts* folder within the *Library* folder on your Mac.

6. If a display comes up stating you already have the font, choose Don't Replace. These fonts will not hurt your computer.

7. Close the windows when you are done. Your fonts are ready for the text exercises. (You can also use the fonts already installed on your computer.)

8. EXTRA: To view fonts and their shapes, you can double-click a font file to open the Font Book. It will display the selected font in all ASCII characters (Figure 2-21).

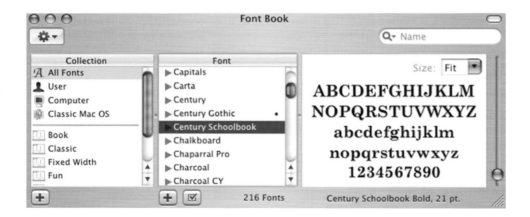

▷ FIGURE 2-21

To view what certain font shapes look like, double-click one of the font icons to open up the Font Book.

Windows 7

In Windows, you would open the *Fonts* folder in the Appearance and Personalization command in the Control Panel; then from the source window just drag the icon into the fonts folder and it will automatically install (Figure 2-22).

1. To install your fonts in Windows, select the Start button, then select the Control Panel.

2. Select Appearance and Personalization link, not the links underneath, then locate the Fonts icon.

DESIGN TIP

Try not to switch back and forth between Mac and PC computers with the same project, because the fonts are not exactly the same on either computer. If you have to switch, try to use fonts with the same name.

3. Click on the Fonts link to open the Fonts folder displaying the fonts on your computer and resize the window to half screen or less.

4. If you download a particular font you like, just drag the icon or the folder onto the desktop. Resize the window display, then all you need to do is drag the new font icon into the display of Fonts folder. It will automatically install.

5. To delete a font, click on the icon and press delete from the toolbar, or right-click the icon and select Delete. Be careful when deleting as it cannot be undone.

6. Close the dialog boxes to get back to the desktop. Your fonts are added to your computer and ready for the text exercises.

▷ FIGURE 2-22

Installing fonts in Windows 7.

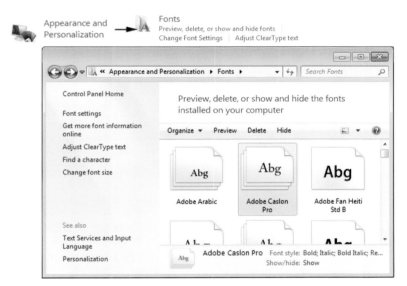

To add font, drag font icon from source to Fonts folder of icons
To delete a font, select font icon and select to delete.

TOOLKIT TIP ClearType is a software technology developed by Microsoft that improves the readability of text on existing LCDs, such as laptop screens, Pocket PC screens, and flat panel monitors. With ClearType font technology, the words on your computer screen are more sharpened and clear. With your home computer, you can turn on and adjust the screen for best readability using ClearType technology. To adjust, select Start Menu > Control Panel > Appearance and Personalization > Fonts > Adjust ClearType text. Then just follow the instructions.

Need additional fun computer graphics tutorials and info, and an additional look at the projects you'll be creating in this book? Check out my Artist's Digital Toolkit website at: **http://www.digitoolkit.com**

IMAGERY

Images are needed to explain ideas, provide further illustration to text in long articles, and strengthen the mood or idea the designer is trying to convey. We are basically visual learners of our environment. When designing with computer imagery, graphics can be categorized as either *vector images* or *bitmap images* (Figure 2-23). **Vector images** are illustrations, logos, drawings, or clip art that can be enlarged to any size without affecting the quality of the original image. **Bitmap images,** or **raster images,** are photographs, paintings, or complex designs that use millions of colors to record subtle gradations of tone in the image. They are not capable of being scaled larger than the original size without deteriorating the quality.

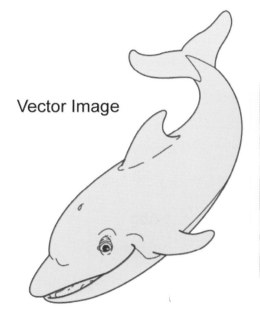

Vector Image

Bitmap (raster) Image

▷ FIGURE 2-23

Computer images are either categorized as vector or bitmap (raster) images.

SAVING GRAPHIC FILE FORMATS

Graphic applications allow the designer to save files in specific universal formats for an intended purpose. The file extension determines the type of graphic format saved and how a file may be used. Saving graphic files in these universal formats—extensions such as .EPS, .TIF, .JPG, .GIF, .PNG, or .PDF—gives them the flexibility to be used with other graphics programs for specific purposes. Specific graphic formats will be discussed in detail throughout this text.

TOOLKIT TIP The Save As command is used when changing a file's extension the first time a document is saved and when saving it with a different name or to a different drive or location. Using the Save command saves a file with the same name, in the same directory or location, or in the same drive.

The table below gives an overview of file formats.

FORMAT	ADVANTAGES	CONSIDERATIONS
.PNG	Records transparencies in bitmap and vector images. Compresses files without losing data. Web use.	Cannot be read by older browsers. Larger size files but can still be used for the web. Cannot be enlarged.
.GIF	Used for vector graphics and animation. Used on the web. Keeps transparencies.	GIF files have only 256 colors. Scalable.
.JPG	Compressed format used in photographic images. Keeps file sizes small. Used for web and ink-jet proof printing.	Data is thrown out each time the image is saved, gradually deteriorating quality. No transparencies. Not for commercial press. Cannot be enlarged.
.TIF	Most accurate recording of detail in photographs. Quality maintains as original regardless of changes. Can be used for commercial printing of photographs.	Largest file size. Not used for the web. Cannot be enlarged.
.PDF	Compresses text and graphics in documents without losing data for electronic distribution and the web. Works best with many documents. Can also be used for soft proofs and commercial printing.	Can also be read in free Acrobat Reader program.
.EPS	Preferred method when combining graphics and type. Vector graphics can be scalable. Used extensively for commercial printing.	Large file size. Not for the web.

DESIGN TIP

It is a good idea to save graphic files in their native formats first to be used as back-up copies for future editing. Using Illustrator and Photoshop for instance, saved in their native formats (.AI and .PSD) allows them to work nicely together, but may cause problems with other applications. That is why you should also save in a universal format afterwards for its intended purpose.

UNDERSTANDING THE IMPORTANCE OF COLOR

Creating a design with appropriate colors is a major factor in client approval. Research on the designer's part is critical to the success of the design. Some colors work better in small quantities than others. A designer must also be wary of design components using dark or light tones in specific quantities that may symbolize positive or negative aspects (Figure 2-24). Complementary background colors or lettering may be used with products extensively in package design. A bag of apples might have green lettering on the package as its complement to highlight the red color of the produce, giving a fresher appearance. When working with advertising agencies, whether on a local or global scale, color is used differently within various cultures. Designers need to be aware of the intended market. For instance, the color of royalty is purple in America and in Europe, but in China it is yellow. We in America look at white as symbolizing purity, and we associate it with weddings, whereas in China red is the usual bridal color.

▷ FIGURE 2-24

The lightness and darkness of tone in a design generates different emotional appeal. Understand the message you want to convey before designing for a particular market.

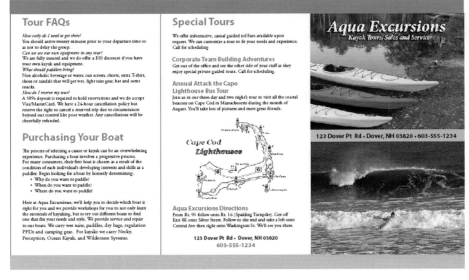

Inside Fold   Back   Front

3-Way Folding Brochure (outside page)

DESIGN TIP

When you specify a color for a design, consider how the final product will be used. Be wary of various themes with specific colors and their tonalities. Darker tones may have a contrary or more adverse impact than lighter tones. Be selective and keep color combinations simple and pertinent to the overall design.

Depending on the intended message, colors can have contrary effects. Here are some general concepts regarding the use of color in our American culture:

• White will usually stand for purity, but can also be utilized to generate a feeling of emptiness. Websites sometimes use white backgrounds as a neutral setting for images and for easier readability of text.

• Black can show value in terms of elegance, such as in tuxedos and gowns. Black can be used as an attention getter as a background with white, or *reversed,* type. Black can also suggest danger or something negative. It is also used as a neutral background in designing web pages that have many photographs.

• Gray (if a very light gray is used) can provide a subtle background on electronic media, leanding a neutral balance for images and colored type. On printed media, it is used very sparingly. Gray can also have powerful negative symbolism, such as stormy weather.

• Red can make the boldest of statements and may draw the viewer's eye more than any other color. Red can be used in small amounts for emphasis. Red can symbolize love (bright or medium red), strength (middle or true red), or anger (dark red) depending on the tone.

• Pink is a color used often in the bakery industry. Pink can also suggest high value in packaged goods and is a feminine color.

• Violet is another color that is generally used in small quantities. Dark violet, for instance, may suggest royalty.

• Blue, as one of the most widely used colors, has different effects. Lighter shades of blue may signify dream-like fantasies. Medium and dark blues may be used to signify honesty, professionalism, and sometimes spirituality. However, in some instances, blue used as the dominant color can adversely signify depression, dreariness, or isolation.

• Green signifies nature and can be used for produce, products related to healing, or for environmental issues. Green is also used to represent wealth, perhaps for banking institutions. Contrarily, green can imply jealousy or greed.

• Yellow can produce feelings of warmth and may be used to signify fast service (taxis, fast food). In contrast, yellow can also suggest danger or caution.

CREATING COLORS ON THE COMPUTER

Millions of light-emitted colors can be created on the computer by mixing the electronic primary colors: red, green, and blue. These **RGB mode** colors are used for electronic display such as web pages. Computers use an additive process to create color from the primary colors. The computer's secondary colors are magenta, cyan, and yellow, or **CMYK mode** (K stands for black, which is used to increase contrast). Mix red and blue and you get magenta. White is theoretically created by mixing red, green, and blue at their full intensity (Figure 2-25). Using computer software, you can convert files from RGB mode to CMYK mode to create colors that will closely match pigment colors used in commercial printing.

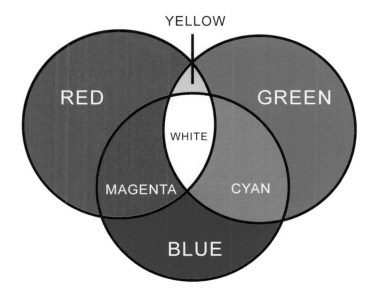

DESIGN TIP

When designing for a client, avoid symbols that are recognizable (road signs, hearts, icons) that may be used as clichés for a product. They can become ineffective if used too often.

▷ FIGURE 2-25

A computer's primary colors are red, green, and blue. Adding these colors creates the secondary colors: cyan, magenta, and yellow. White is created by adding red, green, and blue at full intensity.

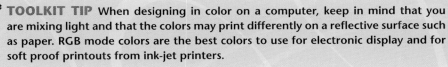

TOOLKIT TIP When designing in color on a computer, keep in mind that you are mixing light and that the colors may print differently on a reflective surface such as paper. RGB mode colors are the best colors to use for electronic display and for soft proof printouts from ink-jet printers.

CLIENT ASSIGNMENT: Designing in Color or Black and White Contrasts

Here is an assignment that will allow you to design a layout that would be used in this book as a two-page spread to make the section "Understanding the Importance of Color" look more appealing by using imagery to complement the text descriptions. In this section, colors are described as having certain effects on a design when used in different tones, shades, or quantity. As part of this layout, with each color description, you are going to include two-color (or you can challenge yourself to use only black-and-white images) contrasting images for emphasis. You need to think how to best portray the colors mentioned. Create a series of three or more sketches to show peers or your instructor—as your clients—the proposed layout of images with text. Using their input, create a final rough at full scale, using your word processor to print out images to be pasted, or create fine detailed drawings as if for final approval before setting up a comp. Have fun!

ACTION ITEMS OVERVIEW

Here is a breakdown of what you need to do:

• Determine the layout of images and text, including spacing and margins, for the final size.

• Research what images will be used and what fonts, styles, and sizes will be used.

• Create three or more thumbnail sketches of how the images will be laid out with the text descriptions (normally, you would create more sketches, but this will do for this exercise).

• Present your thumbnail sketches to your instructor or peers to get their input.

• With the sketches narrowed down, create the final, full-size rough combining elements from various sketches. Then show them to your clients.for approval.

• ADVANCED USERS: Identify design elements and principles in various ads.

CONSIDERATIONS IN THE DESIGN PROCESS

In the following chapters, you will be guided through the designing process to create and complete the assignments using various graphic applications. Here, we will help you work through the process of creating a two-page color (or black-and-white) spread describing color (Figure 2-26).

DESIGN TIP

It is always best to create in the computer's RGB mode first; then, create a duplicate file and convert it to CMYK mode.

▷ FIGURE 2-26

Create a two-page spread with space for margins, text, and images.

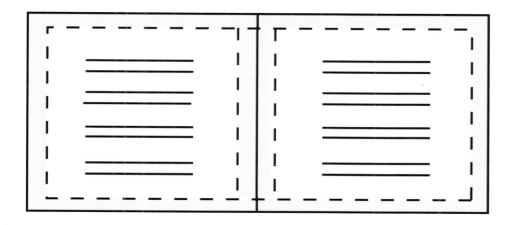

DESIGN TIP

Although you need not be concerned with trimming at this point, just as an FYI, when looking at determining size, it is a good idea to add an extra eighth inch horizontally and vertically for final trimming purposes if a commercial printer will be used. For instance, a final page dimension of 9 3/4 × 7 3/4 inches would actually be set up as printing on a 10-by-8-inch sheet.

TOOLKIT TIP If you have neither Microsoft Word nor a WordPerfect application, both operating systems have basic ASCII word processors. You can open Wordpad in Windows 7 (Start > All Programs > Accessories > Wordpad), or use TextEdit in Mac OS X (Go > Applications > TextEdit).

Here are some considerations.

1. First, as a designer you have to think of portraying color in this book with recognizable images that will be printed in color (or black and white or shades of gray, if you are up to the challenge).

2. Consider one table or column for each page; obviously you would not want text across both pages. Create two separate pages for our purposes.

3. Determine the layout for incorporating text and images, as if it would be used as a two-page spread within this text. Use this book as a guide for measurements (Figure 2-26).

4. Locate the *Color* file in the *Chapter 2* folder (Client > Chapter 2 > Color) on your hard drive, or locate it on the text CD. It contains the text you need, so you do not have to type it over again and can concentrate on designing instead.

5. Open the *Color* file in your word processing program, such as Microsoft Word.

6. Determine what fonts will be used for the title and body of the text. Consider using a sans-serif font, such as Arial or Helvetica, for the title and headlines. Try a serif font for the body of the text. Times Roman, Georgia, or Century Schoolbook fonts provide a good starting point.

7. Highlight the text and make printouts with your chosen fonts at 10- and 12-point sizes to start.

8. Observe the text and its relationship to the rest of the document. Determine the sizes of the title, headlines, and the body text. Leave enough extra blank space for margins all around and between the images and text so they do not appear to run into one another. Try inch-wide margins along the outside to start.

9. Determine what type of images will be used. Will they be photographs, clip art, or your own drawings? Your images may be fairly small, so keep the images simple and basic. Stay consistent when you decide what type of images to use.

10. Research what images you need to best complement each color description. You can use not only images from your word processing program, such as Microsoft Word (Insert > Picture > Clip Art), but you can also cull graphics from the Internet; find websites where you can download free images (see Chapter 1).

 TOOLKIT TIP If you are not sure of the process, in the Chapter 2 folder you will find a text file named Download that describes how to download images off the Internet. Be careful not to use images that are copyrighted (©) or have a visible watermark on the image.

11. Create a series of two or more proportional thumbnail sketches of possible layouts that show where to place contrasting images alongside each description. Include printed images or image descriptions alongside the text description in each sketch. Figure 2-27 gives you a few ideas for layouts.

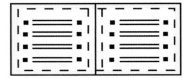 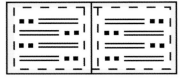 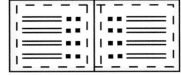

▷ FIGURE 2-27

Here are some layout ideas to position your text and images (lines are text, squares are images).

12. Get feedback from your peers or instructor as to which layout, images, and text would best suit this assignment; then create the final rough.

13. Use your word processor to help position text and possible images or, if you are not comfortable with positioning elements using the computer yet, cut out, arrange, and paste the elements to create a full-size rough. You can also create a detailed, full-size drawing if you want. Draw guidelines, if needed, to help with placement.

 TOOLKIT TIP In the *Chapter 2* folder, you will find a file *PlaceIMG* that describes how to insert images into a word processor document. Open this file in your word processor.

DESIGN TIP

Professional presentations may involve spray mounting your designs onto gray or black matte (illustration or foam-core) board with appropriate margins for a nice, clean look.

14. Go back to your "clients" to get final approval or input on your rough for any last-minute changes. Ask them how they would like the final rough presented, and then present it to your client neatly.

15. Remember: Presentation is an important component in design. It shows professionalism to a client. Designers can present labeled roughs and comps mounted on illustration board for stability, inside a binder encased in transparent sheeting, or by any other method that makes the presentation look clean and neat.

16. Welcome to the world of design!

ADVANCED USER: Identifying Design Elements and Principles in Various Ads

Here is a little exercise to help you think about design principles and elements. Formal design elements that make up the basic building blocks of design are *line, shape, color, texture, value,* and *format.* You are trying to communicate something in each design you create, and these physical elements of design are your tools for communication; knowing when and how to use them is essential to design building. Here, you will identify design elements used in various ads and media and the design principles they employed.

1. Locate four good magazine ads, either half or full page, with graphic imagery and text.

2. Locate two CD covers that you find very pleasing.

3. Find a book cover that looks appealing.

4. Find your favorite website.

5. Define the design elements used in each and the design principles established.

6. Identify the typography used (serif or sans serif, alignment, etc.).

7. Explain how color was used for emotional appeal.

8. Pick one of the pieces and try to design it a little differently, creating three sketches, or roughs, if time allows.

9. Explain to your client, peer, or instructor why you would make these changes.

DIGITAL TOOLKIT EXTRA: Internet Resources

One of the best resources for locating current technologies, tutorials, information, or design concepts is on the Internet. There is a wealth of information that you can print or save as a bookmark. To learn how to create bookmarks of your favorite sites in Internet Explorer, open the file Bookmark in the Chapter 2 folder. We have included a list below for you to access information and download trial versions of the software, to find special applications, and to search for tutorials about each application we are using in this book. You will find these and additional lists of resources in a file called Research in the Chapter 2 folder. Just click on any underlined text links in the document, and it will take you to these websites. Feel free to check out the Goodies folder in your CD for additional assignments and information for each chapter.

INTERNET RESOURCES

To access information, tutorials, software and hardware updates, and to try versions of the applications used in this book, visit these websites:

- To access information regarding Windows 7 and Microsoft products:
  http://www.microsoft.com
- To access information about using Microsoft's Office Suite products on a Mac (OfficeMac) check out the Mactopia site:
  http://www.microsoft.com/mac/default.mspx
- If you are a student or educator, check out these two sites that will give you great discounts on software and hardware:
  http://www.academicsuperstore.com
  http://www.journeyed.com
- For information on Macintosh OS X and software utilities you can download, including iTunes and Quicktime (for movies): *http://www.apple.com*
- For digital imaging (Photoshop), digital desktop publishing (InDesign), and digital illustration (Illustrator):
  http://www.adobe.com

You can also download the free Acrobat Reader application to view any portable document files (PDFs) created electronically, and you can download a free Flash Player and Shockwave to view animations. We will get into these next in the Unit 1 Review. Also, you can check out their library of video tutorials on many Adobe products at **http://tv.adobe.com**

- To get information and ideas in design:
  http://www.graphicdesign.about.com
- For information in all areas of desktop publishing, web design, digital imaging, and illustration, use the About website. It is a great place to start!
  http://www.about.com
- So, you want to download and watch Photoshop TV on your iPod or on the big screen to learn all kinds of great tricks and tips?
  http://www.photoshopusertv.com
- Need additional fun computer graphics tutorials and info, and an additional look at the projects you'll be creating in this book? Check out my Artist's Digital Toolkit website at:
  http://www.digitoolkit.com

CHAPTER SUMMARY

This chapter introduced lots of information to get you prepared to work in the upcoming chapters. You learned about incorporating various design elements and principles to create effective layouts. You were exposed to typography basics and the importance of using the right fonts and spacing for your design. You installed fonts for the text exercises, and you learned how color can affect the message or mood of a piece. In your assignment, you learned to research and use color symbols—and you could attept this assignment in black and white—to complement the text descriptions. You learned the design process with client input. For more projects and ideas, check out the *Goodies* folder on your CD.

REVIEW QUESTIONS

1. Explain the design elements used in graphic design.

2. Explain the principles of graphic design.

3. Describe font, type family, font size, tracking, leading, and four kinds of type alignment.

4. Explain in general terms contrasting symbolism or emphasis for the colors white, black, red, blue, green, and yellow, or when a different shade of a particular color is used.

5. Explain the design process from concept to completion when working with a client.

▷ FIGURE 2-28

Excerpts: Design Elements and Principles, Design Process, Typography, Imagery, and Color. Chapter project involves using design components to lay out contrary color images to match descriptions to be used in a color (or black-and-white) spread.

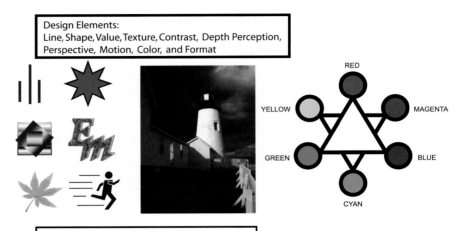

Design Elements:
Line, Shape, Value, Texture, Contrast, Depth Perception, Perspective, Motion, Color, and Format

Design Principles:
Balance, Space, Emphasis, Rythym, and Unity

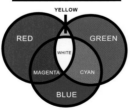

Color and Typography

Book Antiqua (serif type)
Arial **Bold** (sans-serif type)
Papyrus (decorative type)
Brush Script Italic (script type)
❖ ✗ ♌ ♦ ☎ (symbol type)

Getting Ready for Production

This review encompasses some of the topics covered in the first two chapters to get you, as a designer, ready for production. You will install the free Acrobat Reader application from the Adobe website that is used to read universal portable document formats (PDFs). You can also use this application to look at and print additional resources and projects in the *Goodies* folder on your Student Text CD, and additional graphic tutorials from *http://www.digitoolkit.com.* To prepare you for the next unit in Photoshop, you will check for the size and memory space needed on your computer, then go through the process of downloading and installing the tryout software, which you can download from the Adobe site at *http://www.adobe.com,* or see your instructor. You will also sketch and explain how you would improve a particular design and review some basic design techniques to use throughout this book.

CLIENT ASSIGNMENT: Installing Acrobat Reader, Photoshop Tryout, and Improving a Design

You will install the free application (not a tryout version) Acrobat Reader from the Adobe site, which is used to read universal electronic portable document formats (PDFs). You will find additional assignments, resources, and other information in the *Goodies* folder that came with your Student CD. Many of these will be in PDF format. Tryout versions of software work just like the real application and are useful for a set number of days. To get ready for the next unit about Photoshop, you can go through the process to install the tryout version of Photoshop CS5 from the Adobe website *(http://www.adobe.com)* on your computer, or see your instructor to go through the process on your network drive. It is important to first find out if you have the needed system requirements to use the software, such as having enough RAM memory, before installing a large program. You will see where you can find this information on your computer. We will also review some important design points to consider as you go through the exercises in this book.

Need additional fun computer graphics tutorials and info, and an additional look at the projects you'll be creating in this book? Check out my Artist's Digital Toolkit website at: **http://www.digitoolkit.com**

ACTION ITEMS OVERVIEW

• Install Adobe Acrobat Reader to be able to read and print portable documents that you can find in the *Goodies* folder on the student text CD, and at a special website created for you at *http://www.digitoolkit.com*.

• Find information about your computer's memory and system requirements before you install an application.

• Go through the process of installing the Photoshop tryout demo onto your computer. You can also install it to use in the next unit if you do not have the current version installed.

• Review techniques in design and create a sketch of an improved design.

DOWNLOADING AND INSTALLING ACROBAT READER

Macintosh OS X and Windows operating systems contain many programs or applications that allow the user to perform all kinds of operations. They become the coordinators or managers of the applications running within them. There are some free application utilities that can be useful to help you become more productive. One of them is Acrobat Reader, which can be found at the Adobe website (*http://www. adobe.com*). As a cross-platform application, this free application allows both Mac and Windows users to read each other's PDFs, and make comments to communicate with one another, as long as document rights are allowed. Many manuals, support information, and other documentation, including illustrations, are created in PDF form. With the Acrobat Reader, you can e-mail PDF documents. because they are small in file size, and they can be printed. We will be covering PDFs in more detail later. Inside your text CD, in the *Goodies* folder, you will find additional resources and assignments, and we've also added an additional graphics tutorial site, *An Artist's Digital Toolkit*, with more resources and assignments. Much of the documentation is in PDF form. You will also be using the Address bar to not only locate and display folders on your drive, but also to type in the **URL** or website address.

TOOLKIT TIP The space that this program uses is about 50 megabytes, which is a very small amount. There is a also a full retail version of Adobe Acrobat that allows designers to produce, edit, and make comments on PDF documents as part of a team effort. You should also download the free Flash Player and Shockwave Player applications as well to view animations.

In this exercise you will be downloading Acrobat Reader and installing it on your desktop. You will then locate the *Goodies* folder on your desktop, which contains additional assignments and info, and use the Acrobat Reader to display and print a file. You can also find additional tutorials in PDF form at *www.digitoolkit.com*. This is one of those applications that is a must for every computer and is safe to install.

Macintosh OS X

1. Make sure you are connected to the Internet and type in the address bar the site *http://www.adobe.com.*

2. At the first page of the site, or Home page, you will find the button for the Acrobat Reader application.

3. Click on the Get Adobe Reader button.

4. When the Download Acrobat Reader window comes up, select the type of computer platform (if asked), version, and language you want to download. Select Download, which means that you agree to policies of using the software for yourself, and then click Download Acrobat Reader to start the download process onto your computer. Note: The file is usually in compressed format and may ask you what you want to do with the file, use the default application being used. Adobe will provide further instructions if needed for you to follow.

5. The application, which may read *AdbeRdr90_en_us_ppc.dmg*, or something similar depending on the country and language, will download to the desktop (Figure UR1-1).

▷ FIGURE UR 1-1

Downloading and installing Acrobat Reader on Mac OS X.

6. When the downloaded compressed file is completed, an icon will be displayed on the desktop. Double-click on it to decompress the file until a window opens up displaying the icon Acrobat Reader or the application may start to automatically install.

7. Follow the instructions to install the application. That's all there is to it.

8. To check to see if it installed correctly, click on the desktop, and using Finder, select Go > Applications. You will find the Acrobat Reader application among the list of applications.

9. If possible, make an alias of the application by selecting the application, then selecting File > Make Alias, and when the Acrobat Reader Alias appears, drag it to the desktop.

10. Launch Acrobat Reader, then load the text CD and open the *Goodies* folder, where you will find additional info in each chapter. Open the *Chapter 2* folder and select the *Bookmark* PDF document.

11. The Acrobat Reader application should display the document on how to book-mark your favorite sites using Internet Explorer or Safari browsers.

12. Print the document (File > Print) and feel free to look at other goodies in the folder.

13. To keep the desktop clean, drag the compressed Acrobat Reader installer file *AdbeRdr90_en_us_ppc.dmg*, or similar, (not the alias you just made) into the Trash icon on the Dock.

14. To delete the file permanently, click on the desktop screen to bring up the Finder Menu, and select Finder > Empty Trash.

15. EXTRA: Locate the Adobe site and continue the same process to download the free Flash Player and Shockwave Player applications, for viewing annimations.

 TOOLKIT TIP There are a couple ways to install applications in Windows if they do not start automatically. If one has an .EXE extension, it is a compressed file, and you can simply double-click it and it will guide you through a set of screen instructions. The Add and Remove Programs command in the Control panel works well with all applications safely to install or remove programs. With Windows, its a good idea to create a Download folder in order to keep track files downloaded from the Internet in case you may need to reinstall them at a later date.

Windows 7

1. Make sure you are connected to the Internet, and type in the Address bar the site http://www.adobe.com.

2. At the first page of the site, or Home page, you will find the button for the Adobe Reader application.

3. Click the Get Adobe Reader button, then when the Acrobat Reader page opens, click Continue to accept the software agreement and that you will use the free software for your own purposes.

4. When the Download Acrobat Reader window comes up, select the type of computer platform and a language if asked. You can also choose to install a free Google Toolbar to help with your future searching on the Internet. You would then click on Download Acrobat Reader with Google.

5. For our purposes here, only have a check in the box to have the Acrobat Reader downloaded onto your computer. Click on Continue at the bottom of the page.

6. Once the file is downloaded, it will automatically decompress and open up into an installation window to Set Up the application.

7. With the installation or Set Up window open, click on Next, and follow the instructions to install the Reader.

▷   FIGURE UR 1-2

When downloading Acrobat Reader using Windows, you may find a security pop-up on the information bar; just click inside the yellow bar to continue the automatic installation.

8. To check to see if it installed correctly, click Start > All Programs, and see if it is displayed among the list of programs or applications.

9. If possible, make a shortcut of the application by locating the Acrobat Reader application in the Programs list, then right-click once to display a menu.

10. Select Send To > Desktop to place a shortcut on the desktop.

11. Launch Acrobat Reader, then load the text CD and open the *Goodies* folder, in which you will find additional information for each chapter. Open the *Chapter 2* folder and select the *Bookmark PDF* document.

12. The Acrobat Reader application should display the document on how to bookmark your favorite sites using Internet Explorer or Safari browsers.

13. Print the document (File > Print) and feel free to look at other documents in the *Goodies* folder.

TOOLKIT TIP You can also find tutorials in PDF form in the Artist's Digital Toolkit site, which we have set up for students and educators. In addition, you'll find a more visual tutorial for downloading and installing Acrobat Reader on the main page. Connect to the Internet, type the URL *www.digitoolkit.com,* and click on the "Yes I Need Acrobat Reader" link to display the web document. Go play!

DOWNLOADING AND INSTALLING PHOTOSHOP TRYOUT

Many applications will start to install automatically when you insert their CD. You can download tryout or demo versions of the applications used in this text; Photoshop, InDesign, and Illustrator software from *http://www.adobe.com,* or see your instructor. You may install these when you are ready to work on your chapter assignments, if you do not already have the application on your computer. Here you will learn to install a tryout version of Photoshop for the next unit. This tryout version will work as a regular application for 30 days: enough time to complete the next unit.

TOOLKIT TIP If you already have Photoshop installed, you can still go through the process of installing the tryout version and then canceling, which we will show you in the steps below. If you do not wish to install this tryout software, you will find that most of the exercises will work with earlier versions of Photoshop.

TOOLKIT TIP Most school systems have security settings that may allow you to install an application but will not hurt the computer, because the computer automatically resets to its original set state when shut down. This protection avoids any tampering with lab computers to keep a safe environment. Check with your instructor.

Macintosh OS X

Here you will check information about the computer's memory using the Apple Menu, then go through the process to download the Photoshop CS5 Tryout version on you Mac OS X computer, which you can use for the next unit for 30 days. To do this exercise, you need a DSL or cable connection, *not* dial up. The file size is very large, over 1.2 gigabytes for Mac. Adobe also routinely changes their website, so the following steps may not be exactly what you may find, but they will be quite close, and you should have no problem following along.

1. Mac OS X: To find how much memory you have on your Mac computer, select the Apple menu in the corner, and then select About This Mac from the drop-down list. The display will tell you what version you are working in, how much memory you have, and so on. You should have at least 1 gigabyte (1000 MB) of RAM memory, and a 1 gigabyte (1000 MB) processor to continue.

2. Connect to the Internet and in your browser address bar type *http://www. adobe.com.* When the site opens, select Downloads > Trial Downloads, then select Photoshop CS5 icon, and click the TRY link.

3. You may be asked to register to create an Adobe ID free account and password that does not share any personal info but allows you to download future tryouts, updates, and so forth.

4. After posting the information, you will need to select a language and platform (Windows or Macintosh) to download, then click Continue to accept the software policy that you will use it yourself.

5. Print out the instructions.

6. In the newer Mac OS X versions, the installer will automatically download with the application and will be placed on the desktop. If you already have Photoshop CS5 on your computer, then do not install it; drag the icon to the trash to delete the file.

7. If you wish to install the tryout version, locate and double-click the *tryout* folder on your desktop, then double-click the Install Adobe Photoshop icon. When the dialog box pops up, select Continue, then Accept the agreement if you want to install. Follow any instructions and you are ready!

TOOLKIT TIP If you are not sure about the size of the file or the amount of memory you need before installing a large application on your Mac, select the file, and then select File > Get Info to get the information you need. This is a good, safe habit to get into.

Windows 7

Here, you will use the Control Panel to find information about your computer and then install a Photoshop tryout version that you can use for the next 30 days. To do this exercise, you need a DSL or cable connection, *not* dial up. The file size is very large: over 1 gigabyte (1000 MB). Adobe also routinely changes their website, so the following steps may not be exactly what you may find, but they will be quite close and you should have no problem following along.

1. With Windows 7, to find information about your PC, select Start Menu > Control Panel > System and Security > System. When you select the System link, you will find the information you need about your computer. You should have at least 1 gigabyte (1000 MB) of RAM memory, and a 1 gigabyte (1000 MB) processor to continue. More is better.

2. Connect to the Internet and in your browser address bar type *http://www.adobe.com*. When the site opens, select Downloads > Trial Downloads, then select Photoshop CS5 icon, and click the TRY link.

3. You may be asked to register to create an Adobe ID free account and password that does not share any personal info but allows you to download future tryouts, updates, and so forth.

4. After posting the information, you will need to select a language and platform to download, then click Continue to accept the software agreement stating that you will use the program yourself.

5. Print out the instructions. Observe the system requirements for your computer. If acceptable, follow directions at the Adobe site to download the tryout version of the software.

6. When the dialog box asks whether you want to Open or Save the file, you can choose Open if you want the application to install at some default location on

your hard drive. This will work if you are downloading to a home computer. If you wish to download the file to install to the *Photoshop* folder you created in Chapter 1 on a network drive, and you have WinZip as a file decompressor installed (it is a free utility, check in Start > Programs > WinZip), select Save and select the *Photoshop* folder inside the *Toolkit* folder you created earlier. Ask your instructor what will work. If you already have Photoshop on your computer, then select Save to put it in the *Photoshop* folder to complete this exercise, then delete the file.

7. If you choose Open, the application will automatically open and install the application. If you have saved the file to your *Photoshop* folder, and you wish to install, double-click to open the file and WinZip will lead you through installing at its default settings.

TOOLKIT TIP In Windows, you can find information about a file by selecting the file and selecting the Properties command (File > Properties).

Need additional fun computer graphics tutorials and info, and an additional look at the projects you'll be creating in this book? Check out my Artist's Digital Toolkit website at: **http://www.digitoolkit.com**

DESIGN TECHNIQUES

1. Try to find a CD cover or magazine ad design that you would like to make better.

2. Sketch in the changes and identify design elements used and design principles emphasized.

Here are some helpful hints in design techniques to watch for as you go through the text chapters:

• Listen to your client. Research, research, research. Determine your market.

• Use file management techniques to keep your work organized.

• Stay focused on the theme or message. Strive for simplicity.

• Provide a hierarchy of content to lead the viewer through your composition.

• Maintain consistency in fonts, font sizes, and spacing throughout.

• Choose the appropriate font to complement the imagery in the design.

• Typography should enhance a message, not detract from it. Use typefaces that are appropriate to the message. Color of type should also play a vital role in enhancing the visual expression, but should not hinder readability.

• Be wary of various themes with specific colors and their tonalities. Darker tones may have a more negative impact than lighter tones. Be selective and keep color combinations simple and pertinent to the overall design.

• Avoid using recognizable, clichéd symbols (road signs, hearts, or trite icons) for a product.

• Develop a sense of consistency, using the same margins and column layouts on every page; provide consistency in typeface, line spacing, and alignment.

• Always present your designs neatly, professionally, and on time.

UNIT

2

CHAPTER 3

Adjusting Images in Photoshop

CHAPTER OBJECTIVES: To understand the importance of Photoshop's function as an image-editing program to adjust and enhance images, in this chapter you will:

▷ Learn Photoshop's desktop components and how they interact with one another.

▷ Navigate around an image using the Navigator panel, Zoom, and Hand tools.

▷ Use the Image menu to perform adjustments or enhancements to an image.

▷ Use the Auto Color command to remove color casts and the Auto Tone and Auto Contrast commands to adjust and compare contrast to maintain detail in highlight and shadow areas.

▷ Use the Shadows/Highlights command for correcting poorly exposed images.

▷ Learn the importance of resolution in creating images for print and web media.

▷ Adjust image size, resolution, and determine color modes for print and web media.

▷ ADVANCED USERS: Understand the use of histograms, the Histogram panel, and performing detailed adjustments using the Levels adjustment and Curves adjustment.

▷ DIGITAL TOOLKIT EXTRA: Learn to use Adobe Bridge and Mini Bridge to locate, manage, and sort images; learn how to create slide shows and import images from a digital camera.

Digital imaging involves the process of scanning or importing images—photographs, paintings, illustrations, and so on—from scanners, digital cameras, drives, or other devices into the computer so the software can convert them into editable digital images for enhancing, retouching, and restoration. Using Adobe Photoshop CS5, the premier program of the digital imaging industry, a designer or photographer can edit, manipulate, enhance, or apply effects to selected parts of an image or to the entire image. Images can also be combined as composites. Photoshop CS5—the *CS* stands for Creative Suite, a package designed for all types of media that includes Photoshop, Illustrator, InDesign, Dreamweaver, and Acrobat, among others—provides tools that design professionals and photographers need, not only to create images that can be integrated with other Adobe products, which we will explore later in this text, but to create publishable images for both print and web media. In this chapter, you will perform basic image enhancements while exploring some of Photoshop's tools and functions. You will also create images for both print and web media.

Need additional fun computer graphics tutorials and info, and an additional look at the projects you'll be creating in this book? Check out my Artist's Digital Toolkit website at: **http://www.digitoolkit.com**

THE PHOTOSHOP ENVIRONMENT

Photoshop comes in regular and extended versions. The extended version is used for additional work with medical images, video images, and 3D design. The figures shown are from the Photoshop CS5 Extended version, although all projects and assignments can be completed using the standard edition. When you launch Photoshop for the first time, a Welcome screen appears. It provides a "What's New" feature to walk you through some of the new functions in Photoshop's newest version, along with tutorials to learn the basics and advanced features in Photoshop. You can use these tutorials to revive or enhance your skills. If the Welcome screen is not displayed, click on the Essentials (Workspaces) tab menu on the right side bar. When an existing or new file is opened within Photoshop, the Photoshop desktop contains the Title bar, which displays the file title, Menu bar, Tools panel, Tool Options bar, Application bar and panels (Figure 3-1). The Menu bar provides commands to perform almost any type of editing your creative mind can come up with. The Tools panel contains the tools you need to edit your image, with different options for each tool available in the Tool Options bar. The Application bar provides a tabbed interface for displaying multiple images, and a Workspaces menu (Essentials default) for retrieving essential information like basic tutorials and for choosing specific media work space settings, a file-management program icon called *Adobe Bridge* (tutorial in Digital Toolkit Extra section), and a Mini Bridge program that works within Photoshop (new in CS5). Panels provide commands and functions to help you modify and monitor your images. They can be collapsed into labeled icons, or small pictures, to conserve space on your desktop. The Window menu on the Menu bar allows you to display panels, the Tools panel, the Application bar, preset workspaces, and the Tool Options bar. By clicking on the list, you choose which items you want to display. You will find that Photoshop's active features change when you open an existing image, or when you are editing the current image. In working with various Adobe programs, you'll find the interface similar between all applications so that once you learn to navigate around one application, the others will feel quite familiar. Note: If you are using Microsoft Windows, the Application bar is combined with the Menu bar.

▷ FIGURE 3-1

The Photoshop CS5 Desktop.

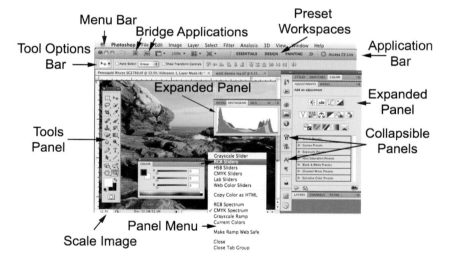

WORKING WITH BITMAP (RASTER) IMAGES

On your computer's monitor, individually colored square dots, or **pixels**, are displayed and are the smallest picture elements on your computer screen. Images created in Photoshop or imported from cameras or other devices into Photoshop are converted into bitmap, or raster images. Bitmap images are the most accurate for recording details in photographic images or paintings and use may millions or even billions of individually colored pixels that determine the details in shading and tonality of the image. These images are *nonscalable*, so a designer or photographer should not add pixels to make the final image larger than the original image size without understanding that he or she may be sacrificing detail. The **resolution** determines the amount of detail in an image. An image's resolution, measured as **dpi** (dots per inch), is used for printing documents; 300 dpi is the norm for high-resolution, quality images for press or photographic output. Images measured as **ppi** (pixels per inch) refer to the screen resolution that you see on your computer monitor. The standard for creating web pages is 72 ppi; the higher the resolution, the more detail there will be in shading, highlights, and tonality—and the larger the file size.

TOOLKIT TIP In Photoshop, when you choose File > New to create a new file, you have a predefined set of document size choices for print, web publishing, mobile devices, and for video, with the resolution already built in. Use this option if you already know the image size or resolution that you will need.

PHOTOSHOP TOOLS PANEL

The **Photoshop Tools panel** provides the tools to select, edit, manage, and manipulate image pixels and to draw or add type to images. On some of the tools, you will notice a small triangle at the bottom right of the tool to indicate there are more related tools that will be displayed when you select the tool and hold the mouse down. The corresponding keystroke to access that tool is also displayed. We will be using the most common tools in the chapters that follow. You can change the shape of the Tools panel from two columns to one column wide to help conserve desktop space by clicking on the double arrows at the top of the Tools panel (Figure 3-2).

Here is Photoshop's Tools panel broken down into various categories of tools with a brief description of each, including the corresponding keystroke in parentheses for each tool group:

• **Navigation** in an image can be done with the Zoom tool (Z) or Hand tool (H). The Rotate View tool provides a different perspective.

• **Selection tools** select and isolate image areas. Marquee tools (M) select rectangular or elliptical selections, while Lasso tools (L) allow you to make freehand selections. The Magic Wand tool (W) and the Quick Selection tool select by similar color. The Move tool (V) technically does not generate a selection, but moves selections onto or within an image. The Crop tool (C) draws rectangular selections inside the image area that trim away what is outside the selection area.

• **Painting and drawing tools** allow you to apply brush or shape effects. The Shape tools (U) are used to create various shapes that help with selections. Brush and Pencil tools (B) are used for painting. The Color Replacement tool (B) replaces colors under the brush with the foreground color while retaining the detail and shading in the image. History and Art History brushes (Y) allow you to go back in time to a previously used brush or apply an effect. Pen tools (P) create paths using anchor points for precise selections. Path and Direct Selection tools (A) are used to select paths created by the Pen tool.

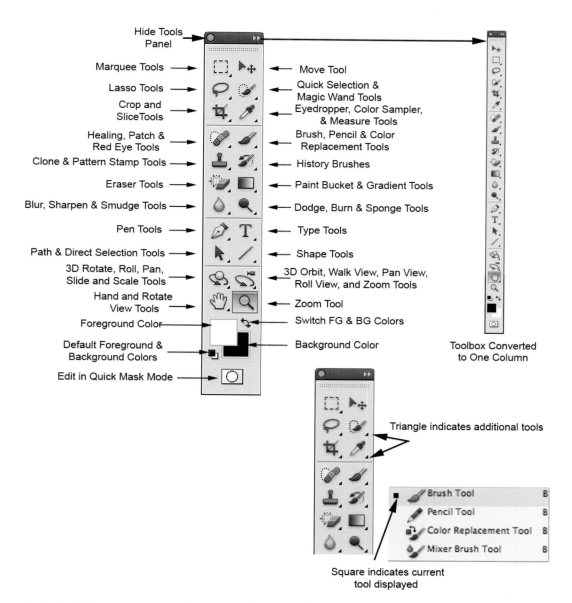

Hide Tools Panel

Marquee Tools → ← Move Tool

Lasso Tools → ← Quick Selection & Magic Wand Tools

Crop and Slice Tools → ← Eyedropper, Color Sampler, & Measure Tools

Healing, Patch & Red Eye Tools → ← Brush, Pencil & Color Replacement Tools

Clone & Pattern Stamp Tools → ← History Brushes

Eraser Tools → ← Paint Bucket & Gradient Tools

Blur, Sharpen & Smudge Tools → ← Dodge, Burn & Sponge Tools

Pen Tools → ← Type Tools

Path & Direct Selection Tools → ← Shape Tools

3D Rotate, Roll, Pan, Slide and Scale Tools → ← 3D Orbit, Walk View, Pan View, Roll View, and Zoom Tools

Hand and Rotate View Tools → ← Zoom Tool

Foreground Color ← Switch FG & BG Colors

Default Foreground & Background Colors → ← Background Color

Edit in Quick Mask Mode

Toolbox Converted to One Column

Triangle indicates additional tools

Square indicates current tool displayed

Brush Tool B
Pencil Tool B
Color Replacement Tool B
Mixer Brush Tool B

▷ FIGURE 3-2

Photoshop Tools panel contains the essential tools for image editing. Other tools also display whenever any tool button with a triangle is depressed.

• **Editing and retouching tools** help to improve or enhance an image. The Healing Brush, Red Eye, and Patch tools (J) blend in lighting and shading of the sampled area to be copied for more detailed precision. The Crop tool (C) trims a rectangular area and can change perspective of an image. The Slice tools (K) delineate and select image components to use for the web, which allow faster downloading. The Eraser tools (E) remove selected pixels or background colors or make the background transparent. The Gradient tool (G) creates a shaded fill from one color to another, while the Paint Bucket tool (G) fills in solid colors. The Blur, Sharpen, and Smudge tools, and the Burn, Dodge, and Sponge tools (O) let you soften, sharpen, lighten, or darken parts of an image. The Clone and Pattern Stamp tools (S) copy over sampled image areas.

• **Type tools** (T) bring text into your images with various type orientations and type masks. They create vector type that can be scaled to any size and still remain sharp. The Type Mask tools create a selection in the shape of type.

• The **Note tool** (N) allows you to leave electronic notes to yourself or other members of your team that can be attached to an image.

• **Color tools** like the Eyedropper and Color Sampler tools (I) are used to sample any color on any image to make a new foreground color by default and provide color information. Below the tools, you will find the Color Picker area, which displays the foreground color for use by color, painting, and retouching tools and the background color used by the Eraser and Gradient tools. You can select and switch between colors (X) and also default to black and white (D).

• **Measuring tools** involve the Measure tool (I) which checks distances and dimensions whereas the Count tool (I) counts objects in an image. In the Photoshop Extended CS5 version, there are **3D tools** that can move and rotate an object on its axis (K), while another set of 3D tools (N) change the view or perspective of an object.

THE TOOL OPTIONS BAR AND APPLICATION MENU BAR

In Photoshop, when you select a tool in the Tools panel, the **Tool Options bar** displays options for that particular tool (Figure 3-3). If the Tool Options bar is not displayed, open it from the Window menu. On the left side there is also a Tool Preset Picker displaying preset tool functions of the current tool or for all tools, which you can create and add at any time. The Tool Presets are also displayed as a panel; this allows you to create preferred settings for your tools to increase your productivity. The Application bar provides a tabbed interface for choosing how images will be displayed, and a Workspaces menu for retrieving essential information like basic tutorials, and for choosing and creating customized specific media work space settings. On Mac OS, you can also work within an Application frame from the Window menu, which keeps all Photoshop's windows and panels together within the single display frame. On the left side of the Application bar, you will find the Adobe Bridge icons, used to locate and manage files. In CS5, you'll find Adobe applications have a Mini Bridge icon to locate and keep images and media files within an open application like Photoshop. Note that if you are using Windows, both the Menu bar and Application bar are combined together.

 TOOLKIT TIP Any changes you make to most of the options on the Tool Options bar will remain in place even after you close Photoshop. Any tool presets you create are saved, so you can have your own group of preset tools for future use until you change them.

PANELS

Panels display many options, and they help modify and control information about your image. Some panels provide thumbnail representations of the image to help with your editing. On the top right side of each panel, you will notice three lines

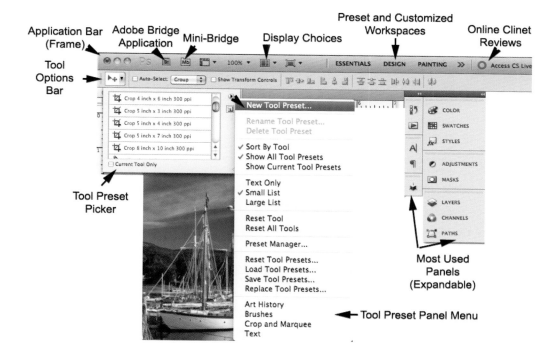

Application Bar (Frame), Adobe Bridge Application, Mini-Bridge, Display Choices, Preset and Customized Workspaces, Online Clinet Reviews, Tool Options Bar, Tool Preset Picker, Most Used Panels (Expandable), Tool Preset Panel Menu

▷ FIGURE 3-3

The Tool Options bar allows you to create and store tool presets, and set tool options. The Application bar allows you locate files (Adobe Bridge), choose display options, and select or customize your workspace.

(Figure 3-4). This is the **Panel Menu button**, which displays commands used for each particular panel. Most of these same commands may be located on the Menu bar as well. To display a panel, you can select it from the Window menu. Panels can be grouped together for easy access by clicking and dragging the panels tab in the top of the display and releasing it on top of the target group. They can also be dragged to the right of the desktop to become collapsible icons that you simply click on to expand; you can click on the panel top bar to contract or expand the panel as well. You can dock or organize your panels to have the ones you use most go in the left column as icons; others could go to the rightmost column displaying the panel name. You can also dock panels on the left side.

TOOLKIT TIP If you are using specific panels for a particular project you are working on, you can save the panels and their arrangement on your workspace when you edit the file in the future by selecting the Workspace (Essentials) button in the Application bar; or select Window > Workspace > Save Workspace, then give it a name so it can be used for similar work.

TOOLKIT TIP Panels and Tools panel looking too cluttered around your image? Press the Tab key and they disappear; press it again and they reappear. To keep just the Tools panel visible and hide the panels, press the Shift and Tab keys together.

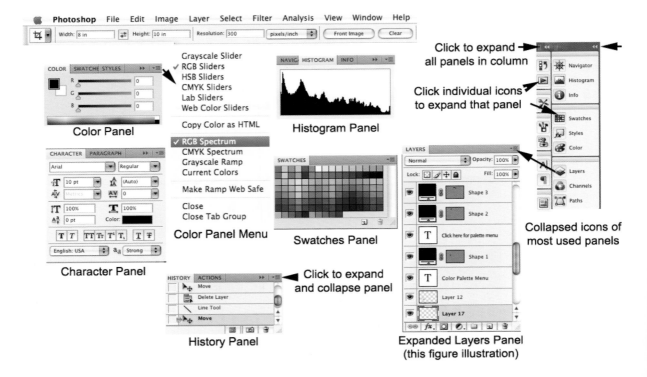

▷ FIGURE 3-4

Click on the top right corner (right arrow in earlier versions) to display each panel's individual menu. To expand, click on the panel icon; to collapse or expand a panel, click on the double arrows.

USING PHOTOSHOP HELP

Photoshop's Help menu allows the designer or photographer access to any information about tools, application features, updates, tasks, and terminology (Figure 3-5). In the Help menu, special wizards walk you through certain popular tasks, like resizing an image for web media or transferring your software activation to another computer. The Photoshop Help menu also displays a list of popular "How To" tutorials for many tasks, and you can create your own tutorial. You can look for topics by searching for keywords, or simply jumping from one topic to another by selecting from a list of text links. The online Adobe Help and Support Center lets you seek help among Photoshop and other Adobe applications in a weblike format, and it provides additional links to resources, documentation, and community support from peers, including video tutorials you can view and get expert product support. Online Help, entitled Photoshop Help and Support, can be accessed by selecting Help > Photoshop Help, or Photoshop Online in the Help menu. You can also download Help PDF's of tutorials and print them for later use. In CS5 there is a new help function called CS Review on the right side of the Application bar, where you can arrange to have your work securely shared and reviewed in real time with a client, or fellow designers.

▷ FIGURE 3-5

The Photoshop Help menu displays popular tasks and tutorials, updates, and online access. It also allows the designer to search by keywords, or online at the support center.

Type in what you are looking for

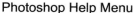

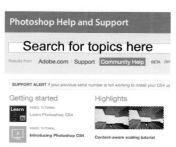

Photoshop Help Menu

Adobe Topic Search

Photoshop Online Support

CLIENT ASSIGNMENT: Basic Image Correction: Saving to Specific File Formats

Your client, Chris Winston, was given three images, two images for a local newsletter story and for a website on lighthouse restoration by a local resident, and one color image of an antique car behind a barn that needs to be converted to a B&W image for a local gallery advertisement in the newspaper. One of the lighthouse images is a low-contrast image and the other is an image that is off color. The car image is fine in color but needs to be converted and adjusted as a quality black and white image. He needs to have all images scanned, enhanced, and resized to be used for both commercial print use and a website. Looking at the images, you notice that both lighthouse images need overall color corrections, and the car image is a good candidate to create a quality black and white toned image. You know all these adjustments can be made by using the Image menu in Photoshop (Figure 3-6). You tell Chris to come around 5 o'clock and pick up his images.

ACTION ITEMS OVERVIEW

As a designer or photographer, you will be taking poorly exposed and off-color images and correcting them for the best color and definition for your client. You will also be taking a properly exposed color image and converting into a well toned B&W image. This assignment will also walk you through adjusting image sizes for print and web media output, along with using special automated commands and techniques in color correction. In you career, your judgment in creating good quality color images and your knowledge of how to use those images for various print and web media is essential to providing the right information and files for your client. You will duplicate the images, adjust both lighthouse images for best color, adjust for best B&W tones in the car image, and set the output resolutions for print and for web media output; then, you will save the images

Originals

Adjust contrast,
shadow, and highlights

Convertng colors for accuate
black and white tones

Auto Color Adjustment

▷ FIGURE 3-6

**Corrected images
using special
commands in the
Image menu.**

with the proper file extensions for use in printing and the web. For images used for the press, you will convert the default RGB color mode to CMYK color mode. This will help you understand the purpose of using various graphic file-format extensions.

Here is what you will need to do:

• Duplicate the images for print and web use, keeping the originals as backups.

• Adjust the tone (Auto Tone) on the low-contrast lighthouse image, compare the results, then adjust the original image again using the Shadows/Highlights command and compare with Auto Contrast for best accuracy of tones and color.

• Apply the Auto Color command to the lighthouse image with a poor color cast to correct it.

• Convert the car behind barn color image to an accurately toned B&W image.

• Convert high resolution RGB images for print to CMYK mode.

• Save the files used for print with .TIF extensions.

• Decrease the resolution of the two duplicated images to 72 dpi for monitor display on the web by using Photoshop's Image > Image Size command.

- Save the files for web media with .JPG extensions.

- The final nine files will be named for specific purposes: *FIXlight1.tif* and *FIXlight2.tif*, and *B&Wcarbarn.tif* for editing and printing, *CMYKlight1.tif*, *CMYKlight2.tif*, and *CMYKcarbarn.tif* for use in commercial printing, and *WEBlight1.jpg*, *WEBlight2.jpg*, and *WEBcarbarn.jpg* for electronic use. There is also an additional option to save images in native PSD format.

CORRECTING IMAGES FOR PRINT

Digital cameras, flash and portable hard drives, and scanned images are still the most popular formats to get an image into your computer. Once images are converted into digital files, Photoshop or any image-editing program can enhance, manipulate, or combine them with other images.

A WORD ABOUT SCANNING AND RESOLUTION

As a designer or photographer, before you scan, you need to determine the image's use. You need to determine whether it will be a high- or low-resolution image, which will dictate the amount of detail required in the image. Scan at a resolution of 300 dpi if you want to print an image ready for commercial press. For the web or e-mail only, scan at 72 dpi, because this is all your monitor needs to keep the file size small for quick downloading. When using a scanner, you need to stay within its **optical resolution** set by the manufacturer, which is what the scanner actually sees (i.e., 3600 dpi) or the original size of the image you are scanning, which can be adjusted and resized in Photoshop later. Scanning an image larger than the optical resolution (i.e., 4400 dpi) may add pixels between the actual pixels. This is known as **interpolation,** and it deteriorates the image sharpness and quality (to learn more about scanning, check out the exercise in the *Goodies > Chapter 3* folder on your text CD). Always edit at the highest resolution you think you will need first.

 TOOLKIT TIP Scanning software allows some basic editing during the preview scan before you do the final scan into Photoshop. Always preview the image first, make adjustments, and then perform the final scan.

NAVIGATING AROUND THE IMAGE

The **Zoom tool** allows you to get in close and then zoom out to observe the whole image. Selecting the plus sign on the Tool Options bar zooms in on an image, while selecting the minus sign allows you to zoom out and observe your work. In CS5, you can check the Scrubby Zoom option in the Tool Options bar to allow you to click and drag to zoom in and out of the image. If the Tool Options bar is not displayed, select it from the Window menu. Using the **Hand tool** is like moving a document with your own hands; it is great for quick positioning (Figure 3-7). The **Navigator panel** helps you see what portion of the image you have zoomed into. There is also the **Rotate View tool** (by the Hand tool) to rotate the image view nondestructively.

▷   FIGURE 3-7

**Use the Zoom and
Hand tools and the
Navigator panel
to find your way
around the image.**

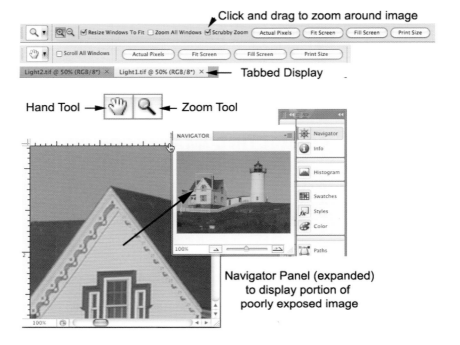

TOOLKIT TIP To quickly zoom out of an image when the Zoom Tool is selected,
press the Option (Mac) or Alt (PC) key. You can also use the View > Zoom In or View
> Zoom Out functions or type in the percentage at the bottom left of the window
to display different percentage amounts. Double clicking on the Zoom Tool goes to
100%, while double clicking on the Hand Tool fits the image in the window.

You will open the original, poorly exposed Light1 and Light2 images in your
Chapter 3 folder, and then you will use the Zoom and Hand tools to navigate
your way around the images.

1. Launch Photoshop and open (File > Open) the two files *Light1.tif* and *Light2.tif*
   in your *Chapter 3* folder inside the *Photoshop* folder you created in Chapter 1;
   or open the files on your Student CD that came with your text (If a dialog box
   displays about ignoring file info data, click OK).

2. In CS5, the two documents should be set as tabbed displays; select the *Light1*
   image. If the images are not set up as tabbed, select the Arrange Documents
   button in the Application bar, and select Consolidate All (first icon-default). In
   earlier versions, minimize the window of the *Light2* image and leave the *Light1*
   window open.

3. Select the View menu in the Menu bar and make sure Rulers is checked to display
   the rulers. Select the Zoom tool, then select the *Light1* image and click until the
   image is at 100% (shown on the Title bar). Using the Navigator panel, note where
   you are on the image by observing the red rectangle around the view area.

4. Use the scroll bars to move around and to observe that any changes you make will show up in the Navigator panel. You can also drag the slider on the Navigator panel to zoom around the image.

5. Select the minus sign on the Tool Options bar and zoom out until the entire image shows on the screen. You can also hold down the Option/Alt key to zoom back out. Remember this is a poor quality image.

6. Now maximize the *Light2* image and select the Zoom tool again.

7. Zoom in to about 200%.

8. Select the Hand tool and click and drag the image around. Notice that the change shows on the Navigator panel.

9. Select the Zoom tool and zoom out (minus sign on the Tool Options bar) until the entire image shows. Make sure the Scrubby Zoom option is checked in the toolbar, then click on the image and drag with your mouse to zoom in and out of the image. Leave both files open for the next exercise.

 TOOLKIT TIP Most images carry a color identity profile, called an *ICC profile*, that defines colors and embeds the color information with the file. If, when you open a file, and a Profile Mismatch dialog box appears, select OK and leave the default; Photoshop will automatically adjust the colors of that image for consistency. It does not cause any problems with your computer and does not adjust any preference settings.

 TOOLKIT TIP Now, it is time for your math quiz. In Photoshop, if the images that you are viewing with the Zoom and Hand tools are at a scanned resolution of 300 dpi, why would they display very large on your monitor? Your monitor only displays at 72 dpi! How much bigger is the 300 dpi image going to be on your 72 dpi monitor at full size? Yep, about four times the size, which is why the image may appear much larger full size (the title bar will read 100% in the title) on the monitor. The percentage of an image's size is displayed in the Title bar of the image window. Remember, the monitor will only display at 72 dpi. To see the actual size, choose View > Print Size.

USING THE IMAGE MENU

The **Image menu** in Photoshop contains commands for all kinds of image enhancements and modifications (Figure 3-8). Some of the commands you will be using are the Mode, Duplicate, Adjustments, and Image Size commands. The **Duplicate command** creates an exact image copy. The **Adjustments command** in the Image menu (Image > Adjustments) gives you the ability to make a variety of color adjustments and editing changes to an image or to selected portions of an image. The **Image Size command** allows you to adjust an image's size while the **Mode command** assigns different color modes and profiles for various media.

▷ FIGURE 3-8

The Image menu is used for most editing of the image or selected portions of the image.

Image

Mode	► ←	Assign color modes and profiles
Adjustments	► ←	Enhancing and modifying the image
Auto Tone	⇧⌘L ←	Adjusts tonal balance of colors for detail in highlights and shadows
Auto Contrast	⌥⇧⌘L ←	Readjusts an image's washed out highlights or blocked shadows
Auto Color	⇧⌘B ←	Adjusts color imbalances by looking for black or white areas
Image Size...	⌥⌘I ←	Adjusts the document and screen size of the image
Canvas Size...	⌥⌘C ←	Placement of the image within the canvas or page
Image Rotation	► ←	Rotation of the entire document (including all layers)
Crop	←	Removes the background outside of the image selection
Trim...	←	Precise removal of background pixels and image edges
Reveal All	←	Reveals position of layer images outside of the page area
Duplicate...	←	Creates an exact image copy
Apply Image...	←	Blend one layer onto another image
Calculations...	←	Blend from multiple sources with varying opacities
Variables	► ←	Used to define which elements in a template change
Apply Data Set...	←	Apply a data set's contents to the base image
Trap...	←	Setting used in printing to prevent gaps between overlapping images

DUPLICATING IMAGES

When you have an image that you want to make changes to, it is a good idea to always make a copy of the original image in case something goes wrong (Figure 3-9). You should always duplicate the original image before applying any changes, because once changes are saved, they may not be able to be undone. The copy serves as a backup. Duplicating an image only makes a duplicate of the displayed image within Photoshop; it does not automatically save the duplicate copy to the hard drive.

▷ FIGURE 3-9

It's a good habit to duplicate an image before making any changes.

In this exercise, you will duplicate the *Light1* and *Light2* files for the next exercises.

1. Select the *Light1* image on the Photoshop desktop.

2. Select Image > Duplicate to create an image copy before making any adjustments; name the copy *FIXlight1*, then select OK.

3. Select the file *Light2* you opened in Photoshop.

4. Select Image > Duplicate to create an image copy before making any adjustments; name the copy *FIXlight2*, then select OK.

5. Close both the original *Light1* and *Light2* TIF files—do not save any changes—to serve as backup copies; leave the *FIXlight1* and *FIXlight2* files open for the next exercise.

CORRECTING IMAGES USING AUTO TONE

You can adjust an image's contrast or its highlights and shadows by using Auto Tone and Auto Contrast from the Image menu (Figure 3-10). **Auto Tone** (Auto Levels in earlier versions) adjusts the tonal balance of colors to show detail in highlights and shadows, which works well by rearranging an image's tones slightly to provide detail in all areas. **Auto Contrast** works with images that need lightening and darkening in highlights and shadows. You will find that Auto Contrast is used when shadow and highlight values need to be adjusted or clipped and readjusted in an image to make the highlights appear lighter and shadows appear darker. It *does not* improve flat, faint, or underexposed images. There are different ways to observe the changes before and after you have applied the effect. You can use the Edit > Undo/Redo commands, or Undo State Change (or Undo "effect name"), or you can toggle the Command/Ctrl + Z keys on your keyboard. The **Fade command** in the Edit menu allows you to adjust the amount of the effect you are applying and blending modes.

TOOLKIT TIP To toggle the changes and see the results before and after the applied effect, hold down the Command (Apple) key on the Mac, or Ctrl key on the PC, and press the Z key. These are great hot-key combos for quick observations.

Here, you will use the Auto Tone (Auto Levels in previous versions) and Auto Contrast commands to enhance a dull image to see which looks best. To observe the changes, you will use the Undo/Redo commands, commands in the Edit menu, and the toggle keys Command + Z (Mac)/Ctrl + Z (PC).

1. Select the *FIXlight1* image of the low contrast lighthouse on the Photoshop desktop. Use the Zoom tool to view the entire image, or press Command/Ctrl 0.

2. Select Image > Auto Tone to adjust the tonal balance. For earlier versions, select Image > Adjustments > Auto Levels. Select Edit > Fade Auto Tone and adjust the amount of the effect you apply for the best overall tone adjustment.

▷ FIGURE 3-10

Photoshop provides the Auto Tone commands to adjust poorly exposed or flat images. You can step through your changes or Fade in your effect in the Edit menu.

3. Select Edit > Undo Fade Auto Tone to see the previous image, then Edit > Redo Fade Auto Tone (or Undo State Change if it displays), to toggle back to the corrected image. You will notice that it makes fairly good color and tonal corrections. Use the Edit menu to Step Backward (twice) the original low-contrast image.

4. Select Image > Auto Contrast (for earlier versions, select Image > Adjustments > Auto Contrast). You will notice in this case that it makes the image too contrasted without enough midtone colors. Usually this command is for increasing contrast in highlight and shadow areas in a well-exposed image; it does not improve flat, faint, or underexposed images.

5. Toggle the keys Command + Z (Mac) or Ctrl + Z (PC) to observe the before and after effects. Go back to the original low-contrast image when you are done.

USING THE SHADOWS/HIGHLIGHTS COMMAND

The Shadows/Highlights command (Image > Adjustments > Shadows/Highlights) is used for carefully correcting poorly exposed (overexposed: too light; underexposed: too dark) areas in photographic images—it is a dialog box that allows you to adjust highlights and shadows in an image (Figure 3-11). When Show More Options is checked, it provides a series of sliders for more advanced detailed adjustments in highlights, shadows, and color correction by adjusting Tonal Width, Pixel Radius, and Midtones. In the Edit menu, the Step Backward and Step Forward commands let you observe changes made in a series of steps, or use the Fade command to adjust the amount of the effect applied.

Here, you will make adjustments to the image until it is visibly accurate to your eye; then, you will move forward and backward through your steps using the Edit menu.

1. With the *FIXlight1* image displayed, select Image > Adjustments > Shadows/Highlights to adjust the tonal balance.

2. When the dialog box comes up, make sure the Preview box is checked to view the results, and drag the dialog box alongside the image.

▷ FIGURE 3-11

The Shadows/
Highlights command corrects
underexposed
and overexposed
images and
flat images more
accurately than
other methods
by precisely fine
tuning highlights,
shadows, midtones,
and color.

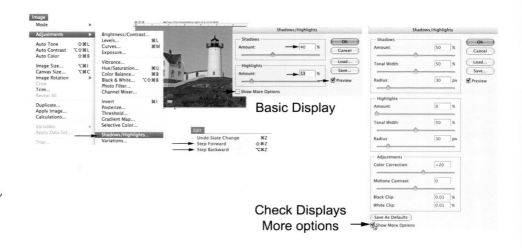

3. Start with 40% in the Shadows area to lighten it up and 15% in the Highlights area. You can either move the sliders, or to be more accurate, type the amounts in the appropriate boxes.

4. Adjust the sliders to make the picture look better, then click on the Show More Options to display more adjustments.

5. Feel free to make slight adjustments with these effects until the image looks best, with details in the shadows and highlights, and visibly accurate color of the white lighthouse set in green grass against the blue sky. Click OK to exit the dialog box.

6. Select Edit > Step Backward to see the previous changes then Edit > Step Forward to observe the changes in the image.

7. Notice that you have much better control with the Shadows/Highlights effect than in the previous exercise with Auto Tone and Auto Contrast.

8. Leave the *FIXlight1* image open for the later exercise in saving as a .TIF file.

CORRECTING COLOR CASTS WITH AUTO COLOR

The **Auto Color command** looks for color casts in an image and adjusts imbalanced colors (Figure 3-12). It looks for a true white and black in an image and any gray to adjust for midtones. If you have an old image, a poorly scanned image, or an image with any color casts that may have been caused by improper digital camera settings, the Auto Color command works quite nicely. In the Edit menu, a designer or photographer can use the Fade Auto Color command for further tweaking of the result. To compare the results, use the Step Forward and Step Backward commands in the Edit menu to go back through a series of steps. The Undo State command also can be used to revert back and move forward to previous states. The command works best in images with black or white areas.

▷ FIGURE 3-12

The Auto Color command removes colorcasts from old or poorly scanned images, and may correct images from a digital camera with an improper color setting.

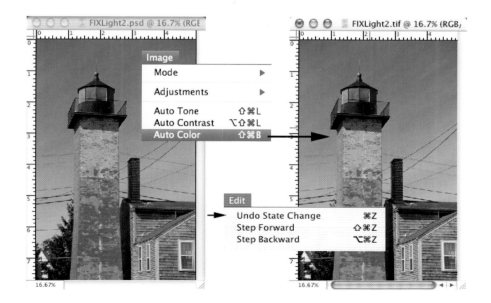

DESIGN TIP

The Auto Color command gives the designer the flexibility to correct many color cast images quickly to check for any color imbalances before performing any other editing tasks. This command also helps when working with many images from many different sources with a variety of colors.

In this exercise, you will use the Auto Color command to remove a red color cast.

1. Select the file *FIXlight2*, which has a red color cast.

2. Choose Image > Auto Color (Image > Adjustments > Auto Color in earlier versions) and watch the red cast change into more normal colors.

3. Select Edit > Undo Auto Color (or Undo State Change if it displays) to see the previous image; then Edit > Redo Auto Color to toggle between the corrected image and the original off-color image.

4. Try Edit > Fade Auto Color and adjust the Opacity setting to tweak the changes in color. Toggle between states until you feel the best color displays; leave the mode set to Normal for now.

5. Leave this file open with the new changes applied. We will save both adjusted images in the next exercise.

SAVING FILES WITH THE .TIF EXTENSION

Files saved with a .TIF extension can be edited repeatedly and still be as accurate as the original image. They can be edited in Photoshop or any graphic application without losing quality, because they are saved in a **universal format** that can be read by any graphic application (Figure 3-13). Graphic files saved with a .TIF extension are preferred in the commercial printing industry; they also generate the largest file sizes, so be aware of the space needed to store these files.

▷ FIGURE 3-13

Save both adjusted images as .TIF extension files for a universal format that can be read by any graphics application.

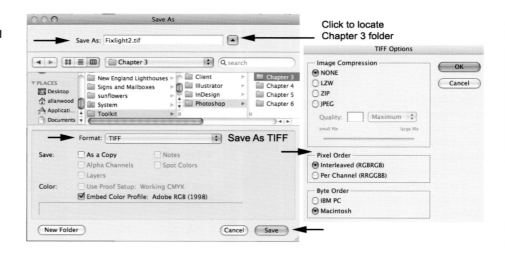

DESIGN TIP

Images that have telephone wires can be made better by removing the wires and other distractions using retouching tools like the Clone or Patch tools in Photoshop. You will learn to use these in Chapter 6.

Here, you will save the two adjusted *FIXlight* files as .TIF files for commercial printing.

1. Select the *FIXlight1* tab and Save As *FIXlight1.tif* in the *Chapter 3* folder on your drive (File > Save As, and keep default settings).

2. When the .TIFF Options window displays, select an Image Compression of NONE for best accuracy, then in the Byte Order section, select your computer (PC or Mac).

3. Select OK and leave the file open for the next exercise.

4. Repeat the same process with the *FIXlight2* image and Save As *FIXlight2.tif* in the *Chapter 3* folder. Select OK after you have entered all settings and, again, leave the file open.

SAVING IN PHOTOSHOP'S NATIVE PSD FORMAT (OPTIONAL)

It is sometimes a good idea to save an image in the application's native format to use as a back-up copy. In the case of Photoshop, the extension is **.PSD** (Photoshop document). As a native file, it can be read by other Adobe products or other Photoshop users and edited with ease without losing quality; but because it is not an extension that can be read by all graphic applications universally, some may not be able to read it. It does provide an accurate back-up copy of the original image for future use. To save in a different identifiable format extension, in a different location, or as a different file name, you would use the Save As command. Whether you save a file as a .TIF extension or its native extention, .PSD, the quality on both is the same. As you save to a new format, PSD for instance, the newly saved format remains open and the previous format (TIF) closes.

TOOLKIT TIP In Windows, you may notice that no other files are displayed in the *Chapter 3* folder when you are saving in .PSD format. That is because only files with the same format extension are displayed, and since there are no other .PSD files in the folder, it appears blank.

Here you will save the corrected images in Photoshop's native .PSD format on your hard drive. You will also display the images with rulers on the top and left sides.

1. Select the *FIXlight1.tif* file. For Mac users, select File > Save As > *FIXLight1.psd*. In the Format drop-down box, select the Photoshop (or PSD in other versions) format to save in Photoshop's native format in the *Chapter 3* folder on your drive. For Windows users, select File > Save As > File name > *FIXLight1.psd*. Select Photoshop as the format and save in the *Chapter 3* folder. Leave all other default settings as they are.

2. Select the other *FIXlight2.tif* and Save As *FIXLight2.psd* in the *Chapter 3* folder, as mentioned in Step 1. Leave all other default settings as they are.

3. For future editing, and to get an idea of the image sizes, select View and make sure Rulers (View > Rulers) is checked to display the rulers.

4. Close the .PSD files to be used as backups, and reopen your TIF files, *FIXlight1* and *FIXlight2,* in your *Chapter 3* folder for the next exercise.

CONVERTING A COLOR IMAGE TO BLACK AND WHITE

DESIGN TIP

Converting a color image to B&W involves looking at all details in an image. Avoid cloudless skies, skin tones in overcast shadow, or images with low or poor contrast.

The Image menu also provides a designer or photographer the ability to make special changes to the pixels in an image. The Adjustments menu (Image > Adjustments) provides a series of commands to modify, enhance, or adjust an image's pixels. The Black and White command inside the Adjustments menu provides a series of color-based adjustments to create a well-toned black and white image from the original color image. The colors act as filters much as are sometimes used by photographers in front of their cameras or in the chemical darkroom. As a guide, increasing the color lightens that B&W tone in the image, and decreasing the color darkens that B&W tone in the image. You can also use a series of preset settings and create your own customized settings, including various color tints for special effect. Welcome to your digital black and white darkroom with no smelly chemicals!

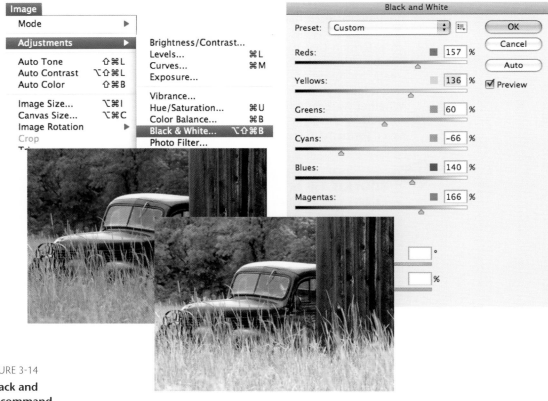

▷ FIGURE 3-14

The Black and White command provides all the adjustments needed to convert color images into well toned B&W images.

This exercise will serve also as a review of what has been covered so far. You will be converting the car behind the barn color image to an image that displays a wide range of black and white tones.

1. Open the file *Carbarn.tif* in your *Chapter 3* folder inside the Photoshop folder you created in Chapter 1; or open the file on your Student CD that came with your text. Make sure the whole image displays 100%.

2. Select Image > Duplicate to create an image copy before making any adjustments; name the copy *B&Wcarbarn.tif*, then select OK.

3. Close the original *carbarn.tif* file you just made a copy of to serve as the original backup copy; leave the *B&Wcarbarn.tif* file open.

4. Select Image > Adjustments > Black & White. Use Figure 3-14 as a starting point for your adjustments. Use the Zoom tool and Navigation bar to look at details of your adjustments. Use the Edit menu to move backward and forward for any adjustments.

5. Make note of your favorite settings, then click on the Presets selections to see other B&W options for the image, or create your own and Save as a Preset. Adjust for the best range of B&W tones. Pretty nice, huh?

6. Select File > Save > *B&Wcarbarn.tif* and keep the default settings.

7. When the .TIFF Options window displays, select an Image Compression of NONE for best accuracy, then in the Byte Order section, select your computer (PC or Mac). Save the file in the *Chapter 3* folder you created. Optional: Feel free to save an additional file in the native PSD extension as shown earlier.

8. Select OK and leave the file open for the next exercise.

SETTING RESOLUTION AND IMAGE SIZE IN PHOTOSHOP

Increasing or decreasing an image's size or resolution, either for print or for the web, is called *resampling.* You can use the Image Size command under the Image menu to do this by changing Pixel Dimensions for electronic media or Document Size for print output. By keeping a check mark in the **Resample Image** box in the Image Size dialog box, you can change the resolution or the image size, which automatically changes the number of pixels and adjusts the file size. Keeping a check mark in the **Constrain Proportions** box allows you to increase or reduce the image size proportionately to avoid distortion. In Photoshop, another box to keep checked is the **Scale Styles** box, especially if you applied any effects on your image; this feature scales the effects proportionately without distortion when you are resizing, so leave this checked as a default. When you make changes to the pixels or the document size, Photoshop adjusts the rest proportionately when all three boxes are checked (Figure 3-14). Interpolation, mentioned earlier, is the action of adding pixels in between pixels to enlarge an image; this seriously deteriorates image quality. Always resample or resize down in an original image to maintain quality—never up. Now we need to adjust the image sizes for print. The resolution is already set in this example for a newspaper submission.

TOOLKIT TIP When resizing a corrected image, you could again create a duplicate, rename it, and save it as a copy of the original corrected file. Also when resizing an image, always set the highest resolution first, then adjust the size.

By leaving Resample Image checked, pixel dimensions change and file adjustments are made

**FIXlight1 (white lighthouse)
resampled down to size**

Now you will resize the corrected images so they will be ready for print.

1. Select the *FIXlight1* tab and choose Image > Image Size in the Menu bar.

2. Make sure Scale Styles, Constrain Proportions, and Resample Image: are checked. The resolution is already set previously for a newspaper.

3. Type a "4" in the Width of the Document Size area and Photoshop adjusts the rest—make sure the units are set to Inches. Click OK.

4. Select the *FIXlight2* tab and choose Image > Image Size, entering a 4-inch Width, as shown in Figure 3-15. Repeat the same process with the *B&Wcarbarn* file. Do not adjust the resolution.

5. You will notice in all three images that the pixel dimensions decreased, which in turn decreased the file size. Actual numbers may be slightly different than shown.

6. Save all three files in your *Chapter 3* folder with their default names, and leave open for the next exercise.

ENLARGING AN IMAGE WITHOUT INTERPOLATION

For good quality prints to be used for commercial press work, you rarely need more than 300 dpi resolution. Scanning at higher resolutions using the same size image is wasteful and creates huge file sizes. However, if you need to enlarge the original image's size and avoid interpolation, you can scan at a higher dpi—like 600 dpi, to double the size of the original image—and then resample the resolution in Photoshop to 300 dpi without adding any pixels.

You can do this by removing the check mark in the Resample Image box and leaving the Constrain Proportions box checked to adjust the file size in conjunction with the resolution proportionately; while maintaining the same number of pixels, it merely redistributes the pixels within the image. Figure 3-16 shows you how it is done; no exercises are necessary. Always remember to adjust the image resolution before resizing the dimensions.

TOOLKIT TIP In Photoshop, with the Image Size dialog box, you will see choices beside Resample Image. Try Bicubic Smoother, which works nicely in creating enlargements; Bicubic is always the default when in doubt.

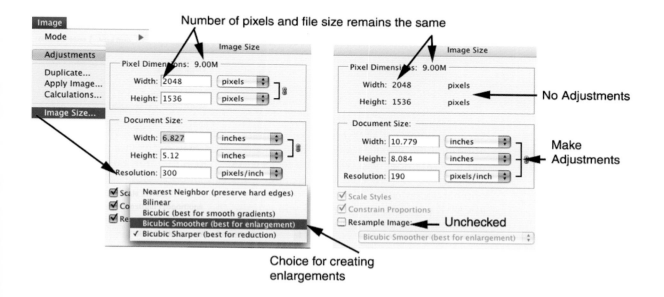

▷ FIGURE 3-16

Unchecking Resample Image rearranges the same amount of pixels to the adjusted resolution, changing only the file size.

USING RGB AND CMYK COLOR MODES

When working with images in Photoshop, it defaults to the RGB color mode; this is because red, green, and blue, when added in different combinations, create all other colors electronically. This is the working color space you normally use with your computer's monitor, because RGB images contain the original image data. Use RGB mode for all initial set up and editing, which we have done in the exercises in this chapter. This mode works fine for designing images for electronic displays, like web pages, computer monitors, e-mail, and for local printing to an ink-jet printer or laser printer. This is good for showing a client proofs of what the final design and layout will look like. Since image files *FIXlight1*, *B&Wcarbarn*, and *FIXlight2* will be printed on commercial press for a newspaper, you should convert the images to CMYK to closely match the ink pigments on the press. The colors cyan (C), magenta (M), and yellow (Y) are used as part of a subtractive process by creating all ink colors as a percentage of these three colors. Black (K) is automatically added for details in the shadows and to provide contrast in ink colors. Commercial printers only use CMYK color, and it is important for you, the designer or photographer, to send them the final images as CMYK (Figure 3-17).

▷ FIGURE 3-17

Images that will be used for commercial printing need to be converted to CMYK color mode.

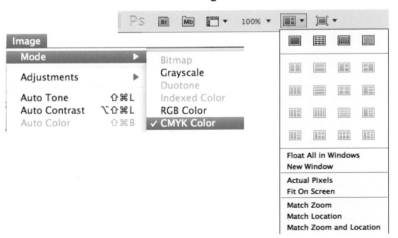

Saving images in CMYK mode before going to the printer helps the designer or photographer visualize any possible changes that may occur in color from RGB mode. Remember, you will still be seeing it on an RGB monitor, but you will have a better idea of how colors will be affected. It is a good habit always to save the original document in RGB mode for future editing and keep a duplicate document in CMYK mode for press. In CS5 you can use the Arrange Documents button on the Application bar to set up the images next to each other for comparison. Go ahead, play!

Here you will convert and save the three adjusted images as CMYK files in preparation for use by a commercial printer.

1. With the *B&Wcarbarn*, *FIXlight1,* and *FIXlight2* images open on the Photoshop desktop, select each image and select Image > Duplicate, leaving the default name as a copy. Select the *FIXlight1 copy* image and then choose Image > Mode > CMYK Color. When a display box opens warning about choosing CMYK, select OK to continue, since you made a duplicate of the *FIXlight1* file. Save the file in your Chapter 3 folder as *CMYKlight1.tif* so that *FIXlight1* remains as the backup RGB file for any future editing. You always want the original edit in RGB mode.

2. Repeat the same process for the *FIXlight2* and the *B&Wcarbarn* files. Use the Arrange Documents button to display all the images next to each other to compare for any color changes; look carefully. Close the CMYK files you just created after they have been saved.

3. Your CMYK files are ready for press. Note: These images are a lower resolution for educational purposes and thus are not the high resolution 300 DPI images you would normally need for preparing for press.

TOOLKIT TIP Most commercial printers, in order to communicate between creators of various documents, use a universally accepted PDF mode (Adobe Acrobat). This is an electronic format that embeds or pastes in documents images and text without the user having to choose the required color mode or font. In the Unit 1 review, you downloaded the universal Acrobat Reader to read any PDF files from any platform. This will be covered more in depth later.

PREPARING IMAGES FOR WEB MEDIA

With the three images adjusted for commercial print output, you can duplicate the corrected images you created earlier in the default RGB format, and saved as "FIX" files, change the resolution settings, and save the file in a compressed format for much smaller file sizes appropriate for web display (figure 3-18).

DUPLICATING AND RENAMING CORRECTED IMAGES

With the three images corrected, you can now make duplicates and rename them so they can be adjusted for web media. The corrections will remain intact in the copies.

In the next exercise, you will duplicate the new enhanced images so they can be adjusted for use on the web.

1. Select the *FIXlight1.tif* image on the Photoshop desktop.

2. Choose Image > Duplicate to make a copy of the image.

3. When the dialog box appears, name the copy *WEBLight1*. Click OK and leave the file open. Close the *FIXlight1* file.

4. Repeat the same process with the *FIXlight2* and *B&Wcarbarn* files, leaving the WEB files open and closing both FIXlight files and the *B&Wcarbarn* file.

ADJUSTING IMAGE SIZE FOR WEB MEDIA

To get the images ready for the web, they need to be resampled down to a resolution of 72 ppi in order to display correctly on a monitor and keep the file size to a minimum (Figure 3-18). When adjusting or measuring images for electronic display, use the Pixel Dimensions area in the Image Size dialog box for adjustments; change the resolution to 72 ppi as the standard size. Remember, always adjust the resolution first, then the image size.

DESIGN TIP

When creating duplicate images that will be used for different media, always start off enhancing the highest resolution image first; then make a copy for other media, such as the web, that can be adjusted in Photoshop. The duplicate will retain the changes used in the original enhanced image.

▷ FIGURE 3-18

Duplicating the adjusted images for web media.

DESIGN TIP

Always scan at your highest resolution size needed first (i.e., 300 dpi for print), and then make adjustments for lower resolution or smaller size images later. When you resize or modify an image in Photoshop to be used for the web, display the image at full size while making changes. When preparing images for the web, make sure they are at the exact dimensions needed; they will always display at full size.

In this exercise, you will take both web-labeled images and resample them down to 72 ppi for use on the web.

1. Select the file *WEBlight1* on your desktop.

2. Select Image > Image Size to display the dialog box.

3. You will notice the resolution is set at 200 dpi as if for print media (for commercial print, you would normally use 300 dpi, but in the previous exercise as it was for a newspaper, we were able to use a lower resolution, which also kept the file size down).

4. Make sure the Scale Styles, Constrain Proportions, and Resample Image: boxes are all checked.

5. Enter 72 in the Resolution box; the pixel dimensions will change automatically, decreasing the file size for the web (Figure 3-19 shows settings for *WEBlight1*).

6. Try choosing Bicubic Sharper, under Resample Image, when reducing image sizes to maintain image clarity. When in doubt, keep the default Bicubic setting.

7. Leave the document size the same and select OK.

8. Zoom the image to 100% (displays in Title bar).

9. Repeat the same process with the *WEBlight2* and *WEBB&Wcarbarn* files. Leave the three files open to save as JPEGs.

TOOLKIT TIP Another safer method to see the maximum size under the resolution you have chosen is to uncheck Resample Image, Constrain Proportions, and Scale Styles so that the dimensions remain unchanged and cannot be edited. Type in the Resolution (highest first), then go back and check all three as shown in Figure 3-19, and then type in the size. The resolution will not change and the pixels will either be redistributed so you can see the maximum size allowed, hopefully without any pixels added, or the pixels will be removed, maintaining maximum image quality.

TOOLKIT TIP In the Help menu, there is a "How to Create Web Images" link that shows you options to use the Save for Web & Devices command to create JPEG images, which you will be exposed to later, and for saving for e-mail to send to someone to give you some tips on sending small files to family and friends. The Help menu is a great resource. Try using this method with one of the original *Light1*, *Light2*. or *carbarn* files, as if you were making images for the web; use 72 ppi to keep the file size minimal for practice. Zoom to 100% before selecting the Help link for online use. When finished, do not save your file.

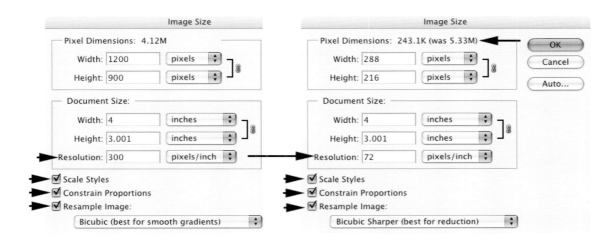

▷ FIGURE 3-19
To set up for web media, with check marks as shown, and type in a resolution of 72 ppi. You can then subtract further pixels as desired.

SAVING IMAGES AS JPEG FILES

Images saved with a .JPG extension generate smaller compressed files and are used primarily for the web or when smaller file sizes are needed. This is a universal format, which can be read by most graphic applications. Images that are saved as JPEGs, however, lose data each time they are compressed and saved. When JPEG images are edited and resaved a number of times, they will start to deteriorate—without necessarily reducing the file size. You can set the quality of the compressed, saved image at the maximum number (12), resulting in the highest quality or accuracy and a larger file size. The lower the number, the lower the quality; however, electronic display of images is pretty forgiving because of the limited number of colors monitors can display.

DESIGN TIP

Remember, you can safely resample down or remove pixels, but enlarging by adding more pixels than those contained in the original image will cause interpolation and seriously deteriorate the image quality.

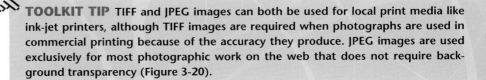

TOOLKIT TIP TIFF and JPEG images can both be used for local print media like ink-jet printers, although TIFF images are required when photographs are used in commercial printing because of the accuracy they produce. JPEG images are used exclusively for most photographic work on the web that does not require background transparency (Figure 3-20).

Here, you will save the new web images as JPEGs for the web to keep the file size down.

1. Select and Save the image *WEBlight1* as *WEBlight1.jpg* in your *Chapter 3* folder (File > Save As > *WEBlight1.jpg,* making sure you select the JPEG format), leaving any default settings (Figure 3-20).

2. Select the High setting of 8 in Image Options for an image that will display nicely on a web page while keeping the file size small for faster downloading.

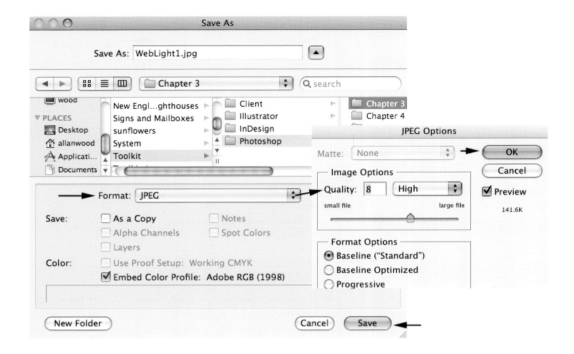

▷   FIGURE 3-20

Saving files in JPEG format helps compress the file size for use in electronic display or the web.

3. Select and save the images *WEBlight2* as *WEBlight2.jpg,* and *WEBcarbarn* as *WEBcarbarn.jpg,* with the High setting of 8, in your *Chapter 3* folder. Leave any default settings.

4. You now have three enhanced images for web display, along with the three you created earlier for commercial print media.

SAVE FOR WEB & DEVICES COMMAND IN PHOTOSHOP

To save images that will be used on the web, Photoshop also has a Save for Web & Devices command (File > Save for Web & Devices). Before using this command, a designer or photographer should have the image dimensions already established for the web to display it at actual size (100 percent). When working

▷ FIGURE 3-21

Using Save for Web & Devices, you select various .JPG, .GIF, and .PNG file extensions to determine the best download time and image quality.

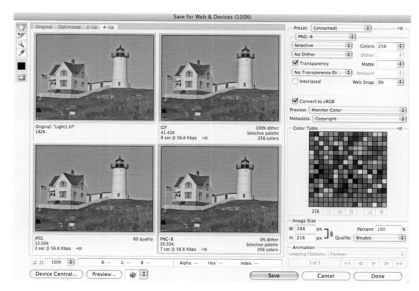

Select image frame, then file format to view

DESIGN TIP

For web images, you usually would not need to save a JPEG with the maximum setting, unless you are planning on further editing. As mentioned before, however, it is not wise to edit and save JPEG images; use the original file and use the Save As command to retain quality. A high quality setting for a large screen image provides all the needed details and keeps the file size smaller for faster download times. Lower quality settings may be useful for smaller image sizes or thumbnails on a web page.

with images for the web in Photoshop, always make sure the image is displayed at 100 percent and is the final size decided upon for display. If the image is too large to be displayed at 100 percent, and you find yourself scrolling around the display, go into the Image menu (Image > Image Size) and adjust the pixel size to 600 pixels or less at 72 dpi resolution, unless the image is to be used as a background image to fill the screen. With the Save for Web & Devices command, a designer or photographer can choose up to four methods of output display in quality (Original, .GIF, .JPG, and .PNG formats) and an approximate download time to observe what works best for the intended purpose (Figure 3-21). If you want, try this command on one of the images, compare different settings in quality and download time, but do not save the file. This will be covered more in depth in Chapter 10.

FILE FORMATS REVIEW

Here is a table to give you an idea of some graphic file extension formats. We have covered TIFF and JPEG, and introduced PDFs so far. The rest we'll be covering in future chapters. When you are creating images for a client, it is crucial to understand how the graphic files will be used.

FORMAT	ADVANTAGES	CONSIDERATIONS
PNG	Records transparencies in bitmap and vector images. Compresses files without losing data. Web use.	Cannot be read by older browsers. Larger size files but can still be used for the web. Cannot be enlarged.
GIF	Used for vector graphics and animation. Used on the web. Keeps transparencies.	GIF files have only 256 colors. Scalable.
JPEG	Compressed format used in photographic images. Keeps file sizes small. Used for web and ink-jet proof printing.	Data is thrown out each time the image is saved, gradually deteriorating quality. No transparencies. Not for commercial press. Cannot be enlarged.
TIF	Most accurate recording of detail in photographs. Quality maintains as original regardless of changes. Can be used for commercial printing of photographs.	Largest file size. Not used for the web. Cannot be enlarged.
PDF	Compresses text and graphics in documents without losing data for electronic distribution and the web. Works best with many documents. Can also be used for soft proofs and commercial printing. Editable in Photoshop and Illustrator.	Can also be read in free Acrobat Reader program.
EPS	Preferred method when combining graphics and type. Vector graphics can be scalable. Used extensively for commercial printing.	Large file size. Not for the web.

Need additional fun computer graphics tutorials and info, and an additional look at the projects you'll be creating in this book? Check out my Artist's Digital Toolkit website at: http://www.digitoolkit.com

THE NEW DOCUMENT DIALOG BOX

In Photoshop, if you are creating a new document from scratch, and you know what specific media it will be used for, you can set the color mode in the New Document dialog box (RGB, CMYK, LAB, or Grayscale), along with other settings, including selecting preset sizes for print, web, and video or for creating a custom size document (Figure 3-22). You will find a Device Central button that creates custom sizes based on whatever mobile media you want to use your images on. Be wary that you should not start out a document in CMYK color mode, unless you are not planning on converting it back to RGB mode. Also, many of Photoshop's filters do not work on CMYK images. Stay in the habit of making all edits in RGB color mode and save a separate file in CMYK mode for press. You can also adjust the resolution, observe the image file size of the document, and create a new document based upon a previous size or an image that has been copied into your clipboard; more on that in Chapter 10.

TOOLKIT TIP **Device Central** enables Photoshop users to preview how Photoshop files will look on a variety of mobile devices. It lists proposed document sizes based on the device or devices you have selected (mobile phones, etc.). You can create a separate mobile document for each display size or try to find one size appropriate for all devices by using either the smallest or largest suggested document size as a common denominator.

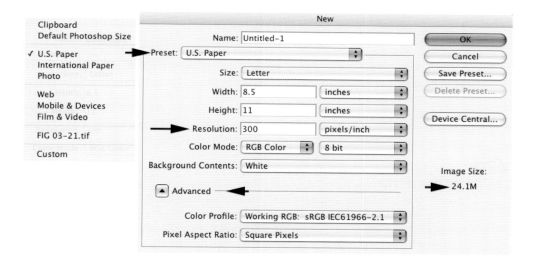

▷ FIGURE 3-22

If you know the media your new document will be used for, you can set the resolution ahead of time and select preset sizes.

Here, you will open a new document and navigate around the dialog box observing settings.

1. To create a new document with the color mode set, select File > New.

2. When the New display window opens, use the Color Mode bar to see your choices.

3. Look around the Preset sizes, adjust the Resolution, and notice the changes in Image size. If you are using Photoshop Extended version you will notice settings for video as well.

4. Click OK and then close the file without saving it.

ADVANCED USER: Using Histograms for Manual Levels Adjustment and Curves for Precise Toning

There are a lot of manual adjustments you can make on your own to enhance an image. One of these, the Shadows/Highlights command used earlier, adjusted poorly exposed images. Another of these is the **Levels command** in the Image menu. This provides more subtlety and precision by making adjustments to details in the highlights and shadows of an image. The Levels dialog box displays what is called a **histogram**, which is a graph that shows the highlight, shadow, and middletone properties of an image. By adjusting the histogram, you can control the amount of detail in the highlights and shadows by redistributing pixels to generate the full range of tones. In Photoshop, there is a **Histogram panel** (Window > Histogram) that displays the before (gray) and after (black) histograms to see the changes made in an image (Figure 3-23). Adjusting the levels of an image brings back hidden details. Many digital cameras can display a histogram in the LCD display, so the photographer can check for proper exposure. When the image is opened in Photoshop, this same histogram is displayed as the image's digital fingerprint when accessed through the Levels dialog box and the Histogram panel. Histograms can be edited in whatever color mode is selected or in the individual channels, R, G, or B or C, M, Y, and K. The Histogram panel allows you to view individual color channels. Photoshop also has a **Curves** adjustment which allows the designer or photographer more precision in adjusting for toning in highlights, midtones, and shadow details using a system of plotting points in those areas that need adjustments.

TOOLKIT TIP Many well-exposed image histograms with details in shadows, midtones, and highlights display a graph across all tones with peaks and valleys. Adjusting "flat" areas on either side of the start and end of a graph "peak" increases details to recreate the actual image. Histograms can also give the designer an indication whether the image is properly exposed. Images that are too dark (underexposed) will show the histogram graph curving up, cutting off at the shadow side while washed out images (overexposed) will have the graph curve up and cut off on the right side. For advanced users, the Histogram panel can also display changes in individual color channels, such as RGB or CMYK, by selecting the All Channels View from the panel submenu and then Show Channels in Color from the panel submenu.

In this exercise, you will open the *Light1* image and use the Levels commands and Histogram to create a better enhanced image.

1. Open the original file *Light1* in your *Chapter 3* folder.

2. If a Profile Mismatch dialog box appears, or a dialog box displays asking whether to ignore file data dialog box, select OK. It will not make any difference on the image here.

3. Duplicate the image so you will be able to see the differences between the original and your altered version, and rename it *LightLVL*. Select the "Float All in Windows" option from the Arrange Documents icon on the Application bar.

4. To display the Histogram panel, select Window > Histogram.

5. Select Image > Adjustments > Levels. The Levels dialog box displays with the image's histogram. Make sure the Preview box is checked to observe the

▷ FIGURE 3-23

Use the Levels command to bring out details in highlights, shadows, and midtones in an image. Use the Histogram panel to observe levels before and after adjustments are applied. This works best with properly exposed images.

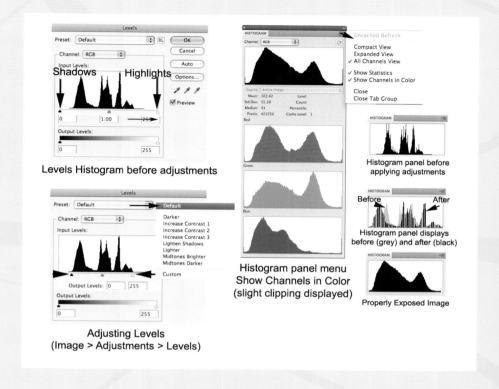

Levels Histogram before adjustments

Adjusting Levels
(Image > Adjustments > Levels)

Histogram panel menu
Show Channels in Color
(slight clipping displayed)

Histogram panel before
applying adjustments

Histogram panel displays
before (grey) and after (black)

Properly Exposed Image

changes and drag the *Light1LVL* image window next to the Histogram panel, which shows what you see in the levels display as a grey mountain. So you can see both open documents.

6. In the Levels dialog box, the default channel displayed is RGB that combines all the colors together, and there are three triangle sliders under the histogram graph. The left is for the shadows, the right is for the highlights, and the one in the middle is for the midtones. You will notice they are positioned below the graph peak with flat areas on both sides. What you want to do is to drag these sliders to the start and ending points of the peaks.

7. Drag the shadow and highlight triangles on either side to the start and end of the graph (see Figure 3-23). The middle triangle will adjust automatically, but you can also adjust that slider separately to adjust the midtones. Notice the difference between the adjusted image and the original image. All the tones are rearranged for a clearer, more accurate color image.

8. Notice the before and after effects in the Histogram panel: the before image is gray, while the after image is black. Try selecting and adjusting the individual red, green, and blue channels to further tweak the levels in the image; use the Channel pop-up menu to select each in turn.

9. Save the file as *LightLVL.tif* in your *Chapter 3* folder. Click the *Light1* image to see the difference in the histograms.

10. In the Levels dialog box there is also a Preset menu containing preset adjustments. Try this with any image.

USING CURVES FOR PRECISION IN TONING

When you open an image and choose to adjust it using Curves, the display will have a slanted line with a faint histogram display in the background which provides a handy guide to maintain proper highlight and shadow detail. The upper portion of the slanted line represents the highlight areas while the bottom left portion of the line represents shadow details, with the middle area for midtones. With Curves you can make incremental adjustments by clicking on the line graph to create a point, then dragging the active point using your mouse very carefully, or you can simply use the arrow keys on your keyboard. This is used for precision adjustments, so a slight adjustment may go along way in making changes to your image. Only one plotted point is active at any given time. To switch from one point to another existing point, simply re-click on it. To remove a point, simply drag it off the graph and it will go away.

1. Open the original file Carbarn in your *Chapter 3* folder.

2. If a Profile Mismatch dialog box appears, select OK. It will not make any difference on the image here.

3. Duplicate the image so you will be able to see the differences between the original and your altered version, and rename it *CarbarnCRV*. Select the "Float All in Windows" option from the Arrange Documents icon on the Application bar.

4. Select Image > Adjustments > Curves. The Curves dialog box displays as a slanted line graph with the image's histogram in the background. Make sure the Preview box is checked to observe the differences (Figure 3-24).

5. At the bottom of the display you'll notice, as in Levels, a white triangle for highlights and a dark triangle for shadows. Drag each, if needed, to the starting and end peaks of the histogram. With this image it may not need to be done.

6. Click on three places on the line graph, in the middle, then on the top right corner of the bottom first square, then the bottom right corner of the top right square. This will allow you to make slight adjustments in the midtone,

▷ FIGURE 3-24

Using Curves adjustments for subtly toning highlights, midtones, and shadows.

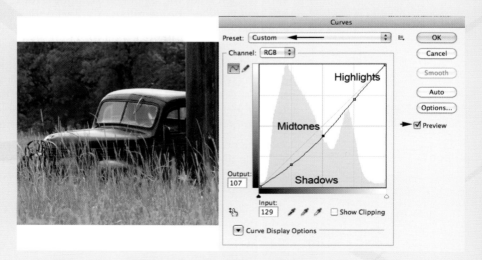

highlights, and shadow areas. Having less plotted points is always better than having too many.

7. You're going to darken the image a little to provide a little more "punch" to the image. Hover your mouse over the middle point, and when you see the cursor change to a black cross with little arrows, click on the middle point. Use your arrow keys and press a few times to bring the graph downwards a little to darken the midtones slightly.

8. Do the same procedure with the bottom point to darken the shadows, then click on the upper point and increase the highlight area slightly. Notice the highlights on the top of the car are being washed out. Click the down arrow key to bring the point slightly below the original line.

9. Click on the Preview button, then click again to see before and after results. You can also use the original *Carbarn* image to see the differences.

10. Use Figure 3-24 as a starting point and make slight adjustments to suit your tastes. Be careful, in that a little adjustment goes a long way. You can plot points anywhere on the line. Again less is better. If you need to delete a point, simply drag it off the graph and it will go away.

11. As with Levels, you can also experiment with customized presets, or create and save your own presets for future projects.

12. Save the file in your *Chapter 3* folder when done.

13. Try this technique with the *B&Wcarbarn* image, the *Light1* image, or one of your own images to practice toning.

DIGITAL TOOLKIT EXTRA: Using the Adobe Bridge and new Mini Bridge for Retrieving and Managing Files

Photoshop has created an easier way to locate, retrieve, preview, and manage your image files; it is called the **Adobe Bridge,** and its folder icon is located permanently on the Application bar along with a new Mini Bridge icon built in every application for more local control. Adobe Bridge is an additional application within Photoshop and other Adobe applications that "bridges" the other Creative Suite applications (Figure 3-25). The Adobe Creative Suite consists of Adobe products for all types of media; Photoshop, Illustrator, InDesign, Acrobat, and Dreamweaver to name a few, and all work together with various types of files. Adobe Bridge is the hub for retrieving and editing files and their information to help with file management and automation between files, various pieces of artwork, and between applications within the Adobe Creative Suite. Although beyond the scope of this text, Bridge contains a file-version management system that works between all applications in the Adobe Creative Suite; this is located in the Bridge's Tools menu, and it is called *Version Cue.* It allows designers and photographers to keep track of versions of files without having to invent complicated file names. You can open Bridge by clicking the Bridge (Br) icon, or select File > Browse in Bridge (File > Browse in earlier versions) within Photoshop; or select File > Close and Go To Bridge if you need to close Photoshop. You can also access Bridge as a stand-alone application through Windows or Mac OS X. The vast amount of information that can be obtained from digital files, especially from cameras and other devices, is all recorded and can be retrieved using Adobe Bridge. Here is a brief list to show you some of Adobe Bridge's features:

• It provides thumbnail previews of multiple image files from which you can select various sizes of displays. You can select how you want the images and information displayed from four workspace view buttons at the top (bottom in earlier versions) of the display (Essentials (Default) View, Filmstrip (Slide) View, and Metadata View). There is an Output button to choose a specific workspace, display. Click and drag the edges of the panels to enlarge thumbnails to check out details.

• Bridge generates and displays data in the Metadata pane about your file: file properties information, camera and exposure data, camera RAW data, GPS information, and editing history. You can also add information and instructions—including copyright, author, source, and creation information—and you can edit the information on multiple files simultaneously.

• Use the Filter panel, where images can be sorted by various file properties and data information; you can flag important files, color code, and rate them. Images can also be rotated, deleted, and automatically batch processed to a set standard, size, color mode, and so on with renaming of multiple files starting with a specified number.

• You can search for, or apply keywords to, one or more files. This is useful for image file management.

• In the Tools menu (Tools > Photoshop > Batch), you can batch process many images, create contact sheets of your images, and send digital images directly to online services for ordering prints, books, and so on. You can also create your own picture package with various combinations of sizes of your images.

• Image previews can be moved around as if they were slides on a light table.

• Use the Compact Mode icon at the top right to create a smaller window display from which you can drag thumbnails into an open Adobe application, such as Photoshop. Double clicking a thumbnail will open the image in the application in which it was created.

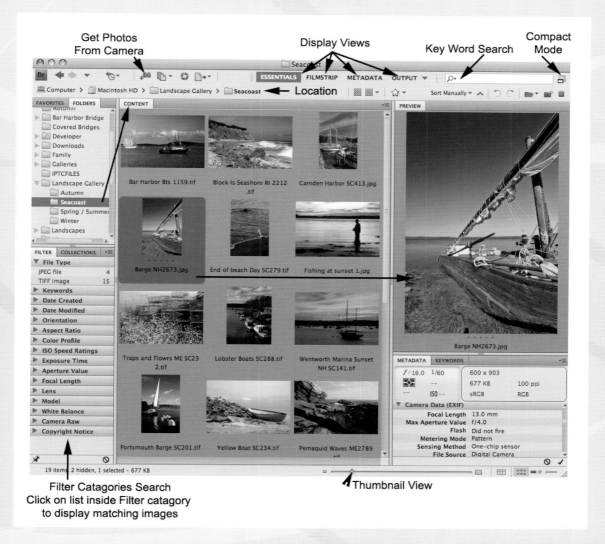

▷ FIGURE 3-25

Use Adobe Bridge to observe, manage, and retrieve all types of graphic files.

In this exercise, you will locate and observe the files you created in this chapter using Adobe Bridge.

1. There are different ways to launch the Bridge application. You can select the Bridge icon "Br" on the Application bar in Photoshop or from the Tool Options bar in earlier versions. To select it as an application on its own,

from the Mac desktop, select Go > Applications > Adobe Bridge CS5, from the Windows desktop, select Start > Programs > Adobe Bridge CS5. In Photoshop, you can also select File > Close and Go to Bridge to open Bridge.

2. Select the Folders Panel and locate the images in your *Chapter 3* folder to display the contents (double-click folders to open them). You can also try to use the Favorites Panel to locate the files.

3. Select the *WEBlight1.jpg* image; you will notice thumbnail images and a lot of file information in the Metadata pane. Notice the file size. Select the *FIXlight1.tif* image and notice the difference in the data. If the files were not properly named, this method of searching through Bridge can help you to locate files by data. You can also color code the images so that, say, all low-resolution images for the web may be color coded blue, which would then allow you to use the Filter panel locate them.

4. Select the other images in the *Chapter 3* folder and notice differences in file size and other properties information in the Metadata pane. You can also try to look for images you may have of your own in another folder.

5. In the Menu bar, observe the many features available. Click the Compact Mode icon to view the Window display option, then bring it back to the original size. Leave Bridge open for the next exercise.

CREATING SLIDE SHOWS USING BRIDGE

Adobe Bridge allows a designer or photographer to create a slide show to display their artwork from any combination of applications they are using. This is a great tool you can use to show your work to a client. You can choose how you want your artwork to display, how long the images are displayed, etc. Before you create a slide show you should have a folder of artwork or images ready.

Here you'll open a folder of images and create a quick slide show of your images.

1. Create a folder for your images and drag your favorite images into that folder, or, you can use your *Images* folder that you created in Chapter 1 Advanced section of Internet images, or, open your *Chapter 3* folder of images you saved; although there will be much repetition, you can still get the idea.

2. Launch the Bridge application by selecting the Bridge icon "Br" on the Application bar in Photoshop, or from any of the other methods described in the previous exercise.

3. Select File > Open and locate the folder of images you want to make into a slide show. In Figure 3-26, you'll notice I went to locate a folder called *Seacoast*; a directory structure is displayed at the top. Thumbnails of your images will then be displayed.

4. To set up your slide show settings, select View > Slideshow Options. Use the settings shown in Figure 3-26 as a starting point, then select Play to test the slideshow. That's it!

5. The settings will remain until you change them another time. Now you can select a folder of your artwork, then select View > Slideshow to show your work with the same settings.

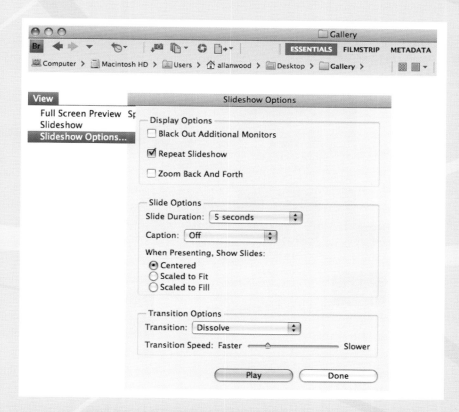

Using Adobe Bridge to create an instant slide show for your artwork.

USING BRIDGE TO IMPORT IMAGES FROM YOUR DIGITAL CAMERA

Bridge comes with a built-in application called Photo Downloader, which can download images automatically from your digital camera. To help with production, it's easier to use Adobe Bridge to view multiple images before opening them in Photoshop or an other application. Adobe Bridge is also useful in renaming files and images, and as a file management system.

If you have images from a digital camera, it doesn't matter what type, you can use Adobe Bridge's Photo Downloader to manage your images. Try the following steps.

1. Create a folder to place your images, either on your hard drive or on the desktop. Name the folder *Gallery*, or *Family*, or whatever you like.

2. Launch Bridge from Photoshop or as a standalone from the Mac or Windows desktop.

3. Select File > Get Photos from Camera, or click on the camera icon. If the program asks whether to use Photo Downloader, select to make it the default for this exercise.

4. Plug your card reader or your camera's USB connection into your computer. When the Adobe Bridge CS5- Photo Downloader display box opens, you have some choices to make. You can batch rename as one name with sequential numbers, have subfolders created that are separated by the shooting dates, etc.

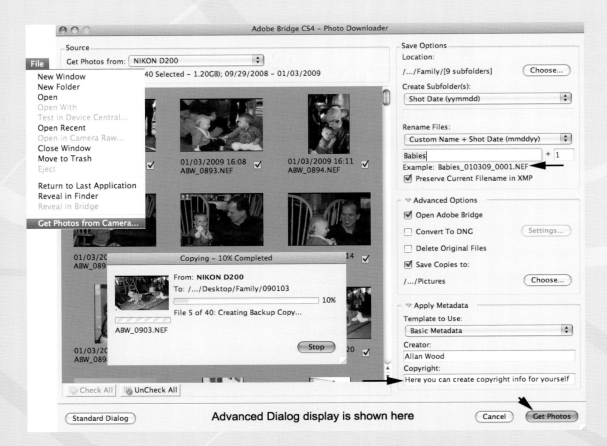

Advanced Dialog display is shown here

▷ FIGURE 3-27

Adobe Bridge's Photo Downloader provides an easy way to import, rename, and manage images from your digital camera or card reader.

This helps in later identifying what event was photographed within a certain date, and keeps images better organized, making it easier to find your images.

5. You can use the default Standard Dialog display window if you want to import *all* the images on your card. Alternatively, you can use the Advanced Dialog display if you want to be able to select the images you want to import; simply remove the check next to those that you don't want to import, as shown in Figure 3-26. This is a great way to make some quick edits on lots of images. Bridge will display graphic images of most extensions, including what are called "Camera RAW" files, or some cameras digital negatives, which will be covered in Chapter 5.

6. Use Figure 3-27 as an example for your settings. One good habit is never to delete the files from your original memory card until you are confident you have imported the selected files. You can also check Save copies to:, choosing another backup folder for your work that makes backup copies of your files from your memory card without renaming.

7. When you are ready to import your images, select Get Photos and the images will be copied to the folder you designate. You can also rename them and apply customized settings for easy access for future projects you created.

8. The new imported folders and selected images will then display in Bridge, allowing you to view them in more detail for further editing. Bridge makes it easy to import your images and manage your files for faster production, so you can get back out and play!

USING MINI BRIDGE

The new Mini Bridge in CS5 is an extension within an Adobe application, like Photoshop. It allows you to work using many of the Adobe Bridge features, especially if you may need to work between different applications using various types of files or documents. You can search for, sort, display thumbnails, batch process for multiple tasks, and also create slideshows from Mini Bridge's panel when you launch the application. The Path bar helps you to navigate in finding your files or folders. Mini Bridge also communicates with the parent Adobe Bridge to create thumbnails, keep files organized and synched, among other tasks.

Here you will use Mini Bridge to look at files.

1. There are different ways to launch the Mini Bridge application. In Photoshop, you can select the Mini Bridge icon "Mb" on the Application bar, or select File > Browse in Mini Bridge, or choose Window > Extensions > Mini Bridge.

2. When you launch Mini Bridge, the Mini Bridge panel will open with a Path bar, and Navigation Pod and Content Pod inside. Use the Path bar (Figure 3-28) to double–click on the drive icon to find the *Chapter 3* folder with all the files you just created, or feel free to locate a folder of images you may have from another location.

3. Scroll through the thumbnails in the Content Pod to view your images.

4. Click on the slideshow icon to display a slideshow of images. Press the ESC key when done.

5. To locate one file, click on the magnifying glass icon to search for one of the files by typing its name (B&Wcarbarn.jpg for instance). It should then display as a thumbnail.

6. To open a file using Mini Bridge, double-click it in the Content Pod. Close when done, don't save.

▷ FIGURE 3-28

Mini Bridge, in CS5, provides the power of the parent Adobe Bridge locally within the Photoshop application for searching, filtering, and displaying files.

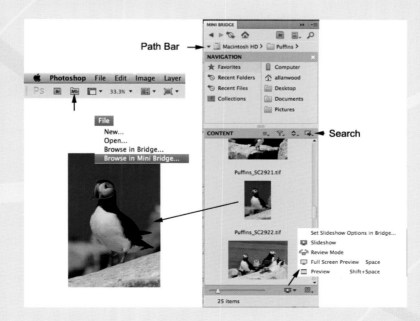

CHAPTER SUMMARY

In this chapter, you were introduced to Photoshop and some of its basic functions and components. You learned about the importance of determining the appropriate resolution of your image for different media. You saved files in .PSD, .TIF, and .JPG formats for specific uses. You learned the purpose of RGB color mode for electronic media and desktop printing and CMYK color mode for commercial press. The Image menu contains commands for enhancing, duplicating, resizing, trimming, and rotating an image. The Edit menu helps you to go back and compare before and after effects when applying a command or effect. Adobe Bridge helps you to search, view thumbnails, identify, sort your images, create slideshows, and import images from your digital camera. For more projects and ideas, check out the *Goodies* folder on your CD or you can also go to *http://www.digitoolkit.com* for more Adobe tutorials and projects.

REVIEW QUESTIONS

1. Explain the use of the Tool Options bar and its components.

2. Explain the purposes of using 72 dpi and 300 dpi resolutions.

3. Explain the differences when saving images in .PSD, .TIF, and .JPG formats.

4. Why does a 300 dpi image appear larger on the monitor when viewed at full size than when it is printed?

5. Explain RGB and CMYK color modes, Auto Color command, Shadows/Highlights command, and Auto Tone command.

6. What is a histogram? What is the purpose of the Histogram panel?

Originals

Adjust contrast,
shadow, and highlights

Convertng colors for accuate
black and white tones

CHAPTER 3
Corrected images using special commands
in Photoshop's Image menu.

Auto Color Adjustment

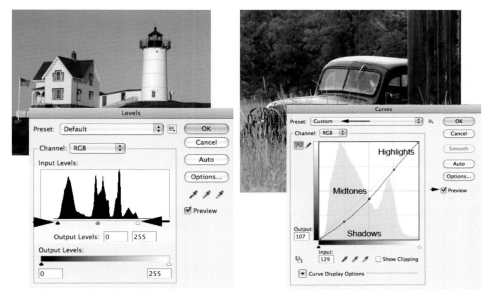

CHAPTER 3 ADVANCED
Using Histograms, Levels, and Curves adjustments in Photoshop to adjust
shadows, midtones, and highlights for quality images.

▷ FIGURE 3-29

Adobe Bridge interface to retrieve, observe,
and manage all types of graphic files.

Using Adobe Bridge to
create an instant slideshow
of your photos or artwork.

Path Bar

Search

Mini Bridge, in CS5, provides the power of
the parent Adobe Bridge locally within the
Photoshop application for searching, filtering,
and displaying files.

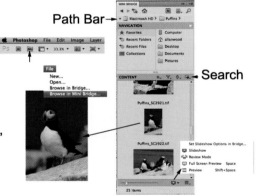

CHAPTER 3 EXTRA
Adobe Bridge, and the new Mini Bridge, which is inside each Adobe application like Photoshop,
allows you to import, retrieve, observe, manage, and edit files, and they can play slide shows.

▷ FIGURE 3-30

Working with Selections and Channels

CHAPTER OBJECTIVES: To understand the importance of using selection tools and techniques in Photoshop, in this chapter you will:

▷ Use the Marquee, Magic Wand, Quick Selection, Move, and Lasso tools for specific selections.

▷ Learn to add, subtract, and intersect selections using the Tool Options bar.

▷ Create selections that can be saved permanently as channels in the Channels panel.

▷ Make complex selections using and combining different selection tools.

▷ Modify and edit selections using the Select menu.

▷ Use the Hue/Saturation command to adjust color while retaining shadows and highlights within an image.

▷ ADVANCED USERS: Create a quick mask selection for working with detailed selections.

▷ DIGITAL TOOLKIT EXTRA: Make a better sky by combining images using either the Paste Into command, or selecting by Color Range using the Masks panel.

When making changes within areas of an image, a designer or photographer usually needs to isolate certain portions of that image, like in case a client decides to change the color of a model's shirt or dress in an advertisement, for instance. Creating selections gives the designer or photographer a variety of ways to isolate those portions of the image that need to be modified, duplicated, or deleted. Photoshop provides tools and techniques for just about any type of selection needed. You can make changes to the selected portion of the image without affecting any areas outside that selection and then save it for later use. In this chapter, we will examine how to create and save selections using some of Photoshop's tools and techniques.

Need additional fun computer graphics tutorials and info, and an additional look at the projects you'll be creating in this book? Check out my Artist's Digital Toolkit website at: **http://www.digitoolkit.com**

PHOTOSHOP'S SELECTION TOOLS

Much of Photoshop's image editing involves making selections within an image area and making changes. Photoshop provides a variety of selection tools and techniques with special purposes to aid the designer or photographer in creating virtually any type of selection needed (Figure 4-1). When you make a selection, you will notice a moving line or dashes ("marching ants") called a *marquee.* Selections use marquees to display the selected areas. When a selection is active, the area inside that selection can be edited; anything outside the selected area cannot be changed, unless the selection is reversed using the Select menu. Photoshop's selection tools are the Marquee (M), Lasso (L), the Magic Wand (W), and Quick Selection (W). The Move tool (V) is also in the category of selection tools, although technically, it does not generate a selection but moves or cuts a selected area. You can access these tools by typing in their specific shortcut keys, shown in parentheses, or by holding down the mouse and selecting the tool you need. The Marquee, Lasso, Magic Wand, and Quick Selection tools have a black triangle at the bottom of the tool to indicate there are more tools in the same category. You can access these tools using the mouse, or you can navigate between each group of tools by holding down Shift and pressing the appropriate letter key.

▷ FIGURE 4-1

Photoshop CS4 selection tools.

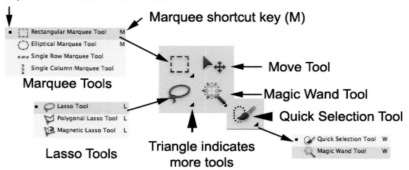

MARQUEE TOOLS

Marquee tools select rectangular boxes, elliptical areas, and single pixel row or column selections. The Rectangular and Elliptical Marquee tools (M) can help the designer or photographer select images that need to be modified, cropped, or resized to a specific dimension. The Single Row and Single Column Marquees are used as temporary pixel-wide guidelines for aligning images and text.

TOOLKIT TIP To make perfect square and perfect circle selections with the Rectangular (squares) or Elliptical (circles) Marquee tools, hold down the Shift key as you drag diagonally with the mouse.

EDITING SELECTIONS WITH THE TOOL OPTIONS BAR

The Tool Options bar provides options for each selection tool. The Marquee and Lasso tools in Photoshop have buttons on the Tool Options bar that indicate each new selection you are making (default) and allow you to add, subtract, and intersect with other selections. You can also create specific basic shape selections by using combinations of these selection buttons, as shown in Figure 4-2. The Crop and Move tools, for instance, will have different options to enter than the Marquee and Lasso tools. You will also notice a **Refine Edge** button on a selection tool's Tool Options bar. This allows you to soften or enhance a selections edge and to preview the results on different backgrounds to see the effect created.

LASSO TOOLS

The **Lasso tools** (L) work well with selections that are needed as either freeform or complex selections (Figure 4-3). When using any Lasso tool, the cursor will display a circle "o" when brought back to the original point. Click and the selection will be completed. You can also double-click the mouse, and the selection will be completed with a line back to the original point.

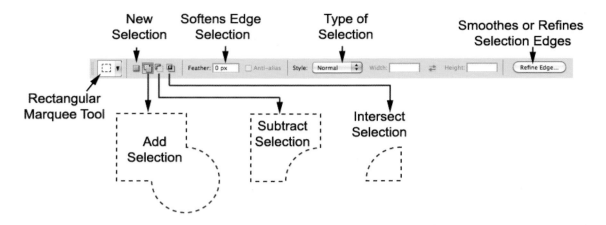

New Selection   **Softens Edge Selection**   **Type of Selection**   **Smoothes or Refines Selection Edges**

Rectangular Marquee Tool

Add Selection   **Subtract Selection**   **Intersect Selection**

▷ FIGURE 4-2

In the Tool Options bar for selection tools, there are options specific to these tools, including the ability to add, subtract, and intersect selections, as well as to soften or refine the edges.

• The *Lasso* tool itself works as a freehand tool; you simply click for a starting point and drag the cursor around any area you choose. It is a useful tool as a starting point for the designer or photographer who needs to make general selections on a large area, as a tool for cleaning up or fine tuning selections, or when making a selection in a small area of an image that is zoomed in close.

• The *Polygonal Lasso* tool is a great tool to make straight-line selections on images such as buildings or products. Every time you click with the Polygonal Lasso tool, a straight line is created from one point to the next.

• The *Magnetic Lasso* tool is useful for image areas that have edges with good contrast. It snaps to the edge of an area, which is helpful when making a detailed selection of images of people, cars, products, or wherever there is good edge contrast.

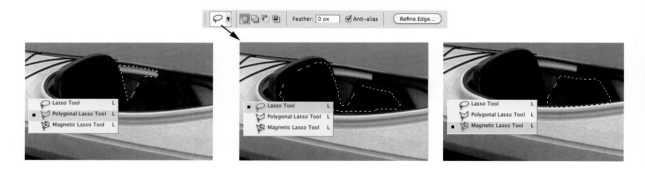

▷ FIGURE 4-3

Lasso Tools.

THE MAGIC WAND TOOL

The **Magic Wand tool** (W) selects parts of an image based on similar tints or shadings of colors (Figure 4-4). This tool is used for areas with difficult outlines or soft edges that cannot be traced with the Lasso tools. It helps the designer or photographer who needs to make selections based on color, like on the blue sky area in an image. The **Tolerance** setting for the Magic Wand in the Tool Options bar is important, because it determines the amount of similar colors selected; the lower the tolerance, the fewer similar colors are selected.

▷ FIGURE 4-4

The Magic Wand tool creates selections based on similar colors.

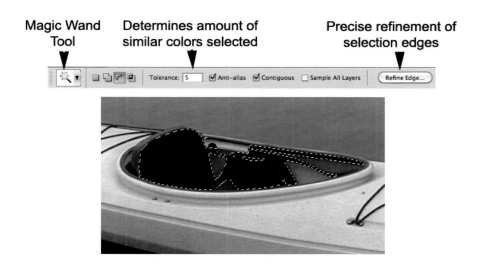

Magic Wand Tool — Determines amount of similar colors selected — Precise refinement of selection edges

 TOOLKIT TIP Deselect selections created by the Marquee, Lasso, Quick Selection, and Magic Wand tools by selecting Command/Ctrl + D on the keyboard or by selecting another tool on the Tools panel and then clicking outside the selected area.

THE QUICK SELECTION TOOL

The **Quick Selection tool** (W), like the Magic Wand tool, selects similar colors, tints, or shadings of color. It allows you to "paint" a selection of a predefined brush width you set in the Tool options bar, then looks for similar adjacent colors and defined edges and shapes as you paint (Figure 4-5). It works well with edges with good contrast, and can save time in creating complicated selections.

▷ FIGURE 4-5

The Quick Selection tool allows you to paint in a selection, following defined edges and shapes.

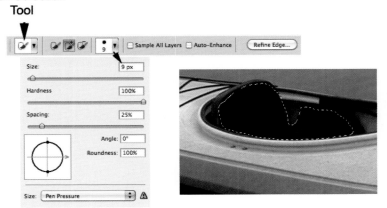

Quick Selection Tool

THE CHANNELS PANEL

Photoshop uses the **Channels panel** to store selections permanently. A designer or photographer can create a variety of complex selections then name and save them as **channels** in the Channels panel for later use. These channels are saved with the document and can be used or edited at any time. Channels also store an image's color mode information in separate color channels (Figure 4-6). For instance, an RGB image will have red, green, and blue channels, which can be edited individually.

▷ FIGURE 4-6

The Channels panel saves selections and an image's color mode information.

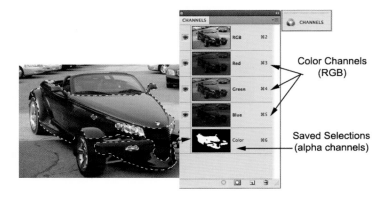

Color Channels (RGB)

Saved Selections (alpha channels)

▷ FIGURE 4-7

Using selection techniques and tools, the original color of the sports car is changed to gold, maintaining complete tonality for realism.

Original Image

Completed Recolored Image

CLIENT ASSIGNMENT: Replacing Color on a Sports Car

Steve Lyons is a local car dealer and enjoys sports cars. His brother Bryan owns a local auto body shop. Steve has a favorite black sports car that is close to having a 25th year anniversary of the car's model in business. He'd like to have his car painted in gold to celebrate the anniversary, have his brother paint it, and also use it to help promote his brother's business. He comes to you with a digital photo of the car and asks you to create a gold color so he can show to his brother what he is looking for. You know this will involve using selections to remove the background and to change the color of the car. You tell him it will be ready the following day.

ACTION ITEMS OVERVIEW

This project shows how a designer or photographer can use selections to create a totally realistic different colored object from the same selected object. Designers or photographers constantly use these techniques with different colored products: clothing, packaging products, and the like. Selections are like building the foundation of a house: they need to be created in accurate detail, and they are essential for the successful completion of the final project. As a designer or photographer, your goal is to create a detailed selection of the car that can be saved permanently with only those portions that should be used for painting, minus the lights, windshield, and hardware. Be wary this is a complicated project and may take a number attempts to create an accurate selection. Provide ample time for corrections.

To create accurate selections of this project, here is what you need to do:

• Create a duplicate copy of the original image to serve as a back-up copy.

• Crop the image to remove part of the background to emphasize the car using the Rectangular Marquee tool.

• Create the initial selection for changing the color by using the Magic Wand, Quick Selection, and Lasso selection tools. Only the areas of the car that are to be changed must be selected; all hardware, lights, windshield, tires, etc. and background must be isolated.

• Use the Tool Options bar, Select menu, and Edit menu to help with editing selections.

• Make the selection permanent by saving it as a channel in the Channels panel for reuse and future editing.

• Create a new color using the Hue/Saturation command.

• ADVANCED USERS: Create a Quick Mask for final detail work on the selections using the Brush and Pencil tools, and then save the masked selections permanently in the Channels panel.

DUPLICATING AND SAVING THE FILE

It is always a good habit to make duplicates of any file you are working on and save as often as possible. Save your images throughout the chapters here with a .TIF extension (File > Save As > *SportscarGOLD.tif*) as a default setting on your computer, so you can edit your image as many times as needed, and the quality will always remain the same (Figure 4-8). You can save Photoshop files in either .PSD or .TIF formats, and you will be able to edit either one and still maintain the original quality. Photoshop's native .PSD format can primarily be read by Adobe applications, whereas **TIF format files** are universally read. In this chapter, you will save and work with this file as a .TIF. If you have room, create a back-up .PSD file in your *Chapter 4* folder for practice. Do not save your file here with a .JPG extension; although using .JPG will compress your file and save space, it would soon degrade the image quality as a result of making multiple changes to the image.

TOOLKIT TIP Most images carry a color identity profile or what is called an **ICC profile** that defines colors and embeds the color information with the file. If you open a file, and a Profile Mismatch dialog box appears, select Use the Embedded Profile and Photoshop will automatically make a slight adjustment to match the colors of that image for consistency. If you choose to open it in the default working space, or if you convert to the current color space on your computer, it will adjust the colors slightly in your default working space. You will notice little if any visual difference, and it will not cause any problems with your computer.

▷ FIGURE 4-8

Before editing the image, make a duplicate of the original and save it as a .TIF extension to maintain accuracy.

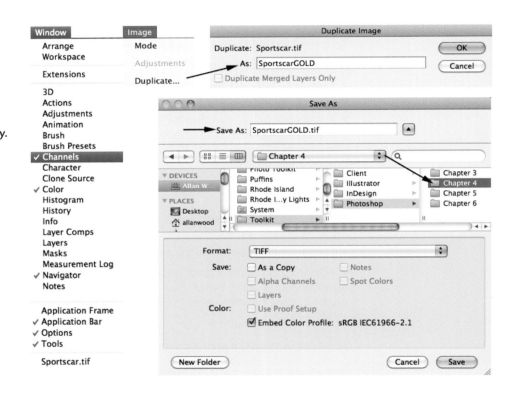

You will check to make sure you have access to panels using the Window menu, then you will create a duplicate copy of the original *Sportscar* file and save it with a new name and a .TIF extension.

1. Make sure to locate the Navigator and Channels panels on the desktop to assist you in creating the ad for this chapter. If they are not open, use the Window menu to select the panel you need; it will put a check mark beside all those panels expanded on the desktop. If you see any additional panels checked, leave them for now. If you see the default workspace as Essentials, leave it. If the Tool Options bar or Tools panel is not displayed, select Options, or Tools, from the Window menu to open them.

2. To bring in the *Sportscar.tif* image, choose File > Open and select the *Sportscar.tif* image located in the *Chapter 4* folder on your drive. If a dialog box opens up regarding reading info or profile matching, just click OK and continue.

3. Create a duplicate image by selecting Image > Duplicate.

4. Name the new copy *SportscarGOLD* and Save As *SportscarGOLD.tif* to your *Chapter 4* folder on your drive with the default settings. The new *SportscarGOLD.tif* file is what you will be working with.

5. If you have extra space, it is a good idea to save the file in Photoshop's native .PSD format to serve as a back-up copy (*SportscarGOLD.psd*). If you save a PSD format of the file, close the file afterwards.

6. Close the original *Sportscar* file.

 TOOLKIT TIP When you get familiar with certain panels you prefer to have open on your workspace, you can save it as a customized workspace (Window > Workspace > New Workspace). You can name it and assign a hot key combination to it.

SELECTING THE SPORTS CAR TO CHANGE COLOR

This selection will be used for changing the car's black painted color to the gold color specified by the client. Here, only the black painted colors of the original sports car are going to be selected; all hardware, lights, tires, windshield, and background must be isolated so they will not change color. Make sure you have enough time to complete this series of exercises so that you can save your selections permanently at the end.

USING RECTANGULAR MARQUEE SELECTION TOOL FOR CROPPING

The Rectangular Marquee tool can be used to make freehand, or specific square or rectangular, selections on an image. These selections can be used to provide an emphasis to an image in creating borders, vignettes, or for cropping a busy looking image. Many times, as you can see with the Sportscar photo, a client will hand a designer a snapshot image to help explain what they are looking for. The Rectangular Marquee tool can create specific or freehand dimensions using the Style button on the Tool Options bar. A Fixed Size dimension can be entered in the Width and Height boxes as a specific pixel (px) or inches (in) amount. A Fixed Ratio option can be entered to meet a specific format indicated by the client. The default Normal Style provides a freehand dimension to be used to isolate outer components of an image, which is what is needed for this image, without worrying about specific dimensions, as the final image will be used as a guide. The Rectangular Marquee tool can also be used to crop an image along with the Image menu (Image > Crop).

In order to focus on the car, you will crop some of the outside cars to be able to keep your attention in working with this car.

▷ FIGURE 4-9

The Rectangular Marquee tool can be used to draw freehand, or specific four-corner selections on an image for cropping and emphasizing selected components.

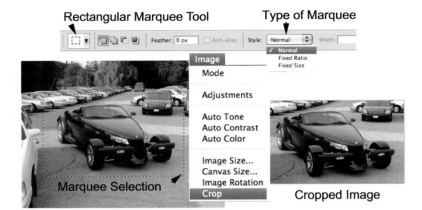

1. With the *SportscarGOLD* image displayed, select the Rectangular Marquee tool, and on the Tool Options bar, select Normal on the Style button (Figure 4-9).

2. Drag diagonally from the top left to the bottom right leaving enough room to work on the car, but removing the side white car and upper background. To redo a selection, click outside the selection and try again.

3. Use the arrow keys on the keyboard to move your selection around accurately.

4. When you are happy with your selection, select Image > Crop to crop your image, removing some of the unwanted background.

5. Save the file in your *Chapter 4* folder and leave open for the next exercise.

USING THE MAGIC WAND TOOL

Since the car is a basic black color, you will use the Magic Wand tool. This tool works well for selecting an image using similar adjacent colors as determined by the Tolerance setting on the Tool Options bar. Make sure the Anti-aliased setting is checked on the Tool Options bar to keep the pixel edges from looking jagged by softening the transition between colors.

Here, you are going to set the options for the Magic Wand tool and start selecting the black painted areas of the car.

1. Zoom in to about 100% with the Zoom tool to get a good, detailed view. Click on the Actual Pixels button, or try using the new Scrubby Zoom option on the Tool Options bar, to click and zoom to get the full view of the car. The percentage the window displays will show on the title bar of the image window.

2. Select the Magic Wand tool.

3. Set the Tolerance to 20 pixels on the Tool Options bar to indicate how many pixels of relatively the same shade of black color should be selected.

4. Place a check in the Anti-alias box in the Tool Options bar by clicking on the box. This setting helps to gradually smooth out square pixels so they will not appear as jagged edges. Finally, check in the Contiguous box to be able to select colors next to one another as shown in Figure 4-10.

5. Select the front hood area of the car. A marquee selection will show on your image.

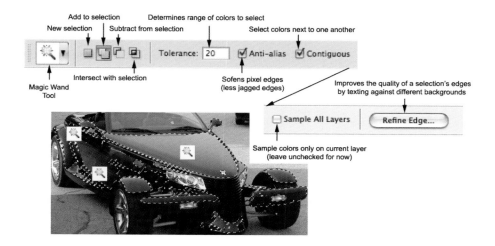

▷ FIGURE 4-10

**Magic Wand Tool
Options bar.**

ADDING AND SUBTRACTING SELECTIONS

The selection tools have buttons on the Tool Options bar that allow you to add, subtract, and intersect with previous selections (Figure 4-10). When you add to or subtract from a selection, you will notice a plus or minus sign under the tool cursor. When the intersect selection button is chosen, an "x" is displayed under the cursor. Use these buttons carefully each time you want to edit your selection.

TOOLKIT TIP If you like keystrokes instead of the buttons on the Tool Options bar, holding down the Option/Alt key will subtract from your selection, and holding down the Shift key will add to your selection.

Follow the steps below using the buttons on the Tool Options bar to add to and subtract from the selection you are making.

1. While your marquee is still showing, and the Magic Wand tool is selected, set the Tolerance to between 10 and 15 pixels.

2. Use the Tool Options bar buttons, or the keystroke shortcuts, to add to and subtract from your selection until you have part of the front hood and side selected, excluding any hardware or background (Figure 4-10). Do not select the background, front radiator area, tires, or windshield area. If you select too much, select Command/Ctrl + Z to undo the selection. Use the Option/ALT key to minus the selection.

3. Work on selecting the front hood and side of the car for now. Adjust the Tolerance to 10 and 5 pixels. Don't worry about stray selections, you'll be cleaning them up later.

4. Keep the selection active, and save your file, but do not close it.

PROBLEM A selection is automatically removed if you have the New Selection button on the Tool Options bar set when making another selection. To remove all selections on the image, choose Select > Deselect. If you make a mistake, choose Select > Reselect. To go back to the last action, choose Edit > Undo State Change, or toggle Command/Ctrl Z.

FINE TUNING WITH THE QUICK SELECTION TOOL

The **Quick Selection tool** can help to paint or add to the selection of the black painted areas of the car, or to delete parts of the selection that may have gone outside the sports car itself (Figure 4-11). It gives you the feeling of being a kid again, when you tried to color the drawings you were working on. Zoom in closer and keep the paintbrush at 10 pixels wide or less to start, using the Add To Selection and Subtract From Selection icons on the Tool Options bar to fine tune your selection.

▷ FIGURE 4-11

Add to the selection by painting it in using the Quick Selection tool.

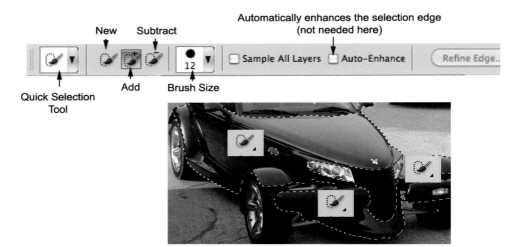

 TOOLKIT TIP You can quickly adjust the brush size of this tool or any painting tool by pressing the bracket keys on your keyboard. The left bracket ([) makes the size smaller and the right bracket (]) increases the size. To save time, you can also use the spacebar instead of the Hand tool to scroll around the image as you work.

1. Zoom in to 100% or closer to observe the detail in the selection area. Use the Hand tool and Navigator panel to move around the image.
2. To select the Quick Selection tool, click on the Magic Wand tool's lower black triangle to display the Quick Selection tool. Select this tool to make it active. With the Quick Selection tool displayed in the Tools panel, set the brush size to 5 pixels wide or less to start. Zoom in close to click and drag selections,

you'll notice it cleans up stray pixels as well. For details, zoom to 200% or more and set pixel size to 1 or 2 pixels to select minute edges. Do the front fender areas last at 1 pixel as they will blend into the color of the tires easily.

3. Now click and drag to paint or to add or subtract from the selection area. Use the Tool Options bar icons to add to and subtract from your selection until you have most of the car's black painted color selected, excluding any hardware or background (Figure 4-11). Understand that being detailed in your work is what it is all about. You will finish fine tuning this selection in the next exercise.

4. In CS5, select the Zoom tool, click on the Scrubby Zoom option in the Tool Options bar, then click on the image and drag to quickly zoom in and out of the image to observe your work, or select the zoom in and zoom out icons. You can also select the Fit screen button to have the image fill your screen. Make any additional adjustments as necessary. Keep the selection active and save it, but do not close the file.

CLEANING UP WITH THE LASSO TOOLS

The Lasso tools can be used to help clean up stray areas not yet selected by the Magic Wand or Quick Selection tools. You can use them to combine with and subtract from selected areas and for straight edge selections. After general selections are made, you can zoom in close and work on detailed areas with the Lasso tool (Figure 4-12).

▷ FIGURE 4-12

Using the Lasso tool for free-hand selections.

In this exercise, you will use the Lasso tools for editing your selections in detail.

1. Using the Zoom tool (Z), zoom to about 200% (or use Command/Ctrl + 0, or select the Fit Screen button on the Tool Options bar if you want to zoom to fit your monitor).

2. Select the regular Lasso tool (L) to make freehand selections on the car's black painted color.

3. Use the buttons on the Tool Options bar for adding to the previous selection made by the Magic Wand and Quick Selection tools (W), and then subtract any part of the selection that included hardware or the background.

4. When you return to the starting point of your selection, indicated by a small circle underneath the cursor, let go of your mouse to close the path. Since you can add to or subtract from a selection at will, it is okay to select or deselect small areas to remain precise.

5. Zoom in to about 200% or closer to start editing the selection near the hardware and alongside the edges of the car. Remember: only the black painted color areas are to be selected. Do not drink any coffee before doing this!

6. Save the file and leave the file open with the selection active.

THE SELECT MENU

The Select menu contains commands to edit selections (Figure 4-13). You still may need to work on selecting small areas of black on the car. The Select menu is a helpful tool for making slight changes in selections and for saving and reusing selections. Using the Select menu, you can increase a selection of similar adjacent colors by choosing Select > Grow, or by selecting similar colors throughout the image by choosing Select > Similar. To clean up stray pixels, the Smooth command (Select > Modify > Smooth) works nicely. You can also choose to select and deselect all layers within a document, or select layers of the same type, such as selecting all layers that contain text.

▷ FIGURE 4-13

The Select menu.

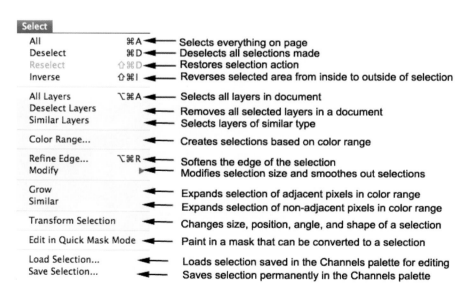

In this exercise, if needed, you will adjust the selections slightly and smooth out any stray areas that need to be included as part of the selection.

1. If you have large places that still need to be selected, select the Magic Wand tool (W), and set the Tolerance to 5 pixels on the Tool Options bar to keep the selection confined to a small amount of black tones of the car.

2. To add to the selection, choose Select > Grow for adjacent pixels or Select > Similar for nonadjacent pixels of similar colors.

3. To fill in stray areas that are not selected, choose Select > Modify > Smooth. Choose a 1- or 2-pixel sample radius; make sure the hardware and the background are *not* selected—the key is making sure all black painted areas have been selected, and no hardware or background is selected, much like a body shop would mask off areas that are not to be painted.

4. Save your file and leave it open with the selections active. It is time to fine-tune the edges of your selection. Do not deselect your work.

SAVING SELECTIONS PERMANENTLY USING CHANNELS

Photoshop uses channels in its Channels panel to save and store selections of an image area permanently called **alpha channels**, so they can be used again. These channels can also be edited at any time. Channels also store an image's color mode information in separate channels like the colors red, green, and blue for RGB color mode. You will notice these are displayed individually on the Channels panel. The Select menu allows you to save a selection to the Channels panel, so you will not lose all that hard work. Choose Select > Save Selection and name a new channel to save your selection. To load a selection already created from the Channels panel, choose Select > Load Selection.

▷ FIGURE 4-14

Save the selection as *Color* in a channel.

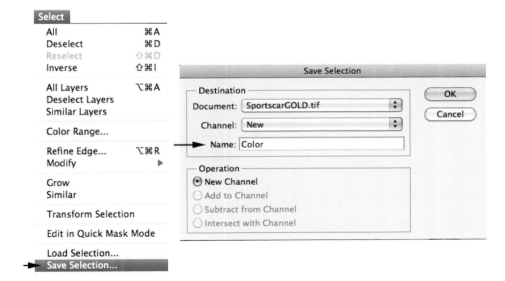

You are going to create a permanent channel in this exercise to save the selection. You will name the selection and save the file.

1. Make sure the Channels panel is displayed by selecting Channels from the Window menu; if it is already on your desktop, click the icon to expand it.

2. Click on Select > Save Selection from the Menu bar; when the Save Selection dialog box comes up, select New Channel and name it *Color* (Figure 4-14). Click OK.

3. Select the Channels panel, and you will notice that a new channel entitled *Color* has been created that actually shows a black and white thumbnail of what is selected. Notice that the separate RGB color channels are displayed, as well (Figure 4-15).

4. The *Color* channel is the new permanent alpha channel you just created. If the eye icon is hidden (not displayed), you will see the image in its normal (RGB) view.

5. In the Channels panel, when you click the box to show the eye icon, a red overlay mask shows the areas that are not to be changed. The normal image areas *without* the red overlay are the selected areas you created earlier that are going to be used to change the sports car's color.

6. Hide the eye icon by clicking the box again next to the *Color* channel to display the color channels' eye icons (RGB). The normal image will display.

7. Save the file again as *SportscarGOLD* again in your *Chapter 4* folder, making sure that the Alpha Channels box is checked for permanent selections. If a dialog box displays asking to replace the file, choose to replace it. Close the file, your selection is now permanent with the image.

▷   FIGURE 4-15

The Channels panel.

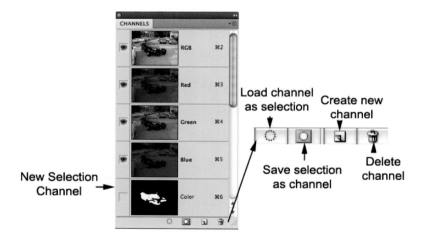

EDITING CHANNELS

You can repeatedly modify and save the changes to your selection by choosing Selection > Save Selection and select Replace Channel in the Channel drop-down menu as the operation. This replaces the old selection with the new, edited selection. If you want to save multiple selections at various stages, choose Select > Save Selection and provide different names to describe different channels.

Here, you will make final changes to the selection and save them in the *Color* channel you created earlier.

1. To check your selection, open the file *SportscarGOLD* in your *Chapter 4* folder (if a dialog box displays about the file, click OK), then choose Select > Load Selection. When the dialog box opens, you will see the *Color* channel. Since it is the only alpha channel you created, it is the only one available to load.

▷ FIGURE 4-16

Loading, saving, and replacing a selection.

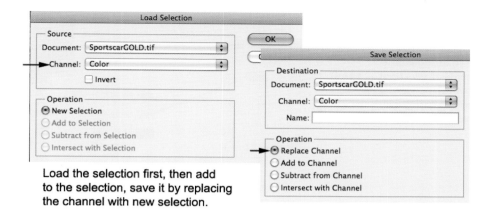

Load the selection first, then add to the selection, save it by replacing the channel with new selection.

2. Select OK. The selection you saved displays on the image showing with a marquee. You can now edit your selection.

3. Go back and use the Lasso tool, Quick Selection tool, or Select menu to complete the selection so that only black painted areas are selected. Zoom in to 200% to check any details.

4. To replace the permanent channel selection with the most recent version, choose Select > Save Selection. (Figure 4-16)

5. Locate the *Color* channel on the drop-down display and select Replace Channel. This replaces the old selection with the new edited selection. Select OK.

6. Continue until you are confident you have all the areas for recoloring the sports car selected.

7. Save the file in your *Chapter 4* folder on your hard drive.

REFINING THE EDGES OF THE SPORTS CAR COLOR SELECTION

With any of the selection tools used, you will notice a **Refine Edge** button in the Tool Options bar. This provides the designer or photographer the opportunity to soften, increase the contrast of, or expand the selection edges, and to test them against various backgrounds for accuracy (Figure 4-17). Pixels are not round: they are square and create jagged edges for selections along curved areas. The Refine Edge feature provides additional minute adjustments to soften selection edges. It has been reconstructed in CS5 to provide more accurate selections with a new series of selection-edge modification controls using enhanced edge detection technologies. You can observe various masks and views that show your selection, and adjust the sliders so the selection will make a smooth softened transition within its surroundings for true realism in your final image. This function can also be used to accurately remove an object from its surroundings. Keep in mind that adjusting the selection edges to soften should be done when you have your final selections completed as accurately as possible.

▷ FIGURE 4-17

The Refine Edge button provides softening or enchancing adjustments of selections that can be viewed on various backgrounds or masks.

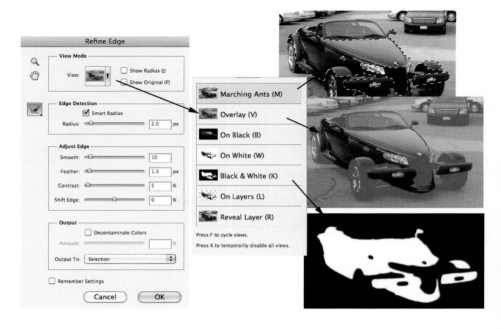

Now that you have finalized your detailed selection for changing the color of the Sports car, you will use the Refine Edge command to soften the edges for the car to blend into the background area of the image, which will make the transition more believable. You will also check the selection against various background masks.

1. With the sports car selection still active, zoom out the car to at least 100% to show the front area, and then select one of the selection tools. Click the Refine Edge button on the Tool Options bar.

2. As a starting point, select the Overlay View in the Refine Edge dialog box to display a red mask around those areas NOT to be painted, and make subtle adjustments using the sliders, starting with those displayed in Figure 4-17.

3. If you find that there are any stray areas that were not selected, or any place over selected (background areas), then you may need to go back and use the selection tools to correct the problem areas. Refine Edge can also help as a guide to check selections closely for accuracy.

4. To continue to check, you can press "P" to toggle the preview of the edge refinements, press "F" to cycle through the various preview modes or masks, or press "X" to disable all views allowing you to view the original image again. Select the Marching Ants (M) View to see your new selection.

5. When the edges seem smooth enough, click OK. Subtlety in making changes is important here. It is easier to come back and add to soften the edges than it is to remove them sometimes.

6. To save your new selection change to replace the existing channel, choose Select > Save Selection > Color Channel > Replace Channel > OK. You are now ready to change the car's color.

7. Save the file.

TOOLKIT TIP **TOOLKIT TIP** Inversing a selection: Sometimes it is easier to select what you do not want at first, because it is easier to select areas that are not as complex; then you can inverse the selection to include the area you actually want to edit. For instance, you have a landscape image with a blue sky, but you want to adjust the tones in the image except for the blue sky. Instead of selecting the landscape area you want to adjust, select the blue sky then choose Select > Inverse from the Select menu to change the selection to surround the landscape—what you really want to edit. You can then save the inverted selection permanently as a channel.

DESIGN TIP

If you were to try to "paint" the car with a brush, even at a low opacity, the shadow areas in particular would appear "filled in" and unrealistic looking. Painting is best done in small areas of an image. Using the Hue/ Saturation command works best with large areas or images with varying shadows and highlights.

ADJUSTING COLOR USING THE HUE/ SATURATION COMMAND

We are now ready to change the color of the sports car using the Hue/Saturation command in the Image menu. The **Hue/Saturation command** lets you adjust the hue, saturation, and lightness of an image or selected areas of an image. It works well with large items that have varying shadow and highlight detail. This technique works wonderfully when changing the color of a car, for instance. You can use the Hue slider to select new colors and the Saturation and Lightness sliders for color purity and intensity. You also have the option to try out various preset settings in the Hue/Saturation panel, or create your own customized preset settings that you can save and access for future projects.

▷ FIGURE 4-18

The Hue/Saturation command blends in colors with tones for a more realistic look on your image.

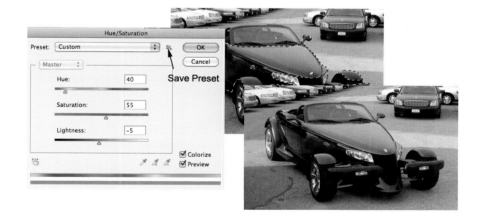

In this exercise, you are going to accurately color the sports car. You will load the completed *Color* channel selection you created, and then you will use the Hue/Saturation command to get the color you want.

1. If you have the selection still active go to Step 2. If not, to retrieve your selection, choose Select > Load Selection > Color > OK. This is the alpha selection channel you created for only those areas of the car that are going to be colored.

2. Select Image > Adjustments > Hue/Saturation and make sure the Colorize and Preview option boxes are checked.

3. Move the dialog box alongside the image so you can see the effects.

4. To change the color of the sports car to gold, start with these settings and adjust the sliders until you have a nice golden color.
Hue: 40, Saturation: 55, Lightness: –5 (minus 5). See Figure 4-18 for settings. To save your color settings, click the Preset Options menu, and choose Save Preset.

5. Name the preset *Gold* in the Hue/Saturation panel. It will be saved as a custom preset.

6. Save your file.

7. Optional: Feel free to duplicate your *SportscarGold* file and make your own colors, the selection will still be saved as a channel. Try candy apple red, turquoise green, or purple as color ideas. Simply adjust the Hue/Saturation sliders to taste.

DESIGN TIP

When scanning images or photograph documents, sometimes an image may appear overly saturated in color, especially in skin tones. You can use the Hue/Saturation command to help to bring back the original colors by decreasing the image's saturation.

PROBLEM If you are not getting close to the color you want, make sure the Colorize box is checked in the Hue/Saturation dialog box.

TOOLKIT TIP When changing a product's colors, or creating multiple products of different colors from the same image, instead of creating different files as shown in this beginner's exercise, you can create what are called adjustment layers to the image and keep the changes all within one file. You'll be using this more effective method in the next chapter.

ADVANCED USER: Using Quick Mask for Masking Selections

Using a **Quick Mask** and saving it as a selection is another method to further edit your selections for more advanced detail work. As you noticed using the Refine Edge function, you observed different masks of the selection you had made of the sports car as a way to check your accuracy and to soften the edge selections. Using the Quick Mask method allows you to create a detailed selection using the brush or pencils tools based on observing the mask as a guide. You may find this a more preferred alternative than using the selection tools covered.

At the bottom of the Tools panel, you will find your image that you are working on, by default, is in normal Standard Mode (bottom icon). You are going to work in Quick Mask mode by simply pressing the same button, which acts as a toggle (Figure 4-19), and paint to add or remove part of the selection. You would paint with white to remove areas of the mask or SUBTRACT from the selection. Painting with black would ADD to the mask or selection (as far as the image goes, remember, white reveals, black conceals). Quick masks, however, are not permanent; after you have set up your selection mask and checked it, you will need to make a permanent selection channel again as done earlier.

As for the Brush and Pencil tools, when you select either tool, you can click on the brush size icon to bring up the tool's Preset Picker of customized tools. You can also use the sliders to determine the size and edge hardness of the tools and create your own preset tool. We'll cover them more in later chapters.

▷ **Masks** are used to protect parts of an image from being changed the same way an auto body shop masks off parts of an auto not to be painted.

▷ **Masks** are great for working in minute detail, maintaining accuracy and providing another way to save a selection.

▷ Using a mask covers areas outside the selected area with a red colored overlay. You noticed a red mask was one of the options when you chose the Refine Edge function.

▷ All exposed areas (unmasked or not red) are part of the selection you made for making changes. Here, you should use the Brush tool for soft edges and the Pencil tool for sharp contrast edges; you will also find that Lasso tools and the Eraser tool work in Quick Mask mode as well.

DESIGN TIP

Here is where a designer can really get into accurate details with a very small brush size. Painting with masks allows you to edit minute details within an image, so there is little room left for mistakes; this attention to detail provides quality workmanship that pays back with customer satisfaction and loyalty.

 TOOLKIT TIP You can quickly adjust the brush size of any painting tool by pressing the bracket keys on your keyboard. The left bracket ([) decreases the brush size; the right bracket (]) increases it.

 TOOLKIT TIP You can switch back and forth between adding to the mask with black and subtracting from the mask with white foreground colors by pressing the X key on your keyboard. Remember, white removes the mask, black will add to the mask. If you use the Eraser, make sure the background color is set to white to delete parts of the mask.

You can add or subtract from a selection mask by painting with the Pencil tool or Brush tool in Quick Mask mode.

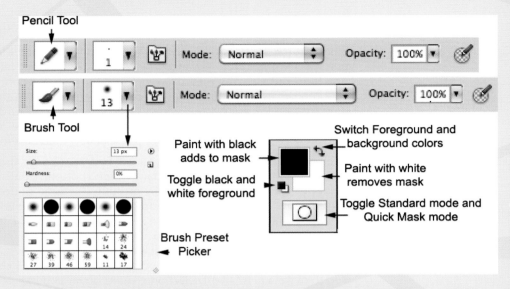

Now you will paint with the Brush and Pencil tools to add to or subtract from the mask. You will then replace the old selections with the new, edited selections by saving the new channel.

1. If continuing with your selections created earlier and your selection is active, go to Step 2. If not, open your *SportscarGOLD* file, then choose Select > Load Selection and select the *Color* channel. If you want to start from scratch, open the original *Sportscar* file or your own image, and make a series of selections on the areas you want to color. Save the selection using Select > Save Selection > New Channel and name the channel *Color*.

2. Click the bottom icon on the Tools panel to toggle from the default Standard Mode to Quick Mask mode (Figure 4-19). You will notice the icon turns red and you'll observe a red overlay indicating what has been masked out. You can also select Edit in Quick Mask Mode in the Select menu.

3. Zoom in to around 200% to 300% to observe what needs editing.

4. Masking and unmasking, use the foreground and background colors in the Tools panel and either the Brush for larger areas or Pencil tool for smaller areas as starting points to paint. White removes the mask, black will add to the mask.

5. Select either a harder edge brush or try the Pencil tool and enter 5 pixels or less brush size to start in the Tool Options bar. You are working with detail here, so a smaller brush size will be easier to work with.

6. On the Tool Options bar, set Mode to Normal and the Opacity settings to 100%.

7. Select the Foreground color as white by clicking the bent arrow above the Foreground/Background color icons so that white displays as the Foreground color (or simply press "X" on the keyboard to switch them). Paint with white to remove areas of the mask to expose any missed black areas of the car (Figure 4-20).

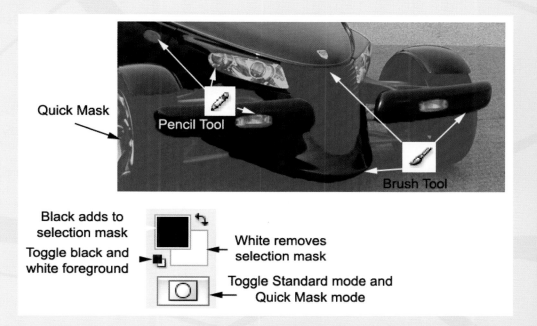

▷ FIGURE 4-20

Completing the mask to make a very accurate selection.

8. Select the bent arrow again—it acts as a toggle—to change the Foreground color to black. Use this to add to the mask. Change brush sizes depending on the size of the area.

9. Work on small details around the lights, tires, background, and seat of the car to edit the mask. Remember, you want to isolate the hardware and background completely from the black area of the car.

10. Toggle between Standard Mode and Quick Mask Mode on the Tools panel to see your new edited selection.

11. Select the Brush tool for painting along the outer edges of the car.

12. When you have everything selected as accurately as possible, select one of the selection tools, then select Refine Edge on the Tool Options bar to check your work. If everything looks great, go ahead and soften the edge selection. Select OK when finished.

13. To replace the alpha channel with the most recent selection, click on the icon at the bottom of the Tools panel to toggle back to Standard mode to view the selected car, then choose Select > Save Selection.

14. Locate the *Color* channel on the drop-down display and select Replace Channel. This replaces the old selection with the new edited selection.

15. When your selection is complete, make sure your selection is active on the image (Select > Load Selection > Color Channel), then select Image > Adjust > Hue/Saturation (make sure Colorize and Preview boxes are checked), adjust for your new color, and save and close the file in the *Chapter 4* folder.

DIGITAL TOOLKIT EXTRA: Make a Better Sky Using Either the Paste Into Command, or the Masks Panel

COMBINING IMAGES USING THE PASTE INTO COMMAND

So you have a nice photo composition on a day with all blue sky. Well, here is a way to change the sky to enhance your image by adding clouds from another image. In this first method, the idea is to Paste the new improved sky into a selection made from the plain sky using the **Paste Into command** (Figure 4-21). You can create all kinds of different image combinations with this technique.

Original Images   Final Image With Clouds

▷ FIGURE 4-21

Using the Paste Into command lets you combine images for dramatic effects.

CROPPING A FIXED SELECTION SIZE

The Marquee tool can create selections based on a fixed width and height set in the Tool Options bar. The area outside the selection can be removed by choosing Image > Crop to make the image a specific size. Of the Marquee tools, cropping a fixed image selection is best done with the Rectangular Marquee tool, which will create a rectangular crop. Since the lighthouse image is slightly larger than the clouds image, you will crop the lighthouse image to size. Both images are the same resolution, so there will be no distortion.

▷ FIGURE 4-22

Enter a fixed size of 7 by 5 inches, then crop the image using the Rectangular Marquee tool.

Rectangular Marquee Tool

TOOLKIT TIP Before you combine images, make sure that the resolution ppi is the same for both images by choosing Image > Image Size and checking the Resolution setting.

Here you will crop the lighthouse image size to match the size of the image of the clouds.

1. Open the *Litehous.tif* file from the *Chapter 4* folder on your drive.

2. Select the Rectangular Marquee tool. In the Tool Options bar, select Fixed Size for Style and enter "7 in" for Width and "5 in" for Height. This creates a fixed, 7-inch by 5-inch selection.

3. Click on the image once to place the marquee, and then use the arrow keys to position the selection so the tank on the left side of the picture is eliminated (Figure 4-22).

4. To remove the area outside of the selection, choose Image > Crop, then remove the selection (Select > Deselect). Leave the image open.

SELECTING TWO IMAGES FOR PASTE INTO

To replace the blue sky with the image of the clouds, a selection of the blue sky needs to be made and then a selection of the entire clouds image. The blue sky selection becomes a cutout, or window, into which you place the clouds image.

You can use the Magic Wand tool and the Select menu to select only the blue sky, and then use the Select > All command (or Command/Ctrl + A) to select the clouds image (Figure 4-23). Both images will have a selection to prepare for the Paste Into command.

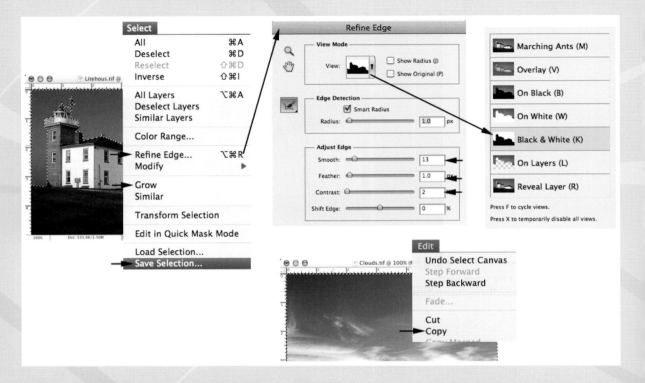

▷ FIGURE 4-23

With selections made in the original image, locate the *Clouds* image and choose Select > All. Copy it before using the Paste Into command.

In this exercise, you will create the selections in both images before using the Paste Into command in the next exercise.

1. Make sure the *Litehous.tif* image is open.

2. Select the Quick Selection tool and enter a Tolerance of 5 pixels in the Tool Options bar. You can also try the same settings with the Magic Wand tool and paint the sky areas to select.

3. Select the blue sky and add to the selection until all of the sky is selected. To add to the selection, you can use the setting in the Tool Options bar, use the Select menu (Select > Grow), or hold down the Shift key while clicking with the Magic Wand tool.

4. Use the Lasso tool, if needed, to add to or subtract from the selection to make sure only the blue sky is selected, not any part of the lighthouse.

5. Save the selection to create an alpha channel by choosing Select > Save Selection and name the new channel *Blue Sky*.

6. You have now created a window to put the clouds image in without affecting any other part of the lighthouse image. Use the Refine Edge function to slightly soften the edges of the selection. Select the Black & White View mask

as a guide. Click the zoom icon on the Refine Edge display to 400% to get close. You can also try feathering the selection by one pixel or less, and leave the rest of the settings as shown. Click on the Zoom icon, hold down the Option/ALT key and zoom back out to 100%, then select OK. Leave the sky selected.

7. Open the Clouds file from your *Chapter 4* folder.

8. Choose Select > All (or Command/Ctrl + A) to select everything in the image. Both images will maintain their selections for the next exercise.

9. Leave both files open with the selections active.

COMBINING IMAGES USING PASTE INTO

With selections made for both images, you will use the Paste Into command to paste the new cloud selection into the selection you made in the lighthouse image. The selection in the lighthouse image becomes a cutout or window that hides the blue sky, so you can paste the clouds image into the window. The Move tool will then help to position the clouds in place (Figure 4-24). The **Move tool** allows you to move a selection or an entire image onto another image or another area of the same image. When moving a selected area to another place within an image, you can use the mouse for basic positioning and the arrow keys on the keyboard for more accurate positioning.

▷ FIGURE 4-24

The Paste Into command pastes a copy of the clouds into the selected blue sky window you created. Adjust with the Move tool.

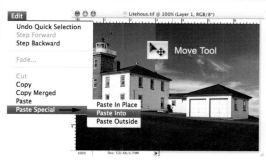

Using the Move tool to adjust the position of the pasted clouds

Completed image with clouds added.

1. With the *Clouds* image active (click on the title bar), choose Edit > Copy to copy the selection to memory in the Clipboard, which is a storage area on your computer's memory. Although you cannot see any changes, the new cloud image is ready to be pasted into the old sky portion of the *Litehous.tif* image.

2. Close the Clouds file without saving it, leaving the *Litehous* file still open. When you click the *Litehous* image, the previous selection of the blue sky on the lighthouse will be displayed.

3. With the sky still selected in the *Litehous* file, select Edit > Paste Special > Paste Into (earlier versions: Edit > Paste Into). Paste Into will paste your new clouds into the blue sky selection covering the original blue sky.

4. Select the Move tool and drag the image to where you want it.

5. Save the file as *NewSKY.tif* using the default settings in your *Chapter 4* folder.

6. To give a slight introduction to layers which we will cover in Chapter 5, select the Layers panel (Window > Layers) and you'll notice the original lighthouse image on the bottom layer, and then another layer on top of it that shows the image of the clouds with a layer "mask" next to it, black to hide the lighthouse, and white to show the sky "window." Whenever you paste or move an image onto another it creates another layer. Try this technique with your own images.

 PROBLEM If you cannot move the clouds, make sure the clouds *Layer 1* is highlighted in the Layers panel (Window > Layers). The layer will be shaded blue. If not, click the layer with your mouse to select it. We will be using layers in the next chapter.

SELECTING BY COLOR RANGE, AND USING THE MASKS PANEL

In Photoshop, as in most applications, there are numerous ways to achieve the same results, some better than others. This technique is a little more advanced but demonstrates another method that also provides a more detailed look using masks and the Masks panel. As discussed in the "Advanced" section, masks are the chosen method for creating the most detailed selections. The **Masks panel** allows you to select by color range or invert a selection, and define the selection edges using the **Mask Edge** function. It then creates what is called a layer mask that sits next to the thumbnail image in the Layers panel. This will also introduce a little about layers, which we will cover in depth in Chapter 5. You will use the same two files *Lighthouse.tif* and *Clouds.tif*, and then compare results from the previous Paste Into tutorial.

SELECTING BY COLOR RANGE

Another more complicated method of selection involves selecting same areas of color and color tones using the **Color Range command** from the Select menu. This works best with either solid colors, or same color tones in same area, such as a bowl of fruit like strawberries that may need to have their color enhanced. You'll find that using the Color Range as a mode of selection helps when you have tiny areas you want to keep away from the selection, like the lighthouse antennae here. This is a little more advanced, but more accurate approach.

Here you are going to use the Color Range function in the Select menu to select the blue sky and save as a selection channel.

1. Open the *Clouds.tif* file, then open the original *Lighthous.tif* file from your *Chapter 4* folder, crop the lighthouse image as indicated in the previous exercise to a fixed size of 7 inches wide by 5 inches high using the Rectangle Marquee tool. Show as much of the sky as possible in your crop.

The Color Range command samples colors and their tones to create colors based selections.

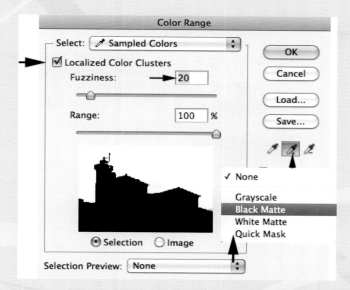

2. Remove the crop selection, by choosing Select > Deselect.

3. Zoom in to 200% to view details. Choose Select > Color Range.

4. When the dialog box opens, check Localized Color Clusters to keep all selection areas adjacent to one another. This keeps the chosen colors from spilling to other unwanted areas of the image.

5. Keep the Fuzziness setting to around 20 to keep the color selection area relatively small, since we only want the blue-sky area. Select the eyedropper with a plus sign to add each selection and carefully paint along the sky area, close to the lighthouse, but don't touch it, even close to the ground area. Use the minus eyedropper if you selected areas other than just the sky. You will see the black and white thumbnail will display the lighthouse as black and the selected blue sky area as white (Figure 4-25).

6. On the Color Range display, choose Black Matte from the Selection Preview list to get an idea of your selected area, take a look at the other types of previews, and then select the default None when you are ready.

7. Select OK to display the new selection areas you just made on the original lighthouse image, use the Lasso tools (subtract selection) to remove or clean up any stray areas of pixels, or choose Select > Grow for any pixels left in the sky.

8. Choose Select > Save Selection and name the new channel Blue Sky as in the previous exercise. Leave the selected blue sky open for the next exercise.

USING THE MASKS PANEL

The Masks panel allows you to sharpen or soften selection edges using various masks, much the same as the Refine Edge command when you were creating selections on the sports car. When you have the edge selection the way you want it, you can paint in areas that have been removed to display (white), or continue in more detail to add to the mask (black) using the Brush tool.

▷   FIGURE 4-26

Using the Masks panel, inverting the selected blue sky removes it.

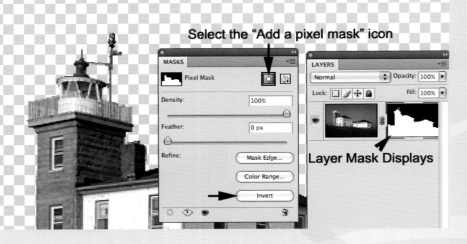

1. Make sure the Masks panel is open (Window > Masks).

2. Click the "Add a pixel mask" icon, which looks like a square with a circle center, on the Masks panel (see Figure 4-26). You will notice the selected blue sky remains and the lighthouse is removed.

3. Click on the Invert button on the Masks panel and the selection is inversed, removing the blue sky. You can see the blue sky background as a black mask that shows not only on the Masks panel, but also as a black "layer mask" next to the thumbnail image on the Layers panel (you'll learn more about layer masks in Chapter 6).

4. Select the Zoom tool on the Tools panel, and zoom in to about 200% showing the top of the lighthouse, as this is the most complicated selection area.

5. To make detailed adjustments for your selection, click on the Mask Edge button on the Masks panel. The thumbnail will show a black mask of the blue sky area and the lighthouse area in white. The black area represents the mask and the white area shows what will be displayed.

6. You'll find a dialog box that looks very similar to the Refine Edge dialog box when you were working with the sports car image except the title bar reads Refine Mask instead. The idea here is to make the transition between the lighthouse edges and the clouds image very believable. Pixels are square, so you want less jagged edges showing.

7. Select the Black & White view mask in the Refine Mask dialog box. Use Figure 4-27 as a guide and make slight adjustments to show a smooth transition. Don't make the edges too smooth or you will lose the detail edges like the top of the lighthouse area. Keep the areas to display as white, and the blue sky to hide as black. Try to make sure the pole on the lighthouse is selected. Remember you are zoomed at 200%. Click on the Marching Ants view (Preview Standard (1st) button in earlier versions) to see the difference and then click OK when you're satisfied.

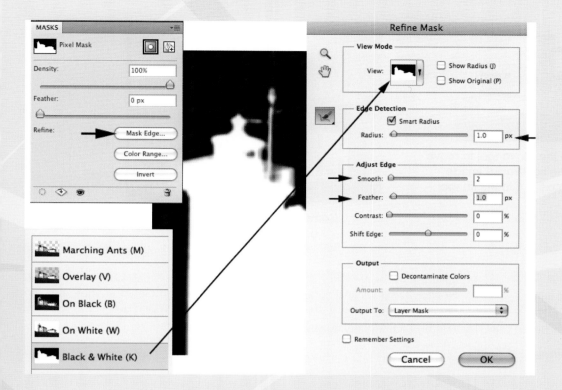

▷ FIGURE 4-27

The Masks panel allows you to adjust the edges of any selection using the Refine Mask display.

8. The lighthouse image now displays without the sky. Zoom at 400% or closer with the Zoom tool for minute details, and then select the Brush tool.

9. It's time to paint using black or white as the foreground color, to add to or subtract from the mask. To paint back those areas that may have been erased make sure the White foreground color is displayed in the Tools panel, to display parts of the lighthouse, not the blue sky. Use the bracket keys on your keyboard to increase or decrease the size of your brush and paint.

10. To add to the mask, removing stray blue-sky areas, make sure the foreground color is set to Black in the Tools panel and paint in. Here is where careful attention to detail shows.

11. Drag the tabs of both image files *Litehous* and *Clouds* to the desktop as separate windows, or select the Arrange Documents button on the Application bar, and choose Float All in Windows. Make sure both windows display at 100% in the title bar.

12. Instead of using Paste Into as before, make sure the Layers panel is displayed, select the Move tool in the Tools panel, and drag the lighthouse image onto the Clouds image. In this way you adjust the lighthouse to lose some of the excess ground to show most of the sky; adjust until you feel satisfied (Figure 4-28).

13. Notice you now have two different layers displayed on the Layers panel, much more on that in Chapter 5 next.

**Use the Move tool to move
the lighthouse image
onto the Clouds image**

**Completed image with clouds
using the Masks panel**

▷ FIGURE 4-28

**Moving the light-
house onto the
clouds image,
completed
composite image.**

14. Save the file as *NewSky2.tif* in your *Chapter 4* folder. Open both NewSky and NewSky2 images and compare detail in the two completed images, also the difference in position of the lighthouse and clouds. Which do you prefer?

15. Try this technique with other images.

CHAPTER SUMMARY

You have now created an accurate complex selection using the Magic Wand tool and Quick Selection tool for similar colors and then the Lasso tools for additional editing. The Tool Options bar and its settings for each tool were used to edit the selections until they were perfect. You have created, named, and saved a permanent selection for changing the sports car's color, and then created a new color using the Hue/Saturation to accurately blend in tones for a realistic effect. Advanced users created masks with Quick Mask mode using the Brush and Pencil tools to make more accurate selections. For more projects and ideas, check out the *Goodies* folder on your CD.

REVIEW QUESTIONS

1. Explain some of the differences and similarities between the Lasso, Marquee, Move, Quick Selection, and Magic Wand tools.

2. Why should you save images as .TIF files for editing instead of saving them as JPEGs?

3. Why is the Tolerance setting important for the Magic Wand tool?

4. Explain how to create perfect circles and squares with the Marquee tools.

5. Explain the purposes of channels and the differences between color and alpha channels.

6. What are some of the uses of the Select menu?

7. How do you save a channel that has been edited?

8. What are Quick Masks and how do they work?

9. What color would you paint to remove part of a mask? To add to the mask?

10. What is the purpose of the Paste Into command in the Edit menu? Explain the purpose of the Masks panel.

▷   FIGURE 4-29

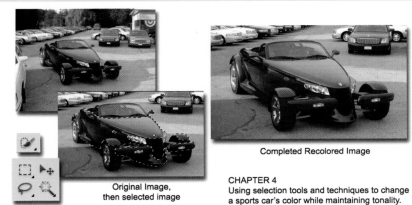

Original Image,
then selected image

Completed Recolored Image

CHAPTER 4
Using selection tools and techniques to change
a sports car's color while maintaining tonality.

CHAPTER 4 ADVANCED
Adding and subtracting selctions
with precision using Quick Mask function,
Brush and Pencil tools.

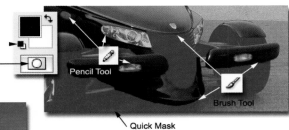

Pencil Tool

Brush Tool

Quick Mask

CHAPTER 4 EXTRA Combining images for dramatic effects, using either the Paste Into Command, or selecting
by Color Range and using the Masks panel for more detail work.

CHAPTER

5

Using Layers

CHAPTER OBJECTIVES: To understand the importance of using layers in Photoshop, in this chapter you will:

▷ Rename, duplicate, and move layers.

▷ Create two permanent selections to duplicate graphics for replication with a variety of realistic colors.

▷ Use the Hue/Saturation command to adjust color while retaining shadows and highlights within an image.

▷ Use layer styles to create drop shadows and specialized effects.

▷ Create type layers and make adjustments.

▷ Record states of layers in various stages of development with Layer Comps.

▷ Merge layers and prepare files for commercial printing and for electronic distribution.

▷ ADVANCED USERS: Prepare Camera RAW files; the new digital negative for accurate toning.

▷ DIGITAL TOOLKIT EXTRA: Image Transformations using Content-Aware Fill and Scale to remove unwanted background elements and resize images, and Picture Package to create photo business cards.

Every Photoshop file contains one or more layers. *Layers* are like stacks of transparent sheets with parts of an image laid one on top of another. Layers are used to modify selected portions of an image and to combine different images, or selected areas, together. Special effects can also be added to each layer, so layers provide the designer or photographer the flexibility to make changes to any precise area of an image to achieve whatever effect is needed. In this chapter, we will explore using layers for duplicating and coloring images, creating special effects, and for adding lines of text.

Need additional fun computer graphics tutorials and info, and an additional look at the projects you'll be creating in this book? Check out my Artist's Digital Toolkit website at: **http://www.digitoolkit.com**

PHOTOSHOP'S LAYERS

Layers can be used by the designer or photographer for a variety of purposes and can be arranged for a variety of effects. When areas of an image are selected, layers can be created to isolate those areas for modification. Layers can also be used to combine images, duplicate selected areas, and create special effects on selected areas. The Layers panel provides thumbnails of layers stacked on top of one another. An effect on one layer may or may not have an effect on the layers below it, depending on the Opacity setting and Blending Mode options chosen. For example, a Normal Mode (default) setting at 100 percent opacity allows you to make changes to an active layer without affecting any layers below it.

DISPLAYING AND HIDING LAYERS

Only one layer can be edited at a time, and that is the active layer, highlighted and shaded in blue. The **eye icon** displayed indicates that the layer is visible. You can hide or show a layer by clicking the eye icon. Layers are part of the new collapsible workspace, where layer panels can be minimized or docked to an icon image, or to an icon with the Layer panel labeled, to allow more work space (Figure 5-1). By clicking on the icon, panels can be expanded for instant display. You can click on the top tab of any panel to collapse it to an icon display.

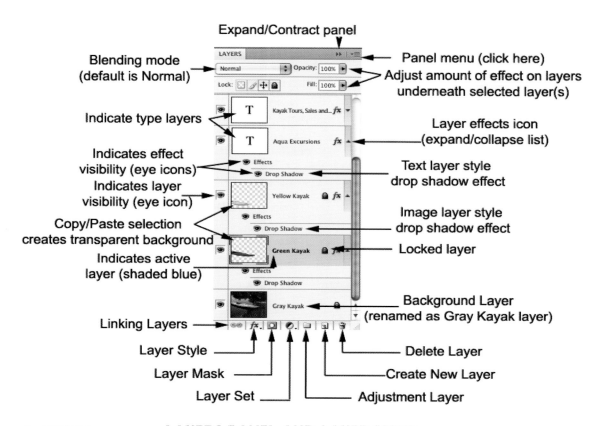

Expand/Contract panel

Blending mode (default is Normal)

Panel menu (click here)

Adjust amount of effect on layers underneath selected layer(s)

Indicate type layers

Layer effects icon (expand/collapse list)

Indicates effect visibility (eye icons)

Text layer style drop shadow effect

Indicates layer visibility (eye icon)

Image layer style drop shadow effect

Copy/Paste selection creates transparent background

Locked layer

Indicates active layer (shaded blue)

Background Layer (renamed as Gray Kayak layer)

Linking Layers

Layer Style

Delete Layer

Layer Mask

Create New Layer

Layer Set

Adjustment Layer

▷ FIGURE 5-1

Layers panel with options.

LAYERS PANEL AND LAYER MENU

You can use either the **Layers panel** or **Layer menu** to display, modify, edit, copy, group, or delete layers, along with other various commands and options for layers and layer effects. The Layers panel allows you to view thumbnails of the content contained in each layer, and you can move layers above or below others for specific effects (Figure 5-2). Selecting the Layers panel submenu or the icons at the bottom of the Layers panel will give you many of the same commands found in the Layer menu. The Layer menu contains additional commands for editing individual layers and effects between selected layers. An arrow pointing to the right at the end of the command indicates that there are more functions to choose from.

THE BACKGROUND LAYER

Every time you open an image or create a new image or blank document, there will always be one special layer to start called the *Background,* which contains the original image or blank canvas. The Background remains locked at the bottom until you double-click the Background layer's name and rename it. It then behaves as a normal layer and can be moved around between other layers.

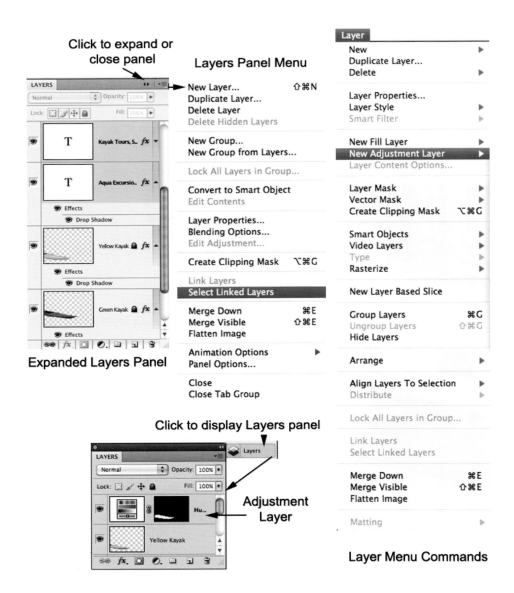

Click to expand or close panel

Layers Panel Menu

Expanded Layers Panel

Click to display Layers panel

Adjustment Layer

Layer Menu Commands

ADJUSTMENT LAYERS

Using adjustment layers (Figure 5-2) within an image allows a designer to create a series of layered effects over the original image that are non-destructable,
so that pixels in the original image are not manipulated. Adjustment layers have
their effects on their own individual layers and can easily be edited. The layer mask
provides a window for the effects as they trickle down through the layers below,
giving total control to the user (this will be covered in more detail in Chapter 6).

THE MOVE TOOL

The Move tool is used to drag selected areas within the image to create additional layers, or to drag selections created from other images onto the image, which automatically creates a new layer. For precision positioning of selections within an image, select the Move tool and use the arrow keys on the keyboard for precise placement of artwork (Figure 5-3).

▷ FIGURE 5-3

Use the Move tool to move selected areas within an image, or move selected images between image windows.

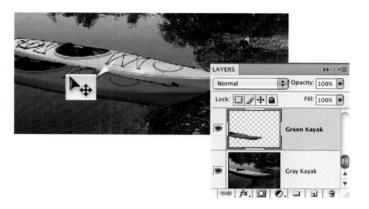

SAVING IMAGES WITH LAYERS

To keep your layers editable, make sure you save the file with Photoshop's native extension, .PSD, or as a .TIF file. Files saved in TIFF or PSD formats maintain the original quality no matter how many times you make changes. Images with a .TIF extension can be read universally by all graphic applications as long as the final image combines all layers into one layer (leave the layers option selected to include all layers); although many applications, like those by Adobe, allow files to be read with multiple layers. If you save the file in a **JPEG format,** you should make sure all layers are combined as one, although data will be discarded each time the file is edited and saved, gradually deteriorating image quality. JPEG files cannot be changed later either. If you need to decrease the file size to distribute it electronically for a client, make a back-up copy of the TIFF file, then combine the layers and save the file with a .JPG extension. Most applications use the universal form of PDF files to communicate; in Photoshop you can save your layered files in the Photoshop PDF format, and anyone can view the image with the free Adobe Acrobat Reader you downloaded in Chapter 1. PDF files retain all the formatting used in the document; and you can also use this method to create "flattened" PDF files for electronic distribution or high-resolution files that can be used for commercial printing.

ACTION ITEMS

This assignment provides a review of selection tools and techniques from Chapter 4. It shows how a designer or photographer can use selections to create multiple colored objects from the same selected object for an advertisement. Selections are essential for the successful completion of the ad. As a designer or photographer, your goal is to create two detailed selections of the original gray kayak that can be saved permanently. One selection will be used to recolor the kayak, without including hardware,

CLIENT ASSIGNMENT: Creating a Multicolor Product Advertisement

Your client, Alyce Powell, who owns a kayak sales and touring service called Aqua Excursions, wants to have a direct mail advertisement created for her customers. The purpose of the ad is to move her current inventory to make room for next year's models and supplies by having a sale for her customers in September. She gives you a call to help her create the ad. When you meet, she informs you that she has a photograph of one gray kayak and wants you to create two other kayaks of different colors. You both decide in addition to the gray kayak, a

hunter green and yellow kayak will also be created. The green and gray kayaks will be marketed to the outdoor enthusiast, while the yellow kayak will cater more to the recreational user. With a lake shoreline as the background, the ad will display the three different colored kayaks (gray, dark green, and yellow) placed diagonally with drop shadows for added realism and depth. The white business title and ad text will be placed in the dark areas of the image, and for emphasis, a yellow text line describes the sale. Alyce leaves excited to see the final layout.

Original Image

Completed Kayak Advertisement

Portion of layers used

▷ FIGURE 5-4

Completed advertisement and some of the types of layers created in this chapter.

straps, or seat. The other selection will be used to include the kayak with all hardware so you can duplicate it to create multiple images. These selections will be used to make layers that allow you to duplicate the kayak image, color it, and position it in the ad. You will then create text layers for each line of type in the ad. Drop shadow layer effects for the type and images will make the text stand out and match the gray kayak's shadow. Finally, you will organize the text layers under one layer set and prepare the file for electronic distribution and commercial printing.

To create the additional images and text for this assignment, here is what you need to do:

• Create a duplicate copy of the original image to serve as a back-up copy.

• Create the first selection for changing the color by using the Magic Wand, Quick Selection, and Lasso selection tools. Only the gray areas of the kayak must be selected; all hardware, seat, cords, and background must be isolated.

• Create a second selection, which will be used for duplicating the entire kayak by *including* hardware, seat, and cords in the selection.

• Use the Tool Options bar, Select menu, and Edit menu to help with editing selections.

• Make the two selections permanent by saving them as channels in the Channels panel for reuse and future editing.

• Select the original kayak Background layer and rename it.

• Load the channel selection (*KayakALL*) for the whole kayak; copy and paste the selection to create a new layer.

• Load the channel selection (*Kayak Color*) for changing the color of the new kayak.

• Create new color (Hunter Green) using the Hue/Saturation command as part of an adjustment layer.

• Load the *KayakALL* channel selection again to select the entire kayak, duplicate it and drag it into position using the Move tool.

• Repeat the same process above to create and position the yellow kayak. Alternative method is to use adjustment layer technique, which will be discussed.

• Apply drop shadows using the layer styles for the green and yellow kayaks to match the gray kayak shadow angle and color. Apply shadows for the text layers.

• Create Layer Comps to record various layer stages in development and to provide variations within the project.

• Decrease the file size by using layer groups, merging layers, and flattening layers to prepare the ad for press.

• Advanced Users: Prepare Camera Raw files, the digital negatives, with proper toning.

CREATING THE KAYAK SELECTIONS FOR COLOR AND DUPLICATION

Selections are essential for the successful completion of the ad. As a designer or photographer, your goal is to create two detailed selections of the original gray kayak that can be saved permanently. You will use those selections to make layers that allow you to color the kayak image, duplicate it, position it, and create realistic drop shadows in the ad.

FIRST SELECTION OF THE KAYAK FOR COLOR CHANGE

The selection will be used for changing the kayak's gray color to the other colors specified by the client. Here, only the gray colors of the original kayak are going to be selected; all hardware, seats, and background must be isolated so they will not change color. Make sure you have enough time to complete this series of exercises so that you can save your selections permanently using channels.

DESIGN TIP

It is a good habit to zoom in with the Zoom tool and work on a small area at a time, and then to zoom out and observe results in the bigger picture, much like an artist would when working on a painting or sketch.

TOOLKIT TIP If you like keystrokes instead of the buttons on the Tool Options bar, holding down the Option/Alt key will subtract from your selection, and holding down the Shift key will add to your selection. You can quickly adjust the brush size of this tool or any painting tool by pressing the bracket keys on your keyboard. The left bracket ([) makes the size smaller and the right bracket (]) increases the size. To save time, you can also use the spacebar instead of the Hand tool to scroll around the image as you work.

▷ FIGURE 5-5

Add/Subtract selections by using the Quick Selection and Magic Wand tools.

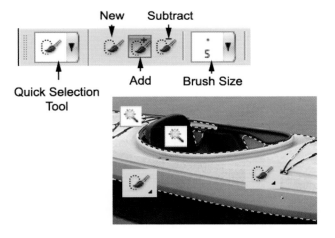

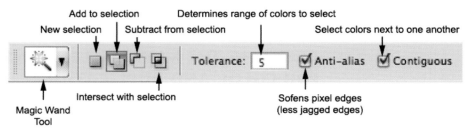

Here, you are going to set the options for your selection tools and start selecting the gray areas of the kayak to be recolored.

1. Launch Photoshop and open the *Kayak.tif* file in your *Chapter 5* folder. Zoom in to about 100% with the Zoom tool to get a good, detailed view.

2. Select the Quick Selection tool (W) and set the Brush Picker box to 5 pixels, and then select the Add to selection icon on the Tool Options bar. (Figure 5-5).

3. Select the front gray area of the kayak. Use the Tool Options bar buttons, or the keystroke shortcuts (try pressing the bracket keys on your keyboard to increase or decrease the brush size), to add to and subtract from your selection until you have a lot of the kayak's gray color selected, excluding the seat, any hardware, or background (Figure 5-5). Decrease the Brush Size setting to 3 pixels to gradually build on your selection.

4. Zoom in to 100% or closer to observe the detail in the selection area. Use the Scrubby Zoom on the Tool Options bar for quick observation (CS5). Make any additional adjustments as necessary. Use the Hand tool and Navigator panel to move around the image.

5. If needed, select the Magic Wand tool and set the Tolerance to 5 pixels wide or less to start, making sure the Anti-alias and Contiguous boxes are checked, to indicate how many pixels of relatively the same shade of gray color should be selected and added (Figure 5-5). Now click and drag to paint or to add or subtract from the selection area, especially inside the straps. Use the Tool Options bar icons to add to and subtract from your selection until you have most of the kayak's gray color selected, excluding any hardware or background.

6. Save the File as *KayakAD* in your Chapter 5 folder.

 PROBLEM A selection is automatically removed if you have the New Selection button on the Tool Options bar set when making another selection. To remove all selections on the image, choose Select > Deselect. If you make a mistake, choose Select > Reselect. To go back to the last action, choose Edit > Undo State Change, or toggle Command/Ctrl Z.

CLEANING UP WITH THE LASSO TOOLS AND SELECT MENU

The Lasso tools can be used to help clean up stray areas not yet selected by the Magic Wand or Quick Selection tools. You can use them to combine with and subtract from selected areas and for straight edge selections. The Select menu allows you to expand, contract, and fill in stray selected areas.

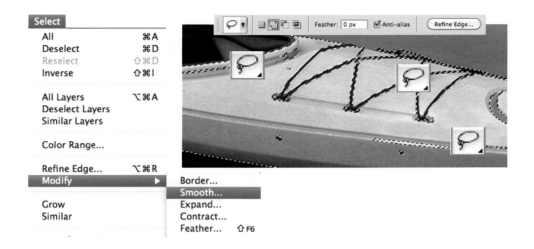

▷ FIGURE 5-6

Using the Lasso tool for freehand selections, and Select menu to enhance the selection areas.

In this exercise, you will adjust the selections slightly and smooth out any stray areas that need to be included as part of the selection.

1. Select the regular Lasso tool (L) to make freehand selections on the kayak's gray color (Figure 5-6). Use the buttons on the Tool Options bar for adding to the previous selection made by the Magic Wand and Quick Selection tools (W), and then subtract any part of the selection that included hardware or the background. For selecting the cords to *subtract* areas of the selection you may want to try the Polygonal Lasso tool (L) to click and make straight edges between points.

2. Zoom in to about 200% or closer to start editing the selection alongside the edges of the kayak. Remember: only the gray painted areas are to be selected, much like a body shop would mask off areas that are not to be painted. Leave the file open with the selection active.

3. To fill in stray areas that are not selected, choose Select > Modify > Smooth, then choose a 1- or 2-pixel sample radius. To add to the selection, choose Select > Grow for adjacent pixels.

4. Save your file and leave it open with the selection active.

 PROBLEM If you have problems with straight edges, try using the Polygonal Lasso tool by clicking at short distance intervals. Select either the Add or Subtract button on the Tool Options bar to edit your selection.

SAVING AND EDITING SELECTIONS AS PERMANENT CHANNELS

When you save your selections as channels, they remain permanent so they can be used for editing in the future. You can create channels using the Select menu, or by clicking the icons at the bottom of the Channels panel. You can repeatedly modify and save the changes. The best way to edit channels is to save the selection and choose to "Replace" the channel. You can view your selection as a selection mask in the Channels panel. A **selection mask** displays areas that are exposed or selected (white); areas that are hidden (not selected) are displayed in black.

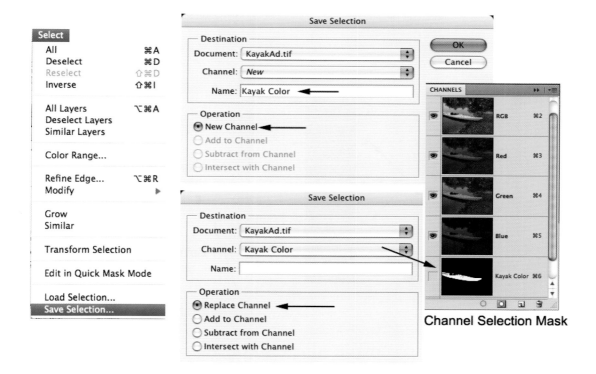

Channel Selection Mask

▷ FIGURE 5-7

Saving and replacing a selection channel.

You are going to create, name, and save a permanent channel in this exercise.

1. With your selection still active, choose Select > Save Selection from the Menu bar; when the Save Selection dialog box comes up, select New Channel and name it *Kayak Color* (Figure 5-7). Click OK.

2. Select the Channels panel, and you will notice that a new permanent selection channel entitled *Kayak Color* has been created. This same selection will display as a mask on the Channels panel (Window > Channels).

3. If you find areas that you have missed, go back using the select tools to make the final selection as accurate as possible. If you need to take a break, with the selection permanent, you can close the file, then reopen it later; choose Select > Load Selection > Kayak Color to get your saved selection to edit.

4. To replace the permanent channel selection with the most recent version, choose Select > Save Selection.

5. Locate the *Kayak Color* channel on the drop-down display and select Replace Channel. Select OK. You can also use the icons in the Channels panel to create, save, and edit selection channels (Figure 5-8).

6. Continue until you are confident you have all the areas for recoloring the kayak selected.

7. Save the file.

▷ FIGURE 5-8

The Channels Panel.

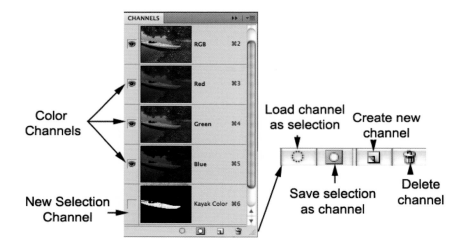

OPTIONAL: USING QUICK MASK FOR DETAILED SELECTIONS

As was shown in the Advanced section of Chapter 4, you can use the Quick Mask option to mask any minute areas of the background, cords, and seat of the kayak that are not the gray color and replace the Kayak Color channel selection with the new edited selection from the mask. This is a great project to try this technique.

Now you will paint with the Brush and Pencil tools to add to or subtract from the mask. You will then replace the old selections with the new, edited selections by saving the new selections in the Kayak Color channel.

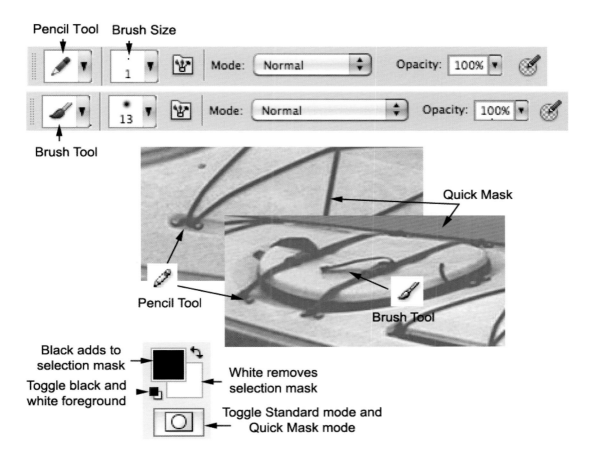

1. If your selection is not active, choose Select > Load Selection and select the *Kayak Color* channel.

2. Click the icon on the Tools panel to toggle to Quick Mask mode (Figure 5-9). You will notice a red overlay indicating what has been masked out. Note: You can also select Edit in Quick Mask Mode in the Select menu.

3. Zoom in to around 200% to 300% to observe what needs editing, masking and unmasking, use the foreground and background colors in the Tools panel and either the Brush or Pencil tool to paint. White removes the mask, black will add to the mask.

4. Select either a harder edge brush or try the Pencil tool and enter 3 pixels or less brush size to start in the Tool Options bar. You are working with detail here, so a smaller brush size will be easier to work with.

5. On the Tool Options bar, set Mode to Normal and the Opacity settings to 100%.

▷ FIGURE 5-9

Using Quick Mask to enhance your selection.

6. Select the Foreground color as white by clicking the bent arrow above the Foreground/Background color icons so that white displays as the Foreground color (or simply press "X" on the keyboard to switch them). Paint with white to remove areas of the mask to expose any missed gray areas of the kayak (Figure 5-9).

7. Select the bent arrow again—it acts as a toggle—to change the Foreground color to black. Use this to add to the mask. Change brush sizes depending on the size of the area. You can quickly adjust the brush size of either tool by pressing the bracket keys on your keyboard. The left bracket ([) makes the size smaller and the right bracket (]) increases the size.

8. Work on small details around the straps, cords, and seat of the kayak to edit the mask. Remember, you want to isolate the hardware and background completely from the gray area of the kayak.

9. Toggle between Standard Mode and Quick Mask Mode on the Tools panel to see your new edited selection.

10. To replace the alpha channel with the most recent selection, toggle back to Standard mode to view the selected kayak, then choose Select > Save Selection.

11. Locate the Kayak Color channel on the drop-down display and select Replace Channel.

12. You can also use this same procedure to remove minute areas of the mask from around any parts of the hardware or the kayak itself in the KayakALL selection channel you'll be creating.

13. When you are all set, save the file *KayakAD* in the *Chapter 5* folder. Leave open for the next exercise.

ENHANCING SELECTION EDGES USING REFINE EDGE

DESIGN TIP

Since the kayak is being duplicated, with drop shadow effects to be applied later, the selection's edges should be softened, so the transition between the change in colors will make the kayak look more realistic next to the background, avoiding a cut-out effect.

Now that you have finalized your detailed selection for changing the color of the kayak, you will use the Refine Edge command to soften the edges for the kayak to blend into the background area of the image, which will make the transition more believable. You will also check the selection against various background masks.

TOOLKIT TIP In CS5, the Refine Edge dialog box contains a new Edge Detection function using Smart Radius. This feature helps to make highly precise selections of complex subjects easily, enabling faster, more accurate combinations of multiple images. You can then use the extra view modes to assist you in previewing the quality of your selections. You can also have any residual background color removed from around your selections using the color decontamination settings.

▷ FIGURE 5-10

Using Refine Edge to check for selection details and soften edges.

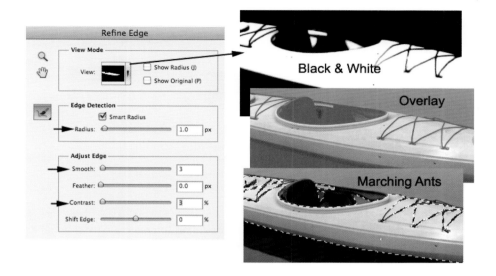

▷ FIGURE 5-10

Here you will slightly soften the edges for a smoother transition to the background.

1. With the kayak selection still active, select one of the selection tools then click the Refine Edge button on the Tool Options bar.

2. Click on the Black & White or Overlay (red) mask view to see if there are any stray areas that were not selected or any place over selected that you may have to go back and fix. If more work is needed, select Cancel.

3. Continue making adjustments with selection tools until you are confident you have all the areas for recoloring the kayak selected. Zoom in to 200% to check any details.

4. When you have all adjustments complete, choose one of the selection tools again, select Refine Edge, then choose one of the views (try Black & White or Overlay) and make slight adjustments. Start with 1 pixel Edge Detection, and 3 for Smooth, 3 for Contrast (Figure 5-10) to slightly soften the edges. Do not click to Decontaminate. Click OK when ready.

5. Click on the Marching Ants view and zoom in to see your results.

6. To save your new selection change, choose Select > Save Selection > Kayak Color > Replace Channel > OK. Save the file.

SECOND SELECTION: THE ENTIRE KAYAK FOR DUPLICATING

The second selection is for duplicating the entire kayak image. You have already done the hard part with the initial *Kayak Color* selection. Now all that is needed is to include all the hardware on the kayak by *adding* to the selection so that it outlines the entire kayak. The new selection will be saved as another permanent selection channel named *KayakALL*. You do not have to start this second selection from scratch. By saving the first selection, *Kayak Color*, again with a new name (*KayakALL*), you can easily build upon that first selection. This selection will be used to make multiple copies of the original kayak for the advertisement.

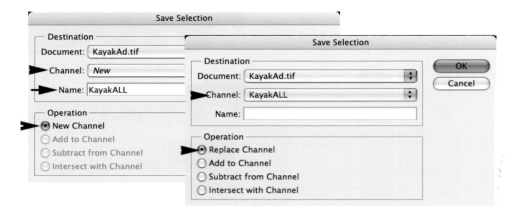

▷ FIGURE 5-11

Saving the second selection of the entire kayak with hardware, *KayakALL*.

In this exercise, you are going to create a new channel *KayakALL* from the first selection *Kayak Color*, where you will name the new channel, and save it. You can then edit this new channel to include all the hardware and then save the new edited selection.

1. Click Select > Load Selection. When the dialog box opens, you will see the *Kayak Color* channel. Click OK.

2. Choose Select > Save Selection > New Channel. Name the new channel *KayakALL*. This will be the second permanent selection (alpha) channel that you will edit for duplicating the entire kayak. Select OK.

3. Zoom in to around 200% with the Zoom tool to search the areas that need to be selected.

4. Use the Lasso tools and the Quick Selection tool, and add to the selection to *include* all the hardware and the seat of the kayak this time. Take your time; again, you need to be very detailed in creating this selection for the final advertisement to look professional.

5. Continue until you are confident you have the entire kayak selected (feel free to try the Quick Mask option mentioned earlier).

6. Select Refine Edge to create a slightly soft edge on the outside of the kayak to make a smooth transition of colors between the kayak and the background. Start with 1 pixel Edge Detection, and 3 for Smooth. Do not choose to Decontaminate for this exercise.

7. Use one of the View Masks as your guide.

8. To replace the channel selection *KayakALL* with your selection involving the entire kayak, choose Select > Save Selection. Locate the *KayakALL* channel in the drop-down display and select Replace Channel (Figure 5-11).

9. Save the file again in your *Chapter 5* folder on your drive.

CREATING THE THREE KAYAK IMAGE LAYERS

Now that you have the selections created for duplicating the entire kayak image and for changing the kayak color, you will see how to put it all together. In the next exercises, you are going to duplicate and change the color of the original kayak to create the green and yellow kayaks, creating a separate layer for each one. Drop shadows will be created on the new kayaks to match the original kayak.

TOOLKIT TIP You can save Photoshop files in either PSD or TIFF formats, and you will be able to edit either one with layers while maintaining the original quality. Photoshop's native PSD format can only be read by Adobe applications, whereas TIFF files are universally read. In this chapter, you will save and work with the file as a TIFF; remember to leave "Layers" checked in the Save As dialog box. As a good practice, if you have room, create a back-up PSD file in your *Chapter 5* folder.

CONVERTING THE BACKGROUND LAYER TO A NORMAL LAYER

The first layer in any document is the **Background layer.** It always displays on the bottom of the Layers panel. As a Background layer, it cannot be moved among other layers. Additional layers, when they are first created, are placed above the selected layer in the Layers panel and can easily be moved around between any other layers for various effects. If a Background layer is converted to a normal layer, it can then be moved between other layers and can also be renamed. Naming layers helps to keep track of each layer for making further changes. You will rename the Background layer as *Gray Kayak,* allowing it to become a normal layer and identifying it as the gray kayak image.

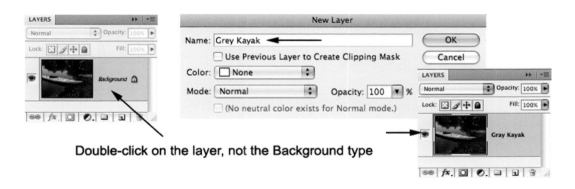

Double-click on the layer, not the Background type

▷ FIGURE 5-12

Changing the background layer to a normal layer for editing and renaming the layer as *Gray Kayak*.

Now you will rename the Background layer *Gray Kayak.*

1. With the *KayakAD.tif* image open, display the Channels, Navigator, Color, and Layers panels. If not displayed, open them by selecting them from the Window menu, or click on their icons to expand each panel. You will use these panels in this chapter.

2. In the Layers panel, double-click on the Background layer to bring up the New Layer display box. You can double-click anywhere in the background layer, even on the layer name, to open the New Layer dialog box.

3. In the Layer Name field, type *Gray Kayak;* leave the other settings at their defaults.

4. Click OK and you will notice the layer name has been changed to *Gray Kayak* (Figure 5-12). It is now a normal layer that can be moved if needed.

PASTING A SELECTION CREATES A NEW LAYER

Each layer is like a clear sheet with all or part of an image on it. When you copy and paste a selection, a new layer is created with those areas that were selected on the image. This displays a new layer, showing all areas that were *not* selected as transparent. These transparent areas display as a checkerboard on the layer thumbnail. To color and duplicate the kayak without the background, additional layers need to be created for each kayak with the background left transparent. Pasting a selection on its own layer gives the designer the flexibility of editing certain areas of an image without affecting other areas or other layers; that is, unless a particular Blending Mode or Opacity level is chosen on the Layers panel.

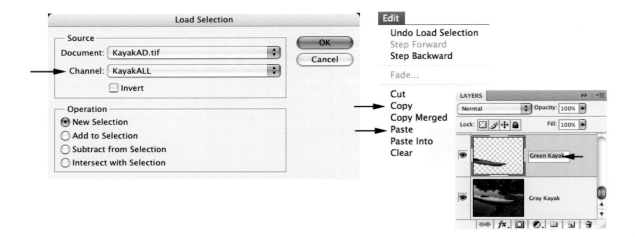

▷   FIGURE 5-13

Duplicating the kayak image for a new layer.

It is time to use the alpha (selection) channel (KayakALL) of the entire kayak you created in the last chapter. In this exercise, we're going to make an additional layer of the original kayak image, removing the background (Figure 5-13).

1. Click the *Gray Kayak* layer in the Layers panel to highlight it.

2. Choose Select > Load Selection > KayakALL > OK. This is the alpha channel you created for the whole kayak by saving your selection. Notice the marquee is displayed along the outer edges of the kayak.

3. Choose Edit > Copy, then choose Edit > Paste. Although you will not notice any change on the original kayak image, you have actually pasted a copy directly on top of the original kayak. When you have pasted an image, it creates a new layer—*Layer 1*—on top of the *Gray Kayak* layer in the Layers panel. You will notice the additional *Layer1* containing the kayak and a transparent background.

4. Now we will rename it. Double-click the text *Layer 1* in the Layers panel and rename it *Green Kayak* (Figure 5-13). If you accidentally double-click the layer,

you will be presented with a Layer Style dialog box; if this happens, just click Cancel and try again.

5. Press the Return/Enter key to accept the change. If you want to see larger thumbnails of your work, click the Layers Panel Menu > Panel Options and click on the large thumbnail.

6. Save the file again (including layers) as *KayakAD.tif* in your *Chapter 5* folder.

ADJUSTING COLOR USING THE HUE/SATURATION COMMAND

We are now ready to change the color of the kayak using the Hue/Saturation command in the Image menu. The **Hue/Saturation command** lets you adjust the hue, saturation, and lightness of an image or selected areas of an image. It works well with large items that have varying shadow and highlight detail. This technique works wonderfully when changing the color of a product, when you need to retain all highlight and shadow tonal details. You can use the Hue slider to select new colors and the Saturation and Lightness sliders for color purity and intensity. You have the option to try out various preset settings in the Hue/Saturation panel, or create your own customized preset settings that you can save and access for future projects.

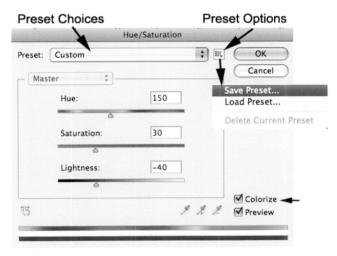

Suggested green color with Colorize button checked

▷ FIGURE 5-14

Creating the green color for the new kayak with the Hue/ Saturation command.

In this exercise, you are going to color the new pasted kayak. You need to use the *Kayak Color* channel selection you created earlier to select only those areas that need to be colored, much like an auto body shop would paint on unmasked areas, and then you will use the Hue/Saturation command to get the color you want.

DESIGN TIP

 If you were to try to "paint" the kayak with a brush, even at a low opacity, the shadow areas in particular would appear "filled in" and unrealistic looking. Painting is best done in small areas of an image. Using the Hue/ Saturation command works best with large areas or images with varying shadows and highlights.

1. In the Tools panel, set the foreground color to the default black. If black is not the foreground color, select the two small squares underneath to toggle to the black foreground.

2. With the *Green Kayak* layer highlighted (shaded blue), choose Select > Load Selection > Kayak Color > OK. This is the alpha selection channel you created for only those areas of the kayak that are going to be colored.

3. Select Image > Adjustments > Hue/Saturation and make sure the Colorize and Preview option boxes are checked.

4. Move the dialog box alongside the image so you can see the effects.

5. To change the color of the gray kayak to hunter green, start with these settings and adjust the sliders until you have a dark green. Hue: 150, Saturation: 30, Lightness: –40 (minus 40). See Figure 5-14 for settings. To save your color settings, click the Preset Options menu, and choose Save Settings. Name the preset *Hunter Green* in the Hue/Saturation panel. Click OK. It will be saved as a custom preset.

6. Save your file.

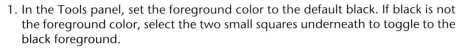

⊗ PROBLEM If you are not getting close to the color you want, make sure the Colorize box is checked in the Hue/Saturation dialog box.

DESIGN TIP

When scanning images, sometimes an image may appear overly saturated in color, especially in skin tones. You can use the Hue/Saturation command to help to bring back the original colors by decreasing the image's saturation.

POSITIONING LAYERS WITH THE MOVE TOOL

The Move tool allows you to move a selection within an image or onto another image file. When you use the Move tool to readjust or position a selection, the new position of the image you are moving will be updated in the layer thumbnail on the Layers panel.

You are now going to select the entire kayak and move the duplicate away from the original and position it.

1. With the *Green Kayak* layer highlighted, choose Select > Load Selection > KayakALL > OK to select the entire kayak to be moved.

2. Select the Move tool (V) and click and drag the green kayak image to move it away from the original. Place it under the original kayak, as shown in Figure 5-15. You will notice as you move the green kayak away, the gray kayak will show underneath.

3. Choose Select > Deselect. Save the file in your *Chapter 5* folder.

PROBLEM If you have the *Gray Kayak* layer selected by mistake, you will end up moving the gray kayak along with the background. Make sure the *Green Kayak* layer is highlighted.

▷ FIGURE 5-15

Using the Move tool to drag the newly created green kayak into position.

CREATING THE YELLOW KAYAK LAYER

It is time to duplicate the third kayak in the ad and color it yellow. Then you will rename the layer and put a drop shadow effect on the yellow and green kayaks to approximate the original gray kayak's shadow.

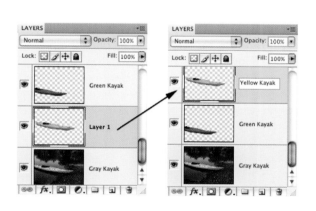

Moving pasted layer and renaming "Yellow Kayak"

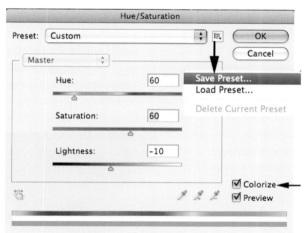

Suggested settings for yellow kayak

▷ FIGURE 5-16

Creating the layer for the yellow kayak and applying color change with the Hue/Saturation command.

In this exercise, you will duplicate the gray kayak again and color it yellow.

1. Make sure the original *Gray Kayak* layer is selected (shaded in blue).
2. Choose Select > Load Selection >KayakALL > OK. This selection will be used for duplicating the whole kayak.
3. Choose Edit > Copy, then choose Edit > Paste to copy the selection in a new layer above the original kayak. Again the new kayak is pasted directly on top of the original.

PROBLEM If you receive an error box displaying Unable to Copy Contents, make sure the *Gray Kayak* layer is selected and not any other layer.

4. Notice a third layer named *Layer 1* is placed between the other two. Photoshop places new layers above the selected one.

5. Select and drag the new *Layer 1* above the *Green Kayak* layer. A black line appears at the top of the Layers panel to show you the position of the layer you are dragging.

6. Double-click the *Layer 1* name and rename the it *Yellow Kayak* (Figure 5-16), then press the Return/Enter key to accept the change.

7. To get the channel selection for just the kayak color, make sure the Yellow Kayak layer is still highlighted, choose Select > Load Selection > Kayak Color > OK.

8. To create the yellow color, choose Image > Adjustments > Hue/Saturation again. Drag (or type in) the settings to Hue: 60, Saturation: 60, Lightness: –10 (minus 10) as a starting point. Make sure the Colorize box is checked. Use Figure 5-16 as a guide. To save your color settings, click the Preset Options menu, and choose Save Settings. Name the preset Yellow Kayak in the Hue/Saturation panel. Click OK. It will be saved as a custom preset.

9. To select the whole kayak again to be moved into position, choose Select > Load Selection > KayakAll > OK. A marquee will display around the kayak's outer edges. This step is very important.

10. With the *Yellow Kayak* layer selected, use the Move tool to drag the pasted yellow kayak below the green one (Figure 5-17).

▷ FIGURE 5-17

Three different colored kayaks.

EDITING INDIVIDUAL PASTED LAYERS

The alpha selection channels you created in the last chapter were based on the original *Gray Kayak* layer. When you paste a copied selection on its own layer and you want to make changes, like adjusting the color on one of the kayak layers, you need to create a selection on that layer. With pasted layers from these exercises, you can:

- Select the *Green Kayak* or *Yellow Kayak* layer
- Select only the hardware and seat
- Invert the selection by choosing Select > Inverse, which would have no effect on the transparent background but will cover only those areas that are to be colored or edited
- Save the selection as a channel that can be called upon anytime on that layer

With individual layers you can make adjustments that only affect that layer, unless you choose to change blending modes or opacity settings that affect layers underneath. With the channel selection created on one of the pasted layers to color the kayak, you can edit the color on that layer whenever the client wants without having to redo the image again.

OPTIONAL ALTERNATIVE METHOD: CREATING ADJUSTMENT LAYERS

Another method to create the same outcome in recoloring the pasted kayak selection is to create an **adjustment layer** of the Hue/Saturation command. Adjustment layers are useful in that you can make all kinds of changes without changing the original image (in this case the pasted gray kayak). Let's say that you finished the design with the layers for the green and yellow colors of the two additional kayaks, but the client wants to change the colors. Having adjustment layers makes the process of changing the colors using the Hue/Saturation command much easier by simply clicking on the icon of the adjustment layers and making the change. At the bottom of the layers panel the icon for making adjustment layers looks like a half moon, or you can use the Layer menu (Layer > New Adjustment Layer) to create an adjustment layer. You will find a variety of adjustments you can create. When you select to create an adjustment layer from a selection, the selection channel mask is also displayed for reference. The trick with this technique in this exercise is that when you need to move the newly pasted image, you must make sure you move the image layer and the adjustment layer in sync together. You will be learning more about adjustment layers in Chapter 6.

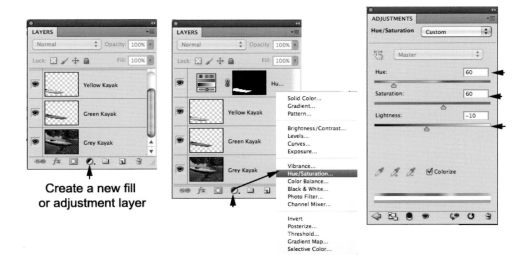

Create a new fill
or adjustment layer

▷   FIGURE 5-18

**Creating Hue/
Saturation
adjustment layer.**

If you want to try this technique, select Edit > Step Backward until you come to the part where you just named the pasted layer *Yellow Kayak*, then follow the steps below.

1. With the last pasted layer labeled Yellow Kayak, you need to get the Kayak Color channel selection for just the color change.

2. Make sure the Yellow Kayak layer is still highlighted, choose Select > Load Selection > *Kayak Color* > OK.

3. Click on the "Create a new fill or adjustment layer" icon at the bottom of the Layers panel (or select Layer > New Adjustment Layer).

4. Select the Hue/Saturation command and you'll find an Adjustments panel will display.

5. Drag (or type in) the settings to Hue: 60, Saturation: 60, Lightness: −10 (minus 10) as a starting point. Make sure the Colorize box is checked (Figure 5-18).

6. To select the whole kayak again to be moved into position, make sure the Yellow Kayak layer is highlighted, not the adjustment layer, and choose Select > Load Selection > *KayakALL* > OK.

7. Use the Shift key and select both the Yellow Kayak Layer and the Hue/ Saturation adjustment layer.

8. With both layers selected, use the Move tool to drag the pasted yellow kayak below the green one as shown previously in Figure 5-17.

9. So that you don't get confused with the rest of the exercises, as this optional exercise is to just expose you to this technique, you could again go backward until you reach the past exercise and redo it to get the yellow kayak again, or keep the new adjustment layer. If you keep the Hue/Saturation adjustment layer, be mindful that it is not referenced in the forthcoming exercises but will be fine when working within them.

LAYER STYLE EFFECT: DROP SHADOWS

When you double-click on a thumbnail image in the Layers panel or select the Layer Style icon (it looks like "Fx" in a circle) at the bottom of the Layers panel, a Layer Style dialog box opens up. Layer styles allow you to create shadows, embossing, bevels, overlays, glow, and stroke effects on selected portions of an image or text. You can create a realistic drop shadow effect by adjusting the distance, size, and angle settings to match the original shadow. Make sure the **Use Global Light** option is checked to cast all the shadows at the same angle so that all shadows in future layers will look like they have the same light source for visual accuracy.

In this exercise you will create a drop shadow on the new kayak layers to add a sense of realism consistent with the original kayak.

1. Double-click the *Green Kayak* thumbnail image you created on the Layers panel, or select the Add a layer style icon at the bottom of the Layers panel. Do not double-click on the text.

2. The Layer Style dialog box will open. Position the display alongside the image to preview the effect.

3. Click the Drop Shadow name under Styles in the dialog box to access the Drop Shadow dialog box.

4. To duplicate the original gray kayak's shadow, set the Angle to 30 degrees, Blend Mode at Normal with Opacity at 100%, and Distance of 100 pixels with a shadow Size of 60 pixels for a soft shadow effect (Figure 5-19).

5. Make sure Anti-aliased, Use Global Light, and Preview are all checked. Click OK to apply the effect. You will find a nice shadow set beneath the green kayak.

6. Notice on the Layers panel, the layer style effect is placed under the *Green Kayak* layer. You can double-click any layer effects for future adjustments. If you do not see the effects, click on the triangle next to the "Fx" at the right end of the layer.

7. To make a drop shadow of the yellow kayak image with the same setting as the green kayak, make sure the *Yellow Kayak* layer is highlighted.

8. Select the Add a layer style icon at the bottom of the Layers panel, then select Drop Shadow from the menu. The Layer Style dialog box opens up.

9. Position the display alongside the image to preview the effect.

10. Set the Angle to 30 degrees, Blend Mode at Normal with Opacity at 100%, and Distance of 100 pixels with a shadow Size of 60 pixels.

11. Make sure Anti-aliased, Use Global Light, and Preview are all checked, and then select OK to apply the effect.

12. Save the file in your *Chapter 5* folder.

DESIGN TIP

To create a sense of realism, especially when duplicating an image, always place a check in the Use Global Light box in the Drop Shadows dialog box for consistent placement and angle of shadows in line with the original image.

DESIGN TIP

Placement of light and dark colors helps achieve balance within an image. With the shadow reflections on the water dominating the upper portion of the kayak image, placing the bright yellow kayak near the bottom and having the dark green kayak in between the light gray and yellow kayaks provides that balance.

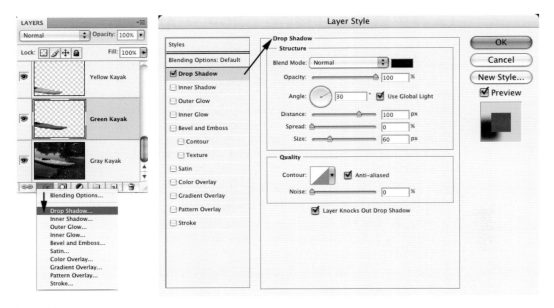

▷ FIGURE 5-19

Applying drop
shadow layer style
effect to new kayaks
to match the original
kayak shadow.

(X) PROBLEM If any of the menu commands are grayed out so they cannot be
selected, chances are the wrong layer is selected. Select the layer you need to work
on, and the commands should display.

TOOLKIT TIP You can copy Layer Style effects created in one layer to another
layer by selecting the effects created in one layer, holding down the Option/Alt key,
and copying the effects to the next layer. Release the mouse first when copying,
then the key.

RECORDING STATES USING THE LAYER COMPS PANEL

The **Layer Comps panel** allows the designer or photographer to capture the
various stages or states of development of a document by recording existing
settings for the visibility or opacity of layers and their effects on the previous
layers, their position in the document, and various blending options. Record

various states of development using the New Layer Comp button, which gives you the flexibility to hide or display layers and to show before and after views when applying effects or making changes. This provides the ability to experiment, and you can show variations of the project to your client, then cycle back through previously recorded stages. You can also include comments to describe the recorded state; states recorded in the Layer Comps panel are permanent for future reference or editing. The Layer Comps panel can be opened using the Window menu.

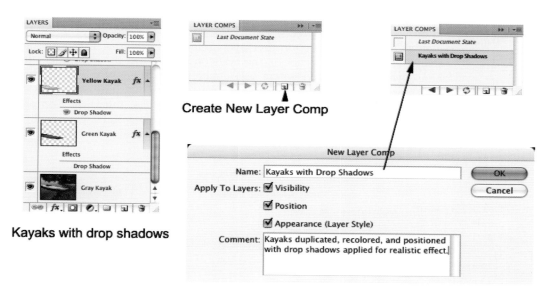

Create New Layer Comp

Kayaks with drop shadows

Layer Comp created to record current state of project.

▷ FIGURE 5-20

Using Layer Comps to record a layer's state or variations of a project.

You will record the state of the three colored kayaks at present in the Layer Comps panel.

1. With all three kayaks in position, make sure all eye icons are displayed in the Layers panel.

2. Select the Layer Comps panel or open it from the Window menu; select the Create New Layer Comp icon on the panel bottom or from the Panel menu (Figure 5-20).

3. When the New Layer Comp dialog box displays, name the layer state *Kayaks with Drop Shadows*.

4. In the Apply To Layers section, check the boxes for Visibility, Position, and Appearance (Layer Style) settings, to record everything thus far.

5. In the Comment section, type "Kayaks duplicated, recolored, and positioned with drop shadows applied," then select OK. Note: if you tried creating

a Hue/Saturation adjustment layer on your yellow kayak in the previous optional exercise, you could create a Layer Comp as an experiment for this technique.

LAYER COMPS RECORD BEFORE AND AFTER EFFECTS

With the Layer Comps panel, a designer or photographer can create various layer configurations to observe before and after effects by selecting the eye icons to display or hide effects. Layer Comps also provide the opportunity to experiment with different layer combinations to observe their effects by simply turning on and off layers and their effects. If you click once on the Effects eye in the Layers panel, all effects are hidden in that layer. Select the eye again and it toggles to display the effects. If you click on the eye icon next to just the individual effect—for instance, the eye icon where you created drop shadow effects in the last exercise—only that effect is hidden or displayed. Recorded states in Layer Comps are permanent so that when you close and save a file, the Layer Comps you created are saved with the image. To observe the various states you saved, click on the box at the left of the layer comp to make it active.

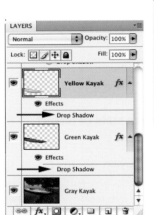

**Kayak layers only to be displayed
(click eye icon to remove
drop shadow effect)**

Select between different states

▷   FIGURE 5-21

**You can also cre-
ate different Layer
Comp configura-
tions and choose
between states
to experiment.**

Next, you will create a Layer Comp of the kayaks without the shadow effects applied earlier to observe the before and after effects of applying drop shadows.

1. In the Layers panel, click on the eye icons beside Drop Shadow to hide the Layer Style drop shadows in the *Green Kayak* layer and the *Yellow Kayak* layer. The eye icon will disappear. Leave the Green, Yellow, and Gray kayak layers displayed.

2. Click on the Layer Comps tab to display the Layer Comps panel.

3. Select the New Layer Comp icon on the panel bottom or from the Panel submenu.

4. When the New Layer Comp dialog box displays, name the layer state *Kayaks Before Shadows.*

5. In the Apply To Layers section, check the boxes for Visibility and Position. There are no layer styles to affect the Appearance setting.

6. In the Comment section, type "Kayaks before Drop Shadows," and then select OK.

7. In the Layer Comps panel, select the boxes to the left of the Layer Comp boxes *Kayak before Shadows* and *Kayaks with Drop Shadows* to make them active individually. Observe the before and after effects of applying the drop shadows. (See Figure 5-21.)

8. Select and leave the original Layer Comp state, *Kayaks with Drop Shadows,* with all eye icons displayed in the Layers panel to show the three kayaks and drop shadows.

9. Save the file in your *Chapter 5* folder and leave it open.

TOOLKIT TIP Try creating different color variations on the kayaks and create additional layer comps to give you an idea of how you could show different versions to a potential client.

LOCKING LAYERS

To prevent inadvertent edits, you can lock layers by selecting the layer to be locked and clicking one of the locking icons near the top of the Layers panel, usually the one that looks like a padlock (Lock All). The lock icon is then displayed on the active layer. This locks all sublayers, like Layer Style effects, under the main layer. To remove a lock, select the lock icon again. It acts as a toggle.

Locks all sublayers within layer

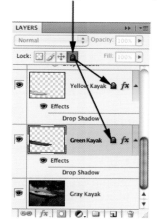

▷ FIGURE 5-22

Locking layers prevents inadvertent editing.

Now that you have all three kayaks positioned, colored, and shaded, you will lock them so they cannot be accidentally edited.

1. Select the *Gray Kayak* layer and then select the Lock all icon. You will notice it looks like a padlock on the right side of the layer (Figure 5-22).

2. Repeat the same procedure for the *Green Kayak* and *Yellow Kayak* layers. This will also lock the Layer Style shadow effects with each new kayak layer. (To hide effects in sublayers, click on that effect's eye icon first before locking.)

3. Save the file.

CREATING TYPE LAYERS

DESIGN TIP

In the Tool Options bar, a good starting point for anti-alias settings for type is to use a Strong setting for text that will be printed, and a Crisp setting for text that will only be displayed electronically, like on the Web. Settings may also vary depending on the font and point size.

When you use the Type tool, a text layer is created specifically for the text. Wherever you click, you can type on a path. To reposition the text, just use the Move tool. Sometimes it helps to have each text line as a different text layer, so they can be moved individually or linked to move together. To start another new text layer, select another tool in the Tools panel, such as the Move tool, then click on the Type tool again. The Type Tool Options bar contains many formatting options for editing type. Photoshop's Character panel can also provide many of the same options and any changes made are reflected in the Tool Options bar.

FORMATTING TYPE IN THE TOOL OPTIONS BAR

In the Tool Options bar for the Type tool, you can change font, color, size, anti-alias method, alignment, and text warp effects. You can change the text orientation (vertical or horizontal) and create special Type tool presets. You can observe what the various fonts look like for making quick decisions on what type to use on a given project. Always start off text with the anti-alias setting turned on as the default. Using the Anti-alias setting helps smooth the transition between different colored pixel edges, keeping them from getting the jaggies. Remember: all pixels are square, so it is important to give the appearance of a smooth transition when working with curved edges. When working with text, it is important to create type that is not fuzzy or jagged in appearance.

 TOOLKIT TIP Use the Move tool to position text. If you need to make any changes to text, select the Type tool again, then select the text layer you want to edit; highlight the text with your cursor to make any changes.

In this exercise, you will format type for the *Aqua Excursions* company.

1. Select/highlight the *Yellow Kayak* layer.

2. Select the Horizontal Type tool.

3. In the Tool Options bar, set the type for 48-point Minion Pro Bold with a Strong Anti-alias (feel free to substitute another wide serif font by selecting it from the dropdown menu under the Font Face field in the Options bar).

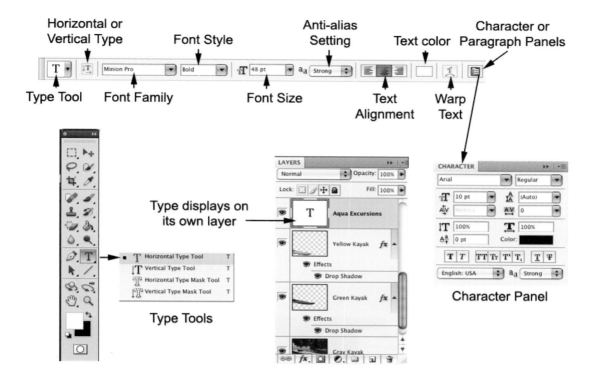

▷ FIGURE 5-23

Select options for type tools using the Tool Options bar or the character panel. Types uses its own layer for editing.

4. Set white as your foreground color. You can click the top left corner within the color box, or you can switch the Foreground/Background color box on the Tools panel for a white foreground (press the X key).

5. Type "Aqua Excursions" near the top left corner of the image.

6. Select the Move tool to center the text between the left and right edges, about one-quarter inch away from the top edge.

7. You will notice a "T" (type) layer is created displaying the text you have typed in the Layers panel (Figure 5-23).

8. Make sure the type layer is located at the top of the Layers panel.

9. Save the file in your *Chapter 5* folder.

 PROBLEM If you do not see any text while typing, make sure the text layer is on top of the other *Gray Kayak* layer. If not, simply click the text layer and drag it to the top.

USING THE CHARACTER PANEL

Photoshop's Character panel contains additional commands for formatting text. Any changes made in the Character panel are reflected in the Tool Options bar and vice versa. Create a new text layer first before making any formatting changes. You can access the Character panel on the Type Tool Options bar using the Character/Paragraph panel button, or from the Window menu. There is also a Paragraph panel in Photoshop for formatting blocks of text, usually as a tab in the Character panel.

TOOLKIT TIP After typing a line of text, selecting another tool like the Move tool then selecting the Type tool again will automatically create a new type layer.

▷ FIGURE 5-24

Format type using the Tool Options bar for the first line, then try using the Character panel for the second line of type.

You will now format the type in the second line of the ad using the Character panel.

1. Select the Move tool to exit the previous type layer, and then select the Horizontal Type tool again to create the next line of type.

2. Click under the *u* in *Aqua* to create a new text layer. A new layer needs to be created *before* you make any changes to the text formatting, otherwise the changes occur on the previous type layer.

3. Make sure the Character panel is displayed (Window > Character or select the Character/ Paragraph button on the Tool Options bar).

4. In the Character panel, change the text size to 18 points, white color, Minion Pro Bold font to make it stand out in the dark portion of the image.

5. Notice the changes made in the Character panel display in the Tool Options bar.

6. Type "Kayak Tours, Sales, and Service."

7. Position the text with the Move tool as shown in Figure 5-24, aligning the top of the line with the bottom of the *q* extension.

8. Save the file in your *Chapter 5* folder.

SELECTING AND LINKING LAYERS

Linking layers allows you to move several layers together for accurate positioning. Layers that are linked can be moved and transformed simultaneously, keeping the alignment and composite layering intact. Once layers are linked, if any minor adjustments need to be made, they will be moved together. You can link any normal unlocked layer to another layer or layers. The Link Layers icon is located at the bottom of the Layers panel; in earlier versions, it is toggled on a box to the right of the layer eye icon. The Select menu contains commands to select Similar Layers, Deselect Layers, and Select All Layers. You can select a group of similar layers, such as type layers, using the Select > Similar layers command and then click the Linking Layers icon to connect them together for easy moving and alignment.

▷ FIGURE 5-25

Link type layers to make any adjustments together.

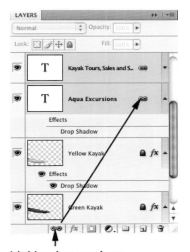

Linking Layers Icon

 TOOLKIT TIP To select adjacent layers, hold down the Shift key and select both layers, then click the Link Layers icon at the bottom of the Layers panel. To select nonadjacent layers, use the Command (Mac) or CTRL key (PC).

Here, you will link the text lines *Aqua Excursions* and *Kayak Tours, Sales, and Service* together. This will keep both layers together for final positioning.

1. Once both lines are in position, click on the *Kayak Tours, Sales, and Service* layer to highlight it.

2. Choose Select > Similar Layers to select both type layers. Click the Link layers icon at the bottom of the Layers panel.

3. Now the *Aqua Excursions* text line is linked to the *Kayak Tours, Sales, and Service* text line. You will notice a link icon is displayed at the right of each layer affected in the Layers panel (Figure 5-25).

4. Select the Move tool and position the two text lines accurately. Use the arrow keys to make small adjustments.

5. You can toggle the link off by selecting one of the linked layers and clicking the link icon at the bottom of the panel. To turn it back on, highlight both layers and click again. Try using Select > Similar Layers to select and link the three kayak images together.

ADDING TYPE USING SEPARATE TYPE LAYERS

To start each line of type on its own layer, click on the Move tool, then select the Type tool, and click in the document image before making any text formatting changes. This allows you to change the text without affecting the existing text. This also makes it easier to move each line into exact position without affecting the other lines.

▷ FIGURE 5-26

Create separate type layers for each line of text.

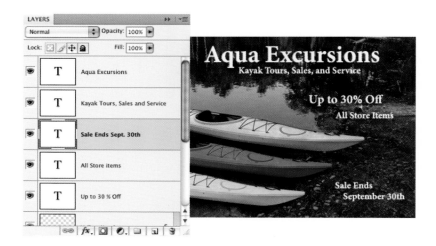

In this exercise, you will create the final three lines of text, creating a layer for each.

1. Select the Move Tool, then the Type tool, and click on the document to create a new type layer.

2. Use either the Tool Options bar or the Character panel to select the white Minion Pro Bold Italic font, and change the font size to 18 points.

3. Click and type "Up to 30% Off" (Figure 5-26).

4. Select the Move tool, then reselect the Type tool, and type in the remaining lines of the ad: "All Store Items" and "Sale Ends September 30th" to create two more type layers. After the words "Sale Ends," press the Return/Enter key to put "September 30th" beneath it. Press the space bar a few times to move it under the *I* in *Sale.*

5. Select each individual text layer in the Layers panel; use the Move tool to position each line as shown in Figure 5-26.

6. Save the file in your *Chapter 5* folder.

EDITING TYPE

Use the Tool Options bar to make changes to type. Simply highlight the text and make the changes. Here, we will make the line "Up to 30% Off" stand out by making it italic for emphasis, increasing the size slightly, and changing the color to match the color of the yellow kayak. With the Color Picker display window open, you can either select colors in the Picker itself, type in the values if you know them, or simply use the cursor and click on any part of the color box to select a color. In this case, we will use the Color Picker to select the yellow color from the kayak.

TOOLKIT TIP You can select multiple type layers and apply changes that effect all type layers at once, like changing fonts, sizes, styles, color, and so on. Use special effects on type sparingly to create more drama.

Next, you will change "Up to 30% Off" to make it stand out as the sale line.

1. Select the Type tool, and click the "Up to 30% Off" layer in the Layers panel to make it active.

2. Highlight the type by clicking and dragging through it with the text tool.

3. Change the font to Minion Pro Bold Italic (or use an itlalic style with your selected font); select a 24-point size.

4. Click the Set the text color box in the Tool Options bar to open up the Set text color display, and then move the window above the the kayak image (Figure 5-27).

5. Position the eyedropper cursor over the darker yellow area of the kayak and click; the eyedropper acts as a color selector. Notice the circle on the color you chose, and remember, your setting may be a little different from the one on Figure 5-27. Click OK to close the Color Picker.

Double-click to open the Color Picker and sample the yellow kayak.

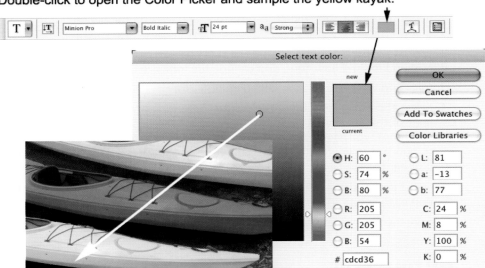

▷ FIGURE 5-27

Use the Text color box to sample the yellow kayak for the text sale line.

6. To see the new color, deselect the type by selecting the Move tool. With the type layer for the sale selected, position the type as indicated in the layout (refer to Figure 5-28).

7. Change the foreground color on the Tools panel back to black as the default color.

8. Save the file.

 TOOLKIT TIP You can also use the Eyedropper tool in the Tools panel to select the color on the darker side of the yellow kayak.

 TOOLKIT TIP If you are using a Color Picker, and a cube displays next to the color you have chosen, it indicates that the color you picked may not display precisely when viewed on the Web. If this happens, and you want to send the color for print, it will be fine. If you observe a yellow triangle with an exclamation point inside, the color will not print on commercial press precisely, but will display on the Web properly. If any of these cautions are displayed, you can click on the cube or triangle icon and Photoshop will display the nearest available color.

TYPE LAYER STYLES AND BLENDING MODES

Type layer style effects can be applied the same way as image effects. Type layer styles help to create special effects to accent type against photographic images and backgrounds or to add special emphasis to text in an image. Another feature in the Layers panel is the use of various blending modes that allow the designer or photographer to determine how pixels in one layer blend with pixels in the underlying layers. Different blending modes produce different results between layers, and these allow you to create a variety of special effects. The default blending mode is Normal. Use the Color Burn mode to darken or burn the text shadows.

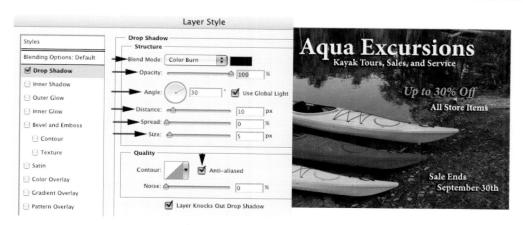

▷   FIGURE 5-28

Drop shadow layer style settings for type lines.

In this exercise, to help accent the light-colored text against the dark background, you are going to create a drop shadow on all the text and use a Color Burn blending mode. While this is not something you would want to do all the time, it is important to learn how to do it, so you can apply the effect in special cases.

1. Click on the *Aqua Excursions* type layer in the Layers panel to make it active. This will be the first type layer we will work on.

2. Click and hold the Layer Style icon at the bottom of the Layers panel. (Click on the Link icon to remove the link between layers if the Layer Styles icon is grayed out.)

3. Select Drop Shadow from the dropdown menu to open up the Drop Shadow Layer Style dialog box.

4. Enter the settings as shown in Figure 5-28. Make sure Use Global Light, Preview, and Anti-aliased are checked.

5. Set the Blend Mode to Color Burn. Color Burn mode creates a very dark shadow under the type. Select OK to create the shadow effect.

6. Select each type layer in the Layers panel and repeat the same procedure to create a shadow for each line of text.

7. Save the file in your *Chapter 5* folder.

LAYER COMPS FOR TYPE AND SPECIAL COMBINATIONS

As was done earlier with the kayak layers, you can also create a Layer Comp that includes Type layers. Layer Comps help when you want to document the stages of your layers in developing your image. They also provide a means to experiment with different layer combinations to display various effects. To hide all layers and sublayers, such as Layer Style effects, click on the eye icon on the main layer, and the sublayers will be dimmed out. To hide just layer effects, click the eye icon next to the Effects sublayer.

Creating Layer Comps combining various layers with type.

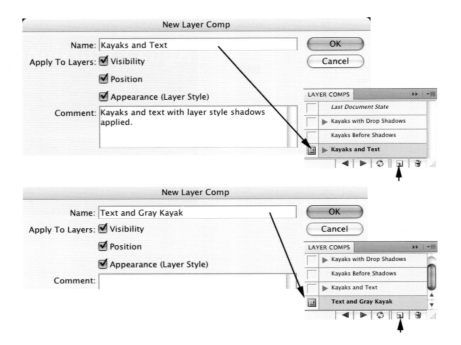

Now you will create a Layer Comp of all the layers in your layout, including type layers; observe all states recorded.

1. Make sure all layers are displayed at this point by having the eye icon on in the Layers panel.

2. Click on the Layer Comps icon to display the panel, or select Window > Layer Comps. In earlier versions it appears on the right side of the Tool Options bar.

3. Select the New Layer Comp icon at the bottom of the panel or from the panel submenu.

4. When the New Layer Comp dialog box displays, name the layer state *Kayaks and Text*.

5. In the Apply To Layers section, check the boxes for Visibility, Position, and Appearance (Layer Style) settings to record everything thus far.

6. In the Comment section, type "Kayaks and text with layer style shadows applied," and then select OK.

7. Hide the yellow and green kayak eye icons in the Layers panel and make sure the eye icons are displayed in the *Gray Kayak* layer and all the Text Layers with effects.

8. Select the Layer Comps tab, and then select the New Layer Comp icon on the Layer Comp panel.

9. Name the layer state *Text and Gray Kayak* and in the Apply to Layers section, check the boxes for Visibility, Position, and Appearance (Layer Style) settings.

10. Leave the Comment section blank, then click OK.

11. Click on the box next to each Layer Comp to display the different states you created in the Layer Comps panel. Observe how each is recorded with certain layers displayed and hidden (Figure 5-29).

12. Select the Layer Comp state Kayaks and Text with all eye icons displayed on the Layers panel to show the three kayaks and the type, along with the Layer Style effects.

13. Save the file as *KayakAD.tif* again in your *Chapter 5* folder.

ORGANIZING LAYERS AND PREPARING THE AD FOR PRESS

When you are finished with your project, or perhaps during various stages of development, you may find the need to streamline your layers to increase productivity and decrease file size. Creating layer groups allows you to assemble several layers within a folder. Merging layers combines layers permanently, while **flattening** layers combines all layers into one without losing any detail. Providing a client with an image flattened into one layer creates the smallest file size for easier portability. Use Adobe Bridge to compare file properties, like file sizes, to determine a which file fits your clients needs.

LAYER GROUPS

Here is a great tool to organize your layers: *layer groups.* Earlier versions of Photoshop called these *layer sets.* A **layer group** allows you to place several layers within one folder. The layer group folder is created above the active layer and can display just the name of the layer group on the layers panel, or, by clicking on the triangle next to the folder, to display all the layers within that group. Click the triangle, which flips down or up, to hide or show the layers included.

 TOOLKIT TIP To select all the Type layers you Select > Similar Layers. To move a layer out of its group, just drag the layer above or below the layer group folder. You can also drag a layer within a group over to another layer group folder.

In the next exercise, you will create a layer group to group all the type layers.

1. If it is not open already, open the *KayakAD.tif* file and highlight the topmost type layer in the Layers panel.

2. Select the Create a new group folder icon at the bottom of the Layers panel, or choose Layer > New > Group from the Layer submenu. A new layer with the default name of *Group 1* and a folder icon will display.

▷ FIGURE 5-30

Grouping all type layers in a layer group folder.

Folder contents displayed

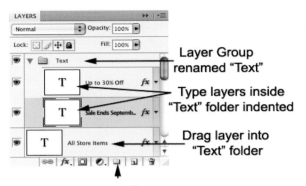

Layer Group "Text" (contains all type layers)

3. Double-click on the *Group 1* name, and rename the layer set *Text*. Press the Return/Enter key to accept the change.

4. Click each type layer and drag it into the *Text* folder.

5. When the folder arrow is clicked to display the contents, the newly positioned type layer inside the *Type* layer group will display as an indented thumbnail beneath the layer group folder (Figure 5-30).

6. When all the type layers are in the *Text* folder, click the triangle to hide the list, displaying only the *Text* folder.

7. Using the default settings, save the file as *KayakAD.tif* in your *Chapter 5* folder. Your file will keep all the layers intact as long as you keep RLE (faster saves, bigger files) selected in the TIF options dialog box.

MERGING LAYERS

When you have finished a series of layers, and you are ready to combine several layers into one, you can merge them. This helps to decrease the file size, since every time you add layers to your document, you increase its file size. **Merging layers** still maintains the image quality and allows you to group any combination of layers together. The Merge Layers function merges only highlighted layers and is one of the safer commands for merging. There are many merge commands, like the **Merge Visible command**, in which only layers that display the eye icon are merged. After merging layers, they take on the name of the bottom layer in the merged group, which you can rename afterwards. Be careful using the various Merge commands because most are final once you save the file and cannot be edited later.

TOOLKIT TIP Warning! When you change how layers are displayed, if you open the Layer Comps panel, you will notice warnings in the various states, because they have been altered. It is a good habit to duplicate a file before making any permanent changes.

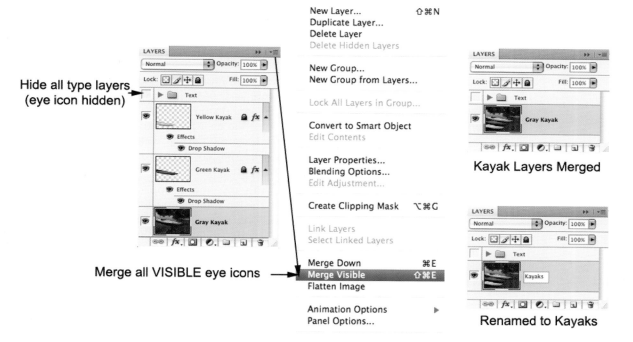

Hide all type layers (eye icon hidden)

Kayak Layers Merged

Merge all VISIBLE eye icons

Renamed to Kayaks

▷ FIGURE 5-31

Merging all kayak layers into one. The type layers are unaffected, because they were hidden when Merge Visible was selected.

In this exercise, you will merge the three visible kayak images and remove the alpha (selection) channels you created since you will not need them anymore.

1. With the *KayakAD.tif* file open, make sure the eye icons are visible on all the kayak image layers, along with their drop shadow effects. Even though they are locked, they can be combined as one image.

2. Duplicate the *KayakAD* file (Image > Duplicate), and name the copy *KayakMERGE*. This leaves the *KayakAD* original with all its separate layers in case any future editing may be needed.

3. Click the eye icon by the *Text* layer group to hide all type layers (Figure 5-31). The eye icon will disappear, along with the text.

4. Select the *Gray Kayak* layer to make it active; this will become the name of the layer of the combined kayak images. You will rename the layer later.

5. Select Merge Visible from the Layers panel submenu or from the Layer menu to merge all the displayed kayak layers and their effects together. The type layers are unaffected, because they were hidden when Merge Visible was selected.

6. Double-click the *Gray Kayak* layer and rename it *Kayaks*. Press the Return/Enter key to accept the change. All the kayaks are now on one layer.

7. To display the text again, click the leftmost box to display the eye icon next to the *Text* layer group folder.

8. Select the Channels panel, and drag the *KayakALL* and *Kayak Color* alpha (selection) channels into the trash; they are no longer needed.

9. Use the Save As command (File > Save As) and save the file in your *Chapter 5* folder as *KayakMERGE.tif* using the default settings. This will provide a thumbnail visual of all three kayak images together on one layer. Close the file; the type layers are unaffected.

FLATTENING THE FILE

Some applications may not be able to read multilayer images, so it is important to duplicate a completed image with layers, flatten it, and save it to show the work to a client. Merging all the layers in a document into a single layer is called *flattening* the image. Although saving a file as a JPEG automatically compresses it significantly into one layer and deletes some data, it is useful for showing the client the final project electronically. Since flattened files are permanent, keep an original image with all layers as a backup in case the client may need changes.

To make sure your file is compatible with any graphic application that your client may be using, you will need to flatten the file and rename it. Since we do not need the alpha channels we used for selections, we will delete them here. Then compare file sizes. Be aware that when you flatten a file with type, it rasterizes the type into a bitmap; this is not good quality for print, only for electronic distribution or for a rough proof on a local printer.

1. Open the *KayakAD.tif* file displaying all the layers and duplicate it; give it the name *KayakFLAT* (Image > Duplicate > As KayakFLAT). Close the *KayakAD* file.

2. Select the Channels panel, and if they are not already deleted, drag the *KayakALL* and *Kayak Color* alpha (selection) channels into the trash.

3. To flatten the entire file, select Layer > Flatten Image from the Layer menu, or select Flatten Image from the Layers panel menu. If you get a dialog box asking to discard hidden layers, select OK (Figure 5-32).

4. To save the file for electronic distirbution, use File > Save As to save the file again as *KayakFLAT.jpg* with maximum quality settings (if a warning displays, select to save it anyway, which will save it as a copy) in your *Chapter 5* folder. Files that are flattened and saved as either JPEG or TIF files can be read by most any graphic application universally.

TOOLKIT TIP Although the final file here is still in RGB color space mode, you can print JPEG and TIF files locally to your ink jet printer for a "soft" proof of your work to check for composition and relative color or to give the client an idea of the completed product. You can also send your JPEG file (still in the computer's default RGB color space mode) to a client electronically. If you are sending files electronically, keep the file sizes under 3 MB to minimize download time; less is better. Understand that the client's computer set up, or the network the client is on, may have a low tolerance for downloading files over 3 MB.

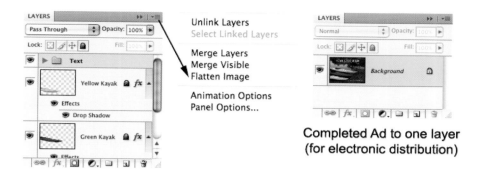

Completed Ad to one layer
(for electronic distribution)

▷   FIGURE 5-32

**Flattening all layers
on one layer.**

PREPARING THE AD FOR PRESS

As a last step, since all editing has been done while in RGB color mode, and the completed ad will be sent to a commercial printer, a duplicate file needs to be created of the *KayakMERGE.tif* file, and it needs to be converted to CMYK color mode. In most instances, a commercial printer will need an image converted to CMYK color, but always keep the RGB image as back-up or for future editing. The printer will also need all image layers merged or combined into one layer for production purposes; always check with them regarding their preferences). To send images to press, only send TIF or EPS files, if you combined text or graphics with your photos images, or PDF files.

TOOLKIT TIP Always make a dupliucate copy of your RGB file before converting to CMYK. When you change the RGB color mode of an image with layers to CMYK or Grayscale, a display may ask to merge layers; if it does, select Merge and the layers will be combined together.

Next, you will learn the procedure to prepare a CMYK file with a TIF extension.

1. Open the *KayakMERGE.tif* file, then select Image > Duplicate, and name the file *KayakCMYK;* select OK. The image layers should already be combined and the text layers grouped but not merged together. Close the *KayakMERGE* file.

2. With the *KayakCMYK* copy displayed, select Image > Mode > CMYK Color to prepare the file for press. If a dialog box displays regarding merging layers, choose to Merge. If another displays regarding your profile, choose to keep the current profile you have on your computer.

3. Save the duplicate file as *KayakCMYK.tif* using the default settings in the *Chapter 5* folder (Figure 5-33).

▷   FIGURE 5-33

**After all editing
is complete,
convert to
CMYK color
mode for press.**

4. Now the ad is ready for press and the RGB file remains as a backup.

5. Although this may seem a little redundant, having back-up copies for specific applications helps to keep you organized. If you performed all the exercises up to this point, you should have these files in your *Chapter 5* folder: *KayakAD*, *KayakFLAT*, *KayakMERGE*, and *KayakCMYK*. You may also have a *KayakAD.psd* file as a backup.

6. Feel free to use Adobe Bridge to compare properties and determine which files would suit your needs for specific purposes.

PRINTING TO YOUR LOCAL COLOR PRINTER

When printing graphic files to your ink-jet printer, you are printing what is called a *soft proof* that hopefully will closely match your monitor's screen. On the Web, search for a monitor calibration screen to check your monitor's accuracy in displaying colors and tones in shades of gray, or purchase monitor calibration software to routinely adjust your monitor's display for color accuracy. Printing graphic files is usually a three-step process with versions earlier than CS3: From the File menu, select Page Setup to determine the page size, which printer to use, and the format (portrait or landscape); then Print With Preview to set up how the color will match for the final proof; with everything set, select to print the file to your printer. Page Setup lets you specify the page orientation and printer: then select Print; the preview screen opens with default selections. This process will be covered in more detail later, but here are a few helpful hints when printing to your ink-jet printer. This is optional if you have access to a color printer, otherwise continue to the next exercise.

1. Calibrate your monitor with software, or find a method to adjust brightness and contrast to display the best tones.

2. Select File > Page Setup in Photoshop to determine paper size, what printer you will print to, and the format.

3. Select File > Print (or File > Print With Preview (earlier versions)), and make selections to specify how your image will be printed.

4. Place a check to keep the image centered on the page; if left unchecked, you can move the image around using the highlighted bounding box. Keep the Show Bounding Box checked if displayed.

5. Your desktop printer will probably have special profiles already installed for the type of paper you are using. You can also find special setting information with the photo or special paper you have purchased. Retain the Printer Manages Colors setting; it will probably be the most accurate.

6. Choose Print if you are printing to your ink-jet printer from RGB mode. Choose Proof if you are planning to print a CMYK proof for press.

7. Keep the rendering intent Relative Colormetric as the default to help preserve more of the original colors for your graphics work. You can also try Perceptual rendering if you are printing a photographic image.

8. Select Print to print the image.

CREATING PDF FILES FOR PRESS AND FOR CLIENT COMMUNICATION

Need additional fun computer graphics tutorials and info, and an additional look at the projects you'll be creating in this book? Check out my Artist's Digital Toolkit website at: **http://www.digitoolkit.com**

Most applications use the universal form of Portable Document Format (PDF) files to communicate. Most commercial press establishments and clients prefer communicating in this format, because anyone can open and see your exact layout, including images and fonts. In Photoshop you can save layered files in the Photoshop PDF format, and anyone can view them with the free Adobe Acrobat Reader you downloaded in Chapter 1 without having to use any graphic applications. PDF files retain all formatting used in the document, and you can also use this method to create flattened PDF files for electronic distribution and as a high-resolution CMYK file that can be used for commercial printing. You can save a PDF file as a CMYK copy without having to worry about going through the Image menu to convert it; and it will automatically produce a CMYK version that can be printed or distributed electronically. We will cover more on PDF files in Chapter 10.

Next, you will create a PDF document in Photoshop for electronic distribution to the client and make a high-resolution copy for the commercial press.

1. Open the *KayakMERGE.tif* file, then select Image > Duplicate, and name the file *KayakPDF,* then select OK. The image layers should already be flattened into one layer, with the text layers grouped but not merged together. Close the *KayakMERGE* file.

2. With the *KayakPDF* copy displayed, select File > Save As >Photoshop PDF. When the display box opens, make sure you check Save As a Copy, Use Proof Setup: Working CMYK, and Embed Color profile U.S. Web coated (SWOP) to create a CMYK copy ready for press (Figure 5-34).

3. Click to save in your *Chapter 5* folder. If you get a warning dialog box about overriding current settings, just click OK to continue.

4. When the Preset dialog box opens, select to save as Press Quality if you are sending the file to a commercial printer, and uncheck where it asks about preserving Photoshop's editing capabilities, which will prevent someone from inadvertently editing it. It will save so that someone who has an earlier version of Acrobat Reader (version 5) will be able to read it.

5. Click Save PDF to convert the file. Go ahead and locate the file and double-click it to open the Adobe Acrobat Reader application and take a look at it.

6. Now the ad is ready for press and the RGB file remains as a backup.

▷ FIGURE 5-34

Saving final files as press quality PDFs for commercial press.

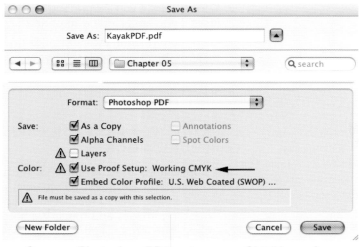

Save as Photoshop PDF set up as a CMYK proof

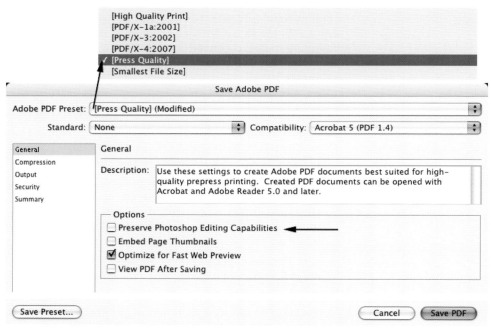

Saving for Press Quality preset when ready for commercial press.

7. To send the same file to a client electronically, you would repeat steps 1 through 4 and select Smallest File Size to create a low-resoultion version. Go ahead give it a shot, and save it as *KayakPDF2*.

8. Select High Quality in the Presets and print a quick, high-quality soft proof on your desktop printer if you have access to one, otherwise save and close the file. Have fun, this is the most popular method used in the industry today.

TOOLKIT TIP If you choose Photoshop Editing Capabilities, and you get a dialog box indicating this function is incompatible with earlier Photoshop versions, in most cases it is safe to click OK to continue.

TOOLKIT TIP If you download the latest free version of Acrobat Reader, you have several options. You can add comments to documents, upload the file to be printed and sent through FedEx/Kinkos, and much more.

ADVANCED USER: Prepare Camera Raw Files: The Digital Negative

Most digital images created in moderately priced and professional digital cameras are either set to process the images automatically or to create images as **Camera Raw files,** which lets photographers and designers interpret the image data themselves, rather than letting the camera make adjustments and conversions. Here are some options and information regarding these files:

• A Camera Raw file contains unprocessed picture data from a digital camera's image sensor.

• Only Camera Raw image files contain the actual data captured by the sensor without any in-camera processing.

• Working with Camera Raw files still lets you set the white balance that reflects the lighting conditions under which the photo was taken, tonal range, contrast, color saturation, and sharpening, or you can shoot automatically and adjust those aspects later. The original RAW file is never adjusted permanently, always a copy is saved after adjustments. You can easily default back to the original settings and start over.

• Think of Camera Raw files as your photo negative. You can go back and reprocess the file to achieve the results you want. Camera Raw files always remain pure recordings, like a film negative or transparency.

• Your camera saves files in its own raw file format. When you download the files from the camera, they will have file extensions such as .NEF (Nikon), or .CRW to identify their own raw format.

• You can save various versions of these files with special adjustments, the same as you would save different prints or experiment with different exposures. You can save to Adobe's universal digital negative (DNG) version, especially if you are downloading raw files using different cameras on the same computer. You can also save to Photoshop's PSD format, JPEG, and TIF formats after you have made your adjustments. Camera Raw files always remain pure: you open up your image and save it to a file format after you make changes, and the Camera Raw plug-in makes a digital copy of the edited image. You can always default back to the original settings.

• Camera Raw is a free Photoshop plug-in that you can download from the Adobe website; follow the simple instructions to place it inside the appropriate folder inside your Photoshop application folder. In current versions, it is automatically installed for you. If you purchase a new camera, you should check the Adobe website for the newest version of Camera Raw.

• When you open a raw file, it will open in the Camera Raw application within Photoshop. Even though it may look flat or off color, it contains all unprocessed information, just like a digital negative. Use this application as your new digital darkroom with no chemicals. You will find in the Camera Raw dialog box, in addition to other controls, White Balance, which sets the color balance for various lighting conditions; the Temperature control, which controls the color temperature; and Tint to compensate for green or magenta tints in photos. Moving the temperature slider to the left, for instance, makes the color a cooler, bluer tone; moving the slider to the right warms the image. You also notice plenty of additional tools and controls you can play with to achieve the best image (Figure 5-35).

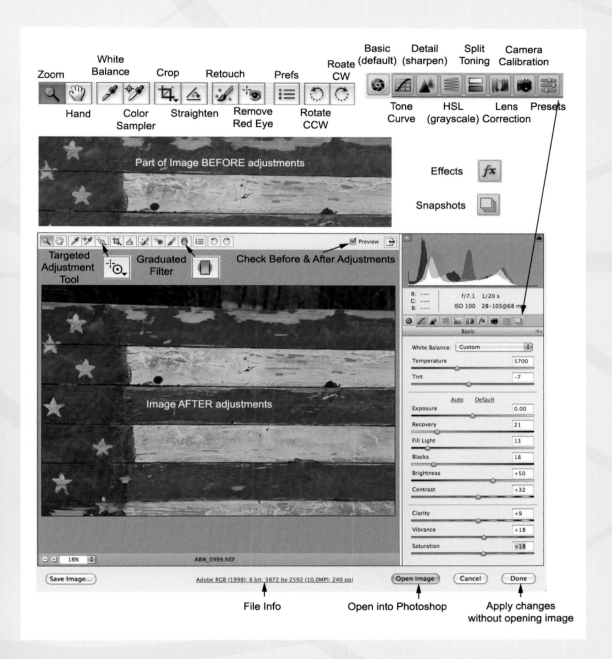

▷ FIGURE 5-35

Camera Raw image and dialog box before and after adjustments: the digital negative.

Next, we will open an image and play.

1. Launch Photoshop and open the *ABW0099.NEF* file in your *Chapter 5 folder*.

2. When you open the image, you will notice the Camera Raw dialog box open, if the plug-in is loaded on your computer; if it does not appear, you will need to download and install it. This is a raw image made on a very overcast day with very flat lighting; it has been saved in a NEF format with a Nikon camera.

3. This dialog box is your digital darkroom, where you can experiment with your digital negative. You will notice the White Balance settings are As Shot, which uses the camera's settings, the same as the auto setting that many people use on their cameras. Select other White Balance options to see some interesting color adjustments, then go back to As Shot. Notice the color temperature changes as you select various White Balance settings.

4. Adjust the Temperature slider to see the effects. Try increasing the saturation and other options, until you have an image representing what the scene might look like to show more vibrant colors. Use the settings in Figure 5-35 as a starting point. Select the icons above the "Basic" display for more adjustments.

Go ahead and make a good, publishable image.

5. You will notice that when you select the Shadows and Highlights buttons, they will indicate areas with no detail. Check the shadows mostly in this image.

6. Save the final image in JPEG format, using the default settings in your *Chapter 5* folder. Print the final image using a desktop printer.

TOOLKIT TIP Along the top of this window, next to the hand tool, you will notice the **White Balance tool** (I) which you can use if you have a very tinted image. This only works well when you have an image that contains a neutral gray or neutral white color. You will notice it will probably create a cool effect in this particular image. To balance the color, try using pavement, rocks, and other neutral gray tones, if they are in your image. When making edits, keep an eye on your histogram to make sure that both sides for shadows and highlights of the histogram show the bottom or start and end of the peak to avoid what is called *clipping* of highlight and shadows.

DIGITAL TOOLKIT EXTRA: Image Transformations Using Content-Aware Fill and Picture Package

Sometimes you need to make radical changes to your image to make it stand out. You may find parts of the image may be distracting and need to be removed. You may have need for the image to fit a client's specific dimension, which may involve accurately stretching or shrinking the image without ruining the original components. You may also want to use additional programs that you can download from the Adobe site and run. Picture Package is one of these programs that allow you to create multiple images within a page automatically. Photoshop has many tools to suit your needs. You will play with a few in the following exercises.

USING CONTENT-AWARE FILL IN REMOVING BACKGROUND DISTRACTIONS

New in CS5, **Content-Aware Fill** has the ability to remove an image element and replace it with details that blend in closely to match the lighting, tone, and noise of the surrounding area. It is used when you decide to select the area you want to remove, press the delete key, and choose the Content-Aware Fill option in the dialog box. This new technique works best with cluttered or open backgrounds that don't have a pattern, such as background trees, or sky area. You can use Content-Aware Fill in conjunction with the Spot Healing Brush for optimum results. The **Spot Healing Brush** analyzes the parts of the image and blends into surrounding pixels. This tool will be covered in depth in the next chapter. You can see its usefulness and its limitation with this exercise. In many cases, it is best to have all color adjustments and toning already done before removing.

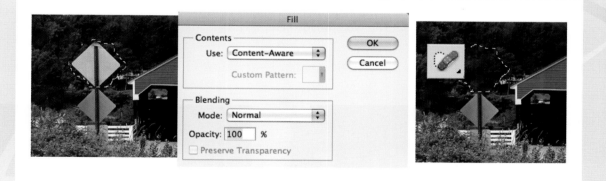

▷ FIGURE 5-36

The Content-Aware Fill technique used with the Spot Healing Brush removes elements and fils in with surrounding background elements.

Here you have a rather complex photo that needs a lot of removal of distracting components. You will select certain areas, and use the Content-Aware Fill option to remove most of these problems. Be aware that the final results will not be perfect.

1. Open the file *Badbridge.tif* from your *Chapter 5* folder. You will notice lots of distractions. Duplicate the image (Image > Duplicate) and save the file as *BadbridgeFILL.tif* in your *Chapter 5* folder. Close the original *Badbridge* file.

2. Using your Lasso Tool, make a close selection around the left top sign as shown in Figure 5-36. Less is better when using this technique.

3. Press the Delete key on your keyboard, and when the Fill dialog box comes up, choose Content-Aware, then click OK. You will find the sign replaced with the surrounding trees. Deselect when done. It is not perfect, but shows what can be done.

4. Select the second sign down and repeat the process. You may find that you may want to undo (Cmnd/Ctrl + Z, or Edit > Step Backward) a few times to try practicing to get this technique more accurate. Deselect when done. The sign in front of the fence will not work well because it is a pattern that Content-Aware Fill will not adjust to accurately so it will have to stay.

5. Select the Spot Healing Brush, with a 15 pixel brush for starters, and simply click inside or around the outside area that was filled and you will find it starts to help to blend in nicely. You can increase the size of your brush if needed. You may find again that it will take frequent attempts to get it realistic looking (love the undo functions!). Avoid having repetitive patterns from the brush and try to keep the background blending in nicely.

6. You can use the Spot Healing Brush to delicately cover the bottom portion of the left sign with copied flowers, and hide a portion of the left side house behind the bridge. Be careful you don't copy the bridge edge, or just undo and try again.

7. You can use the Content-Aware Fill feature to initially remove selected telephone wires, the house on the right side and the sign (remember to select individual elements to remove), then use the Spot Healing Brush to fill in the edges. You can see the right side is much easier and looks probably more realistic initially (Figure 5-37). Deselect when done.

8. This technique takes a lot of patience and practice but can help to make a better image. In Chapter 6, you'll learn other methods of retouching images where you can come back and use to tweak this image. When you feel confident with your image here, save and close the file.

▷ FIGURE 5-37

Using the Content-Aware Fill and Spot Healing Brush to remove unwanted distractions in an image.

USING CONTENT-AWARE SCALE FOR IMAGE RESIZING

Where normal scaling affects all pixels uniformly, The Content-Aware Scale function allows you to resize an image without changing the important elements like people, buildings, animals, etc., by affecting pixels in areas that aren't visually important. This handy tool may help you get out of a jam with a client if the image needs to be a slightly reduced dimension, say from an 8 × 12 inch full size to 8 × 10 inch standard size image. Content-Aware Scale allows you to drag the vertical handle of a selected image and the image's horizontal pixels are blended in without affecting the vertical elements of an image. The opposite holds when dragging the horizontal handle, only the vertical elements are blended. Content-Aware Scale works on layers and selections. As with the Content-Aware Fill function mentioned earlier, the success of this technique depends on the type of image you want to use. Images with simple backgrounds work best.

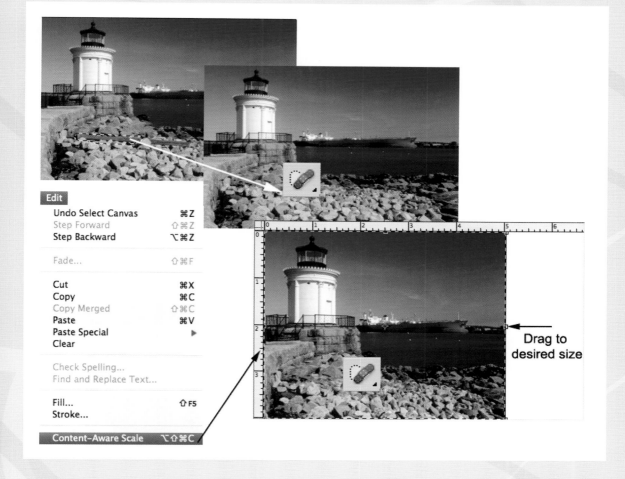

For this exercise, you will first use the Content-Aware Fill described in the last exercise to remove a distraction, then you will adjust an original image that is roughly 4 × 6.5 inches, to an image that is 4 × 5 inch format.

1. Open the file *Ship.tif* from your *Chapter 5* folder, duplicate the image (Image > Duplicate), and save the copy as *SCALEShip.tif* in your *Chapter 5* folder. Close the original *Ship* file.

2. Make sure Rulers are displayed; View > Rulers.

3. Oh look, you have a nasty board that's ruining the foreground. Go ahead and select the part divided up by a large rock (Figure 5-38), press the Delete key, and select the Content-Aware fill as done in the previous exercise.

4. Use the Spot Healing Brush to help fill in the area with realistic rocks. Repeat the same process with right side of the board. More practice! Avoid making the area look repetitive.

5. To scale your image, use the Rectangular Marquee tool and select the entire image or choose Select > Select All (or Cmnd/Ctrl + A).

▷ FIGURE 5-39

Using Content-Aware Scale to create images larger than the original by creating a new document canvass to move the image onto, then stretch to taste.

6. With the entire image selected, choose Edit > Content-Aware Scale and you will find the selection with handles in the corners and middle of each side.

7. Click on the middle vertical handle on the right side and drag inward until you reach the 5-inch mark on the ruler guide (Figure 5-38). Notice the pixels in the horizontal red ship and sky adjust to the change but the vertical lighthouse remains accurately displayed, although it too has been slightly adjusted.

8. Press the Return/Enter key to accept the change. You may need to tweak the area where the board was removed using the Spot Healing Brush. Save the file.

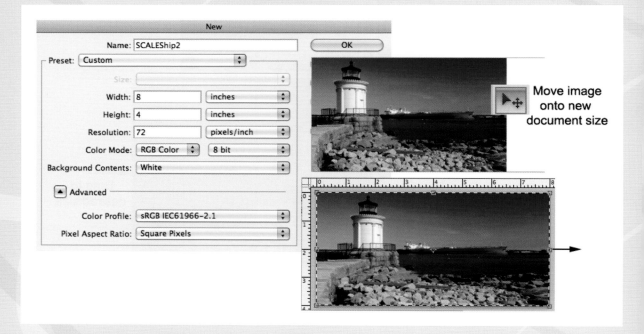

Move image onto new document size

To create a panoramic 4 × 8 inch image, or one that is longer than the original image, you'll need to create an image canvass to the size, then move your original image as a separate layer, and then stretch it.

1. Create a new custom document, which will be at Web resolution for our purposes here (File > New > Preset Custom, Width 8 inches, Height 4 inches, Resolution 72 pixels). Click OK to get your blank document (Figure 5-39).

2. Open the file *Ship.tif* from your *Chapter 5* folder, duplicate the image (Image > Duplicate), and save the copy as *SCALEShip2.tif* in your *Chapter 5* folder. Close the original *Ship* file.

3. Resize both windows of both documents next to one another, select the Move tool, and drag the *ScaleShip2* image onto the blank canvass aligning it along the left side edge (Figure 5-39). Use the keyboard arrow keys if needed.

4. You'll notice two layers displayed on the Layers panel. Make sure the "Layer 1" is active, then choose Select > Select All (or Cmnd/Ctrl + A).

5. With the entire image selected, choose Edit > Content-Aware Scale.

6. If it does not automatically fit into the new dimensions, click on the middle of the vertical handle on the right side and drag outward until you reach the 8-inch mark on the ruler guide (Figure 5-39). Notice again, the pixels in the horizontal red ship and sky adjust to the change but the vertical lighthouse remains accurately displayed, although it too has been slightly adjusted.

7. Press the Return/Enter key to accept the change.

8. Feel free to get rid of that board again if you want more practice using Content-Aware Fill and the Spot Healing Brush. If you had tried to stretch the other *SCALEShip* image you just created with the board removed, in most cases, it would probably have needed to be redone anyways due to adding too many pixels.

9. When you are ready, flatten the layers (Layer > Flatten Image), and then save the file *SCALEship2* in your *Chapter 5* folder closing the file.

CREATING PHOTO BUSINESS CARDS WITH PICTURE PACKAGE

DESIGN TIP

Our eyes read from left to right, top to bottom. Providing an introduction line to the right, then your name and occupation, leads the reader's eye into who you are.

The Adobe site has opportunities not only to provide help and training, but also to download additional FREE features, tools, and functions to its products. **Plug-ins** are additional small applications that can run within the major application like Photoshop. Picture Package is a Photoshop plug-in you can download from the Adobe site and easily install. To download this plug in, go to *http://www. adobe.com/* and use the Search box for CS5 Photoshop plug-ins. They may also be located in the "Downloads" section at the site. The install directions are also in the Text CD in the Goodies > Chapter 5 folders. If you have a home computer and you purchased Photoshop or the CS5 suite of applications, in the purchased CD's there should be a Goodies folder containing a variety of additional plug-ins with installation instructions as well. Picture Package is a great function in Photoshop that allows you to create different sizes of an image: this used to require several steps, especially with multiple layers. Under File > Automate, the **Picture Package** command allows you to combine several images onto one sheet that can be printed. The images are automatically created on separate image and text layers, which can then be flattened into one layer (if the Flatten All Layers box is checked) or it can be created showing all the layers involved. This project will show you how to create your own unique photo cards. All that is needed is to make the first photo business card, insert the image in the Preview layout, and the command will perform the rest.

TOOLKIT TIP Picture Package is a Photoshop plug-in for CS5. Plug-ins are additional small applications that can run within the major application like Photoshop. If you need to install this fun plug-in and others, including simple instructions, you wiil find them in the Goodies folder of your Text CD (Chapter 5). You can download Picture Package and others from the Adobe site below (or type "CS5 picture package" in the search box in the Adobe help site).

Windows: http://www.adobe.com/support/downloads/detail.jsp?ftpID=4048
Mac OS: http://www.adobe.com/support/downloads/detail.jsp?ftpID=4047

DESIGN TIP

Sometimes changing the orientation of the card will make it stand out. Using a vertical format gives a little more individual attention compared to traditional business cards. Creating shadowed yellow text provides depth to the image and warms up the complementary blue tones in the image.

CREATING THE INITIAL BUSINESS CARD

Photographic business cards are a great visual tool to attract attention. The normal size for a business card or wallet-size photo is 2.5 inches by 3.5 inches (but sometimes, a ¼ inch less). The size for this exercise is already created for a wallet-size photo. As a review of some of the past exercises, you will type in information for the business card then apply a drop shadow effect to make the text stand out in the photograph. Even if you use a larger image, the Picture Package command will automatically convert it to the smaller size you determined from a list of preset Layout sizes. This is also a great tool for portrait packages and holiday cards.

TOOLKIT TIP When using an image for the Picture Package command, do not use an image that needs to be enlarged more than your intended size, since this may cause pixel problems. You can always make a smaller image from a larger image, but do not ever make a larger image from a smaller one.

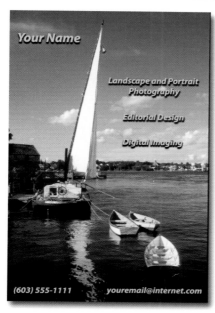

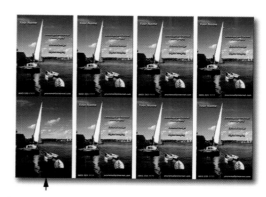

Select another image
to substitute

Completed sheet of photo business cards with
Picture Package

Completed photo business card

▷ FIGURE 5-40

**Creating multiple
business cards from
one image using
Picture Package.**

DESIGN TIP

As italicized text
should be minimized
for emphasis, a more
traditionally accept-
able approach would
be to have only the
name italicized.

In this exercise, you will create the type lines for the business card in the photograph.

1. Open the *Photocard* file from your *Chapter 5* folder in Photoshop. Make sure the Layers panel is showing.

2. To adjust the overall color, choose Image > Auto Color.

3. Select the Type tool in the Tools panel; on the Tool Options bar, choose a 12-point Minion Pro Bold Italic font, or something similar, with a yellow-gold color from the Color bar. Another great way to choose a color is to sample from the actual image; it creates a nice continuity in the design. The color inside one of the dinghys is nice.

4. Click on the left side of the sail, as shown in Figure 5-40, and type "Your Name" or use your own name. If you are using a long name, create two lines with the last name indented under the first name, or decrease the font size to 10 points.

5. Click the Layer Style icon on the bottom of the Layers panel (Fx), and create a drop shadow with the settings shown in Figure 5-41.

6. With the Type layer selected, use the Move tool to position the line. To create a separate type layer, select the Move tool then select the Type tool again, and click on the image to type. Here you can choose to continue with italics, or stay traditional with the name only in italics and the rest as Minion Bold text.

7. Decrease the Minion Bold Italic (or Minion Bold) font size to 8 points and select center align on the Tool Options bar.

▷ FIGURE 5-41

Layer style settings for a drop shadow on type.

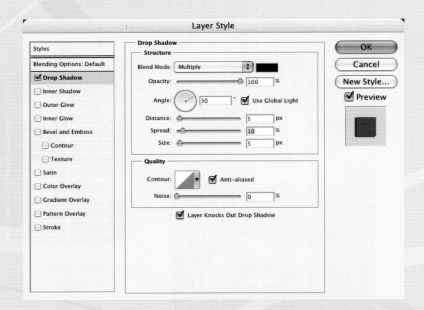

8. Type the line "Landscape and Portrait Photography" in two lines by pressing the Return/Enter key after *Portrait.* Use the Character panel to adjust the leading for better spacing. Apply the same drop shadow Layer Style effect as you did before; you can Option/Alt drag the effect in the Layers panel to apply it to another layer.

9. To create another type layer, Editorial Design, select the Move tool, then the Type tool, and click on the image to type.

10. Again, apply drop shadows to this text with the settings shown in Figure 5-41.

11. Create separate type layers for the lines "Digital Imaging," "(603) 555-1111" and "youremail@internet.com." Use 8-point Minion Bold Italic with the same settings for the drop shadow (Figure 5-41).

12. Save the file as *PhotoDONE.tif* using the default settings in your *Chapter 5* folder. You now have completed your business card.

CREATING MULTIPLE BUSINESS CARDS WITH PICTURE PACKAGE

Now that you have created the initial business card, you will use Picture Package to create a sheet of business cards. You can also substitute images in the layout sheet you create by clicking on the image to be replaced and locating the substitute image.

It is time to create a sheet of business cards from one card. You will substitute one of the images to see how that is done.

1. Make sure the *PhotoDONE* image is open and active.

2. Select File > Automate > Picture Package.

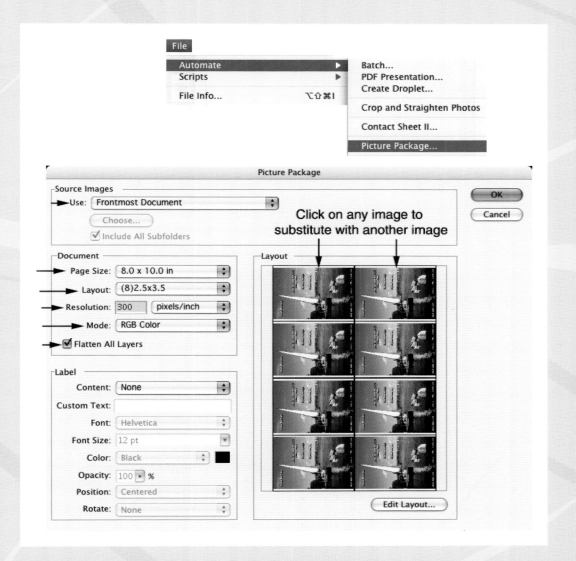

▷ FIGURE 5-42

Creating business cards using automate > picture package.

3. When the Picture Package dialog box comes up, select Use > Frontmost Document, which uses the current *PhotoDONE* image. (If you wanted to use a different image, you would select Use > File, then Choose to locate it.)

4. Enter the other settings shown in Figure 5-42 for eight 2.5 × 3.5 business cards.

5. Before clicking OK, click to select one of the images to substitute and locate the original Photocard image as the replacement (or use one of the kayak images); it will display as substituted for the business card image.

6. Click OK in the Picture Package dialog box and watch Photoshop do its magic. When it is done, you will have created a sheet with eight wallet-size images.

7. Save the file as *BusCARDS.tif* using the default settings in your Chapter 5 folder.

TOOLKIT TIP Check out some of the other features under the Automate command, like fitting images to size, creating a Web photo gallery, or creating a contact sheet of your images. You can also automatically crop and straighten photos, create panoramic compositions, or use the Edit Layout function within Picture Package to create your own customized layouts from the preset layouts.

SHARPENING THE IMAGE USING SMART SHARPEN OR UNSHARP MASK

A good habit to aquire, when combining multiple images, images that have been scanned, or images that have been edited, is to apply a little sharpening using either the Smart Sharpen filter or the Unsharp Mask filter when the work is completed. The Smart Sharpen and the **Unsharp Mask** filters in the Filter menu provide precision sharpening of an image or selected portions of an image. The **Smart Sharpen filter** provides more sharpening controls than the Unsharp Mask filter. You can also control the amount of sharpening that occurs in shadow and highlight areas by setting the controls in the Sharpen tabs. The Amount sets the amount of sharpening. A higher amount increases the contrast between edge pixels, giving the appearance of greater sharpness. The Radius setting determines the number of pixels surrounding the edge pixels that affect the sharpening. The greater the radius value, the wider the edge effects and the more obvious the sharpening. Adjust the Amount of sharpness using a low Threshold with a 1-pixel Radius to start with. With the Preview button checked, you can click on the image window to see the effect.

TOOLKIT TIP Apply a little sharpening at a time, because this filter is permanent. When looking at the preview in the dialog box, if the image edges appear to have a "halo" effect, the image has been sharpened too much.

Here you will apply the Unsharp Mask filter to the *BUScards* image.

1. With the *BUScards* file open, select Filter > Sharpen > Smart Sharpen (or use Unsharp Mask)

2. When the dialog box appears, drag it close to your *BUScards* file to view the results. Enter the settings as 70 for Amount, 2 for a Threshold, with a 1-pixel Radius (Figure 5-43).

3. Click on the Preview image and move the image around to find sharp edges on the sailboat for reference. You can also look at your *BUScards* file to see the results.

4. There should only be a slight change. To make more dramatic changes, increase the amount; but be careful not to oversharpen, otherwise it may look unrealistic. It is better to apply changes incrementally in small amounts. Select OK to accept the changes, then save the file and print it when you are done.

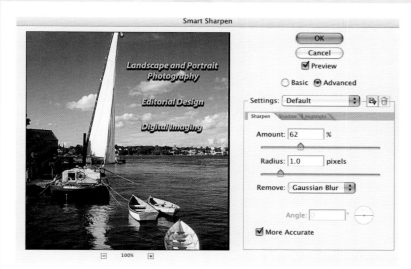

Smart Sharpen dialog box

Unsharp Mask Filter dialog box

▷ FIGURE 5-43

**Smart sharpen
and unsharp mask
filter settings.**

CHAPTER SUMMARY

In this chapter, you completed a rather complex project that gave you quite an overview of Photoshop's use of selections, layers, and text. With the selections created, the original kayak was duplicated and pasted into separate layers, which allowed you to change the colors on the kayaks separately using the Hue/Saturation command; then the kayaks were moved into position. You were able to rename layers, move layers, duplicate layers, and use layer styles to create realistic drop shadows for the kayaks and to the text for added dimension. The final image was saved as a TIF file with all layers intact for future editing. You created a layer group (set) to combine all the type layers, then you merged the kayak images together onto a single layer. The ad was then duplicated and flattened to one layer, decreasing the file size and allowing you to send an electronic proof to the client. The advertisement was then converted to CMYK color mode, ready for press. In the advanced section you got a taste of working with Camera Raw files as pure digital negatives. For more information and projects check out the *Goodies* folder on your CD.

REVIEW QUESTIONS

1. Explain the procedure used to duplicate and recolor the kayaks.

2. Explain how using the Hue/Saturation command is helpful for changing color on large-scale products.

3. Explain Anti-alias settings, Layer Style effects, and layer groups.

4. Explain how to use Layer Comps.

5. Explain the differences between flattening an image using Photoshop's Layers panel and saving a file as a JPEG, which automatically flattens an image's layers.

6. What is the purpose of using Camera Raw files?

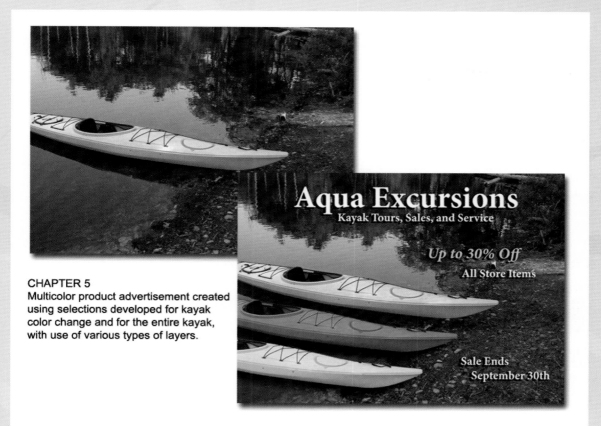

CHAPTER 5
Multicolor product advertisement created using selections developed for kayak color change and for the entire kayak, with use of various types of layers.

CHAPTER 5 ADVANCED
Taking a flat raw file captured in a digital camera and making precise adjustments using the Camera RAW function in Photoshop. The new digital darkroom.

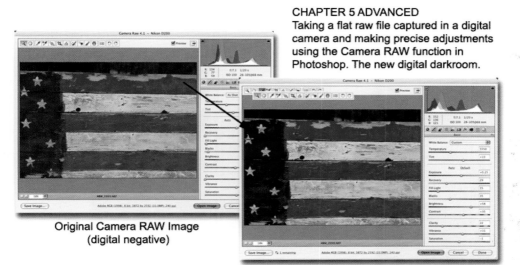

Original Camera RAW Image
(digital negative)

Chosen Adjustments to RAW Image

▷ FIGURE 5-44

CHAPTER 5 EXTRA
Using the Content-Aware Fill and Spot Healing Brush to remove unwanted distractions in an image (top).

Using Content-Aware Scale to resize unimportant image elements with accuracy.

Creating Photo Business cards using Photoshop's Picture Package plug-in (bottom).

Completed Photo Business Card

Completed Sheet of Business Cards

Restoring and Coloring a Black and White Photograph

CHAPTER OBJECTIVES: To understand Photoshop's tools and techniques for image restoration and retouching, in this chapter you will:

▷ Use the Dust and Scratches and Gaussian Blur filters and the Blur tool to smooth out or replace imperfections.

▷ Use the Clone Stamp, Patch, Healing Brush, and Spot Healing Brush tools to repair parts of an image.

▷ Use the History panel to avoid mishaps and create snapshots at certain points in the editing progress and save them.

▷ Use the painting tools and color panels to select, sample, and paint realistic colors on a black-and-white image.

▷ Learn the importance of RGB, CMYK, and Grayscale color modes.

▷ ADVANCED USERS: Color cast correction by neutralizing shadow and highlight areas using the Threshold feature Levels sample points, and Info panel.

▷ DIGITAL TOOLKIT EXTRA: Special creations with the Masks panel and Adjustments panel, using adjustment layers and layer masks.

One of the things that Photoshop is best known for is its arsenal of **editing and retouching tools** that can help repair and reconstruct images. As a designer or professional photographer, whenever you receive an image, you will need to examine it thoroughly for imperfections, defects, or color problems, and then retouch the image to make it publishable. In your profession, you may find yourself involved with a lot of minor and major retouching (and painting) projects for clients. In this chapter, you will get a taste of some of the tools and special panels that provide you the necessary equipment to take on most retouching tasks.

TOOLS AND PANELS FOR EDITING

Retouching tools can be used for all kinds of restoration and image enhancement projects, which may involve replacing image components, editing selected areas, and trimming outside portions of an image. Painting tools and special panels allow you to sample and apply color from images, store colors, create new tool settings and brushes, or paint back to a previous state in a document.

TOOLKIT TIP Getting to know the appropriate shortcut or "hot key" for most used tools will make a designer or photographer more productive by saving time.

 Need additional fun computer graphics tutorials and info, and an additional look at the projects you'll be creating in this book? Check out my Artist's Digital Toolkit website at: **http://www.digitoolkit.com**

RETOUCHING TOOLS

Retouching tools are the most widely used tools for restoration and retouching projects (Figure 6-1); their shortcut keys follow the tool name in parentheses.

• Healing Brush, Spot Healing Brush, Red Eye, and Patch tools (J) restore damaged sections of an image by sampling pixels from a good area and then blending in lighting and shading; they are great for working on portrait restorations and old photos.

• The Color Replacement tool replaces the color underneath the brush cursor with the foreground color.

• The Clone Stamp and Pattern Stamp tools (S) copy sampled image areas, replacing the target area with the same pixel information.

• The Crop tool trims a rectangular area, while the Slice tools split an image into many components of a Web page for links and rollovers.

• The Eraser tools (E) consist of the Eraser, Background Eraser, and Magic Eraser; these remove selected pixels, background colors, or make the background transparent.

• The Gradient tool (G) creates a shaded fill from one color to another, while the Paint Bucket tool (G) fills in solid colors.

• The Blur, Sharpen, and Smudge tools (R) let you soften or sharpen selected parts of an image. The Burn, Sponge, and Dodge tools (O) lighten, darken, or saturate the tones of color in an image.

▷ FIGURE 6-1

Photoshop retouching tools.

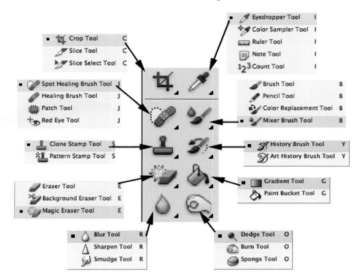

PAINTING TOOLS, SPECIAL TOOLS, AND PANELS

Painting tools allow you to apply selected colors and effects. The Tool Presets panel is where you can create custom tools with specific options and save them for later use.

• Brush, Color Replacement, and Pencil tools (B) are used for painting. The Brushes panel allows you to select from an array of regular and custom brushes of varying sizes and shapes.

• The Shape tools (U) are used to create various shapes that help with selections.

• The Pen tools (P) create paths using anchor points for precise selections.

• The Path Selection and Direct Selection tools (A) are used to select paths created by the Pen tools (Figure 6-2). Slice tools (C) divide an image into smaller images that can then be reassembled on a web page.

• The History Brush and Art History Brush (Y) tools allow you to go back in time to a previous brush used or to apply an effect. The History panel records all actions as states and snapshots. It allows the user to easily revert to previous states.

• The 3D object tools (K) change the position or scale of a 3D model. The 3D camera tools (N) are used to change the view of the scene (Photoshop Extended version only).

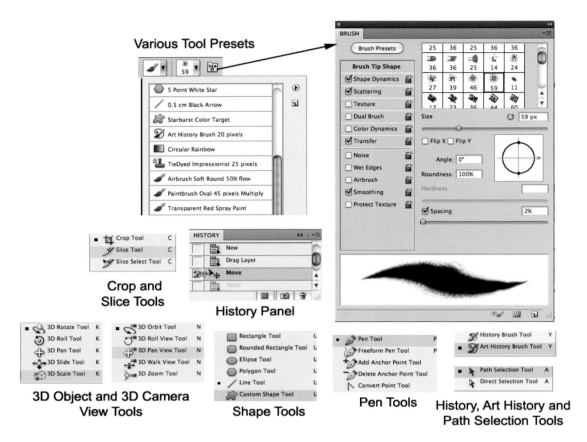

▷ FIGURE 6-2

Painting tools, special tools, and panels.

COLOR TOOLS, SWATCHES, AND COLOR PANELS

Color tools like the Eyedropper and **Color Sampler tool** (I) are used to sample any color in an image and provide color information (Figure 6-3). You will also find within the same tool area Ruler and Count tools for measuring with precision for more complex projects. You can select colors or sample colors with the **Color panel** and create or use preset colors in the Swatches panel. Below the tool buttons, you will find the **Color Picker** icons, where you can select and switch between foreground and background colors (X), and also default to black and white (D).

SPECIAL FILTERS

Photoshop has an arsenal of filters, most in the Filter menu, to enhance or apply special effects to selected portions of an image like applying special artistic effects, or create special distortions and lighting effects. Some additional filters can be provided by third-party developers and are available as plug-ins. It also has special filters to help with the retouching and enhancing process (Figure 6-4). To get rid of dust and scratches or clean up solid color areas, like the blue sky in an image, use the **Dust and Scratches filter** or the **Median filter**. To soften a

▷ FIGURE 6-3

Color and measure-
ment tools, Color
panel, Swatches
panel, and
Color Picker.

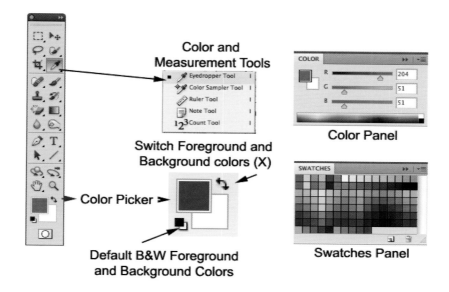

▷ FIGURE 6-4

Some special
retouching filters:
Smart Sharpen,
Dust and Scratches,
Gaussian blur, and
photo filters.

portrait image or a scanned image that was printed on a matte surface, use the **Gaussian Blur filter**. For precision in sharpening images or their components, the **Unsharp Mask filter** is a designer's special digital tool. The **Smart Sharpen filter** precisely locates areas that need to be sharpened. There is also the **Filter Gallery** under the Filter menu to preview and apply various filter effects on an image. There is also the Photo Filter function under the Image menu (Image > Adjustments) to simulate the effect of standard photographic lens filters. You can control the amount of effect by adjusting the density.

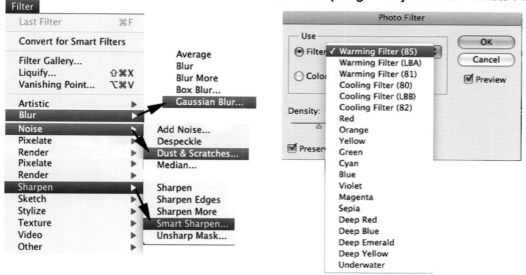

CLIENT ASSIGNMENT: Retouching and Coloring a Black and White Photograph

Your client, Elizabeth Roberts, has an old black-and-white photo of two brothers that has been damaged over the years. She wants to have the image restored and an additional copy colorized to give to the brothers at their family reunion. When you discuss possible colors, she mentions the baby boy's clothing was light blue. The older brother was wearing a dark green vest, and the background was a light blue. You tell her you will also try to match the flesh tones by using another photo of children with the same basic skin tones. She is excited about the project, and you tell her you will have it done by the end of the week.

ACTION ITEMS OVERVIEW

▷ FIGURE 6-5

Before and after restoration.

This job requires two important phases: First, to maintain the image quality, you need to restore the black-and-white image as close to its original state as possible before applying any effects or colors. The second phase is to make a realistic color painting using color from the Swatches and Color panels and to apply the colors using painting tools with a low opacity brush. The Color Sampler tool will also be used in sampling skin color tones to apply to the B&W image. Because painting will involve a special brush, a custom brush will be created for more accurate work on the image (Figure 6-5).

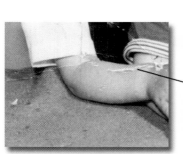

Enlarged view of part of
image area to be restored

Original Image

Restored Image (colored)

Here are some things you will learn to do in this chapter:

- Duplicate the image, one for restored black and white and another for color.
- Soften and replace background imperfections using the Dust and Scratches filter.
- Use the Clone, Patch, Healing Brush, and Spot Healing Brush tools to remove the cracks and defects in the photo.
- Use the History panel for multiple undos and to save previous editing changes.
- Soften the matte surface of the image slightly using the Gaussian Blur tool.
- Change the Grayscale color mode to RGB to add color.
- Create a new brush in the Tool Presets panel for carefully painting the image.
- Select colors from the Swatches panel to paint the clothing, blanket, and background using a low opacity setting with the **Brush tool**.
- Sample skin tone color from a color image using the Color Sampler tool and paint with a low opacity setting to make realistic flesh tones.
- ADVANCED USERS: Correct colors casts using the Threshold Adjustment Layer, Levels sample points, and the Info panel.

RESTORING THE IMAGE

Before adding color to a black-and-white photo, it has to be restored to the best quality possible. This is done by selecting the areas that will be adjusted, then editing with special retouching tools and the Dust and Scratches filter to help remove and replace any imperfections, cracks, and dust spots. This part of the process involves a lot of trial and error to create an accurately restored image. Using the **History panel** helps to avoid problems by providing multiple undos and saving recorded actions or states during the editing process, which are called snapshots.

DUPLICATING AND SAVING THE IMAGE FILE

It is always a good habit to make duplicates of any file you are working on and to save your work frequently. Save your images throughout this chapter with a .TIF extension (File > Save AS > *FIXBoys.tif*) so you can edit your image as many times as needed without compromising the quality.

You will create a duplicate of the original file *Boys* and save it with a new name.

1. Choose File > Open and select the *Boys.tif* image located in the *Chapter 6* folder.
2. Make sure the Navigator, History, Color, and Swatches panels are displayed on the desktop to assist you. If not, use the Window menu to access the panels you need.
3. The Tool Presets panel is located at the left side of the Tool Options bar.
4. Create a duplicate image by selecting Image > Duplicate.
5. Name the new copy *FIXBoys* and save it as a TIF file using the default settings in your *Chapter 6* folder. Now you have a back-up copy. Leave the *FIXBoys* file open and close the *Boys* file.

DESIGN TIP

The Dust and Scratches filter is a great tool when a designer is given dirty or grainy slides and negatives with blue skies or solid background colors. Try also using the Median filter, another pixel-softening filter that works nicely, especially with single color blue skies. Applying these filters softens the details in selected areas without losing sharpness in the rest of the image.

MAKING SELECTIONS AND APPLYING THE DUST AND SCRATCHES FILTER

With any image or image selection, such as a solid color background or blue sky with slight imperfections or dust spots, the Dust and Scratches filter in the Filter menu can help to smooth out pixels to blend them in and remove small dust spots. This will provide a nice review of using selections.

▷ FIGURE 6-6

Use the selection tools and the Dust and Scratches filter to smooth out background imperfections.

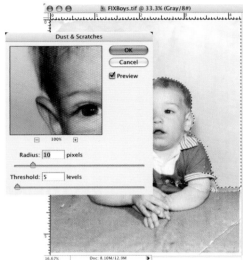

In this exercise, you will select the background area of the image with the Magic Wand and Lasso tools and blur the pixels to smooth out the stray selections; then remove dust marks and imperfections using the Dust and Scratches filter or the Median filter.

1. Select the Quick Selection tool and set the Brush size to 5 pixels in the Tool Options bar. Click on the Add to selection button, and then select the background, making sure the boys' ears are not selected. Feel free to try the Magic Wand tool to paint in your selections at a tolerance of 5 pixels to add to the selection.

2. Use the Lasso tool for editing the selection if needed. Use the Tool Options bar buttons to add to and subtract from selections. Feel free to click the Quick Mask icon in the bottom of the Tools panel for fine-tuning.

3. To eliminate any stray pixels from inside your selection, choose Select > Modify > Smooth > 2 > Pixels.

4. Save the selection as an alpha selection channel using Select > Save Selection. Name the channel *Background*. Now you will be able to edit this saved selection if needed.

5. With the background selected, choose Filter > Noise > Dust and Scratches. Click and drag the image in the dialog box to show part of the selected background. If you inadvertently deselect the background, use Select > Load Selection and choose your background alpha selection channel.

DESIGN TIP

The key to removing cracks and imperfections accurately is to zoom in very close and start working with a brush size just a little larger than the defect size; gradually increase the brush size to smooth out details.

6. Drag the Dust and Scratches window next to the image and enter these settings: Radius at 10 pixels, a Threshold of 3 levels, and check the Preview box (Figure 6-6). You can also try the Median filter (Filter > Noise > Median) and see which works best.

7. You will notice the matted surface of the scanned image when you zoom in on the image. Not to worry; we will adjust that later.

8. Toggle the Preview on and off to see the before and after of the applied effects on the background, or click and hold inside the preview image to see the original; let go to see the revision. Click OK when you are satisfied.

9. Click on the background to select it, then click the Refine Edge button on the Tool options bar and select the Black & White View Mask icon to smooth out the edge pixels. Try the settings shown in Figure 6-7 for starters, including placing a check in Smart Radius for increased accuracy, and click OK when done. To see the edge effects, click on the Show Original Preview button. You will blend in the imperfections next.

10. Save the file and leave it open.

TOOLKIT TIP In CS5, the Refine Edge dialog box contains a new Edge Detection function using Smart Radius. This feature helps to make highly precise selections of complex subjects easily, enabling faster, more accurate combinations of multiple images. You can then use the extra view modes to assist you in previewing the quality of your selections.

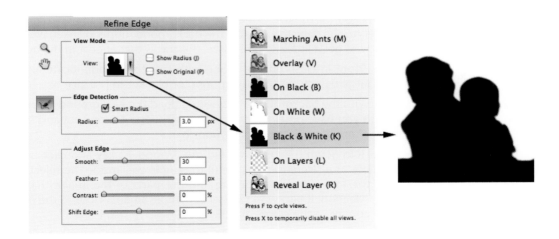

 FIGURE 6-7

Use the Refine Edge command to soften the selection edges.

THE CLONE STAMP TOOL

The **Clone Stamp tool** allows you to sample a group of pixels from a source area and transfer or clone those pixels to another area. This tool works great for replacing difficult spots and scratches in an image. To use the Clone Stamp tool successfully, hold down the Option (Mac)/Alt (Windows) key and click a clean area to sample from. This becomes your reference point. Click within the area to be replaced, making a short stroke with the mouse, and the sampled pixels replace the defective parts of the image. You need to continually sample and set different reference points to provide a final realistic effect.

TOOLKIT TIP Making realistic restorations with the Clone Stamp tool is accomplished by holding down the Option (Mac)/Alt (Windows) key and clicking on good areas and then applying those over the defective area by dragging the mouse in short movements. If you know you have just made a mistake, use the Command/Ctrl Z undo, or you can use the Edit > Step Forward and Step Backward commands.

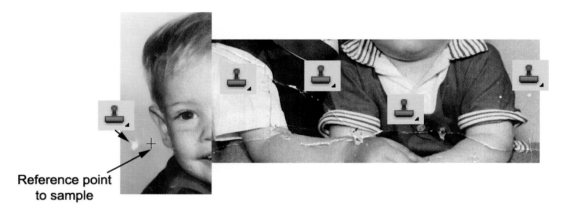

Reference point
to sample

▷   FIGURE 6-8

Use the Clone tool to practice replacing imperfections in the background, then replace the cracks on the shirts. Do not use the Clone tool on the skin.

Here, you will use the Clone Stamp tool to sample the source pixels and clone those pixels to the defective areas in the background, upper blanket, and—when you feel ready to get a little more precise—the cracks that appear in the boys' clothing.

1. Zoom in close on the image with the Zoom tool; locate any white spots or large defects on the background or blanket to practice on.

2. With the background still selected (load the Background channel as a selection if you have deselected it), select the Clone Stamp tool and enter a brush size of 40 pixels in the Tool Options bar.

3. Hold down the Option (Mac)/Alt (Windows) key and click on a good spot to use as a reference. Be careful to sample well inside the selected area, because the tool will also recognize and use parts of the image that are outside the selection. It also works better to sample an area close to the piece you want to correct so the colors match.

4. Drag a short stroke with the mouse on the area you want to replace, and you will notice a crosshair that shows the area you referenced, along with your brush icon as you replace the defective area with the pixels you sampled.

5. Continue Option/Alt clicking for new reference spots to replace the dust spots and general defects in the background. Sample inside the selection and constantly resample a good reference area.

6. To undo or redo previous actions, select Edit > Step Forward and Step Backward.

7. To sweep the background with a consistent shade, select a large, 100-pixel brush and use the Clone Stamp tool to make short sweeping motions.

8. Deselect the background.

9. Zoom the picture back to see the effects. When you are satisfied and feel comfortable working with the Clone Stamp tool, zoom in close on the white shirt on the boy on the left; you will notice a crack in the image (Figure 6-8).

10. Start the Clone Stamp tool brush size at 15 pixels, adjust as needed, and continue Option (Mac)/Alt (Windows) clicking periodically to consistently reference the sampled area, and replace the cracks on the boy's white shirt sleeve and on the blanket next to his elbow. If you find you cannot edit this area, make sure the background is deselected.

11. Be careful to constantly resample and use short strokes to maintain a realistic look.

12. Do not work on any skin areas yet; you will use the Healing Brush for that.

13. Save the file and leave it open.

 PROBLEM If the Clone Stamp tool does not seem to work, or you get a dialog box that indicates no pixels were selected, make sure you Option (Mac)/Alt (Windows) click the reference area first.

THE HISTORY PANEL

Say you started working on an image, but went too far and feel you may have to start over. With the History panel, your previous actions are recorded in what are called **states,** so you can go backward in a series of steps, as if going through multiple undos. You can click on a previous state or drag the most recent states into the Trash. You can save a state as a **snapshot** for later editing as long as the document remains open. You can create a new document from a snapshot and save it for later use. A snapshot allows you to record an image's state at a particular time in the editing process, and you can go back to that snapshot at any time as you experiment. Warning! As soon as you close a file, all those history states are removed, because they are not permanently saved. The amount of states displayed is limited, so it is a good habit to create a snapshot when an area is completed.

 TOOLKIT TIP The History panel is your quickest way to get out of potential trouble by dragging mistakes into the Trash or by selecting and saving a previous state layer. If you know you have just made a mistake, use the Command/Ctrl Z undo, or you can use the Edit > Step Forward and Step Backward commands.

The History panel allows you to go back and observe previous actions.

1. Select a previous state on the History panel to see some of the past actions you took. Notice that the more recent actions are undone (Figure 6-9).

2. Select the most recent action again, and continue your work with the Clone Stamp tool.

3. Continue using the Clone Stamp tool at 15 pixels or less to replace the cracks in the boy's plaid vest and the baby's shirt.

▷ FIGURE 6-9

The History panel allows you to select previous commands and to create snapshots at specific points in the most recent development of your work.

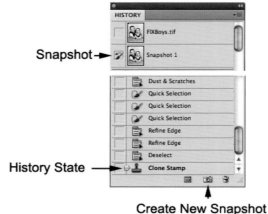

4. When you have completed the Clone Stamp tool exercise and feel comfortable with the work, click on the state layer of the most recent action at the bottom of the panel, then select the Create New Snapshot icon there. The snapshot thumbnail will appear on the top panel area under the original image, and it will be named *Snapshot 1;* you can leave the name as is or double-click it to rename it something more intuitive.

5. Save the file when you are finished, and leave it open.

THE PATCH TOOL

The **Patch tool** samples patterns and textures in an image. It analyzes the texture and lighting and matches the source pixels to blend in with a destination area. You drag around a selection the size of the area you want to replace, or a little smaller, click and drag it over to the defective area, and watch the source area blend into the defective area with the corrected texture, lighting, and color. Very cool! You can also choose and load preset patterns using the Tool Options bar for special effects.

In this exercise, you will use the Patch tool to replace the cracked area of the blanket; you will notice the lighting and texture will blend right in.

1. Select the Patch tool (it is underneath the Healing Brush if that tool is displayed) and choose the Destination setting on the Tool Options bar. This will allow you to select a good sample area and replace the defective destination area. Make sure transparent is *not* checked.

2. Scroll to the blanket area on the bottom right of the image where you will notice another crack in the image. Zoom in to observe the changes.

3. Make a freehand selection, much like you would with the Lasso tool, of an area near the defective area (Figure 6-10).

4. Click and drag the selection over the cracked area and, voila, the crack is gone! To deselect the Patch tool, choose Select > Deslect.

5. Save the file and leave it open.

▷ FIGURE 6-10

Using the Patch tool, create a freehand selection on the source to be sampled, then drag over the defective area to blend in the pixels.

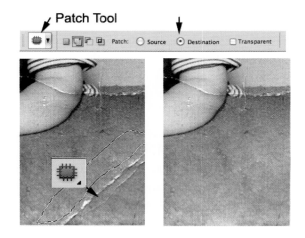

Create selection to sample and drag over area to patch

Crack replaced

THE HEALING BRUSH AND SPOT HEALING BRUSH

▷ FIGURE 6-11

The Healing Brush and Spot Healing Brush analyze and correct shading and textures to blend in pixels.

The **Healing Brush** tool works the same way as the Clone Stamp tool: by selecting a reference area using the Option/Alt key to establish a source, then clicking and dragging the mouse using a short stroke over the area you want to replace. The Healing Brush also works like the Patch tool: it analyzes the texture, lighting, and color and blends them in. These tools are wonderful for restoring portrait images. The **Spot Healing Brush** allows you to simply click on smaller areas that need to be replaced without having to use the Option/Alt key to set a sampled area. It makes the change automatically.

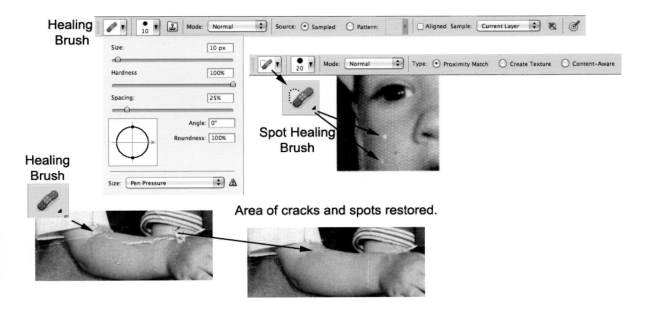

Area of cracks and spots restored.

TOOLKIT TIP In CS5, you'll find a Content-Aware button on the Tool Options bar that allows you to select an area to be replaced with the Spot Healing brush and then, when removed, can be filled in with the (content-aware) surrounding background. This was demonstrated in the Chapter 5, Digital Toolkit Extra exercises.

In this exercise, you will use the Healing Brush to replace the cracks and dust spots in the boys' arms and faces.

DESIGN TIP

Inverting a selection comes in quite handy when you cannot select a complex image too well. Select a same color area instead, then invert the selection to apply your effect. The Gaussian Blur filter is also a great tool for softening skin pores and blemishes in portrait images.

1. Use the Zoom tool to get in close to the boys' arms.

2. Select the Healing Brush with a brush size of 10 pixels to start. Leave the default settings in the Brush panel.

3. Option/Alt click a good reference area on one boy's arm and apply the Healing Brush effect with short strokes (Figure 6-11).

4. Zoom out to view the image, then zoom in to work on small areas. You can also use the Command/Ctrl followed by the plus sign or dash key to zoom in or out quickly.

5. Change the brush size as needed (remember you can use the bracket keys to do this quickly) and continue Option/Alt clicking different reference areas and applying the Healing Brush, watching how the texture and shading blend in nicely.

6. Use the History panel to help with any problems or save snapshots for reference.

7. Continue until the cracks are blended away.

8. Select the Spot Healing Brush tool, and with a brush size of about 10 pixels, just click on the dust spots on the boys' faces and the small areas on the arms to repair them. There is no need to Option/Alt click first with this tool.

9. When you have completed the restoration, zoom out to see your work. Save the file again as *FIXBoys.tif* in your *Chapter 6* folder.

TOOLKIT TIP You can use the Clone Source panel (Window > Clone Source) with the Clone tool or Healing Brush tools to set cloning from five different sources. There is an Overlay option that allows you to precisely position, rotate, and transform the destination brush stroke. This can also be used in working with video and animation projects.

SOFTENING A SCANNED MATTE SURFACE WITH GAUSSIAN BLUR AND THE BLUR TOOL

With the restoration complete, you will notice that the image of the boys shows the matte surface of the scanned image. To soften this matte surface, you can invert the background selection to select everything except the background, and then apply a **Gaussian Blur filter**. To help soften the edges so the boys do not look like cutouts, use the **Blur tool** on the edges with a 20-pixel brush and 50 percent strength (Figure 6-12) or use the Refine Edge function and soften the edges. Photoshop has an arsenal of filters to enhance, distort, or create special effects on selected portions of images.

TOOLKIT TIP If you want to invert any selection, you can choose Select > Inverse.

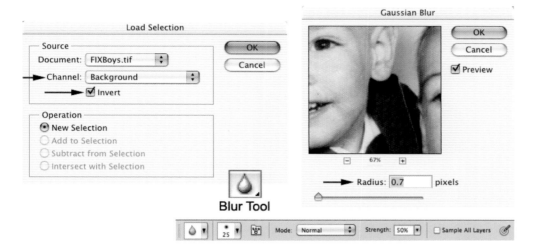

▷   FIGURE 6-12

Softening the matte surface of the scanned image by inverting the back- ground selection and applying a Gaussian Blur effect. You can also soften edges using the Blur tool to avoid a cutout effect.

Now you will select the boys and soften the matte surface.

1. With the *FIXBoys* file open, choose Select > Load Selection and select the *Background* channel you created earlier. Zoom in close to see the effect.

2. Make sure the Invert box is checked to reverse the selection, which will include everything except the background. Click OK (you can also choose Select > Inverse).

3. With the boys selected, select Filter > Blur > Gaussian Blur.

4. In the dialog box, select 0.7 Radius for affected pixels; check the Preview box to see the effect, which should be slight.

5. By applying a slight amount of blur, the image remains relatively sharp and the indentations of the old matte surface are significantly reduced. To view the before and after effects on the preview image, click and hold, then let go. Then select OK. Zoom back out when done.

6. With the boys still selected, use the Blur tool on the edges with a 20-pixel brush and 50% Strength to start softening the edges to avoid the cut-out look. It will show slightly when you paint later.

7. Save the file.

TRIMMING WITH THE CROP TOOL

The Crop tool (C) allows you to trim an image. You simply make a rectangular selection and the area outside the selection becomes shaded, so you can observe what will be removed. You can then move the selection around by clicking inside the selected area and dragging, or by using the arrow keys on the keyboard. If you need to adjust the size, click and drag from one of the control points on the marquee.

 TOOLKIT TIP You can also crop a selection using the Marquee tool and then choose **Image > Crop** to remove the area outside the selection.

▷　FIGURE 6-13

Final trim with the Crop tool.

Here, you will enter a set size in the Tool Options bar and select the area to remove with the Crop tool. Cropping the image will center the boys in the image area.

1. Select the Zoom tool and zoom out until the entire image displays. Make sure Rulers are displayed (View > Rulers).

2. Select the Crop tool and enter 4.0 inches for the Width setting and 5.0 inches for the Height in the Tool Options bar. These settings will create a proportionately sized selection when you drag your selection.

3. Click in the upper-left corner of the image and drag diagonally until it reaches 4 inches wide. You will see the outside selection area shaded. Use the arrow keys to position the selection area accurately.

4. Click the Crop tool icon again and select Crop to trim the image, or simply double-click inside the marquee (Figure 6-13). If you make a mistake, select Don't Crop.

5. Save the file. The image is now restored close to its original form.

COLORING THE BLACK AND WHITE IMAGE

The second part of this chapter deals with using color tools and panels to apply color to your black-and-white image. This involves converting the image color mode from Grayscale to RGB color, then selecting areas to be painted. You can create your own custom brush sizes and options in the Tool Presets panel, and you can select colors from the Swatches and Color panels.

COLOR MODES

Any image you are working with has a color mode. Images that are shades of gray are set in Grayscale mode, which is the color mode of your original restoration image. When you need to apply RGB colors to a Grayscale image, all you have to do is create a duplicate of the original and change the mode from Grayscale to RGB color. The default working color mode you would use initially while working on your computer is usually RGB color, which is also used as the default color mode for electronic display, as in web design, and for printing on desktop printers. If you were sending an image to a printing press, you would convert the RGB (red, green, blue) image to CMYK color (cyan, magenta, yellow, and black) for reproduction.

TOOLKIT TIP As mentioned in earlier chapters, when changing color modes, always make a file copy of each. When you are working with color in Photoshop, start with the default RGB color; then, if you need to convert to CMYK color for press, make a duplicate file of the RGB image, and convert the duplicate to CMYK color. It is a good idea to wait until all editing is complete before converting to CMYK, because many functions in Photoshop are disabled in CMYK mode. Now, you have two files for different purposes. Do not try to convert an image back from CMYK to RGB; it usually muddies up the colors.

▷ FIGURE 6-14

Changing the color mode from Grayscale to RGB to color the black and white image.

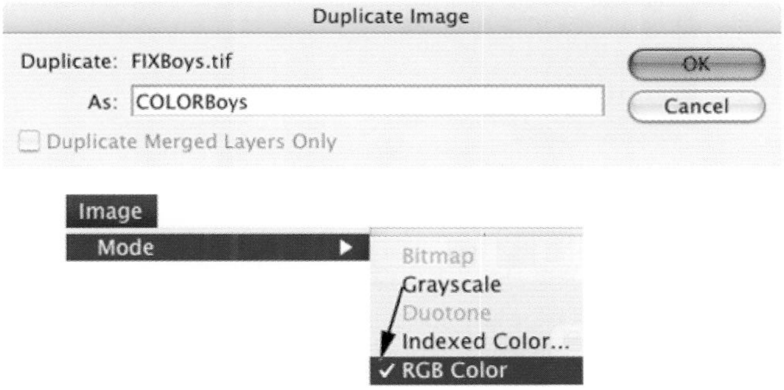

Here, you will duplicate the image and convert the Grayscale image to RGB color, so you can apply colors.

1. Select Image > Duplicate to make a copy of the black-and-white image.

2. Name the file copy *COLORBoys and save it.*

3. Close the *FIXBoys* file.

4. Select Image > Mode > RGB Color (Figure 6-14). Now you are ready to apply colors.

TOOLKIT TIP If you want to create an overall color cast in an image, try using one of the Photo Filter options (Image > Adjustments > Photo Filter). To create an old-fashioned sepia tone of the black-and-white image of the boys, duplicate the *FIXBoys* image again, change the mode from Grayscale to RGB color mode, then select Sepia from the Photo Filter options (see Figure 6-4). Adjust the Density setting to the desired effect. These filters can be used on individual layers as well for special effects.

PAINTING COLORS USING THE SWATCHES PANEL

The **Swatches panel** is a selection of predefined colors from which you can select a color and paint. When selecting a color from the Swatches panel, the Color Picker's foreground color on the Tools panel changes to that color. The Color panel will display the color mode settings for that color. You can also create your own color and add it to the Swatches panel. The key to painting is to use a sweeping motion with the Brush tool at a low opacity setting (Figure 6-15).

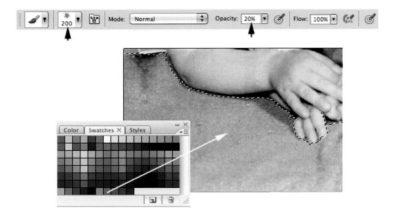

Here you will use the Swatches panel to select colors for the background and blan-ket, and you will paint using a large brush with sweeping strokes.

1. Select the blanket area using the Magic Wand tool with a Tolerance of 10 pix-els and Lasso tools for adding to and subtracting from the selection.

2. Choose Select > Modify > Smooth > 2 pixels to include any stray, unselected pockets. Click on the Refine Edge button on the Tool Option Bar, select the black mask, and soften the selection edges.

3. Choose a light brown color from the Swatches panel (see Row 8, Column 7).

4. Select the Brush tool (B) and select a soft-edge brush size of 200 pixels at 20% opacity for a much larger sweep. Make a few sweeps across the blanket. Use the History panel to track your progress.

5. To color the background, load the Background channel selection you created earlier (Select > Load Selection > Background), and then select a dark blue color from the Swatches panel with a larger, 600-pixel soft-edge brush at 20% opacity. Make a few sweeps across. Use the History panel to track your progress.

6. To soften the selection edges for a smooth color transition, use the Clone tool with a 30-pixel brush to start; Option/Alt click near the edges of the boys, then carefully outline those edges with the background and the blanket to fill in uncolored or stray pixels. This may take a number of tries, but it adds more realism.

7. Save the file in your *Chapter 6* folder when you feel comfortable with the image.

CREATING A CUSTOM BRUSH IN THE TOOL PRESETS PANEL

▷ FIGURE 6-16

The Tool Presets panel allows you to create and save your own custom brushes and other settings for tools.

Another panel in Photoshop is the Tool Presets panel. You can create a custom brush with special options, which you specify in the Tool Options bar. You can then save the customized brush for future images. Once you create your special tool, you can select it from either the Brush panel or the Brush tool's Preset Picker in the Tool Options bar. When you create a tool in the Tool Presets panel, give it a name that describes the settings or options for that tool.

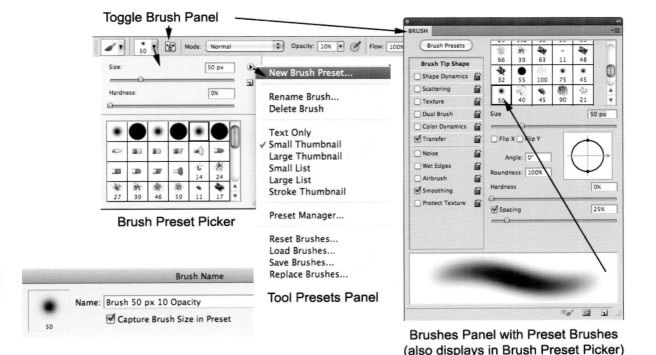

Toggle Brush Panel

Brush Preset Picker

New Brush Preset...

Rename Brush...
Delete Brush

Text Only
✓ Small Thumbnail
Large Thumbnail
Small List
Large List
Stroke Thumbnail

Preset Manager...

Reset Brushes...
Load Brushes...
Save Brushes...
Replace Brushes...

Tool Presets Panel

Brush Name

Name: Brush 50 px 10 Opacity
☑ Capture Brush Size in Preset

Brushes Panel with Preset Brushes
(also displays in Brush Preset Picker)

Here, you will create a large custom brush to paint with a low opacity using the Tool Presets panel.

1. Select the Brush tool and enter a Brush Size of 50 pixels with an Opacity setting of 10% in the Tool Options bar (Figure 6-16).

2. Click the arrow in the Brush pixel box to open the Brush Presets Picker. Select a soft edge brush and click on the panel menu to display the Tool Presets menu, then select New Brush Preset.

3. Name the tool *Brush 50 px 10 Opacity* and click OK. You now have a new custom brush that will be displayed in the Brush Presets Picker, and when you click on the Brush panel icon in the Tool Options bar, you'll find it is added to the Brush Panel, and the Brush Presets panel.

PAINTING WITH A CUSTOM BRUSH

After creating a custom brush that includes brush size and opacity settings, you can apply colors with these settings to any selected area. To color the black-and-white clothing of the two boys, you will select and create individual channels for each boy's clothing, select the colors, and paint using sweeping strokes.

 TOOLKIT TIP Only color over an area a few times, otherwise it will start to fill in too much and may look flat and unrealistic. Use the History panel to track and edit your progress.

Now you will select each boy's clothing, create channels to save the selections, and paint with the custom brush you created.

1. Select the boy's vest using the Magic Wand tool with a Tolerance of 10 pixels and Lasso tools for adding to and subtracting from the selection.

2. Choose Select > Modify > Smooth > 2 pixels to include any stray selected pockets.

3. Create a channel and name it *Vest* (Select > Save Selection > Name: *Vest*). Use the Refine Edge function to soften the selection edges slightly.

4. Select the Darker Green color from the Swatches panel (see Row 7, Column 7).

5. Select the Brush tool, and from the Tool Preset Picker in the Options bar, select the *Brush 50 px 10 Opacity customer brush* you just created (Figure 6-17). Click to place a check mark in the Current Tool Only box to reduce the list of presets. If you do not see the text description, select "Text Only" from the panel submenu to provide that option. If it does not show in the Preset Picker, look in the Brushes panel.

6. Sweep over the selected area of the vest with the mouse a few times.

7. Make sure the Add to Selection is deselected, then select the baby's shirt with the Magic Wand (with a 10-pixel tolerance) and Lasso tools the same way you selected the boy's vest.

8. Create a channel and name it *Baby Shirt* (Select > Save Selection > Name: *Baby Shirt*).

▷ FIGURE 6-17

To colorize a grayscale image, select the area to be painted, then select the new brush preset with low opacity. Choose the color from the Swatches panel, and apply a sweeping stroke over the selected area.

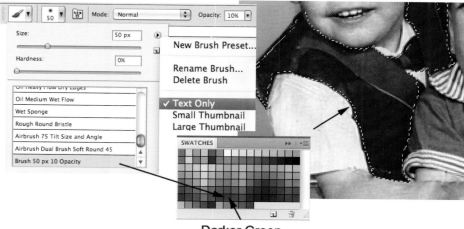

Darker Green

9. Choose a blue color from the Swatches panel (see Row 6, Column 11). Make a few sweeps across the shirt. Use the History panel to track progress or select Edit > Step Backward.

10. If you want to work in a smaller area, zoom in close to the stripes on the baby's shirt; select the stripes with the Magic Wand tool at a low tolerance, such as 5 pixels, and paint with the same light blue color from the Swatches panel.

11. Create a state snapshot on the History panel to return to this spot after the next exercise. Name the snapshot *Color Clothing*.

12. Save the file and try printing to a color printer.

USING THE COLOR REPLACEMENT TOOL

The **Color Replacement tool** replaces the color of a selected area with the foreground color. Although it is a little too vibrant for the subtle colors of the clothing just painted with the brush, it is a great tool to observe different colors on the same selected product, clothing, or other material. Instead of flat painting over a selected area, it also takes into account highlights and shadows and blends these in for a realistic look. But the Color Replacement tool does not blend colors together; it just replaces any color in a selected area. To paint colors more faintly, try using Edit > Fade Color Replacement Tool. The Fade command allows you to determine the amount of a color opacity being applied.

Now you will use the Color Replacement tool to apply the same colors to the boys' clothing.

1. With the *ColorBoys* file open, select the Darker Green color from the Swatches panel for the boy's vest.

2. Load the *Vest* channel selection (Select > Load Selection).

3. Select the Color Replacement tool with settings as shown in Figure 6-18 and paint with a 100-pixel brush. A very dramatic green color will display, replacing the subtle green you painted previously.

▷ FIGURE 6-18

The Color Replacement tool replaces selected colors and blends in highlights and shadows of the selected area.

Color Replacement Tool

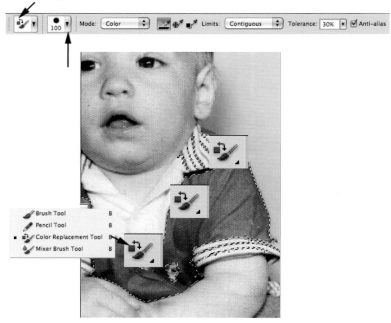

▷ FIGURE 6-18

4. Select a red color and paint over the selected vest again with the Color Replacement tool. The green color of the vest is replaced automatically with the red color. With the Color Replacement brush tool directly on the photo, try selecting Edit > Fade Color Replacement Tool at 75 Opacity to adjust it.

5. Select Edit > Step Backward to step back to the green color on the boy's vest. If you have used up more than 20 steps, you can revert to the snapshot you took in the previous exercise by clicking on it in the History panel.

6. For the baby's shirt, select a light blue color from the Swatches panel.

7. Load the *Baby Shirt* channel selection (Select > Load Selection). Use the Refine Edge function to slightly soften the selection edges.

8. Select the Color Replacement tool with settings as shown in Figure 6-18, and paint with a 100-pixel brush. Select a new color and paint again to see the difference.

9. Use the History panel to go back to the *Color Clothing* snapshot state you created in the last exercise.

TOOLKIT TIP If the History panel was not available, or you closed the file in the last exercise, you can select File > Revert to have the file brought back to the last time it was saved. Remember, when you close the file, the History panel does not permanently store states or snapshots.

SAMPLING AND APPLYING SKIN TONES

Sampling for skin tones and painting them on a black-and-white image is a little tricky, because you are still trying to create a realistic effect. To do this, you need to select only the skin areas first, not the eyes or mouth, on the black-and-white image. You can then use the Eyedropper tool to sample a closely matching skin tone color from another color image. The color must be applied carefully in a few sweeps with a large brush size and low opacity setting to avoid overlapping the color stroke lines.

SAMPLING AND PLACING COLOR WITH THE EYEDROPPER TOOL

The **Eyedropper tool** is used to sample and place a color in the Color Picker. It can sample color from a current image or another image. The sample will show its color mode information in the Color panel, if you need to record it. Once you have a sample color displayed in the Color Picker, you can add that color to the Swatches panel for later use by selecting the Create New Swatch of Foreground Color icon at the bottom of the Swatches panel.

In this exercise, you will sample a skin tone and save the color in the Swatches panel, then use the color on the selected skin areas of the boys.

1. Open the file *Myboys* in the *Chapter 6* folder.

2. Select the Eyedropper tool and click on the cheek of one of the boys. You will notice that the color is displayed as the foreground color in the Color Picker.

3. Select the Swatches panel and click the icon button Create New Swatch of Foreground Color to save the color. If you open the Color panel, you will notice the RGB values of the skin tone (Figure 6-19). If CMYK values are displayed, select RGB Sliders from the Color panel menu. Your values may differ. You can also click on the Color Picker, and when the display opens, select Add to Swatches button. The skin tone color will remain permanently on the

▷ FIGURE 6-19

You can sample colors of skin tones from other images with the Eyedropper tool, and then apply a wide brush over the selected areas of the image. You can then add the color sample as a swatch in the Swatches panel.

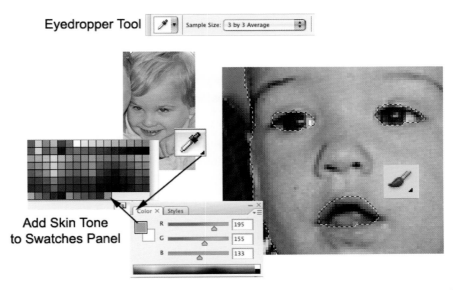

Eyedropper Tool

Sample Size: 3 by 3 Average

Color × | Styles

R | 195
G | 155
B | 133

Add Skin Tone to Swatches Panel

Need additional fun computer graphics tutorials and info, and an additional look at the projects you'll be creating in this book? Check out my Artist's Digital Toolkit website at: **http://www.digitoolkit.com**

Swatches panel. You can just click in the Swatches panel to add the color. Clicking inside the panel also lets you name your swatch.

4. Close the *Myboys* file; it was needed just to sample colors here.

5. Using the Lasso tool and the Magic Wand tool set at a 10-pixel tolerance, edit the selections; select the boys' faces and arms, excluding eyes, nostrils, and mouths. Use the Refine Edge function to soften the selection edges along the hair lines using the Black and White View.

6. Select the Brush tool set to 10% opacity, and use a large, soft-edge brush size of about 150 pixels to sweep a uniform color across the selected areas.

7. Use the History panel to keep track. This may take a number of attempts.

8. Save the file in your *Chapter 6* folder; if you have access to a color printer, print your work. You now have a nicely restored black-and-white image that has also been colored for a realistic effect (Figure 6-20).

▷ FIGURE 6-20

Colors including skin tones applied to restored B&W image.

Image Restored and Recolored

TOOLKIT TIP A new feature in CS5 involves a tool called the Mixer Brush. Let's say you completed painting in your predetermined colors using a regular brush as is being done in these exercises. For a painterly effect to your image, you can use the Mixer Brush to provide extensive control over a brush's wetness, define multiple colors on a single tip, mixing and blending to taste on your image, and select choices as to whether to clean or refill your brush, much as an artist would approach their painting. Photoshop's painting tools have Bristle Tips and Bristle Qualities incorporated to give you more control when painting. Go ahead and play with this tool when you have a chance.

ADVANCED USERS: Color Cast Correction by Neutralizing Shadow and Highlight Areas

Many images may have a color cast to them, whether from old age, or from incorrect color exposure or white balance with a digital camera. There are a variety of ways to correct this issue. One quick way that you will learn in this exercise is to find the darkest shadow black parts of the image and a highlight area with detail and remap the pixels using the black and white components as a guide to accurately bring all colors in the image. This same technique can also be used for old images that have a colorcast. The file provided is a digital image of flowers that had the wrong white balance setting. It was mistakenly set to incandescent light that would normally be used to photograph indoors with normal tungsten lights without a flash (would normally make images have an orange cast); however, the same setting used outdoors makes the image a blue cast. This problem happens quite often when people forget to adjust their digital camera settings.

Original Color Cast Image

Corrected Image

▷ FIGURE 6-21

Neutralizing shadow and highlights to correct color cast image.

FINDING HIGHLIGHT AND SHADOW DETAILS USING LEVELS

This technique again uses the Levels command described in the "Advanced Users" section in Chapter 3, but takes it a step further in that you can sample the highlight and shadow areas by setting their point as black and white which adjust all the pixels to those samples. Understand that this technique involves trial and error; if you find it bounces way off in tones, then cancel and try another area. The key is to first locate a shadow of darkest color areas with slight detail, then locate a highlight area with detail. In working with digital images, be careful when selecting highlight detail that it is not a pure white without detail. Otherwise your image may appear very washed out. In digital always look for highlight detail, as pure white cannot be corrected.

TOOLKIT TIP To neutralize shadow and highlight areas the key is to have the RGB channels the same number, the lowest for the shadow, and the highest for the highlight. When using highlight or the whitest area decide if you need to use an area that may have specular highlights or pure white, or highlights that need to have detail in the brightest areas. Works best with product and food photography, or old photos.

THE INFO PANEL

The Info panel is useful in looking at color from a numerical standpoint. You can move the eyedropper over an area and the RGB (or CMYK) values are displayed. The lower the numbers the more towards shadow detail, the highest numbers represent the highlight detail. The numbers range from pure black at "0" to pure white at "255" with mid-tones in between (120–140). An image with proper color balance will have the RGB numerical values close together in both the shadow and highlight areas. An image with a colorcast as in the *Bluecast* image you will be working on will obviously show an abundance of blue and green in the RGB values since the white balance setting was set incorrectly. Use the Info panel as a guide with the Levels eyedropper samplers to find the shadow and highlight areas that can be neutralized.

▷ FIGURE 6-22

Using the Info panel to find RGB values, setting the shadow black point with the Levels dialog box. Results display in Info panel.

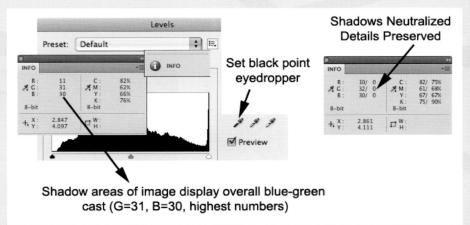

Set black point eyedropper

Shadow areas of image display overall blue-green cast (G=31, B=30, highest numbers)

TOOLKIT TIP Sometimes it's a good practice to neutralize the shadow areas first, taking care to watch for blocked up or black shadows in areas where there should be some slight detail, then neutralize the highlight detail, making sure glare or light refractions are not chosen. There needs to be some detail in the highlights, especially with digital images. When shooting images with a digital camera, always expose for the highlights first for detail, shadows are easier to readjust.

Here you will neutralize the shadow detail area first on the image.

1. Launch Photoshop, then open the file *Bluecast.tif*, duplicate the image (Image > Duplicate) and save in your *Chapter 6* folder as *BluecastADJ.tif*. Close the original *Bluecast* file and display the new *BluecastADJ* file it at 100%.

2. Select the Info panel ("i" in circle icon) to display, or select Window > Info.

3. Select Image > Adjustments > Levels and move the display next to the image.

4. Select the black eyedropper on the Levels display that indicates "Sample in image to set black point" and hover over the image observing the RGB values on the Info panel. You will notice most values display with an abundance of blue and green values, which you can easily see in the image itself (Figure 6-22).

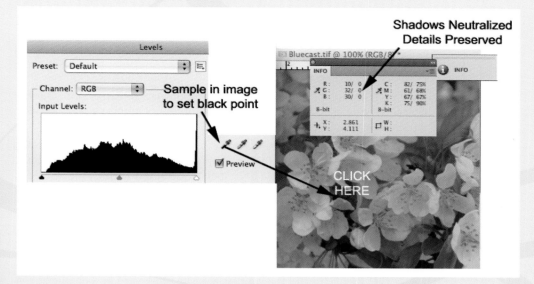

▷ FIGURE 6-23

Locating and neutralizing the shadow detail areas of the image.

▷ FIGURE 6-24

Setting the highlight or white point to readjust the colorcast to its correct colors.

5. Locate a shadow area under one of the flowers or leaves, or on the branch behind the leaves. Notice no values display a pure black "0" which is good, always look for shadow details that display in the "teens" for numerical values.

6. When you think you have pretty much the lowest number, click the spot to remap the RGB pixel values to "0" or close to the lowest number so that shadow details are not "clipped" away and are neutralized or spread out. Now the "0" or lowest number doesn't mean all your shadows are a pure black, the details are simply pulled out and remapped so that now the lowest number still indicates shadow detail (Figure 6-23).

7. If everything looks too dark or black, hit CMD + Z or your Mac, or Ctrl + Z on your PC to undo and try again.

8. Select the white eyedropper on the Levels display that indicates "Sample in image to set white point" and hover over the image observing the RGB values on the Info panel.

9. To set the highlight detail, find a white lower area that shows detail in the highlights. Use the Info panel to spot a white area closest to 255 here, which you'll probably find in the blue channel because of the colorcast.

10. Click on the bright white area of one of the flowers. You'll notice the RGB colors will be remapped to "255" each or close to that number (Figure 6-24).

11. If everything looks too bright, hit CMD + Z or your Mac, or Ctrl + Z on your PC to undo and try again. Select the highlight sample tool and try again, you can use the Preview button to observe the before and after effects.

12. When you look at the histogram on the Levels dialog box, you want the least clipping on both the highlight (far right) and shadow areas (far left) to show. You want as close to the entire "mountain" histogram as possible to show with little if anything cut off.

13. The final corrected image should not show any blown out highlights. Save the image in your *Chapter 6* folder. Feel free to open up the original *Bluecast* image to make comparisons. This technique also works great with old colorcast images as well.

TOOLKIT TIP Highlights are the trickiest areas to work with in digital imagery. When searching for highlights, make sure they are not metallic reflections or pure white that show no highlight details, or on the other side, shadow areas, otherwise clicking on these areas will wash out or block colors. The same goes for whether you are working with older images or recent digitally captured images.

NEUTRALIZING SHADOW AND HIGHLIGHT AREAS USING THE THRESHOLD COMMAND

Sometimes our eyes adjust very quickly to subtle changes in color, or as designers you may have received an image from a client who may not have as well-calibrated a monitor as you may have, or perhaps your own monitor may not be adequately calibrated. You can use the Info panel to see if there is any slight colorcast, and neutralize shadows and highlights by finding an image's black and white points to sample and remap the pixels. One feature that has been around in Photoshop for a while is called Threshold, which can be used to find true black and white areas with no guessing. It is found in the Adjustments section (Image > Adjustments > Threshold) or as an adjustment layer in the Layers panel (discussed in the following Toolkit Extra section). You may find this technique used by perfectionists working in the commercial or advertising industries where color is critical. Again the trick is finding black and white points, and all other colors will remap to those colors.

THE THRESHOLD COMMAND AND THE COLOR SAMPLER TOOL

The **Threshold command** works in conjunction with the Color Sampler tool. You use the Threshold command to find the darkest blacks and whitest whites, while **the Color Sampler tool**, although is used to sample colors, can also be used to create reference points for the black and white areas of an image that are transferred onto the Info panel. You can sample a series of adjacent sample areas too. After creating the reference points for optimum shadow and highlight areas,

Before   After

▷ FIGURE 6-25

Precision in neutralizing color casts using the Threshold command, Color Sampler tool, and Levels command.

you then use the Levels command black and white sampler eyedropper to click on the reference points to remap the shadows, highlights, and accurate color tones.

Here you'll use the Threshold command and the Color Sampler tool to sample the correct shadow and highlight areas. Make sure the Info panel is displayed. You'll find the shadow area first.

1. Launch Photoshop and open the *Plate.jpg* image. Make a duplicate image (Image > Duplicate) and save as *PlateADJ.jpg* in your *Chapter 6* folder.

2. Zoom in at 200% and use the Hand tool to position the image area to the front side of the plate.

3. Select the Color Sampler Tool. The Color Sampler tool is the eyedropper icon with a bullseye on it (Figure 6-26). It may be located where you may just see an eyedropper on the Tools panel.

4. In the Tools Option bar, select a 3x3 Average pixel Sample Size from the drop down menu for sampling adjacent colors. This is a good starting point so you don't select a stray off-color pixel.

▷ FIGURE 6-26

Using the Threshold command to find accurate shadow areas of the image. The Color Sampler tool is used to create point samples for reference.

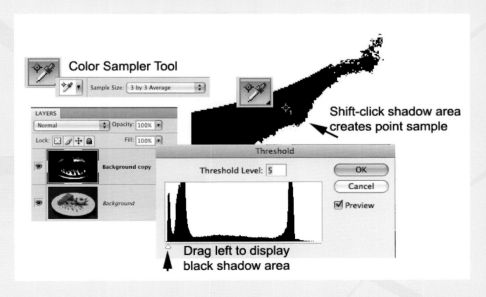

5. In the Layers panel, drag the *Background* layer onto the "Create a new layer" icon to duplicate the *Background* layer. Leave as the default *Background* copy. Make sure that the *Background* copy layer is selected.

6. Select the Threshold command in the Image menu (Image > Adjustments > Threshold). The *Background* copy layer thumbnail will appear black and white only along with your image.

7. You'll notice a histogram with a sliding arrow underneath in the middle. If you slide the arrow icon to the left it will display only darkest shadow areas, slide it to the right and it will display the highlight areas of the image.

8. To find the darkest shadow area, which will appear under the plate, drag the arrow slider from the default middle area to the left (Figure 6-27).

9. Shift-Click in the shadow area to set the color sample point #1 on that portion of the image area. It will display in the Info panel as #1 before and after number values with RGB color channels. DO NOT click OK.

10. Drag the slider to the right to find the highlight with detail that does not display bright light reflections as at the plate edges. Select the white area near the icing of the food and Shift-Click to set the color sample point on that portion of the image area. It will display in the Info panel as #2 for highlight RGB color channels (Figure 6-27). Select OK.

11. Click the eye icon next to the B&W Background copy thumbnail to see the #1 and #2 reference points on the image.

12. If you need to move either of the sample reference points you just made, move the cursor over the point (or Shift-click in earlier versions), the cursor turns into an arrowhead, and drag the point spot to move into place.

13. When you feel comfortable with reference points made, drag the Background copy layer with the Threshold adjustment into the Trash. The non-printable reference points will still display on the image.

▷ FIGURE 6-27

Locating the highlight area, no light reflections. Both #1 and #2 reference sample points indicated on the Info panel.

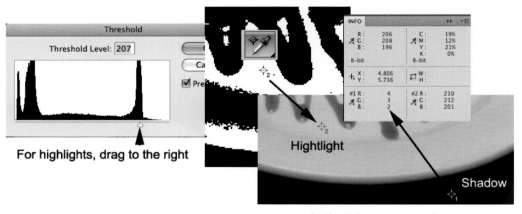

For highlights, drag to the right

Hightlight

Shadow

Shift-click to create reference point with Color Sampler tool

NEUTRALIZING COLORS WITH LEVELS SAMPLE POINTS

With the extra steps you just made creating the shadow and highlight reference points, all you need to do is use the eyedropper point samplers in the Levels display box to Shift-click on the points you created and Photoshop will remap highlights and shadows and all color toners to the black and white reference points with precision.

1. To neutralize the colors using Levels, still zoom in on the image about 200%, and select Image > Adjustment > Levels.

2. Select the Sample in image to select black point eyedropper icon and click over the #1 sample point (shadow).

3. Select the Sample in image to select white point eyedropper icon and click over the #2 sample point (highlight). You'll notice a major change here.

4. The color should be neutralized. Click the Preview button to see you before and after work. Click OK when satisfied. Notice how the adjusted white of the plate makes the food stand out better (Figure 6-28).

5. You may also notice on the histogram that the highlights show clipping or are cropped at the end, this represents the area of pure white on the plate from bright light reflections, and as long as the rest of the plate isn't "glowing" you have accurately remapped your image for best tonal representation.

6. To remove the reference points, drag the points as the mouse becomes an arrowhead out from the edge of the image. The point references will also be removed from the Info panel.

7. Save the file in your *Chapter 6* folder.

▷ FIGURE 6-28

Using the Levels command black and white sampler icons to click on reference points and accurately remap all tones and colors.

DIGITAL TOOLKIT EXTRA: Special Creations with the Masks Panel and Adjustments Panel

Here is a project that uses the concept of **layer masks**, which allow parts of an edited image to display (white area of mask), and block portions of an edited image from displaying (black area of mask) with various layers. This project also involves the use adjustment Layers, using the Adjustments panel to create layers of special adjustments without editing any pixels on the original layers. Using adjustment layers allows you to experiment with various effects without harming the original image. A designer or photographer would then create various layer masks to isolate the effects on certain selected areas of an image. In this project you are going to select the flag, increase the vibrancy of the colors, save the selection, then invert the selection to convert the background into an accurately B&W toned image, to emphasize the colors of the flag (Figure 6-29).

▷ FIGURE 6-29

Using adjustment layers and masks to create special compositions.

ISOLATING FLAG USING SELECTION TOOLS OR PAINTING QUICK MASK

Here you'll create a selection of the flag area using selection tools or try painting a mask using the Quick Mask tool on the Tools panel.

1. Launch Photoshop and open the *Patriot.tif* file from your *Chapter 6* folder. Make sure the Adjustments, Masks, Layers, and History panels are displayed.

2. Create a duplicate of the file and name it *PatriotADJ.tif*. Save in the *Chapter 6* folder.

3. Zoom in at 200%. Use either the Quick Select, Magic Wand and Lasso tools to start selecting the flag.

4. Create an alpha channel selection (Select > Save Selection) of the selected flag and name it *Flag*.

5. To continue on the fine details of your selection, make sure the flag is still selected, then go ahead and select the Quick Mask at the bottom of the Tools panel (Figure 6-30), select a Brush at 100% Opacity to paint Black as the foreground color to "add to" (red overlay mask) the selection of the flag, and White to remove areas that should not be part of the selection.

DESIGN TIP

In advertising, or in good design, there are always different techniques for emphasizing a subject. Use of color is one of the most effective ways. This project emphasizes the color of the flag against a B&W background to make the colors of the flag stand out for a sense of patriotism.

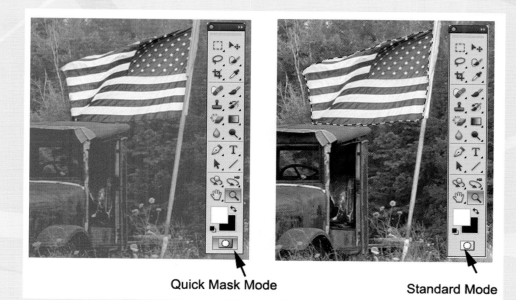

Quick Mask Mode   Standard Mode

▷ FIGURE 6-30

Use the selection tools, or Quick Mask as shown to paint in the flag selection.

6. Use the bracket keys on your keyboard for selecting quick brush sizes. Remember painting with white reveals, and painting with black conceals or masks the effect.

7. In using the Quick Mask option, to display the selection, just toggle the button to get back to Standard mode (earlier versions have two buttons at the bottom of the Tools panel), watch for the red mask and the red portion of the flag.

8. When all areas of the flag are selected accurately, save the selection again as *Flag* (Select > Save Selection) to replace the previous Flag selection channel.

9. Toggle the Quick Mask button to display the Standard mode, with the flag showing the selection marquee (Figure 6-31).

10. Select the Refine Edge button on the Tool Options bar. Choose the Black & White View mask and create a fairly sharp edge for the contrast between the color flag and the new B&W background you are going to create. Use the settings as a guide. Click OK.

11. Choose Select > Save Selection and choose the Flag channel you just created, making sure Replace Channel or Add to Channel is selected. Click OK.

CREATING ADJUSTMENT LAYERS AND LAYER MASKS WITH THE NEW MASKS AND ADJUSTMENTS PANELS

Using **adjustment layers** within an image allows a designer to create a series of layered effects over the original image that are non-destructible, so that the pixels in the original image are not manipulated. Adjustment layers have their effects on their own individual layers and can easily be edited. The **layer mask** provides a

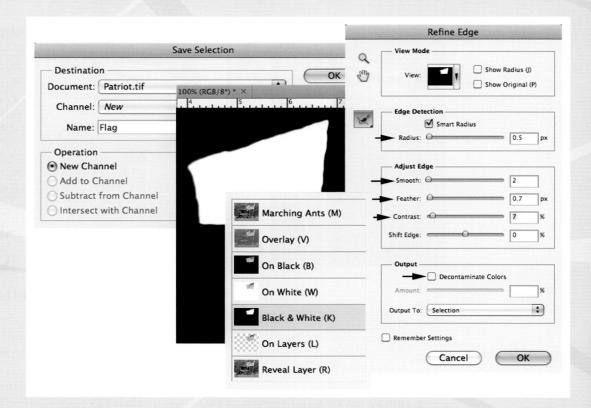

▷ FIGURE 6-31

**Saving the selection
and adjusting the
edge of the mask
of the flag.**

window for these effects as they trickle down through the layers, giving total control to the user. The **Adjustments panel** works alongside the Masks panel in
that as the Adjustments panel creates adjustment layers of a selected area, which
displays as the white area, and as a part of a layer mask on the Masks panel. Both
adjustment layer and layer mask of the selected area are displayed in their own
layer on the Layers panel. The Masks panel shows the pixel or vector mask on the
highlighted or selected layer. It can select by color range too so that a designer can
adjust the same color tones in an image. The Masks panel can invert or reverse a
selection, and it defines the selection edges using the Mask Edge function.

The **Vibrance command** adjusts color saturation on selected portions of an
image. Vibrance controls the intensity of saturated colors. It adjusts the saturation
so that clipping is minimized as colors approach full saturation. There is also a
Vibrance command in the Adjustments menu (Image > Adjustments > Vibrance).

TOOLKIT TIP If you are using an older version of Photoshop, the Layers panel has
adjustment layers and masks you can create by selecting the appropriate icon at the
bottom of the panel. The process is relatively the same as discussed in these exercises
using the Adjustments and Masks panels in CS4- and CS5 these new panels just make
the workflow much easier than was done previously using the Layers panel.

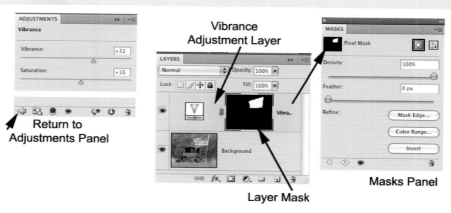

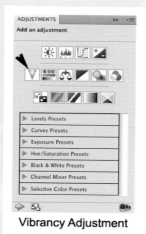

Vibrancy Adjustment

▷ FIGURE 6-32

Adjusting the vibrancy of color in a selection using the Adjustments panel. The mask selection displays in the Masks panel.

Here you will increase the saturation and vibrancy of the selected flag image.

1. Make sure the flag is selected. Select > Load Selection > Flag.

2. Select the Adjustments panel, and then select the new Vibrance icon. You'll notice a layer mask of the flag next to the thumbnail image on the Layers panel.

3. Increase the saturation and vibrancy of the colors (Figure 6-32). The background outside the selection layer mask is not affected.

4. When you have the color tones to your liking, click the "Return to adjustment list" arrow at the bottom of the panel.

5. Since both the Vibrance adjustment layer and the layer mask are on the same layer, you can click on the Vibrance icon to further edit the effect, and click on the layer mask, and you can paint the image black or whiter to add or remove part of the mask.

6. Deselect the selection on the image when done. Notice the pixel mask still displays on the Masks panel.

👆 **TOOLKIT TIP** It's best to start out thinking of using the Masks panel as first creating the selection and saving it as a channel within the image itself, then use the Adjustments panel to generate the desired effect, and then use the Masks panel to identify the layer mask that is created from the selection and adjust the mask edges for the transitioned effect. On the Masks panel, the Density slider controls how much of the image if at all shows through the mask, where 100% blocks the image area entirely. Feather controls the gradation of the selection edges. You might increase the Feather adjustment when lightening or darkening an area of a portrait so the transition of the effect is very gradual.

USING THE ADJUSTMENT PANEL'S "HAND TOOL" FOR PRECISE TONING

You can add many different adjustment layers as needed for various effects on the Layers panel. The Adjustments panel, in addition to providing many different effects to choose from, also provides preset settings, and the ability to customize your own presets on many of these effects. The Adjustments panel has a special "hand" tool on some of its display boxes that when following the indicated arrows, lets you make tonal adjustments over a small area that you drag over in the direction of the arrows. This allows you to make quick accurate adjustments on the fly with little effort. You can call this the "Adjustment Hand Tool" if you like. The Masks panel allows you to invert or reverse a selection area or mask.

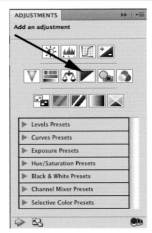

Select Black & White Icon

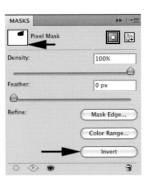

Invert the Flag Selection to Display Background

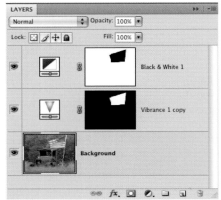

Adjustment Layers and Layer Masks Created Over Original Layer Image

▷ FIGURE 6-33

Adjustment and Masks panels create adjustment layers and layer masks on individual layers to control desired effects.

In this exercise, you are going to invert the selection using the Masks panel, and create a well-toned B&W background using the Adjustment panel's hand tool.

1. With the image open, load the Flag selection you created earlier (Select > Load Selection).

2. Select the Black & White adjustment layer icon from the Adjustments panel. Don't worry if the flag is black we're going to invert the selection.

3. With the Black and White adjustment layer created and highlighted on the Layers panel, select the Invert button on the Masks panel (make sure you have the pixel layer mask of the flag showing) to inverse the flag selection to become the background selection (Figure 6-33).

4. The background should be B&W and the colors of the flag should remain.

5. You can choose one of the B&W presets on the Adjustments panel, or find the "Hand tool" in the Black and White adjustments panel (not the Tools panel), select on a small area and drag sideways as indicated by the arrows, and create

your own visual B&W toning. You can also drag the sliders for each color, but the hand tool already senses color tones in an image and will lighten and darken those tones you drag within a small area; to cover all selected tones in the image (Figure 6-34). Very cool!

▷ FIGURE 6-34

Creating a well-toned black and white background using the Black & White Adjustment panel's hand "Adjustment tool".

6. When you have the black and white tones to your liking, click the "Return to adjustment list" arrow at the bottom of the panel.

7. Save the completed image as *PatriotADJ.tif* with its layers in your *Chapter 6* folder.

8. With the adjustment layers and layer masks saved, you can come back to the image at any time and edit the adjustment icon by clicking on it, or the mask itself by clicking on it.

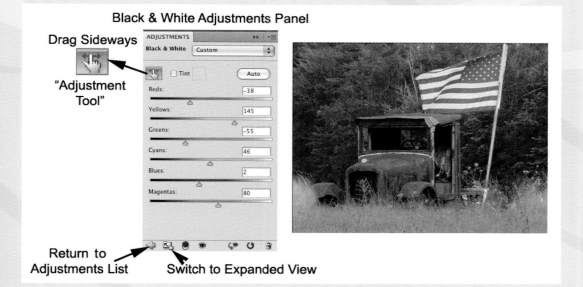

Black & White Adjustments Panel

Drag Sideways

"Adjustment Tool"

Return to Adjustments List   Switch to Expanded View

TOOLKIT TIP Just as was done years ago in a chemical darkroom, slightly lightening and darkening on selected parts of an image can be done digitally using the Dodge, Burn, or Sponge tools. Photoshop has greatly enhanced these tools to provide accurate lightening, saturating, and darkening of the tones of an image. Go ahead and try these tools on either the new *PatriotADJ* file you just created, on the original color *Patriot* file, or on your own work to see how you can carefully and precisely tone an image using these improved tools!

CHAPTER SUMMARY

Well, you have completed the restoration and retouching of an image in Photoshop. With so many tools available, you have almost limitless abilities to perform any restoration or editing procedure with confidence. You learned to repair cracks and defects with the Clone Stamp tool, the Patch, and various Healing Brush tools. You sampled colors and saved them in the Swatches panel, created a custom brush to add color to a balck-and-white image, and painted through previous states using the History Brush tool in the History panel. You also sampled skin tone colors from a color image and applied them to a black-and-white portrait. In the Advanced section you learned how to neutralize shadows and highlights to correct color casts, using the Threshold command, Levels command, and Color Sampler tool. In the Extra section, you learned how to use the new Adjustments and Masks panels to make spacial creations in adjusting color and B&W tones.

REVIEW QUESTIONS

1. Explain the difference between the Healing Brush tool and the Clone Stamp tool.
2. Explain the process of cloning a crack in an image.
3. Explain Grayscale, RGB, and CMYK color modes.
4. Explain how to create a custom brush in the new Tool Presets panel.
5. Explain how the History Brush tool is used with the History panel.

▷ FIGURE 6-35

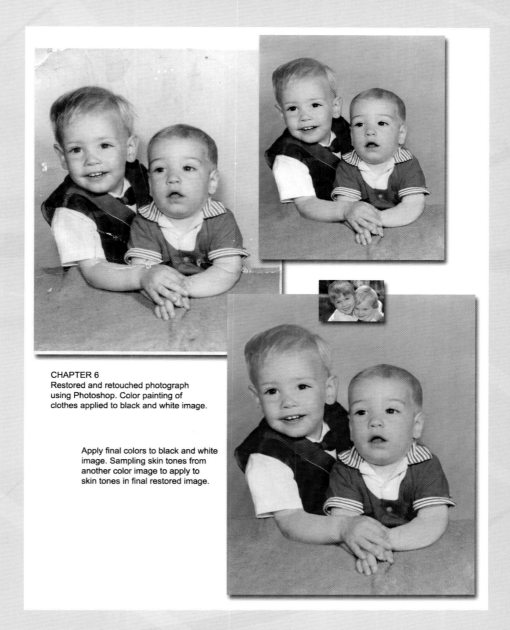

CHAPTER 6
Restored and retouched photograph
using Photoshop. Color painting of
clothes applied to black and white image.

Apply final colors to black and white
image. Sampling skin tones from
another color image to apply to
skin tones in final restored image.

▷ FIGURE 6-36

Original Color Cast Image

Corrected Image

Before

After

CHAPTER 6 ADVANCED
Neutralizing shadow and highlights to correct color cast images.

CHAPTER 6 EXTRA
Using adjustment layers and masks
to create special compositions.

2

Digital Image Editing: Adobe Photoshop CS5

Ever wonder how to put together a CD cover? Photoshop is the corner-stone of the digital editing industry, and you will use a lot of the tools, techniques, and functions that you learned in the preceding chapters in the making of this CD cover. You will also use a few new tools and tech-niques that will be introduced in this project to further your learning. You will be working with multiple images to create final composite CD cover images, and getting comfortable with managing display windows and images on your desktop to avoid too much clutter. Have fun!

CLIENT ASSIGNMENT: Creating a Music CD Cover

An alternative rock band called the Pundits is recording a CD of good old rockabilly and rhythm and blues in their own style, entitled *Back to Rock*. They schedule a meeting with you to discuss some ideas they have for their CD. After running through a series of thumbnail sketches, a final concept has been decided upon. The main cover image of a tunnel carved out of rock with a paved road going through it will be provided by the guitarist. The front cover will have an older car coming out from the tunnel, with the *Back to Rock* title engraved above the tunnel entrance, in the same basic curve pattern as the tun-nel. The back cover will have the tunnel image and CD title flipped, with a sports car parked facing toward the tunnel. The song titles on the back cover will be left aligned. The band members decide on a photo of a friend of theirs in his old '64 rambler and another photo the drum-mer has of his favorite sports car. You tell the excited band that by using these photos, you will be able to bring all the images and effects together and make the final image look realistic (Figure UR2-1).

Front Cover

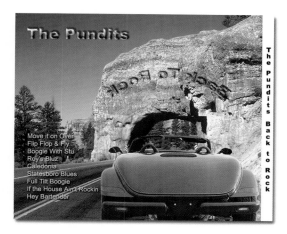

Back Cover

▷ FIGURE UR2-1

Front and back of the CD cover with spine.

Need additional fun computer graphics tutorials and info, and an additional look at the projects you'll be creating in this book? Check out my Artist's Digital Toolkit website at: **http://www.digitoolkit.com**

ACTION ITEMS OVERVIEW

Before putting all the elements together, this project is going to involve some detail work on the images. The image of the rock tunnel is old and needs some basic retouching, and it will also be cropped on the left side for the CD format. The cars need to be selected carefully and taken out of their backgrounds to be moved into the rock tunnel image later. The windshields of the cars need to be "clear" to show the road and background of the tunnel image they are being put into. The images will then be placed together and the text for the title of the band and CD name will be placed on the image.

For this project using Photoshop, here is what you need to accomplish:

- Create duplicates of the original images.
- Use the Crop tool to trim the tunnel image for the CD format.
- Clean the blue sky in the tunnel image with the Dust and Scratches or Median filter, and replace the oil mark on the road with the Clone Stamp, Patch Tool, and Brush tools.
- Use the selection tools to select and remove the cars from their backgrounds.
- "Clear" the glass in the windshields of the old Rambler and the sports car using the Eraser tools, so the background image shows through.
- Create the text for the CD title and the band name using Layer Style effects, and then create a duplicate image for the back cover and reverse the image.
- Place the car images on the front and back CD covers.
- On the back cover, place the song titles to the side of the sports car, and rotate the text line for the CD spine with the band's name and the title of the CD.
- Use the Unsharp Mask or Smart Sharpen filters to sharpen the final image.

DUPLICATING AND SAVING THE FILES

To make sure the original images are kept for backup copies, you need to make duplicate files of all three images that are going to be used in this project. Since there will be a lot of edits, save each file with a TIF extension to ensure image quality through all the changes you are going to make.

In this first exercise, you will open all three images, make duplicates, and save the new files. You will then close the original files for safekeeping.

1. Use Adobe Bridge to open the files *Tunnel*, *Oldcar*, and *Newcar* in your *Unit 2 Review* folder. Once you have opened them, you can quit Bridge.

2. Launch Photoshop. Duplicate each image (Image > Duplicate) and name the new images *TunnelCD*, *OldcarCD*, and *NewcarCD* respectively.

3. Save each image with a TIF extension with default settings for your computer in the *Unit 2 Review* folder.

4. Close the original *Tunnel*, *Oldcar*, and *Newcar* files, leaving the new files open. Use the Application bar's icon, Arrange Documents default setting (Consolidate All) to keep the files on their own tabs.

5. Select the *TunnelCD* tab to work on first, or in earlier versions, minimize the *OldcarCD* and *NewcarCD* windows on the desktop.

PREPARING THE TUNNEL IMAGE

To make the *TunnelCD* image ready, it needs to be cropped to CD size, sky areas must be cleaned, the oil mark on the road removed, and the pavement restored, so as not to detract from the final image.

CROPPING AND ADJUSTING THE IMAGE COLOR

The *TunnelCD* image needs to be cleaned and adjusted for color then cropped to size for the back cover first, since it is larger than the front cover size. You will use the Rectangular Marquee tool and place a fixed-size selection on the image and crop it using the Image menu. The edited image will then be duplicated and cropped later for the front cover size.

TOOLKIT TIP To adjust color casts, you can also try Image > Adjustments > Variations to see various color versions of the image. Check Photoshop > Help to play with this function. It allows you to click on a certain color cast of an image to bring in other options to add color to balance out the color cast.

In this exercise, you will select the sky with the Magic Wand tool and use the Dust and Scratches filter to clean it. Here are some options to try also.

1. Make sure the *TunnelCD* image is open.

2. To adjust the colors, because there is slight magenta color cast, select Image > Auto Color to restore the original colors to this old photo; or try Image >

Adjustments > Color Balance, and add 5 points of green and 5 points of blue for starters, or simply adjust to create a blue sky and grey pavement.

3. Select the Magic Wand tool, set the Tolerance to 30 pixels, and select the sky; then use the Lasso tool to add to the selection any stray areas. Use the Refine Edge function to soften the transition edges a little, setting the Smart Radius at .5 pixels, and Smooth at 1 pixel. Click OK.

4. To smooth out and remove the graininess in the sky select Filter > Noise > Dust and Scratches with a setting of 5 pixels Radius and 3 levels Threshold to clean and smooth out the sky area. You can also try Filter > Noise >Median with a setting of 5 pixels. Compare which works best and apply. Save the selection as SKY (Select > Save Selection> New Channel> SKY). Deselect the selection.

5. To crop the image, select the Rectangular Marquee tool and enter a Fixed Size Style with a Width of 5.75 inches (5.75 in) and Height of 4.75 inches (4.75 in) in the Tool Options bar (Figure UR2-2).

▷ FIGURE UR2-2

Marquee fixed-size settings to crop for CD back cover.

6. Click to display the selection on the right side of the image and move into place using the arrow keys on your keyboard. Use Figure UR2-1 as a guide.

7. Select Image > Crop, and Save the file as TunnelCD.tif. You can also choose to use the Crop tool instead; make sure you use the appropriate dimensions in the Options bar. Click Select > Deselect.

FIXING THE ROAD

When given an image, it is important for the designer to carefully observe and repair any defects and remove distractions that may draw a viewer's attention

▷ FIGURE UR2-3

Use the Patch tool to replace the oil mark, the Clone Stamp tool to replace smaller detail areas, and then paint in the white stripe with the Brush tool.

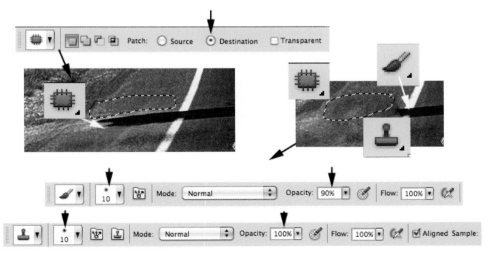

away from the intended message of the final image. In this section, you will remove the distracting oil stain on the pavement and finish painting in the white stripe using the Patch, Clone Stamp, and Brush tools. The Patch tool is located with the Healing Brush tools as one of the retouching tools.

Next, you will use the Patch, Clone Stamp, and Brush tools to remove the oil slick and paint in the white line on the road.

1. To remove the oil mark on the road on the left side of the image, zoom in to about 200% with the Zoom tool (click and drag around the area you want to work on).

2. Select the Patch tool with Destination checked in the Tool Options bar to make a freehand selection of a good portion of the pavement (Figure UR2-3). Do not select the white stripe area—you will deal with that in a minute.

3. Drag the selection over the stain and watch the new pixels blend in nicely. Deselect the selection when done (Select > Deselect). Repeat this process until the road looks natural to its surroundings.

4. Use the Clone Stamp tool with a brush size of 10 pixels to replace the rest of the pavement next to the white stripe. Option/Alt click frequently to sample new pixels of the pavement on both sides of the white stripe without selecting the stripe itself. If it still looks a little unnatural, use the Patch tool again to blend in.

5. Use the History panel to undo and redo your work and save snapshots if needed.

6. Zoom in to 300% to paint in the white stripe, then sample the color of the white stripe by clicking on it using the Eyedropper tool.

7. Select the Brush tool and enter a brush size of 10 pixels with 90% Opacity. Paint in the white stripe with the white, sampled foreground color to match the rest of the road.

8. When you feel comfortable with the road repair, zoom out to full view again.

9. Save the *TunnelCD* file in TIF format with the default settings.

USING SMART SHARPEN

Smart Sharpen pinpoints those fuzzy areas then need to be brought back into sharp focus. You will notice that the tunnel entrance is a little soft due to the scanning of an old slide film image that may have been slightly curved. This is where a designer would look at details from scanned images for anything that may need further adjustments or enhancements.

You will select this area and use Smart Sharpen to sharpen that area.

1. Select the Quick Selection tool and, with a 5 pixel brush size, drag around the soft roof area of the tunnel.

2. Select Filter > Sharpen > Smart Sharpen, and use the settings in Figure UR2-4 as a guide. You don't want to over sharpen, but to sharpen enough so it matches the surrounding rock. Click OK when done.

3. Deselect the selected rock and save the file.

▷ FIGURE UR2-4

Use Smart Sharpen to sharpen those soft areas of an image.

PREPARING THE CAR IMAGES

The car images need to be completely removed from their backgrounds, and the windshield glass "cleared" so they look realistic in front of the tunnel. You will use the various selection tools and eraser tools to prepare the images, and save each car selection as a channel.

SELECTING THE VEHICLES

As with selecting the kayaks earlier, use the selection tools to remove the two car images from their backgrounds and permanently save the selections as channels.

TOOLKIT TIP Try clicking on the toggle icon to display Quick Mask mode at the bottom of your Tools panel; you normally work in Standard mode. Zoom in to about 200% to look for details of any part not selected. Using mostly the Pencil tool with a 5-pixel brush size or smaller, paint with white to remove the mask in any areas within the car. Paint with black to add to the mask in the background. Select Standard mode to see the original image.

Here you will select the cars and save the selections as channels (Figure UR2-5).

1. Select the *NewcarCD* tab, or in earlier versions open the window you minimized previously.

2. Use the Lasso tools to select most of the car (try using the Polygonal Lasso tool to select straight edges), then use the Magic Wand or Quick Selection tool with a small brush setting to add to or subtract from the selection until the entire car is selected.

3. Use the History panel to help with your editing.

4. Save the selection as a channel with the name *NewSELECT* (Select > Save Selection > NewSELECT), then click OK.

▷ FIGURE UR2-5

Saving the selections of both new and old car images as permanent channel selections.

5. Zoom in to 200% and make sure the entire car is completely selected, no shadows. Continue resaving the selection in the *NewSELECT* channel until completed.

6. Save the file as *NewcarCD.tif* with default settings for your computer in your *Unit 2 Review* folder.

7. Select the *OldcarCD* tab to work on the classic Rambler.

8. Repeat the same procedure and save the selection as a channel named *OldSELECT*. Remember: you are only saving the selection.

9. Save the file as *OldcarCD*.tif in your *Unit 2 Review* folder and leave it open.

CLEARING THE WINDSHIELDS

In order to bring in the car image and have it look realistic, the windshield needs to be "clear" to show the background of the image it is being moved into. You need to subtract from your selection to delete the windshield area. To remove background area behind the windshield, you will need to delete the windshield from the car selection, then invert the selection to include the background and windshield. This requires attention to detail.

▷ FIGURE UR2-6

Selecting the windshield and removing the background to make the image composite realistic.

In this exercise, you will use the selection tools again to select the windshield area and add to the channel selections on both images.

1. Make sure that the background color on the Tools panel Color Picker is set to white and the car is still selected. If it is not, use Select > Load Selection and use the *OldSELECT* channel to make it active again.

2. With the file *OldcarCD* open, select Subtract from the Selection button on the Tool Options bar and use the Magic Wand tool (10 pixels) to select the

windshield, and finish up with the Lasso tool. Do not worry about the vent windows in our example.

3. Save the combination car and windshield selection (Selection > Save Selection) and select the channel *OldSELECT* again, replacing the previous channel selection in the Channels panel.

4. Invert the selection (Select > Inverse) to include the background and windshield. Use the Refine Edge function with a Black and White mask to soften the edges by roughly 1 pixel, to determine if you need to paint to add to or subtract from the selection.

5. Press the Delete key to remove the background and windshield; the background and windshield should appear white, if the Fill dialog box appears (CS5) choose Background color (white). Make sure no areas of the car are removed when you delete the background (Figure UR2-6). If there are, undo the action (use the History panel to go back to a previous state, or Command/Ctrl Z) and keep editing and saving the selection. Deselect the selection when done.

6. Save the file in your *Unit 2 Review* folder when the selection is complete.

7. Repeat the same process with the *NewcarCD* file (Figure UR2-7).

8. Save the file in your *Unit 2 Review* folder. Leave both images open.

THE MAGIC ERASER TOOL AND THE HISTORY BRUSH

One of the retouching tools is the **Magic Eraser tool.** It simply erases a single color background on the image to make it transparent. Use this tool when you want to bring different images together without any backgrounds. This way, when you bring the images into the tunnel image, the road of the tunnel image will display through the windshields. The **History Brush** is used in conjunction with the Eraser tools and other retouching tools, and is useful for painting back original areas that had been mistakenly erased by one of these tools.

▷ FIGURE UR2-7

Background removed and windshield cleared using various selection tools, the History Brush tool, and the Magic Eraser.

Here, you will use the Magic Eraser tool and History Brush tool to make both the background of the cars and the windshields transparent.

1. Select the *NewcarCD* file and double-click the background layer to make it a normal layer with a transparent background. If it does not show, name the new layer *Background*.

2. Zoom in 200%. Select the Magic Eraser tool with a Tolerance of 10 pixels to make the rear windshield of the car and background transparent; it should look like a checkerboard. (See Figure UR2-6.)

3. Click on the white background areas until all areas outside of the selection are transparent. Use the History Brush to carefully paint back any parts of the original image if needed starting with a 5 pixel brush.

4. Repeat the same process for the *OldcarCD* file (Figure UR2-7). Crop the image to just show the top portion of the car, beginning at the top of the bumper (Figure UR2-8).

5. Save both files.

6. Minimize the *NewcarCD* and *OldcarCD* images. You will be bringing the cars into the tunnel image soon. Maximize the *TunnelCD* file window for the next exercise.

▷ FIGURE UR2-8

Using the Selection and Magic Eraser tools to remove the background and windshield area.

 TOOLKIT TIP Try with the NewcarCD image area selected, to load the selection again and use the Masks panel. With the selections, click on the Add to pixel mask and a selection mask will be created removing the background automatically. You can then paint areas of the mask for best accuracy. Try this technique with the Old car image to experiment. The Masks panel is a very powerful tool.

CREATING THE TITLES AND CROPPING THE COVERS

Here you will create the CD title *Back To Rock* and make it look like it is chiseled into the rock of the tunnel using a combination of Layer Style effects, the Create Warped Text function, and the Screen blending mode. Blending modes affect the way layers blend with one another. The Screen blending mode on the Layers panel screens or lightens the colors of the layers above—in this case, the lettering will blend with the background layer to make them appear chiseled in the rock. The band's name, The Pundits, will be placed in the sky area of both the front and back covers with Layer Style effects. Then the *TunnelCD* file will be duplicated, cropped to size, and reversed with "Back To Rock" backwards for the back cover, but the band's name will read correctly. The spine where the band and CD titles are placed will use vertical type.

CHISELING EFFECT USING WARPED TEXT, LAYER STYLES, AND SCREEN BLENDING MODE

The type tools have a warped text function to bend or curve type lines to a specific shape. In this exercise, you will use the warped text feature to match the curvature of the tunnel and apply the special Layer Style effects, Bevel and Emboss, and use a Drop Shadow to make it look like it is chiseled. **Blending modes** in the Layers panel dictate how one layer blends onto the layer below it, by contrast, tonality, or color for all kids of special effects. In this exercise you will apply a Screen Blending mode to make the lettering take on the color of the rocks and appear to blend into the rock.

▷ FIGURE UR2-9

Using the Create Warped Text command to bend the type line.

Here is how to create the effects.

1. With the *TunnelCD* file open and zoomed to 100%, select the Horizontal Type tool and set the font to 24-point Arial Black Regular with a Strong Anti-alias in the Tool Options bar. Make sure the Foreground text color is set to black.

2. Click above the tunnel and type "Back to Rock," then highlight the text.

3. Select the Create warped text button on the Tool Options bar to bring up the dialog box (Figure UR2-9).

4. Choose the Horizontal Arc Style with a 50% Bend, then select OK.

5. Select the Move tool and drag the type line into place above the tunnel entrance.

6. Click the Add a layer style icon at the bottom of the Layers panel ("fx" icon) to apply a Drop Shadow effect as shown in Figure UR2-10, including entering the angle of *minus* 126 degrees and other settings shown.

7. Make sure Layer Knocks Out Drop Shadow is also checked in the middle of the display. After creating the drop shadow layer style settings, place a check in the Bevel and Emboss style *before* you create the next layer style.

8. Without exiting the layer style dialog box, double-click the Bevel and Emboss option and match the settings in Figure UR2-10 to create a chiseled look in the rock. Click OK when you have finished.

9. To make the effect of chiseling into the rock, select Screen blending mode in the Layers panel.

10. Save the file.

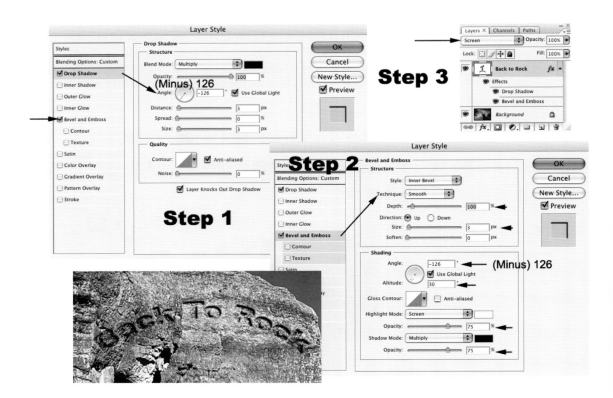

▷   FIGURE UR2-10

Using layer style settings and Screen Blending mode for the chiseled effect in the CD title.

CREATING THE BACK COVER AND SPINE

Now that all the editing has been done to the tunnel image, the image needs to be duplicated to be used as the back cover with a spine added for the band's name and CD title and for the front cover. The back cover image will also be flipped so the CD title reads backwards. Flipping or rotating an image is done in the Image menu. To type the title of the CD and band's name vertically on the spine of the back cover image, you will use the Horizontal Type tool, then rotate the text line using the Transform command. The **Transform command** in the Edit menu allows you to move, rotate, reflect, scale, skew and flip an image or text in specified degrees or amounts.

It is time to duplicate and flip the tunnel image, reverse it for the back cover, and create the type for the band's name and CD title on the spine.

1. Select Image > Duplicate to copy the *TunnelCD* file. Name the copy *Backcover*.

2. Make sure the *TunnelCD* image remains active; you will use it for the front cover later.

3. Make sure the *Backcover* image is displayed.

▷ FIGURE UR2-11

**Rotating text
to create the
CD spine.**

4. Select Image > Image Rotation (Rotate Canvas in earlier versions) > Flip Canvas Horizontal to reverse the image. The chiseled "Back To Rock" line will also appear reversed. Yep, the client wants this effect.

5. To create a space for the spine, select the Rectangular Marquee tool and select the Fixed Size Style in the Tool Options bar. Type in a fixed size of ".25" in Width and "4.75" in Height and use the arrow keys to position the selection to the rightmost edge of the image. Don't go beyond the image area.

6. Select the *Background* layer on the Layers panel and press the Delete key to remove the background. In CS5, if the Fill dialog box displays, select Background Color (white).

7. To make the vertical text spine for the CD back cover, select the Horizontal Type tool, using 14-point Arial Black in the Tool Options bar. Select black for the color and click on the Center Text icon on the Tool Options bar. Leave Strong for the anti-alias.

8. Type in "THE" (space bar twice) "PUNDITS" on the sky area; then hit the space bar nine times and type "Back To Rock" placing two spaces between words. Select Edit > Transform > Rotate 90 degrees CW to make the text line vertical. Use the Move tool and arrow keys to position the vertical text line centered in the white area at the right.

9. Save the file as *Backcover.tif* in your *Unit 2 Review* folder using the default settings. Click on the Move tool to deselect the text.

CROPPING FOR THE CD FRONT COVER

The front cover is narrower than the back cover and needs to be cropped to fit the front cover case. You can use either the Rectangular Marquee tool or the Crop tool to trim the TunnelCD image to size. Here, you will use the Crop tool.

▷ FIGURE UR2-12

**Cropping the image
for the front cover.**

Here is where you will crop the *TunnelCD* to size for the front cover (Figure UR2-12).

1. To crop for the CD front cover size, select the *TunnelCD* file.

2. Select the Crop tool, entering the Width to 4.75 inches and Height to 4.75 inches in the Options bar to allow a little room to be able to close the case. Click in the top left corner, then drag right all the way to the bottom of the image.

3. Use the arrow keys to move the marquee to the top and right side of the image.

4. Click on the Crop tool again and click Crop.

5. Save the *TunnelCD* file. This will now be your front cover.

CREATING THE BAND NAME

It is time to create the type for the band's name and apply Layer Styles on both the *Backcover* and *TunnelCD* files.

1. Maximize the *Backcover* file and select the Horizontal Type tool. Use 24-point Arial Black Regular with a Strong Anti-alias in the Tool Options bar.

2. Type "The Pundits" in the sky area (Figure UR2-13). Keep the Type layer highlighted on the Layers panel.

3. Click the Add a layer style icon at the bottom of the Layers panel to apply the effects and settings as shown in Figure UR2-12. Start by selecting the Drop Shadow Layer Style, determine your settings, and then double-click on the Bevel and Emboss option to establish those settings. Then just add a check in Gradient Overlay to complete the effect. Go ahead and experiment if you want, creating your own type style.

4. Position the type with the Move tool and Save the file. Minimize the *Backcover* window.

5. Select the *TunnelCD* (front CD cover) and repeat steps 1 through 4.

6. Save the *TunnelCD* file. Leave the file open for the next exercise.

▷ FIGURE UR2-13

Layer style settings for the band name, the Pundits.

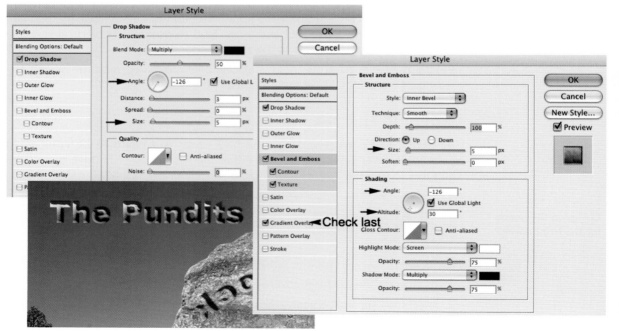

COMBINING IMAGES AND ADDING SONG TITLES

Now that you have done the hard part, it is time to put these images together. The front cover will have the old car and the back cover will be reversed showing the sports car. In the final exercise, you will add the song titles, and then you will be done!

▷ FIGURE UR2-14

Placing the car images onto the CD cover and adding song titles.

Move it on Over
Flip Flop & Fly
Boogie With Stu
Roy's Bluz
Caledonia
Statesboro Blues
Full Tilt Boogie
If the House Ain't Rockin
Hey Bartender

In this exercise, you will position the cars for the CD covers as shown in Figure UR2-14 and sharpen the final image with the Unsharp Mask filter or try the Smart Sharpen filter.

1. Open the image *TunnelCD* and maximize the *OldcarCD* window. Resize and position the windows next to each other.

2. Select the Move tool and drag the *OldcarCD* image onto the front cover *TunnelCD* image, positioning it as shown in Figure UR2-14. Do not show the tires. The old car will automatically be placed on its own layer. Rename the layer *Old car*.

3. To sharpen the tunnel image, select one of the image layers at a time, then select Filter > Sharpen > Unsharp Mask and enter settings of 70 for Amount, 1 for the Radius and 2 for Threshold. Click OK. To try to use the Smart Sharpen Filter instead, select Edit > Undo before saving. Then select the Smart Sharpen filter (Filter > Sharpen > Smart Sharpen) and judge how you want it to look: not to make it too sharpened that it looks obvious. Check the Preview and decide which method works best.

4. Save the *TunnelCD* in TIF format in your *Unit 2 Review* folder.

5. Close both the TunnelCD and OldcarCD files. The front cover is finished.

6. Maximize the *Backcover* image window and open the NewcarCD image.

7. Select the Move tool and drag the *NewcarCD* image into the *Backcover* image, positioning it to the right of the image as shown in Figure UR2-14; do not show the tires.

8. Close the *NewcarCD* file and leave the *Backcover* file open.

> **TOOLKIT TIP** Create layer comps that show "Back To Rock" placed on the tunnel, the tunnel image with the car, and the tunnel image by itself. This will help you understand the process. The Dodge, Burn, and Sponge tools have been greatly enhanced so a designer can apply slight variations of toning in lightening, darkening, or saturating parts of an image using these tools as brushes without having to select first. Try these tools on your own images. Welcome to the digital darkroom!

ADDING SONG TITLES

 Need additional fun computer graphics tutorials and info, and an additional look at the projects you'll be creating in this book? Check out my Artist's Digital Toolkit website at: **http://www.digitoolkit.com**

In this exercise, you will enter the song titles on the back cover and create a drop shadow effect.

1. Make sure the *Backcover* file is open.

2. Select the Horizontal Type tool and use 10-point Arial text. Select white for the color, then select Left Align in the Options bar.

3. Click on the left side and type "Move it on Over."

4. Select the Layer Style effect Drop Shadow (Layer > Layer Style > Drop Shadow) and use its default settings or create your own. If this is affecting other layers, make sure the layers aren't "linked" together.

5. Continue typing the following songs and the drop shadows will automatically be created: "Flip, Flop, and Fly," "Boogie with Stu," "Roy's Bluz," "Caledonia," "Statesboro Blues," "Full Tilt Boogie," "If the House Ain't Rockin," and "Hey, Bartender" (Figure UR2-14). If drop shadows are not created automatically, Option/Alt copy the effects from one line to the next.

6. To sharpen the composite image a little, select one of the image layers at a time, then select Filter > Sharpen > Unsharp Mask and enter settings of 70 for Amount, 2 for the Threshold, and 1 for the Radius. Or, you can use the Smart Sharpen filter instead for a little more control. Select OK when you choose which method works best.

7. The back cover is done. Save the *Backcover* file in TIF format with default settings in your *Unit 2 Review* folder.

> **TOOLKIT TIP** To experiment with the car images, feel free to use the Adjustments panel to add "Vibrance" to the red car image, or try making the new car image a "Black and White" image, or, select the color as done in Chapters 4 and 5 and paint a candy apple red color. Try making your own image composites for a CD cover. You can also create custom sizes for CD's (File > New > Preset-Custom). More Photoshop tutorials and info in the Goodies folder in your text CD.

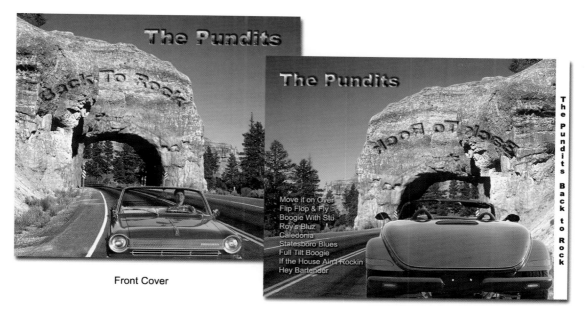

Front Cover

Back Cover

Images used for CD covers

UNIT II REVIEW
Creating the CD covers (front and back)
from multiple images using Photoshop.

▷ FIGURE UR2-15

Creating Shapes with Illustrator

CHAPTER OBJECTIVES: To understand Illustrator's basic functions in digital illustration, in this chapter you will:

▷ Learn Illustrator's desktop components and how they interact with one another.

▷ Switch between Preview and Outline views to observe and evaluate precision work with paths and the entire image with colors.

▷ Apply and edit stroke and fill colors.

▷ Learn to create, color, combine, transform, and align basic shapes precisely.

▷ ADVANCED USERS: Build a lighthouse from complex shapes with precision adjustments and alignments.

▷ DIGITAL TOOLKIT EXTRA: Create playing cards by making custom shapes using shape and selection tools, and the new Shape Builder tool.

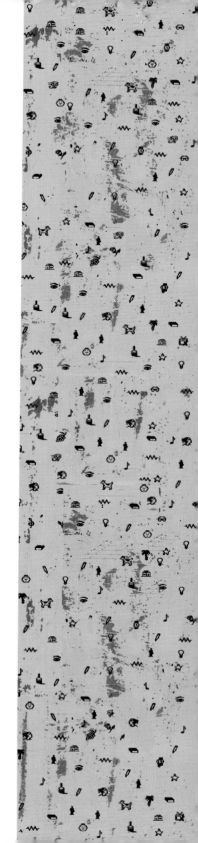

Illustrator is the premiere application for creating and editing vector-based digital illustrations. Artwork drawn on paper can be scanned into the computer through Photoshop and placed into Illustrator to be "traced over" and scaled up or down without compromising image quality. Digital artwork can also be created on the computer using Illustrator's tools, which allow for precise placement of individual objects, application of colors, transformations, and so on. Complex illustrations can be created by applying various layers on top of one another. Artwork from other drawings created in other applications can have individual components modified in order to create a new composite image. Adobe Illustrator CS5 is the newest version of this premiere program of the digital illustration industry, which provides tools design professionals need not only to create scalable images and type that can be integrated into other Adobe products, like Photoshop and InDesign, but to create images for print, web, mobile devices, and other media. In this chapter, you will learn to work with basic shapes and coloring and to understand the importance of accurate placement and alignment.

Need additional fun computer graphics tutorials and info, and an additional look at the projects you'll be creating in this book? Check out my Artist's Digital Toolkit website at: **http://www.digitoolkit.com**

THE ILLUSTRATOR ENVIRONMENT

The Illustrator desktop shares many similarities with Photoshop's tools, panels, and menus, since they are both created by Adobe. When you work on your **artwork,** or illustration, created in Illustrator using shapes, tools, paths, and panels, you will notice that there is a rectangle on the document. The area inside the rectangle is called the **artboard,** which is where you will create and modify all your illustrations. Illustrator CS5 provides designers the ability to work with multiple artboards for creating a variety of things such as multiple page PDFs, printed pages with different sizes or different elements, etc. The area outside the artboard area is called the **scratch** area. This is a nonprintable area that you can use to store artwork components in case you need them; place elements you might want to use again here, rather than deleting them. The panels are used to monitor, arrange, and make changes to your artwork. The **Tools panel** contains all the tools to select, create, and manipulate objects. Various selection tools are used to select colors, shapes, and paths. The **Control panel** in Illustrator, like the Tool Options bar in Photoshop, provides options related to a selected tool, and information regarding object dimensions and location, fill and stroke colors, opacity, and selecting the Bridge application. A **bounding box** is made when selecting objects to move or resize, which can also be toggled to be hidden in the View menu. The Illustrator CS5 work space is shown in Figure 7-1.

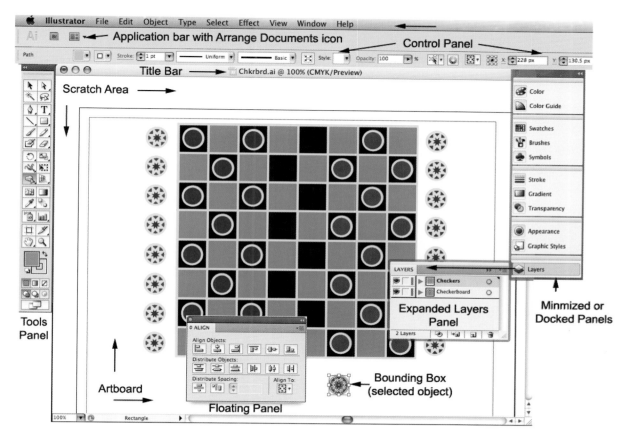

▷ FIGURE 7-1

**Illustrator
CS5 workspace.**

WORKING WITH VECTOR IMAGES

Illustrator creates vector images used for illustrations, drawings, CAD images, video, and clip art. In Illustrator, vector images are created as **objects** or **paths** that have starting and ending points and determine the shape of an image. These paths can be closed like circles or open like lines. Paths contain nonprinting **anchor points** that define where line segments begin and end. **Segments** are curved or straight lines between anchor points (Figure 7-2). All vector images can be scaled to any size the designer needs, because they use mathematical formulas to calculate distances between points as they are resized, rather than inventing pixels as in raster or bitmap images. The quality stays the same, with smooth crisp edges no matter what size is used. Illustrations have a lower **color depth,** because they usually use fewer total variations of color, and therefore the file sizes of vector images are small.

▷ FIGURE 7-2

Vector images consist of open and closed paths using anchor points between path segments.

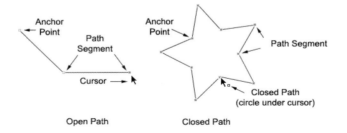

ILLUSTRATOR VIEWS

Illustrator provides different ways to view your artwork. When you open a file, it first displays the artwork in full color **Preview view**, showing all the colors and how it will look when printed. Otherwise, choose View > Preview to see all the artwork. You can also choose to display just the outlines of shapes as **Outline view** by selecting View > Outline (Figure 7-3). There are other views available, and you can save views to help with your work production.

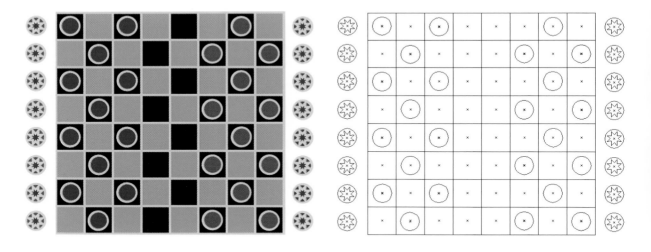

Preview View   Outline View

▷ FIGURE 7-3

Preview and Outline views.

THE ILLUSTRATOR TOOLS PANEL AND CONTROL PANEL

The Tools panel in Illustrator contains all the tools you need to create and modify objects and their individual components. It contains selection tools, drawing and painting tools, shape and liquefy tools, gradient tools, editing and viewing tools, transformation tools, and the Fill and Stroke color selection boxes. Many of the tools in Illustrator create paths or shapes like the Pen tools, Line Segment tools, Shape and Liquefy tools, Brush and Pencil tools, and Symbolism tools. Like the tools in Photoshop, any tool that displays a triangle will show other tools hidden underneath, when you click and hold the mouse on the tool icon. If the mouse hovers over the tool icon, the name of the tool and the corresponding keystroke are displayed. For tool buttons that have hidden tools, you can isolate the tools from the Tools panel by clicking and dragging the Tearoff bar on the right side to make it a separate toolbar panel. To access options on several of the tools, select the tool first; then, click on the artwork area, and a dialog box will be displayed to enter settings.

The Control panel, located below the Menu bar, is displayed to provide options pertaining to a selected object or tool, including color stroke and fill information; it provides information regarding object size and location. The Control panel is used to combine some of the most used functions of some of the more popular panels to minimize work space. It contains a panel menu on the far right that allows toggling to display commands and to dock the panel either on the top or bottom of the screen (Figure 7-4).

▷ FIGURE 7-4

Illustrator CS5 Tools panel and Control panel.

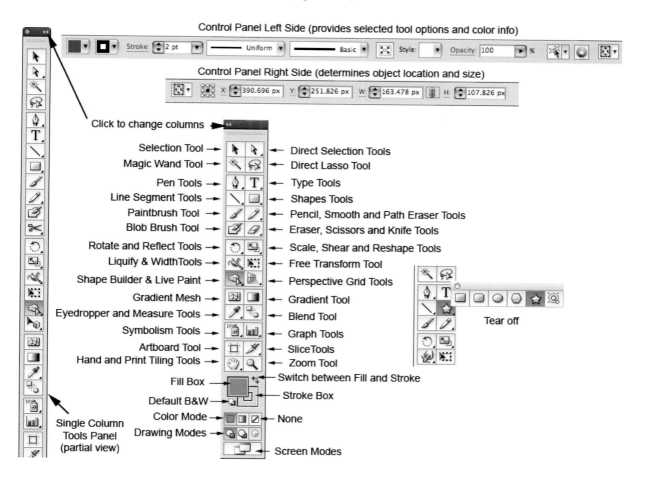

FILL AND STROKE BOXES AND PANELS

On the Toolbar, below the small tool icons, you will find the larger Color Picker, which contains the Fill and Stroke boxes. You can sample colors in the Color panel or use preset colors and save new ones in the Swatches panel. The Swatches panel in Illustrator has a feature that allows you to save a set of colors as a group, view the grouping structure, and take out those colors used in a selected piece of artwork as a group. The **Fill box** in the Color Picker is used to fill color inside an object, whereas the **Stroke box** is used to define the outline or edge of the object. The stroke thickness is determined by entering the stroke weight in the **Stroke panel**, which is also used to determine how stroke lines are joined, capped, or changed to dashed strokes, or in the Control panel. In CS5, you can also use the Stroke panel to create variable width strokes and custom arrowheads. A Fill or Stroke box with a red line through it indicates no color or transparency. **Color modes** below the Fill and Stroke boxes determine how color is applied to either the fill or stroke of an object or path, although you cannot use a gradient or blend of colors in a stroke (Figure 7-5). They are the *Color* (default), *Gradient,* and *None* (red line) modes. As in Photoshop, you can minimize or expand your panels by clicking on the double arrows on the panel name tab, the icon if it is docked on the side, or by using the Window Menu.

▷ FIGURE 7-5

Stroke characteristics are defined in the Stroke Panel. Selecting Stroke and Fill colors for object is made through the Tools, Color or Swatches panels.

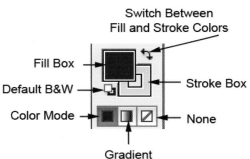

Switch Between
Fill and Stroke Colors

Fill Box

Default B&W

Color Mode

Stroke Box

None

Gradient

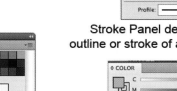

Stroke Panel determines how the
outline or stroke of an illustration displays

Swatches Panel contains preset
individual colors and groups of colors

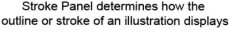

Color Panel allows you
to select any color

 TOOLKIT TIP To switch between fill and stroke colors, press the X key on your keyboard; to switch to the default black stroke with white fill, click to toggle the default icon or press the D key. These are the same keystroke shortcuts used in Photoshop.

THE WELCOME SCREEN WINDOW

In Illustrator, there is a **Welcome window** that automatically appears when you open Illustrator (if not, select Help > Welcome Screen). It provides a quick shortcut to create a new document, open an existing document, or create a new document from a template (Figure 7-6). It also provides information about Illustrator and tutorials to revive or enhance your skills. You can check out the Template link to find samples, such as brushes, special templates, special actions, and so on. Feel free to check out the tutorials to learn about some of the tools and techniques in Illustrator CS5. If you are using Illustrator CS5, you can click the Resources link to find tutorials, videos to download and learn from, and other cool links. There is a link called New Features that you can browse through to see what new features are offered in CS5. Illustrator is a versatile program for all types of media, including print, web, video, film, basic CMYK and RGB documents, and special mobile devices. CS4 and CS5 provide the user with start **profiles**, which determine what color will display most accurately based on which media the final image will be exported to. When you select a link to find a tutorial, you are brought into the Adobe Help and Support center.

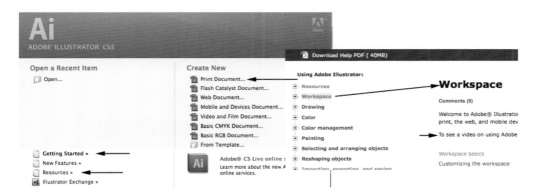

▷ FIGURE 7-6

Adobe Illustrator CS5 welcome screen allows you to select media profiles, open and create documents, and select links to access help and videos to learn about this versatile program.

Optional Exercise: Here you will learn how to use the Resources link to look at online videos and also how to use the Video Workshop to learn about the Illustrator work space.

1. Launch Illustrator; if the Welcome window is not displayed, select Help > Welcome Screen. (The Help menu also contains tutorials.) If you are using Illustrator on your school network, make sure you are able to download information.

2. Select the Getting Started link at the bottom left of the window, which will open the Adobe Help Viewer, displaying the Workspace title.

3. Select the video link above the list of related links, which will take you to the Adobe website to get an idea what Illustrator is about. If you are using Illustrator on your home computer, you may have a CD of videos to look at on the Learning CD; Adobe has a video website for podcasts or computer video tutorials at www.tv.adobe.com you can check out. You must have the free Flash player installed to view the videos.

4. When you are finished checking out the video options, take a look at the From Template section in the Welcome screen to get more ideas.

THE ADOBE HELP AND SUPPORT CENTER

Illustrator's Help menu allows the designer access to any information about tools, application features, updates, tasks, and terminology, along with information about transferring your software activation to another computer and access to the **Adobe Help and Support Center** on the web by selecting the Illustrator Help link. The Help and Support Center displays tasks, index help, and bookmarks of previously visited help areas. You can look for topics by searching for keywords, using the alphabetized index, looking through a table of contents, or simply jumping from one topic to another by selecting underlined text links (Figure 7-7). The online Adobe Help and Support Center also lets you seek help from other Adobe applications in a weblike format and provides additional links to resources and support, and video tutorials.

Here you will look up how to use the Help and Support Center.

1. Launch Illustrator CS5 and select Help > Illustrator Help from the Menu bar. It will then take you into the Adobe Help and Support Center on Adobe's website.

2. In the website, select the Learn Illustrator CS5 video tutorial link, and select the Getting Started 01 tutorial, Create a New Document and watch one of the new features in creating multiple artboards.

3. In the Help and Support box, type in Color Guide, a feature regarding matching colors, and choose from a list a tutorials and videos.

4. Look around other links or other new features described using the Adobe Help Center.

▷ FIGURE 7-7

Using Illustrator Help to find information about the Color Guide feature.

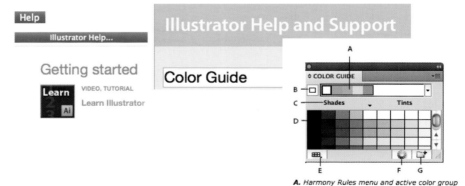

A. Harmony Rules menu and active color group

LIVE COLOR IN ILLUSTRATOR

One great feature in Illustrator is the ability to look at color groups and assign new colors to selected art work on the fly, called Live Color, along with a new Color Guide panel. The Kuler panel as part of Live Color is used by designers to find colors that complement one another or to experiment with colors in their art work and then create custom groupings of colors. You can create and reuse groups of colors to help enhance your productivity and work flow. The **Color Guide panel** provides quick access to color groups. The Swatches panel in Illustrator allows a designer to save a set of colors as a group, view the grouping structure, and save those colors used in the artwork as a group. Finally, there is a Recolor Artwork

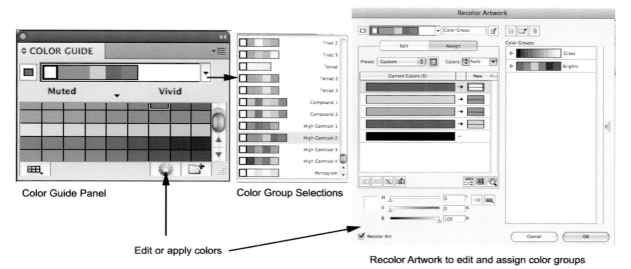

▷ FIGURE 7-8

Color panel, and Recolor Artwork display to select, define, and assign color groups.

dialog box that helps the designer edit or rearrange various color combinations using preset color groups, individual colors, or by using an interactive color wheel to define and save those custom color groups (Figure 7-8). It also helps to constrain your selections within specific color spaces, such as web colors or Pantone print colors.

Color Guide Panel

Color Group Selections

Edit or apply colors

Recolor Artwork to edit and assign color groups

CLIENT ASSIGNMENT: Creating an Electronic Checkerboard Game for E-mail

A good friend of yours, Thomas Mate, wants to be able to play checkers through e-mail with a friend who has moved away. He comes to you and wants you to create a checkerboard and pieces that can be sent back and forth through e-mail. After discussing colors, you both decide to use black and light blue colors for the checkerboard, with deep blue and deep red colors for the checkers, to be more distinctive. You know this project should be created in Illustrator since it involves creating basic shapes and using the selection tools to move the pieces (Figure 7-9). You find out that both Thomas and his friend have Illustrator on their computers and can easily play the games that way. You tell him you will have it ready the next day.

ACTION ITEMS OVERVIEW

As a designer using Illustrator, you need to have a basic understanding of the importance of creating shapes and the alignment or placement of objects precisely. First, the checkerboard itself is created by copying, combining, and accurately aligning squares to make the board. Next, the colored checker pieces are constructed for both players.

▷ FIGURE 7-9

**Completed
checkerboard.**

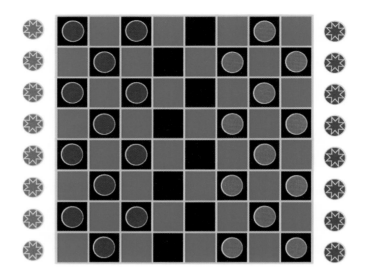

Here is what you need to do:

• For the checkerboard, create two different colored squares with a yellow stroke (RGB Color mode).

• Group the two squares and align them, and then copy the squares and align to make rows, and then copy and align again until the checkerboard is completed.

• For the checkers, create blue and deep red perfect circles with a yellow stroke.

• Copy to make 12 pieces for the board and place these centered in the appropriate playing squares to begin the game.

• Use the Color Guide panel to find harmonious color combinations to change colors on the board.

• Combine and transform shapes to make the crown pieces.

• Advanced Users: Create complex shapes together in building a lighthouse.

CREATING CHECKERBOARD SQUARES

Creating illustrations can start with building upon basic shapes then editing them or modifying them to create other shapes. In this phase, you will be creating the checkerboard by creating, copying, and aligning the two different-colored squares into a checkerboard that is eight rows by eight columns. A document can be set up as either a vertical portrait orientation (default) for normal documents or as a landscape orientation, displaying the document lengthwise horizontally. This document will be created in landscape orientation.

CREATING A NEW DOCUMENT

In Illustrator you can always create a new document, open an existing document, or open a template. When you set up a new document, you need to determine its dimensions, orientation (portrait or landscape), and color mode (RGB or CMYK). Illustrator's default color mode is in CMYK. If you use the Welcome window, you can start a new document there as well. For new documents created using the Web document profile, a new option in CS5 is Align new objects to pixel grid. This feature, when enabled, allows an object to have its vertical and horizontal paths aligned to the pixel grid, which remains with the object even when it is later modified. It helps maintain a crisp appearance of pixel-aligned strokes for all web documents.

TOOLKIT TIP Set up your color mode when you create a new document using the Welcome window. If you later need to convert it to a different mode, go to File > Document Color Mode. You can also create a new document as always using the File > New command, and you will get the same New Document dialog box.

Next, you will set up a new electronic document for the checkerboard using the welcome screen, which is the first screen to appear in Illustrator.

1. Launch Illustrator; if the welcome screen is not displayed, select Help > Welcome Screen. (The Help menu also contains tutorials.)

2. Select Create New > Web Document on the right side.

3. Create the new web document in Landscape Orientation using 1024 × 768 pixel size with settings shown, since it will be used for electronic display (Figure 7-10). Click on the Advanced arrow to make sure Color Mode is set to RGB Color. The new document should automatically be set up in RGB color mode. You will also notice you can have more than one artboard displayed, leave at 1 for this project. Place a check in the Align new objects to pixel grid box.

4. Name the document *Chkrbrd*, then select OK. The new blank document will display.

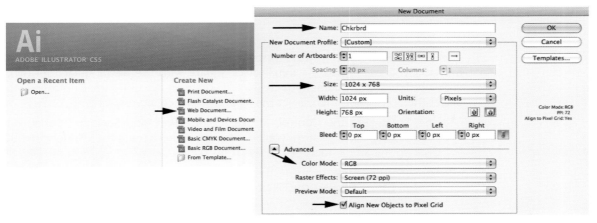

▷ FIGURE 7-10

Setting up the new electronic document using the Welcome Screen.

TOOLKIT TIP Most computers today can easily handle a screen size of 1024 x 768 pixel display. The concept for this assignment is to create a project that can be used as a full screen display. If you only have access to a computer more than seven years old, change the size to 800 × 600 pixels. Screen displays measure at 72 pixels per inch to be printed, remember that 72 pixels equals an inch; in this case, pixels will be the unit of measurement.

USING FILL AND STROKE COLORS WITH SHAPES

DESIGN TIP

Illustrator works in CMYK as the default color mode, which is used for images that are going to press. For creating artwork with colors that will be used primarily for electronic display like the web or e-mail, a designer should create the project with RGB Color.

When working with basic shapes, the new Shape tools provide an initial starting point from which to build upon. There are different methods in Illustrator for selecting fill and stroke color and weight. The **Fill** is the color selected to fill the inside of an object. The **stroke** is the outline of the object, and the **stroke weight** determines its thickness. The outline of the shape, or stroke, is determined by selecting the Stroke box in the Tools panel or Color panel, selecting the color, and then determining the stroke weight in the Stroke panel. In CS5, you can also create strokes of variable widths. You can also find these options in the Control panel. The fill color of the shape is determined by selecting swatches from the Control panel, or by selecting the Fill box on the Tools panel, then choosing a color from either the Swatches panel, which contains preset colors, or the Color panel, where colors are sampled or mixed. For black and white colors, you can select preset squares from the Control panel's Fill and Stroke swatches, or from the Swatches panel or Color panel.

TOOLKIT TIP Before creating shapes or selecting a drawing tool, set up the Fill and Stroke colors in the Color Picker or the Control panel first. The Control panel is most useful in editing selected objects that are already created.

There are several different ways to select fill and stroke colors in Illustrator. In this exercise, you will create the initial black square with the Rectangular tool (M), with a yellow stroke outlining the square. If you want, try using the Control panel. Select the object first, then select the fill and stroke color you want.

1. First, make sure the Control, Stroke, Color, Align, and Swatches panels on your desktop are displayed, you can also select them using the Window menu. Click on the Shape tools box in the Tools panel.

2. To make the black square of the checkerboard, select the Fill button on the Control panel, or select the Fill box in the Tools panel to bring it forward in the Color Picker.

3. Select the black color from either the swatches displayed in the Control panel or from the Swatches panel to make the fill color black, or you can select the black rectangle in the Color panel (Figure 7-11).

4. Select the Stroke button on the Control panel, or the Stroke color box on the Tools panel, and select a yellow color from the displayed Swatches panel.

5. Enter 4 points Weight in the Control panel, or use the Stroke panel to enter 4 points Weight (Figure 7-11).

6. Select the Rectangle Shape tool (M) and click—do not drag—in the upper-left area of the artboard to display the dialog box (Figure 7-12).

7. Enter 75 pixels for both Width and Height, (if you see inches in your display, you can type "75 px" in the fields, even if it is measuring in inches; Illustrator will convert the number). Select OK. Notice how this information displays in the Control panel. You have a 75 px × 75 px black square with a yellow 4-point stroke weight.

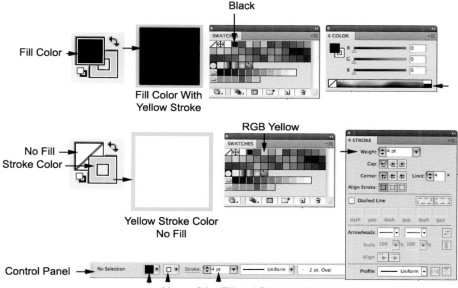

▷ FIGURE 7-11

Stroke and Fill settings for the black color and yellow outline of the checkerboard.

Many of the Fill and Stroke options can also be applied using the Control Panel.

TOOLKIT TIP Dragging a shape tool diagonally while holding down the Shift key also creates proportional objects, such as perfect circles and squares (Figure 7-12). Holding down the Shift key while dragging a corner point from a selected object scales the size proportionately. To create objects with precise dimensions, click once with the tool to access the dialog box.

▷ FIGURE 7-12

Creating a perfect square with the rectangle shape tool.

ILLUSTRATOR SELECTION TOOLS

Selection tools allow the designer to select a specific path, its segments, or an entire object (Figure 7-13). The **Selection tool** selects objects, creating a bounding box around them; use the View menu to hide or display the bounding box, if needed. A bounding box around a selected object has handles in its corners and can be used to reshape, copy, or rotate that object. The **Group Selection tool** (with a plus sign) selects paths in a group. The **Direct Selection tool** selects anchor points and segments on a path, whereas the **Magic Wand tool** selects objects with similar attributes, such as color, and the **Direct Select Lasso tool** selects path components. The Selection tool and Direct Selection tool are the most widely used selection tools.

▷ FIGURE 7-13

Selection tools.

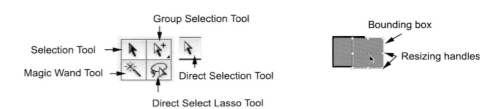

TOOLKIT TIP Holding down the Option/Alt key while an object is selected makes a copy of the image. Make sure to release the mouse first and then the Option/Alt key. Holding down the Shift key and the Option/Alt key moves the copy in alignment with the original.

COPYING SELECTIONS USING THE OPTION/ALT KEY

Copying an object is done by first selecting the object with the Selection tool, then holding down the Option/Alt key while clicking and dragging the selected object. You can also select an object and move it using the Selection tool.

In this exercise, you will use the Selection tool to select the square, copy it by holding down the Option/Alt key, change the fill color, and then select both squares to create a bounding box that will be used to make multiple copies.

▷ FIGURE 7-14

With the Selection tool, Option/Alt click and drag to make a copy of the selected square; change the color to red using the Swatches panel.

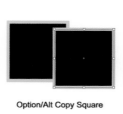

Option/Alt Copy Square

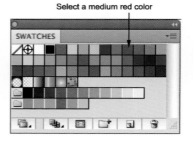

Select a medium red color

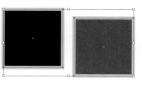

Shift select both squares to create bounding box

DESIGN TIP

One method to accurately place one object within another is to use the handles on the bounding box created by the Selection tool as a guide for centering and positioning.

1. To duplicate the black checker box you just created, choose the Selection tool, then select the box and hold down the Option/Alt key while dragging to the right to make a copy. If you want, try to also use the Shift key with the Option/Alt key to keep the boxes aligned (Figure 7-14).

2. With the copy still selected, click the Fill box in the Tools panel so that it appears in front of the Stroke box, and then select one of the red colors—something easy on the eyes—from the Swatches panel. Leave the stroke the same yellow color. You now have the two colored squares for the checkerboard.

3. Hold down the Shift key; with the Selection tool, either click on each square or drag across them both to select them. This will create a bounding box for the next exercise. If you don't get a bounding box, go to View > Show Bounding Box and click it if it is displayed.

THE ALIGN PANEL AND SMART GUIDES

The **Align panel** is used to align multiple selected items along a horizontal or vertical axis. The Align panel can also be used to evenly space the distance between multiple objects. The Align panel can be used to align to a selection, an artboard from its multiple artboards feature, or a key object as one specific object in a selection of multiple objects. Illustrator also uses **smart guides**, which are guides that display when the centers of two or more objects are properly aligned or intersected for visual reference.

TOOLKIT TIP To select multiple objects easily with the Selection tool, click and drag diagonally over the objects you want to include.

Now you will use the Align panel and arrow keys to position the first two squares. Then, using the Selection tool and the arrow keys on your keyboard, you will copy and align three more pairs and position them precisely to make the first row of the checkerboard.

1. With both squares selected and the bounding box visible, make sure the Align panel is displayed (Window > Align is checked). To enable smart guides, select View > Smart Guides, then zoom in to 200%.

2. Select the Vertical Align Top icon on the Align panel to put both squares on the same X axis.

DESIGN TIP

Using the arrow keys with any object selected will move it one pixel at a time (default) for precise alignment. Changing the image to Outline View in the View menu helps with alignment of lines.

3. Zoom in to 200%–300%, then with the Selection tool, click outside the squares to deselect them, then select only the red square on the right. Use the arrow keys on the keyboard to move it, so the yellow strokes overlap by 4 keystrokes to keep the stroke the same width (Figure 7-15). You can check also by using Outline View (View > Outline) then check back to Preview View.

4. To copy the squares, zoom back out to 100%, then select both black and red squares with the Shift key, then hold down the Option/Alt key while dragging the selected boxes to the right. You will notice the smart guides will display that align with the center of each group of squares to visually help keep your squares aligned vertically.

▷ FIGURE 7-15

Use the align panel to align the squares, then use the arrow keys for precise placement of squares.

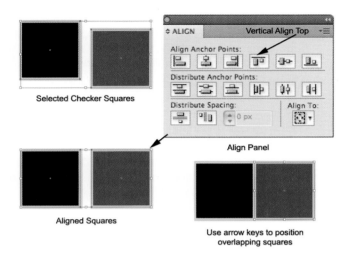

Selected Checker Squares

Align Panel

Aligned Squares

Use arrow keys to position
overlapping squares

5. Repeat twice more so that you have a total of eight squares showing (Figure 7-16). Select all squares using the Selection tool.

6. Select the Align panel, then select the Vertical Align Top icon again to align the squares into a row.

7. Use the Navigation panel (Window > Navigation) or Zoom tool to move in close—200% to 300%—to check placement.

8. To combine all the pairs of squares together, select pairs and use the arrow keys for precise placement, overlapping the edges by 4 pixels to create the same yellow stroke throughout. Zoom out when done.

▷ FIGURE 7-16

Creating the first row of squares for the checkerboard.

Smart guides for visual center alignment

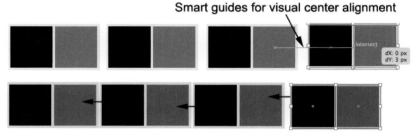

Shift select each pair and use the arrow keys on the keyboard
for precise placement to make sure the stroke is equal throughout.

First row of eight squares completed

USING OUTLINE VIEW TO CHECK ARTWORK

One of the best ways to check for precise placement of shapes is the Outline view option. Look for overlapping, misshapen, broken, or missing lines.

1. To check whether all the boxes are properly aligned, select View > Outline.

2. Make sure that all squares meet together as single lines, as shown in Figure 7-17.

3. If not, realign the squares using the Selection tool and left and right arrow keys on your keyboard. Zoom in for more precision.

4. When all squares are aligned perfectly, switch back to the artwork by selecting View > Preview.

▷ FIGURE 7-17

Using Preview view and Outline view to check accuracy of alignment.

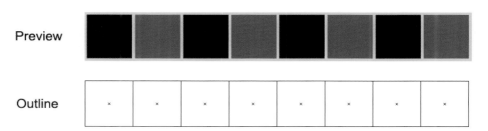

Preview

Outline

SAVING ILLUSTRATOR IMAGES

Illustrator images can be saved in a variety of formats, and Illustrator can read many graphic file formats. Graphic file formats are determined by the particular ways they represent graphic information.

• Illustrations saved with **Encapsulated PostScript (EPS)** extensions are used in page-layout programs for print, especially when graphics and text are combined.

• The **Portable Document Format (PDF)** is used for electronic publishing that can be read by Adobe Acrobat Reader or Adobe applications. The PDF format is universally accepted for commercial printing, as a proofing mechanism for layout of imagery and type, and can also be viewed in other graphics applications. It can also be used as the final proof in commercial printing establishments.

• Saving an Illustrator file in **FXG** format is useful when the need involves preserving maximum appearance and availability for accurate editing, and for animation purposes using Flash Catalyst.

• **Scaleable Vector Graphic, or SVG**, is a vector format that describes images as shapes, paths, text, and filter effects. The resulting files are compact and provide high-quality graphics that are used in the development of web pages.

• Artwork can be converted for web use by using **Save for Web and Devices**. It can also be saved for mobile devices.

• The **Save as Template** option allows you to save documents as templates for future projects. It has an **.ait** extenson. For duplication, use the **Save a copy** feature.

• When saving illustrations within Adobe applications, you can use the application's native format; in the case of Illustrator, this is an **.AI extension**. Saving a document in Illustrator's native format provides a good back-up file for future editing.

• You can save files with *backwards compatibility,* so someone who may not be using the same version as you can open and work on it. Be aware that when you save to earlier versions, Illustrator warns you that some operations or functions may not be backwards compatible.

TOOLKIT TIP For the purposes of this assignment, you will save artwork in Illustrator's native format (Figure 7-18) and later as a GIF document for web use. You can also save the checkerboard file as a PDF or SVG file (be sure to embed all elements) and still be able to move the checkers with the Selection tool. Saving as a PDF is the most universal method and allows you to use the file in other graphic applications or use the free Acrobat Reader from the Adobe website.

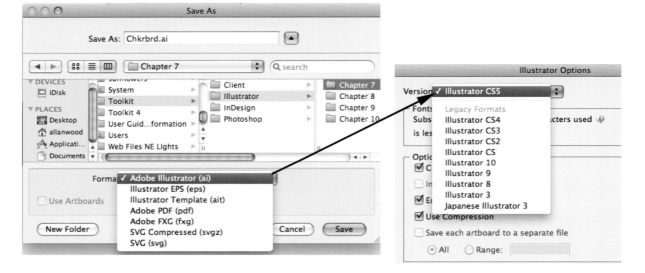

▷ FIGURE 7-18

Saving Illustrator artwork in its native format.

In this exercise, you will save the file in Illustrator's native file extension.

1. Save the file as *Chkrbrd.ai* (File > Save As > Adobe Illustrator Document), using the default settings, in your *Chapter 7* folder.

2. Leave the file open to continue creating the checkerboard.

THE OBJECT MENU

The **Object menu** is used for editing, combining, and transforming objects. With the first row of the checkerboard created accurately, the squares will be grouped together; then a copy will be rotated 180 degrees so the red squares are below the black squares, creating the pattern for the rest of the checkerboard.

TOOLKIT TIP By grouping the squares together, you can use the Selection tool to select the whole group at once. To select each square individually, use the Direct Selection tool. For accuracy, when lines are overlapping, make sure they appear as one line in Outline View. Sometimes it is easier to adjust objects in Outline View. You can flip back and forth between Outline View and Preview View using Command/ Ctrl Y.

DESIGN TIP

In Illustrator accuracy and the alignment of objects is important. Use Outline View frequently to check your work. Lines or paths that are overlapping, as in the case of the checkerboard, need to be viewed as a single line in Outline View for precise measurment.

▷ FIGURE 7-19

Use the object menu to group and rotate objects. Control panel can help with alignment.

In this exercise, you will use the Object menu to group and rotate squares for two rows.

1. Select the eight squares by dragging diagonally over all squares with the Selection tool, which will create a bounding box.

2. Select Object > Group to combine all eight squares together.

3. With the squares still selected, use the Selection tool and hold down the Option/Alt key to make a copy of the row, and drag it below the first row. Use the arrow keys on the keyboard to position it accurately.

4. Using the Control panel's Align icons, or the Align panel, with both rows of squares selected, click the Horizonal Align Left to align the rows. Use Outline View (View > Outline View) to check for accuracy and adjust the rows as needed. In Outline View, all lines should be single lines (Figure 7-19).

5. To rotate the second row 180 degrees, so that the red squares are under the black squares and vice versa, select Object > Transform > Rotate > 180 degrees.

6. To group the two rows together, select both rows with the Selection tool and choose Object > Group.

7. You now have the basic pattern for the rest of the board.

TOOLKIT TIP In all versions of Illustrator, you can also rotate the squares using the bounding box made by the Selection tool; this is done by moving the cursor to the corner until it becomes a bent arrow and then dragging.

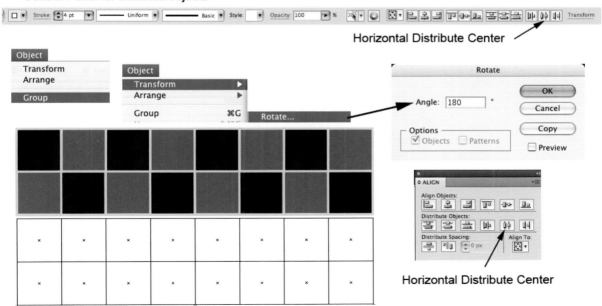

DUPLICATING AND ALIGNING THE REMAINING ROWS

With the two rows created and aligned perfectly, all that remains is to copy the two rows three more times, align them, and place them snugly together to make the checkerboard of eight rows by eight columns (Figure 7-20).

▷ FIGURE 7-20

Final checkerboard.

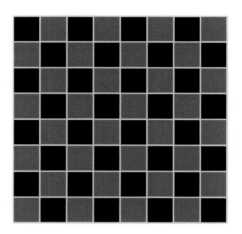

Preview View

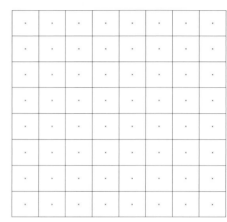

Outline View

1. Select the two rows you just created with the Selection tool, then hold down the Option/Alt key to click and drag a copy, placing it below the selected rows.

2. Use the arrow keys to position these new rows precisely. Use Outline View to check for final accuracy then make additional adjustments as needed. When you have all four rows aligned precisely, select them all with the Selection tool and group them using the Object menu.

3. With the Selection tool, select the four rows you just created, then hold down the Option/Alt key to click and drag a final copy below the four selected rows.

4. Zoom in and use the arrow keys and the Selection tool to ensure precise positioning. To check your work to make sure all the boxes are aligned, select View > Outline and zoom in; all lines must be displayed as single lines for accuracy.

5. When everything is aligned perfectly, switch back to the artwork by selecting View > Preview.

6. Select Object > Group to group all rows into one checkerboard.

7. Save the file inside the *Chapter 7* folder.

DUPLICATING AND LOCKING LAYERS

The Layers panel in Illustrator works much the same way as in Photoshop. Layers can be renamed, duplicated, moved, and locked (Figure 7-21). To keep the checkerboard from being moved or edited by mistake, the layer can be duplicated for placing the checker pieces, and then the original layer can be locked for prevention.

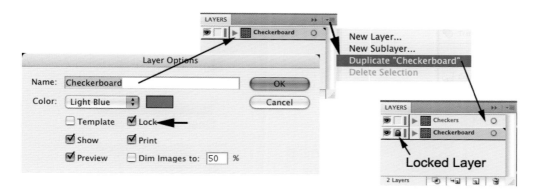

▷ FIGURE 7-21

Duplicating, renaming, and locking layers.

With the squares on the checkerboard aligned precisely, you will duplicate the layer in the Layers panel and then lock the original layer. The layers will be renamed to identify them.

1. Make sure the Layers panel is displayed (Window > Layers) or click on the icon in the dock.

2. Double-click the Layer 1 text; when the Layer Options dialog box displays, enter "Checkerboard" in the Name area and then check the Lock option as shown (Figure 7-21).

3. Click OK.

4. Select the Layers panel submenu and click on Duplicate "Checkerboard."

5. Double-click the new layer *Checkerboard copy*, and rename it *Checkers*, making sure that Lock is unchecked in the Layer Options box to add the checkers. To lock any layer on the Layers panel, just click on the blank box next to the eye icon. To unlock, click on the lock to toggle off.

6. Save the file in your *Chapter 7* folder.

CREATING THE CHECKERS

With the checkerboard completed, it is time to make the light and deep blue checker pieces, using the Color panel. The checkers are going to be created with the Ellipse tool, colored, copied, and centered on all the playing squares of the checkerboard.

ELLIPSE TOOL AND COLOR PANEL

Any oval or circle can be created by selecting the Ellipse tool (L) in the Shape tools area of the Tools panel; click once on the artboard and enter the options in the dialog box by clicking and dragging diagonally or by drawing outward from the center while holding down the Option/Alt key. Holding down the Shift key will create a perfect circle as you drag. The Color panel provides the designer with plenty of color choices to experiment with. Colors can be either selected randomly, or their values can be typed in. All colors in RGB mode are combinations of red, green, and blue, with values that range from 0 to 255 for each.

DESIGN TIP

There is a preset limited color selection with the Swatches panel; but with the Color panel, there is much more freedom to select or create a color. Double-clicking on the Stroke or Fill box in the Tools panel will display the Color Picker for plenty of experimentation.

Creating the checker pieces.

Ellipse Tool

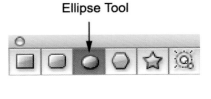

Deep Blue Checker

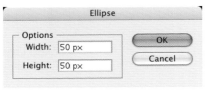

Precise dimensions
using the Ellipse tool

Light Blue Checker

To make the checkers, you will use the Ellipse tool to create the circles with a yellow color stroke, and then select the two different blue colors from the Color panel by entering the appropriate RGB settings (Figure 7-22).

1. To make the deep blue checker for the board, first select the *Checkers* layer, then select the Ellipse tool and click—do not drag—on the artboard to display the dialog box.

2. Enter 50 pixels Width and 50 pixels Height for the circle and select OK.

3. With the circle still selected, use the Stroke box in the Swatches panel and choose a yellow color (yellow may still be selected from before, when we created the squares).

4. Open the Stroke panel and enter 2 points for the stroke weight.

5. Select the Fill box within the Color Picker to change the fill color.

6. Select the Color panel or double-click on the Fill box to access the Color Picker and enter the settings R=51, G=51, and B=153 to make the fill color a deep blue. You can use the Tab key to move from one field to the next.

7. To make the second checker piece, choose the Selection tool, then select the circle and hold down the Option/Alt key and drag to make a copy.

8. Select the Fill box in the Tools panel and select the Color panel. Enter the settings R=102, G=153, and B=204 to make a light blue color. You now have two checker pieces for the checkerboard. If RGB values do not appear, click the double vertical arrow on the Color panel to expand.

9. Use the Selection tool to move both pieces outside the checkerboard.

PLACING THE PIECES ON THE BOARD

With the two colored checker pieces created, each piece now needs to be copied and centered on the black squares. This will give you a little review of using the Selection tool, copying the circles by holding down the Option/Alt key, and then placing the circles aligned precisely in the black squares. Another option for alignment is using smart guides again.

Next, you will duplicate the checker pieces and center them accurately inside the squares.

1. Select the light blue checker with the Selection tool and drag copies to the first three columns of black squares on the board's left side using the Option/Alt key.

2. Continue until all 12 pieces are copied onto the squares as shown (Figure 7-23).

3. Select each circle piece and position it exactly in the center with the arrow keys. You can also be precise by matching the centers of the circles with the centers of the squares in Outline View, or you can turn on smart guides (View > Smart Guides) and move the piece until it reads "Intersects" which indicates the center of the square intersecting with the center of the circle.

4. Repeat the same process with the deep blue checkers for the right side of the board.

5. For pieces that need to be "crowned" during play, you can change the color of the checker in the next exercises, or create and use crowned checkers in the Advanced Users section coming up.

6. Save the file in your *Chapter 7* folder.

DESIGN TIP

Sometimes when a color is chosen, a small cube displays to indicate that it will not display accurately for the web. Click on the cube and Illustrator will change the color to the closest web-safe color. (Figure 7-24).

▷ FIGURE 7-23

Checkerboard before adjusting colors.

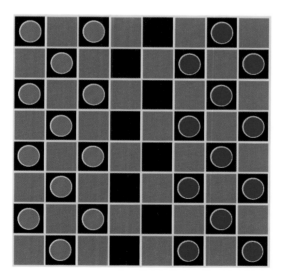

CHANGING COLORS OF THE BOARD

Time to play with the colors! Select the red squares with the Magic Wand tool and change the fill color to light blue or some other mellow color to replace the bright red color. When selecting a color and a small cube appears, it is a warning that the color you have chosen may not display correctly on the web. Click on the cube to display web-safe colors (Figure 7-24). Go ahead, break the traditional-color barrier!

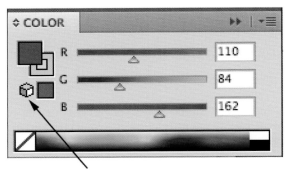

Click on cube to make it RGB Web safe

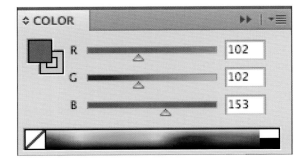

Color is now accurate for Web use

▷   FIGURE 7-24

The cube indicates a color that is not web safe. Clicking the cube allows Illustrator to choose the correct RGB colors for electronic display.

SELECTING WITH THE MAGIC WAND TOOL

The Illustrator Magic Wand tool allows you to select similar attributes, like fill colors, stroke colors and weights, blending modes, and opacities. Adjust the Tolerance in the **Magic Wand panel** to determine the amount of similar color that will be selected, much like setting the Magic Wand Tolerance in Photoshop. Use the Magic Wand tool to select a color area by just clicking on the color. All colors on the checkerboard that are the same will be selected as long as the Fill Color box is checked in the Magic Wand panel (Figure 7-25). To access the panel, double-click on the Magic Wand tool, or select Window > Magic Wand.

TOOLKIT TIP To select a single color area, make sure the Fill Color box is *not* checked in the Magic Wand panel. To select all of the same color in a document, make sure the Fill Color box *is* checked.

It is time to select all the red squares and apply a different color.

1. Double-click the Magic Wand tool to display the Magic Wand panel (or select Window > Magic Wand). If the display does not show as in Figure 7-25, click the double arrows left of "Magic" on the panel. Make sure the Checkers layer is selected and unlocked on the Layers panel.

2. Make sure the Fill Color box is checked in the Magic Wand panel to select all similar colors on the document. Enter 5 pixels for Tolerance and leave all the other defaults as is (Figure 7-25). You can leave this panel open.

▷   FIGURE 7-25

The Magic Wand tool selects all the same colors in the image when the Fill Color box is selected.

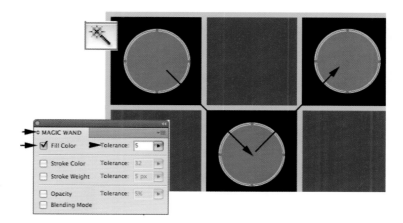

3. Select the Fill box in the Tools panel, then select one of the light blue checker circles on the checkerboard. By clicking on one circle, they all should become selected.

4. Use your cursor to select another color from either the Swatches panel or the Color panel; the selected objects' colors will all change. Go ahead and try using other colors, selecting the checker squares with the Magic Wand tool.

5. If you want to keep your choices, save the file with a different name, such as *Checkerbrd2*, because we are going to use the *Live Color* feature to create different harmonious colors for our checkers.

FINDING HARMONIOUS COLORS USING THE COLOR GUIDE

A nice feature in Illustrator is **Live Color,** along with the Color Guide panel. Designers can use this feature to find colors that complement one another and experiment with colors. Along with this comes the option to create custom groupings of colors. The **Color Guide panel** provides quick access to finding color groups. Use the Color Guide panel (Window > Color Guide) as a use for color inspiration while you create your artwork. The Color Guide panel suggests harmonious catagories of colors based on the current color in the Tools panel. You can use these to color artwork or you can save them as swatches. On the Control panel, you will also find an icon to edit colors within artwork (or select Edit > Edit Color > Recolor Artwork).

To find colors that may be appealing for your checkerboad and its checkers, you will use the Color panel to select various combinations of colors that go together.

1. If it is not still open, open the *Chkrbrd* file you saved before using the Magic Wand tool. Make sure the Checkers layer is selected.

2. Open the Color Guide panel (Window > Color Guide) and select a light blue checker or one of the checkers with a light color.

3. Click on the color icon at the top left of the Color Guide panel to create a set of colors (set base color to the current color) based on the color you have selected (Figure 7-26).

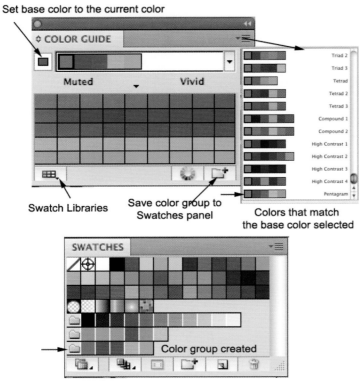

Set base color to the current color

Swatch Libraries

Save color group to
Swatches panel

Colors that match
the base color selected

Saving a Color group in the Swatches panel

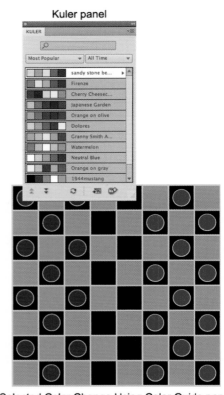

Kuler panel

Selected Color Change Using Color Guide panel

Color group created

▷ FIGURE 7-26

**Using the Color
Guide panel to
create colors that
work well together
in an illustration.**

4. Select the drop down arrow next to the color field to see other combinations of colors that work with the color you selected. Select the Pentagram combination at the bottom of the list (you will have to scroll down—there are so many options).

5. Use the Magic Wand panel again, with Fill Color selected and a tolerance of 5 pixels, and use the Magic Wand tool to select all checkers of the same color.

6. Click the blue box in the Color Guide panel to see a set of colors that work with the selected checkers. Go through and select combinations of both checker-board squares and checkers that match the color scheme of Pentagram, or try another group of colors from the list to see what works for you. Check out the "Swatches Library" for themes color choices on the Color panel, or the Kuler panel (Window > Extensions > Kuler), an online group of colors and themes from professional designers.

TOOLKIT TIP With the *Checkers* layer locked in the Layers panel, you will find that you can alter objects all you want on that layer, but the locked layer of the original colors underneath will not change. Select the checkerboard with the Selection tool and slightly move to see the original underneath, then select Edit undo. Duplicating the checkerboard layer is like a safety net; it allows you to bounce back to the original image.

7. When you have made your color choices, save the file as *Checkerboard3* and look at the other color combinations from other checkboards you created.

8. To save the color group, click the Save Color Group to Swatches panel at the bottom of the Color Guide panel (it looks like a folder). It will then be displayed as a group of colors in the Swatches panel for future projects.

DESIGN TIP

Color has a way of stimulating us and can provide pleasing and not so pleasing combinations. Using the Color Guide can help you in the creative process to find colors that work together. Look at the various combinations available based on a color you choose from the Swatches panel.

TOOLKIT TIP Illustrator has a Kuler panel (Window > Extensions > Kuler) which provides more color groups or themes created by a community of designers accessible online.

SAVE FOR WEB AND DEVICES FOR ELECTRONIC DISTRIBUTION

To use Save for Web and Devices (Save for Web in earlier versions), choosing File > Save for Web and Devices provides quick formatting options for eletronic media and mobile devices (Figure 7-27). You can choose to format a file as simply optimized, if you know exactly what you want to use for a file extension; or you can select various format options and see up to four variations of your artwork.

▷ FIGURE 7-27

Using Save for Web to optimize the artwork for web and electronic (e-mail) use.

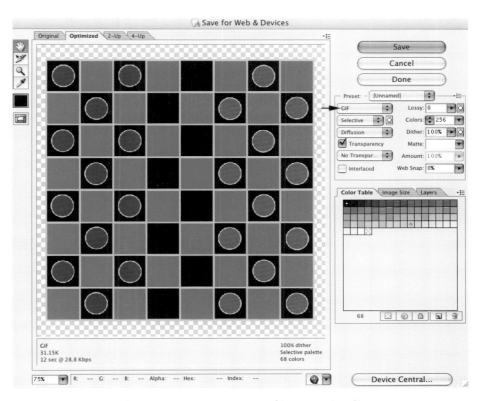

Saving the illustration as a GIF extension file

Each version includes information as to what your image will look like using those formats, a rough idea on how long your artwork may take to download with a 56.6k modem, and the file size. One method of choosing a file extension for artwork is to save the artwork as a **GIF** file: it does not use more than 256 colors and artwork can contain no applied gradients, but it allows transparency within the artwork and creates a small file size compared to a JPEG format. You can use Save for Web and Devices to see if your artwork displays properly as a GIF file. GIF files are also the base files used in some animations. This will be covered later in later Chapter 10.

TOOLKIT TIP As you look at the Save for Web and Devices dialog box, you will also notice the option for a PNG extension. PNG files are sometimes used on the web in place of JPEGs, because they can handle millions of colors, and they can handle transparencies. JPEGs cannot display graphics with transparencies. The drawback depends on your market: the files can be larger, which slows download time; and older browsers, such as Internet Explorer 4.0 or earlier, cannot read these files.

Need additional fun computer graphics tutorials and info, and an additional look at the projects you'll be creating in this book? Check out my Artist's Digital Toolkit website at: **http://www.digitoolkit.com**

Here you will use the Save for Web & Devices command to view the checkerboard and optimize it to be saved as a GIF to keep the file size small.

1. Open your favorite checkerboard file from those you created. Select File > Save for Web and Devices and choose the Optimized tab at the top left of this window to display just the artwork.

2. Select the GIF preset settings; observe that it does not alter the quality of the image, and note the file size and download time. If it displays at 28.8 kbps (kilobytes per second), or 28k at 12 seconds download time, you figure the download time of someone using a 56k dial-up modem would be cut in half—to about 6 seconds or less.

3. Click Save to save the file as a GIF in your *Chapter 7* folder. Because it has a different extension, the other files in Illustrator's native format will not be affected. Observe the slight differences in file sizes and quality, which you may find easier to do using Bridge, if there is any difference close up.

COMBINING COMPLEX SHAPES: CROWNED CHECKERS

Illustrator's Shape tools can be modified for all kinds of purposes. You can reshape, combine, or remove portions of objects to create new objects. You can also create complex artwork by laying paths on top of one another. As a continuation of the checkerboard project, you will see how to combine shapes to create other objects creating crowns for the checkers by combining shapes. You will use the Transform command in the Object menu to scale shapes to size.

USING THE STAR TOOL

The **Star tool** will be used to create a pointed star shape for the crown pieces that will be used when a player reaches the end zone. To determine the star shape, you enter an outside radius, an inner radius, and the number of points for the star.

Here, you will create the crown shape with the Star tool.

1. Open the checkerboard you saved previously as a GIF. In the Tools panel, set a Fill of None and a Stroke of Black. Set the stroke to 1 point in the Stroke panel if necessary. Select the Star tool, then click (don't drag) inside the artboard to access the dialog box.

2. Enter a Radius 1, the outside radius, of 150 pixels; enter 2 inches if you are using inches. Enter a Radius 2, the inside radius, of 75 pixels, or 1 inch. Then, adjust the number of Points to 8 (Figure 7-28); you will resize it later. NOTE: Radii 1 and 2 are interchangable—the larger number is automatically set as the outer radius, and the smaller number is automatically set as the inner radius.

3. Use the Selection tool to click on the star to display the bounding box.

4. Move the cursor to the lower-right corner until a bent arrow displays, then rotate until two points are standing vertically (Figure 7-28).

▷ FIGURE 7-28

Create an eight-point star for the crown checker piece.

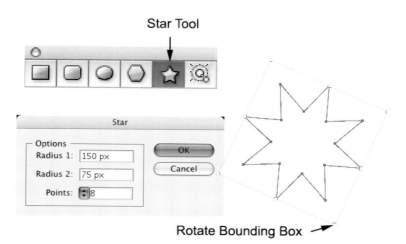

Star Tool

Star

Options
Radius 1: 150 px
Radius 2: 75 px
Points: 8

OK
Cancel

Rotate Bounding Box

THE TRANSFORM COMMAND

The **Transform command** under the Object menu allows you to move, rotate, reflect, scale, or shear an object in specified degrees or amounts. Since the star shape will be very small, the stroke color will be changed to yellow, and the width will be adjusted to 2 points. The fill color will be set to None to make the inside of the star transparent.

To create the crowned checker, you will scale the star shape to fit inside the checker piece, then make aligned copies placed outside of the checkerboard (Figure 7-29).

▷ FIGURE 7-29

Scaling and placing crowns inside the checker pieces.

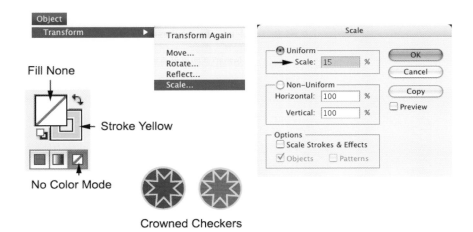

Crowned Checkers

1. Option/Alt copy one checker from each side of the checkerboard; drag them to the pasteboard and deselect them by clicking in a blank area of the artboard. Use the Eyedropper tool from the Tools panel to sample the colors from one of the checkers.

2. With the eight-point star selected, sample one of the checkers, and then set the fill to none. Make sure the Stroke box in the Tools panel is set with a yellow stroke at 2 points on the Stroke panel.

3. To scale down the star, choose Object > Transform > Scale and enter 15%. Click OK.

4. Use the Selection tool to drag the star inside the one of the checkers. If it does not fit inside the checker, undo (Edit > Undo or Command/Ctrl Z) and try scaling it again in increments of 5%.

5. With the Selection tool, use Option/Alt to copy the star and drag it to the opponents' checker.

6. When both crown pieces are complete, group each by selecting the checker and the star and choosing Object > Group.

7. Use the Selection tool while pressing the Option/Alt key to copy each opponent's crowned checker seven more times; place them along the opponent's side of the board, outside the checkerboard area. Do not worry about aligning them perfectly yet—we will cover that next.

HORIZONTAL AND VERTICAL ALIGNMENT

The Align panel allows you to align objects in either a horizontal or vertical fashion. You can also align objects so that they are distributed evenly along an axis.

To complete the checkers, you will align them evenly along the outsides of the checkerboard (Figure 7-30).

Use settings on the Align panel to align and evenly distribute crowned pieces.

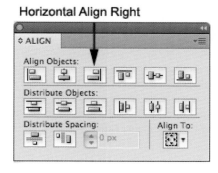

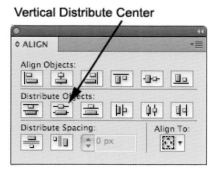

1. For more precise placement, use the Selection tool and Shift-select all the crowned pieces on one side of the checkerboard to display a bounding box.

2. Open the Align panel and click the Horizontal Align Right icon to align the pieces along the vertical side of the bounding box, then select the Vertical Distribute Center icon to evenly distribute the pieces.

3. Repeat the same process for the opponent's crowned checkers.

4. Use the Save for Web & Devices command again (File > Save for Web and Devices), and save the file as a GIF file again. If you want, you can also save the file as *Chkrbrd.ai* for a back-up copy in your *Chapter 7* folder. You can also save as an Adobe PDF file (File > Save As > Adobe PDF). When the Save Adobe PDF dialog box comes up, choose Adobe PDF Preset: Smallest File Size. Leave the rest at their default settings. Save as *Chkrbrd.pdf* in your *Chapter 7* folder.

5. Use the Selection tool to select each checker and group together (Object > Group). Now you can move the pieces to play the game (Figure 7-31). Have fun! Close file when you are done.

Completed checkerboard, checkers, and crowned checkers.

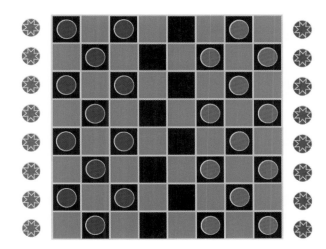

ADVANCED USERS: Building a Lighthouse

Here are some more advanced methods for making complex shapes using the Direct Selection tool and positioning selected anchor points precisely with the arrow keys on the keyboard. This graphic will be used as a symbol in the next chapter as part of a map. You can create images or shapes that are composites of multiple shapes and group them using the Object menu. Using guides helps to create perfectly symmetrical shapes. You can use the Color panel or Swatches panel to sample colors, including pure black and white colors (Figure 7-32). You will also scale the lighthouse using the Transform command.

TOOLKIT TIP When rulers are visible on the sides of your document, you will notice the position of the cursor always displays as a dotted line on each ruler. This helps with measuring distances and positioning objects.

▷ FIGURE 7-32

Selecting pure white or black is easy using the Color panel.

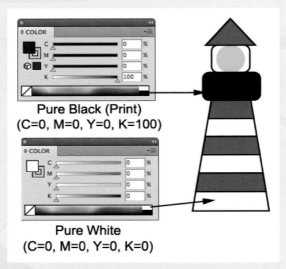

Pure Black (Print)
(C=0, M=0, Y=0, K=100)

Pure White
(C=0, M=0, Y=0, K=0)

DESIGN TIP

One method used to center objects on top of one another is to use the center point of the selected object's bounding box. You can also use the vertical and horizontal alignment options in the Align panel.

SHAPING THE LIGHTHOUSE TOP

The upper portion of the lighthouse is made by combining various shapes created by the Rounded Rectangle tool, the Ellipse tool (L), and the Polygon tool; this will help you understand how to combine basic shapes into complex artwork. Creating shapes on top of one another is like having each shape on its own clear sheet of acetate; you can rearrange the position of these shapes behind or in front of one another using the Arrange command, use smart guides to help with alignment, then group them together as one object using the Group command.

TOOLKIT TIP Before selecting another shape with a different fill and stroke, always deselect the previously selected object. To do this, either select the Selection tool and then click an empty area on the artboard, or choose Select > Deselect from the Select menu.

Next, you will create and position objects with various shapes to make the lighthouse top.

1. Use File > New to create a new, letter size Print file with portrait orientation and CMYK color. Set measurement Units to inches. Leave Align New Objects to Pixel Grid unchecked for this assignment.

2. Name the file *Light* and click OK.

3. Make sure to display the ruler guides (select View > Rulers > Show Rulers) and smart guides (View > Smart Guides).

4. For the lighthouse roof, select a Fill of red from the Swatches panel (or try C=0, M=100, Y=100. K=0 in the Color panel), and a 2-point Stroke of black. Use the Control panel to set the color and width of the Stroke.

5. Select the Polygon tool, then click on the artboard to access the dialog box. Enter a radius 0.75 inch and 3 Sides. Click OK. You will build the lighthouse from the top down to the base (Figure 7-33).

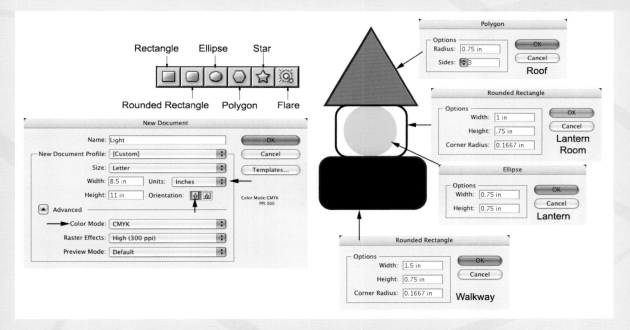

6. Deselect the roof shape before continuing (Select > Deselect).

7. To make the lantern room, select a Fill of None and a black Stroke of 2 points.

8. Select the Rounded Rectangle tool, then click once on the artboard.

9. Enter a 1 inch Width and a 0.75 inch Height. Leave the Corner Radius at its default, and click OK.

10. Using the arrow keys on the keyboard, center the shape below the triangle roof. Deselect the shape.

11. For the light, select a Stroke of None and a Fill of yellow or orange.

12. Select the Ellipse tool, then click on the artboard and enter 0.75 inch for both Width and Height. Click OK.

13. Center the light inside the rectangle with the arrow keys, then select Object > Arrange > Send to Back to position the light behind the rectangle. Deselect the shape. (If the shape disappears, it means the rounded rectangle did not have a Fill color of None. Select it and correct the Fill color using the Options panel.)

14. To make the walkway, set the Fill to black and use a 2-point black Stroke.

15. Select the Rounded Rectangle tool again, and click once on the artboard area.

16. Enter a 1.5 inch Width and a 0.75 inch Height with the Corner Radius at its default. Click OK. Center it under the lamp.

17. Using the Selection tool, select all the shapes by dragging diagonally over them to display a bounding box.

18. Select Object > Group, and then Save the file as *Light.ai* in your *Chapter 7* folder, using the default settings.

TOOLKIT TIP The CMYK color mode for printing is a **subtractive process** using percentages of ink: cyan (C), magenta (M), yellow (Y), and black (K). When you are creating pure white or pure black colors using the Color panel or Swatches panel, a pure black would be C=0, M=0, Y=0, and K=100 (most designers and illustrators actually add 50% cyan to create a "rich" black). A pure white would be the absence of color or C=0, M=0, Y=0, and K=0. RGB—which stands for red, green, blue—is an additive process with 255 as the highest number for each color. For pure black, all RGB colors would be set at 0; for pure white, they would be set at 255.

GUIDING THE LIGHTHOUSE

When creating custom shapes, it helps to use nonprintable guidelines created from ruler guides to position anchor points and path segments with accuracy. Guides can be created by clicking and dragging them into position from either the horizontal or vertical rulers.

TOOLKIT TIP You can use the Selection tool to click on guidelines individually (shows as a square under the cursor), and then use the arrow keys to move them precisely into place. Guides can be locked and unlocked in the View menu (View > Guides > Lock Guides).

Here, you will draw guidelines for making accurate angles for the base.

1. Make sure the rulers are visible (View > Rulers > Show Rulers).

2. Drag a guide from the left Vertical ruler, and drag it to the 4 inch mark on the Horizontal Ruler; this will be the center of the lighthouse.

3. Use the Selection tool to select the grouped shapes you created, you can also try using smart guides to help with alignment of your individual object pieces. With the arrow keys, move the them so they are centered on the guide. Use the center resizing handle of the bounding box as a guide. Deselect it when it is in position.

4. To make guidelines for the base, drag vertical guidelines to the 3.0, 3.5, 4.5, and 5.0 inch positions (Figure 7-34). Now you are ready to create an angle base.

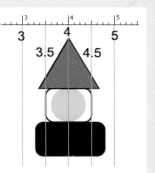

▷ FIGURE 7-34

Setting guides for placement of the lighthouse base and additional adjustments.

SHAPING THE LIGHTHOUSE BASE

You can adjust the shape of any object by moving its anchor points. The **Direct Selection tool** allows you to select and move individual anchor points or path segments. After creating the basic shape for the lighthouse base, you will use the Direct Selection tool to select anchor points and move them into position using the arrow keys on the keyboard to make fine adjustments (Figure 7-35). When the Direct Selection tool is hovering over an anchor point, the anchor point will enlarge so you can select it easily.

DESIGN TIP

When guides are unlocked, you can use the Options panel to type in an exact position.

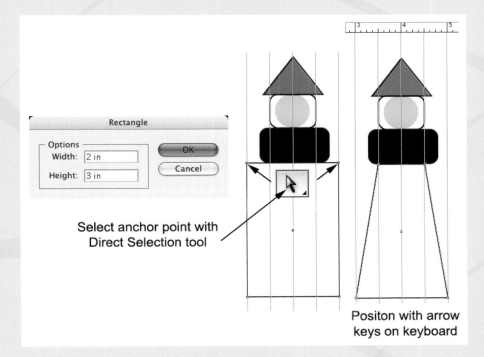

Select anchor point with Direct Selection tool

Positon with arrow keys on keyboard

▷ FIGURE 7-35

Use guides to lay out custom angles, the Direct Selection tool to select individual anchor points, and the arrow keys on your keyboard for positioning.

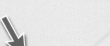

TOOLKIT TIP When using the Direct Selection tool, always click on the artboard first before selecting the anchor point or path segment you want to edit.

DESIGN TIP

For the most accurate positioning of anchor points, select individual anchor points with the Direct Selection tool, and then use the arrow keys to move around.

It is time to adjust the roof and create the angled base using the Direct Selection tool and arrow keys.

1. To adjust the lighthouse roof, select the Direct Selection tool (A) and click on the artboard. Click the top anchor point of the roof. A large square displays under the cursor; once the anchor point is selected, the anchor point will turn solid, but the rest will remain white.

2. Tap the Down arrow key 20 times to minimize the roof angle. Deselect the roof. (You can also hold the Shift key down and press the arrow key twice instead. Holding the Shift key while using the arrow keys moves a selected point or path 10 times the normal increment.)

3. For the base, set a Fill of White and a black Stroke of 1 point; try typing the letter D, which resets the colors to this default.

4. Select the Rectangle tool, click once on the artboard, and enter a Width of 2 inches and a Height of 3 inches. Click OK.

5. Center the box below the upper portion of the lighthouse, between the outer guidelines, using either the Selection tool or the arrow keys.

6. Select the Direct Selection tool and click on the artboard to deselect the rectangle, then click the upper-left anchor point of the rectangle to select it.

7. Use the right arrow key to move the anchor point to the 3.5-inch guide. (You can also enter 3.5 in the X value in the Control panel instead.)

8. Click on the artboard again, and select the upper-right anchor point.

9. Use the right arrow key to move the anchor point to the 4.5-inch guide.

10. The base outline is completed; now it is time to add the stripes (Figure 7-36).

MAKING THE LIGHTHOUSE STRIPES

To further your skills in making angled shapes (trapezoids) using the Direct Selection tool and the arrow keys, you will create three stripes on the lighthouse base. When creating angled shapes for precise placement on top of other objects, it is easier to work in Outline view.

Here you will create three stripes at angles to match the lighthouse base.

1. First, click on the red roof then click on the artboard to deselect it. Doing this will reset your stroke and fill colors to match the roof, so the stripes will also be red with a 1-point black stroke.

2. Select the Rectangle tool, then click on the artboard once.

3. Enter a 2-inch Width and 0.5-inch Height in the display box. Select OK.

4. Move the first red rectangle at the top of the base with the Selection tool.

5. Use the Selection tool and Option/Alt drag down to make two more copies of the red stripe. Make sure the bottom rectangle is placed at the bottom of the lighthouse base. Select all three stripes (Shift and click each one) and use the Align panel to distribute them evenly if needed, or use smart guides (Figure 7-36).

6. To ensure precision, switch to Outline view (View > Outline).

7. Select the Direct Selection tool and click on the artboard before selecting a corner anchor point. This will avoid moving the whole object.

8. Use the arrow keys to move each corner point alongside the angled base until they are all aligned with it (Figure 7-36). You want the blended lines to display as one to avoid incorrect overlapping.

9. Drag the second rectangle down a half inch under the top stripe, and use the Direct Selection tool and arrow keys to select and drag the corner points in as before.

10. Repeat this process for the middle and bottom rectangles.

11. To group all the elements together, choose the Selection tool and drag a box diagonally over the entire lighthouse.

12. Select Object > Group. The lighthouse is now one object.

13. Scale the lighthouse to size for the next chapter using Object > Transform > Scale > 10%. Place a check in Scale Strokes and Effects, then click OK.

14. Save the file as *Light* in your *Chapter 7* folder.

15. Feel free to experiment with color choices using the Color Guide (Window > Color Guide) panel or the Kuler panel (Window > Extensions > Kuler). Enjoy!

▷ FIGURE 7-36

Sometimes positioning accurate points is best done in Outline view. Select anchor points with the Direct Selection tool, and position precisely with the arrow keys.

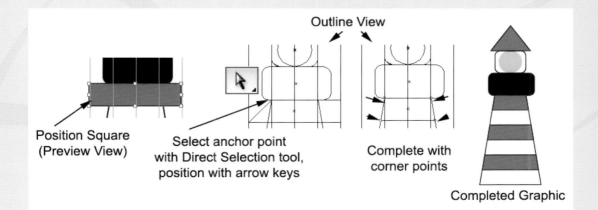

Outline View

Position Square (Preview View)

Select anchor point with Direct Selection tool, position with arrow keys

Complete with corner points

Completed Graphic

DIGITAL TOOLKIT EXTRA: Custom Shapes
to Create Playing Cards

This assignment involves using the new Shape Builder tool in CS5 to create complex shapes out of a series of separate shapes. In creating the Ace playing cards, you'll use various shape tools, then combine with the Shape Builder tool to create a diamond, club, spade, and heart shape. You will also learn to use the Direct Selection tool which allows you to select parts of either an object's anchor points or path lines to accurately adjust using the arrow keys on your keyboard. You will get familiar with the Ellipse, Polygon, Rounded Rectangle, and Rectangle shape tools for your cards. The Transform command is also used here to reflect, rotate, and scale shapes and adjust the "Ace" font character.

▷ FIGURE 7-37

Creating playing cards using custom shapes, Transform command, and the Shape Builder tool.

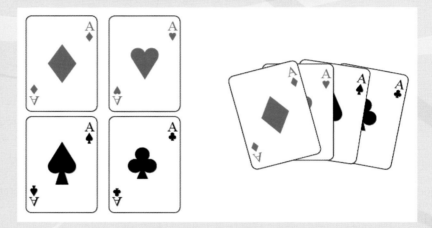

CREATING THE CARD OUTLINE WITH THE ROUNDED RECTANGLE TOOL

The Rounded Rectangle shape tool does exactly what its name implies, rounds the corners of a square or rectangle. Professional playing cards have rounded corners, which is what you will create for this exercise. You will also set your document for printing and use the Control panel to create the stroke outline for the cards.

You will set up the document as a print document, measuring in inches, and create the card outline.

1. In Illustrator, create a new Print document by selecting Create New > Print from the Welcome Screen or by selecting File > New > Document Profile – Print.

2. Change the Units measurement to Inches instead of points and change the orientation to Landscape, 11 inches Width by 8.5 inches Height. Keep all other default settings (Figure 7-38). Name the document *Cards* and click OK.

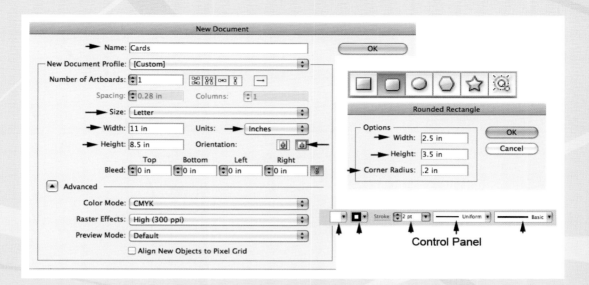

▷ FIGURE 7-38

Creating the playing cards outline using the Rounded Rectangle Tool.

3. Select the Rounded Rectangular shape tool and click on the artboard to bring up the dialog box. Create a size 2.5 inches Width by 3.5 inches Height, by 0.2 Rounded Corners. Click OK.

4. With the selected shape on the document, use the Control Panel to make sure the Stroke is black with a 2-point thickness and the Foreground is white.

5. Make sure Smart Guides, Snap to Point, and Rulers are checked in the View menu.

USING TYPE IN ILLUSTRATOR

As you learned in Photoshop, Illustrator also has a Type tool and a Type menu to select from a font list. The list displays the fonts as thumbnail representations of what the font will look like to help you in your selection. You can also use the Control panel once the Type tool is selected to also make selections. In Illustrator you can use the Type tool to click anywhere on the artboard and begin typing normally. You then use the Selection tool (black arrow tool) to position the type character(s) the same way you would with any shape object. This will be covered more in depth in the next chapter.

In this exercise you will select a serif font, type and position it, then make a copy and flip it using the Transform command.

1. To choose a regular font in Illustrator, select Type > Font > and select from the list of fonts displayed. Choose a slender serif font like Georgia, Garamond, or Times New Roman. For this example we are using Times New Roman. Official playing cards use their own custom font, so we will improvise here.

2. Select Type > Size and choose a 36-point size, then set the Foreground color to black. You will also notice you can also make these settings using the Control panel as well.

DESIGN TIP

In most cases, especially in traditional design, you want to allow ample space between type and the edge of the document, and, in the case of creating these playing cards, between the type and the shapes you are creating.

▷ FIGURE 7-39

Using the Type menu and Type Tool to make the character for the playing cards.

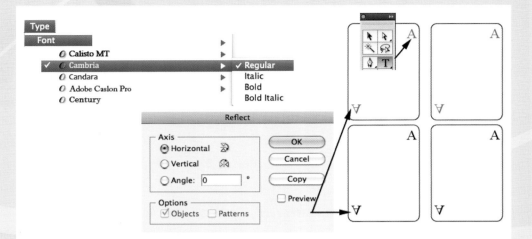

3. Select the Type tool and type an uppercase "A" in the upper-right corner of the card, allowing about a one-eight inch space from the right edge and a quarter inch space from the top. Use the Selection tool or arrow keys to position your letter.

4. Select the character and copy it by holding down the Option/Alt key and dragging it to the bottom left of the card with the same spacing from the edge as you made in the upper-right corner.

5. You need to flip the character in the bottom left by selecting the character, then select Object > Transform > Reflect. When the Reflect dialog box displays, select Axis > Horizontal. Click OK. Reposition your character.

6. Now that you have one card outline completed, use the Selection tool and drag diagonally to select the card outline and contents, and either use the Edit menu to copy and paste three more cards, or use the Option/Alt key and drag three times to make three copies.

7. Position the cards apart from one another on the left side of the artboard, two on top, two on bottom, using the smart guides as practice for even alignment. The right side of the artboard will be used as a work area for creating your shapes (Figure 7-39).

8. Select the "A" character on the top left card, and choose a red color from the Swatches panel. Change the color of the other characters on the two top cards to the same red color.

9. Save the file in Illustrator CS5 format as *Cards.ai* in your *Chapter 7* folder.

CREATING THE DIAMOND SHAPE USING THE DIRECT SELECTION TOOL

In the previous exercises, you have been using the Selection tool, which is the black arrow icon to move entire objects or shapes. Next to the Selection tool is the **Direct Selection tool**, which is displayed as a white arrow icon. This tool is used to select parts of a path, or an object's anchor point described in the beginning of this chapter, and move or adjust only that component. In creating the diamond shape, a square will be created, rotated, and then adjusted using the Direct Selection tool. Again this tool will be used more in depth in the next chapters. You can also choose to have a Stroke color of None displayed by choosing the Stroke color icon in the Tools panel, then either selecting the None icon which displays as a box with a red line through it below, or through the color or Swatches panels.

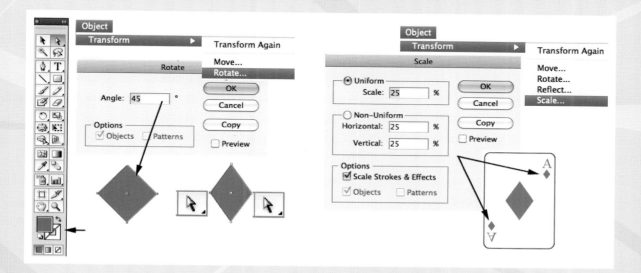

▷ FIGURE 7-40

Creating the diamond shape using Direct Selection Tool and Transform command.

Here you will use the familiar Rectangle Tool used in the checkerboard assignment to make the square, and then rotate it 45 degrees using the Transform command. The sides will be adjusted using the Direct Selection Tool.

1. On the Tools panel, select the red Foreground color from the Swatches panel, and select the None icon (red line through square) for the Stroke color. You can also do this using the Swatches panel. Make sure Rulers is still checked (View Rulers).

2. Select the Rectangle tool and click on the black space on the right side of the artboard. Enter a 1-inch Width and Height. Click OK.

3. To rotate, select Object > Transform > Rotate. Enter 45 degrees, in the display box and then click OK.

4. Click on the artboard to deselect the object. Click on the Direct Selection tool and click on the left point of the diamond object to access the anchor point. When you have an anchor point selected, or when the cursor hovers over an anchor point the white arrow displays a white square underneath.

5. Press the right arrow key on your keyboard 15 times, then select the anchor point on the right side and press the left arrow key 15 times. This will slender down the diamond shape accurately.

6. Click on the artboard to deselect the diamond from the Direct Selection tool, then select the Selection tool (black arrow) and select the shape again. Using the smart guides to assist you, position the shape in the center of the top left card when you see the intersection lines appear.

7. To create the little diamond shapes that will appear underneath the "A" character you created, with the diamond selected, hold down the Option/Alt key and drag twice to create two copies (or you can use the Edit command to copy and paste the object twice).

8. For each, select Object > Transform > Scale > and enter "25" in the display dialog box (Figure 7-40) to scale down one-quarter the original size.

9. Use the Selection tool and move each under the "A" character centered with some space as shown in Figure 7-40. A good rule of thumb is to use the space of an anchor point from the bounding box to the bottom of the character.

10. To flip the bottom left diamond shape (although it wouldn't be noticeable for this shape), select it and choose Object > Transform > Reflect > Horizontal.

11. Your first card, the Ace of Diamonds, is finished.

12. Save the file in your *Chapter 7* folder.

TOOLKIT TIP You can also rotate an object at 45-degree increments by selecting the object using the Selection tool, and hover the cursor over the bottom right corner until a bent arrow appears as a cursor. Hold down the Shift key and drag to the left or right and the object will turn in 45-degree increments. Release the mouse when you are done.

CREATING THE HEART SHAPE USING SHAPE TOOLS AND SHAPE BUILDER TOOL

One of the new tools in Illustrator CS5 is the **Shape Builder tool**. This tool allows you to create one complex shape out of a group of selected shapes. The default setting for this tool is to merge shapes together. It can also be used to help fill in gaps with color. To change or adjust settings, you can double click on the tool and make your changes, but we will keep the default settings for this exercise. You can also use the Direct Selection tool to select not only anchor points, but path lines as well, and then adjust using the arrow keys.

Here you will use the Ellipse and Polygon shape tools, and the Shape Builder tool, to create the heart shape for the next playing card.

1. To create the top of the heart shape, make sure the Foreground color is red with a Stroke of none. Select the Ellipse tool, click on the blank right side of the artboard, and enter a 0.5-inch Height and Width.

2. Use the Option/Alt key and hold down the selected shape creating another copy to move to the right of the first circle with the inside edges touching.

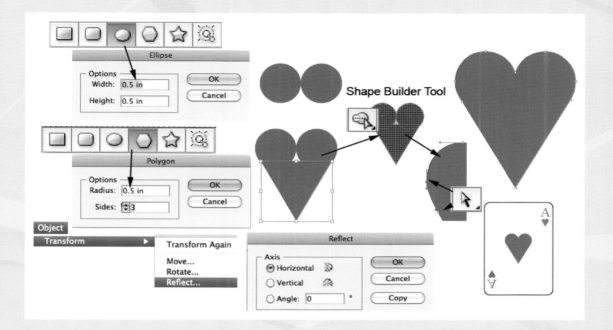

▷   FIGURE 7-41

Creating the heart shape using Ellipse, Polygon, and Shape Builder tools.

3. To create the point area, select the Polygon tool, click on the artboard, and create a 3-sided object at 0.5 Radius.

4. To flip the triangle, select it and choose Object > Transform > Reflect > Horizontal.

5. With the triangle object selected, use the Selection tool and drag underneath until the two circle edges blend visually with the side as accurately as possible (Figure 7-41). You will notice a gap is between the three shapes.

6. Select all three shapes with the Selection tool, and then select the Shape Builder tool. Shapes must always be selected first. Note: If you DO NOT have CS5 with the Shape Builder tool, you can create a third circle to fill in the gap, then select Object > Group, and then skip to Step 9.

7. Click on the left circle shape and drag across diagonally to blend in the other shapes. You will notice the highlighted shapes have a cross mesh displayed. When you let go the shapes start to merge together and the gap between the shapes will also be filled in.

8. Continue until the heart shape is blended together as one shape.

9. OPTIONAL: The shape will probably not be perfect at this stage of your learning, but you can use it for the rest of the exercises. There are many more advanced ways to make adjustments, which you'll learn later. One way, if you want to attempt it, is to zoom at 300% and use the Direct Selection tool and click on the path line, or the anchor point, near the left edge of the circle and then click the right arrow key only one or twice to adjust the shape to make it more accurate (Figure 7-41), then try on the other side. If it doesn't work you can always undo the action (Edit > Undo).

10. Click on the artboard to deselect the heart shape, and then select the Selection tool (black arrow) to select the shape again. Using the smart guides to assist you, position the shape in the center when you see the intersection lines appear.

11. To create the little heart shapes that will appear underneath the "A" character you created, select the heart shape, then hold down the Option/Alt key and drag to create a copy.

12. Select and choose Object > Transform > Scale > and enter "25" in the display dialog box to scale down one-quarter the original size.

13. Use the Selection tool and move each under the top right "A" character centered with some space, using the smart guides for proper alignment with the previous card. A good rule of thumb is to use the space of a square anchor point from the bounding box to the bottom of the character.

14. With the little heart selected, hold down the Option/Alt key to create a duplicate and drag to the bottom left under the upside down "A. "

15. To flip the bottom left heart shape, select it and choose Object > Transform > Reflect > Horizontal. Reposition if needed using the smart guides.

16. Your second card, the Ace of Hearts, is finished.

17. Save the file in your *Chapter 7* folder.

TOOLKIT TIP Although a little advanced for now, you can use the Direct Selection tool to select the path line, not the anchor point, and slightly curve inward the heart shape (and the previous diamond shape as well), as would be done in professional playing card shapes. You will find little lines coming out of the anchor point, which are called directional lines and can also be used to more accurately change the shape of the curve as well. The trick is to make sure they are both accurate on both sides. This will be covered more in depth in Chapter 9.

COMBINING SHAPES TO CREATE THE SPADE SHAPE

To create the spade shape, you can flip the heart shape you just created, and then add a triangle underneath, and adjust using the Direct Selection tool. This allows you to then use the Shape Builder tool to create another custom shape.

Here you will create the spade shape built upon the heart shape you just created.

1. Using the Selection tool, select the heart shape create a duplicate copy by holding down the Option/Alt key and dragging to a blank workspace on the artboard.

2. Change the Foreground color to black with a Stroke of none, using the Swatches or Color panel. The new color will display on the Tools panel.

3. To flip the heart shape upside down, select it and choose Object > Transform > Reflect > Horizontal.

▷ FIGURE 7-42

Creating the spade shape using the Shape Builder tool. Making adjustments with the Direct Selection tool.

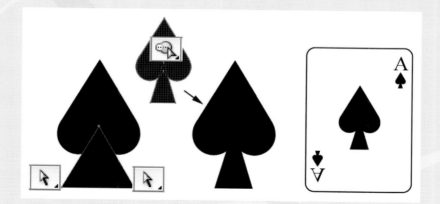

4. To create the bottom portion of the spade, select the Polygon tool, click on the artboard, and create a 3-sided object at 0.5 Radius.

5. With the triangle object selected, use the Selection tool and drag underneath the center of the upside down shape about a third of the shape overlapping as shown in Figure 7-42.

6. Select the Direct Selection tool and click on the left bottom anchor point and click the right arrow key 15 times to slender the shape size. Do the same with the right side anchor point using the left arrow key.

7. Select both shapes with the Selection tool, and then select the Shape Builder tool. Shapes must always be selected first. Note: If you DO NOT have CS5 with the Shape Builder tool, you can select both shapes, then select Object > Group, then skip to Step 9.

8. Click on the upside down heart shape and drag downward to blend in the two shapes. You will notice the highlighted shapes have a cross mesh displayed. When you let go the shapes start to merge together.

9. Click on the artboard to deselect the spade shape, and then select the Selection tool (black arrow) to select the shape again. Using the smart guides to assist you, position the new spade shape in the center of the bottom left card when you see the intersection lines appear.

10. To create the little spade shape that will appear underneath the "A" character you created, with the spade object selected, hold down the Option/Alt key and drag to create a copy.

11. Select and choose Object > Transform > Scale > and enter "25" in the display dialog box to scale down one-quarter the original size.

12. Use the Selection tool and move under the top right "A" character centered with some space, using the smart guides for proper alignment with the previous card. Use the space of a square anchor point from the bounding box to the bottom of the "A" character.

13. With the little spade object selected, hold down the Option/Alt key to create a duplicate and drag to the bottom left under the upside down "A".

14. To flip the bottom left heart shape, select it and choose Object > Transform > Reflect > Horizontal. Reposition if needed using the smart guides.

15. Your third card, the Ace of Spades, is finished.

16. Save the file in your *Chapter 7* folder.

CREATING THE CLUB SHAPE USING THE SHAPE BUILDER TOOL

The final shape, the club, provides a nice review of some of the shape tools, and in using the Shape Builder tool again. This time, with the shapes a bit further away from one another, you will hold down the Shift key with the Shape Builder tool to make this custom shape. When all four cards are completed, you can save the document as a template for creating future cards. Templates have an "ait" extension.

▷ FIGURE 7-43

Creating the Ace of Clubs using the shapes tools and Direct Selection tool.

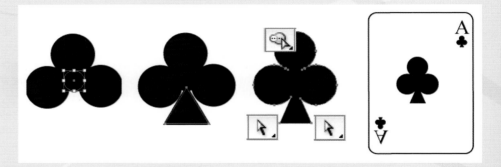

Here you will complete the last card, the Ace of Clubs.

1. Set the Foreground at a black color and Stroke of none.

2. Select the Ellipse shape tool and click on the artboard. Enter a Height and Width of 0.5 inches to make a circle.

3. Hold down the Option/Alt key and copy two more circles, placing them with the Selection tool to the bottom left and right and touching the original circle, using the smart guides for proper alignment.

4. Create another smaller circle with the Ellipse tool at 0.25 × 0.25 inches, and then using the Selection tool, place the circle in the center underneath the three larger circles (Figure 7-43).

5. Select the Polygon tool, then clicks on the artboard, and create a 3-sided object at 0.3 Radius.

6. With the triangle object selected, use the Selection tool and drag underneath the center of the upside down shape overlapping slightly.

7. Select the Direct Selection tool and click on the left bottom anchor point and click the right arrow key 5 times to slender the shape size. Do the same with the right side anchor point using the left arrow key.

8. Select all five shapes with the Selection tool, and then select the Shape Builder tool. Shapes must always be selected first. Note: If you DO NOT have CS5 with the Shape Builder tool, you can select all shapes, then select Object > Group, then skip to Step 10.

9. Since this is a rather complex shape with components further away, hold down the Shift key and drag from the middle circle to the other shapes to include all shapes. When you let go the shapes start to merge together. Repeat if necessary.

10. Click on the artboard to deselect the new club shape, and then select the Selection tool (black arrow) to select the shape again. Using the smart guides to assist you, position the shape in the center of the bottom right card when you see the intersection lines appear.

11. To create the little club shape that will appear underneath the "A" character you created, with the club object selected, hold down the Option/Alt key and drag to create a copy.

12. Select and choose Object > Transform > Scale > and enter "25" in the display dialog box to scale down one-quarter the original size.

13. With the little spade object selected, hold down the Option/Alt key to create a duplicate and drag to the bottom left under the upside down "A."

14. Use the Selection tool and move under the top right "A" character centered with some space, using the smart guides for proper alignment with the previous card, and the space of a square anchor point from the bounding box to the bottom of the "A" character.

15. To flip the bottom left club shape, select it and choose Object > Transform > Reflect > Horizontal. Reposition if needed using the smart guides.

16. Your fourth card, the Ace of Clubs, is finished. Remove the excess shapes in the workspace area you created, by selecting with the Selection tool, then pressing the delete key.

17. Save as a template file for future cards by selecting File > Save as Template in your *Chapter 7* folder. It will have an "ait" extension.

18. Save the file again as the normal Illustrator file *Cards.ai* in your *Chapter 7* folder.

POSITIONING THE PLAYING CARDS USING THE OBJECT MENU AND SELECTION TOOL

In this final exercise, you'll use the Object menu to group each individual card's components as one unit, and then arrange the cards. The Object menu allows you to take selected objects or groups of objects and place them in front of or behind one another. You will then use the Selection tool to move the selected cards at angles to one another so they appear as a hand of cards.

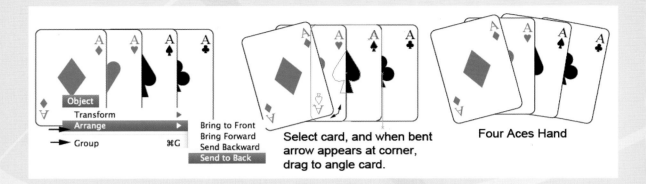

Object
  Transform ▶
→ **Arrange** ▶   Bring to Front
→ Group   ⌘G   Bring Forward
   Send Backward
   Send to Back

Select card, and when bent arrow appears at corner, drag to angle card.

Four Aces Hand

▷ FIGURE 7-44

Creating a four aces hand.

Here you will use the Object menu to place the cards overlapping one another, then use the Selection tool and arrow keys to move the card corners.

1. Before moving the cards, you will need to make them as individual groups. To make sure each card's components are grouped together, use the Selection tool and select the first Ace of Diamonds card, then select Object > Group.

2. Repeat the same with the other three cards individually. You can now move around each individual card with all its objects as one using the Selection tool.

3. Move the cards around so they overlap one another by about half a card.

4. Select the cards where needed, and select Object > Arrange >Send to Back, or Send to Front so they appear in order shown in Figure 7-44.

5. Select the Ace of Diamonds card, and then hover the cursor over the bottom right corner until a bent arrow appears, then click and drag to move the card at an angle. Use the arrow keys for further positioning.

6. Repeat the same process with the other cards as needed.

7. Save the file again as *Cards.ai* in your *Chapter 7* folder.

8. Go ahead and create some other cards using the template you just created with all the shapes completed. Enjoy!

CHAPTER SUMMARY

Illustrator is a digital illustration program that creates scalable vector images. In this chapter, you learned the importance of precise alignment, creating and modifying basic shapes, and grouping shapes together to create more complex objects. You used the Selection tool combined with Option/Alt and Shift keys to select multiple objects and to copy objects. You found using the Direct Selection tool helpful in editing path segments or anchor points. You learned how to select fill and stroke colors using the Swatches, Color Guide, and Color panels. For more information and projects, check out the *Goodies* folder on your CD, or go to *www.digitoolkit.com*.

REVIEW QUESTIONS

1. Define objects or paths, anchor points, path segments, and the artboard area.
2. Explain the characteristics of vector images.
3. Explain how to copy an object.
4. Explain the purpose of Preview view and Outline view.
5. Explain the difference between the Swatches, Color, and Color Guide panels.
6. Explain four graphic file formats or extensions in which Illustrator files can be saved.

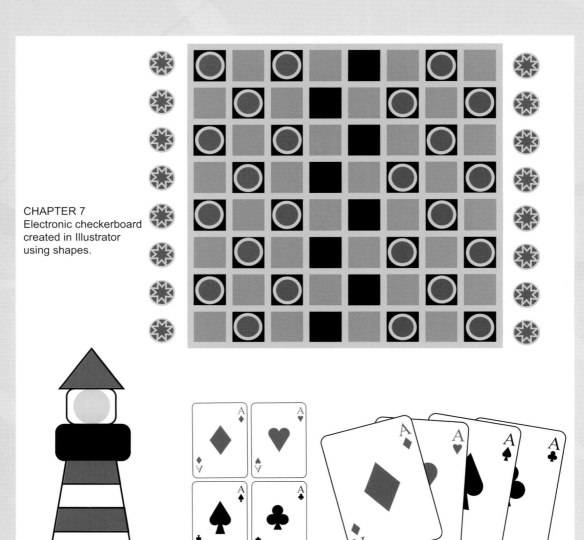

CHAPTER 7
Electronic checkerboard
created in Illustrator
using shapes.

CHAPTER 7 ADVANCED
Building a lighthouse
by creating and combining
complex shapes in Illustrator.

CHAPTER 7 EXTRA
Creating playing cards using custom shapes,
Shape Builder tool, and Object menu.

▷ FIGURE 7-45

CHAPTER

8

Working with Brushes, Symbols, and Layers

CHAPTER OBJECTIVES: To understand the importance of using Illustrator to create images from basic sketches, in this chapter you will:

▷ Use a sketch or line art in Illustrator as a template to make artwork scalable and sharp with Illustrator's drawing tools.

▷ Learn to trace an image accurately using Illustrator's drawing tools and the Live Trace tool.

▷ Create and apply brushes, place symbols, and format text by applying styles.

▷ Create symbols to add to the Symbols panel.

▷ Work with Symbolism tools and symbol libraries.

▷ ADVANCED USERS: Place a logo created by the Blob Brush tool onto multiple artboards.

▷ DIGITAL TOOLKIT EXTRA: Create 3-D objects and map labels using various types of brushes.

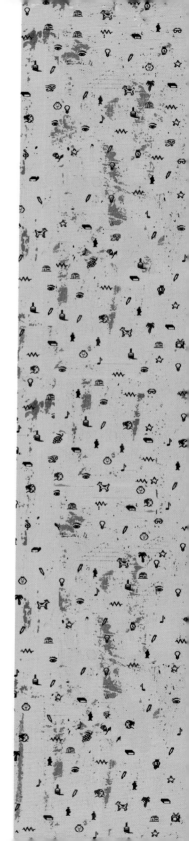

A digital illustration can be started from scratch or by tracing an image drawn on paper and scanning that image into the computer. A template is then made from that graphic that can be traced and modified with a variety of drawing tools and functions. As in Photoshop, using layers for various parts of the image allows the designer to work on one area at a time without affecting the other layers. Layers can be moved around for a variety of effects. Brushes and symbols in Illustrator allow the designer to apply all kinds of strokes, artwork, and other effects with ease. In this chapter, you will learn how to trace images and create and apply brushes and symbols. You will be creating a simple map to demonstrate some of the basic skills a cartographer, a map illustrator, would use.

MAKING DIGITAL ILLUSTRATIONS FROM DRAWINGS

When drawings are scanned in a digital imaging application, like Photoshop, and then traced and recreated in Illustrator, they can be scaled to any size and edited without losing their sharp edges. A nonprintable template can be created from a scanned image, traced, and edited using many of Illustrator's drawing tools, such as the Pen, Pencil, Smooth, Eraser, Direct Selection, and Blob Brush tools. Any graphic can also be saved as a symbol for later use on a document, and brushes can be applied to any path created. Illustrator also uses type, which can be formatted with various commands or style panels.

CREATING TEMPLATES IN ILLUSTRATOR

One of the nice features of illustration programs like Illustrator is that you can trace any image or drawing very accurately by creating a nonprintable **template**. A template is a faded version of the original image that acts as a guide for recreating it (Figure 8-1). A new working layer for using these drawing tools is created on top of the template layer. A new vector drawing is made using the template, which can be modified and resized while retaining its image clarity.

▷ FIGURE 8-1

Tracing over a template.

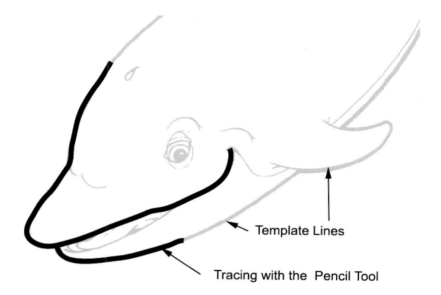

Template Lines

Tracing with the Pencil Tool

THE PENCIL, SMOOTH, BLOB BRUSH, AND PATH ERASER TOOLS

The **Pencil tool** allows the designer to draw freely, or trace from a template, any drawing or image. As a line is drawn, a path is automatically created with anchor points when the mouse is released. One of the benefits of the Pencil tool is that you can create joining open paths, allowing you to stop and start again along the way. As long as you start on the ending anchor point, the paths should join together. The **Smooth tool** moves and deletes anchor points to smooth out crooked freehand path segments created by the Pencil tool. The **Eraser tool** removes anchor points and path segments (Figure 8-2). The Blob Brush tool creates clean vector paths and shapes, even when strokes overlap one another. This tools works in conjunction with the Direct Select, Path Eraser, and Smooth tools creating paths that can be merged as filled shapes of the same color. In Illustrator CS5, you can create variable widths to your stroke paths, or use the default Uniform Profile for a consistent stroke.

▷ FIGURE 8-2

Pencil, Smooth, Path Eraser, and Blob Brush Tools.

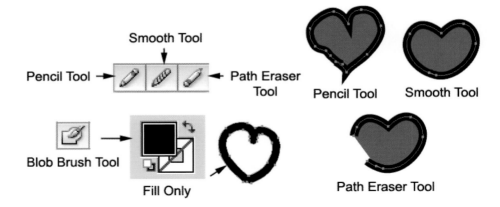

THE DIRECT SELECTION TOOL

In addition to using the Selection tool, which creates a bounding box around selected paths, there is also the Direct Selection tool, which is used when you need to select specific segments, anchor points, or objects (Figure 8-3). You can then drag and reposition these selected paths and anchor points.

▷ FIGURE 8-3

The Direct Selection tool selects individual path segments, objects, and anchor points.

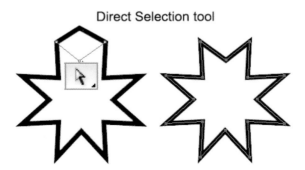

SYMBOLS, SYMBOLISM TOOLS, LIBRARIES, AND THE SYMBOLS PANEL

One of the nice features in Illustrator is the ability to create symbols, store them in the Symbols panel for later use, and modify them in your document with the various Symbolism tools in the Tools panel. **Symbols** are art objects that you can create from combinations of paths, text, images, or groups of objects, and you can save them for later use in the Symbols panel in your document. Symbols can also include brush strokes, special effects, blending of colors, and more. The **Symbols panel** is used to place, store, and create symbols. You can create repeating symbols or **symbol instances** of a particular symbol within a document. After a symbol is created, any instances on the artboard can be edited and changed if necessary. Using symbol instances in your artwork minimizes file size, because they are set up as links to the original symbol in the Symbol library. You can modify the size, color, and distribution of symbol instances using various **Symbolism tools** (Figure 8-4). Illustrator comes with a wide variety of preset symbols organized in collections called **symbol libraries**. When you open a symbol library or any library, it displays in a new panel. To add symbols, select from the symbol library and drag to the Symbols panel, or select Add to Symbols from the Library panel menu.

▷ FIGURE 8-4

Symbols, Panel Menu options, Symbol Library panels, and Symbol Instances.

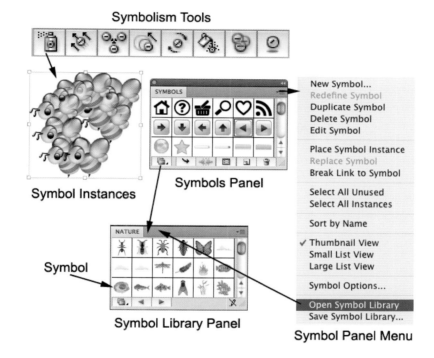

BRUSHES, BRUSH LIBRARIES, AND THE BRUSHES PANEL

Brushes allow you to apply freehand strokes of artwork in various ways to paths or objects. You can apply brushes to existing selected paths or use the Brush tool to create a path. Illustrator comes with a variety of preset brushes organized as **brush libraries**, which appear in a new panel (Figure 8-5). You can create new brushes by selecting the object you have created in your document and dragging it to the Brushes panel. To apply a brush stroke with the Paintbrush tool, select the tool first, along with fill and stroke settings, and then select a brush style from the Brushes panel. You can also select an existing path drawn by any tool, and then choose a brush style from the Brushes panel. You can create your own brush artwork and add it to the **Brushes panel** or use predefined brushes in five different categories: **Calligraphic Brushes, Scatter Brushes, Art Brushes, Bristle,** and **Pattern Brushes.** In Illustrator CS5, the new **Bristle brush** style allows you to create brush strokes with the appearance of a natural brush with bristles. You can either select the Brushes panel from the Window menu (Window > Brushes), or from the Control panel when a brush stroke is selected.

▷ FIGURE 8-5

Brushes panel, Panel Menu options, and Special Brush panels stored in a brush library to add to the Brush panel.

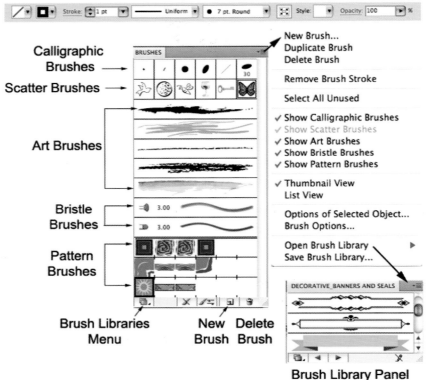

Brush Library Panel

WORKING WITH TYPE

The Type tools provide many functions in Illustrator (Figure 8-6). You can select the normal horizontal Type tool, make selections from the Type menu, and then click anywhere to start typing normally. There are also Type tools that allow you to type vertically, along a path, or within a shape. Type-related panels found under the Window menu (Window > Type) allow adjustments in character or paragraph formatting, tabbing, and creating and applying automatic formatting or styles to selected text. The Character panel and Character Styles panel apply formatting options to selected type. You can also apply formatting options to selected type by using the Control panel.

▷ FIGURE 8-6

Type tools and Type menu, Character and Character Styles panels, and Control panel for type.

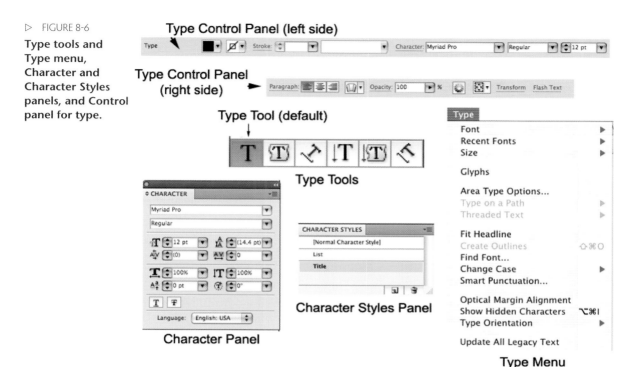

CLIENT ASSIGNMENT: Creating a Tourist Map

The owner of Magic Bus Tours, Mike Nelson, wants you to help him create a map of Cape Cod lighthouses in Massachusetts that he wants to print on parchment-type paper for his summer bus tours. He wants to use it as a visual reference for his clients, showing lighthouse locations with some cities and towns labeled. Symbols of lighthouses would be placed around the map and numbered so they could be identified in a list placed beneath the map for reference. The two main highways to the Cape, U.S. Highway Route 6 and State Highway Route 28, would be placed on the map for further reference. He gives you a sketch of Cape Cod with lighthouse locations marked with an "x" to scan into your computer and a document for the text information to include for each lighthouse. Knowing this would be best done in Illustrator, you tell Mike you will trace the map and create lighthouse and highway symbols, then place the list of lighthouses beneath the map shape. You tell Mike it will be ready at the end of the week.

ACTION ITEMS OVERVIEW

To use a sketch, a designer must first scan the sketch into Photoshop and save it in Grayscale mode to be used as a template to trace. Color is not important here, because the template will be grayed out for tracing. This has already been done, and the template is in your *Chapter 8* folder. In Illustrator, the image needs to be traced with drawing tools, and symbols and brushes must be created and applied for the map elements (Figure 8-7).

Here is what you need to do:

• Place the scanned image in a new Illustrator print document using portrait orientation and the default CMYK color mode.

• Trace the document using the Pencil tool and adjust the paths with the Smooth, Eraser, and Selection tools.

• Create the highway roads as brushes and apply them to the highway template outlines.

• Create the U.S. Highway symbol using the Live Trace tool.

• Place lighthouse and highway symbols.

• Type in titles, numbers, and lighthouse descriptions on the map. Use formatting techniques and apply styles for consistency.

▷ FIGURE 8-7

Creating a tourist map from a drawing sketch.

• Edit symbol instances with Symbolism tools.

• ADVANCED USERS: Illustrator freestyle creations with the Blob Brush tool. Working with multiple artboards.

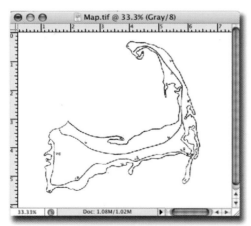

**Sketch of Map
of Cape Cod, Massachusettes**

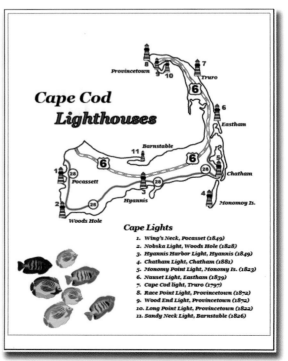

Completed Map

PREPARING THE MAP IMAGE FOR TRACING

Before tracing and applying brushes and symbols to the map, it needs to be brought into Illustrator as a template to use as a guide for tracing. Since the template will be dimmed when placed in Illustrator, you can scan the image into Photoshop and save it in Grayscale mode to keep the file size down.

SCANNING LINE ART INTO PHOTOSHOP

Line art can be any drawing or sketch created by traditional drawing utensils, like pencil, pen, charcoal, and so on. To bring line art into the computer to use in Illustrator, it still needs to be scanned and imported into an image-editing program like Photoshop. The image can then be "placed" into a new document created in Illustrator.

DESIGN TIP

If you are scanning a pencil or charcoal sketch, use the Grayscale Mode option (Image > Mode > Grayscale) in Photoshop or on your scanner to capture the subtle shading of these types of drawings and to keep the file size down. With line art, you can scan at 300 dpi.

▷ FIGURE 8-8

Scanning line art or sketches into Photoshop as 8-bit grayscale.

TOOLKIT TIP When scanning for image size, it is always better to resize (resample) down than to increase the size. You can resize by percentage or by inputting a specific physical size. Use inches to specify printed sizes. Use pixels to specify screen display sizes. Another idea is to scan at a higher ppi than you need, and then reduce the ppi while enlarging the image in Photoshop using the Image Size function.

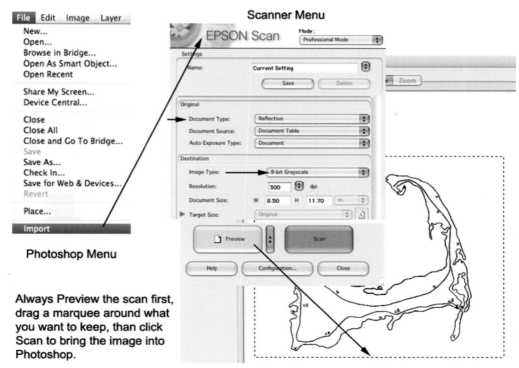

Optional Exercise: In this exercise in scanning line art, you can print the *Map* file from your *Chapter 8* folder, then scan and adjust the image into Photoshop. If you do not have access to a scanner, you can proceed to the next exercise, "Clearing the Background...", and just use the same prescanned map.

1. Open Photoshop and open the *Map* file in the *Chapter 8* folder within the *Illustrator* folder on your drive (Illustrator > Chapter 8 > Map).

2. Print the sketch using the default portrait orientation, which displays the document vertically (File > Print > Portrait Orientation). Your printer settings may be worded differently.

3. Place the printed document of the map in your scanner face down; using Photoshop, select (File > Import > Scanner name, or Twain).

4. Make sure you have Reflective, or Document, as the document setting— something indicating you are scanning a document for print, not transparency or film, because this indicates scanning slides or film negatives—and that you are scanning as 8-bit or 256 colors of gray (grayscale), and set the resolution of your scanner to 300 dpi (Figure 8-8).

5. Select Preview: when the image is displayed, drag the marquee around the map sketch area to delete as much white space as possible, and click Scan to bring the image into Photoshop.

6. In most cases, you can close the scanner software and you will find the image in Photoshop. If your scanner software is different, save as a TIF file to your *Chapter 8* folder, then launch Photoshop to open it. Leave the image open in Photoshop for the next exercise.

CLEARING THE BACKGROUND WITH THE MAGIC ERASER TOOL IN PHOTOSHOP

When scanning line art, most of the cleaning up of the paper background and spots should be done in Photoshop before placing the image in Illustrator. Using the **Magic Eraser tool** removes the unwanted background colors and spots to make the background transparent.

TOOLKIT TIP Drawings or sketches that are scanned into Photoshop to be used in Illustrator are generally saved as TIF files, which are better for tracing, because they are the most accurate when recording detail.

DESIGN TIP

Using the Magic Eraser tool in Photoshop allows the designer to remove the white paper background, or any single colored background, so that when the line art is placed into Illustrator, it is "clear"; only the line art is displayed.

Now you will use the Magic Eraser tool to clear out the background area.

1. If you completed the previous optional exercise, the scanned *Map* file should be open and displayed on the Photoshop desktop. If you did not complete the previous exercise in scanning, launch Photoshop and open the *Map* file in the *Chapter 8* folder within the *Illustrator* folder on your drive (Illustrator > Chapter 8 > Map).

2. Select the Magic Eraser tool entering a Tolerance of 32 pixels; click all the white areas of the map to make them transparent or absent of color, so the background does not interfere with painting in colors later (Figure 8-9).

3. To darken the drawing lines, adjust the Brightness to minus 30 and the Contrast to 30 (Image > Adjustments > Brightness/Contrast).

4. Check to make sure the mode is set to Grayscale (Image > Mode > Grayscale). Do not forget it is going to be a gray template anyway, so color does not matter. Use the Crop tool to crop the image down to just the map itself.

5. Save the file *as MapSCAN.tif* in your *Illustrator* folder (*Chapter 8*) with default settings. If you get a message that saving as a TIF with layers will increase file size, click OK.

6. Close the file, then quit Photoshop. It is time to bring your map into Illustrator.

▷ FIGURE 8-9

Making the background transparent with the Magic Eraser tool, and adjusting the brightness and contrast for clarity.

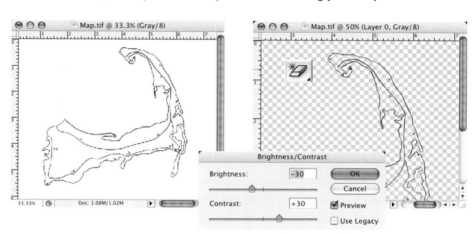

SETTING UP FOR CMYK COLOR IN ILLUSTRATOR

In Illustrator, color defaults to the CMYK mode, which is used mostly for illustrations going to press. RGB colors are the colors best used for electronic display and for limited printouts from an ink-jet printer. When there will be a large quantity printed, leaving the default CMYK mode intact allows the map to be printed fairly inexpensively by a local print shop.

You will now create a new document for print in portrait orientation with CMYK color mode.

1. Launch Illustrator and create a new document in CMYK Color, one (1) Artboard, Units of Inches for measurement, set at Portrait Orientation, and Letter Size, with no Bleeds for this project (see Figure 8-10). Click on the Advanced arrow if all the display box is not displayed.

2. Name the file *MapPRINT.* Click OK.

3. Make sure Rulers are displayed (View > Rulers > Show Rulers), and leave this document open for the next exercise.

▷ FIGURE 8-10

New document in CMYK color.

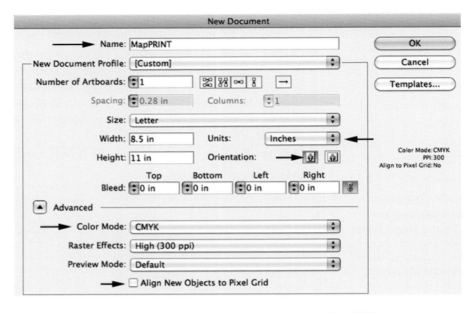

▷ FIGURE 8-10

New document in CMYK color.

PLACING THE DRAWING AS A TEMPLATE LAYER

Before an image is traced, a template layer must be created, which dims the image. **Template layers** are nonprintable representations that allow you to trace a sketch or drawing. By using the **Place command**, any sketch or drawing can be made into a template for tracing manually by either the Pencil or Pen tool. When the Place dialog box comes up, and the Template option is checked, the scanned image can be placed in a new document created in Illustrator and is automatically dimmed 50 percent. A drawing layer is automatically created on top of the template layer for tracing the drawing. You can lock and unlock the template layer or any other layer by clicking on the Lock Icon to the left of the active layer. Layers can be named and options set by double-clicking on a layer's name.

▷ FIGURE 8-11

Placing the map sketch as a template.

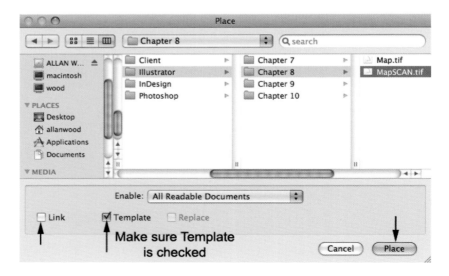

TOOLKIT TIP When placing files in a single page document or small job, which may be sent to a service provider for printing, leave the Link box unchecked (unless increasing the overall file size is a problem). This way, the graphic will be embedded in the document, and you will not have to worry about remembering to supply the original as well. Linked files need to have the original template file along with the document, but this keeps the document size smaller. Make sure you have the placed template or object where you want it before accepting its position. You can unlock a template layer and move the scan around. Even if you link the scan, you can always delete the template layer when you are done with the image. When the placed object or template is accepted, it becomes a permanent part of the document, or it can be deleted if no longer required.

Need additional fun computer graphics tutorials and info, and an additional look at the projects you'll be creating in this book? Check out my Artist's Digital Toolkit website at: **http://www.digitoolkit.com**

1. In Illustrator, make sure the Layers panel is displayed. If not, make sure it is checked in the Window menu (Window > Layers), or open it from the panel icon at the right. Click on the Selection tool on the Tools panel.

2. With the *MapPRINT* file open, select File > Place and locate the *MapSCAN* file created in the *Chapter 8* folder in the last exercise. Select the *MapSCAN* file.

3. Make sure that the Template box is checked in the Place dialog box when the file is selected to create a template layer for tracing. Leave the Link box unchecked to embed the file (Figure 8-11).

4. Select Place in the dialog box. If a TIFF dialog box displays, choose to "Flatten Layers to a Single Image," then select OK. The image will be centered in the new document and automatically dimmed, with a drawing layer named *Layer 1* added above the *Template* layer in the Layers panel. A template layer is identified by the triangle, circle, and square icon in the far left column of the layer panel.

5. To move the map image, you will notice a lock on the *Template* layer in the Layers panel; click on the lock to make the layer editable, then select the *Template* layer itself (Figure 8-12).

6. With the Selection tool, select the map; use your mouse or the arrow keys to move it until the top is about 1-1/2 inches from the top of the document. Remember, you can always drag a guide from the top ruler to ensure accuracy.

7. Click the lock icon again in the template layer to prevent accidently drawing on the Template layer or moving the template image.

8. Double-click the *Layer 1* text above the *Template* layer to display the Layer Options dialog box.

9. Name the layer *Map Outline* (Figure 8-12). Leave the default settings as they are, and click OK.

TOOLKIT TIP Any layer can be a template layer by double-clicking the layer thumbnail. When the Layer Options dialog box comes up, check the Template box and the image will gray out. You can also turn a selected layer into a Template layer using the Layers panel submenu. To create a working layer above the template layer for tracing, click the Create new layer icon at the panel bottom.

▷ FIGURE 8-12

Layer options, renaming layers, and moving and locking layers.

TRACING THE MAP OUTLINE USING DRAWING TOOLS

The Pencil tool allows the designer the freedom to draw complex outlines of images by creating paths. These paths can then be modified with any of Illustrator's tools and features that apply to paths. There is no worry about making an outline in one stroke when using the pencil tool. When you finish drawing a section and you are ready to continue, simply move the Pencil tool close to the still-selected path (the *X* below the Pencil tool cursor should disappear) and continue drawing to add to the path.

TRACING WITH DRAWING TOOLS

When tracing an image, the Pencil tool allows you to create freehand paths. You can modify a path by drawing over the path with the Pencil tool again, which replaces the existing path with the newly drawn path. The Smooth tool is used to edit or smooth out crooked path segments, while the Eraser tool will remove path segments. Use the scroll bars (or hold your spacebar) to move around your image and take your time tracing the outside of the map. If you mess up, use Edit > Undo Pencil to delete that portion of the path, redraw it, and then use the Smooth and Eraser tools to adjust and complete the basic outline, if needed. In Illustrator CS5, the default Uniform Profile is used for a consistent stroke path, whereas you can also create variable widths.

DESIGN TIP

When using the Smooth tool, the amount of smoothing can be controlled more precisely when you zoom in on an image's path, creating more subtle results. When the image is zoomed out, the Smooth tool deletes more points.

TOOLKIT TIP Be careful if you need to use the Eraser tool, because it might remove paths and anchor points that you need. Save the file frequently, and zoom in to at least 200 percent or closer in a given area to view the results.

In this exercise, you will trace the map image with the Pencil tool.

1. Select the *Map Outline* layer on the Layers panel.
2. Zoom in to 200% or even closer for more detailed work.
3. Set your workspace settings from the default Essentials on the Application bar (or frame) to Painting to bring up common panels for painting. Select the Pencil tool.

4. Select a Fill of None and a black Stroke of 2 points. Use the default Uniform Profile to keep a consistent brush stroke path. This will allow you to trace the template without a fill color, which could cover your template as you draw.

5. Start at the upper left and draw carefully, staying close to the template lines.

6. Continue tracing the outline of the map with the Pencil tool. If you stop, you can resume where you left off. Trace only the outline as a single shape, do not include the roads.

7. Start another path by clicking on the ending anchor point of the selected path. That way you will be creating a series of connected paths (Figure 8-13). Keep saving the file.

8. Use the Smooth tool to go over crooked lines to help smooth them out; use the Eraser tool to remove any clusters of anchor points that may be generated.

  FIGURE 8-13

The pencil tool creates open freehand paths. To continue with the path, start at the end anchor point and keep drawing.

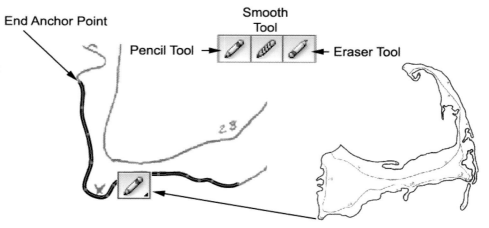

 PROBLEM If you start a new or additional path with the Pencil Tool and the previous path disappears, select Command/Ctrl Z, or Edit > Undo, and start again. Make sure when you start again that you click on the last anchor point to begin where the previous path had ended. Remember, the path you want to add to must be selected for this to work.

FINE-TUNING WITH THE DIRECT SELECTION TOOL

The Direct Selection tool allows the designer to select single path segments or anchor points and move them around independently of the rest of the path. Dragging the **direction lines** extending from anchor points modify a curve or path with precision. Use this tool to fine-tune and accurately match the template outline.

TOOLKIT TIP When using the Direct Selection tool, always click outside the path first to deselect it, and then select the path segment or anchor point to work on.

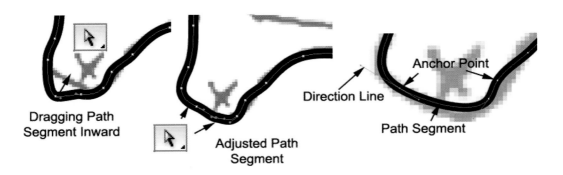

Dragging Path
Segment Inward

Adjusted Path
Segment

Direction Line

Anchor Point

Path Segment

▷ FIGURE 8-14

The direct selection tool allows you to select individual anchor points, direction lines, or path segments to make adjustments.

Here you will use the Direct Selection tool (A) to make any final adjustments.

1. For fine-tuning, zoom in to 300% or better, select the Direct Selection tool, and click away from the path. Then click on the portion of the path you want to edit to display the anchor points and direction lines from those points.

2. Drag anchor points and direction lines to make the path match the outline of the shape template. Direction lines help to steer a path segment's bending direction (Figure 8-14).

3. Save the file in your *Chapter 8* folder on your drive in the native Illustrator .AI extension format.

WORKING WITH LAYERS AND SUBLAYERS

When you use drawing tools, every time you create a closed or open path, a "path" layer or sublayer is created under the initial layer in the Layers panel. You can select the circle to the right of the sublayer thumbnail to select that particular path to work on. A template layer is locked (which can be toggled on or off), and it displays a shapes icon instead of the eye icon in the Layers panel. To hide the template, click the shapes icon to toggle the template view off, then click again to see it.

DESIGN TIP

If you are concerned whether all paths are connected to make one complete path, a good indicator is to check the subpaths layers. Click the triangle next to the layer to see sublayers. If your paths are all connected, you will see one path displayed, rather than multiple, disjointed sublayers.

TOOLKIT TIP To select large areas or combinations of paths, drag a diagonal box over the area with the Selection tool, or use the Lasso tool to draw a freehand selection intersecting the paths to be highlighted.

Next, you will hide the Template layer to see your progress, and then observe how to select paths you created.

1. To see the progress of your outline by hiding the template display, click on the shapes icon on the *Template* layer.

2. Select the *Map Outline* layer and then select the arrow on the left side, where you will notice a series of path sublayers. If you connect the entire map outline, it will display as one large closed path, with the island as an additional closed path (Figure 8-15).

3. To highlight a path to display, select the circle to the right of the thumbnail. It displays a bounding box around the path on that sublayer.

4. To make your outline more accurate, select the various paths you want to work with and edit them with the Direct Selection, Smooth, and Pencil tools.

5. Save the file in your *Chapter 8* folder when you have completed the outline.

▷ FIGURE 8-15

Displaying and hiding the template layer and selected paths.

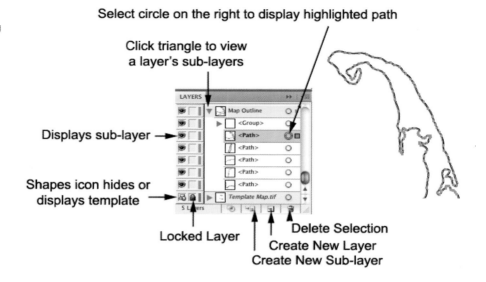

CREATING AND APPLYING BRUSHES

In the Brushes panel, you can create your own brushes or use predefined brushes in four different categories: Calligraphic, Scatter, Art, and Pattern. You can apply any brush stroke with the Paintbrush tool to create a path or apply brush strokes to existing selected paths by choosing a brush style from the Brushes panel. Any special stroke or combination of shapes and lines can be created and saved in the Brushes panel to be applied as a brush style.

CREATING U.S. AND STATE HIGHWAY ART BRUSHES

One of the techniques a cartographer might use in Illustrator is to create various brushes of topographic mapping elements or symbols for roads, railroads, waterways, and boundaries, using a combination of various tools and shapes, and then saving them in the Brushes panel to use again. The Line Segment tool is used to create straight lines at any angle. The Stroke panel is used to change the properties of lines, including their weight and style, and comes with the option to create dashed lines. In Illustrator CS5, you can create stroke paths with variable widths and precise arrowheads, and control the alignment of dashes, including around corners. The default stroke profile is the Uniform setting on both the Stroke and Control panels. A single line element can be copied by selecting the line with the Direct Selection tool, then dragging while holding the Option/Alt. Saving artwork as an Art brush stretches it evenly along a path.

DESIGN TIP

If the panels temporarily seem to get in the way as you are drawing, press the Tab key to remove them, then press again to toggle them back on to display.

DESIGN TIP

When first creating brush styles, it is a good idea to keep the initial stroke weight to a minimum; when you need to apply the brush, you can alter it at that time.

▷ FIGURE 8-16

**Using the Line
Segment and the
Direct Selection
tools to create the
U.S. Highway brush.**

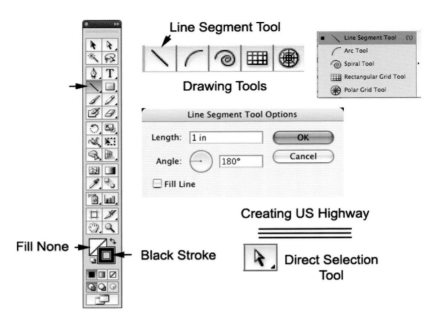

▷ FIGURE 8-16

**Using the Line
Segment and the
Direct Selection
tools to create the
U.S. Highway brush.**

Now you will create two different highway brushes and save each in the Brushes panel.

1. To create the U.S. Highway brush, zoom in to 200%. Make sure nothing is selected.

2. Set the Fill to None and the Stroke to black with a 1-point Weight.

3. Select the Line Segment tool and click once, away from the map image (Figure 8-16), to access the Line Segment Tool options.

4. For the first line, enter 1 inch for the length and 180 for the angle; click OK.

5. To make two more copies underneath one another, use the Direct Selection tool to select the line; then, while holding down the Option/Alt key, select and drag twice to copy two more lines directly underneath the original.

6. Make the lines equal distances apart but close together. Use the arrow keys for positioning. You can try to use the Align panel to make the distance between each equal or to make sure the left/right sides are aligned.

7. To create a dashed centerline, use the Direct Selection tool to select the middle line and set the Stroke to 1 point with 10-point gaps and 10-point dashes with a Uniform Profile (Figure 8-17). If the dashed line options are not showing, select Show Options from the Stroke panel's submenu, or click the arrows at the top right to toggle through the layer views until they appear.

8. To group all three lines together, Shift-select all three lines with the Direct Selection tool, or drag through the lines with the Lasso tool.

9. Select Object > Group.

10. With all three lines selected, select the Brushes panel and select the New Brush icon at the panel bottom or from the Brushes panel menu.

11. Select New Art Brush in the dialog box and click OK.

▷ FIGURE 8-17

**Using the Stroke
panel to create a
dashed line for the
highway's center.**

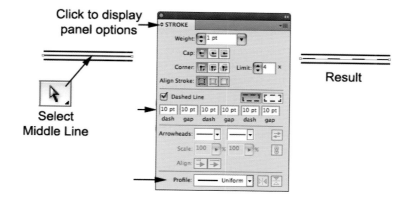

▷ FIGURE 8-17

**Using the Stroke
panel to create a
dashed line for the
highway's center.**

12. When the Art Brush Options dialog box appears, name the brush *US Highway;*
choose the right arrow in the Direction section, leaving all the other defaults as they
are, and then click OK (Figure 8-18). The brush will display in the Brushes panel.

13. Delete the selected graphic on the artboard. It is now saved in the Brushes
panel. Save the file.

14. To create the state highway in red, set the Fill to None and the Stroke to red
with a 2-point width. Set the dashes and gaps in the Stroke panel back to zeros.

▷ FIGURE 8-18

**Creating
highway brushes.**

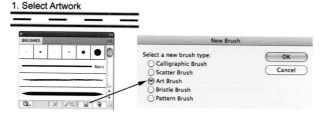

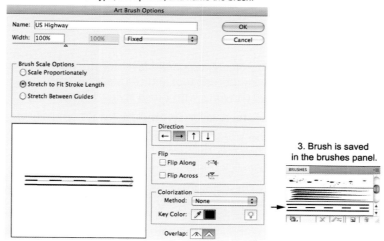

15. Select the Line Segment tool, click on the artboard to display the dialog box, and enter a 1-inch segment with 180-degree angle line.

16. With the new line selected, open the Brushes panel and select the New Brush icon at the panel bottom or from the panel's submenu. You can also simply drag the selected line into the Brushes panel.

17. Select New Art Brush for the type and name the brush *State Highway.* Choose the right arrow in the Direction section, then click OK.

18. Delete this line graphic on the artboard and save the file.

DESIGN TIP

Before selecting drawing tools or brushes, set the stroke and fill colors first, then set the stroke weight in the Stroke panel or Options bar.

APPLYING BRUSHES

Creating paths with brush styles usually involves the Paintbrush, Pencil, or Pen tools. To apply brushes using the Paintbrush tool, you choose a brush from the Brushes panel first and then draw the paths you need. You cannot use a brush style with the Pen tool or the Pencil tool until you draw a regular path first and then apply the brush style to it. You apply brushes to existing paths by selecting the path first; then choose a brush in the Brushes panel.

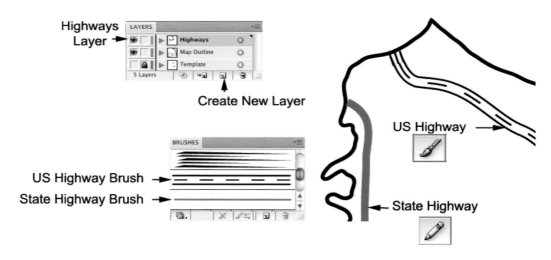

▷   FIGURE 8-19

Painting the highways with Paintbrush and Pencil tools.

It is time to create a separate layer for the highways, then paint the U.S. highway using the Paintbrush tool and the state highway using the Pencil tool, so you can see how each works with brush styles (Figure 8-19).

1. To create a layer for the highways, make sure the *Map Outline* layer is highlighted, and select the Create New Layer icon at the bottom of the Layers panel. Make sure the Map template layer is turned on.

2. Double-click this layer and name it *Highways.*

3. Select the Paintbrush tool, then click on the new *US Highway* brush in the Brushes panel. Carefully trace over Route 6 on the template. To continue to add to the path, click on the end anchor point of the previous path. Once you have completed the path, choose Select > Deselect.

DESIGN TIP

You can drag artwork into the Brushes panel to make it a new brush as well. If you want to color a brush, it needs the fill and stroke colors set up before it is applied. You can also use the Colorize option in the Art Brush Options panel—set it to Hue Shift—and then you can select a brush stroke or path and change the color.

4. For the state highway, select a Fill of None and a black Stroke of 2 points, then select the Pencil tool.

5. Trace over the Route 28 on the template.

6. To apply the red *State Highway* brush, click on the *State Highway* brush in the Brushes panel to apply the red color brush. To remove a brush stroke, in the Brushes panel, choose Remove Brush Stroke from the panel menu, click the Remove Brush button at the bottom of the panel, or, in CS5, you can select Basic Brush from the Brushes panel or Control panel.

7. Toggle the shapes icon on the *Template* layer to see the results of the map. Use the Direct Selection tool to create the lines to accurately follow the template.

8. Save the file and then minimize the document window.

CREATING AND APPLYING CUSTOM SYMBOLS

In Illustrator, a designer has the ability to create symbols. Symbols can be any graphic that you create that can then be used as repeated symbol instances on your document. Symbols are not applied to paths and do not create paths like brushes; these repetitive symbols are placed onto a document with the Symbol Sprayer tool. Symbol instances on the artboard can be edited and changed if necessary, using the various Symbolism tools. This allows you to create variations of the same basic symbol on your document. Symbols are saved for later use in the Symbols panel. You will be making lighthouse and highway symbols to be placed on the map.

USING THE LIVE TRACE FUNCTION TO MAKE THE U.S. HIGHWAY SIGN.

Symbols can also be created from scanned drawings or sketches or with Illustrator's tools. A sketch can be traced, scaled to size, and saved in the Symbols panel for future use. Illustrator has a **Live Trace** function that interprets the contours and outlines of drawings and bitmap images, translating them into vector drawings. The Tracing Options dialog box offers presets to trace a variety of images, including sketches, drawings, photos, and even templates. You also have the ability to set your own options for tracing. Live Trace is located in the Object menu. In order to trace any object it has to be selected first. To convert the tracing outline to a series of connected paths, you select the **Expand command**. You will be using some more of this powerful new function in Chapter 10. Although the Live Trace function does a nice job in accurately reproducing a sketched outline, you can modify any path it generates with the Direct Selection tool. This tool is used to edit anchor points and direction lines that determine the shape of the path line segment.

Using the Live Trace function, you will trace a template file of a U.S. highway sign. Remember to make sure the object is selected before applying the Live Trace function.

1. To create the U.S. highway sign, open the *Sign* file in your *Chapter 8* folder. You can trace this even though it is set up as a template.

2. Select the Zoom tool and zoom in 200% to 300%.

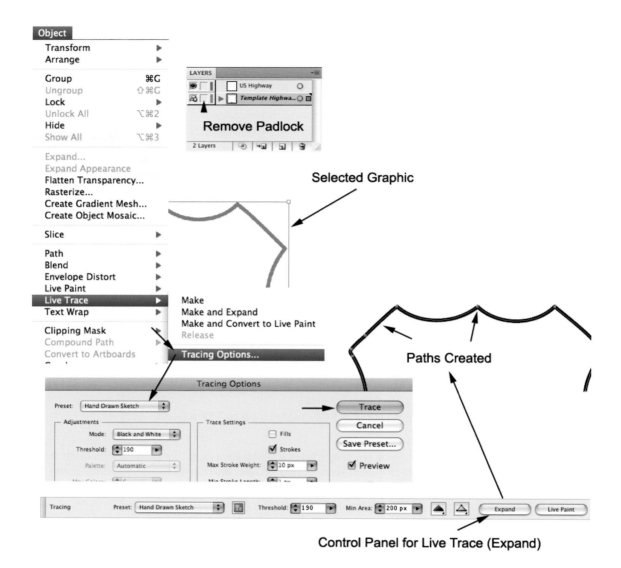

Control Panel for Live Trace (Expand)

▷ FIGURE 8-20

In Illustrator, the Live Trace command allows you to trace over preset drawings, sketches, and bitmap images for accuracy.

3. To trace the *Template* layer in this document, in the Layers panel, click on the padlock to unlock the template layer, and make sure that layer is highlighted.

4. Select a Fill of White and a Stroke weight of 2 points; then with the Selection tool, select the drawing, which will display a bounding box around it.

5. Select Object > Live Trace > Tracing Options to bring up the Live Trace dialog box.

6. Select the Hand Drawn Sketch option in the presets area and leave other settings as shown in Figure 8-20.

7. Select Trace and the sign will be outlined. If the Trace button is not displayed, you don't have the Template Highway layer selected, or did not remove the padlock icon. Because it is on the *Template* layer, it will not print, but it does

demonstrate how well the tracing was made. It should trace the outline of the sign very accurately.

8. To convert the tracing to paths, select Expand from the Control panel, or use Object > Live Trace > Expand. You will notice a closed path line with anchor points ready to be edited or selected.

9. To make sure all the paths are connected, select Object > Group. You will notice the the original artwork has disappeared from the *Template* layer.

10. With the U.S. Highway sign selected, copy it (Edit > Copy).

11. Close the *Sign* file (File > Close). Do not save the file.

12. Maximize the *MapPRINT* window to display the map document again.

13. Paste the *US Highway* graphic outside the map outline (Edit > Paste). Leave it selected.

14. To scale down the selected graphic, select Object > Transform > Scale and enter a Uniform scale of 40%. Uncheck the Scale Strokes and Effects box to keep from scaling the stroke weight (Figure 8-21). Click OK.

15. Optional: If you wish to modify the path outline, zoom in 200% to 300% and use the Direct Selection tool by selecting outside the graphic to deselect the bounding box, then selecting one of the path line segments to edit (see Toolkit Tip).

16. Save the file as *Map* again in your *Chapter 8* folder and leave it open for the next exercise in creating symbols.

TOOLKIT TIP Although it will not be necessary here, if you needed to modify the highway shape, you can select a path then click and drag individual anchor points or click and adjust the shape of line segments using the Direct Selection Tool. You do this by clicking outside the path to deselect everything, then select the portion of the path to display anchor points and direction lines. Drag anchor points and direction lines to make adjustments. Feel free to experiment then choose File > Revert to have Illustrator go back to the previous save.

TOOLKIT TIP When scaling an object to a smaller size, sometimes it is better to leave the Scale Strokes and Effects option unchecked to avoid creating hairlines that may not print well. When enlarging an object, place a check in the Scale Strokes and Effects for consistency and sharpness. Sometimes, however, the lines get so fat compared to the rest of the image that they obliterate it.

DESIGN TIP

When creating headings or basic labels, it is good practice to use a universal sans serif font, like Arial Black, that can easily be viewed.

USING TYPE IN SYMBOLS

The Type tools contain many functions in Illustrator. You can select the default horizontal Type tool, make selections from the Type menu, and then click anywhere to start typing normally. You can type inside an area and type vertically as well. Type can also be used in a graphic and made into a symbol. In all Illustrator CS versions, you can see what the font looks like before you use it in your project.

Here you will add text to the U.S. Highway Route 6 sign and create the State Highway Route 28 sign as well.

DESIGN TIP

You can also create outlined type by selecting a white or colored Fill with a different colored Stroke if you have a large enough size text.

1. To create the U.S. Highway Route 6 sign, select the Type tool, then select the Type menu to find an Arial Black font with a Size of 36 points.

2. Click inside the U.S. highway sign and type the number "6."

3. Use the Selection tool to select the text and center it with the arrow keys.

4. Press the Shift key and select both text and shape to display a bounding box around both.

5. Select Object > Group to combine both text and shape together as one.

6. To scale down the *US Highway* graphic further to be used as a symbol, select Object > Transform > Scale and scale the image to 40% Uniform. Keep the Scale Strokes and Effects unchecked. Click OK, then choose Select > Deselect.

7. To make the State Highway Route 28 sign, choose a Fill of white and a black Stroke of 2 points, and then select the Ellipse tool.

8. Click on the artboard to display the dialog box, and then enter a 1-inch by 1-inch circle.

9. Select the Type tool and use the Type menu to select Arial Black with a Size of 36 points.

10. Click inside the circle and type "28" (Figure 8-21).

11. Repeat steps 3 through 5 to group the type and shape.

▷ FIGURE 8-21

Use the Type tool to type the route numbers in 36-point Arial Black.

12. To scale down the *State Highway* graphic, make sure it is selected and use Object > Transform > Scale and scale down the image to 30% Uniform (not shown). Keep the Scale Strokes and Effects unchecked.

13. Save the file.

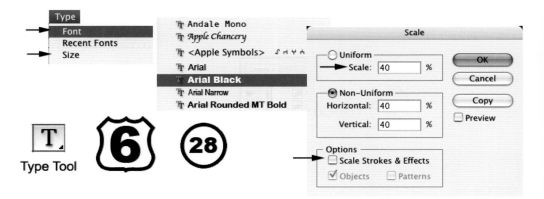

MAKING HIGHWAY SIGNS AND THE LIGHTHOUSE GRAPHIC SYMBOLS

A designer can create a graphic, copy it, and then paste it into another document. The selected graphic can then be saved as a symbol in the Symbols panel for later use. Any object can be made into a symbol, which can then appear as a graphic thumbnail in the Symbols panel (Figure 8-22). Once a symbol is created, it stays in the Symbols panel for use whenever it is needed in the document. You can create multiple versions of the symbol, called *symbol instances*, by dragging it from the Symbols panel to the artboard. Once it is placed in your document, you can resize or edit it. Illustrator allows you to name your symbol and determine whether it will be used as a graphic or as part of a video or animated sequence.

DESIGN TIP

Storing graphics as symbols is a great way to create and reuse artwork for multiple projects without having to recreate the same artwork over again. Since they are stored as vector images, they can be resized to fit any dimensions needed.

TOOLKIT TIP Keeping documents arranged as tabs, or by minimizing windows in earlier versions, helps you to concentrate on one active document at a time. You can also select various active documents within Illustrator from the Window menu, which indicates the active document with a check mark.

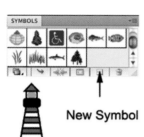

New Symbol

Select Graphic

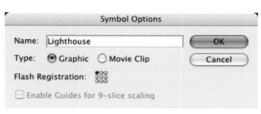

Choose as Graphic and Symbol Name

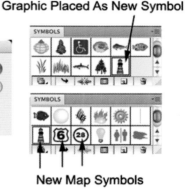

Graphic Placed As New Symbol

New Map Symbols

▷ FIGURE 8-22

Symbols panel with new symbols created for the map.

Now that you have created the highway signs, you will turn them into symbols. You will then bring in the copy of the *Light* graphic of the lighthouse that you created in Chapter 7 (Digital Toolkit Extra), and paste it into the *MapPRINT* file to be used as a map symbol. If you missed that exercise, open the *Light2* graphic in the *Chapter 8* folder and use that instead.

1. Select the U.S. Highway Route 6 graphic with the Selection tool.

2. Open the Symbols panel and select the New Symbol icon at the bottom of the panel. When the Symbol Options display opens, select the "Graphic" option, and then name the symbol *Hwy 6* and click OK. You will notice a thumbnail representation of the U.S. Highway Route 6 symbol in the Symbols panel.

3. Repeat the process to make the State Highway Route 28 sign (name it *Hwy 28*), then deselect the Route sign and reset the Fill box to black on the Tools panel.

4. To make the *Light* graphic a symbol, open the *Light* file you created in last chapter's Digital Toolkit Extra in the *Chapter 7* folder. If it is not available, open the *Light2* graphic in the *Chapter 8* folder instead. You can also select File > Open Recent Files to locate the file.

5. Use the Selection tool to select the lighthouse.

6. Copy the graphic (Edit > Copy), then close the *Light* file without saving it (File > Close).

7. Paste the selected lighthouse graphic outside the map outline in the *MapPRINT* file (Edit > Paste).

8. With the lighthouse graphic still selected, select the Symbols panel and click on the New Symbol icon at the bottom of the panel. Name the graphic *Lighthouse.*

9. You now have a lighthouse symbol and the two highway signs that will be used on the map later. Delete the lighthouse graphic and the highway signs from the artboard—they are now permanent symbols in this file.

10. Save the file *MapPRINT.*

PLACING THE HIGHWAY SYMBOLS

Before placing the symbols you created onto the map, it is a good idea to create another layer for just the symbols. Placing symbols is done by dragging the symbol onto the artboard or by using the Symbols panel Place Symbol Instance icon. The placed symbols, called *symbol instances,* can be resized using the bounding box or modified with the Symbolism tools. Although not needed here, in CS5, you can also create sublayers for symbols in symbol editing mode.

TOOLKIT TIP You can stack symbol instances by selecting the Place Symbol Instance icon at the bottom of the Symbols panel then dragging each to its appropriate location with the Selection tool (Figure 8-23).

▷ FIGURE 8-23

Dragging symbols from the Symbols panel and placing them on the map image.

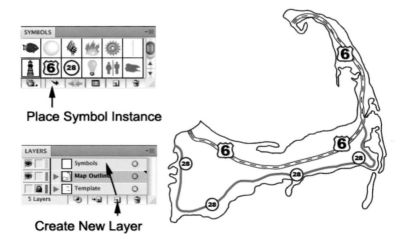

In this exercise, you will create a layer for the symbols and place both highway symbols as instances on the map.

1. With the *MapPRINT* file open, select the *Highways* layer in the Layers panel; then click the Create New Layer icon at the bottom of the panel. Make sure the new layer is the topmost layer; if not, click and drag it to the top.

2. Rename the new highlighted layer *Symbols.*

3. Select the *State Highway Route 28* symbol from the Symbols panel and drag it into position on one of the places where 28 is written on the template

(or use the Place Symbol Instance icon on the Symbols panel). This creates an instance of the symbol in your artwork. Drag additional instances of this symbol on the map as indicated in the template. You can also click on the symbol and copy it by holding down the Option/ALT key.

4. Repeat the same process for the *US Highway Route 6* symbol.

5. Delete any extra highway symbols outside the map area and save the file.

PLACING AND NUMBERING THE LIGHTHOUSE SYMBOLS

Need additional fun computer graphics tutorials and info, and an additional look at the projects you'll be creating in this book? Check out my Artist's Digital Toolkit website at: **http://www.digitoolkit.com**

An instance of the lighthouse symbol needs to be dragged from the Symbols panel and placed on each *X* on the map. Consecutive numbers will be typed next to each lighthouse, starting from the top left side and positioned counterclockwise around the map outline until all the lighthouses are numbered. These numbers are important, because they refer to the numbered list that will be placed under the map for the viewer to follow.

For this exercise, you will create an instance of the lighthouse symbol, number it, and then place it by each *X* on the map.

1. Click and drag the lighthouse symbol onto the artboard or use the Place Symbol Instance icon on the Symbols panel.

2. Use the Option/Alt key to copy the selected graphic and drag the instance to the first *X* on the left side of the map near the Route 28 symbol.

3. Use the Option/Alt key to make copies; repeat the same process until lighthouse instances are placed on all eleven marks (Figure 8-24).

4. Select the Type tool (default setting) with a Fill of a deep blue color and a Stroke of None.

5. In the Type menu, select the Arial Black font at 14 points.

6. Type the number "1" to the left of the first lighthouse; position it with the Selection tool.

7. Select the number and use Option/Alt to copy it, moving the copy over to the second lighthouse position, as shown in Figure 8-24.

8. Select the Type tool, highlight the number *1* and type "2".

9. Continue the same process, numbering all the lighthouse symbols consecutively (Figure 8-24).

10. To resize the lighthouse graphics as shown in Figure 8-24, select the graphic to be resized with the Selection tool which will place it inside the bounding box (View > Show Bounding Box), and press the Shift key while dragging inward or outward to resize it proportionately.

11. Save the file.

LABELING THE MAP

Using text in an image can provide contrast to the artwork as well as adding information about the image. Labeling the map defines the map as a reference tool. This map is going to be used by tourists with a focus on lighthouses, indicated

**Placing and number-
ing the lighthouse
symbols along
the map.**

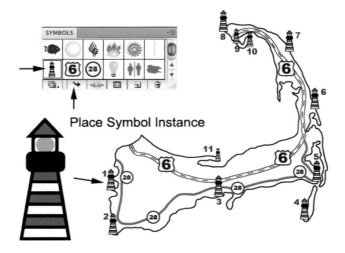

by the map's title "Cape Cod Lighthouses." Because of Illustrator's capability to use stroke and fill colors for text as well as graphics, lettering can be enhanced to provide focus. Labeling some of the cities and towns on the map will help to give it perspective and distance. The list of lighthouses to be visited, already created in a word processing application, will be "placed" below the map image. You can then format the list for consistency using Illustrator's Character panel.

TYPING THE TITLE, TOWNS, AND CITIES

The main title of the map will be placed diagonally within the empty area inside the cape "elbow," as shown in Figure 8-25. Since the emphasis is on the lighthouses, making the word *Lighthouses* red with a darker black stroke color italicized will help to bring focus to the purpose of the map. The towns, cities, and the lighthouse list will be labeled with the same Georgia font in Bold style for continuity. In Illustrator, a designer can get a quick visual of the font in the Character panel or using the Type > Font menu before selecting one to use in the document.

DESIGN TIP

Since the map image is made of lots of curved paths, using a serif font like Georgia for the title and labels complements the image.

TOOLKIT TIP You can also use the Control panel to apply type formatting commands easily.

Next, you will create the main title, headline, and label the cities and towns.

1. To create a layer for text, select the *Map Outline* layer in the Layers panel and click the Create New Layer icon at the bottom of the panel.

2. Select the *Layer 5* text in the new layer and rename the layer *Text*.

3. Select the Type tool, and use the Type menu to select Georgia Bold (or something similar) in a 36-point size. You can also use the Control panel.

4. Click in the elbow area of the map and type *"Cape Cod,"* then press the Return/ Enter key to make a new line.

▷   FIGURE 8-25

**Labeling title,
headline, cities,
and towns.**

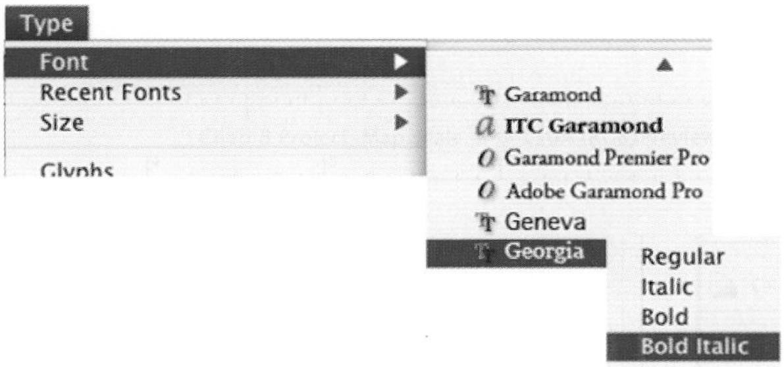

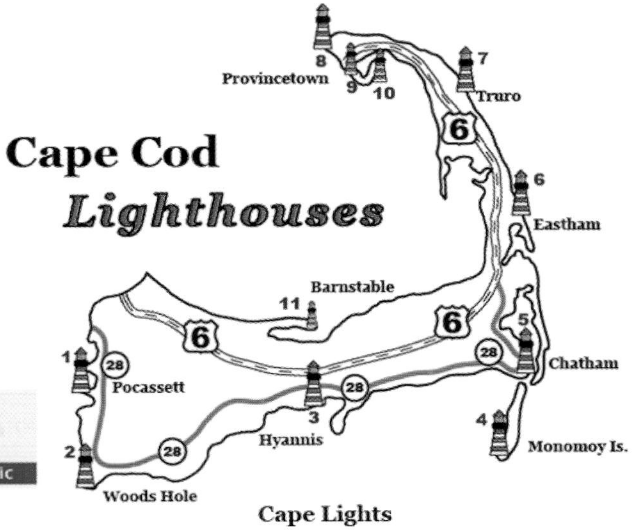

DESIGN TIP

Because of the long list of imported text, positioning it to the right side adjacent to the title helps to balance the overall map. With some empty space to the left, placing and modifying symbols as described in the Advanced section will add color and personality to the map.

5. Select the Type tool, and choose the Georgia Bold Italic font with a red Fill and a black Stroke; type "Lighthouses," tabbing over to offset it (Figure 8-25). To provide some space between the characters, you can select the Character panel (Window > Type > Character) and put in a tracking of 75 for starters. Deselect the text.

6. To label the towns, change to Georgia Bold with a Size of 12 points. Change the color to a stroke of None with a black fill.

7. Type counterclockwise around the map the towns: *Pocassett, Woods Hole, Hyannis, Monomoy Is., Chatham, Eastham, Truro, Provincetown,* and *Barnstable* without having the type overlap the lighthouses or route symbols. To stop typing one line to start the next, select another tool, such as the Selection tool, then select the Type tool again to start another type line. When clicking on the map with the Type tool, be careful not to click too closely to any highways or paths or the text will align itself to the path.

8. To place the headline *Cape Lights* under the map for the lighthouse list, select the Type tool and type "Cape Lights" in 18-point Georgia Bold using the Hyannis town label as a guide for position.

9. The *Template* layer is no longer needed, so drag it to the Trash icon at the bottom of the Layers panel.

10. Save the file. The map is labeled; now it is time to bring in the lighthouse list.

PLACING AND FORMATTING IMPORTED TYPE IN ILLUSTRATOR

Creating bulleted or numbered lists is difficult within Illustrator. To solve this problem, Illustrator allows you to import text from other documents created in Microsoft Word (**DOC**), as plain text files (**TXT**), or Rich Text Format files that maintain formatting commands (**RTF**). Using the **Place command** for text imports the copy into its own text block so it can easily be moved into position and edited. Illustrator has a Character panel and a Paragraph panel to format selected type. This is helpful when you need to format large amounts of text or specialized titles and headlines. In the Character panel, you can apply character formatting techniques to selected characters or lines of text, while in the Paragraph panel, you can apply paragraph formatting commands to selected paragraphs.

To finish the map, you will place the lighthouse list from a Word document into the *MapPRINT* file. You will then format the text using the Character panel.

▷ FIGURE 8-26

Using the Place command to import a text document into the Illustrator document.

1. Use File > Place > *Lighthouses.doc* to place *Lighthouses.rtf* from your *Chapter 8* folder into the *MapPRINT* document. Use the Selection tool to move under the map.

2. In CS2 or earlier versions, if the Text Import Options dialog box displays, select either Windows or Mac Encoding (whichever OS you are using) and ANSI Character Set. Accept all the defaults for Microsoft Word options and choose OK (Figure 8-26).

PROBLEM If the list is spread out horizontally, you will need to select the Type tool, click before each number on the list, and press the Return/Enter key to create a numbered list. Continue until all eleven lighthouses are set up as a list.

3. Use the Selection tool to select the text block; use the resizing handles to shrink the box and crop out the blank space below the text if needed,. If the text block resizes, use the Type tool and click at the end of the last line, then press the delete key continually until the extra space below is removed.

4. Move the text box to the right side under the *Cape Lights* heading.

5. Make sure the Character panel is displayed (Window > Type > Character).

6. With the type box still selected, select Georgia, with the Font Style as Regular, Size 14 points, Tracking at 25 to separate the letters a little, and Leading at 18

points in the Character panel. Leave the other settings at their defaults, and deselect the type to see the formatted type lines (Figure 8-27).

7. Save the file. You now have an easy-to-read map.

▷ FIGURE 8-27

Using the Character panel to format selected type.

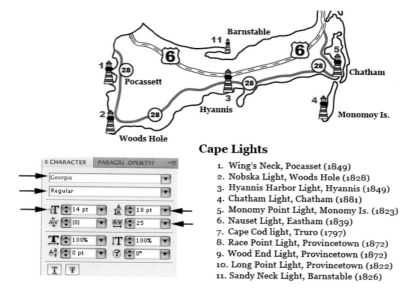

Cape Lights

1. Wing's Neck, Pocasset (1849)
2. Nobska Light, Woods Hole (1828)
3. Hyannis Harbor Light, Hyannis (1849)
4. Chatham Light, Chatham (1881)
5. Monomy Point Light, Monomy Is. (1823)
6. Nauset Light, Eastham (1839)
7. Cape Cod light, Truro (1797)
8. Race Point Light, Provincetown (1872)
9. Wood End Light, Provincetown (1872)
10. Long Point Light, Provincetown (1822)
11. Sandy Neck Light, Barnstable (1826)

THE UPDATE LEGACY TEXT COMMAND

Illustrator includes the Update Legacy Text command, or Legacy Text command, which uses the new Adobe text engine to provide the highest quality text output. If your intention is to edit or modify text elements from a document created in a previous version of Illustrator, the text needs to be updated for consistency. When you open an older file containing text, a dialog box usually displays, asking whether to update the legacy text (this will also occur when opening older files with type in Photoshop). When a previous version of text is updated, you may notice various changes in character position or words shifting. To avoid these changes, you can choose not to update the text if you do not plan to make any changes. This command is also located under the Type menu. As a general rule, it is better to update the type in your project when sending it for proofing or to a commercial printer. When in doubt, if the dialog box comes up, choose to update your text.

USING SYMBOLISM TOOLS AND THE SYMBOL LIBRARY

You can select symbols from a variety of preset symbols organized in collections called *symbol libraries*. Illustrator has provided a vast selection to choose from. When you open a symbol library from the Symbols panel menu, it displays in a new panel. To add symbols to the Symbols panel from the library, just select it in the symbol library; it will automatically be placed in the Symbols panel. Placing symbols on the artwork creates symbol instances, which can be resized and modified using the various Symbolism tools. To make any changes to a symbol instance, it needs to be selected first. To adjust the size of a graphic, you can use the **Symbol Sizer tool.** The **Symbol Spinner tool** is used to vary the direction of the selected symbol instance. You can change the color of symbol instances with the **Symbol Stainer tool,** and apply other effects to symbol instances with the other Symbolism tools. You can experiment with the Color Guide panel or the Kuler panel as part of the Live Color feature to change color combinations on various selected symbols.

TOOLKIT TIP Always select the symbol instance before using any Symbolism tool. Placing symbols individually allows the designer to modify each differently. Short clicks on the symbol instance works well with some of the Symbolism tools since they change the properties of symbol instances rapidly.

ⓧ

PROBLEM If the Symbolism tools are not working, make sure that the graphic is selected. After applying a Symbolism tool on a selected symbol, choose the Selection tool again before choosing another Symbolism tool or symbol instance.

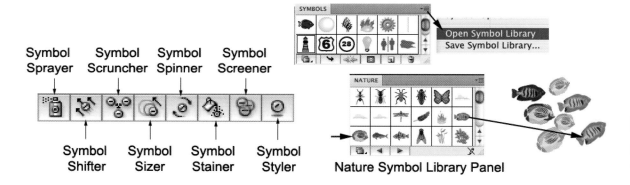

Nature Symbol Library Panel

▷ FIGURE 8-28

Symbolism tools and symbol libraries.

Next, you will place and adjust a few fish symbol instances from the Nature Symbol library using some of the Symbolism tools. Feel free to practice this exercise in a new document before adding the graphics to the *MapPRINT* file.

1. From the Symbols panel, use the panel submenu to select Open Symbol Library > Nature (Figure 8-28).

2. Select the Fish 2 symbol to place the symbol in the Symbols panel. (If you are using Illustrator version 10, select the Blue Tang fish symbol in the Symbols panel instead.)

3. Drag the symbol to the left of the list of lighthouses. Repeat this until you have placed four fish on the artboard.

4. Select a fish with the Selection tool, select a fill color, and then select the Symbol Stainer tool to change its color. The color changes the whole fish. The Symbol Stainer tool can be found in the Tools panel underneath the Symbol Sprayer tool.

5. Select two fish and vary their size using the Symbol Sizer tool. Hold the Option/ Alt key to decrease the size.

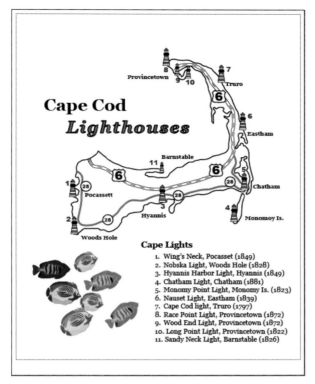

▷ FIGURE 8-29
Completed map.

6. Select one or two fish and try the Symbol Spinner tool to vary their direction.

7. Drag a couple of the Fish 1 symbols by the other fish; select and make adjustments with the Symbolism tools.

8. Experiment with other libraries and symbols, but be careful not to be overdo it—less is usually more. Feel free to experiment with the Color Guide panel or the Kuler panel to find other interesting color groups to change the fish symbols into.

9. Save the file *MapPRINT* again in the *Chapter 8* folder when you have finished playing with the Symbolism tools and libraries.

10. Print the map with the fish additions. You are now a cartographer! (Figure 8-29).

SAVING YOUR ARTWORK IN EPS FORMAT

Saving Illustrator files in EPS format allows them to be viewed universally by many graphics applications (Figure 8-30). EPS files handle text and graphic elements very well and are used predominantly in the commercial press industry, especially when vector graphics are needed to maintain sharpness and clarity. You can also save individual artboards as separate EPS files. You can include options like embedding fonts and displaying thumbnail previews, although doing so will also increase file size. You can save EPS files using the current CS5 version or earlier versions. If you save to an earlier version, you may see various warnings and functions grayed out in the dialog box; this is because some of Illustrator CS5's features may not have been available in a previous version.

DESIGN TIP

For files used in the printing industry, save files as EPS whenever graphic objects, illustrations, and text are used in the same graphic. You can edit an EPS file the same way you would an AI file. For photographic images only, saving files in TIF format is universally used.

Here you will save the file in EPS format with default settings.

1. Choose File > Save As > and navigate to your *Chapter 8* folder.

2. Name the file *MapPRINT* and select Illustrator EPS for the format, then click the Save button.

3. When the EPS dialog box comes up, save to the version you are working with or to the default CS5 if you are using the current version. If you save to an earlier version, you may see some warnings regarding possible editing or font issues. Do not worry about this for this assignment. With most all versions, select an 8-bit color TIF Preview to display a thumbnail preview of the document. Leave the rest at the default settings (Figure 8-30).

4. Select OK to save the file in the *Chapter 8 folder* as *MapPRINT.eps.* You now have a map ready for print with the EPS extention and a backup in Illustrator's native. AI extension.

▷ FIGURE 8-30

Saving the document in the universal EPS format with options.

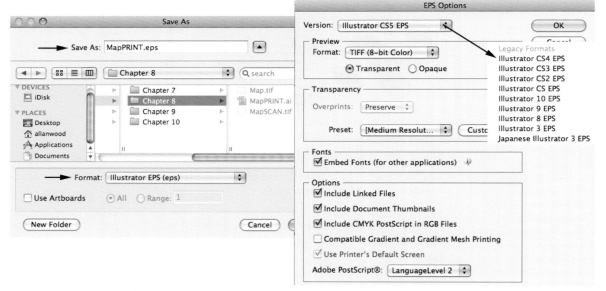

 TOOLKIT TIP If you are saving to an earlier version for use on your school or work network or at home, save to the earliest version you are using. It will not affect this assignment; it usually affects complex editing or special tools and functions that may have been created with the current version (CS5) and which earlier versions cannot read.

PRINTING ON COLORED PAPER

To create an interesting map, you can print on colored paper instead of filling in the map with color. With this particular map, printing the map outline and symbols on parchment paper, which you can get at any stationery store, provides a "treasure map" background without wasting much of your ink supply.

ADVANCED USERS: Placing Logos Created by the Blob Brush onto Multiple Artboards

Suppose you have a client who is developing a successful kid's play center and wants a simple kid-like logo on various pieces of media for advertising and on letterhead. Illustrator has a couple of cool features that just invite you to play and increase your production workflow. The Multiple Artboards feature allows a designer to create up to 100 multiple artboards to show a potential client various sizes and types of media that the artwork created can be used for. Whereas the Brush, Pen and Pencil tools create stroke paths and anchor points from the inside out, the Blob Brush tool creates paths of a Fill color with no stroke with paths and anchor points on the outside creating shapes from anything you draw.

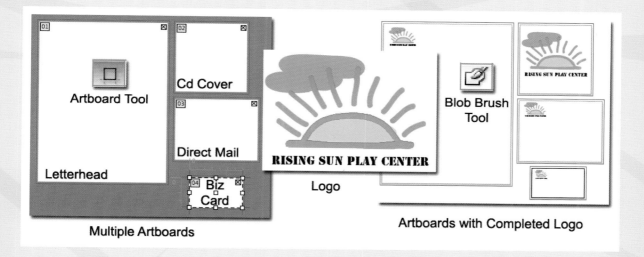

Multiple Artboards

Artboards with Completed Logo

▷ FIGURE 8-31

Using multiple artboards to place logo created by the Blob Brush tool.

USING MULTIPLE ARTBOARDS

Multiple artboards are useful for creating a variety of things such as multiple page PDFs, printed pages with different sizes or different elements, independent elements for websites, etc. Designers can use and save multiple artboards within one document, or export each artboard to its own file. Double-clicking the Artboard tool opens the Artboard Options dialog box, and then clicking Artboard Options button in the Control panel. You can adjust dimensions of a selected artboard using the Control panel, or by using the Artboard tool (Figure 8-31). You can also have independent ruler guides set up for each artboard to help with your sizing.

You can create multiple artboards for your document, but only one can be active at a time. Each artboard is numbered for easy reference. You can edit or delete an artboard at any time, and you can specify different artboards each time you print or export. In CS5, you can specify custom names for your artboards using either the Control panel or new Artboards panel.

In the New Print Document dialog box, you can set the bleed of your artboards so if they were going to be sent to a commercial printer, the **bleed** would be used as a trimming guide to avoid problems if there was a slight shift in paper going through the press (may appear as a white line on color background print). A good default setting for documents is 0.125 or one-eight inch bleed. With this project you really don't need to set a bleed here, but it's good practice. The bleed shows as a red box outside the document area. Using the multiple artboards feature allows a designer to define uniform bleed for all artboards being created.

THE ARTBOARD TOOL

The **Artboard tool** (Shift + O) controls how you move, resize, and edit artboards, with one artboard selected at a time. To set an artboard as the active artboard, click it. When you have multiple artboards defined, you can view them all by selecting the Artboard tool. Double-clicking the Artboard tool opens the Artboard Options dialog box, as does clicking the Artboard Options button in the Control panel.

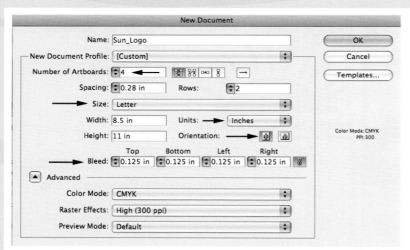

Create New Illustrator Document with Multiple Artboards and Bleed

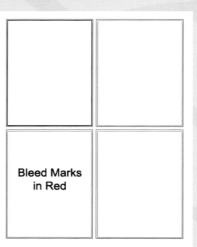

Four Artboards Created

▷ FIGURE 8-32

New document settings for four artboards with bleeds.

To start off your new document, you are going to create four artboards for a logo you will later create with the Blob Brush. The artboard sizes will be for a letter head, CD front cover, business card, and direct mail piece. You will also have a 0.125-inch bleed around each artboard document as if the artboards were going to press. A **bleed** extends beyond the trim edge of a document to ensure good color coverage at the edges of printed material. This is especially useful when artwork contains solid color boxes or artwork itself extends to the edge of the document. It is a good habit to get used to, even though, as in this exercise, it may not be totally necessary.

1. First we want to make sure measurements are set in inches for this project. Select Illustrator > Preferences (Mac), or Edit > Preferences (PC). Select Units, and then select Inches in the General section. Leave all the rest as defaults.

2. To create a new print document, select File > New >New Document, or choose "Create New > Print Document" from the Welcome Screen.

3. In the display, choose to create 4 artboards, which you'll adjust later (Figure 8-32). Use a bleed of 0.125 inches all around.

4. Name the document Sun_Logo and click OK. Your 4 artboards will display as equal sizes.

5. We want rulers and guides displayed. To have the artboard rulers display for each selected artboard, choose View > Rulers > Show Video Rulers. Make sure Smart Guides is also checked in the View menu (View > Smart Guides).

6. Select the Artboard tool (Shift + O) and click on the top left artboard designated as number 1 in the top left area. We'll use that as the main artboard to create the logo on. Notice the ruler guides display for that artboard along the edge of the document. This will be the letterhead artboard at 8.5 x 11 inches so we won't make any adjustments here.

7. To create the CD cover dimensions, with the Artboard tool selected, click on the number 2 artboard to the right and notice the ruler guides now display for this artboard. Drag for the CD cover using the ruler and smart guides, which will display as you drag so that you have a square measuring 4.75 by 4.75 inches. Notice the bleed follows along with the changes you make.

8. To create the direct mail piece, click on the number 3 artboard and drag to create a 4.25 Height x 5.5 Width dimension.

9. To create the business card, click on the number 4 artboard and create a 2.0 Height and 3.5 Width.

10. You can move artboards around, not with the Selection tool, but also with the Artboard tool. Click on the direct mail piece and drag underneath the CD cover, then click on the business card and drag under the mail piece to maximize the work space (Figure 8-33).

11. As an additional note, you can also use the Artboard tool to click and drag on the grey canvas and automatically create an artboard. To remove an artboard just click on the "X" in the upper right corner of the artboard.

12. Save the file as Sun_logo.ai in your Chapter 8 folder. All the multiple artboards can be saved as one document.

▷ FIGURE 8-33

Using the Artboard tool to select, edit, resize and move artboards to suit various client needs.

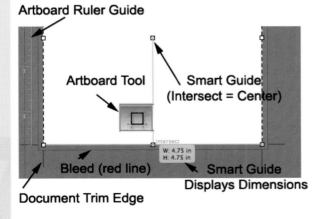
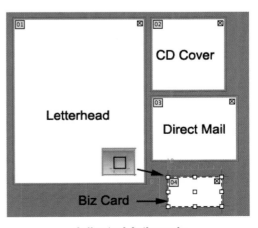

Resizing Artboard

Adjusted Artboards

TOOLKIT TIP You can also use the Control Panel to resize an artboard, by specifying new Width and Height values. To move an artboard and its contents, click to select the Move/Copy Artwork With Artboard icon on the Control panel, and then position the pointer in the artboard and drag. Or, specify new X and Y values in the Control panel.

NAMING THE ARTBOARDS AND USING THE ARTBOARDS PANEL

In Illustrator CS5, you can use the Artboards tool to name and orient your artboards using the Control panel. There is also a new Artboards panel, which allows you to create new artboards, reorder artboards, rearrange artboards, and create duplicate artboards. This helps to keep track of your artboards and edit your work quicker.

Here you will use the Artboard tool to rename each artboard using the Control panel. You can then see the names displayed on the Artboards panel for quick reference to access your work.

▷ FIGURE 8-34

Using the Artboard tool to name each artboard or create orientation. The Artboards panel provides your individual artboards.

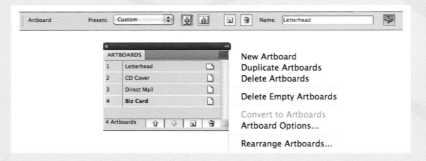

1. With the *Sun_logo.ai* document open, show the Artboards panel by selecting Window > Artboards.

2. Select the Artboard tool, and then select the letterhead artboard you created. It is labeled up in the top left corner as the default *Artboard01*.

3. You will notice that the same name displays on the Control panel. Type in the box Letterhead, then press the Return/Enter key. You can also adjust each artboard's orientation, which is not needed for this exercise. You will notice the name will automatically change in the Artboards panel from *Artboard01* to *Letterhead*.

4. Repeat the same so that all four artboards are labeled correctly.

5. As you see in the Artboards panel, all four artboards are labeled. You can then select an artboard from the panel to highlight it to edit. Check out the panel menu and see the options available with this new feature (Figure 8-34).

6. Save the file when done.

ILLUSTRATOR'S NEW DRAWING MODES AND THE BLOB BRUSH TOOL

▷ FIGURE 8-35

DESIGN TIP

Mulitple artboards in Illustrator allow designers more creative freedom to display their work to a potential client with additional ideas or variations of ideas for new media outlets. The client can also view artboards as individual web like PDF pages.

Illustrator's **Blob Brush tool** (Shift + B) allows a designer to draw merged paths as fill shapes. Instead of a regular paintbrush stroke you get a filled compound path. You can use the Blob Brush tool to paint filled shapes that you can intersect and merge with other shapes of the same color. The key here is same color shapes. The Blob Brush tool uses Fill colors with a Stroke of none. Different colors create different or independent shapes or object paths. The Blob brush works alongside the Direct Selection, Smooth, and Path Eraser tools to smooth out or erase parts of the shape paths created by the Blob Brush. To see brush options, double-click on the Blob Brush tool. In CS5, near the bottom of the Tools panel, you have new Drawing mode options. You have been working in the default Normal Drawing mode all along. Using the Draw Behind mode, you can draw behind all artwork on a selected layer if no artwork is selected, otherwise if artwork is selected, the new object is drawn directly beneath the selected object. Draw Inside mode allows you to draw inside a selected object.

Using the Blob Brush tool to create freestyle shapes.

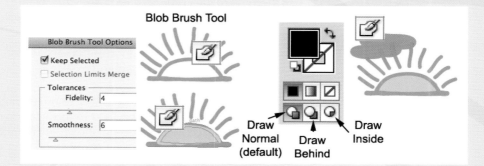

In this exercise you'll be creating a simple playful logo using the new Blob Brush tool, place a playful font underneath, then copy, resize and place your logo on all the arboard media you created.

1. Set your workspace settings from the default Essentials on the Application bar (or Application Frame) to Painting to bring up common panels for painting.

2. Double-click the Blob Brush tool to bring up the Options display. Make sure Keep Selected is checked so you can see the shapes you are creating. Leave all the rest of the settings as shown. The lower half of the display shows brush settings mainly with a graphics tablet. Select OK.

3. Select the first top artboard and zoom in at 100%.

4. Select an orange color stroke with a fill of None. Select the Blob Brush tool and paint a sun outline rising over the horizon as shown in Figure 8-35. Don't worry about the size of your logo since you'll resize it later. Notice that any shapes of the same color merge together as one shape and those not touching any shape have their own individual shape.

5. To paint the yellow sun, deselect the orange outline you created, choose the Selection tool and click on the artboard, area, then select the yellow stroke color.

6. Select the Blob Brush tool and paint inside the sun outline. Notice the new yellow color creates a whole new shape that does not blend with the orange color. Feel free to get more creative if you like.

7. If the yellow color overruns the orange, just select the yellow shape you created with the Selection tool, and select Object > Arrange > Send to Back. Use the Path Eraser, Direct Selection, and Smooth tools to adjust as you like it.

8. To create a cloud behind the sun, using the new Draw Behind mode in CS5, deselect the selected shapes by choosing the Selection tool and click on the artboard, then select a light blue color, select the Draw Behind mode near the bottom of the Tools panel, and paint again with the Blob Brush. The cloud should appear behind the sun as shown in Figure 8-35. Use the bracket keys on your keyboard to adjust the size of the brush to fill in the color of the cloud. Before creating a different colored shape, remember to deselect the shape you just created. Select the default Normal Drawing mode in CS5 when done.

9. If you are using earlier versions, of if the cloud is still in front of the sun, choose Object > Arrange > Send to Back.

10. Use the Direct Selection (with the arrow keys), Path Eraser and Smooth tools to refine your creation to the way you like it for a simple logo. Go ahead and play!

11. Use the Type menu (Type > Font) to see what all fonts look like. Find a fun font for this logo. We chose a sans-serif font called Stencil.

12. Type Rising Sun Play Center underneath.

13. You can now select the whole logo with the Selection tool and choose Object > Group to put everything together.

14. Hold down the Option/ALT Key and copy the logo to the other artboards, or with the selected logo, choose Edit > Copy, then Edit Paste. With the logo selected hold down the Shift key and drag the corner to resize the logo proportionately to each media piece as shown in Figure 8-36. Feel free to put in appropriate text lines for each type of media on your own.

15. When finished, save your work as *Sun_Logo.ai* again in the *Chapter 8* folder.

16. Feel free to create a symbol of the logo you created, as you learned in the previous map project, for future use.

▷ FIGURE 8-36

Simple logo created with Blob Brush tool, copied, resized, and placed in artboards.

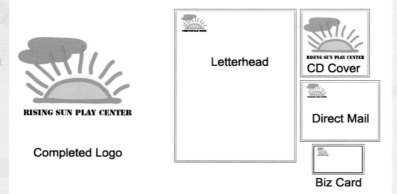

 TOOLKIT TIP Note: In Illustrator CS5, new options called Paste in Place and Paste on All Artboards, paste the object at the same position as the copied objects referenced from the active artboard at the time of copying, which would not work for this exercise.

SAVING AND PRINTING MULTIPLE ARTBOARDS

When saving multiple artboards you can save, as you have been doing, as one document, which will display as multiple pages in Bridge. If you save to earlier versions like CS3 it will create separate documents from each artboard, not all within one document as in CS4 or CS5. There can be up to 100 artboards displayed. You can also export a range of different artboards, or choose individual pages. Saving your work as PDF file will display multiple artboards within the same document name.

When you create a document with multiple artboards, you can print the document in a variety of ways. You can ignore the artboards and print everything on one page, or you can print each artboard as an individual page. In Illustrator CS5, you can have artboards automatically rotated to print to a particular media size. There is also a feature called 9-point referencing that allows you to set reference points for artboards to hinge a corner or center of an artboard while it is being changed. When you print artboards as individual pages, you can choose to print all artboards, or a range of artboards. To print all artboards as separate pages, select File > Print > All. You can see all the pages listed in the preview area in the lower left corner of the Print dialog box. To print a subset of artboards as separate pages, select Range, and specify the artboards to print. To print the artwork on all the artboards together on a single page, select Ignore Artboards. If the artwork extends past the boundaries of the page, you can scale or tile it. You can also specify other print options, and then click Print.

▷ FIGURE 8-37

Options for printing multiple artboards.

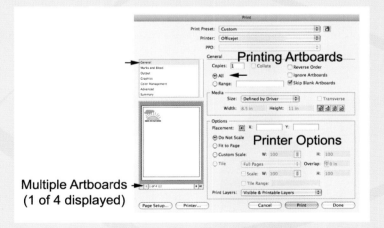

Here you'll print all the completed artboards as separate pages for a potential client.

1. With the multiple artboards saved as Sun_Logo in Illustrator's CS5 format, select File > Print.

2. Select the General tab on the left side, then select the printer you are using.

3. Make sure All is selected under Copies and leave the rest as defaults for now (Figure 8-37). We'll cover more of these settings in depth in future chapters.

4. Select Print to print your copies as separate pages.

DIGITAL TOOLKIT EXTRA: Using 3-D Effects and Map the Label

Here is a great function in Illustrator that you will really enjoy. You can now create 3-D effects from 2-D artwork. You can also control the appearance of 3-D objects by adjusting the lighting, shading, rotation, and other properties. To create these effects, use the Effects > 3-D menu where you can **Extrude** a 2-D object, like a circle, into a cylinder; **Rotate** a 3-D object; and **Revolve** a 2-D outline along an open or closed path around an axis to create a 3-D object. In addition, you can map artwork onto each surface of a 3-D object to design packaging and other 3-D objects. **Mapping artwork** is done in the 3-D Options dialog box to precisely match the artwork to the contours of the 3-D surface. The **Appearance panel** is used to edit the appearance attributes of an object, group, or layer. Strokes, fills, and corresponding effects are stacked in order for future editing. The Appearance panel also displays properties of selected 3-D objects. Any characteristics of an object, from its color to special effects, can be edited directly in the Appearance panel. Click on links, and display boxes from previous commands regarding fill, stroke, or effects are automatically opened up for editing without having to open up their corresponding panels. For this assignment, you will create a 3-D wine (or juice) bottle, using the 3-D Revolve function; then create the label, using symbol and brush library graphics; and map the label to the wine bottle surface (Figure 8-38). The Color Picker lets you select an object's fill or stroke by choosing from a color spectrum, defining colors numerically, or clicking a swatch.

▷ FIGURE 8-38

Creating the 3-D Revolve effect on the outline of the bottle.

CHOOSING COLOR IN THE COLOR PICKER AND OUTLINING THE BOTTLE

To prepare for creating any 3-D effects, an outline needs to be created of half of the shape in order to create the 3-D effect. Use the **Line tool** while holding down the Shift key for straight lines and the Pencil, Pen, and Selection tools to create and adjust the curves. When this is completed, you will have an open path before applying the 3-D effect.

TOOLKIT TIP When creating the path for a 3-D effect, use a Stroke color with no fill for most work. If you revolve an open path that has a fill, the fill s revolved in addition to the stroke color and may produce unexpected results. The process of applying the effect may also slow down your system significantly.

 Need additional fun computer graphics tutorials and info, and an additional look at the projects you'll be creating in this book? Check out my Artist's Digital Toolkit website at: http://www.digitoolkit.com

Here you will trace a template already created of the wine bottle.

1. Launch Illustrator and Open the file *Wine* located in your *Chapter 8* folder. The image has already been scanned and a template created for tracing; if you want, feel free to draw your own, scan it, and place the scanned image into Illustrator.

2. Select View > Rulers > Show Rulers if the rulers are not displayed, and make sure Smart Guides is checked in the View menu. If they are displayed as points, select Illustrator > Preferences (Mac) or Edit > Preferences (Windows). Select Units, and in the General box, switch to inches for this exercise. You can also Option/Right-click in the ruler and select inches from the contextual menu.

3. Select the *Wine* layer to use as the working layer, not the Template layer (Figure 8-39).

4. Zoom in 100% or closer and drag a vertical guideline from the left side ruler to the left side of the wine sketch to be used as the axis for the 3-D revolve.

5. Double-click the Stroke box to display the Color Picker and select a deep purple, 1-point Stroke with no fill; there should be a red line through fill square. The Stroke becomes the fill when revolving a 3-D object.

TOOLKIT TIP You can click on any color, or move up the color scale to choose a color, and it will display its six-digit identity number, although this number is used mostly for colors for the web. Make sure the color will display for the intended output: if a yellow triangle displays it may not print accurately; if a box displays, it may not display properly on the web. By selecting either warning icon, the display will select the next closest color.

6. Zoom in to 200%. Select the Line tool and hold down the Shift key to create straight lines to trace over the bottle base, starting on the guideline. Release the shift key first, then the mouse. Click on the endpoints as you continue to draw to keep the path a single element. Do not draw to the left side of the guideline (Figure 8-39).

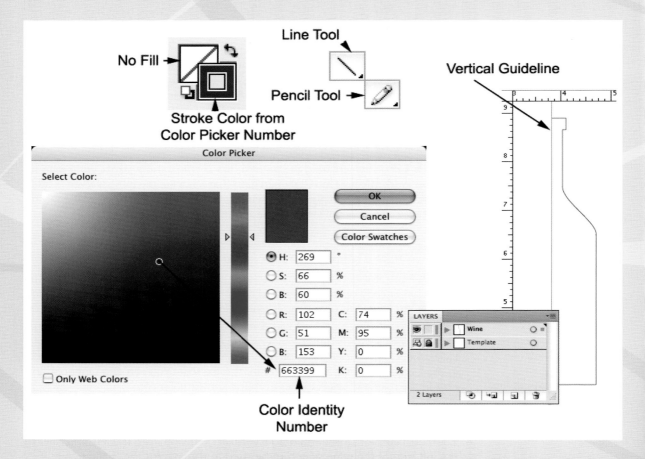

▷ FIGURE 8-39

**Creating the outline
of the bottle with the
Line and Pencil tools.**

7. Select the Pencil tool to draw the curve and adjust with the Direct Selection tool using the arrow keys. Use the Smooth tool if needed to lengthen the direction lines and decrease the amount of anchor points.

8. Select the Line tool again and hold the Shift key to complete the bottle neck, then use the Pencil tool to adjust the curve if needed. Use the smart guides to find the anchor points and for aligning the bottom of the bottle with the top edge. This may take a few attempts to get it right, so be patient.

9. When completed, zoom back out and Save the file as *Wine.ai* in Illustrator's native format in your *Chapter 8* folder, using the default settings for whichever version you are using.

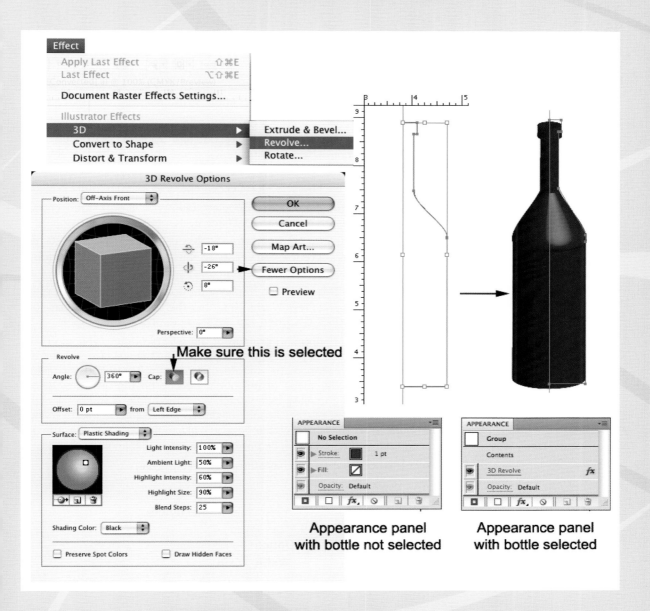

▷ FIGURE 8-40

Creating the 3-D Revolve effect on the outline of the bottle.

APPLYING 3-D EFFECTS

You can revolve an open or closed path around an axis up to 360 degrees for a closed, solid object or make it appear that a slice is removed by using less than 360 degrees. The 3-D Revolve Options dialog box allows the designer to not only preview the effect but also control lighting, shading, and other properties.

▷ FIGURE 8-41

DESIGN TIP

Objects that are revolved around an axis for 360 degrees appear solid, and objects less than 360 degrees will appear sliced or cut into. In the 3-D Options dialog box, select Revolve Cap On to make the object appear solid through-out; select Revolve Cap Off to make the object appear hollow.

Creating the label background.

TOOLKIT TIP When you want to make any changes or delete the 3-D object you created, select the 3-D object and then double-click the effect in the Appearance panel. With the bottle still selected after applying the Revolve effect, you can experiment with applying different colors in the Stroke box.

The process of having the computer figure out and apply a 3-D effect to an outline is called *rendering*. Use the Appearance panel to open the 3-D Revolve Options dialog box if you need to make any changes.

It is show time! Next we see how this 3-D effect can be used for your future projects.

1. With the entire bottle path selected, select Object > Group, then choose Effect > 3-D > Revolve to display the 3-D Revolve Options dialog box.

2. Use the settings shown in Figure 8-40 to create your wine bottle or use the default settings. Make sure the "Turn cap on for solid appearance" button is selected to apply a solid effect to the wine bottle.

3. Select the More Options button to display light qualities and other properties you can apply. Click the Preview box to render the sketch and see what your bottle will look like. Click OK when you are ready to accept the graphic.

4. To experiment with lighting and position of the selected bottle, you can make adjustments while creating the effect, or click the 3-D Revolve link in the Appearance panel to reopen the 3-D Revolve Options pane. You can adjust the lines to change the shape of the bottle directly on the artboard. In our example, we created a small lip below the neck of the bottle. If you deselect the bottle, you'll find the Appearance panel will display Stroke and Fill links to change colors on the fly if you want. Any changes you make to the object on the artboard are recognized and re-rendered. Be patient while it is rendering each change.

5. Deselect the bottle when you have finished. Save the file.

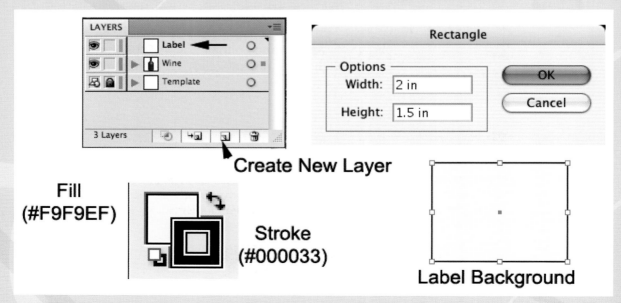

CREATING THE WINE LABEL USING SYMBOL AND BRUSH LIBRARIES

Here you will use a special symbol and brush from their respective libraries to create the components of the wine label. The Transform command in the Object menu can be used to reflect and copy any object to create a symmetrical design. Symbol and brush libraries store graphics under specialized categories for future use. To apply a straight decorative Art brush from the brush library, you will need to create a straight path using the Line tool, while holding the Shift key to make a straight line. Before mapping the label to the 3-D bottle, it has to be made as a symbol.

Here is a little review of using some symbols and brushes by creating a simple wine label (or feel free to change the label for juice, cider, soda, etc.).

1. Create a new layer in the Layers panel for the wine label and name it *Label*. Click OK (as shown in Figure 8-41, previous page).

2. Double-click the Fill box in the Tools panel, and select a very light cream color in the Color Picker display. Double-click the Stroke box; select a deep blue, and set the stroke to 2-points in the Stroke panel as shown in Figure 8-41.

▷ FIGURE 8-42

Creating the label for the wine bottle using symbol and brush libraries.

3. Select View > Rulers > Show Rulers if they are not displayed, and select the Rectangle tool.

4. Click (don't drag) on the document above the wine bottle and enter a 2-inch Width by 1.5 inch Height, select OK, and zoom in to 200%.

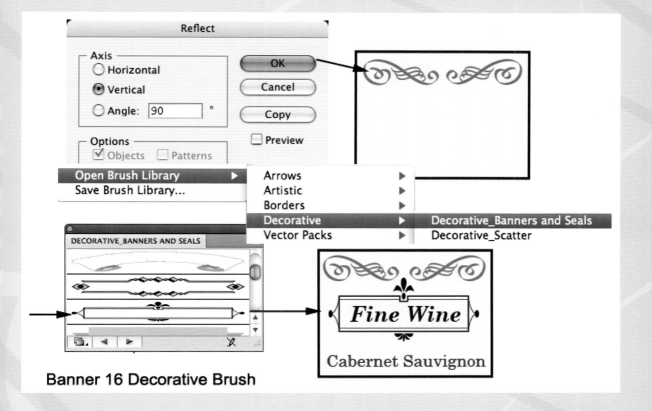

Banner 16 Decorative Brush

DESIGN TIP

For small text (less than 24 points, depending on the font) avoid using any stroke colors, so the type does not appear blotchy and hard to read.

5. Select the rectangle with the Selection tool to display a bounding box. Drag a vertical guideline to the center point of the rectangle (Figure 8-41).

6. Open the *Decor.ai* file in your *Chapter 8* folder, which contains the Arabesque 4 symbol; select and copy the symbol, and then paste it onto your wine document. You can also locate a different graphic if you want, or you can create your own in a separate file. Select the graphic you will use and then click the New Symbol icon in the Symbols panel to add the symbol to your Symbols panel.

7. Position the graphic along the top right edge of the rectangle, then hold down the Shift key and resize it from the right corner toward the middle of the label. Make sure the graphic does not touch the stroke borders.

8. To create the other side, choose Object > Transform > Reflect.

9. From the dialog box, select a 90 degree Vertical Axis rotation, and then click Copy, but *do not* click OK.

10. Drag the copy with the Selection tool, and position it at the left side of the label.

11. To apply a decorative Art brush, select Open Brush Library from the Brushes panel submenu and select Decorative, then select the Decorative Banners and Seals library.

12. Select the Banner 16 brush to place it automatically in the Brushes panel, or choose something similar in style.

13. To apply the brush, select the Brush tool. While holding the Shift key to make a straight line, draw across the label about two thirds of the way up. You can also try to use the **Line Segment tool** and apply the brush style to it afterward.

14. Reposition the sizing handles to center the graphic as shown in Figure 8-42.

15. To enter the text, select the Type tool and click outside the label, not on the brush. Use the Character panel and choose a Century Old Style (Mac) or Century Schoolbook (Windows) font, or another serif font, in Italic style. Set the size to 18 points, with a black Fill and no Stroke.

16. Type "Fine Wine," or create your own title, and use the Selection tool to drag the text on top of the Art brush graphic. Deselect the text.

17. Select the Type tool, click on the artboard, and change the Fill color to deep red with no Stroke; set the Size to 14 points with a Regular Style. Type "Cabernet Sauvignon" below the brush graphic in the wine label and center it.

18. Select all the elements in the wine label with the Selection tool and choose Object > Group.

19. To make the label into a symbol, click the New Symbol icon in the Symbols panel. Make sure, in the Symbol options, you set it as a graphic, not a movie clip.

20. Delete the label if you want, or leave it next to the bottle for comparison or in case you want to modify it later.

21. Save the file. Your wine label is finished and ready to be placed on the bottle.

OPTIONAL: CREATING YOUR OWN DECORATION USING THE BRISTLE BRUSH

In Illustrator CS5, a new type of brush library is called Bristle brushes. Bristle brushes create brush strokes with the appearance of a natural brush with bristles, and you can also vary the width of a stroke, or select from a preset group of variable width brushes. When working with brushes, keep the fill color to none and choose colors for Stroke only. In this exercise, try to create a decorative piece of artwork that can be used as a symbol, using the *Decor* artwork file as a guide for starters. You will use the new Bristle brush library of brushes. To display options for making adjustments to your brushes, just double-click on the Definition box that shows your brush.

This exercise will show you how to select and use the new Bristle brushes. We'll start off making a copy of the *Decor* file, which has an elegant series of lines.

1. In Illustrator, open the *Decor.ai* file, and then create an additional new printable document with one artboard and leave the rest as default settings.

2. Resize both windows so they are next to one another. If you don't want to draw freehand, you can Place the *Decor* file as a template (File > Place > Template) and paint on top of it.

3. Select the Paintbrush tool and choose a Fill color of None and a Stroke color of dark blue, deep red, or golden.

4. To select from the Bristle Brush Library of brushes, make sure the Brushes panel is open (Window > Brushes), and from the panel menu, select Open Brush Library > Bristle Brush > Bristle Brush Library. You can also select Window > Brush Libraries > Bristle Brush > Bristle Brush Library.

5. With the selection of brushes, you can see there are quite a few different brush styles. Hover your cursor over each brush to display each one's name. Choose Cat's Tongue, Angle, or Dagger style brushes for starters, and you'll see the brush style displayed in the Control panel's Brush Definition box.

6. Double-click on the brush icon in the Control panel to display the many brush options available for this new type of brush (Figure 8-43).

▷ FIGURE 8-43

You can select preset variable stroke widths, or create and save your own. Double-click the Bristle brush definition box to display plenty of options.

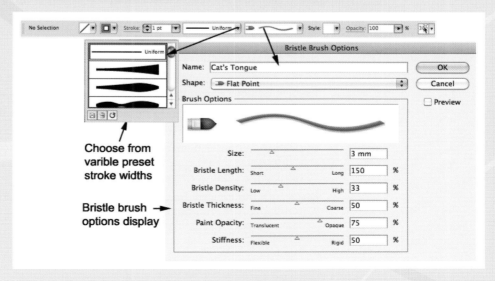

Choose from varible preset stroke widths

Bristle brush → options display

7. To choose a variable stroke width, select the Profile 1 preset variable width (located directly under the Uniform width).

8. The rest is just playing. Try to duplicate the style of the *Decor* file, play with different brush styles. Don't forget to use the Eraser, Smooth, and Direct Selection tools to help you create the path shapes you are looking for. If you are happy with your new artwork, save as a new symbol, and drag onto your wine bottle project.

9. Save the file as *Decor2* in your *Chapter 8* folder.

10. To save your brush with its settings, choose Save Brush Library from the Brushes panel menu, and place the new library file in the Bristle Brush library so that it will appear in the Brush Libraries menu when you restart Illustrator.

MAPPING ARTWORK TO A 3-D OBJECT

Mapping artwork involves wrapping the artwork around the projected surface of an object to match what it would look like on an actual 3-D product. This process can be used when designers are showing products packaged in containers or applying labels to bottles and so on. In Illustrator, any artwork to be mapped onto a 3-D surface has to be stored in the Symbols panel. You can apply any artwork that has been converted into a symbol around any surface of any 3-D object. The Map Art feature is located in the 3-D Revolve Options dialog box and is easily accessed by double-clicking on the 3-D Revolve effect in the Appearance panel. The Appearance panel allows editing directly from the panel itself. Click on links from previous commands regarding fill, stroke, or effects and the corresponding display windows are automatically opened up for editing without having to open up their corresponding panels. You can also adjust the opacity settings for each effect applied and have direct access to live effects to see results on the fly.

TOOLKIT TIP To edit 3-D objects, the object must first be selected to display attributes and properties on the Appearance panel. Double-click on the 3-D list item in the Appearance panel to make changes, like adding mapped artwork to the object, changing lighting, and adjusting object properties.

Now you will Map the label to the wine bottle.

1. Select the wine bottle with the Selection tool.

2. In the Appearance panel, double-click the 3-D Revolve link to open the 3-D Revolve Options dialog box; drag it to the side so you can see the bottle.

3. Click the Map Art button. Do not worry if the color on the bottle disappears. Be patient, as it takes a while to render all the surfaces.

4. Click the Next Surface arrow to page through the surfaces. Select the Surface that displays as a light gray gridline on the right side, as shown in Figure 8-44, to display the front of the wine bottle.

5. Make sure the Preview box is checked to view the results and that the Shade Artwork box is checked to display the label correctly.

6. In the Map Art dialog box, select the new layer symbol from the Symbol drop-down menu and position the bounding box to align the label on the bottle; observe the preview to check the effect.

 PROBLEM If it is taking very long to process, you may have saved the Label symbol as a movie clip instead of a graphic.

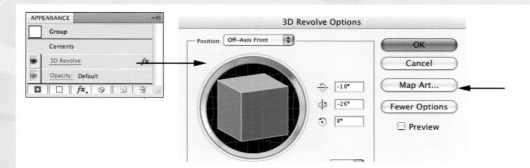

Select the Label Symbol Just Created

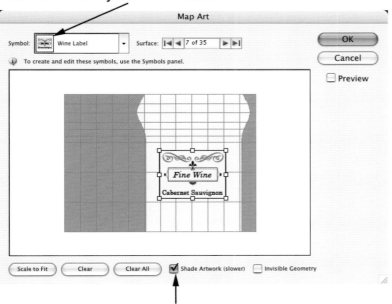

This needs to be checked to display all shading

Indicates Area   Label
for Mapping (red)   Mapped

▷ FIGURE 8-44

Mapping the wine label to the 3-D bottle.

7. If you make a mistake, just select the Clear button on the display box and repeat steps 3 through 5 until you have it positioned the way you want it.

8. When you are satisfied, click OK to exit the Map Artwork window, then click OK again to return to your document and observe your work. Pretty cool, huh? Delete the Template layer when your work is finished.

9. Save the file in the native Illustrator AI format as a backup, then use File > Save As to save it again as an EPS file in your *Chapter 8* folder. Print it using the default settings.

10. You are now designing in 3-D!

PROBLEM If the text on your bottle appears faint or disappears, the Shade Artwork box in the Map Art dialog box was not checked to display the text correctly. Double-click the effect in the Appearance panel to fix it.

TOOLKIT TIP Try experimenting with different lighting settings to get the look you want. You can also apply 3-D effects using the 3-D library from the Graphics Style panel. 3-D objects can be rotated using the Rotate command in the Effect menu (Effect > 3-D > Rotate). The Graphic Styles panel has been greatly enhanced, so you can preview applied styles on the fly on a large thumbnail display to determine if an effect works for you. You can also save your 3D effect for future use in the Graphic Styles panel. Use the Help menu to find more ways to use 3-D effects and lighting.

CHAPTER SUMMARY

In this chapter, you learned that you could trace any sketch or image brought into the computer by creating a nonprintable template layer that dims the image so you can trace the outline on a second layer. Creating various elements on separate layers isolates them, so they do not affect other layers unless you choose. Brushes allow the designer to apply strokes with predesigned brushes, brush libraries, or custom brushes that can be created and saved in the Brushes panel. Graphics can be made into symbols and added to the Symbols panel, or they can be selected from various preset symbol libraries. Symbols can be placed repeatedly on a document to create symbol instances, which can be modified with the Symbolism tools. Illustrator also allows the designer to create or place text from other documents into the artwork. Text can be edited by applying formatting commands. Illustrator gives the designer the ability to create 3-D objects from 2-D drawings and apply lighting and shading properties. Artwork can also be mapped to 3-D surfaces for precise alignment for packaging and design applications. For more information and projects, check out the *Goodies* folder on your CD.

REVIEW QUESTIONS

1. Why would you use Grayscale mode when scanning line art?
2. Explain the EPS formats when saving Illustrator files.
3. Explain two ways templates can be created.
4. Explain uses of the Pencil, Smooth, Eraser, Selection, and Direct Selection tools.
5. Explain the differences between using symbols and brushes.
6. Describe styles, symbol instances, and libraries.
7. What is the purpose of the Appearance panel for 3-D effects?
8. Explain mapping.
9. What is the difference between paths created by the Paintbrush or Pencil tools and those paths created by the Blob Brush tool?
10. Explain the purpose of the Artboard tool.

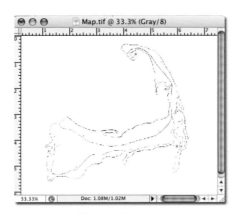

Sketch of Map
of Cape Cod, Massachusettes

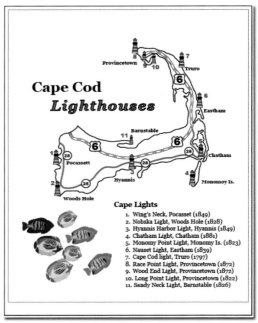

Completed Map

CHAPTER 8
Creating a scaleable tourist map from a drawing
sketch in Illustrator. Using symbols for visual
enhancement.

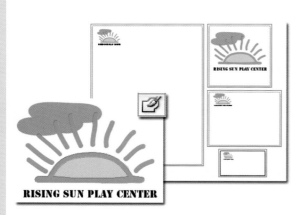

CHAPTER 8 ADVANCED
Freestyle shapes with the Blob Brush.
Placing logo on multiple artboards.

CHAPTER 8 EXTRA
3-D bottle shape with label
created and mapped onto
bottle.

Precision with the Pen Tool

CHAPTER OBJECTIVES: To understand the use of the Pen tool as a precision instrument, and to see how it is used with other drawing tools, in this chapter you will:

▷ Master the use of the Pen tool to create straight lines and Bézier curves.

▷ Combine paths created with the Pen tool and other drawing tools to create complex shapes.

▷ Connect separate paths using the Lasso tool, then align and join end points with Average and Join commands.

▷ Create special shape combinations with the Pathfinder panel and adjust opacity with the Transparency panel.

▷ Learn to create and adjust type on paths.

▷ Save files in Illustrator's native format as a backup and in EPS format for commercial printing.

▷ ADVANCED USERS: Create professional business cards.

▷ DIGITAL TOOLKIT EXTRA: Create a clock face using guides and gradients.

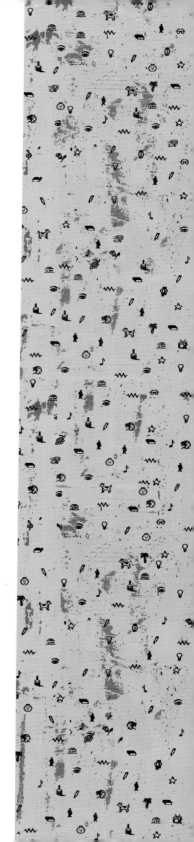

Although the Pencil tool is easier for drawing lines and editing free-hand lines, the Pen tool is used for creating paths that demand precision. With the **Pen tool**, the designer can create perfectly straight lines between anchor points, by clicking from one point to the next, and can also create complex shapes from special Bézier curves of path segments. **Bézier curves** are created by setting anchor points with the Pen tool and dragging the mouse to define the shape of the curve. Special purpose Pen tools can be used to add and delete anchor points, to change smooth curves into sharp corners, or to change sharp corners into smooth curves.

PEN TOOL BASICS

The Pen tool allows the designer to work on images that require precision paths. It takes a little getting used to, but it becomes a very useful tool to the digital designer. The Pen tools are also used in Photoshop and other applications as well. Pen tools can be used in conjunction with other drawing tools to combine paths. Pen tools work well for tracing outlines of complex shapes and images and for creating complex lines from scratch. Pen tools have symbols under the pen cursor to provide feedback as to what function you are about to perform (Figure 9-1). For instance, an *X* by the Pen tool indicates you are starting a new object, and a circle indicates a path will become closed. You will find many adjustments with anchor points and paths can be done using the Control panel with selected tools. If you like, open the template file called *Pentools* in your *Chapter 9* folder and practice.

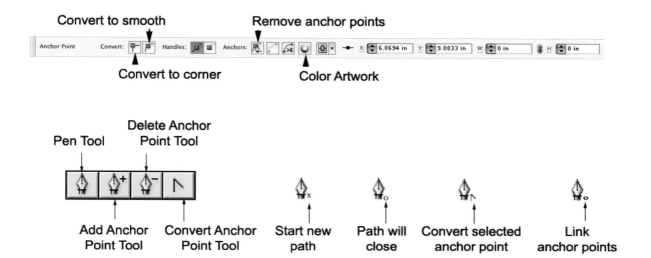

▷ FIGURE 9-1

Pen tools and cursor feedback: Control panel options.

CREATING STRAIGHT LINES

When you click the first time with the Pen tool, the first anchor point is created. When you click a second time, a caret—an upside down *V*—appears next to the Pen tool cursor, indicating that you can continue creating more anchor points. If you click the secondary point without dragging, a single straight line is created (Figure 9-2). When using any of the Pen tools, you must end the path before you can draw other lines that are not connected to the path. To end any path with the Pen tool, select the Pen tool icon again or hit the Return/Enter key.

DESIGN TIP

To create perfect horizontal or vertical straight-line segments or perfect straight lines at 45 and 90 degree angles, hold down the Shift key before clicking the next anchor point.

TOOLKIT TIP You can also end a path with Select > Deselect (Command/Ctrl Y), or by selecting the Command/Ctrl key and clicking away from the line you created. The Command/Ctrl key toggles from the selected tool to the last-used selection tool. If you select Edit > Undo Pen or press the Delete key, it will remove the last selected path segment.

▷ FIGURE 9-2

The Pen tool creates straight lines between anchor points when clicking from one point to another.

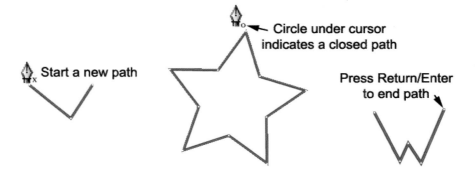

DRAWING BÉZIER CURVES

You can make Bézier curves by setting anchor points with the Pen tool and dragging the mouse to define the shape of the curve (Figure 9-3). Instead of dragging the Pen tool to draw the curve, as you would with the Pencil tool, you drag it to set the starting point or anchor point and the direction of the curve. Path shapes are then created when the anchor point is dragged in a specific direction creating **direction lines**. Dragging two anchor points in the same direction creates an "S" curve, while dragging two anchor points in the opposite direction creates a "C" curve. The anchor points and direction lines do not print with the artwork. Use the Direct Selection tool to edit your paths for even more precision.

TOOLKIT TIP You can set Preferences of how anchor points and paths are displayed in the Selection and Anchor Point Display option. When you select a point, Illustrator now selects the closest point.

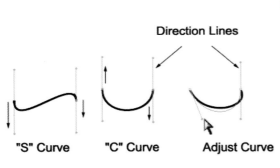

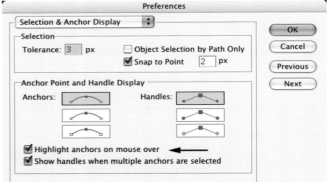

▷ FIGURE 9-3

**The direction an
anchor point is
dragged deter-
mines the shape
of the curve.
You can set
preferences for
accessing anchor
points and paths
in Selection
and Anchor
Point displays.**

MAKING CORNERS FROM CURVES

A smooth curve anchor point can be converted into a corner point and vice versa with the **Convert Anchor Point tool**. A corner point can be created from a smooth point by clicking again, not double-clicking, on the last anchor point drawn with the Pen tool (Figure 9-4). You will notice the convert symbol under the Pen tool cursor; it looks like an upside down V.

TOOLKIT TIP Holding down the Option/Alt key converts any Pen tool into a Convert Anchor Point tool.

Curves can be made into corners and vice versa with the Convert Anchor Point tool or by clicking a second time over the selected anchor point using the Pen tool to display the convert symbol underneath.

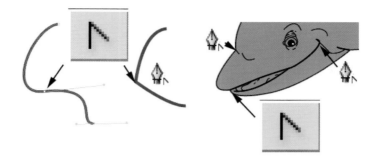

DIRECT SELECTION AND LASSO TOOLS

The **Direct Selection tool** works in conjunction with the Pen tool to precisely adjust the shape of a path the Pen tool creates by adjusting its anchor points and direction lines. The **Lasso tool** is great for quickly making a freehand selection in a small area between endpoints of paths to be joined (Figure 9-5).

The Direct Selection tool adjusts the shape of a path, and the Direct Select Lasso tool selects path segments and anchor points.

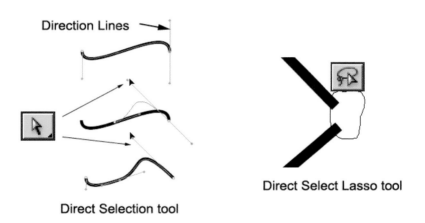

Direction Lines

Direct Select Lasso tool

Direct Selection tool

PATH TYPE TOOLS

In Illustrator, there are two **Path Type tools** that allow the designer to place type on any path created. One allows the type to be placed horizontally along the path, and the other allows placement vertically (Figure 9-6). These tools provide plenty of flexibility to apply type along any path, shape, or object created.

▷   FIGURE 9-6

Horizontal and vertical Path Type tools.

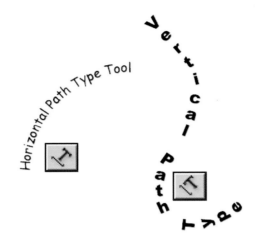

CLIENT ASSIGNMENT: Creating a Logo

The manager of the Crystal Sands Aquarium, Richard Zeigler, needs a new, scalable logo created that can be used for various promotions and signage for the new aquarium. He is looking for an image of an animal for their logo; he wants something geared toward family fun. You discuss possible animals and decide to use a dolphin because of its universal appeal with children. You sketch about a dozen drawings of dolphins for the next meeting. Jack finds the drawing he likes, a smiling dolphin, and he chooses a light blue color for the dolphin image. A slogan for the logo is chosen: Come Play! A playful wide font is chosen for the aquarium's name to match the curvature below the smiling dolphin's body. After summarizing how the logo will look, an appointment is made for the final logo approval (Figure 9-7).

ACTION ITEMS OVERVIEW

The drawing has been scanned and a template created for recreating the image in Illustrator. All the lines outlining the dolphin need to be joined together, so a fill color can be put inside the image. The Pen tool will provide the outer lines, and most of the inner lines will be created by the Pen and Pencil tools for smooth lines and curves with most adjustments made with the Direct Selection tool.

Here is what needs to be done:

• Use the Pen tool to create smooth lines and curves and adjust them with the Direct Selection tool.

- Join separate paths and endpoints of the outline using the Average and Join commands in the Object menu.

- Create paths connected to other paths with the Pen and Pencil tools for the details in the drawing.

- Color the dolphin a light blue by adjusting the color opacity.

- Create the type along horizontal and circular paths to complete the logo.

- Save in EPS format to be used by various applications.

- ADVANCED USERS: Make the logo into a business card and use the Transform command to scale, copy, and position graphic elements accurately for a sheet of business cards.

OUTLINING THE TEMPLATE IMAGE

The purpose of creating an outline in Illustrator is to be able to generate smooth, sharp lines, which are vector images that can be scaled to any size needed. Creating long, smooth lines with the Pencil tool is pretty difficult, whereas the Pen tool can do this with ease. In order to fill the outline shape with color, all separate paths must be connected to make one closed path. It is important to make a complete outline as a closed path for applying color before adding paths for the rest of the drawing.

▷ FIGURE 9-7

Completed logo.

TOOLKIT TIP When using the Direct Selection tool to select anchor points or direction lines, use the tip of the arrow cursor.

DESIGN TIP

If you have too many anchor points, the path will appear choppy or segmented. Remember, you are looking for long smooth lines with the Pen tool. Using fewer anchor points is better. If there are too many anchor points, use the Delete Anchor Point tool.

BASIC BÉZIER CURVES

Before tracing, make sure you are creating your drawing on the working layer above the italicized template layer. To make a path outline of the left half of the tail, start with the Pen tool; click first, then drag in the direction you plan to go and continue clicking and dragging to match the template. The Pen tool will take some practice, so plan on making a few attempts to get it right. When the path looks good, save it.

TOOLKIT TIP If the path is way off or you make a mistake, press the Delete/Backspace key to remove the last path segment. Click on the end anchor point or end of the path with the Pen tool (an *X* is displayed by the cursor) to start again.

TOOLKIT TIP You can adjust the template opacity by double-clicking on the template layer thumbnail in the Layers panel and changing the Dim percentage.

▷ FIGURE 9-8

Create Bézier curves for the left tail portion of the dolphin by dragging anchor points with the Pen tool; adjust with the Direct Selection tool.

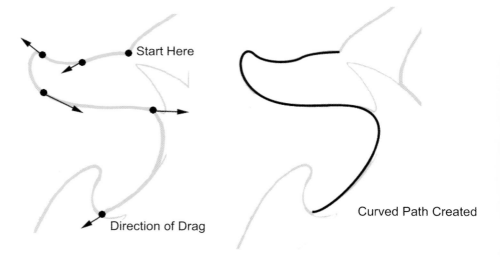

In this exercise, you will set up the dolphin template for tracing, then use the Pen tool to create the left side of the tail following the arrows in Figure 9-8.

1. Open the *Dolphin* file located in your *Chapter 9* folder. It is already set as a template file in CMYK color mode, because it will be used in a variety of publishing media. You are now going to rename the working layer.

2. Double-click *Layer 1* above the template layer and rename it as *Outline* to use as the working layer where you will draw the lines.

3. For the outline of the dolphin, set the Fill to None and the Stroke to 2 points in black. If the stroke is too thick, the paths may look jagged or overlapping.

4. Select the Zoom tool and zoom in to 400% to get in close for accuracy.

5. To create the left portion of the tail, select the Pen tool and click once on the center tip of the tail, as shown in Figure 9-8.

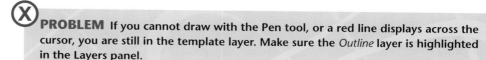

PROBLEM If you cannot draw with the Pen tool, or a red line displays across the cursor, you are still in the template layer. Make sure the *Outline* layer is highlighted in the Layers panel.

6. Halfway over, click again and drag a short distance to the left side.

7. Click and drag again, keeping the path segments close to the template line.

8. Continue until you reach the fin and click once.

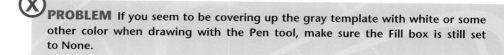

PROBLEM If you seem to be covering up the gray template with white or some other color when drawing with the Pen tool, make sure the Fill box is still set to None.

9. Press the Return/Enter key to end the path.

10. Use the Direct Selection tool to make adjustments by clicking outside the path first; then select the direction line or anchor point to adjust the curve's shape.

11. Save the file as *DolphinOK.ai* in your *Chapter 9* folder when drawn to the point indicated in the illustration.

TOOLKIT TIP When adjusting a path with the Direct Selection tool, selecting a path segment (a black circle displays by the cursor) will display the direction lines from the anchor points on either side of that path segment.

PROBLEM If the entire path moves when using the Direction Selection tool, instead of just the intended anchor point of the path segment, press Command/Ctrl Z immediately, or select Edit > Undo Move. Click outside the path area to deselect the object, and then select the path segment again.

DESIGN TIP

Curves are adjusted by altering the angle of a direction line with the Direct Selection tool, changing the length of the direction line as well.

BÉZIER "C" CURVES

If you had a chance to practice on the *Pentools* practice sheet provided in the *Illustrator* folder (*Chapter 9*), you would notice that to create a "C" curve, you need to drag one direction line one way and the other the opposite way. Now you will put this idea to use by creating the two dolphin fins. You will be adding to these paths later, but for now you are continuing the outline.

▷ FIGURE 9-9

Creating Bézier "C" curves with the Pen tool to complete the fins.

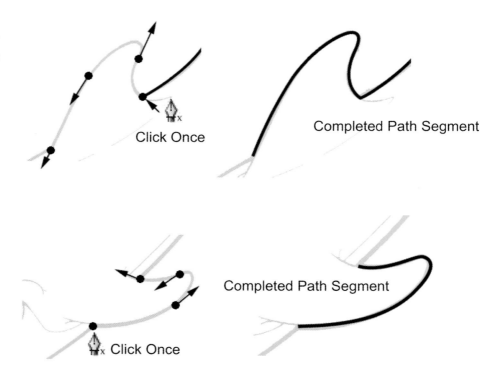

Now you will start a new path in your *DolphinOK.ai* file by clicking on the end-point of the previously drawn path segment so an *X* displays by the Pen tool cursor. Then you will create a "C" curve (Figure 9-9). If you have trouble continuing the path, start a new one; you will learn how to join the two later.

1. Select the Pen tool.

2. Click at the end of the last path when you see an *X* next to the Pen tool cursor.

3. Click near the upper side of the fin and drag upward, then click halfway down on the other side and drag downward to make the "C" curve.

4. Click and drag slightly downward again at the end of the fin. To undo mistakes, press Command/Ctrl Z.

5. Press the Return/Enter key to end the path.

6. For the right fin, click on the bottom corner and drag to the right with the Pen tool.

7. Click on the other side and drag in the opposite direction toward the belly, then click on the other corner and press the Return/Enter key to end the path.

8. Adjust the paths of both fins with the Direct Selection tool.

9. Save the file again, when the new paths for each fin match the template.

TOOLKIT TIP If you find the anchor points are difficult to place exactly where you want them, turn off Snap to Point under the View menu.

DESIGN TIP

For accurate positioning of individual anchor points selected with the Direct Selection tool, use the arrow keys on the keyboard.

CORNERS AND CURVES

Making long, smooth corners is done best with the Pen tool, but making sharp corners can also be done with the Pen tool if, after drawing a direction line, you click the last anchor point again; a convert anchor point symbol is displayed under the Pen tool cursor. You can also use the Convert Anchor Point tool to turn smooth lines into sharp corners and vice versa.

TOOLKIT TIP To change a smooth anchor point to a corner point with the Pen tool, hold down the Option/Alt key and click the point. You will notice a convert anchor point symbol under the Pen tool cursor.

▷ FIGURE 9-10

Creating Bézier curves and corners with the Pen and Convert Anchor Point tools (note symbols by the cursor). To connect different paths, a link symbol shows under the pen tool cursor.

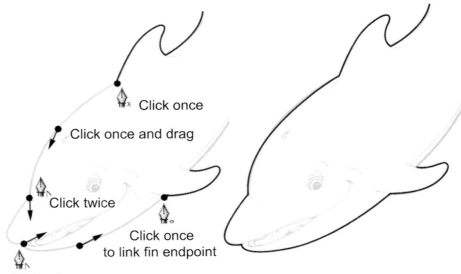

Creating the the dolphin's head involves making a long line using two anchor points, a sharp corner at the snout, and small curves around the outer edges of the mouth. You will be adding details to the image later.

1. Select the Pen tool with a 2-point black Stroke and a Fill of None; click the endpoint of the top fin when an *X* appears on the cursor.

Need additional fun computer graphics tutorials and info, and an additional look at the projects you'll be creating in this book? Check out my Artist's Digital Toolkit website at: **http://www.digitoolkit.com**

2. Halfway down from the top, click and drag downward, then click at the beginning corner of the snout and drag to match the template curve, as shown in Figure 9-10.

3. To make a sharp corner, move the mouse over the last anchor point and you will see the convert anchor point symbol under the pen cursor to indicate that this will make a corner point. Click that anchor point again, or hold down the Option/Alt key to temporarily change the Pen tool to the Convert Anchor Point tool.

4. Click at the edge of the mouth and drag to match the template. Make the anchor point at the edge of the mouth into a sharp corner.

5. Click halfway under the jaw and drag toward the fin to match the template.

6. At the corner of the fin, when you see a circle symbol displayed next to the Pen tool cursor, click once to connect the two points.

7. Press the Return/Enter key to end the path and finish the outline of the head.

8. Make final adjustments with the Direct Selection tool.

9. Save the file; you will be finishing the dolphin outline in the next exercise.

COMBINING CURVES AND CORNERS

Finishing the outline of the belly and the rest of the tail involves creating the long lines of the belly with the Pen tool, making a corner point, and then making short curves to end the tail (Figure 9-11). This also reviews how to make curves and corners. Feel free to try the options displayed in the Control panel in smoothing paths, out or converting paths to corners.

It is time to finish the dolphin's outer outline by completing the belly and tail and closing the path at the beginning point of the tail.

1. Select the Pen tool and click at the corner of the fin.

2. To make a long curve, click on the beginning of the tail and drag to match the template. It is a long direction line, but it makes one perfect curve!

3. Move the cursor back over the anchor point until the convert anchor point symbol appears next to the Pen tool cursor, and click to make a corner point. You could also hold down the Option/Alt key to toggle to the Convert Anchor Point tool, and then click. You might also try using the Control panel options.

4. Click and drag around the tail to the beginning point; when the Pen tool cursor displays an *O*, click to close the path, and then Save the file.

5. Zoom in to 400% and, with the Direct Selection tool, adjust the path around the dolphin so that it matches the template as closely as possible.

6. Where necessary, use the Smooth tool to generate clean, smooth lines.

7. If you were not successful in connecting your paths, make sure to bring path end points as close together as possible with the Direct Selection tool.

8. Save the file in the *Chapter 9* folder.

▷ FIGURE 9-11

Creating curves and corners with the Pen tool to complete the outer dolphin outline.

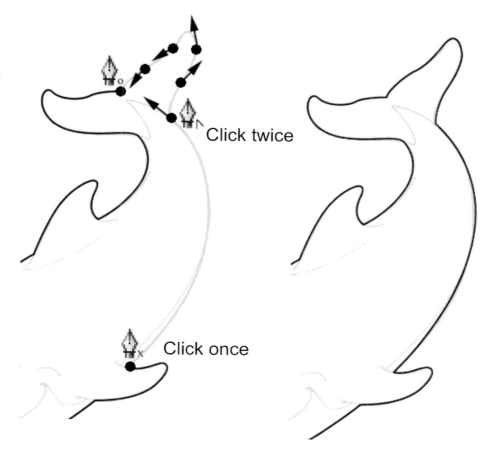

Click twice

Click once

AVERAGING AND JOINING PATH ENDPOINTS

Use the Object > Path menu to connect the end points of paths to make a large, closed path. To connect path end points and make a single smooth path, use the **Average command** (Object > Path > Average) in the Object menu. The **Join command** (Object > Path > Join) makes sure that end points from multiple open paths are joined together as one. To select just the end points of the two paths to be joined together, draw a freehand selection around both end points with the Lasso tool (Figure 9-12). Illustrator CS5 provides the option to join two or more open path segments using the Selection tool to select the open paths, and clicking Object > Path > Join. You can also use the keyboard shortcut Ctrl + J (Windows) or Cmd + J (Mac). Illustrator adds a line segment to bridge the paths to join.

DESIGN TIP

It is a good habit to use the Average command first to align end points on top of one another, and then to use the Join command if needed, to join them correctly as one anchor point. If you do not average the points first, Illustrator simply draws a straight line between the two selected end points.

TOOLKIT TIP Before starting on your drawing, try practicing creating open paths, then practice averaging and joining path segments and endpoints to get a feel for these functions. A good rule of thumb is to use the Average function to connect endpoints, and use the Join function to connect separated path segments as a direct line segment, or for ones that are overlapping.

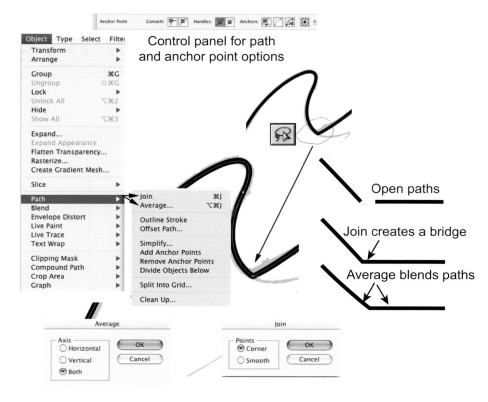

Selecting endpoints with the Direct Select Lasso tool. Averaging and joining endpoints using the object menu.

Control panel for path and anchor point options

Open paths

Join creates a bridge

Average blends paths

Here you will go over the path segments and combine any suspected gaps between paths.

1. Zoom in to 600% to look closely at the paths. Use the scroll bars and Navigation panel to keep track of your position, and scroll to the upper fin area.

2. If you find a gap between the two endpoint of paths, select the Lasso tool and draw a freehand circle around the open area between the two paths, including the end points, to make a selection.

3. Select Object > Path > Average. When the Average dialog box pops up, select Both to let the distance be averaged on both the horizontal and vertical axes.

Ⓧ **PROBLEM** When you are trying to join end points and an Error dialog box comes up when you apply either the Join or Average commands, just click OK. It means the end points are already connected; it could also mean more than two anchor points are selected (not in this image, but for future reference). Move on to the next area.

4. With both points overlapping, use Object > Path > Join to make sure they are joined properly as one point. In most cases, you will receive a display box indicating it is not necessary. When the Join dialog box displays, choose Corner or Smooth, depending on the type of path you are connecting. Feel free to use the Control panel; it contains the same settings and is easier to access.

5. In Illustrator CS5, you can use the Selection tool to select open path segments. If you select Object > Path > Join, Illustrator adds a line segment to bridge paths together. Repeat Steps 2 through 4 to connect any isolated paths to create a single, solid outline.

6. Save often.

7. Use the Direct Selection tool for final adjustments (Figure 9-13).

8. When you have a completely closed path of the dolphin outline, save the file.

TOOLKIT TIP To see if you have a completely closed path after you have connected them all, select the entire image with the Selection tool and change the Fill to a color instead of None. If the color displays inside the outline you just created, congratulations! If not, check for open paths. You will be adding color to this in later, so switch the Fill back to None when you are done.

▷ FIGURE 9-13

Completed closed path, the outer outline of the dolphin image.

COMBINING DRAWING TOOLS

Now it is time to test your drawing skills and your nerves. Here is your chance to continue reviewing and practicing with the drawing tools to make accurate paths by working on the inside area of the dolphin. By clicking on a path with either the Pen or the Convert Anchor Point tool, you can start a new path to branch out from an existing path segment. Again, make fine adjustments using the Smooth and Direct Selection tools. Remember, the Pencil tool works better for short freehand lines, whereas the Pen tool works better when smooth curves or straight lines are needed. Start new paths when an *X* symbol is displayed by the Pen tool cursor.

TOOLKIT TIP Remember that the Pencil tool redraws a line when you go over a path again. Use it for short paths that do not necessarily need to be connected.

▷ FIGURE 9-14

Completed outline.

To start working on the inside area of the dolphin, create the larger details with the Pen tool, and then finish with the Pencil tool. Use Figure 9-14 as your guide and keep practicing.

1. Select the *Outline* layer and make a new layer for the dolphin's details by selecting the Create New Layer icon at the bottom of the Layers panel.

2. Name the new Layer *Inside*. Use this layer as your working layer for inside the drawing. You might want to lock the *Outline* layer so you do not inadvertently draw on it or alter it.

3. Use the Pen tool with a 2-point black Stroke and a Fill of None to work on the mouth area. To create a new line, select another tool like the Select tool to end the path, then select the Pen tool again.

4. To work on the tongue, eyes, blow hole, fin, and tail section, change the Stroke to 1-point black with a Fill of None, and use either the Pen or Pencil tool. Try using the Control panel options in handling paths and anchor points.

5. Do not forget to press the Return/Enter key to end a path, and save frequently.

6. If you use the Pencil tool and a dialog box pops up, just select OK as the default and keep going.

7. Save your file when each new path is created, and undo errors by pressing the Command/Ctrl Z keys.

8. To make the dolphin's eyeball, create the larger circle with a black Fill and another inner circle with a white Fill. Use a Fill of None for the remaining paths. Keep the Stroke at 1-point black.

9. Adjust the new paths using the Direct Selection tool. Try to match the template and allow them to blend into one another, when needed, to keep them visually pleasing.

10. When all the paths are done (it may take a number of attempts), drag the template layer into the Trash icon on the Layers panel since you will not need it, or toggle the visibility box off.

11. Deselect any paths and Save the file again as *DolphinOK.ai*. You are now a Pen tool pro!

CREATING TYPE ON PATHS

With Path Type tools in Illustrator, you can place type along any path or shape created by drawing tools. The Path Type tools let you click on a path and set the text to flow along the perimeter of the path. When type is placed on the path, the path itself loses its Stroke and Fill colors and is nonprinting. It simply becomes a guide for the type to follow. To reposition the beginning of the text, use the Direct Selection tool to drag the path type I-beam, which looks like a vertical line. Formatting type can be done either by using the Type menu, the Type Control panel, or by selecting the Character panel from the Window menu (Window > Type > Character).

TOOLKIT TIP The Arc tool is another Illustrator tool that can be used for specific curved paths. Once the path is created with the Arc tool, the Direct Selection tool can be used for selecting and editing the path by adjusting the direction lines. The Arc tool can be found under the Line Segment tool.

TOOLKIT TIP When making any adjustments to a path of selected type, select only the I-beam and drag carefully with either the Direct Selection tool or Selection tool. You will know when you are clicking on the right place when a small *T* appears next to your cursor.

First you will create a new layer for text, then using the Type tool, you will type the introduction line *Come Play!* Then you will type the *Crystal Sands Aquarium* title using the Path Type tool along a circular path created by the Ellipse tool.

1. In your *DolphinOK.ai* file, select the *Outline* layer in the Layers panel, and click the Create New Layer icon at the bottom of the panel.

2. Rename the new layer *Text*. This will be your text layer to add and edit type.

3. Select the normal Type tool, click on your artboard, and then select a red Fill with a Stroke of None for the introduction line.

DESIGN TIP

To create a playful look for the logo, choices for wide serif fonts can include bold and italic styles. On a Mac, look at these fonts: Gadget, Baskerville, Bookman Old Style, Goudy Heavyface, Minion Pro, and Minion Black. For Windows, try Goudy Stout or Minion Pro, also in bold style. These can be used as informal fonts.

4. Select Bookman Old Style Bold Italic (Mac) shown in Figure 9-15, or choose a wide type font like Goudy Heavyface Italic, Minion Standard Black, or Goudy Stout Italic (Windows). Select a 36-point size from the Type menu, Control panel, or the Character panel (Window > Type > Character). Remember the Character and Control panels contain most of the formatting commands you may need for your text.

5. Type "Come Play!" and position it as shown in Figure 9-15 with the Selection tool. Deselect the text.

6. To make the Crystal Sands Aquarium name, select the Ellipse tool. Make sure you choose a Fill of None and a black Stroke, and then click once on the art-board to bring up the dialog box.

7. In the dialog box, enter a Width and Height of 6 inches (or 440 points) for the circular path.

8. Position the circle, using the Selection tool and arrow keys, so that the dolphin fits inside, as shown in Figure 9-15.

9. Select the Type on a Path tool, and click on the left side of the circle. Try the same font you chose in the intro line, but if the characters are touching, try a narrower font, like the Minion Pro Bold used in this example.

Ⓧ PROBLEM If the type is positioned outside the circle instead of inside, select the middle I-beam with the Direct Selection tool and drag the line of type carefully inside the circle.

▷ FIGURE 9-15

Using type tools to create type on paths and to format the type using the Character panel or Control panel.

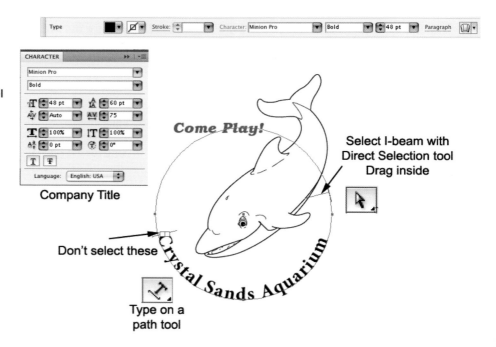

10. Using the Character panel, Type menu, or Control panel, set the point size to 48. You may need to adjust the tracking to add space between characters, depending on the font you use. Select a black Fill and a Stroke color of None and type "Crystal Sands Aquarium" along the path.

11. Select View > Rulers > Show Rulers, then drag a horizontal guideline along the bottom of the word "Play" to help balance out the title along the curve.

12. Zoom back out, and with the Direct Selection tool, select the vertical I-beam that appears on the type path. Make sure the cursor looks like an upside down *T*, then drag along the curve to balance the type line. This may take a few tries.

13. When everything is positioned, choose the Selection tool to drag a diagonal box around all type and paths to select all.

14. Save the file again as *DolphinOK.ai* in the *Chapter 9* folder.

APPLYING COLOR IN A SEPARATE LAYER

DESIGN TIP

When designing logos with type and graphics, having components near or overlapping each other helps to form a connection within the composition.

Color can be selected from the Color Picker, as in Photoshop, and dragged into the Swatches panel for future use. The opacity of a particular color can be adjusted using the Transparency panel in Illustrator. By creating a duplicate outline layer for color, only the color of that layer is affected, while the black outline of the original layer remains solid. Layers work independently of one another, unless the designer chooses otherwise.

TOOLKIT TIP You can take any color displayed in the Fill box and drag it over to the Swatches panel to be saved for later use.

CREATING A CUSTOM COLOR SWATCH

As in Photoshop, you can create your own custom color swatches in Illustrator to reuse whenever you want. You can select a color through the Color panel or by double-clicking the Stroke or Fill color boxes on the Tools panel to bring up the Color Picker. You can create CMYK colors by selecting percentages of CMYK in the Colors panel. Once the color is selected, you simply drag it from the color box on the Tools panel onto the Swatches panel (Figure 9-16).

▷ FIGURE 9-16

Saving color for later use in the Swatches panel.

Set color for dark blue

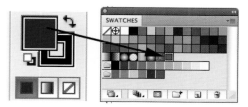

Saving color as new swatch

In this exercise, you will enter settings for a blue color from the Color panel for the type and the dolphin graphic.

1. Make sure the Color, Swatches, and Transparency panels are displayed.

2. Click on the Fill box in the Color panel. If RGB colors are displayed in the Color panel, click on the top right corner (with lines) of the Color panel to display the Color panel menu and select CMYK. Enter the settings C85, M60, Y18, and K2 for a blue color, or choose your own blue from the color ramp. If the CMYK settings are not displayed, click on the double arrows on the Color tab to expand the panel.

3. To save the color, click the Fill box and drag it into an empty area in the Swatches panel (Figure 9-16). That's all there is to it!

 TOOLKIT TIP In order to maintain a black outline around the outside of the dolphin, creating a duplicate layer (not a new layer) of the outline allows you to adjust the duplicate's color and opacity without affecting the original Outline layer.

USING THE TRANSPARENCY PANEL TO LIGHTEN COLOR

In this exercise, you will duplicate the *Outline* layer to add color, and use the Swatches panel to apply the custom color to the dolphin graphic. To show the dolphin's inside lines, you will adjust the Opacity setting in the Transparency panel to lighten the blue color to 20% of its original color.

▷ FIGURE 9-17

Duplicating the outline layer to use as a layer for adjusting color will not affect the black outline color in the original outline layer.

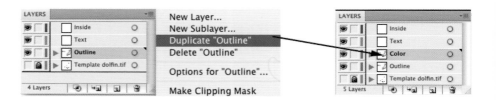

1. Make sure you can access the Color, Swatches, and Transparency panels.

2. Select the *Outline* layer and select Duplicate Outline from the panel submenu to make a duplicate outline layer as shown in Figure 9-17.

3. Name the new *Outline copy* layer *Color*. This layer will be used for applying color and effects without affecting the black outline of the graphic.

4. Using the Direct Selection tool, click on a portion of the outline of the dolphin graphic to select it. The dolphin changes to the blue color in the Fill box.

5. To lighten the color, adjust the Opacity setting in the Transparency panel to about 20% to show the inner lines (Figure 9-18). Notice the outline is still black, because it is on the *Outline* layer and is not affected by changes in the *Color* layer.

6. Experiment with different Opacity settings and different colors on the dolphin if you like. Feel free to use the Brush tool to color the tongue, or create another closed path over the tongue outline.

7. Save the file in your *Chapter 9* folder.

▷ FIGURE 9-18

Selecting the outline with the Direct Selection tool. Adjusting the opacity of color in the Transparency panel.

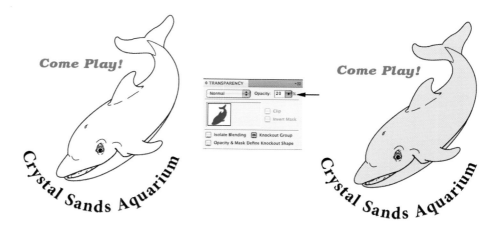

DESIGN TIP

With Illustrator, layered shapes are placed on top of one another with different fill and strokes to create composite illustrations. You can try to add a white underbelly or red tongue on the dolphin for additional colors by drawing closed paths on top on the dolphin outline then using fill colors on separate layers. The trick is to make sure that overlapping paths are adjusted with the Direct Selection tool, so they look like they are as one stroke weight. You could also use a stroke of None, as long as the original paths remain intact.

Ⓧ **PROBLEM** If you find when you select the outline, some color spills outside the dolphin, you may have a couple of paths that have not connected. Select the Anchor points with the Direct Lasso tool and use the Average and Join commands in the Object menu.

TOOLKIT TIP As long as the dolphin outline is selected, you can select any colors from the Color panel with the same Opacity setting to see how they appear on the graphic.

SAVING IN EPS FORMAT

Saving an illustration in EPS format allows the designer to use the graphic universally in most graphic applications. This format works well with scalable vector graphics that are going to press, and along with other options, it can provide thumbnail previews and permanently embeds the fonts, so the viewer does not need the actual fonts. In Illustrator, a designer can save to a previous version, although some editing features may not be backwards compatible. Warnings will display if you save to an earlier version, especially when type is involved. For the purposes of this exercise, save to your current version of Illustrator.

TOOLKIT TIP It is always a good habit, when space allows, to keep a back-up copy of a file in its native format, such as Illustrator's .ai format, before saving in other formats.

▷ FIGURE 9-19

**EPS format
options settings.**

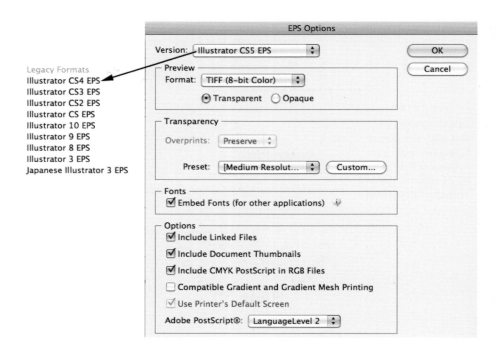

To save the file in EPS format, here is all you have to do.

1. Select File > Save As > Illustrator EPS.

2. Save the file in your *Chapter 9* folder as *DolphinOK.eps* in the version of Illustrator you are using.

3. Use the default options settings, as shown in Figure 9-19. Include thumbnails and document fonts to embed any information to a CMYK PostScript printer.

4. Print the file with the default settings. You now have a logo for future use.

ADVANCED USERS: Creating Professional Business Cards Using Logo Just Created

DESIGN TIP

Many logos for business cards are either one or two colors. Before placing the dolphin logo, you can change the red Fill in the words "Come Play!" to black to turn this into a two-color graphic; then save the file with a different name, and proceed with the exercise below.

Here is where you will put the logo to good use. As long as the completed drawing is saved in either Illustrator's default format (AI) or the universal Illustrator EPS format (EPS), it can be scaled to any size needed by the client. To create a logo for a business card, you only need to scale down the image using the Scale command in the Object menu (Object > Transform > Scale). Other sizes can be used for other promotional materials. To properly align these cards with text lines and the logo, drag horizontal and vertical guidelines. Using guidelines promotes consistency in the layout of the design. Remember, they are nonprinting. Once you position the lines of type and the graphic, you can modify them to balance out the card. We will show you some variations of the same theme.

TOOLKIT TIP Besides using the Transform command to scale objects, you can also double-click the Scale tool in the Tools panel to bring up the same dialog box. The Scale tool scales from a center default reference point of the selected object. Option/Alt clicking with the Scale tool lets you position the reference point for scaling.

With the logo elements all grouped together, you can resize everything at once. Here you will resize the logo, then create a page of business cards. The file will be saved in EPS format.

1. Create a new CMYK color document 8.5 × 11 inches, portrait orientation, named *Fishcard.* Set the view to 100%.

2. Display the rulers for making guides (View > Rulers > Show Rulers).

3. Place the *DolphinOK.eps* file into the new document (File > Place).

4. With the graphic and text selected, choose Object > Transform > Scale.

5. Make sure the Scale Stroke and Effects option is checked to adjust line weights as the graphic is resized to maintain continuity throughout (Figure 9-20).

6. Enter 20% in the Uniform box to scale the graphic proportionately. Select OK and then deselect the graphic.

▷ FIGURE 9-20

Scaling the logo to size.

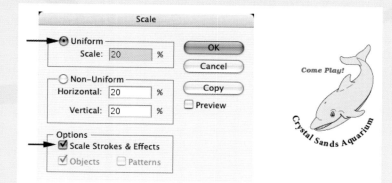

PROBLEM If an error comes up, make sure the graphic is grouped (select all elements, Object > Group and retry), or use the Selection tool and the corner resizing handle, while holding down the Shift key to keep the graphic scaled proportionately, and drag inward until the image height is 1.5 inches.

7. To help with positioning the cards and the left margin for text, drag vertical guides to the 3/4-inch and 1-inch marks on the horizontal ruler to mark the positioning of the card edge and start of type lines.

8. To position cards and lines of text, zoom in to 200% and drag horizontal guides to 10, 9-3/4, 9-1/2, 9-1/4, 9, 8-3/4, 8 1/2, 8-1/4, and 8-inch vertical ruler marks. As you can see, the vertical ruler reads from 11 inches downward, as shown in Figure 9-21.

9. Lock the guides once you have them all laid out (View > Guides > Lock Guides).

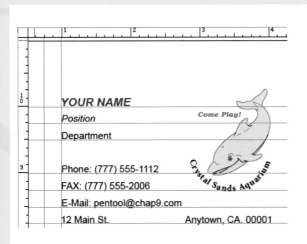
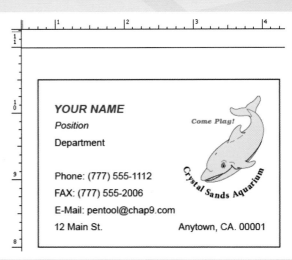

▷ FIGURE 9-21

Using guides to align the logo, card, and text.

TOOLKIT TIP Many business cards can be made a little smaller in height and width with dimensions of 2.25 inches by 3.25 inches. You can also create cards with these dimensions if you prefer.

10. Select the Rectangle tool with a Stroke of 1-point black and a Fill of None. Click on the document to bring up the dialog box.

11. Enter 3.5 inches Width and 2.5 inches Height for a business card-size rectangle. Select OK.

12. Using the arrow keys or Selection tool, carefully move the box into the upper left corner of the document, as shown in Figure 9-21.

13. Select the resized logo with the Selection tool and position it in the right corner of the box. Deselect the logo.

DESIGN TIP

A person's name is the most important line on the business card; it should always stand out by either changing the size, style, and/or color of the font. Some logos display the company name in large letters, while others are subtle—to make the viewer pay attention to the card, as has been done in this project. Another option would be to remove the business name under the dolphin, and place it along the belly lengthwise or on the left side of the business card as shown in Figure 9-22.

14. To make the *Your Name* line, select the Type tool and choose a deep blue or deep red 14-point Arial Italic Bold font from the Character panel, the Type menu, or the Control panel.

15. Type your name on the top line.

16. Choose black 10-point Arial Italic for the Position line. For all other lines of text, use black 10-point Arial Regular from the Character panel. Feel free to substitute your own information and make changes. After each line of text, click the Text tool in the Tools panel, then start another line. This allows you to select each line separately in case you need to make changes later.

17. Fill in the remaining lines as shown and align them flush left at the 1-inch vertical guide.

18. To view your work without guides, select View > Guides > Hide Guides.

19. Now you have a business card. You can select individual text lines with the Selection tool, or highlight them with the Type tool, and type in new information. You can also move the type around, making adjustments to balance out the card.

20. Take a look at the other options shown in Figure 9-22. Create, combine ideas, or copy what you feel makes the best card design using the graphic logo, title, and intro lines.

21. When you have completed the card you want to use, save your file before the next exercise, in which you will create a sheet of these cards.

Option A: Remove title and place to the left side for balance. Same font used as intro line. Adjust intro line and move graphic to provide more room.

Option B: Create another type on path place title alongside underbelly. Adjust intro to grab attention. Adjust color.

▷ FIGURE 9-22

Other options to create business cards based on the same principle logo design.

DESIGN TIP

Keep the use of fonts to a minimum of two or three for a more unified design.

DESIGN TIP

By scaling down the logo with text for a small business card, the title of the business under the dolphin may seem to fight with the type in the rest of the business card. Placing the business name elsewhere on the business card provides a better balance.

TOOLKIT TIP You can also move type around and make adjustments to balance the design of the card. Use the Selection tool to select a group and the Direct Selection tool for individual objects; you may have to Ungroup areas using the object menu (Object > Ungroup), then Group again afterwards. Some examples are shown in Figure 9-22. The type under the belly may seem too distracting from the original logo for such a small document, so try some some other options.

TOOLKIT TIP Part of designing is coming up with possible alternatives, because creating a logo or other graphic image may not work appropriately with all types of media. In the case of the business card, the title under the belly may not seem to balance with the rest of the card, or the font used may be too distracting. Creating alternatives in addition to what the client has asked for, as shown in Figure 9-22, gives them a chance to become more involved in the process. We are choosing to remove the type under the belly and place it elsewhere on the card. Feel free to modify your card now before creating a sheet of cards.

THE TRANSFORM COMMAND

To make multiple copies of the business card to fit on a letter-sized page, use the **Transform command** in the Object menu to accurately position copies vertically and horizontally.

▷ FIGURE 9-23

Use the Transform command to copy the card vertically and horizontally.

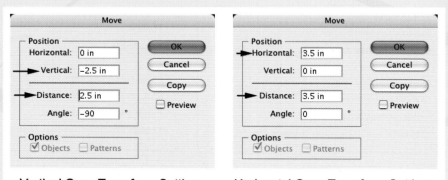

Vertical Copy Transform Settings   Horizontal Copy Transform Settings

Now you will use the Transform command to copy and paste the card to make eight copies.

1. Select the rectangle that defines the size of the business card, and change the stroke from black to None. To move all the elements in the business card, choose the Selection tool and drag diagonally over all the text and objects, including the now-invisible rectangle. Make sure the guides are still hidden, or locked.

2. Group them together (Object > Group). Make sure the card stays selected.

3. Select Object > Transform > Move to get the dialog box. Since the height of the card is 2.5 inches, the card will be copied vertically downward (minus) −2.5 inches.

4. Since you are going to copy downward vertically, type "−2.5 inches" in the Vertical field of the dialog box. Keep the other settings as shown in Figure 9-23. Click inside Distance and both of the other settings will automatically appear.

5. Click Copy (not OK) to place a copy below the original. A duplicate will be made.

6. While the new card is still selected, choose Object > Transform > Transform Again.

7. If a dialog box appears to copy, select Copy with the same settings to make the third card, otherwise continue to Step 8.

8. Repeat Step 6 for the fourth card and select Copy with the same settings once more to make four cards on the left side. If you select OK by mistake, it will only move the card, rather than creating a duplicate.

9. To make four cards on the right, Shift-select all four cards with the Selection tool.

10. Select Object > Transform > Move to open the dialog box. Since the width of the cards is 3.5 inches, the cards will be copied to the right across 3.5 inches. Enter 3.5 inches in the Horizontal dialog box, and 0 inches in the Vertical dialog box, and hit the Tab key for the rest to appear.

11. Click Copy to duplicate the cards to the right.

12. You now have eight aligned business cards (Figure 9-24).

13. Select the Name line with the Selection or Direct Selection tool, and then select the Type tool to highlight and type in the new information. That's it!

14. Save the file in the Illustrator EPS format as *FishCARDS.eps* using the default settings and the version of Illustrator you will be using most often. Leave it open for the next exercise.

SEPARATIONS PREVIEW PANEL

You can preview CMYK color separations and overprinting using the new Separations Preview panel. Previewing separations on your monitor lets you preview spot color objects in your document, and check for rich blacks or process black (K) ink mixed with color inks for increased opacity and richer color. The panel also checks for overprinting when the color CMYK plates are laid on top of one another to observe blending and transparency effects for the particular output device. To observe the dolphin cards you just created, select the Separations Preview panel (Window > Separations Preview) then select the Overprint Preview icon to observe CMYK plate effects. The CMYK plates display as separate layers on the panel. To hide a separation ink on screen, click the eye icon to the left of the separation name, then click again to view the separation. To view all process plates at once, click the CMYK icon. To return to normal view, deselect Overprint Preview. Previewing separations on your monitor can help you detect problems without the expense of printing separations, it does not let you preview trapping, emulsion options, printer's marks, and halftone screens and resolution. Previewing CMYK inks to be visible or hidden on screen in the Separations Preview panel does not affect the actual separations process—it only affects how they appear on your screen during the preview. This will be covered more in depth in the Unit 3 Review.

CREATING A PROOF SHEET FOR PRESS

In Illustrator, there is a very detailed print dialog box, specifically designed to generate any information a service provider in a commercial press environment might need. Since a sheet of business cards has been created, the next step for a designer would be to generate a proof for client approval, which can also be used as a guide for the service provider (Figure 9-25). This proof sheet will be larger than the document to show the necessary printer's marks including:

DESIGN TIP

Any files that are to be used for commercial printing must be saved as either EPS, PDF, or TIF files and must be set up in CMYK color mode. There are functions in the Print dialog box that can be set for commercial printing as well. (Getting files ready for press will be covered more in depth in Chapter 12).

• The position of the **registration marks**, which will allow for precise placement of individual color plates.

• **Trim marks** to show where the document will be trimmed.

• **Color bars** to show the accuracy of colors to be used.

• Other page information to help with the printing process.

• **Bleeds**, which extend solid color boxes of graphics beyond the trim edge of a document to avoid any paper color lines (not needed for this project).

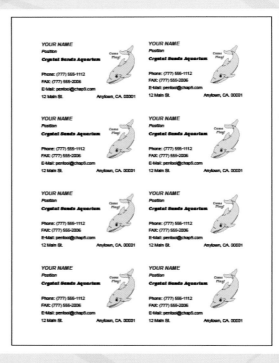

▷ FIGURE 9-24

Completed business card and sheet of cards.

Here you will create a basic proof sheet with printer's marks included in the document.

1. Place an 11 × 17 inch sheet of paper in your printer; you will need the larger size to display the printer's marks.

2. With the *FishCARDS.eps* file open, select File > Print to display the Print dialog box.

3. Select the Marks and Bleed option, then select the Page Setup button. If you get a warning about using the Adobe Print dialog box, click continue.

4. Set the Paper Size to tabloid (11 × 17 inches). Select the color printer you want to print to. Click OK to close the Page Setup window.

5. Click on the Printer's Marks box to select all the basic information for the proof sheet. Leave the other settings at their defaults.

6. Select Print to print the proof sheet. That's all there is to it!

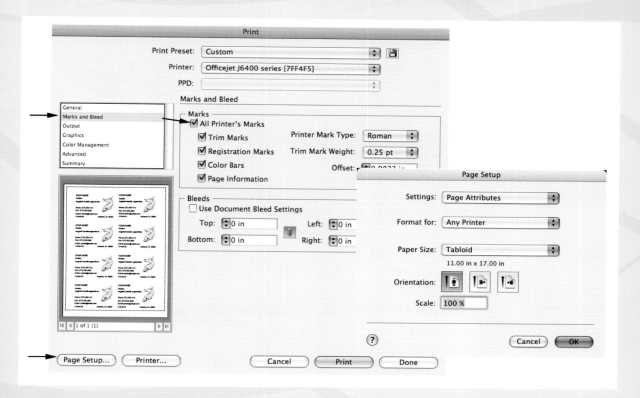

▷ FIGURE 9-25

Creating a proof sheet to include printer's marks.

DIGITAL TOOLKIT EXTRA: Creating a Clock Face

Here is a simple method of using guidelines and shape tools to create the numbers on a scalable clock face (Figure 9-26). The hands are created using the Pen and Ellipse tools. The **Pathfinder panel** will be used to create custom shapes. You will also learn to work with gradients, which transition one color to another—a necessary ingredient in any digital designer's toolkit.

▷ FIGURE 9-26

Creating a scalable clock face using guides, drawing tools, and the Gradient tool and Gradient panel.

CREATING THE CLOCK HANDS WITH PEN AND ELLIPSE TOOLS

The hands of the clock are made by making straight lines for the minute hand and by combining straight lines and Bézier curves with the Pen tool for the hour hand. The circular point that connects the two hands together is made with the Ellipse tool.

▷ FIGURE 9-27

Using the Pen and Ellipse tools to create the hands.

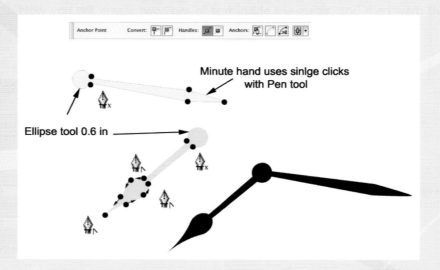

Here is how to create the hands using the Pen and Ellipse tools.

1. First you will create a working layer for drawing above the template layer. In Illustrator, open the file *Hands template.tif* in your *Chapter 9* folder for the dimmed template of the clock hands that you will trace with the drawing tools. In the Layers panel, create a duplicate layer, which will be used to draw on. Select the original Hands template layer and select Template from the panel menu to create a template layer that can be locked in place. Select the new layer above and name it *Hands*. Now you are ready to draw.

2. Select the Ellipse tool and click on the document to enter a 0.6-inch Width and Height with a black Stroke and Fill.

3. Place the selected circle on the minute hand and Option/Alt copy the second circle onto the hour hand.

4. For the minute hand, click straight lines with the Pen tool, then select and group the paths with the circle (Object > Group).

5. For the hour hand, follow the guides in Figure 9-27 to create the straight lines and Bézier curves.

6. Adjust the curves with the Direct Selection and Smooth tools to make them symmetrical.

7. Using the Selection tool and arrow keys, move both hands so the ellipses are overlapping, and then group them together (Object > Group).

8. Save the file as *Hands.eps* in the *Chapter 9* folder, using the default settings.

9. Minimize the document window, leaving the file ready for the next exercise.

SPACING FOR NUMERALS: USING GUIDELINES AND THE POLYGON TOOL

To create the clock face and set up accurate placement of the clock numerals, you need to use guides. Guides help to place objects in a document with precision. They can be locked, shown, or hidden from view to help you with your document layout. Guides can also be created using shapes to position text or graphic elements and then removed after everything is set. You can create a shape with any number of equidistant sides outlining a particular radius with the **Polygon tool**.

DESIGN TIP

When centering a selected shape, use the resizing handles of the bounding box to help position it on a guide. To copy selected objects, hold down the Option/Alt key with the Selection tool.

▷ FIGURE 9-28

Aligning shapes and guidelines for placing numerals.

1. Create the two twelve-sided shapes with the Polygon tool

2. Select and rotate bounding box to align points on guidelines

3. Drag guidelines along inner points for placement of numerals

In this exercise, you will place guidelines to position and type the numerals and add the hands.

1. With the *Hands* file minimized and out of the way, create a new CMYK color document, letter Size with portrait Orientation. Name the file *Clock*.

2. Make sure rulers are displayed; if not, select View > Rulers > Show Rulers.

3. Select the Polygon tool (Shape tool), and set a black, 1-point Stroke with no Fill.

4. Click once on the artboard and enter 12 Sides and a 2.5-inch Radius in the dialog box. This will be the outer shape.

5. With the Selection tool, select the shape to show the bounding box and center the shape inside the document.

6. Drag a vertical guide and a horizontal guide through the center points on each side of the bounding box to mark the center of the shape, as shown in Figure 9-28(1).

7. To make the inner shape, select the Polygon tool again, and use a black, 1-point Stroke with a Fill of None. Enter 12 Sides and a 2-inch Radius this time.

8. Select the new polygon and center it using the guides, as shown in Figure 9-28(1).

9. Hold down the Shift key and select both shapes with the Selection tool.

10. Group the polygons together (Object > Group).

11. Use the Selection tool and move the cursor to just outside one of the corners of the bounding box to display a bent arrow, then click and drag to rotate it until the points of the shape rest on the guidelines, as shown in Figure 9-28(2).

12. Ungroup the two polygon shapes (Object > Ungroup) and deselect them.

13. For placing the numbers, drag horizontal and vertical guidelines along each point in the inner shape, as shown in Figure 9-28(3).

DESIGN TIP

Using the vertical and horizontal guides, the arrow keys on the keyboard, and various shapes as guides such as the Polygon tool provides the designer the ability to position any element within the artwork with true precision. A keystroke option to turn the polygons into guides here is Command/Ctrl 5.

TOOLKIT TIP Here is an advanced way to use shapes as guides. Designers can create guides from shapes and lines, not just from the rulers. Another way to create guides for the numbers would be to draw a vertical line, and then use the rotate tool to make a copy, rotated to 30°; use Command /Ctrl D (redo) a few times to create six lines like spokes (you could use the Align panel to center them to each other if necessary). Select them all and press Command /Ctrl 5 to turn them into guides.

14. Create a new layer in the Layers panel and name it *Numbers*. This way, you can adjust the numbers later without affecting any other layers. Lock the bottom layer with the polygons and guides so as not to accidently alter or draw on it.

15. Select the Type tool and choose 36-point Arial Black, or some other font, and align it centered. You can use the Paragraphs panel or the Control panel to set the paragraph alignment.

16. On the top guide, where the number 12 should go, type "3" instead, and position the middle of the number accurately on the guidelines, using the Direct Selection tool and arrow keys. This number works great for the initial set up.

17. Option/Alt copy the number 3 and place copies all around the clock accurately. See Figure 9-29.

18. When all the 3s are positioned, select the Type tool and type in the proper numbers all around. Select the numbers 10, 11, and 12; reposition them slightly, as shown in Figure 9-29.

19. When completed, choose View > Guides > Clear Guides to remove the guides. If the guides do not clear, unlock the layer and then clear the guides.

COMPLETING THE CLOCK FACE

To complete the clock face, we will reopen the minimized window of the clock hands created earlier. The hands will be copied and pasted into the clock face document, and then resized proportionately to fit the clock (hold the Shift key while dragging one of the corner resizing handles inward to resize proportionately). Use guides to position the hands exactly as desired.

DESIGN TIP

Whenever a designer needs to resize a graphic from its original size in perfect proportion, hold down the Shift key while clicking and dragging the graphic.

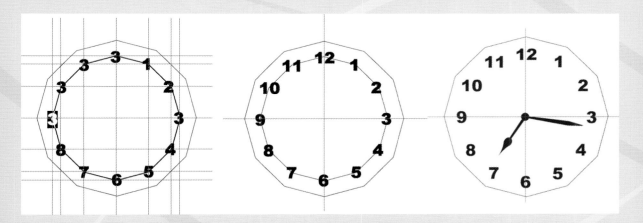

▷ FIGURE 9-29

Placing numbers and hands to complete the clock face.

To complete the clock face, you will position the hands.

1. To set up guides for placing the hands, drag a vertical and horizontal guide from the rulers, intersecting the center of the clock again.

2. Open the *Hands* file by selecting it at the bottom of the Window menu; select and copy (Edit > Copy) the hands, then close the *Hands* file.

3. Paste (Edit > Paste) the hands artwork onto the *Clock* document.

4. To resize the hands to fit inside the clock face, use the Selection tool and hold down the Shift key. Click near a corner-resizing handle, and drag inward.

5. Use the Selection tool and arrow keys to move the hands into position.

6. Unlock the original layer and delete both polygon radius shapes; you will not need them anymore.

7. Select all the numbers and clock hands and group them so any editing can be done to all the numbers at once (Object > Group). Deselect everything.

8. Save the file as *Clock.eps* in your *Chapter 9* folder.

CUSTOM SHAPES USING THE PATHFINDER PANEL

The Pathfinder panel allows the designer to combine various shapes by adding, subtracting, excluding, or intersecting overlapping shapes to create a composite shape. Once the shape is created, it can be filled with gradients or solid colors.

▷ FIGURE 9-30

Using the Pathfinder panel to create the outer portion of the clock.

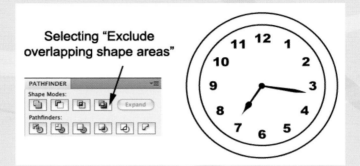

Now that you have created the clock face, let us create the outer clock body using the Pathfinder panel.

1. Make sure you can access the Layers, Swatches, Color, and Pathfinder panels.

2. With the *Clock* file open, create a new layer in the Layers panel called *Outershape*.

3. Select the Ellipse tool, set with a 1-point black Stroke and a Fill of None. Click on the artboard and enter a 6-inch circle for the outer dimension.

Ⓧ **PROBLEM** If the clock face is covered, the Fill is not set to None.

4. Use the Selection tool to select the center point of the circle (not the bounding box) and position so that it is centered where the guides meet. The cursor will display as an arrowhead.

5. Select the Ellipse tool again, with a black Stroke of 1 point and a white Fill to view what happens next.

6. Click on the artboard and enter a 5-inch circle. Position it so that it is centered inside the larger circle. If you Option/Alt click in the center, the circle will be automatically centered.

7. Use the Selection tool to select both circles while holding down the Shift key.

8. Open the Pathfinder panel and, with both circles selected, select the Exclude Overlapping Shape Areas option (first row, fourth icon from the left) to remove the inner clock face area. (See Figure 9-30.)

USING THE GRADIENT PANEL AND TOOL

Gradients provide one of the more artistic tools in a designer's digital toolkit. A **gradient** is a transition or blend of one color into another. There are two types of gradients: *linear* and *radial*. **Linear gradients** are applied in a straight line at a given angle, while **radial gradients** spread out from an inner position to the outer edges of an object. Gradients can be created using the Gradient tool and then selecting a linear or radial gradient type from the Gradient panel. The **Gradient panel** is the control center for creating the gradients. Gradients can be faded into transparency. Colors can be selected from the Swatches or Color panels and dragged into the gradient bar to create color gradient sliders, which can be adjusted to blend in special colors. You can choose from a few preselected gradients in the Swatches panel and modify them. You can even select a gradient color mode to work in from the Tools panel.

DESIGN TIP

Gradients can also help to indicate the direction of light on an object. Applying gradients in opposite directions creates a recessed look in overlapping shapes.

TOOLKIT TIP You can create gradients at any angle, depending on the direction in which you drag with the Gradient tool.

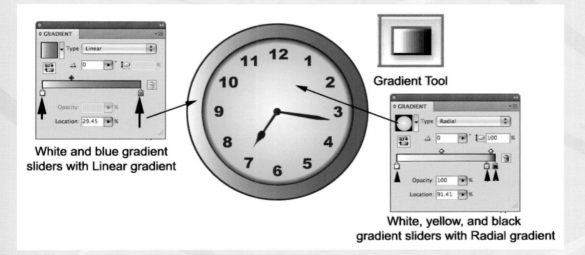

White and blue gradient sliders with Linear gradient

Gradient Tool

White, yellow, and black gradient sliders with Radial gradient

▷   FIGURE 9-31

Adding color and dimension to the clock with gradient colors from the Gradient panel and using the Gradient tool.

Adding gradients will provide a sense of depth to the clock.

1. To make sure the Gradient panel is displayed, select Window > Gradient, double-click on the Gradient tool in the Tools panel, or click the gradient box under the Color Picker in the Tools panel. To display all the gradient options, click on the double arrows at the top left of the tab.

2. Make sure the Color and Swatches panels are also open, and then select a deep blue color from the Color panel using the color spectrum bar at the bottom.

3. To add the blue color to the gradient bar, click and drag the blue color from the Fill box of the Tools panel to the right side of the gradient bar on the Gradient panel (you will notice a small square displays), then release the mouse. It will appear as a new color gradient slider next to a black gradient slider. The Fill box in the Tools panel will display the new gradient (Figure 9-31).

4. Select the Linear Gradient type in the Gradient panel.

5. Click and drag the black color gradient slider down and off the bar of the Gradient panel. This will create a linear gradient with white on the left side and blue on the right. If there is a black gradient slider in addition to the white and blue sliders, drag it downward to remove it.

6. To apply the gradient, select the circles, and click on the gradient in the Gradient panel. This will create a light highlight on the left side of the clock, fading to the blue on the right. You can adjust the direction of the gradient by selecting the the circles, selecting the Gradient tool, and dragging across a new direction to apply the new gradient. Deselect the object when you have finished with the gradient.

7. For the inner clock face area, select the Ellipse tool and create a 5-inch circle, 1-point black Stroke with a Fill of None, and drag it on top of the other 5-inch circle. Use the arrow keys to position it precisely.

8. Drag the *Outershape* layer below the *Numbers* layer to position it behind the numbers (You can rearrange individual objects using Object > Arrange >).

9. Select the black swatch from the Swatches panel and drag it to the right side of the gradient bar. The left side should have a white color slider. If no colors display, select the Default CMYK library from the Colors panel submenu.

10. Select a yellow color from the Swatches panel, and it drag onto the right side of the gradient bar next to the black slider color to give a slight shadow (Figure 9-32).

11. Select Radial gradient for the gradient Type, and click on the center of the clock to make a central radius (Figure 9-31).

12. Use the Selection tool to drag a diagonal across the whole clock face to select it, and then choose Object > Group to group all elements together.

13. Save the completed file as *Clock2.eps* and print the file using the default settings.

14. This can serve as a template for any clock face with different fonts, outer shapes, and colors. Experiment with different gradient settings and combining different shapes with the Pathfinder panel. Have fun!

▷ FIGURE 9-32

Creating gradients that can be saved in the Swatches panel. Dragging color from the Swatches panel to create color stops for gradients.

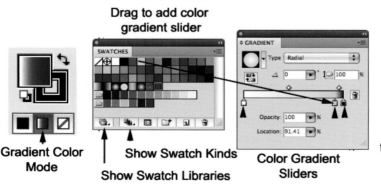

Drag to add color gradient slider

Gradient Color Mode

Show Swatch Kinds

Show Swatch Libraries

Color Gradient Sliders

Double-click on gradient slider to choose other colors from display

SAVING AND OPENING TEMPLATES

Illustrator has the ability to save documents as templates and to open these templates to use as new documents (File > Save As > Template). This function lets you develop documents with common settings and design elements, which can include symbols, imported artwork, brushes, libraries, and document window settings, without having to start from scratch each time. Illustrator templates are saved with an Adobe Illustrator Template **AIT extension.** To create a new document using a template, use the New from Template command (File > New from Template). Illustrator creates a new document with the template settings, while leaving the original template file in its original location. Illustrator includes many preset templates in a variety of layouts and formats that a designer can select from in the Templates folder.

To save a template copy of the clock face, here is all you have to do (Figure 9-33).

1. Make sure all panels, the document window, and the desired artboard size are set up for the workspace you want to save as a template.

2. Select File > Save As Template, or File > Save As > Template in earlier versions, to save the file as *Clock Template.ait* in your *Chapter 9* folder. The template is now saved and can be used as a guide for future documents.

3. Feel free to look at the variety of preset templates by selecting File > New from Template and locate the Templates folder (Adobe > Illustrator > Cool Extras > en_US (your own country and language) > Templates). These templates can be opened and edited to suit a designer's needs.

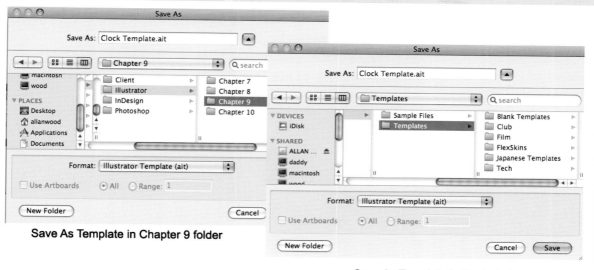

Save As Template in Chapter 9 folder

Save As Template in Illustrator's Template folder with preset templates

▷ FIGURE 9-33

Saving the clock as a template.

CHAPTER SUMMARY

Some of the most important universal tools a designer can learn to master are the Pen tools. By using the Pen tools in combination with other drawing tools, any curve or line can be changed into a path or group of paths to create complex shapes. The Direct Selection tool plays an important role in shaping paths created with the Pen tools by adjusting path segments, anchor points, and direction lines. Illustrator documents, when saved in the universal EPS format, can be used in most graphic applications and can provide previews. Type tools can place text along any given path or shape. Guides are nonprinting and provide consistency and accuracy in the layout of any image. The Gradient tool and Gradient panel are used to create a transition or blend of colors within a shape. Documents can be saved as templates to be used for future artwork. For more information and projects, check out the *Goodies* folder on your CD, or go to *www.digitoolkit.com*.

REVIEW QUESTIONS

1. Explain when to use the Pen tool and when to use the Pencil tool.
2. Explain the purpose of the Average and Join commands in the Object menu.
3. What is the difference between using the Direct Selection tool and the Lasso tool?
4. Describe the "feedback" for the four cursors displayed by the Pen tool.
5. Explain how to adjust the position of type placed on a given path.
6. What is the purpose of saving Illustrator documents as EPS files?
7. Explain the use of the Transparency, Transform, and Pathfinder panels.
8. Explain how to create gradients using the Gradient tool and the Gradient panel.

▷ FIGURE 9-34

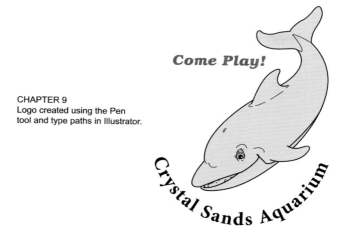

CHAPTER 9
Logo created using the Pen
tool and type paths in Illustrator.

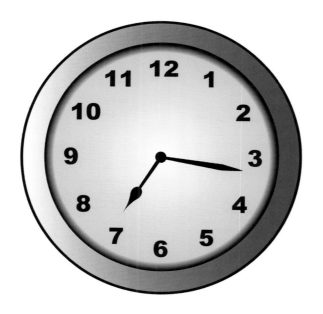

CHAPTER 9 EXTRA
Clock face created in Illustrator
using guidelines and the
Gradient tool.

▷   FIGURE 9-35

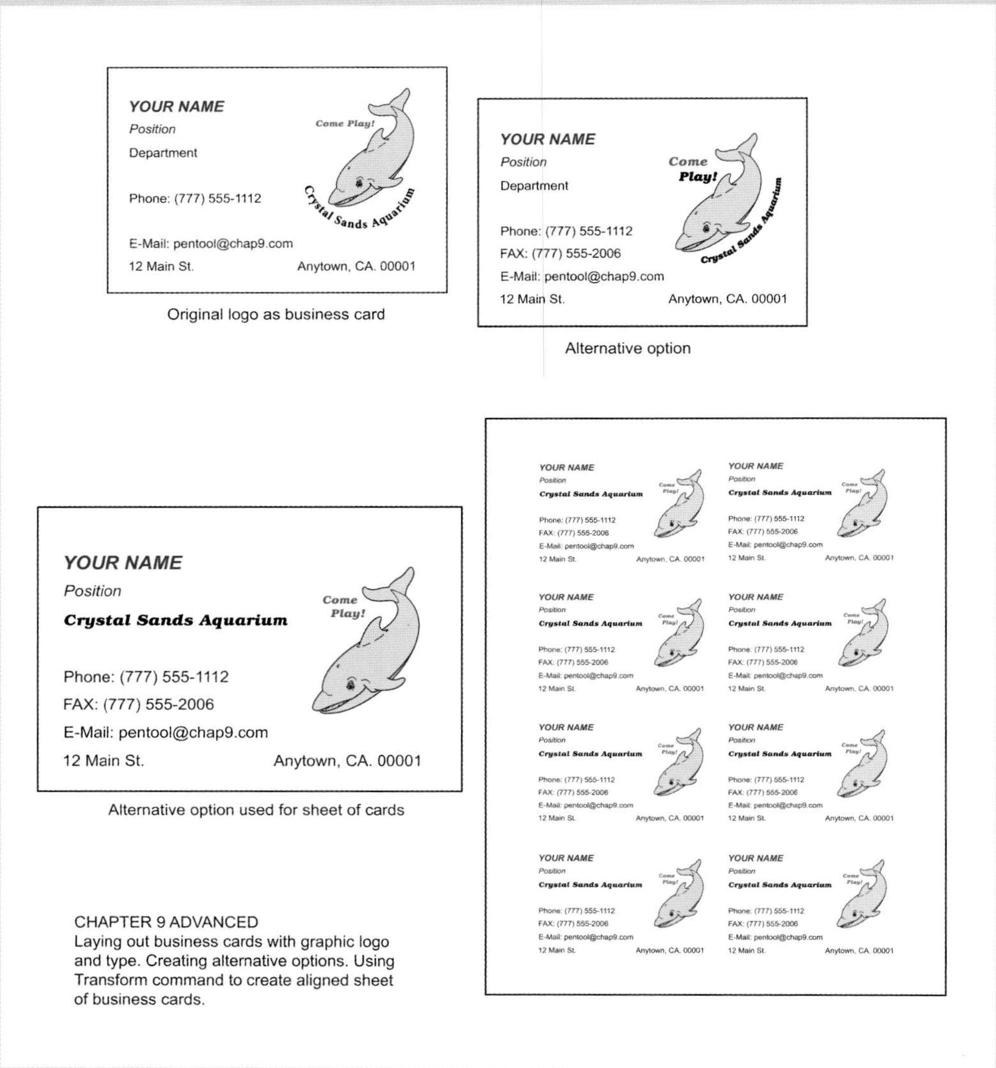

Original logo as business card

Alternative option

Alternative option used for sheet of cards

CHAPTER 9 ADVANCED
Laying out business cards with graphic logo
and type. Creating alternative options. Using
Transform command to create aligned sheet
of business cards.

Integrating Photoshop and Illustrator Files for Web Use

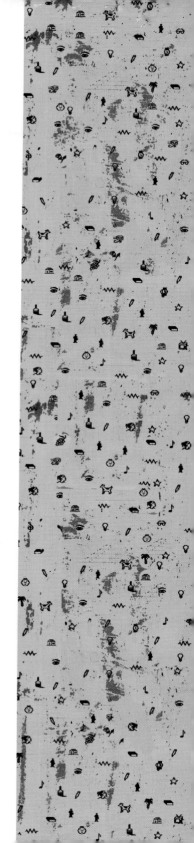

CHAPTER OBJECTIVES: To understand how to integrate Photoshop and Illustrator files and to learn what their possibilities and limitations are, in this chapter you will:

▷ Understand the difference between linking and embedding images.

▷ Work with gradients within both applications.

▷ Place, paste, and export graphic images that have varying opacity and transparency.

▷ Set up web-safe colors, and optimize composite images for use on the web.

▷ Save in various graphic file formats for specific purposes.

▷ ADVANCED USERS: Save files in PDF and EPS formats.

▷ DIGITAL TOOLKIT EXTRA: Use Live Trace and Live Paint to convert bitmap images into scalable vector artwork.

Integrating Illustrator and Photoshop gives a designer the flexibility to combine bitmap artwork and line art into composite images for a variety of effects. Bringing Photoshop's images into Illustrator allows the designer or photographer to trace and create compound paths and apply stroke and fill effects that transform these images into scalable line art. The designer can also bring Illustrator's vector-based line art into Photoshop to apply a variety of special Layer Style effects. In this chapter, you will set up composite web banner images using both applications and become familiar with the more common uses and considerations of each. This chapter is a review of some of the techniques and functions in each application as well.

COMBINING ILLUSTRATOR AND PHOTOSHOP GRAPHICS

Before combining graphics from these applications, it is important to decide what factors will affect the final product. The designer needs to know what media the final design will be used for. The image's final size (dimension), resolution, and color depth should be determined ahead of time, as this may affect the size of the file. Back-up copies should always be made. The graphic format or extension in which the file is saved determines the file size, how it can be used, what components can be edited, and how it will record details for use in various media. Careful planning creates a much easier work flow along the way.

VECTOR IMAGES VERSUS BITMAP IMAGES

Illustrator creates vector graphics that contain sharp, crisp lines that define shapes or objects. A designer can create artwork that uses a limited number of colors in Illustrator, so the file size remains small. Illustrator is used for illustrations, logos, and type that can be scaled to any size based on mathematical calculations. In general, use Illustrator if you need to create scalable graphics or when working with type or outlines that need clean, crisp lines. Photoshop creates pixel-based bitmap images and have a high color bit depth (millions of colors) to display subtle gradations of color. This typically generates larger file sizes. These images, usually photographs or paintings, are called **continuous-tone images**. They cannot be enlarged without adding pixels between existing pixels through a process called *interpolation.* With interpolation, the images start to deteriorate in quality and may appear jagged. Use Photoshop for images that require a large color depth, such as photographs, and for editing pixels and creating special effects, such as drop shadows, beveling, and embossing (Figure 10-1).

▷ FIGURE 10-1

Vector images are scalable to any size for illustrative work, whereas bitmap images are nonscaleable and cannot be enlarged but are better for continuous-tone images, like photos.

Vector Image enlarged 300% of original size

Bitmap image enlarged 300% of original size

SETTING UP FILES FOR THE WEB

When creating files to be used for the web, the measurement settings should be in pixels, the color mode in RGB color, and the orientation is usually landscape mode. Using a measurement of pixels instead of inches makes it easier to lay out graphics for web documents. This can be set ahead of time in the Preferences area (Illustrator/Photoshop > Preferences for Mac; for PC, use Edit > Preferences). Determining the size of the web page itself will also help to create the final composite graphics, such as the web banner. Computer screen resolutions in measurements of 640 × 480, 800 × 600, 1024 × 768 pixels, and 1600 × 1200 pixels (the first number represents width) are the most standard settings. Screen displays have changed with the introduction of wide screen displays. Screen resolution still always displays at 72 pixels per inch, so if you increase your screen resolution,

DESIGN TIP

Although scrolling vertically is acceptable, a user should not have to scroll horizontally through a well-designed web page.

you will notice the icons and images all get smaller. The more pixels being displayed the smaller images become to fit 72 ppi. web pages can be created to grow and shrink to a user's screen size by setting the tables within the page to shrink and expand based on percentages, depending on the monitor screen being used. Graphics that extend across the screen horizontally will need some marginal blank space on both sides, usually about 5 percent of the screen size, so as not to cut off the graphic. The table below displays the maximum width allowed for horizontal graphics for various computer screen resolutions.

COMPUTER RESOLUTION	MAXIMUM HORIZONTAL WIDTH
640 x 480 pixels	600 pixels
800 x 600 pixels	760 pixels
1024 x 768 pixels	980 pixels
1600 x 1200 pixels	1520 pixels

WEB COLORS

Files to be used on the web are usually set up in landscape orientation and in RGB color to display accurate colors on the web. Technically, only 216 colors can be displayed on the web, so it is important to set up images to display in web-safe colors. If non-web-safe colors are used in an RGB image, colors are substituted to simulate the missing colors in the web panel. This process, called **dithering**, can result in a spotty-looking appearance and should be avoided. To make sure all colors are web safe, set the initial document to RGB color mode; then in the Color panel menu, select Web Color Slider in Photoshop or Web Safe RGB in Illustrator (Figure 10-2).

▷ FIGURE 10-2

Selecting Web Safe RGB (Illustrator) or Web Color Slider (Photoshop) in the Color Panel menu ensures web-safe colors. If a cube is displayed, simply click it to find the nearest web-safe color.

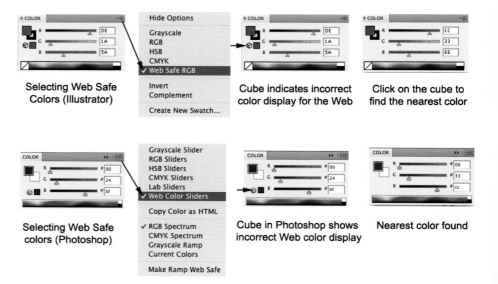

Selecting Web Safe Colors (Illustrator)

Cube indicates incorrect color display for the Web

Click on the cube to find the nearest color

Selecting Web Safe colors (Photoshop)

Cube in Photoshop shows incorrect Web color display

Nearest color found

SAVING GRAPHIC FILE FORMATS

Using Illustrator and Photoshop files saved in their native formats (AI and PSD respectively) allows them to work nicely together and maintains layers for further editing, but native file formats may not be able to be imported or placed in other applications. Still it is a good habit to save a file in its native format as a backup and for future editing when necessary. Saving Illustrator files in universal formats (SVG, EPS, and PDF) and Photoshop files (EPS, TIF, JPG, GIF, PNG, and PDF) gives these files more flexibility when used with other graphics programs. Although they have larger file sizes, EPS and TIF files work best for desktop publishing, while JPG, GIF, and PNG files are used to compress file sizes for use on the web. For artwork with limited flat colors (no continuous tones or gradients) that may be used for the web or in animation programs, save as either a GIF or SVG file. PDF files are used mainly in electronic distribution of documents.

The table below gives an overview of the most common file formats.

FORMAT	ADVANTAGES	CONSIDERATIONS
JPG	Compressed format used in photo images or images that need detail in shading and tones. Universal format read by all graphic applications and browsers. Used for web and proof printing (before going to press).	Data is thrown out each time the image is saved and may gradually deteriorate the quality. Flattens layers in files. Does not support background transparencies. Not recommended for use when documents will be printed commercially.
PNG	PNG files can include detailed transparencies in files without losing detail. Used in photo images.	Cannot be read by older browsers. Larger size files images record detail most accurately. Compressed for the web.
GIF	Used for logos, illustrations, and animation. Compress without losing data. Records with transparency settings. Read by most graphic applications.	GIF files have only 256 colors. Not suitable for continuous-tone images or gradients.
SVG	Used in vector-based graphics for the web and animation. Files can be enlarged on screen without sacrificing sharpness. Embeds fonts for the web. Cannot be read or created in Photoshop.	Limited color depth. Files are not compressed and can be edited in Illustrator.
PDF	Embeds fonts and graphics for electronic distribution and the web. Can be read by most graphic applications or read with the free Acrobat Reader. Can sometimes be edited in Illustrator. Compresses files without losing detail.	Adding embedding and preview characteristics may increase file size. Cannot be edited, only viewed by other applications (except Illustrator, where it can still be edited).

FORMAT	ADVANTAGES	CONSIDERATIONS
TIF	Most accurate record of detail in continuous-tone images. Nonscalable. Used primarily for print output.	Largest file size. Not used for the web.
EPS	Can be imported by most graphic applications and still edited in Illustrator. Vector graphics can be still be scalable. Preferred method when combining graphics and fonts. Used extensively for print output.	Large file size. Does not handle transparency in files created in older versions of Illustrator or Photoshop. Not used for the web.

TOOLKIT TIP When saving graphic files with an older version Mac OS, it is a good habit to check the Append File Extension setting, which will add the graphic format's file extension to the file name. Saving a graphic with an extension on the Mac also allows universal graphic files to be viewed on the Windows platform, which uses extensions to identify documents.

CLIENT ASSIGNMENT: Creating Web Banners

The marketing manager of E-Music Corporation, Christine Santelli, comes to you to design a couple of web banners (or leaderboards) to choose from to promote their classic rock radio station. After listening to her describe the station and creating a number of sketches and roughs, two possibilities are decided upon. You summarize the conversation to confirm her needs. Both banners will have a black to deep blue gradient background. The first web banner, initially created in Illustrator, will have the characters of the station title, with a rock image inside each character. The same banner will have a glowing image of a guitar photo, enhanced in Photoshop, placed in the banner and rotated. "Classic Rock!" and "All the Time!" will be typed in two lines along a slanted path to match the angle of the guitar neck. The second web banner, created initially in Photoshop, will have the station title and the intro line "We are Talking . . ." added to the graphic using a chiseled layer style effect created in Photoshop. A guitar photo, traced in Illustrator and filled with a black, red, and yellow color gradient with the slogan "Classic Rock" typed inside the guitar, will be brought into Photoshop and a drop shadow effect added. Both banners need to be optimized for the smallest file size for quick download while maintaining quality. Christine cannot wait to see the banners and leaves very excited (Figure 10-3).

Banner 1 integrating Photoshop images and effects with Illustrator

Banner 2 integrating Illustrator graphics into Photoshop

▷ FIGURE 10-3

Completed web banners.

ACTION ITEMS OVERVIEW

• Create a gradient black-to-blue color background for each web banner, also referred to as a leaderboard.

• For the first banner, create a rock image in Illustrator in the shape of the letters of the station title by creating a clipping mask of the type and the rock photo.

• Create a glow effect on the guitar photo in Photoshop, and save in PNG format so that transparency and effects are retained in Illustrator.

• Place the image into Illustrator, then rotate it inside the banner for an angled effect.

• Create a path with the Pen tool along the guitar neck; type the lines "Classic Rock!" and "All the Time!"; reposition them to complement the guitar.

• Save as *Banner1* in Illustrator's native format, then optimize the file for the web.

• For the second banner, use the Layer Style effects in Photoshop to create chiseled type of the station title and the intro line for the guitar illustration.

• Use the Pen tool in Illustrator and trace a closed path for the guitar, filling it with a black, red, and yellow gradient.

• Type the slogan "Classic Rock!" with a yellow fill and black outline, then warp it inside the guitar graphic to match the guitar shape.

• Export the new guitar image into Photoshop.

• Save in Photoshop's native format, then optimize the second banner for the web.

• ADVANCED USERS: Save graphics in EPS and PDF formats for later use.

INTEGRATING PHOTOSHOP IMAGES WITH ILLUSTRATOR

Web banners are the titles across the top of web pages that identify the page and the site. They are the eye-catcher that makes someone decide whether it is interesting enough to explore the page or site or go to another site. Photographic images or paintings brought into Illustrator are brought in as bitmap images. Before bringing an image from Photoshop into Illustrator, adjust the size and the resolution in Photoshop's Image > Image Size menu. You can then create a template in Illustrator to use as a guide for tracing images and placing type. You will be creating scalable compound paths with Illustrator's drawing tools.

SETTING PREFERENCES AND CUSTOM SIZE IN ILLUSTRATOR

Illustrator takes the guesswork out of what you will need for universal settings for various media. A designer can select preset document profiles for Print, web screen (full size), Mobile and other Devices, Video and Film, as well as basic RGB and CMYK profile settings; and you can also create your own custom size profile, which we will do here for your web banner, also referred to as a leaderboard. Setting up your document for RGB color and measuring in pixels helps to ensure the accuracy of your electronic artwork.

TOOLKIT TIP Here we are creating an older standard size for all computer screens. If you were to design for an entire web page, you would choose a preset document profile of 800 × 600 pixels or 1024 × 768 pixels to accommodate many computer screens. This size banner can be integrated into any web page adjusting to the web page size, providing the web designer adjusts to percentages within tables being created for the web page. To measure dimensions for the web, use pixels. Graphics that extend across the screen horizontally will need some blank space on both sides so as not to cut off the graphic; allow about 5 percent of the screen size. Screen displays are constantly changing with the introduction of wide screen displays.

Here is what you need to do to set up a new document in Illustrator for the web banner:

1. Launch Illustrator and select the Illustrator menu in Mac OS X or the Edit menu in Windows.

2. Select Preferences > Units; change the General measurement to Pixels, because we are creating for the web (Figure 10-4). Click OK.

3. If the Welcome screen displays, select Create New > Web Document, or select File > New to bring up the dialog box.

4. Type in a custom banner size of of 468 pixels Width by 60 pixels Height (Figure 10-4). This provides some margins when placed in the client's web page. This will accommodate older and newer computers.

5. Select Pixels as the Units from the drop-down menu.

6. Select RGB Color, and then select the Landscape orientation icon. Do not select Align New Objects to Pixel Grid for this assignment.

7. Name the file *Banner1*, then select OK.

8. To make sure the rulers are displayed, choose View > Rulers > Show Rulers. You also should make sure Smart Guides (View > Smart Guides), and Snap to Grid (View > Snap to Grid) are checked to help with quick alignment.

9. Zoom to about 200%, click on the vertical ruler and drag a vertical guide to about the 12-point mark for aligning text later.

10. Open the Color panel, then select Web Safe RGB from the panel submenu.

TOOLKIT TIP The Align to Pixel Grid feature in Illustrator CS5 only works with web based objects that have straight vertical of horizontal path segments that can be aligned, as was used in the Checkerboard assignment in Chapter 7. You cannot pixel-align objects that contain special effects like drop shadows, or text objects because such objects do not have real paths, as will be created for this assignment. If an object with the Align to Pixel Grid option is selected, and the pixel-aligned object is moved or transformed using the Transform panel, the object is then realigned to pixel grid according to its new coordinates.

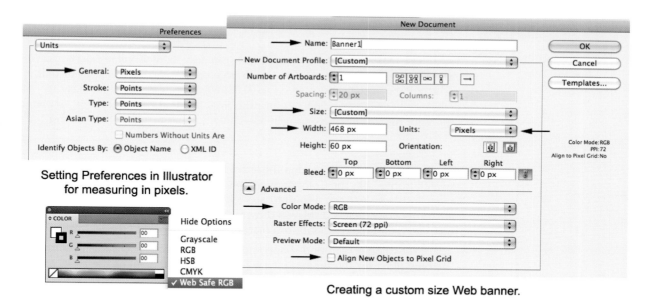

Setting Preferences in Illustrator for measuring in pixels.

Creating a custom size Web banner.

Setting up the file for use on the web with a customized banner setting in the New Document dialog box.

TOOLKIT TIP Do not worry if you see dotted lines on the banner; they are only guides and will not display on the actual web page. This can be changed in Preferences.

CREATING A GRADIENT WEB BACKGROUND IN ILLUSTRATOR

Gradients provide variety in color shapes and backgrounds. The Gradient panel is the control center for creating gradients. You can select colors from the Swatches or Color panels and drag them to the gradient bar to create color Gradient Sliders

DESIGN TIP

If you are using the standard RGB color mode, rather than Web-Safe RGB, in the Color panel, and a cube displays, it is a warning that the chosen color may not display accurately on the web. Click on the cube to automatically find the nearest replacement color. Selecting Web-Safe RGB from the Color panel eliminates this problem.

that can be adjusted to determine how colors are blended. You can even select a gradient color mode to work in on the Tools panel. In Gradient color mode, you can double-click on any color slider to display the Color panel; select another color, and that color will replace the previous color slider (see Figure 10-5). But first you need to create a shape the size of the banner to place the color in.

Here you will create the web banner's background using gradients and the Gradient tool.

1. In Illustrator, select Gradient from the Window menu (Window > Gradient) to display the Gradient panel. Click on the right side of the color bar to display gradient sliders where you will place a new color (Figure 10-5). Click on the right side gradient slider.

2. Select the Gradient color mode at the bottom of the Tools panel, if it isn't already selected, under the Fill and Stroke color boxes.

3. Double-click the Fill color in the Tools panel to display the Color Picker.

4. Select a deep blue color on the color bar. (Try entering #0000FF), then click OK. The right color slider on the Gradient panel will now become the deep blue color. If not, just drag the new blue color displayed in the Fill color box in your Tools panel to the color stop at the right in the gradient panel.

TOOLKIT TIP For web-safe colors you can use six-digit color selections. For instance, if you enter 0000FF for a deep blue color number, it will mean that in the RGB Color panel, it displays as R=00, G=00, B=FF. Note, you will likely see an exclamation point in a yellow triangle; this indicates that the color might not *print* well. Since we are working on a web-based image, you can ignore the warning.

5. On the Gradient panel, click on the left side gradient slider then select the black swatch from either the Color or Swatches panel to change the left side gradient slider to black. You can also drag a black swatch to the left side instead. Drag any other color sliders displayed downward to remove them from the gradient bar. You will find a gradient from black to blue displayed in the fill box.

6. Adjust the middle, diamond-shaped position slider about two thirds over toward the blue slider for the desired effect. Select Linear Gradient as the type. Notice the gradient color also displays on the Tools panel fill box.

7. To apply the gradient, select the Rectangle tool, and click on the top left corner on the artboard to display the dialog box.

8. Enter the same size as the banner, 468 pixels Width and 60 pixels Height; click OK to display the gradient rectangle, and position it over the banner with the Selection tool if necessary. You may notice that the blue gradient color shown in the figure in your text may look quite different than what is shown on the screen, because this book was printed using CMYK color, while your screen is displaying RGB.

9. If the rectangle does not display the new gradient, select the Gradient tool and drag from left to right.

▷ FIGURE 10-5

Creating a gradient for the web banner's background in Illustrator.

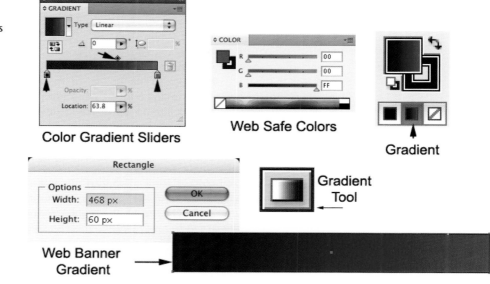

Color Gradient Sliders

Web Safe Colors

Gradient

Gradient Tool

Web Banner Gradient

TOOLKIT TIP Solid colors can be selected in the Color panel or from the Color Picker and simply dragged onto the Gradient panel to become color sliders.

LINKING FILES OR EMBEDDING FILES

Files from Photoshop can be opened, copied, pasted, or placed in an Illustrator document. Photoshop images placed in Illustrator can be either **linked** or **embedded**. The main benefit of linking a Photoshop file before placing it into Illustrator is that when you update the image in Photoshop, any changes made are automatically updated in the linked file in the Illustrator document. This also keeps the file size small. The only drawback is that if you move the location of the linked file, the link will be broken, and changes cannot be updated easily, unless you place the image again. Also, if you are sending the file to another person, both the Photoshop and Illustrator files must be included. **Embedded files** are added permanently, which will increase the file size, and any changes made to the image in one document will not be updated in the other (Figure 10-6). The advantage of embedding is that there is no need to worry about dealing with linked files.

▷ FIGURE 10-6

Embedded documents paste graphics, and changes can only be made on the document itself; linked documents update together when changes are made.

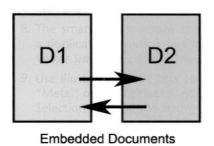

Embedded Documents

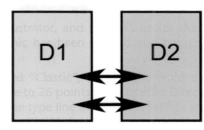

Linked Documents

PLACING PHOTOSHOP IMAGES INTO ILLUSTRATOR

To bring Photoshop files into an Illustrator document, the Place command may be the preferred method (File > Place). When an image is placed, it can be rotated and resized before pressing the Return/Enter key. You can do this with a pasted image as well; pasted images are automatically linked. Browse to find the Photoshop file, and check the Link check box in the Place dialog box to link the placed file for future editing. Uncheck the Link check box to embed the image into the Illustrator document (Figure 10-7). You can also copy illustrator artwork into a Photoshop document as a "Smart Object" (and vice versa) that can be edited as a linked object. This will be covered in depth later.

TOOLKIT TIP If you are working in a smaller document size, crop the images to the smaller size before placing them into the banner document. Do not place images larger than the banner size; you may have problems with excess space beyond the document size if its used in a regular web page. The Rock image was first cropped to the size of the web banner in Photoshop to avoid problems.

▷ FIGURE 10-7

Placing an image as embedded (link unchecked).

DESIGN TIP

For images to be used on the web, set the resolution of the image width to 72 dpi (or ppi) as the standard resolution, and display the image at 100% in Photoshop when making any changes. **Browsers** like Microsoft's Internet Explorer, AOL, Safari, or Netscape display web images full size. While you can alter the image size in a web file, it is best practice to create the image in the exact size needed.

Placed Rock image (embedded)

In this exercise, you will place a Photoshop image into the Illustrator document and type the banner title over the image with the Type tool before clipping the image.

1. With Illustrator open, select File > Place and locate the *Rock* image inside the *Chapter 10* folder within the *Illustrator* folder.

2. In the dialog box, make sure the Link box is unchecked, so the image will be embedded and can be transported without needing the original image. The file size is small enough that embedding will not affect download time. Click Place.

TOOLKIT TIP If an error comes up about an Embedded Profile Mismatch, select the Use Embedded Profile option and Illustrator will closely match the colors in the file. It will have no effect on your screen. Whenever saving an image, check the ICC Profile—if it displays—in a Save dialog box. An **ICC profile** describes a file's colors so that Illustrator can interpret the profile and keep the colors consistent throughout.

DESIGN TIP

One of the concerns a designer needs to keep in mind is the download time of images. Keeping file sizes to a minimum is one of the best ways to achieve this.

3. Select the image with the Selection tool, and move it to the left side of the banner so the blue sky at the top left is off the left side of the banner, as shown in Figure 10-8. Deselect the image. Drag a vertical guide to the 24-pixel mark to start typing.

4. Select the Type tool (T) and choose a wide, rigid font, such as Arial Black, from the Type menu; if you want to try another wide, rigid font instead, try Franklin Gothic Heavy or ITC Eras Bold).

5. Use a black Fill and a Stroke of None.

6. Select a Size of 36 points for the title text.

7. Starting on the left guide, type in capital letters, "ROCK 99.2"; press the Return/Enter key to start a new line (Figure 10-8).

8. Select a Size of 18 points and type "WABW" or any four capital letters starting with a "W."

9. Select the text lines with the Selection tool and position the bounding box along the guides, as shown in Figure 10-8.

10. If needed, select the rock image and reposition it so that it is behind the text.

 FIGURE 10-8

Type positioned over the image.

TOOLKIT TIP In Mac OS, placed files may be linked by default; in Windows OS, placed files are embedded by default. Pay attention to the Place dialog box settings.

MAKING TEXT IMAGES: CREATING A CLIPPING MASK IN ILLUSTRATOR

In Illustrator any shape, type, or closed path placed on top of a graphic can become a window to the image underneath. To do this, you create a **clipping mask** of the selected images (Figure 10-9). Clipping masks can be created from any closed path shape. They can also be created from text typed into the document, so the image fills the shape of the letters.

▷ FIGURE 10-9

Creating a clipping mask to make text images.

Next you will create a clipping mask by using the type to create a window through which you will see the rock image.

1. Select the text lines with the Selection tool, and then Shift-click to select the rock image underneath and not the blue gradient box.

2. Select Object > Clipping Mask > Make to combine the two into a text image.

 PROBLEM If you created the type on two separate lines, only one will become the mask. You have to type both lines as a single type entity using the Enter or Return key for the second line.

3. Position the new type image, if needed, with the Selection tool, then deselect by clicking outside the image. Remove the guides by selecting View > Guides > Clear Guides.

4. Save the text image as *Banner1.ai* in Illustrator's native format in your *Chapter 10* folder.

5. Leave Illustrator open, and minimize the window of the banner image on the desktop.

Need additional fun computer graphics tutorials and info, and an additional look at the projects you'll be creating in this book? Check out my Artist's Digital Toolkit website at: **http://www.digitoolkit.com**

PASTING AN IMAGE COMPONENT TO A SELECTED SIZE IN PHOTOSHOP

For images that only need to be duplicated or copied into another document, or when only a portion of an image needs to be copied, the Paste command works well. When an image is pasted into a new document in Photoshop, it is on its own separate layer and can be edited independent of the background. In Photoshop, when an image is selected with the Rectangular Marquee tool and copied, a new document can be set to the same size as the copied selection, and the selected image can be pasted into this new document. When a selected graphic is copied, it is stored in a temporary place in the computer's memory called the computer's clipboard, mentioned in earlier chapters. It remains there while the computer is on until something new is copied to replace it. You can then paste the selection into various documents.

In Photoshop, you will select a guitar from a photo with the Rectangular Marquee tool and copy it, then paste it into a new document the same size as the selection (Figure 10-10).

1. Launch Photoshop and open the *Guitars* file in your *Chapter 10* folder.

2. Draw a diagonal marquee selection around one of the guitars with the Rectangular Marquee tool (we chose the middle one).

3. Select Edit > Copy to copy the one guitar, then close the *Guitars* file.

4. To paste the guitar into a new document the same size as the selection, select File > New, name the file *Guitar,* and select OK to the Preset > Clipboard settings that match the size of the selection.

5. Select Edit > Paste to paste the guitar into the new document.

6. Save the file as *Guitar* in Photoshop's native PSD format in your *Chapter 10* folder, which will keep the two layers in this file intact.

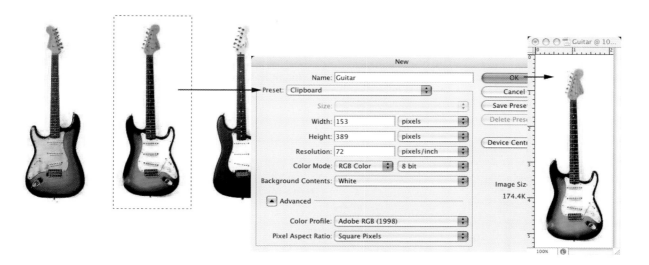

▷   FIGURE 10-10

Copy and paste the selected guitar into a new document the same size as the selection.

TOOLKIT TIP If you receive a dialog box warning about maximizing compatibility, leave the Maximize Compatibility unchecked, then select OK. Usually, if file size is an issue, or if you are opening your files only in Photoshop, unchecking or turning off Maximize Compatibility reduces the file sizes significantly. Leaving it checked saves a composite (flattened) image along with the layers of your document. If you edit or save an image using an earlier version of Photoshop, unsupported features are discarded.

APPLYING EFFECTS AND TRANSPARENCY IN PHOTOSHOP

Designers need to make sure that backgrounds of objects intended as transparent maintain their transparency when brought into web pages. The background needs to be removed to make it transparent in Photoshop before it is placed in a document. Layer Style effects can then be applied to the Photoshop image before placing into Illustrator. If, when using the Magic Eraser tool to remove the background, part of the image to keep is removed, you can select the History Brush in Photoshop to paint back areas to their previous state.

In this exercise, you will make the background transparent and apply an Outer Glow Layer Style around the guitar image.

1. You will notice that the *Guitar* file you just created has two layers; one contains the guitar and the white *Background* layer. Drag the *Background* layer into the Trash icon in the Layers panel; it is not needed.

2. Select the Magic Eraser tool with a tolerance of 20 pixels, and click on the white area. The background is now transparent. If you notice part of the guitar is missing, select the History Brush with a few pixels and paint back what was removed.

3. Zoom in to 500% to paint over any white areas left, outlining the guitar with the Eraser tool using a brush size of 1 to 3 pixels and 50% opacity, which will apply the brush gradually. Observe very closely, especially up near the top of the guitar neck, as this will affect the details in the glow effect you are going to create.

▷ FIGURE 10-11

Applying layer style effects to create an outer glow effect.

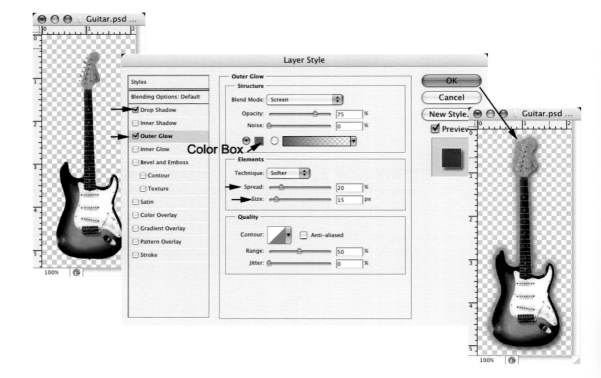

DESIGN TIP

Saving graphic elements that contain transparency and gradient settings as PNG files preserves these effects. If the guitar graphic was saved as a JPEG, the background would be automatically converted to white.

DESIGN TIP

If a designer uses a lot of images on a web page, checking the Interlaced box causes the images to display in successive detail, as if coming into focus as they download. This helps to keep the viewer's interest without having to wait for the entire image to download. Because an entire banner usually displays quickly, however, the choice here would be to select None when the PNG Options box comes up.

4. Save the file when you are done.

5. Zoom back out to observe the effect you are going to apply on the guitar.

6. To make a red glow around the guitar, click the Layer Style ("fx") icon at the bottom of the Layers panel, and drag to select the *Outer Glow* layer style.

7. When the Layer Style display box opens, click the color box next to the Gradient bar to display the Color Picker. Select an orange red color, making sure no cube appears to warn of web-color issues; if it does, click on the cube to display the nearest color match. Enter the settings shown in Figure 10-11 to create an outer red glow effect (Spread 20%, Size 15 pixels). This gradient fades from the red color to transparency.

8. Before you click OK, check the Drop Shadow box in the Styles display to add a little depth to the guitar. Click OK. If there are any white areas after the glow effect has been applied, zoom in to around 300% and use the Eraser tool with a small brush to drag over and remove the white areas around the guitar.

9. Save the file as *GuitarGLO.psd,* and leave it open for the next Photoshop exercise.

SAVING IN PNG FORMAT IN PHOTOSHOP

The **PNG format** supports varying levels of transparency and also preserves gradients. It is effective at compressing continuous-tone images without losing detail, called **lossless compression**, but it may create a larger file size than JPEG compressed images. JPEG uses a **lossy compression**, where details are thrown out every time the image is edited and saved. The disadvantage of PNG formats is that they cannot be read by older browsers, which may be a consideration when you are advertising to a particular market. Saving the file in PNG format saves the image as a Copy and leaves the original where you saved it originally; the PNG can be saved to a different location. Later, you will use the Save for web command to observe different settings for various graphic extensions, including PNG.

The guitar image contains a transparent background and various levels of opacity in the guitar glow effect. You will save the image in PNG format to preserve these effects (Figure 10-12).

1. In Photoshop, use Save As (File > Save As) to save the file as *GuitarGLO.png* in your *Chapter 10* folder, then click Save in the dialog box. This will keep the background transparent and the Layer Style settings accurate.

2. When the PNG Options dialog box comes up, leave the default of None for Interlacing options, because this will be part of the web banner and should display at once. Click OK.

3. It will automatically be saved as a copy of the original in the *Chapter 10* folder. The original *GuitarGLO.psd* file will still be open in Photoshop.

▷ FIGURE 10-12
Saving a document of varying opacity and effects with the PNG extension.

PLACING LINKED PHOTOSHOP IMAGES INTO ILLUSTRATOR

Placing layered Photoshop images into Illustrator re-creates those layers in the Illustrator document, leaving them intact for making further changes. When these images are ready for the web, all the layers will need to be combined as one, or flattened, to keep the file size small. Linking images makes the file size even smaller, especially with rasterized or bitmap images like the guitar; so linking helps speed up the download time, as long as the linked image is stored in the same place on the host server for the website as the original image. In Illustrator CS5, you can double-click on the selected graphic to display **Isolation mode** in the Layers panel, where surrounding graphics are faded out. Isolation mode allows you to edit a symbol or graphic. On the Control panel, you will find the selected graphic as linked, options for editing, and you can isolate it as well.

DESIGN TIP

When images are linked, the designer needs to make sure the original image is stored in the same place as the linked image. If not, an X will appear where the graphic should be when the web image is displayed in the browser.

TOOLKIT TIP If changes need to be made to the placed file that is linked, you can select the Photoshop image in the Illustrator document and select Edit > Edit Original. This will launch Photoshop. You can then make the changes and save the file in Photoshop. The new changes will appear in the linked Photoshop image in Illustrator. You can also use the Link panel to do this.

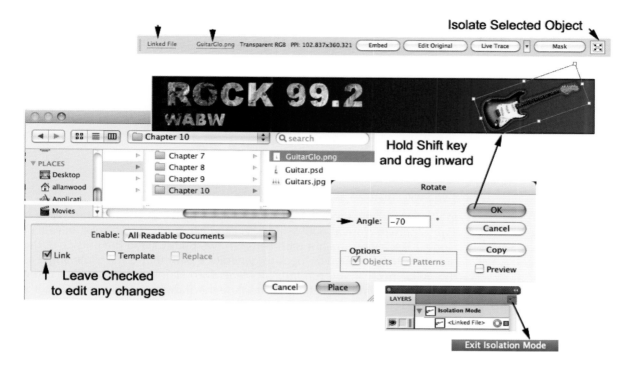

▷ FIGURE 10-13

Place the guitar image linked, scale the image, and rotate it -70 degrees.

DESIGN TIP

You can always make a raster or bitmapped image smaller than the original size and still maintain quality, but you cannot make it larger or the quality deteriorates.

Now that you have created the guitar in Photoshop, it is time to put the image into the Illustrator web banner.

1. Open the Illustrator window with the *Banner1* document (Launch Illustrator if it is not open), zoom to 200% and select File > Place.

2. Locate and select the *GuitarGLO.png* file you just created; leave the Link option checked to provide a link in case you need to make changes to the guitar image later; click Place. The large image will appear inside a bounding box.

3. *Do not* press the Return/Enter key until the guitar image is resized and positioned exactly where you want it, as shown in Figure 10-13. You can do this by selecting one of the corner bounding box handles with your mouse or the Selection tool, then holding down the Shift key and dragging inward as you resize the box to keep it in proportion.

4. Rotate the selected guitar -70 degrees (Object > Transform > Rotate > -70 degrees > OK) and position as shown in Figure 10-13.

5. Drag the guitar up to the banner's right side with the Selection tool or use the arrow keys. Resize it to fit inside the banner by holding the Shift key down and dragging inward on one of the bounding-box handles to constrain proprtions.

6. Optional: With the graphic selected, double-click to display it in isolation mode in the Layers panel. Notice the surrounding graphics are faded out. You won't be editing here, so select the Exit Isolation Mode option in the Layers panel menu.

7. Save the file as *Banner1.ai* in Illustrator's native format in the *Chapter 10* folder. Deselect.

TEXT PATHS IN ILLUSTRATOR

Illustrator's variety of drawing tools provides the means to create a path to place type on. The Pen tool not only creates precise curves; it also creates straight lines between two points (two clicks).

▷ FIGURE 10-14

Placing type on a path so that it aligns with the guitar neck.

Next you will create an angular path for the slogan type to follow.

1. In Illustrator, create a new layer in the Layers panel for the text and name it *Type*. Zoom in close at 600% and select the Pen tool with a Stroke and Fill of None. Click a long straight path between two points along the outside of the guitar to match the guitar neck to generate a path that is the same angle as the guitar neck. If you run into problems with aligning the path, select the path with the Direct Selection tool and use the Transform command (Object > Transform > Rotate) to rotate by 1 degree (or minus one degree) increments. You can even rotate be decimals (.5 for example).

2. With the Direct Selection tool, select the path only and position it to the left of the guitar. Then select the path and hold down the Shift key to enlarge the bounding box proportionally to make a diagonal longer path line across the banner from top to bottom; longer than necessary is okay.

3. Zoom out to 200% and select the Type on Path tool, click on the bottom of the path you created with the bottom diagonal line of the type tool cursor aligned with the path you just created, then select a red Fill and a Stroke of None. Then pick the same font you chose for the *ROCK 99.2* title; we used Arial Black.

4. Change the Size to 14 points from the Type menu or Options bar.

5. Type "Classic Rock!" (or your favorite type of music) along the path. It may appear upside down; the direction that you draw the path will determine if the text is upside down or not. The text will run from the first endpoint to the last endpoint of the path. If, after you type not all the type displays, and you see a plus icon at the end of the path, the path is too short and you will need to either lengthen it, select the type and minimize to 12 points, or change the title.

6. You can also use the Direct Selection tool to reposition the text by dragging the middle I-beam, which looks like a vertical line on the path. If the text is upside down, drag the I-beam to the other side of the baseline to flip it. Save the file.

7. Make sure the path line is selected, and hold the Option/Alt key, dragging downward to make a copy of the angled line.

8. Select the Type Path tool again and change the words to "All the Time!"

9. Position the paths and guitar as shown in Figure 10-14.

10. After the guitar and text are all positioned accurately, with the Selection tool, Shift-click on all the objects in the banner and group (Object > Group). The banner is ready to be saved as one unit.

USING THE SAVE FOR WEB AND DEVICES COMMAND IN ILLUSTRATOR

Illustrator and Photoshop both provide a Save for Web and Devices command (Save for Web in earlier versions) to optimize a flattened copy of the file with the fastest download time while maintaining image quality for web display. Using this feature allows the designer to preview the results of up to four different settings at a time to determine image quality before they are applied and to view the download times for each setting at 28K or 56K per second, the slowest modem downloads. Layers are flattened on the saved copy to keep the file size small. The original layered image is not affected.

Here you will save the file in PNG format to maintain the transparency settings in the guitar glow effect. PNG format provides the best accuracy for images of varying opacity or transpency.

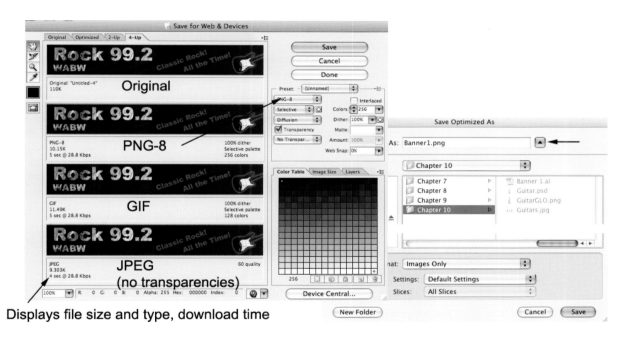

Displays file size and type, download time

▷ FIGURE 10-15

Optimizing the banner by saving it as a PNG file to preserve transparencies.

1. In Illustrator with *Banner1.ai* still displayed, save in Illustrator's native AI format first as a backup, then select File > Save for Web & Devices.

2. Select the 4-Up tab on the dialog box to compare quality and download times with four different settings for the banner image. Download time is displayed on the lower left edge, and settings are displayed on the lower right.

3. Zoom in to 200%, then use the Hand tool to drag one of the images to display the guitar, as shown in Figure 10-15.

4. Select the gray area under the second image, then try different settings using the options at the right. Observe what happens to the image, especially in the glow around the guitar. Observe the download times displayed in the lower left area of the dialog box.

DESIGN TIP

File size on a web banner should be no more than 12K to keep download time minimal. All bitmap images need to be set at 72 dpi (ppi) resolution for web use. When optimizing a web banner, one of the things a designer needs to keep in mind is that using a bitmap image within the graphic can increase the size of the file, because it generally uses more colors, as opposed to using all vector graphics.

5. Select PNG-8 to save the image and preserve all opacities, gradients, and transparencies. The quality is acceptable here, but you can try PNG-24 also. You can look at GIF, but you may notice the glow around the guitar may be too choppy looking. The JPEG has a white background,, because it cannot record transparent backgrounds.

6. Zoom to 100% to see the actual size; make sure the PNG preview is selected, then click Save.

7. Save the file name as *Banner1.png;* choose Images Only for the format, and if PNG Options displays, leave it set at None; this will tell the browser to display the banner all at once. This is a copy, saved for use on the web in your *Chapter 10* folder, while the original is still open in Illustrator.

8. Save the original image in your *Chapter 10* folder as *Banner1.ai.* Using the AI extension will preserve all the layers intact for editing, and the file can be used as a back-up copy. You now know how to place images with effects from Photoshop into Illustrator.

TOOLKIT TIP Illustrator's **Raster effects** are effects that generate pixels on bitmap mages, rather than vector images. Raster effects include all of the effects in the bottom section of the Effect menu, and the Drop Shadow, Inner Glow, Outer Glow, and Feather commands in the Effect > Stylize submenu. The **Resolution Independent Effects (RIE)** capability in Illustrator CS5 makes it possible to make changes with these effects resulting in very little, if any, change in the appearance of the effect. This will only work with embedded files, not linked graphics as was done in this project. For example, this might have been helpful if the client wanted to change the size of the banner, in which case you would have had to embed the guitar graphic instead of linking it. For this project, the linked guitar graphic can also be adjusted and edited in Photoshop, with the new linked graphic displayed in the banner.

INTEGRATING ILLUSTRATOR IMAGES INTO PHOTOSHOP

Any Illustrator graphic placed in Photoshop will become rasterized and cannot be enlarged after that point without losing quality. Because Illustrator uses paths to outline objects, and sharp lines are needed for type, a designer must create this art in Illustrator first, then export that graphic as a PSD file to keep the layers and effects intact. For this second web banner, you will create the gradient background and banner in Photoshop. You will then export a composite guitar graphic with outlined type created in Illustrator to be added to the Photoshop web banner. Special layer style graphics will be used in Photoshop to enhance the illustration.

SETTING PREFERENCES FOR PIXELS IN PHOTOSHOP

You will need to set the Photoshop banner to the same size it was in Illustrator. Since you will be creating the same size banner in Photoshop, you will need to enter the settings using the Custom preset. Photoshop provides a wide selection of preset sizes, not only for web pages and print but also for film, video, and for mobile electronic devices.

TOOLKIT TIP In the Advanced section, you will notice settings at various Pixel Aspect Ratios, depending on the media format. For our purposes, we will stay with Square Pixels format.

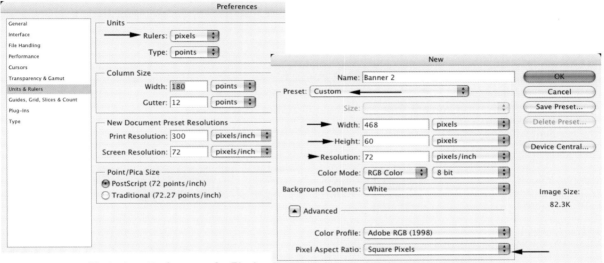

Photoshop Preferences for Pixels   Custom Web banner size

▷ FIGURE 10-16

Setting preferences for web measurements and setting banner size.

First you will set the preferences and set a custom web banner size in Photoshop.

1. Launch Photoshop, and then select the Photoshop Apple menu in Mac OS X or the Edit menu in Windows.

2. Select Preferences > Units & Rulers. Change the Rulers measurement to pixels, then click OK to return.

3. Select File > New; choose a preset size of Custom, and enter 468 Width by 60 Height in pixels. Click on the Advanced section; in the Pixel Aspect Ratios area, select Square Pixels format for our purposes here.

4. Select a Screen Resolution of 72 pixels, RGB Color Mode, and white for background contents in the dialog box (Figure 10-16). Name the file *Banner2* and click OK.

5. Make sure View > Rulers is checked in the Menu to display the ruler.

6. When the document displays, zoom to 200%.

CREATING THE WEB BANNER USING GRADIENTS IN PHOTOSHOP

Gradients in Photoshop use a transition from foreground to background colors. To apply gradients in Photoshop, select colors and apply them with the **Gradient tool** (G). The colors have to be selected in the foreground and background color boxes before using the Gradient tool. When the Gradient Color bar is clicked in the Gradient Options bar, the **Gradient Editor** dialog box displays to select various preset gradient combinations, which can also be customized. You can adjust, add, and remove **Color Stops** in the Gradient Editor to create custom gradient combinations. **Opacity Stops** vary the amount of color applied.

▷ FIGURE 10-17

In Photoshop, selecting a Foreground to Background gradient from the Gradient editor, then applying the gradient with the Gradient tool.

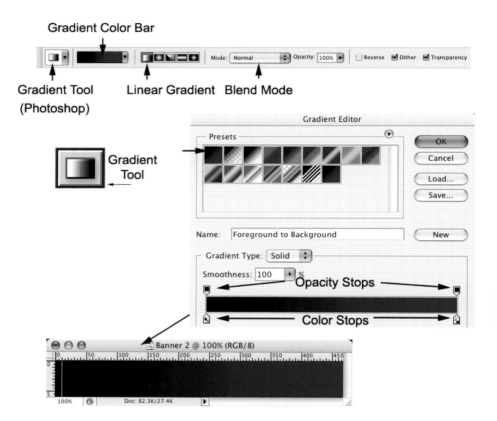

In this exercise, you will create the gradient background for the banner (referred also as a leaderboard) by selecting the foreground and background colors for the gradient, using the Gradient Editor to set up the type of gradient, and then applying the gradient using the Gradient tool.

1. Make sure the Color panel is set to Web Color Sliders. Click the Foreground color box on the Tools panel to display the Color Picker, and select a black foreground color (#000000) first.

2. Click on the bent arrow to display the background color box or press the X key to switch to the Background color, and click to select a dark blue background

color from the Color Picker (try #0000FF, which was used in Illustrator). Do not forget: the bright RGB color blue on your screen will display differently than the blue you see in CMYK mode in this textbook.

3. If the cube displays, click it to find the closest web color, or check the Only Web Colors box in the Color Picker. Press the X key to bring the black Foreground color in front of the blue Background color. Do not worry if a triangle displays; that is for printing.

4. Select the Gradient tool to display the Gradient toolbar in the Options bar. If the Paint Bucket tool is displayed in the Tools panel instead, hold down the mouse on the Paint Bucket icon to access the Gradient tool.

5. Select Linear Gradient with the Blend Mode set to Normal in the Gradient Options bar.

6. Click the Gradient Color bar in the Options bar to open the Gradient Editor, and select the Foreground to Background Preset box (first box, top left). Click OK (Figure 10-17).

7. With the colors displayed in the Tools panel, click and drag the gradient across the banner from left to right to display the gradient. Hold the Shift key to ensure you are dragging the gradient horizontally.

8. You can click the Gradient Color bar in the Options bar to adjust the color stops in the Gradient Editor the way you want, then use the Gradient tool to drag the new gradient.

9. Zoom in to 200% and drag a vertical guide to the 10-pixel mark as a guide for setting the radio station title in the next exercise.

10. Save the file as *Banner 2.psd*, Photoshop's native format, in your *Chapter 10* folder for editing; if you get a Maximize Compatability warning, click OK for now. We will adjust the file size for Web use later.

Need additional fun computer graphics tutorials and info, and an additional look at the projects you'll be creating in this book? Check out my Artist's Digital Toolkit website at: **http://www.digitoolkit.com**

CREATING TYPE EFFECTS IN PHOTOSHOP

A large variety of special effects can be created using Photoshop's Layer Style effects in the Layers panel, including effects on type as well as images brought into Photoshop. These effects can also be applied to type and objects from Illustrator.

For this exercise in Photoshop, you will create a chiseled effect on type to identify the rock station and the intro line to the guitar illustration, which will be brought in later.

1. In Photoshop, with *Banner 2* open, select the Type tool and set the font to 36-point Arial Black in black with a Strong Anti-alias; you can also try fonts like Eras Bold ITC or Franklin Gothic. Make sure the paragraph alignment is set to align left.

2. Click on the 10-pixel guide and type "Rock 99.2." With the cursor still blinking after typing the "2," change the size to 14 points; press the Return/Enter key to start a new line, and type "WABW," or choose your own call letters beginning with *W*.

3. Make sure the text layer on the Layers panel is highlighted, and use the Move tool to position the text as shown in Figure 10-18.

4. Select the Add a Layer Style icon at the bottom of the Layers panel, then select Bevel and Emboss from the drop-down list to bring up its dialog box.

5. Select an Inner Bevel Style with a Chisel Hard Technique and a Gloss Contour of Cone to give a chiseled effect to the type (Figure 10-18). Set the Depth to 100%, the Size to 5 pixels, and then select OK. Feel free to experiment. Click on the Drop Shadow box to add dimension to the type.

6. To create an intro to the upcoming graphic, select the Move tool, then high-light the Background layer. Select the Type tool again to create another type line. Use the same type font, but change the size to 18 points; if the text layer is still selected, choosing a different point size will change the existing text.

7. Click to the right of the number *99.2* and type "We are" for the first line; press the Return/Enter key for the next line, and type "Talking...."

8. Highlight the two lines of type, and create the same layer effects used in steps 4 and 5 to create the same chiseled effect for consistency. You can also select the effects you just created using the Layers panel; hold down the Option/Alt key, and drag the effects in the *Rock 99.2* layer to the new type layer.

9. Remove the left vertical guide (View > Clear Guides) and save the file.

10. Minimize the *Banner2* document window.

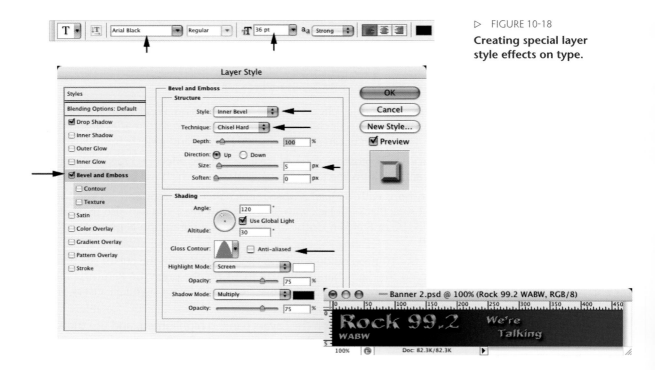

▷ FIGURE 10-18

Creating special layer style effects on type.

CREATING THE GUITAR GRAPHIC IN ILLUSTRATOR

Illustrator creates paths for complex shapes using a variety of drawing tools. The Pen tool is the most effective tool for drawing smooth lines and curves. Here is a little review for using the Pen tool. In Illustrator, you will use the Place command to import the guitar image from Photoshop and then trace the guitar to create a graphic of the guitar. Gradients will be applied, and text created along a path will be placed inside the guitar; the new graphic will then be brought into Photoshop.

TOOLKIT TIP If you are working in Illustrator, and you are using the Place command to import a Photoshop (PSD) or layered image, a Photoshop Import Options dialog box will open up, allowing you to choose to flatten all layers or convert layers to objects to edit in Illustrator. Illustrator will also allow Photoshop images with Layer Comps to be imported.

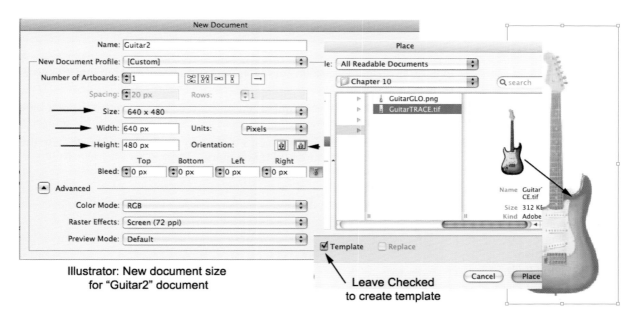

Illustrator: New document size
for "Guitar2" document

▷ FIGURE 10-19

Setting up the document to place the guitar image as a template.

TOOLKIT TIP Remember, to edit paths in Illustrator, click on the circle to the right of the layer or sublayer to select that path to edit.

It is time to crop one of the guitars in Photoshop to use as a template in Illustrator. You will use the Place command to set the guitar image as a template to trace with the Pen tool in Illustrator.

1. Launch Photoshop and open the *Guitars* file in your *Chapter 10* folder.

2. Use the Rectangular Marquee tool (M) to drag a rectangular marquee around the first guitar; then select Image > Crop to remove the other guitars in the image.

3. Save the file in your *Chapter 10* folder as *GuitarTRACE.tif;* accept the default settings and Click OK. This image will be used as a template. Close the both *GuitarTRACE* and *Guitars* files.

4. Launch Illustrator; create a new web document, RGB Color, 640 x 480-pixel landscape orientation. Name this document *Guitar2; it will be used to place the GuitarTRACE* template image in the next exercise. Click OK.

5. In Illustrator, with the *Guitar2* document open, locate and Place (File > Place) the *GuitarTRACE.tif* file from your *Chapter 10* folder as a template (check the Template box and uncheck the Link box). This will create a dimmed template layer with a working layer above it (Figure 10-19).

TOOLKIT TIP When placing images as templates, it is a good idea to use flat-tenened files. If you are using Illustrator, and the Photoshop Import Options dialog box displays, select the option **Flatten Photoshop Layers To A Single Image** before placing the file in Illustrator.

6. In Illustrator, double-click on *Layer 1* in the Layers panel and rename it *Outline*. Deselect the guitar.

7. With the new *Outline* layer highlighted, select the Pen tool with a 2-point blue Stroke and a Fill of None.

8. Place anchor points along the guitar's outline to create a closed path. Use the dots on the image in Figure 10-20 as a guide.

▷ FIGURE 10-20

Tracing an outline of the guitar image using the Pen tool, Direct Selection, and Smooth tools.

Guitar image traced by the Pen tool

9. Edit with the Direct Selection and Smooth tools to get a good outline. Zoom in close for editing details.

10. To join end points, use the Direct Select Lasso tool to select the end points.

11. Using the Object menu, select the Path command to Average, then Join any end points (Object > Path > Average > Join). There is a cool shortcut for this—Command Option Shift J—that does both in one step.

12. When you have created a closed path for the guitar, select it with the Selection tool. It is time to apply the gradient effect.

APPLYING GRADIENTS IN ILLUSTRATOR

In Illustrator, the Gradient panel is the control center for creating custom gradients. Select colors from the Color or Swatches panels, and drag these colors to the gradient color bar to create gradient color sliders. These sliders can be moved around to vary the amount of colors for different effects. In Illustrator, you can have gradients that can be adjusted to fade to transparent, apply special gradients in real time, and move them around. You select the object, then the Gradient tool, and click. A gradient bar displays to edit the gradient effect by dragging and rotating the gradient bar around the selected object. The new gradient can be saved in the Swatches panel. You can also make edits from the Appearance panel.

With the guitar graphic selected as a closed path, you will apply a gradient color inside the graphic.

1. In Illustrator, open the Gradient panel, then select the Gradient Color Mode in the Tools panel.

2. Select a red Foreground color from the Swatches or Color panel, and drag it to the middle of the gradient bar on the Gradient panel (Figure 10-21).

3. Select a yellow Foreground color and drag it from the Swatches panel to the right side of the gradient bar on the Gradient panel (Figure 10-21).

4. Drag a black swatch onto the gradient slider to the left, and drag any other color sliders downward to remove them.

5. Select the Gradient tool and drag across the guitar from bottom to top.

6. Adjust the gradient sliders for desired effect on the guitar outline (Figure 10-21). You can edit the gradient by rotating or dragging the gradient bar, and by adjusting the gradient sliders. Select the guitar, then the Gradient tool, and click.

7. Drag the Template layer onto the Trash icon in the Layers panel to delete it from this file.

8. Save the file as *Guitar2.ai* in the *Chapter 10* folder. You can also save it as a symbol for future use in the Symbols panel.

DESIGN TIP

Applying a stroke outline on type can work nicely as long as the type is over 18 points in size; it must provide enough width for both fill and stroke elements.

▷ FIGURE 10-21

Applying gradients for the guitar illustration.

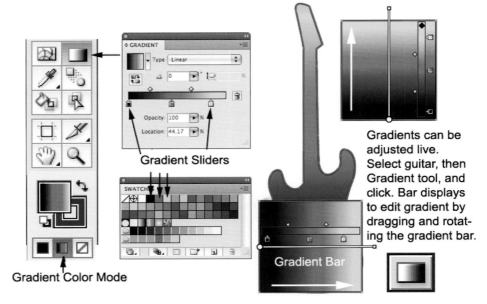

Gradient Sliders

Gradient Color Mode

Gradient Bar

Gradients can be adjusted live. Select guitar, then Gradient tool, and click. Bar displays to edit gradient by dragging and rotating the gradient bar.

WARPING TYPE IN ILLUSTRATOR

Although type can also be warped in Photoshop, in this case using a light-colored type with a black-stroke outline in Illustrator helps to make it stand out within the guitar's gradient color. With Illustrator's stroke colors, type can be easily outlined in any color and weight. To warp type in Illustrator, you can use either the Effect menu (Effect > Warp), or use the Object > Envelope Distort > Make with Warp command. To make the identity of the radio station stand out, the words *Classic Rock!* will be typed inside the guitar and warped using the Flag effect to match the guitar shape.

Now you will create two lines of text inside the guitar, and then warp them to match the guitar's shape (Figure 10-22).

▷ FIGURE 10-22

Warping type to match the inside of the guitar shape.

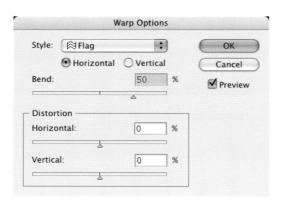

1. In Illustrator, select the *Guitar2* image with the Selection Tool.

2. Rotate the selected guitar minus 90 degrees to make it horizontal (Object > Transform > Rotate > Angle -90 degrees). Resize if necessary.

3. Select the Create New Layer icon on the Layers panel, and rename the new layer Type to use it as a text layer.

4. Select the type tool, click the artboard, and then set the type to 24-point Arial Black with a Fill color of yellow and a 1-point black Stroke using the Type menu and the Color panel.

5. Type the word "Classic," then select the type line with the Selection tool and position it within the guitar body.

6. Select Effect > Warp > Flag. Drag the Horizontal Bend arrow to the left until it matches the curve at the top of the guitar. Check the Preview box to see what is happening while you make the adjustments. Click OK, then deselect the text.

7. Select the Type tool to make a separate second line and click just below the guitar.

8. Select a 36-point Arial Black with a Fill color of yellow and a 1-point black Stroke outline from the Type menu.

9. Type "Rock!" or another type of music you listen to; select the type and position it within the guitar, toward the bottom, with the Selection tool.

10. Select Effect > Warp > Flag. Position the Horizontal Bend so that it matches the bottom curve of the guitar. Keep the Preview box checked. Click OK when you are satisfied.

11. Use the Selection tool and hold down the Shift key to select the guitar and the text.

12. Use the Object menu to Uniform scale the guitar and text to 40% (Object > Transform > Scale > 40%). It is a good idea to scale it before it is brought into Photoshop.

13. Save the file again as *Guitar2* in Illustrator's native format. This will be the back-up copy as you prepare to bring the artwork into Photoshop in the next exercise.

EXPORTING ILLUSTRATOR ARTWORK TO BE OPENED IN PHOTOSHOP

Not only can you open layered Photoshop files in Illustrator, you can also save layered Illustrator files and open them in Photoshop. If a designer wants to work with an Illustrator file in Photoshop, it can be exported in Photoshop's PSD bitmap format. Here are some considerations when exporting files from Illustrator into Photoshop.

• Exporting Illustrator files in the Photoshop format saves most Illustrator layers so they can be edited; it maintains background transparency and gradients so long as the Write Layers option is selected in the Photoshop Options dialog box when you export. With Illustrator, you can export multiple artboards as well.

• You can open the new exported file, edit layers, copy, and paste it into the artwork.

• Resize and rotate the image as needed *before* exporting it into Photoshop, which converts images into unscalable bitmap images.

• Exporting the guitar graphic or any artwork with layers allows the graphic and text to be edited for special effects using Photoshop's Layer Style effects.

TOOLKIT TIP To keep the Illustrator type layer editable in Photoshop, it must be on the topmost layer by itself and not on a layer containing other artwork. Area type, type on paths, or multicolored type in Illustrator can then be exported to Photoshop to be edited.

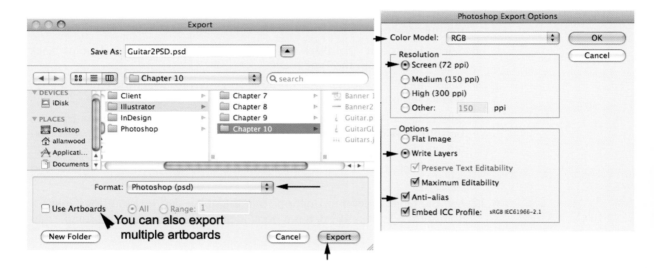

▷ FIGURE 10-23

Exporting Illustrator files into Photoshop to include layers, text, and color information.

Here you will export the resized and rotated guitar image with separate text layers created in Illustrator into Photoshop for special effects.

1. In Illustrator, make sure the original guitar image is saved as *Guitar2.ai* in your *Chapter 10* folder in case it needs to be resized or edited later.

2. To export the *Guitar2* file to Photoshop, select File > Export > Photoshop PSD > and save it in your *Chapter 10* folder. Name the file *Guitar2PSD.psd* and click the Export button.

3. When the Photoshop Export Options dialog box comes up, choose RGB Color Model, set the Resolution to 72 dpi, and place checks next to Anti-alias and Write Layers to include all layers. If Export As displays (in earlier versions), select the current version you are using.

4. Select OK and the PSD version will be placed in your *Chapter 10* folder, while the original *Guitar2.ai* will remain open.

5. Save and close the *Guitar2.ai* image. You are ready to open the new file in Photoshop.

OPENING ILLUSTRATOR ARTWORK IN PHOTOSHOP VERSUS PLACING ARTWORK

DESIGN TIP

Always save the Illustrator file in its native AI format, or use the universal formats EPS or PDF before having the image exported to Photoshop, and you will always have a back-up copy for editing the artwork. Once the image is rasterized in Photoshop, it cannot be enlarged or have pixels added, other- wise the quality may deteriorate (Figure 10-23).

You have created a guitar graphic with layers and type in Illustrator. You exported the file as a Photoshop PSD file including all layers. Now it is time to bring the guitar artwork into the Photoshop banner you created earlier. You can either Open the artwork or Place it into the Photoshop document. We have chosen to open the artwork to preserve the layers. Here are some considerations to help you decide whether you want to open or place artwork created in Illustrator into Photoshop:

• When you use the Open command in Photoshop to open an exported PSD file, Photoshop only rasterizes the vector objects created in Illustrator and keeps the background transparent.

• When using the Open command in Photoshop, the illustration should also be resized *before* bringing it into Photoshop to avoid having to enlarge it as a con- verted bitmap, creating pixeling issues.

• When using the Open command in Photoshop, most of the layers made in Illustrator are editable in Photoshop. Once you make changes to any layers in Photoshop, you can use the Copy Merge command in the Edit menu to paste a flattened copy of those edited layers as a new layer in the Photoshop image with- out affecting the original exported PSD file.

• Placing files in Photoshop (File > Place) automatically flattens all layers into one, preventing any future editing. However, it does allow you to resize the surround- ing bounding box before pressing the Return/Enter key.

▷ FIGURE 10-24

Completed web banner in Photoshop.

Since the image has already been scaled to the correct size, you will use File > Open to open the *Guitar2PSD.psd*, create a drop shadow effect in the outline layer, and then copy and paste it into the web banner; you can also just drag the guitar image onto the banner.

1. Open the *Banner2* image in Photoshop.

2. Open the *Guitar2PSD.psd* file that is in your *Chapter 10* folder. You will notice the background remains transparent, and all graphics are intact, as well as the Illustrator layers.

3. Highlight the *<Path>* sublayer underneath the *Outline* layer in the Layers panel, (or if the Path sublayer does not display highlight the Outline layer), then click and hold the Add a Layer Style icon at the bottom of the Layers panel.

4. To give the guitar image a little depth, add a Drop Shadow effect with a Size and Distance of about 5 pixels. Click OK.

5. Select the entire image (Ctrl A, or choose Select > Select All).

6. Use the Copy Merge command to copy a flattened version of the image (Edit > Copy Merged). This does not affect the actual layers in the document.

7. Click on the right side of the *Banner2*, then paste it (Ctrl V or Edit > Paste). This will create a new layer.

8. Use the arrow keys to position the banner using Figure 10-24 as a guide. Minimize the window for the next exercise.

CREATING SMART OBJECTS FROM ILLUSTRATOR INTO PHOTOSHOP

Smart Objects in Photoshop are layers that contain image data from raster or vector images, such as Photoshop or Illustrator files. These allow a designer to make changes while preserving an image's source data with all its original characteristics, enabling you to perform nondestructive editing to the layer. The command is found under the Layer menu. Here are some characteristics of Smart Objects.

• Smart Objects allow a designer to scale, rotate, and warp Illustrator vector images without fear of pixeling or degrading the artwork.

• Illustrator images placed or pasted into Photoshop as Smart Objects remain live and scalable, allowing future edits made in Illustrator to automatically update in the Photoshop document.

• You can place a variety of EPS and PDF formats into a single layer or paste Illustrator's native format onto a single layer.

• You cannot alter pixel data such as painting, dodging, burning, or cloning, unless the Smart Object is converted into a regular layer, which will rasterize the artwork.

• Smart Objects are like Illustrator symbols: editing one linked copy will update all other linked copies automatically.

• Smart Objects can be created in Photoshop in five different ways.

1. Convert existing selected layers.

2. Place files inside an existing smart object.

3. Duplicate Smart Objects to generate multiple versions.

4. Drag and drop PDF and Illustrator artwork into a Photoshop document.

5. Copy existing Illustrator artwork and paste it into Photoshop as a Smart Object.

TOOLKIT TIP For changes made in Illustrator to display in a Photoshop Smart Object layer, you need to first select the Smart Object layer to be edited in Photoshop, then choose Edit Contents from the Layer menu (Layer > Smart Objects > Edit Contents). You can then make additional changes in Illustrator and save them. When the changes are saved, the image will be updated in the Photoshop document. The edited image may create a new Illustrator file called *vector smart object1.ai*.

▷ FIGURE 10-25

To create a smart object layer, copy the selected Illustrator graphic and paste it as a smart object into Photoshop.

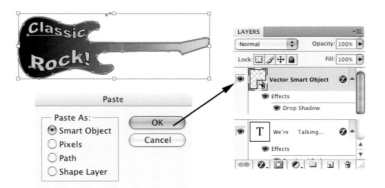

OPTIONAL EXERCISE: In this exercise, you will open the *Guitar2.ai* file you created, paste the artwork into Photoshop as a Smart Object, and create a drop shadow effect. You will then make changes to the graphic in Illustrator and save the Smart Object file to observe the linked change to the Photoshop document.

1. In Illustrator, open the original *Guitar2.ai* file that is in your *Chapter 10* folder.

2. With the Selection tool, hold down the Shift key and select the guitar and type. Use Edit > Copy to copy the selected objects.

3. In Photoshop, make sure the *Banner2* file is open, make a duplicate copy of the Banner2 image (Image > Duplicate), and move the guitar graphic you had created in the previous exercise off to the side to make way for this new guitar graphic.

4. Select Edit > Paste. When the dialog box opens, select to paste as Smart Object (Figure 10-25). Click OK. You will notice a new layer is created labeled as Smart Vector Object. Do not press the Return/Enter key yet.

5. With the graphic still selected, hold the Shift key and drag inward to make the graphic small enough to fit inside the banner. Use the arrow keys to position it. Press the Return/Enter key once the guitar is scaled and positioned accurately.

6. To add a drop shadow layer style effect, keep the Vector Smart Object layer selected; click the Add A Layer Style icon on the Layers panel, select Drop Shadow, and choose a Size and Distance of about 5 pixels.

7. To observe the effect of using Smart Objects by editing the graphic, high-light the Vector Smart Object layer and choose Layer > Smart Objects > Edit Contents (Figure 10-26). A dialog box opens reminding you to save your changes, notifying you that the changes will be reflected upon returning to the smart object. Click OK.

8. The smart object is now linked back to Illustrator, and you will notice that a duplicate document of the *Guitar2* graphic has been created and named *Vector Smart Object1* by default.

9. Use Illustrator's Type tool to select the word "Classic"; change the word to "Metal" or another word. Adjust the type size to 26 points, then use the Direct Selection tool and the arrow keys to move the type line into place. Feel free to make any additional changes to experiment with this feature.

10. Select the graphic, choose File > Save As, and choose to save the default *Vector Smart Object1* file as a native AI Illustrator file with the default options in your *Chapter 10* folder. The original *Guitar2* file is not affected.

11. With the new Smart Object document saved, switch back to the Photoshop banner image; you will notice that the linked smart object now appears with the changes you made in Illustrator.

12. Save the new, adjusted duplicate Photoshop *Banner2 copy* file with the different name in the guitar as *Banner2B* in your *Chapter 10* folder. Close this file and leave the original Banner2 file open.

TOOLKIT TIP Because you have created a Smart Object graphic in Illustrator that is linked to the Smart Object layer in the Photoshop document, both files must be kept in the same folder—in this case, *Chapter 10*—for existing and future edits, or you may not see any changes. Always keep files in the same location for links to work correctly.

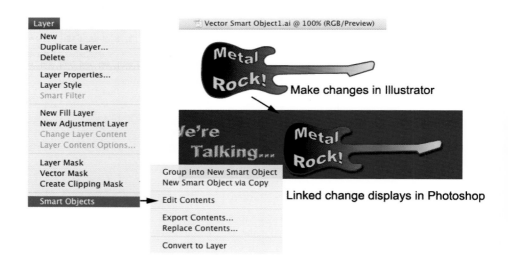

▷   FIGURE 10-26

To edit a Smart Object layer, choose Edit Contents; make changes in Illustrator, save the new graphic, and observe the linked change in Photoshop.

ILLUSTRATOR'S GRAPHIC STYLES PANEL

Designers can use the Graphic Styles panel (Window > Graphic Styles) to create, name, and apply effects to graphic objects or text in conjunction with the Appearance panel. You can create the effect in the Appearance panel and drag the thumbnail, say the guitar gradient, as a new Graphic Style in the Graphic Style panel. You can also choose effects for objects and text from graphic style libraries, which are collections of preset graphic styles. When you open a graphic style library, it appears in a new panel, much like the Swatches panel. You select the object, graphic, or text before applying the style then select the style to apply. Try creating a copy of the guitar graphic, then choose the Image Effects library and start applying various styles for fun. Select the type line and try different effects using the Type Effects library.

USING THE SAVE FOR WEB AND DEVICES COMMAND IN PHOTOSHOP

The process for saving in Photoshop is about the same as in Illustrator, using the Save for Web and Devices (CS3-CS5) or Save for Web (earlier versions) command in the File menu. In Photoshop, the choices are .GIF, .PNG or .JPG. Any one of these formats will automatically flatten the *Banner2* file and save it as a copy of the original file, leaving the original file with its layers still open and intact. Since there are no transparencies used in this banner, the JPEG option is the best choice for maintaining the quality and keeping the file size minimal. JPEG images are compressed, but cannot handle transparencies. You might also notice that since no continuous-tone images (photographs) were used, *Banner2* has a smaller file size than *Banner1*.

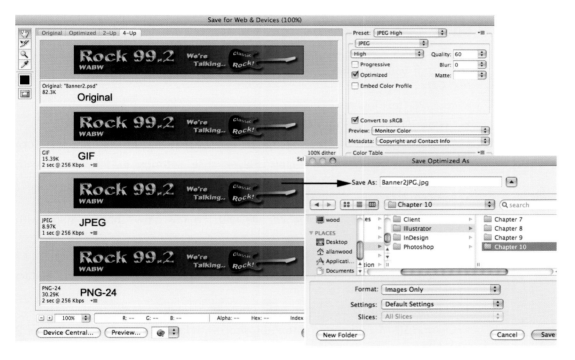

▷ FIGURE 10-27

Optimizing the Banner2 image, observing different formats for quality and file size, and selecting the JPEG option.

TOOLKIT TIP If an image like the guitar graphic, which has a curved outer edge, is saved as a JPEG file, the background would become white instead of transparent. This is why it is important to understand how to save a graphic for its intended purpose. GIF and PNG files allow transparent backgrounds, but JPEG images do not.

Next you will look at the different format options for optimizing the banner, then save it as a JPEG.

1. In Photoshop, select the File > Save for Web & Devices command, choosing the 4-Up tab. If the banner is not fully shown, select the original tab, then select the 4-Up tab.

2. Select the gray box under each image one at a time, and change the settings to PNG-24, JPEG High, and GIF to observe the differences in the image, the file sizes, and download times compared to the original image.

3. Select the gray box with the JPEG High option; it has the fastest download time and will display all graphics accurately inside the banner. Each of these formats will flatten the banner image. (PNG may also be the same size; if so, either would do.)

4. Save the file as *Banner2JPG.jpg* in your *Chapter 10* folder. The original *Banner2* file remains intact with all its layers (Figure 10-27).

5. Compare the file sizes of the *Banner1* and *Banner2* images. You will see that when the file contains a bitmap, the file size increases. Compare the various files.

FILES AND FORMATS CREATED

In your *Chapter 10* folder on your drive, you will find the following 13 files you created, if you completed all the exercises including those that came with the text CD:

• *Rock.JPG* (text low res CD file)

• *Guitars.JPG* (text low res CD file)

• *Guitar.PSD* (pasting selected guitar photo in its own document, Photoshop backup)

• *GuitarGLO.PNG* (creating "glow" layer style settings in Photoshop with tranparency)

• *Banner1.AI* (created in Illustrator for back-up file with layers)

• *Banner1.PNG* (final web *Banner1* file with "guitar glow" photo image with transparency)

• *Banner2.PSD* (file created in Photoshop with layers for backup)

• *GuitarTRACE.TIF* (seleted image of one guitar taken from image of three guitars to be used as template for tracing)

• *Guitar2.AI* (created illustration from photo and applied gradients)

• *Guitar2PSD.PSD* (exported into Photoshop with layers to be placed in Banner 2 with effects)

• *Banner2JPG.JPG* (final web *Banner2* flattened image containing all illustrative artwork)

• If you completed the "Creating Smart Objects" exercise, then you will have two additional files, *Vector Smart Object1.EPS* and *Banner2B.JPG,* which you created to show how you can edit and have the change linked from one application to another.

These files you have been creating for these exercises have various purposes. Now you can compare various files and also see how you would organize them to set up a productive work flow. In the world of graphics, you will be creating and working with many types of files. You can also use Bridge or use the each application's Mini Bridge function to quickly observe info about each file and get a visual thumbnail representation of each.

ADVANCED USERS: Understanding PDF and EPS Files

Two universal graphic formats, PDF and EPS, can be read by most other graphic applications, which comes in handy if someone does not have the same application in which the original document was created. Documents saved as either EPS files or PDF files have very much the same characteristics; it is up to the designer to decide what media they will be used for. In general, EPS files are used in the commercial printing process and for vector graphics that use text and images. PDF files are most useful in sharing documents over the web, through e-mail, on CDs, and where minimal file size is needed. It should also be noted that with improved technology these days, many commercial printers can accept documents created from the original applications like Adobe products. PDF files are also used as proofs for commercial printers to check document layouts, fonts, and graphics, and these can also be used in the actual printing. This text was communicated between myself and the production team electronically from low res PDF documents and then was printed from high resolution PDF files.

SAVING PORTABLE DOCUMENT FORMAT (PDF) FILES

If you want to save your files for distribution via e-mail, on CDs, on the web, or for electronic documents, Portable Document Format (PDF) files can be saved and read by most applications. If an application cannot read them directly, PDF files can be read on any computer using Adobe's free Acrobat Reader program, which you installed as part of Chapter 1 of this text. Anyone can download it from Adobe's website (*http://www.adobe.com*) and install it easily. In Illustrator, the PDF Options dialog box provides many options for specifying compression, Marks and Bleeds for commercial printers, security, file summary, and advanced settings for color management. You will find the same display in the general section for both Illustrator and Photoshop with universal options in each (Figure 10-28). We will concentrate on the General functions. Here are some great features regarding all PDF files:

• When saving a PDF file, all fonts can be automatically embedded so that the viewer can read the document clearly without having the actual fonts installed on their computer.

• PDF files retain any transparency information in the file.

• To display web options, choose Optimize for Fast Web View (or Screen Optimize in earlier versions) from the Adobe PDF Options dialog box.

• When you check the Preserve Illustrator Editing Capabilities box in the Adobe PDF Options dialog box, the file can still be opened and edited as an Illustrator file.

• A Photoshop PDF file can be brought into Illustrator with type made into outlined paths if the Use Outlines for Text box is checked.

• Many commercial printers also prefer to receive files in PDF format from their clients as guides, proofs, and for the printing process itself.

• You can save to earlier versions of Acrobat Reader with a description of considerations. The drawback of this option is that there are no editing capabilities in older versions.

• PDF files use lossless compression; no data is thrown out.

TOOLKIT TIP If you are not sure that the intended viewer has the most current version of Acrobat Reader to view your PDF document, you can save your PDF document to an earlier version of Acrobat Reader.

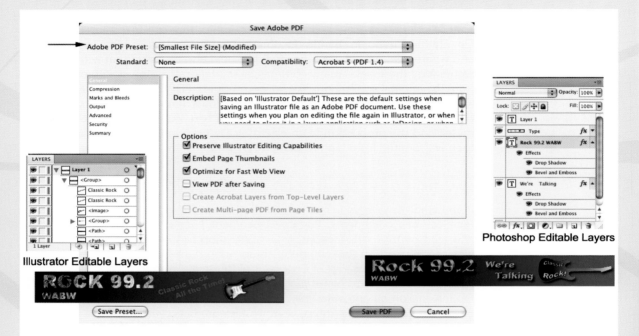

The PDF Save options are the same for both Illustrator and Photoshop
where a designer can create PDF files and maintain editing capbilities.

▷ FIGURE 10-28

**Creating PDF files
in Illustrator or
Photoshop. Using
options that allow
future editing.**

Let us bring in the banners you created and save them as PDF files to compare. As long as you select the option to Preserve Editing Capabilities, you can make adjustments to various layers later.

1. Launch Illustrator and locate the *Banner1.ai* file in your *Chapter 10* folder and Save As Adobe PDF (earlier versions will display Save As Illustrator PDF). Select the General settings.

2. In the Adobe PDF Preset field, select the smallest file size; notice you can set for high-resolution and press-quality documents here. Make sure Preserve Illustrator Editing Capabilities, Embed Page Thumbnails for previews, and Optimize for Fast Web View boxes are all checked (Figure 10-28). The setting will add "modified" to the Preset, since you have changed some of the defaults.

3. Name and Save the file as *Banner1PDF.pdf* in your *Chapter 10* folder.

4. Notice that all layers are editable, and vector type and gradients are still scalable. The guitar image is still a bitmap that can be scaled smaller but not enlarged.

5. Launch Photoshop and open the *Banner2.psd* created earlier; choose Save As Photoshop PDF, making sure that Save: Layers and Color: Embed Color Profile are both checked. Click Save, and another dialog box will pop up with the settings shown in Figure 10-28; these options are identical in Photoshop and Illustrator.

6. To include editing capabilities for type and graphics in earlier versions of Photoshop, make sure you check the boxes next to JPEG, Include Vector Data, and Use Outlines for Text; click Save PDF.

7. Name the file *Banner2PDF.pdf*. Notice the individual layers and sublayers are still separated, except for the guitar layer, which has been combined.

TOOLKIT TIP Photoshop also provides a Scripts function (File > Scripts) to send Layer Comps to clients, team members, or your boss. Layer Comps can be sent as specific files, electronic PDF files, or as exported layers to multiple files. This comes in pretty handy for those who need to document the progress of their project. It is also a time-saver when creating graphics for animation and rollover buttons for the web. Illustrator CS5 provides the option to save a document in the smallest file size as a compact PDF. When saving to PDF in the Save Adobe PDF dialog box, select the Smallest File Size option from Adobe PDF Preset. Make sure that you deselect the Preserve Illustrator Editing Capabilities check box to avoid saving the Illustrator resources along with the document.

ENCAPSULATED POSTSCRIPT (EPS) FILES

Encapsulated PostScript (EPS) files create file sizes that are too large for web use. EPS files are useful for documents that will be used in the commercial printing industry, when the image involves a combination of type and graphics. Here are some features of EPS files.

• EPS files can be imported into and read by most graphic programs. Documents saved as EPS files from other illustration programs can be edited in Illustrator and then saved as an Illustrator document.

• In Photoshop, files saved in EPS format are saved as copies to a designated location, while the original file remains open.

• The EPS file format is a good choice if you want to import graphics into a page layout program, word processing program, or other drawing programs when you are not sure what application the intended receiver is using.

• EPS files do not use compression; they produce large file sizes with precise accuracy, which is why they are used in printing but not for web design.

• EPS files are well suited when you need to combine bitmap and vector graphics. Photoshop, however, rasterizes its EPS files into nonscalable bitmapped graphics that cannot be enlarged but still maintain image quality.

INTEGRATING PHOTOSHOP AND ILLUSTRATOR PDF FILES

Documents saved as either EPS files or PDF files have very much the same characteristics. The designer needs to know what media the document will be used for. There is more flexibility bringing Photoshop PDF or EPS files into Illustrator than Illustrator files into Photoshop, especially with type. Here is a quick breakdown of what happens when you integrate PDF or EPS files in either Photoshop or Illustrator.

• Although Illustrator will flatten the Photoshop layers from either a PDF or EPS document, type is treated as individual outlined paths, which can be edited with the Direct Selection tool.

• Illustrator PDF and EPS files can be brought into Photoshop, but they are rasterized and flattened into a one-layer bitmap image with a transparent background: Layer Style effects can only be applied to the whole image.

▷   FIGURE 10-29

Photoshop PDF and EPS files can have type converted to outlined graphics in Illustrator.

Here you will see that there is more flexibility integrating Photoshop PDF files into Illustrator than there is integrating Illustrator PDF files into Photoshop.

1. In Illustrator, open the *Banner2PDF.pdf* file created in Photoshop. You will notice when you open it in Illustrator and click on one of the circles to the right of a sublayer, the type is outlined as a graphic and can be selected with the Direct Selection tool to be edited. The graphics are combined as a single image.

2. In Photoshop, open the *Banner1PDF.pdf* file created in Illustrator. The file will be rasterized onto one layer. Any effects will be applied to that layer.

3. Try saving the *Guitar* and *Guitar2* graphics in PDF and EPS formats, and observe what happens when you open them in Illustrator and Photoshop.

4. As you can see, more flexibility is provided when working with PDF and EPS files in Illustrator if any rescaling or editing is needed, especially with type, while PDF and EPS files in Photoshop are useful for optimal detail in a certain preset size.

5. Go ahead; play around and see what you can and cannot do. Do not forget to take a look at the file sizes of the PDFs you just created, and compare them to the file sizes of the originals.

DIGITAL TOOLKIT EXTRA: Converting Bitmap Images to Vector Artwork Using Live Trace and Live Paint

In Illustrator there is a function that allows the designer to trace various types of bitmap images called Live Trace. It automatically follows the contours and outlines of drawings and various shades of bitmap images to create vector drawings consisting of many closed paths. It provides much more precision than the Auto Trace tool used in earlier versions. The Paint Bucket tool in previous versions has been replaced with a more accurate Live Paint Bucket tool that creates Live Paint groups of closed paths for adding fill colors. The hours of work required to generate a complex set of paths can now be done quickly live. Creating vector illustrations from bitmap images enables them to be scaled to any size.

TOOLKIT TIP Live Trace and Live Paint are very powerful functions in Illustrator, and can be quite complex in their operations. For an introduction about these functions or as a review, go into Illustrator Help, search either Live Paint or Live Trace, and click on the links; or go to the Adobe website and view live video tutorials if you have a high-speed Internet connection.

LIVE TRACING DIFFERENT BITMAP IMAGES

Live Trace, in Illustrator, automatically follows the contours and outlines of drawings and various shades of bitmap images to create vector drawings consisting of many closed paths. The more detailed the selection, the more complex the paths, depending on the tracing options you choose. Choosing certain tracing options can also create special effects. To trace any object, it must be selected first. To trace the image using the default tracing options, click the Live Trace button in the Control panel, or choose Object > Live Trace > Make. To set tracing options before you trace the image, select presets from the Tracing Options dialog box, which provides a variety options for different types of images, sketches, drawings, and photographs. You can also set up your own custom tracing parameters. To convert the tracing outline to a series of connected paths, select the **Expand** command (Object > Live Trace > Expand).

TOOLKIT TIP If you know in advance that you plan to use the Live Paint Bucket tool to add color to fills and strokes, you can select the Live Paint button in the Control panel after selecting the tracing option.

TOOLKIT TIP Instead of using the Open command to open TIF and JPG files in Illustrator, you can create a new Illustrator document and use the Place command instead, then save the document as an Illustrator file.

▷ FIGURE 10-30

Using Live Trace in Illustrator to create vector illustrations from bitmap images.

Here you will trace a scanned-in painting as one type of bitmap image that can be used for Live Trace. You then will select the Expand command to create connected paths. In order to trace any object it has to be selected first. (If you were to attempt this using the Auto Trace tool in earlier versions, it would work very poorly).

1. Launch Illustrator and open the *Sailboat* file in your *Chapter 10 > Toolkit Extra* folder. This is a scanned file of a kitted cloth that, once traced, will allow you to change various colors to show different versions of the image as an illustration.

2. Select the image with the Selection tool.

3. Set the color boxes in the Tools panel to the default black Stroke with a white Fill for neutral starting colors.

4. In the Control panel, select the down arrow next to the Live Trace button to display the Live Trace options. You can also choose Object > Live Trace > Tracing Options, where you will see the same presets listed.

TOOLKIT TIP You can also select a tracing option on bitmap images to create certain effects. Try bringing in a photograph and selecting Detailed Illustration or the Hand Sketch option to observe the changes.

5. Select the Photo Low Fidelity option to capture details in the shading. You will notice that the colors will appear to be painted in, however, the masts holding the sails need to be filled in more (Figure 10-30).

6. In the Control panel, change the Min Area of pixels from the preset of 10 pixels to 30 or more pixels for a better tracing. It will now display as a Custom Preset setting.

7. Select the Expand button to create the paths. If you select the Live Paint button on the Control panel, it will automatically create ready-to-paint paths for the entire image, although it will make the paths difficult to individually edit.

8. Leave this file open for the next exercise.

TOOLKIT TIP The more complex the tracing option, the longer it will take to convert to paths. The Photo High Quality option will take quite a long time to convert an image due to the complexity of reading shades and tones. Avoid using this unless you have plenty of time to wait for it to render.

LIVE PAINTING FACES AND EDGES

Live Paint detects and corrects gaps to create closed paths for fills and strokes for painting. It treats all paths as if they were on the same canvas without any layering. By creating a **Live Paint group,** all paths are fully editable, and fills can be adjusted as individual paths are adjusted. If you remove a path or adjust it with the Direct Selection tool, the color simply fills in wherever changes were made. Live Paint groups can be painted along edges, like strokes, where the portion of the path intersects with other paths or inside faces, which would be the filled areas for color. You can select colors from the Color panel or various swatch libraries to get the tones of color you are looking for. In Illustrator, the **Live Paint Bucket** tool replaces the older paint Bucket tool and is used to create Live Paint Groups and to fill in the faces or color the edges. **Faces** are the inside areas, and **edges** are the stroke or outlined areas of the path. To paint faces and edges with the Live Paint Bucket tool, you need to create a Live Paint Group first. Use the Paint Bucket cursor to paint in the faces. To paint the edges with stroke colors, hold down the Shift key to change the Live Paint Bucket to a Brush. You will find a vast selection of **Swatch libraries** for specific color combinations. Any colors you select are placed in the main Swatches panel for future use. These can be found by clicking on the Swatch panel submenu and selecting Open Swatch library. The **Live Paint Selection** tool lets you select and then delete faces and edges of a Live Paint group. When paths are deleted with the Live Paint Selection tool, the color of the surrounding paths fills in the deleted path.

TOOLKIT TIP Once a Live Paint Group is created, you cannot delete a component path of a closed path very easily. Make path deletions and adjustments before creating the group to paint. You can use the Live Paint Selection tool to help select and delete faces and edges of a Live paint Group. Before applying any colors with the Live Paint Bucket tool, always select the fill or stroke colors first, then select the tool.

Live Paint Bucket tool
Click sail to make Live Paint Group

Sail is filled with color,
and as you drag the mouse over
you'll see paint groups highlighted in red

Live Paint Selection tool to
delete extra dark remnants

Completed painted sail image
with lighter toned colors painted in

▷ FIGURE 10-31

Using the various Live Paint techniques to make a lighter-toned image.

In this exercise, you will use the Live Paint Bucket tool to fill in edges and faces with color. Then you will use the Live Paint Selection tool to remove paths to fill in adjacent colors.

1. In Illustrator, open or maximize the window of the traced and expanded *Sailboat* image, and zoom in at 150% to 200% to observe the many paths created.

2. Make sure the image is selected with the Selection tool to select all paths.

3. Select the Live Paint Bucket tool and click on the brown sail to make the entire image part of the Live Paint group. (If a dialog box displays that you will not be able to edit the paths after a Live Paint group is applied, select OK). As you move the cursor over the image, you will find various closed paths highlighted in red. The brown sail will be filled in white.

4. In the Swatches panel menu, choose to Open Swatch Library and select the System swatch that matches the type of computer you are using, Macintosh or Windows, or choose another swatch library.

5. Select a light blue color to change the color of the sky. Select the Live Paint Bucket tool and click on the faces of the sky Live Paint group to apply the lighter blue tone.

6. Zoom in to 200% and click any dark remnants inside the red Live Paint group with the Live Paint Selection tool; it will look like a dotted patch. Press the Delete key to remove it and keep the overall sky light blue. You also notice that both Fill and Stroke have defaulted to None.

7. Continue changing the face colors on the sails, if you like, for a lighter toned image (Figure 10-31). You now have another version of this graphic. Be careful not to change the colors of the edges unless that is what you are planning to do. Use the Lasso tool to Average paths together in the Object menu

(Object > Path > Average > Both) to paint smaller areas, and use the Live Paint Selection tool to remove fills and edges. Have fun and experiment!

8. Save the final sailboat image in your *Chapter 10* folder, then print the before and after images.

TRACING AND PAINTING COMPLEX DRAWINGS AND PHOTOS

Here is where the creative fun comes in. You can use Live Trace and Live Paint to save you hours of tracing scanned images using the Pen or Pencil tools. You can also trace a photograph to use as a starting point for artwork or to create special effects. You can take a complex scanned drawing and use Live Trace to set up the initial paths. Keep in mind that before creating Live Paint Groups or applying colors with the Live Paint Bucket tool, the image first needs to be selected and traced with one of Live Trace's options to create the paths.

TOOLKIT TIP If you want to paint the stroke edges, hold down the Shift key. As you move the cursor over the edges, it will turn from a paint bucket to a brush. Click on the edge to apply the stroke. If the brush displays an *X* in the cursor, you are over a face area and cannot apply the color.

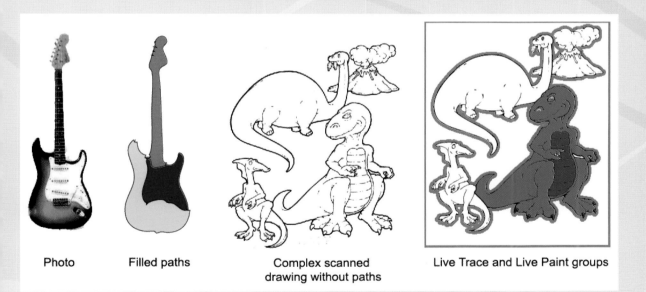

| Photo | Filled paths | Complex scanned drawing without paths | Live Trace and Live Paint groups |

▷ FIGURE 10-32

Tracing a photo for effects and applying Live Paint groups to complex drawings.

For more practice, you will open the guitars photo and trace and color it. Then you will open a complex drawing, trace it and create Live Paint groups and add color as you see fit (Figure 10-32).

1. In Illustrator, open the *MyGuitar* photo image in your *Chapter 10* folder.

2. Select the image with the Selection tool.

3. Choose to Live Trace as Detailed Illustration or Hand Drawn Sketch to see the special effects you can create.

4. Select the Live Paint Bucket to create the Live Paint groups and have some fun.

5. For the grand finale, open the *Dinos* image in your *Chapter 10* folder. Select the image with the Selection tool, and select the Live Trace button on the Control panel to let Live Trace choose the best way to interpret it. Click OK if a dialog box displays. This is a complex drawing that would have taken quite some time to recreate in Illustrator. You will notice the image has been traced quite nicely with good contrast in images.

6. Select the Live Paint Bucket tool and click on the image to generate lots of paint groups.

7. Go ahead and get creative adding color to the paths. Experiment with different fills. Do not forget: if you want to paint the edges, hold down the Shift key. As you move the cursor over the edges, the cursor will turn from a paint bucket to a brush; just click on the edge to apply the stroke. If the brush displays an *X* in the cursor, you are over a face area and cannot apply the color.

8. Save both images in your *Chapter 10* folder, and print them to see your work.

CHAPTER SUMMARY

In this chapter, you were introduced to various methods of saving and importing graphic files and images between Illustrator and Photoshop. Here is a brief list to summarize what was covered; use this as a guide for projects you may do in the future.

• Always try to save Illustrator and Photoshop files in their native formats for a backup.

• Embed images when you do not want to worry about locating the original image. Understand that you may have a larger file size as a result, especially with bitmap or raster images.

• Use linking if you can keep the Illustrator file in the same place as the linked graphic, which will minimize the file size.

• Use the Place command when bringing Photoshop images into Illustrator, making sure you have created the final size in Photoshop first.

• Graphics saved as PNG files preserve transparency settings, whereas images saved as JPEGs do not; however, JPEG files are smaller in size.

• Export Illustrator files into Photoshop as PSD files to maintain the most layers and keep the background transparent.

• Photoshop will always rasterize images from Illustrator, so export at a larger size that can be reduced if necessary.

• Illustrator EPS and PDF files can be edited in Illustrator and saved in Illustrator's native format, whereas Photoshop EPS and PDF files are flattened.

• You can create text outlines in Illustrator as individual closed paths; Photoshop PDF and EPS files can have type converted to outlined graphics in Illustrator.

REVIEW QUESTIONS

1. As a designer, you want to maintain a transparent background in your image. What file formats would you choose in Illustrator to keep this effect? What format would you save in if you needed to bring an Illustrator file into Photoshop?

2. What command in Illustrator allows the background transparency of a bitmap image to be transferred from Photoshop to Illustrator?

3. Explain the difference between bitmap and vector images.

4. Explain the difference between placing and pasting a document within either application.

5. Describe the difference between linking and embedding an image and when one would be more appropriate over the other.

6. Explain when to use EPS and PDF files for each application.

CHAPTER 10
Web banners created by integrating
elements from Photoshop and Illustrator.

CHAPTER 10 ADVANCED
Understanding PDF and EPS files

Original scanned image

Live Trace to create paths

Live Paint Bucket to apply new colors

CHAPTER 10 EXTRA
Using Live Trace and Live Paint in Illustrator
to generate editable paths from various types
of images and apply color.

3

Digital Illustration: Adobe Illustrator CS5

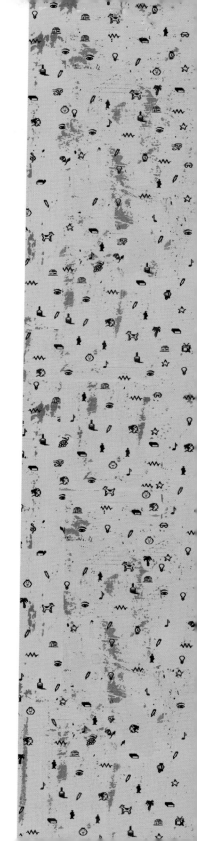

Most drawings created in Illustrator are combinations of various paths. Here you will learn the importance of layering paths to create compound shapes, how to use layers to isolate graphic components, build your skills using the Pen and Pencil tools, and use the Object menu for various edits. You will be creating an illustration from a sketch, building layered paths, and making type paths on a dark mug as part of a promotion. In this case, you will be creating a multicolor logo.

CLIENT ASSIGNMENT: Making a Promotional Mug Logo

Louise Ambler is the owner of Stage Fright Café, a local coffee shop where local musicians come and play on the weekends to entertain the crowds. She wants to promote the café and its local entertainment by creating promotoional coffee mugs to be used at the café and for sale and marketing purposes. She brings you a very rough sketch of an acoustic guitar. She discusses with you how she wants the mug to be a royal blue color with the café name in yellow or yellow gold lettering in a circular path with the guitar in the center of the name. The guitar will be a gradient blend of yellow and orange with red and black details. You meet again with Louise to discuss how she will be given a proof of the logo inside a royal blue square that represents the mug color, and how you will also provide a 3-D rendition of what the logo may look like when applied to the mug surface. You also discuss how you can show her what the logo may look like on other promotional pieces like a CD cover, business card, and direct mail piece. She leaves, excited to see the final results ready for press by the end of the week (Figure UR3-1).

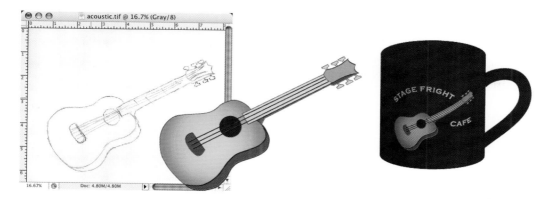

▷ FIGURE UR3-1

Start from a sketch, create a multishape guitar graphic, then create a 3-D mug to map the logo on.

ACTION ITEMS OVERVIEW

After tracing the sketch using Illustrator's drawing tools, primarily the Pen tool, you will need to create a series of shapes to create the guitar graphic. You will then create the business name, Stage Fright Café, on circular paths separate from the guitar graphic. Once you save the graphic as a symbol, you will create a 3-D view of the mug with the logo in it. Here is a breakdown of what needs to be done:

• Clean up the scanned sketch in Photoshop using the Magic Eraser tool and adjusting the brightness and contrast in the Image menu.

• Place the sketch as a template in Illustrator, and create working layers for different portions of the image.

• Use the Pen tool and the other drawing tools to create layered paths and various strokes and fill combinations for the logo.

• Add the Stage Fright Café name in capital letters using the Path Type tool within circle paths, and adjust the position of the text with the Direct Selection tool.

• Create the symbol of the logo for future use.

• Scale the logo to fit the mug and also create a symbol of the logo.

• Create a 3-D mug illustration, and map the logo to the mug's surface.

• Apply the finished logo in multiple artboards format to include a CD cover, business card, and direct mail piece.

TRACING THE BASIC SKETCH LOGO

If an image is to be traced in Illustrator, there usually needs to be some preliminary work in Photoshop. If a sketch or drawing is on tracing or lightweight paper, the scan can create a very "dirty" background. Before scanning an image that is on tracing paper, use a copy machine to copy the traced image onto regular white paper to get rid of much of the background interference. When the image is scanned into Photoshop, adjust it by selecting Image > Adjustments > Brightness/Contrast, or Auto Contrast, or try Levels adjustments (Image > Adjustments > Levels) to further remove the background shadows. Use the Magic Eraser and Background Eraser tools to remove the background from the image, so only the actual drawing is left to be placed into Illustrator for tracing. This will prep the image to be placed in Illustrator for using drawing tools to create the basic acoustic guitar logo.

TOOLKIT TIP Because the image was scanned in Grayscale mode, you have access to the same adjusments as you would with a color scan. If it was scanned as black and white, you would find little or no adjustmemts could be made.

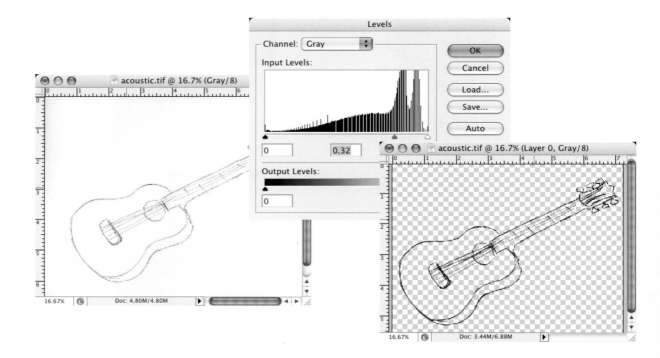

▷ FIGURE UR3-2

Prepping the scanned, sketched image first using Photoshop's tools for cleaning up the image before bringing it into Illustrator for use as a template.

Next, you will take an image that was drawn on tracing paper, copied, scanned, and prepped in Photoshop to be placed in Illustrator for tracing.

1. Launch Photoshop and open the file *Acoustic.tif* in your *Unit 3 Review* folder.

2. Select Image > Auto Contrast to darken the lightly scanned-in lines. You can also try the Brightness/Contrast option in the Adjustments menu.

3. Zoom in to 200% and use the Magic Eraser tool to remove any excess spots so that the image can be traced in Illustrator. Clear out any white areas so that only the lines will show. Be careful not to delete the lines themselves.

4. In Photoshop, select Image > Adjustments > Levels and increase the midtone slider in the Levels dialog box to the right. This will darken the lines significantly, and you can see if there are any dust spots to clean up, too. To remove dirty edges, use the Crop tool and select only the guitar area; crop out any extra space outside the guitar (Figure UR3-2).

5. Save the file in your *Unit 3 Review* folder and minimize the window. Do not be concerned with the roughness of the lines; this is a sketch we will bring into Illustrator as a template to create the required paths.

6. Launch Illustrator and create a new document. Select CMYK color, portrait orientation, letter size, 4 artboards with a 0.125 (1/8) inch bleed, and inches as the Units measurement. Name the document *CafeMug*. Click OK. When the four artboards display, choose the number 1 artboard to create the logo.

7. In Illustrator, use File > Place to place the *Acoustic.tif* image you just fixed in the new document, first artboard. Make sure the Link box is unchecked and the Template box is checked to create an embedded template layer and a working layer, *Layer1*, above it (Figure UR3-3). If a dialog box displays to convert or flatten layers, choose the default Flatten Layers. After you click OK, check your Layers panel to ensure that you have two layers.

8. Save the file as *CafeMug.ai* using the default options in your *Unit 3 Review* folder.

▷ FIGURE UR3-3

In Illustrator, placing the guitar image as a template.

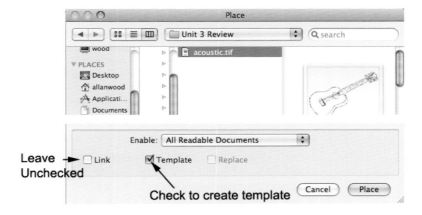

CREATING THE GUITAR FACE USING THE PEN TOOL AND BÉZIER CURVES

Yep . . . it's baaack! That's right: the best tool for most of this job is the Pen tool. Use this tool for smooth connecting lines and placing paths on top of one another, and you will realize just how great this tool really is. It is important to create closed paths when you want them to have a fill color. For making nonconnecting lines, like the turn screws or keys on the neck of the guitar, the Pencil tool may come in handy, or you can still use the Pen tool. In CS5, you can also experiment by using the Draw Behind drawing mode to bring selected path lines behind one another. The Draw Behind mode allows you to draw behind all artwork on a selected layer if no artwork is selected. If the artwork is selected, the new object is drawn directly beneath the selected object.

TOOLKIT TIP If you want to know which path you are selecting, check the Layers panel; you will notice a colored square will display next to the selected path sublayer. If not enough space for this toolkit tip, feel free to put this in the following page.

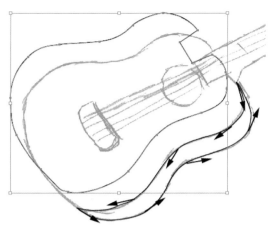

Use the Pen tool to Drag curves that meet the shape of the guitar

To combine shapes that may appear next to or on top of one another, move the closed path away and create the next shape, then use the Selection tools and arrow keys to position closed paths

▷   FIGURE UR3-4

Creating overlapping closed paths using the Pen and Selection tools and arrow keys.

First you will create the guitar shape, making sure that it is a closed path.

1. Rename *Layer1* above the template layer *Guitar Shape*.

2. Zoom in to about 200% and start using the Pen tool with a 1-point black Stroke and a Fill of None to be able to see the paths you create. Create your Bézier curves carefully (refer to Chapter 9).

3. Create an outer outline (Figure UR3-4) by clicking and dragging with the Pen tool. Use the Backspace key, or Command/Ctrl Z to go back a step, and make sure the Pen tool cursor has an *X* showing to continue the path. To make corner points, use the Pen tool with the convert cursor or the Convert Anchor Point tool. When you approach the bottom neck of the guitar, just click to make straight lines. The last point will indicate an *O* on the Pen tool cursor to indicate that you are about to close the path.

4. To check to see if you made a closed shape, select a Fill color to see if it stays inside the path. If so, select None again to remove it for now. Save when you have made an accurate path.

5. Use the Direct Selection tool to adjust path components by clicking outside the path, then select anchor points and direction lines to adjust them.

6. If needed, zoom in to 300% and select open end points with the Lasso tool, then use Object > Path > Average > Both to join them into one path.

7. Check again to make sure the path is closed by selecting a fill color. Change the Fill back to None once this step is complete.

8. To create the side of the guitar, use the Selection tool to select the closed path you just created of the front of the guitar, and move it off to the side. You can choose, instead, to select Draw Behind mode instead from the bottom of the Tools panel to try to draw behind the guitar face instead of having to move it. Use the Pen tools to create a closed path of the guitar side. Try not to use too many anchor points, and keep saving the file periodically.

9. When you have checked to make sure you have a closed path for the side of the guitar, if the Draw Behind option worked it should locate directly behind the guitar face, otherwise use the Selection tool to move back the guitar front over the side path you just created. Keep a black Stroke and Fill of None at this point to show your paths.

10. Do *not* group the two paths; keep them separate. Save the file in Illustrator's native AI format.

TOOLKIT TIP When working with paths laid on top of one another, sometimes it helps to move the paths aside as you create the next one to avoid selecting and combining the wrong paths or path segments. When you are done. select the original path and place it back in its original position.

CREATING PRECISE OVERLAPPING PATHS FOR THE GUITAR FACE AND SIDE

Next, you will place part of one path on top of another. The key to good artwork is to do this without changing the width of the original stroke. This takes some adjusting with the Direct Selection, Selection, and Smooth tools to complement the paths created by the Pen tool. The key when making overlapping paths is to zoom in close and adjust them so that the overlapping paths appear as one (Figure UR3-5).

DESIGN TIP

The key when making overlapping paths is to zoom in close and adjust them with the Direct Selection tool so that the overlapping paths appear as one. Viewing as Outline (View > Outline) can be a great help in aligning two paths.

▷   FIGURE UR3-5

Using the Direct Selection tool and arrow keys to adjust the direction lines and anchor points for precise placement of overlapping paths.

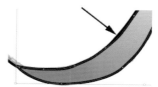

Testing closed path with fill color, check overlapping path.

Overlapping Path

Next, you will create overlapping paths so they appear as one.

1. Use the Selection tool to make sure the guitar face and side are in place, matching the template. Save frequently.

2. With the guitar face selected using the Direct Selection tool, refine paths by adjusting the direction lines, and move anchor points so the paths start to line up where they meet at the side. If you are comfortable using the Draw Behind mode mentioned earlier, you may not have to make hardly any adjustments.

Need additional fun computer graphics tutorials and info, and an additional look at the projects you'll be creating in this book? Check out my Artist's Digital Toolkit website at: **http://www.digitoolkit.com**

3. Use the Direct Selection tool to select the side piece, and make adjustments as needed to create one path where they overlap.

4. Use the arrow keys to move anchor points into place. Save frequently.

5. Continue to check for closed paths by applying a fill color. Change Fill back to None, and leave the Stroke as black to outline the paths.

6. Select View > Outline to see if the overlapping paths are close to looking like a single path. You can then select View > Preview to go back to the original state.

7. If you want, select the guitar side with the Selection tool and then select Object > Arrange > Send to Back to place it underneath the guitar face (see Adjusting the Arrangement of Layers), if again, you were unable to use the Draw Behind function.

8. Feel free to group the two paths together for coloring later. You can always add fill by selecting each piece with the Direct Selection tool, even if they are grouped.

9. Save, save, save!

TOOLKIT TIP Although you may be tempted to use the Live Trace function, it will not work well in this assignment due to the roughness of the lines. If you want to attempt it, duplicate the file, then place the graphic (File > Place) in a new document, select the graphic with the Selection tool, choose the arrow next to the Live Trace button in the Control panel, and select Hand Drawn Sketch from the Preset options; accept the default settings. Click the Expand button to create paths, then use the Live Paint Bucket tool and click in the drawing to make a Live Paint group. Use the Live Paint Bucket for fills or faces, and hold down the Shift key to paint the edges with strokes of color; this works best with closed paths.

ADJUSTING THE ARRANGEMENT OF LAYERS

You can use the Object menu to rearrange objects in any order. With Illustrator, objects are placed on top of one another to create a composite illustration. The Arrange function (Object > Arrange) provides the option to rearrange the stacking order of objects. If you select Send to Front or Send to Back, the object is brought either directly in front of the all the other objects or directly behind all the other objects. If you choose Send Backward or Send Forward, you are sending the objects backward or forward one sublayer at a time. You can also send an object to a different highlighted layer by selecting the Send to Current Layer option.

TOOLKIT TIP You can also use the Layers panel to select objects on sublayers and drag them to another position.

CREATING THE GUITAR NECK WITH STRAIGHT AND BÉZIER PATHS

To create the guitar neck, you will use the Pen tool to click for straight lines, click and drag to create Bézier curves, and use the Convert Anchor point (or hold down thet Option/Alt key with Pen tool) to create corners. It may take a few tries, but mastering this technique will be a huge asset in your digital aresenal.

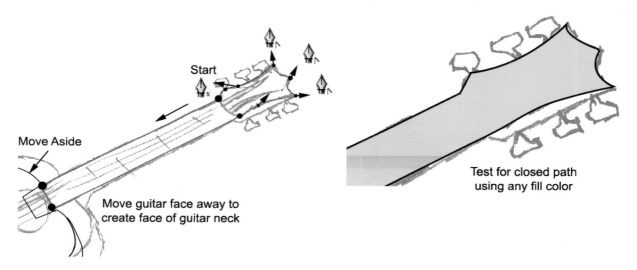

Start

Move Aside

Move guitar face away to create face of guitar neck

Test for closed path using any fill color

▷ FIGURE UR3-6

Creating the face of the guitar neck using the Pen tool to create straight lines, Bézier curves, and the Convert Anchor Point tool.

Now you will create the neck face of the guitar using the Pen tool.

1. Use the Selection tool to Shift-select or drag diagonally across both guitar shapes you created, and move them downward so you can work on the guitar neck. If you had previously tried the Draw Behind mode, click on the Normal Draw (defualt) mode in the Tools Panel.

2. In the Layers panel, add another layer above the *Guitar Shape* Layer and call it *Neck*.

3. Zoom in to 300% and start at the upper back end of the neck, placing anchor points until you reach the other side of the upper neck area (Figure UR3-6). Save the file.

4. Here is where you challenge yourself: Try to create curves at the beginning of the head, then create a corner point using the Convert Anchor Point tool, or select Option/Alt with the Pen tool; add another curve, another corner point, then curve back to the original starting anchor point. If you are having problems with the Convert Anchor point, then just create straight lines instead.

5. Use the Direct Selection tool to adjust path components by deselecting the path, then select anchor points to adjust their position and direction lines.

6. Zoom back in to 300% and select any unjoined end points with the Lasso tool; use Object > Path > Average > Both to overlap the selected points.

7. Check to make sure you have a closed path by selecting a Fill color. When the path is closed, change the back Fill to None.

8. Keep saving your work frequently.

USING THE SCISSORS TOOL TO REMOVE SELECTED PATHS

Here is another fun challenge. In this exercise, we want to create another shape the same as the head piece at the top of the neck of the guitar, called the *headstock*, then close it and put it on top of the neck to apply a different color. You are going to copy the complex guitar neck you just created and use the Scissors tool to delete the portion of the path you do not need. You will use the Pen tool to close the path for the head to create another closed path and apply a different Fill color. The Control panel has a Cut Path at Selected Anchor Points function, too.

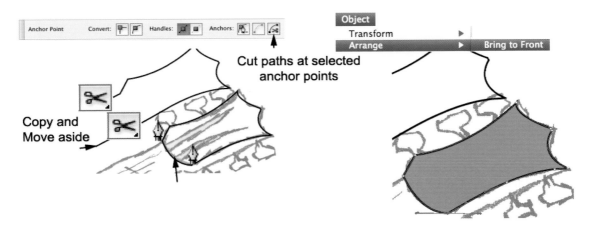

Cut paths at selected anchor points

Copy and Move aside

Use Object menu to join paths, then bring object to front. Use Fill color to test closed path,

▷ FIGURE UR3-7

Copying a complex object, using the Scissors tool to remove paths, then using the Pen tool and Object menu to close the new path shapes.

First, you will use the Option/Alt key to copy the selected guitar neck object you just created, then use the Scissors tool or the Control panel to cut the paths to isolate the complex head path. You will then use the Pen tool and Object menu to close the path.

1. Select the neck face you just created with the Selection tool, then hold down the Option/Alt key and drag a copy to the side. Save your file.

2. Select the original neck face to see its anchor points.

3. Use the Scissors tool located behind the Eraser tool, and click the straight path of the neck as shown in Figure UR3-7 under the tuning keys. When you split the path in the middle of a segment, the two new end points appear on top of the other, and one end point is selected.

4. Do the same on the other side; or you can use the Direct Selection tool to select the anchor point where you want to split the path, and then click the Cut Path At Selected Anchor Points button in the Control panel. When you split the path at an anchor point, a new anchor point appears on top of the original anchor point, and one anchor point is selected.

5. Select the unwanted portions of the neck and use the Delete key to remove them. You now need to close the path, so you can apply a different fill color.

6. Use the Direct Selection tool to select the path, then zoom in to 600%. Use the Pen tool to click on the back end of the path; it should have a slash icon indicating you are about to start drawing from that anchor point, and drag across the bottom edge to create a curve that matches the template. This make take a few attempts. Hit the Return/Enter key or select another tool to end the path segment.

7. If you did not close the path, select the two end points with the Lasso tool, then select Object > Path > Average > Both to overlap end points.

8. Check to make sure you have a closed path by selecting a Fill color. When the path is closed, change the Fill back to None.

9. Drag the guitar neck you copied earlier back into position over the template, and use Object > Arrange > Send to Back to ensure it is behind your new head. Save your file.

CREATING THE UNDERSIDE OF THE GUITAR NECK

Here is where you may find you need to improvise a little. Sometimes clients cannot think in three dimensions when creating sketches, as is the case of this guitar. You still need to create an underside to the neck face so that it balances with the side of the guitar front. You will then need to overlap both neck paths or shapes. Again, the key here is trying to make the stroke weight as consistent as possible when paths overlap. Remember: the template is just a guide for the drawing.

TOOLKIT TIP If you are nervous about moving the artwork to create the underside of the guitar, another option for those who want a little challenge would be to just create the second shape to overlap the neck, and then use the Pathfinder panel to divide it into the two pieces as you did in the Digital Toolkit Extra exercise in Chapter 9, to make the clock. If you do this, you can skip steps 1 through 3 below.

It is time to create the underside of the guitar neck using the Pen tool and the Direct Selection tool to overlap the paths accurately, as you have already done with the guitar face and side.

1. Using the Selection tool, move the neck face you just created aside to create the underside closed path, or, select the Draw Behind mode in the bottom Tools Panel.

2. Start underneath at the head end with the Pen tool and a 1-point black Stroke and a Fill of None; start heading down the neck, placing anchor points a little beyond the line in the sketch to improvise an edge shape, then work your way back up, as shown in Figure UR3-8.

3. Create a Bézier curve to match the curve on the guitar head, then click to close the path.

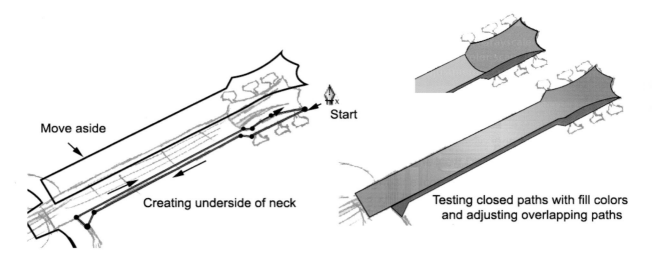

Move aside

Start

Creating underside of neck

Testing closed paths with fill colors
and adjusting overlapping paths

▷ FIGURE UR3-8

Creating the under-side of the neck using the Pen tool with a little impro-vising. Making overlapping paths and adjust-ments and testing closed paths.

4. Use the Direct Selection tool to adjust the paths by deselecting the path, and then select the anchor points and direction lines to refine the path. Use your arrow keys as well.

5. If needed, zoom in to 300% and select open end points with the Lasso tool, then select Object > Path > Average > Both.

6. Check to make sure the path is closed by selecting a Fill color. When the path is closed, change the Fill back to None.

7. Use the Selection tool to move the guitar neck back next to the neck side you just created. Keep saving frequently.

8. With the neck selected with the Direct Selection tool, refine the paths by adjusting the direction lines and anchor points, so the paths start to line up alongside the side piece.

9. Use the Direct Selection tool to select the underside piece, and make adjust-ments as needed to create one path line where they overlap.

10. Use the arrow keys to move anchor points into place. Save frequently.

11. Check the closed paths by applying fill colors to see if any areas are "leaking" through.

12. When you are finished, change the fill back to None and leave the stroke black so you can see the paths. Select View > Outline to see if the overlapping paths are close to looking like a single path. Select View >Preview to toggle back to the original.

13. Group the two paths together for coloring later. If needed, select the neck underside with the selection tool, and then select Object > Arrange > Send to Back to place it underneath the neck face.

14. Keep on saving!

CREATING TUNING KEYS WITH THE PEN OR PENCIL TOOLS AND THE TRANSFORM COMMAND

In this exercise, you can choose to use the Pen and Pencil tools to create the tuning keys. You will use the Selection tool to select and move the keys into position under the neck; use the Option/Alt key to copy the keys to make them consistent. The Transform menu can be used to reverse the object to use it on the other side of the neck.

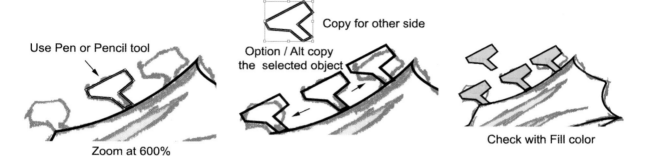

Use Pen or Pencil tool

Zoom at 600%

Copy for other side

Option / Alt copy the selected object

Check with Fill color

▷ FIGURE UR3-9

Creating a tuning key and copying it for consistency.

Now you will create the tuning keys using either the the Pen or Pencil tool, Option/Alt copy for consistency, then use the Transform menu to flip the keys for the other side of the neck. You will only need to make one tuning key. You will use this tuning key to create the rest. Don't worry about matching the template sketch since it's just a guide, and accuracy is more important.

1. You may not need to move aside the neck, but feel free if it is easier. Zoom in to about 600% and either using the Pen or Pencil tool, with a black, 1 point Stroke, and a fill of None, create the middle key of the guitar. Because this is a very small detail, you can be forgiving as to how the key looks.

2. Use the Direct Selection tool to adjust anchor points and direction lines. Use the arrow keys as well.

3. If needed, zoom in to 300% and select any open end points with the Lasso tool, then select Object > Path > Average > Both.

4. Check to make sure the path is closed by selecting a Fill color. When the path is closed, change the Fill back to None, and keep the Stroke black.

5. Using the Selection tool, select the closed path of the tuning key, and hold down the Option/Alt key to drag copies to each side, as shown in Figure UR3-9. Create an additional copy to be reflected for the other side.

6. To reflect the key for the other side, select Object > Transform > Rotate > 180 degrees to flip the object, as shown in Figure UR3-10.

7. Positon the reflected key, then use the Selection tool and the Option/Alt key to make the two additional copies.

8. Use the Selection tool to move the keys into place. To place the keys behind the stroke of the guitar neck, select Object > Arrange > Send to Back. Zoom back to 100% to check your work. There is no need to match the template sketch of the keys underneath. Keep saving frequently.

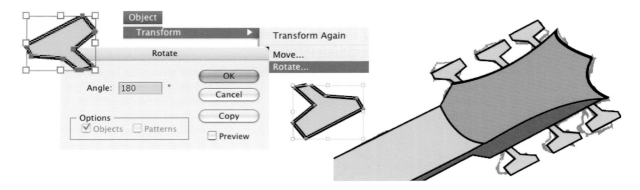

Using the Object menu to rotate the tuning key, copy, and position as shown.

FINSHING DETAILS WITH THE ELLIPSE, PEN, AND PENCIL TOOLS

The hard parts are done, so now it is time to use the Pen, Pencil, and Ellipse tools to provide the finishing details. First you will create the guitar sound hole with the Ellipse tool, then the bridge that holds the strings with the Pen or Pencil tool, and the strings themselves using the Pen tool.

1. Using the Selection tool, move the guitar face and side together over the guitar neck you just created, matching the template for position, then select Object > Arrange > Bring to Front, so these objects are on top of the guitar neck.

2. Use the Direct Selection tool to adjust any paths as needed. Add fill colors to check for accuracy, then select a Fill of None when done.

3. With a Fill of None you can see the template below. Select the Pen or Pencil tool (the Pen tool may work best), and with a 1-point black Stroke and a fill of None, outline the bridge. If you use the Pen tool, create a straight line across the top, then use the Convert Anchor Point tool at the corner to create the curved bottom portion; or with the Pen tool selected, hold down the Option/ Alt key. Use the Direct Selection tool to adjust the curves. Test with a Fill color to make sure the path is closed (Figure UR3-11).

4. To create the sound hole, select the Ellipse tool and click on the hole area. When the dialog box comes up, create a .75-inch circle, and move it below the neck as shown.

5. Select both the sound hole and the bridge, and select Object Arrange > Bring to Front to make sure they are on top of the guitar surface.

6. Add a light fill color to the neck, so you can see how the strings will look, and use the Pen tool with a black, 2-point Stroke and no Fill. Click from the bridge to the upper neck as shown in Figure UR3-11, then press the Return key to end the path, so you can create the next string. Create only three strings, and keep them spaced equally. Remember: this will be used in a much smaller version on a mug, so you do not want many lines. If this were going to be for a poster, then you would create all six strings. You may find that no strings may look better, once you scale it down to fit the mug.

7. Open the Layers panel, and drag the Template layer to the Trash to remove the template. Save the file.

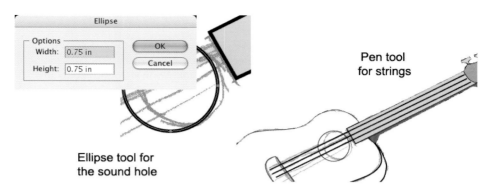

Uusing Pen tool
for string holder

Ellipse tool for
the sound hole

Pen tool
for strings

▷ FIGURE UR3-11

**Creating the string
holder, sound hole,
and strings using
the Pen, Pencil, and
Ellipse tools.**

APPLYING COLOR AND GRADIENTS WITH THE SWATCHES PANEL

You can use the Swatches panel and select from the existing colors, or use the Swatches panel submenu to open up other swatch color libraries, and choose to add the swatches to the main Swatches panel. For instance, choose Open Swatch Library > Nature > Beach; you will find various matching color groups. Command/Ctrl click to select the individual swatches you want to add, and select Add To Swatches from the library's submenu, or drag one or more swatches from the library panel to the Swatches panel. You can also automatically add all the colors from selected artwork to the Swatches panel to create your own customized color group.

Now it is time to play with color. Since the background will be a deep blue, we want to use lighter colors for balance and contrast. For the neck and keys, a yellow or yellow gold may work fine. Use an orange color for the head. Select a deep red for the side of the neck, the bridge, and the side of the guitar. Use a radial gradient of yellow and deep orange for the guitar face. The sound hole will match the blue of the mug itself (Figure UR3-12).

▷ FIGURE UR3-12

**Applying fill colors
and gradients for
the final guitar
illustration.**

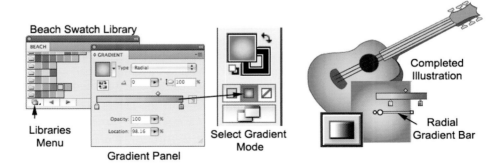

Beach Swatch Library

Libraries
Menu

Gradient Panel

Select Gradient
Mode

Completed
Illustration

Radial
Gradient Bar

TOOLKIT TIP Selecting stroke and fill colors for closed paths can be done with the Direct Selection tool. If you grouped objects together and used the Selection tool to apply color, the color would be applied to all objects instead of to individual objects. If you do not know where the color you have selected is located on the Swatches panel, just select it and the swatch will be highlighted for you.

1. With all objects in position, it is time to fill in color. We will keep the 1-point black stroke for all the objects. You can use the Swatches panel submenu to select Open Swatch Library and choose from various options for colors. Use your own combinations of colors if you like, but keep them light and balanced against the blue color of the mug. To add swatches from any open swatch library to the Swatches panel, just drag them from the library to the Swatches panel.

2. Use the Direct Selection tool to select and apply a yellow Fill color to the keys and neck face (try C5, M0, Y90, or K0).

3. Select the headstock with the Direct Selection tool, and apply an orange fill (try C0, M50, Y100, or K0).

4. Select the side of the neck, the bridge, and the side of the guitar face and apply a reddish color (try C15, M100, Y90, or K10), or try a deep orange tone instead.

TOOLKIT TIP In Illustrator, you can have gradients adjusted to fade to transparent, apply special gradients in real time, and move them around. You select the object, then the Gradient tool, and click. A gradient bar displays to edit the linear or radial gradient effect by dragging and rotating the gradient bar around the selected object. The results are viewed live. The new gradient can be saved in the Swatches panel. You can also make edits from the Appearance panel.

5. To create the radial gradient for the guitar face, use the Gradient panel first (Window > Gradient), and select the colors you want from the Swatches panel; stick with those you have already used for consistency. Drag one to each side of the Gradient panel to create gradient sliders. Select Radial for Type, and adjust the upper gradient slider to preview what it will look like. You can edit the gradient by rotating or dragging the gradient bar, and by adjusting the gradient sliders. To display the bar, select the guitar, then the Gradient tool, and click.

6. Select the guitar face with the Direct Selection tool, and click the Gradient Mode button or the Fill color picker to apply the gradient.

7. For the sound hole, select the circle you created and apply a royal blue color Fill that will be the same used for the mug (try C100, M100, Y25, or K25). If the hole is above the strings you created, select Object > Arrange > Send Backward; this will send it back one sublayer at a time. Keep doing this until it is under the strings but not under the guitar face.

8. After you have chosen and applied all your colors, you can save them as a group (Figure UR3-13). Just select the entire guitar graphic with the Selection tool, and click the New Color Group icon at the bottom of the Swatches panel.

9. Name the color group *Guitar Colors*, click OK, and you will find your color group in the Swatches panel. Save the file.

TOOLKIT TIP To group all your objects together as one guitar graphic, use Select > All, then Object > Group. You would have created a vector graphic that can be scaled to any size. However, remember that grouping objects from several layers combines them all onto one layer, so saving your file first before grouping keeps the layers separate to provide further opportunity for editing.

▷ FIGURE UR3-13

Creating a new color group from the selected guitar graphic.

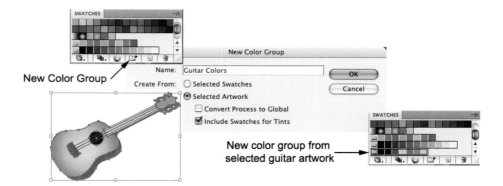

TOOLKIT TIP Not sure what colors to use together? In CS3 and CS4 versions, select the colors using the Color panel, or open swatch libraries to display various color groups that work nicely together. You can also play with the Color Guide panel (refer back to Chapter 7).

SCALING THE LOGO AND SAVING IT AS A SYMBOL

Now that you have spent some time creating you artwork, you can save it as a symbol to reuse whenever the need arises. Saving artwork as symbols allows you to create your own library of reusable, scaleable artwork (Figure UR3-14).

Here is where you can save all your hard work as a symbol for future projects.

1. To make the graphic a little smaller, use the Selection tool to select all objects, then use Object > Transform > Scale > 90%.

2. Select the guitar graphic, then click the New Symbol icon at the bottom of the Symbols panel.

3. Name the symbol *Guitar*, select Graphic, and click OK.

4. You will find a thumbnail of the guitar symbol in the Symbols panel.

TOOLKIT TIP After this project, try dragging the Guitar symbol out and play with the new Graphic Styles panel to observe preset effects applied that could be used as variations of the logo graphic you just created. You can also create your own effect and save it for future projects. In CS5, you can also specify 9-slice scaling in Illustrator so that the symbols scale appropriately when used for specialized media like video.

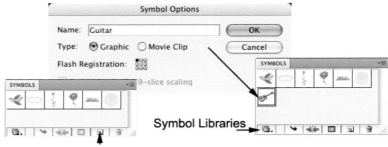

CREATING THE TITLE ON CIRCULAR PATHS

With the guitar graphic complete, you will add the Stage Fright Café name on two separate circular paths to complete the logo. You will use a yellow color or another light color you may have used on the guitar for consistency, and place the text around a 6-inch diameter circle.

First we will create an 8-inch by 8-inch blue background, twice the mug size, to preview the type and logo to see how they will look on the mug, Then, we will put the Stage Fright Café name on a circular path.

1. In the Layers panel, add a new layer and call it *Type*. Move the *Type* layer under the *Guitar Outline* and *Neck* layers to make sure it will appear under the guitar illustration.

2. Select the Rectangle tool, and create an 8-inch square in the same blue that will be used for the mug (we used C100, M100, Y25, and K25).

3. With the Selection tool, select and drag the guitar illustration you created over the background. It should display on top. If it does not, use the Object > Arrange > Bring to Front option.

4. Select the Ellipse tool, click on the artboard, and create a 6-inch circle and a 2-point yellow or other light color Stroke with no Fill to use temporarily as the type path; it will disappear once you start typing. Use the Selection tool to move the circle into position as shown in Figure UR3-15.

5. Select the (Horizontal) Type on a Path tool using 48-point Copperplate Gothic Bold or another bold font in order for it to stand out against a dark background, and type "STAGE FRIGHT." Drag the vertical I-beam with the Direct Selection tool to center the type.

6. To make the other part of the title "Café" line, you need to create a new 6 × 6 inch circular path with the Ellipse tool using same settings. Position it as shown in Figure UR3-15.

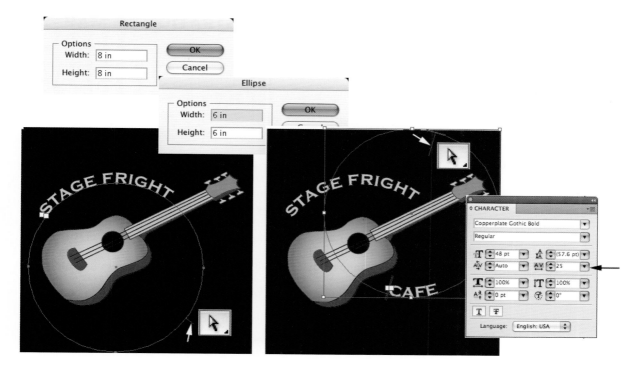

▷ FIGURE UR3-15

Create a background, place the graphic, and create a type path for the title.

7. Select the (Horizontal) Type on a Path tool using the same 48-point Copperplate Gothic Bold Type, or whichever font you chose for the Stage Fright title. Type "CAFÉ"; use the Direct Selection tool to center the I-beam at the bottom of the circle. Drag the I-beam toward the inside of the circle to make sure the type is right side up.

8. To increase separation between characters, you can adjust the Tracking, which is located on the right side of the Character panel. Select the type with the Type on a Path tool, and use 25 as a starting point in the Tracking settings on the Character panel (Figure UR3-15).

9. Make adjustments using the Selection tool to position the type and graphics. Feel free to save and experiment. As you can see, "Café" has been moved up closer to the neck of the guitar for a more pleasing effect.

10. Select all the objects, including the background (Select > All or Command/Ctrl A), and choose Object > Group to combine all objects together.

11. Use the File menu to Save As, and name this Illustrator backup version *CafeMug.ai*.

12. Now to scale the graphic to fit the mug, Select Object > Transform > Scale > 40%. Make sure the Scale Strokes and Effects option is checked for consistency. Click OK.

13. Open the Symbols panel, then Option/Alt copy the graphic with text and background grouped together into the Symbols panel. Name the new symbol Guitar Mug. This prepares the graphic to be mapped to the 3D mug that you are about to create and will be used for the other three artboards.

CREATING A 3-D MUG ILLUSTRATION TO MAP THE LOGO

One of the best features in Illustrator is the ability to create 3-D objects and map 2-D objects to 3-D surfaces (see Chapter 8, Toolkit Extra). Since the logo has been completed, you can show your client what it would look like on a mug. This feature will be a great asset for those who venture into the field of package design. Before placing the graphic onto a 3-D object, it has to be made into a symbol.

TOOLKIT TIP When using the 3-D Revolve effect, draw half of the intended object. In this case, the width of the mug is 3 inches, so you would draw horizontal lines at 1.5 inches before applying the effect. The height is the axis that the effect will use to revolve around and should be drawn at full length. You can adjust the size of the 3-D effect using the Selection tool and the bounding box's resizing handles. To remove guides, hold down the Ctrl key on your Mac and click, or right-click on the guide in Windows. Select Undo Ruler Guides or Hide Guides to temporarily hide the guides.

Now that the logo is created, it is time to see how it will look on a 3-D mug surface.

1. Make sure the *CafeMug.ai* file is open and the logo selected with the Selection tool, then move the logo so that there will be enough space to create the mug full size at about 5 inches tall.

2. Leave the logo on the artboard as a guide. The colors used in the logo should display in the Swatches panel, and the graphic itself is safely stored in the Symbols panel if you delete it by mistake.

3. Select View > Rulers > Show Rulers and drag two vertical guides, one to the 4-inch mark and another at 2.5 inches to set up the lines for the mug. Then drag two horizontal guides, placing them 4 inches apart.

4. To create the blue mug, make sure Fill is set to None, then select the blue that you used for the sound hole in the guitar from the Swatches panel for the Stroke color. Use a 4-point Stroke weight. You can also reverse this and have a Fill color blue with a stroke of None. Either way will work.

5. Select the Line tool, then while holding the Shift key down, draw a vertical, 4-inch line along the vertical guideline at the 4-inch mark; then draw two horizontal lines at either end to the 2.5-inch guideline; hold the Shift key to ensure the lines are straight (see Figure UR3-16).

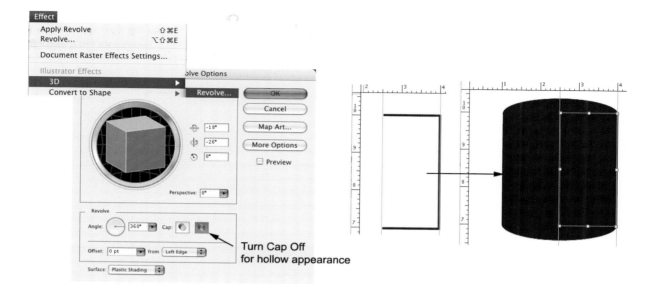

Turn Cap Off
for hollow appearance

▷ FIGURE UR3-16

Create a 3-D mug of royal blue color by applying 3-D effect using the 3-D revolve function.

TOOLKIT TIP You can also try using the Pen tool instead, while holding down the Shift key, for straight lines; adjust with the Direct Selection tool. This will eliminate the need to join end points.

6. Use the Lasso tool to select the corners, then select Object > Path > Join > Corner to make sure the corners are connected. Make sure the path is still selected.

7. Select Effect > 3-D > Revolve to display the 3-D Revolve Options dialog box. Select the Turn Cap Off for Hollow Appearance icon to make the mug appear hollow inside, and leave all other settings at their defaults.

8. Click OK to apply the effect.

TOOLKIT TIP Before selecting OK to apply the 3-D effect, you will notice that a warning may appear stating that spot colors will be converted to process colors. This will have no effect on the outcome of this project; the 3-D effect is only used to give the client an idea of what the final product will look like.

PROBLEM If the mug cylinder displays as broken shapes, the paths are not connected. If it is taking considerable time to apply the effect, make sure the Fill and Stroke boxes do not both have color: one has to not be displaying any color. If you find this, cancel the operation, adjust, and apply again. The revolve process may actually be faster with the Fill color applied and a Stroke of None.

MAPPING THE LOGO TO THE MUG SHAPE

Once artwork is converted to a symbol in the Symbols panel, it can be mapped around any 3-D object you create. The Appearance panel is used to display a hierarchy of fills, strokes, graphic styles, and applied effects. To edit 3-D objects, the object must be selected so its attributes and properties are displayed in the Appearance panel. You can then double-click on the 3-D item in the Appearance panel to make changes to the object, including mapping artwork, lighting, and object properties. The key to having the mapping operation work is to make sure the artwork to be mapped is saved as a symbol first.

Now you will map the logo to the mug surface.

1. To apply or map the logo to the mug surface, double-click the 3-D Revolve item in the Appearance panel (Window > Appearance) to display the 3-D Revolve Options dialog box again. Drag the window to the right side so you can view the mapping effect.

2. Click the Map Art button. Do not worry if the color on the mug shape disappears.

3. Use the arrows to find the surface that matches Figure UR3-17; it will display as a light gray gridline on the right side.

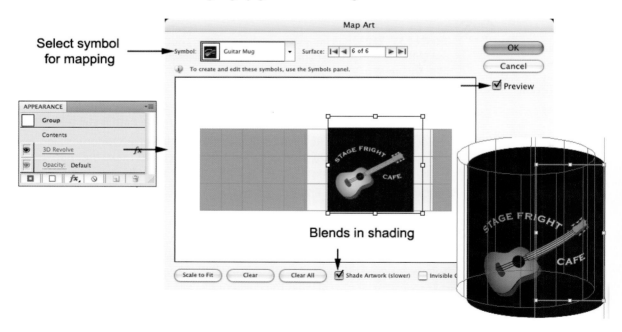

▷ FIGURE UR3-17

Mapping the guitar label onto a 3-D representation of the mug.

4. Make sure the Preview and the Shade Artwork boxes are checked to display the text correctly, along with the lighting properties.

5. In the Map Art dialog box, select the new symbol you created from the Symbols drop-down menu, and position the bounding box to align the logo while observing the preview to check the effect. Do not worry about the guides created by the Ellipse tool for your type; they will not display on the mug.

6. If you make a mistake, select the Clear button on the dialog box, and repeat the previous steps until you position it the way you want it. Select OK when you are satisfied.

PROBLEM If the logo in your mug appears faint, the Shade Artwork box in the Map Art dialog box was not checked to display the text correctly.

7. Select OK, then OK again when you are done; observe your work. Pretty cool, huh?

8. To add a handle for your mug shape, select the New Art Has Basic Appearance icon in the Appearance panel to turn off the 3-D effects and start a new art shape, (Figure UR3-18). It toggles on and off.

9. Make sure the mug is not selected, and use a Fill color of None and a 25-point blue Stroke. Create a path for the handle using one of the drawing tools and the Smooth tool.

10. Use the Direct Selection tool for any path and anchor point adjustments that need to be made. When you have finished, select the mug and the handle, and group everything together (Object > Group).

11. Double-click 3-D Revolve (Fx) again in the Appearance panel, and play with different views and lighting styles by selecting More Options in the 3-D Revolve Options dialog box.

12. Save the file in your *Unit 3 Review* folder. Time for coffee!

▷ FIGURE UR3-18

Use the Appearance panel to reset for new artwork to add the handle to the mug for the final 3-D project.

EDITING THE LOGO ARTWORK WITH MULTIPLE ARTBOARDS

The Multiple Artboards feature allows a designer to create up to 100 multiple art-boards to show a potential client various sizes and types of media that the artwork created can be used for. One of the nice benefits to this new feature is it allows a designer to make variations of the artwork to show to a client with ease, and they can be rotated, edited, and printed individually for a potential client. They are also useful for creating a variety of things such as multiple page PDF's, printed pages with different sizes or different elements, etc. Designers can use and save multiple artboards within one document, or export each artboard to its own file. Double-clicking the Artboard tool opens the Artboard Options dialog box, and allows you to move, resize, and edit artboards, with one artboard selected at a time. You can adjust dimensions of a selected artboard using by using the Artboard tool (Shift + O), or the Control panel. You can also have independent ruler guides set up for each artboard to help with your sizing. Each artboard is numbered for easy reference; each can also be given custom names. In CS5, the new Artboards panel helps you to keep track of multiple artboards, reorder and rearrange artboards, create new artboards and duplicate artboards. You can paste objects at a particular location on the artboard and paste artwork on all artboards at the same location using the new Paste in Place and Paste on All Artboards options. Multiple art-boards can be saved as individual artboards with an Illustrator extension, available in the Illustrator Options dialog box. You will resize the three remaining art-boards for a CD front cover, business card, and direct mail piece (Figure UR3-19). With the graphic already saved as a symbol, you can copy it over and resize or edit as needed.

▷ FIGURE UR3-19

Displaying edited versions of artwork logo on multiple art-boards resized with the Artboard tool for specific uses.

1. Before you resize the remaining three artboards, make sure rules and guides displayed. To have the artboard rulers display for each selected artboard, choose View > Show Artboard Rulers. When you click on an artboard, the ruler guides should show for that artboard. Make sure Smart Guides is also checked in the View menu (View > Smart Guides).

2. To create the CD cover dimensions, with the Artboard tool selected, click on the number 2 artboard to the right and notice the ruler guides now display for this artboard. Drag for the CD cover using the ruler and smart guides, which will display as you drag so that you have a square measuring 4.75 by 4.75 inches. Notice the bleed follows along with the changes you make.

3. To create the direct mail piece, click on the number 3 artboard and drag to create a 4.25 Height x 5.5 Width dimension.

4. To create the business card, click on the number 4 artboard and create a 2.0 Height and 3.5 Width.

5. You can move artboards around, *not* with the Selection tool, but with the Artboard tool. Click on the direct mail piece and drag underneath the CD cover, then click on the business card and drag under the mail piece to maximize the work space.

6. To make the CD cover, select the flat graphic with the Selection tool, not the final mug graphic, if you still have it displayed and Option/ALT copy it to the CD cover piece. Hold down the Shift key to adjust proportionately to adjust slightly larger than the bleed area.

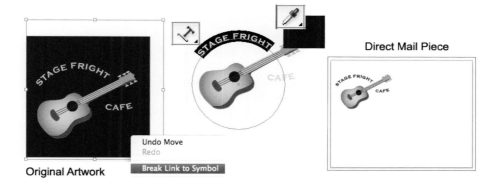

▷ FIGURE UR3-20

Using multiple artboards to create variations of artwork for a potential client.

7. Symbols can be edited by breaking the linked graphic components. To create the direct mail piece, open the Symbols panel (Window > Symbols) and drag out the Guitar Mug symbol from the Symbols panel onto the direct mail artboard or near to it.

8. Here you are going to remove the blue background from the symbol by selecting the entire graphic with the Selection tool, then CTRL + click (Mac) or right-click (PC), and select Break Link to Symbol to create individual components of the artwork (Figure UR3-20).

9. Click outside the artwork to deselect, and then use the Direct Selection tool to select the blue background and drag away from the graphic.

10. To change the yellow text color to match the blue background, select the Type on Path tool and highlight the Stage Fright title.

11. Select the Eyedropper tool and click on the blue background to change the color of the type. Choose the Selection tool and click outside the graphic to deselect and make sure the type is the deep blue color.

12. Repeat the same process with the Café type line using the Type on Path tool and the Eyedropper tool (Figure UR3-20).

13. Select the new artwork with the Selection tool and choose Object > Group. Drag into Direct mail piece, and then resize holding down the Shift key and dragging inward. Adjust for space in the top left corner.

14. You may find you may need to readjust the type to bring it closer to the guitar. Click on the type path with the Direct Selection tool making sure the path vertical I-beams display and not the direction lines. Adjust using the arrow keys on your keyboard.

15. To create a new symbol with the new changes, drag the graphic into the Symbols panel and name it Café Logo as another variation of the original graphic.

16. For the business card, resize the graphic and Option/ALT copy it to drag it into the artboard. Feel free to experiment with the type. You may want to resize the type only to make it 10-point size as shown. You can always remove the circular type paths and type in the title as horizontal text, your call. You can use the Artboard tool to draw additional artboards to show other variations of the same logo. With CS5, you can now go in and label each artboard to keep track of each one, then use the Artboards panel to click each artboard and play. Go ahead and experiment!

17. Save the file when you are satisfied with your efforts.

THE SEPARATIONS PREVIEW PANEL

In Illustrator, you can preview CMYK color separations and overprinting using the new Separations Preview panel. Previewing separations on your monitor lets you preview spot color objects in your document, and check for rich blacks or process black (K) ink mixed with color inks for increased opacity and richer color. The panel also checks for overprinting when the color CMYK plates are laid on top of one another to observe blending and transparency effects for the particular output device. In this exercise you should only find CMYK ink plates.

To preview your artwork in CMYK in the Separations Preview panel:

1. Select the Separations Preview panel (Window > Separations Preview) then select the Overprint Preview icon to observe CMYK plate effects. The CMYK plates display as separate layers on the panel (Figure UR3-21).

2. To hide the separation ink on screen, click the eye icon to the left of the separation name, and then click again to view the separation. You can see what the artwork looks like at various stages of laying out CMYK plates, or without a particular color.

3. To view all process plates at once, click the CMYK icon.

4. To return to normal view, deselect Overprint Preview.

5. Save the entire file with multiple artboards as CafeLogo.eps, selecting the version of Illustrator you are currently using. This would be the file format you would use to give the file to a commercial printer, although many commercial printers are accepting native Adobe formats as technology improves.

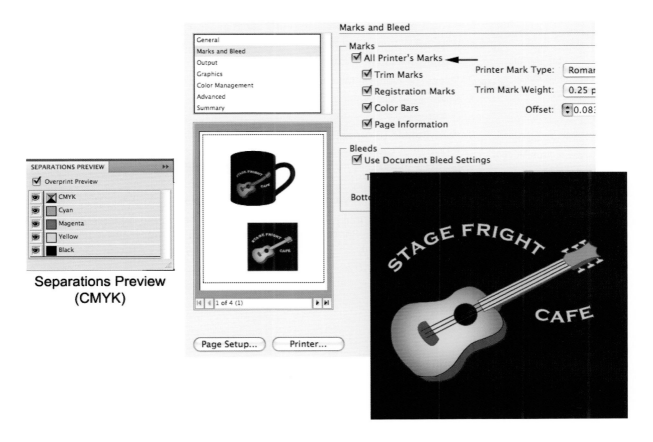

▷ FIGURE UR3-21

Completed graphic ready with multiple artboards for printing as a soft proof to show the client.

SAVING AND PRINTING MULTIPLE ARTBOARDS

When saving multiple artboards you can save, as you have been doing, as one document or as multiple individual documents, which will display as multiple pages in Bridge. You can also export a range of different artboards, or choose individual pages. Saving your work as PDF file will display multiple artboards within the same document name, or you can set to save as individual artboards.

When you create a document with multiple artboards, you can print the document in a variety of ways. You can ignore the artboards and print everything on one page, or you can print each artboard as an individual page. When you print artboards as individual pages, you can choose to print all artboards, or a range of artboards. To print all artboards as separate pages, select File > Print > All. You can see all the pages listed in the preview area in the lower left corner of the Print dialog box. To print a subset of artboards as separate pages, select Range, and specify the artboards to print. To print the artwork on all the artboards together on a single page, select Ignore Artboards. If the artwork extends past the boundaries of the page, you can scale or tile it. You can also specify other print options, and then click Print.

Need additional fun computer graphics tutorials and info, and an additional look at the projects you'll be creating in this book? Check out my Artist's Digital Toolkit website at: **http://www.digitoolkit.com**

Here you'll print all the completed artboards as separate pages for the client.

1. With the multiple artboards saved as CafeLogo.eps in Illustrator's current format, select File > Print.

2. Select the General tab on the left side, then select the printer you are using.

3. Make sure All is selected under Copies and leave the rest as defaults for now (Figure UR3-21).

4. Print the file using default printer's marks, as if you were going to show it to a potential client as a soft proof (File > Print > Marks and Bleed, then check Printer's Marks (Figure UR3-21). We'll cover more of these settings in depth in future chapters.

5. Select Print to print your copies as separate pages.

6. To print as additional PDF's select File > Print > then in the General tab, choose Adobe PDF as the Printer, print All copies to print all pages, and leave all other settings as default.

UNIT 3 REVIEW
Create guitar graphic from sketch.
Set up logo for mug.
Create 3-D version of promotional mug
with shading and lighting applied.
Edit artowrk on multiple artboards for
various uses.

▷ FIGURE UR3-22

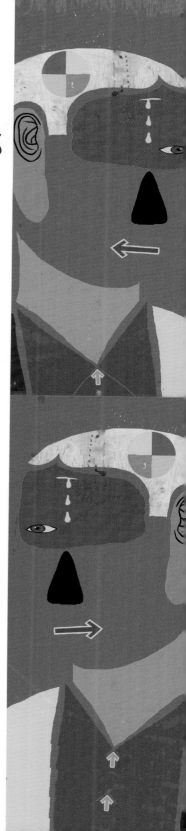

CHAPTER

11

InDesign Fundamentals

CHAPTER OBJECTIVES: To understand the importance of InDesign CS5's function as a desktop publishing program, in this chapter you will:

▷ Learn procedures to set up preferences for special settings with InDesign documents before bringing in graphic and text objects.

▷ Layout guidelines for accurate placement of text and graphics.

▷ Place graphics and format type characters and frames using the Control panel and InDesign menus.

▷ Format spacing within a text frame and align vertically using the Text Frame Options dialog box.

▷ Apply color to selected type and stroke of frames.

▷ Save as the original document and as a template for future editing.

▷ ADVANCED USERS: Preflight, package, and print the final document for press.

▷ DIGITAL TOOLKIT EXTRA: Create a desktop photo calendar using tables.

InDesign is a high-end desktop publishing program used in today's print industry. Desktop publishing programs allow designers to bring in text and graphic objects or elements from other applications and assemble and lay out these items accurately inside boxes called **frames** in an organized manner. InDesign is used to create and prepare documents, brochures, and books for commercial printing. This chapter will focus on the basics of InDesign, techniques to create documents for press, and the importance of layout using text and graphics.

Need additional fun computer graphics tutorials and info, and an additional look at the projects you'll be creating in this book? Check out my Artist's Digital Toolkit website at: **http://www.digitoolkit.com**

THE INDESIGN ENVIRONMENT

InDesign is Adobe's premiere desktop publishing program used in the printing industry (Figure 11-1). Documents saved for printing using InDesign documents have an **INDD extension** to identify them. Here are some key components that make up the InDesign work space environment.

• The Menu bar provides commands to create and edit your documents. In the Menu bar, the Type and Object menus allow the designer to make modifications to text and graphic items and adjust the formatting of paragraphs, characters, and other elements within the page itself.

• InDesign's Layout, View, and Window menus allow you to create and navigate between various layout spaces, display different document views and guides, and access panels and special windows.

• The Tools panel contains the tools you need to create and lay out your document. As you select a paticular tool, its options are displayed in the Control Panel above the Tools panel.

• InDesign panels provide commands and functions to help you modify your projects. As with all Adobe products in the CS5 suite, panels can be docked and minimized to conserve work space and expanded when needed by clicking on the panel icon.

• The Application bar provides a tabbed interface for displaying multiple images, and a Workspaces menu (Essentials default) for retrieving essential information like basic tutorials, and for choosing specific media work space settings.

• In the document window, you can view the **Pasteboard,** which is a space to store graphics and text outside the document page area; you can change the viewing size, measure with rulers, and navigate between pages.

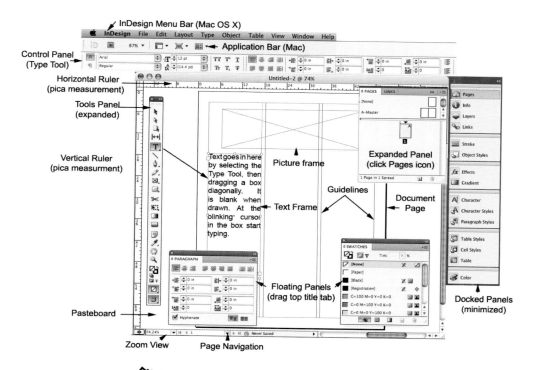

▷ FIGURE 11-1

**InDesign CS5
work space.**

TOOLKIT TIP Windows can read InDesign documents created on a Mac, and Macs can read InDesign documents created in Windows. Due to differences in fonts, it is wise to stay with the same operating system in which you create your document to avoid any problems later. For outputting to a commercial press, create your work on the Mac if possible for consistency; most commercial presses use Macs.

DESKTOP PUBLISHING VERSUS WORD PROCESSING

There is a difference between a **desktop publishing program** and a **word processing program**. To create documents of formatted text for reports, short articles, or single page brochures with fixed inserted graphics that will be distributed in a very small volume (with the exception of electronic distribution over the Internet), a word processing program works best; but they are usually not suitable for printing on a commercial press, where high-volume printed material is needed for distribution for home or office use. Desktop publishing involves placing items from a more diverse group of source applications into boxes for text and images called *frames*. These **frames** serve as "containers" that can be easily resized, repositioned, reshaped, combined, and in the case of text, linked into other frames on other pages. When you look at a newsletter, articles may be continued to other pages to lead the reader on to other articles. Creating documents for mass production, advertisements, books, and other multipage documents is best done using a desktop publishing program. It becomes a place to lay out and reposition items and edit and format contents in a more controlled work space ready for publishing.

TOOLKIT TIP When creating documents with lots of text, it is easier to use your word processor and then import the text into your InDesign document. Although you can type in InDesign, it is a lot slower and works best with single paragraphs.

MEASURING IN INCHES AND POINTS

Desktop publishing and word processing programs use points as a default measurement for sizing type fonts and spacing between characters and lines of type. Although many designers lay out text and graphic items using fractions and inches as standards of measurement, sometimes, on a commercial press, the preferred units of measurement are picas and points. Font sizes and spacing are measured in points; because 72 points is the equivalent of one inch, and 36 points equals one-half inch, you can see why using points is a more precise method of measuring for the smaller measurements. This will be covered more in detail in the following chapter.

THE INDESIGN CS5 TOOLS PANEL

Look at the Tools panel: you should be familiar with some of these tools since some are the same as those used previously in Photoshop and Illustrator. Tools with a small black triangle display other tools when held down with the mouse (Figure 11-2).

▷ FIGURE 11-2

InDesign CS5 Tools panel.

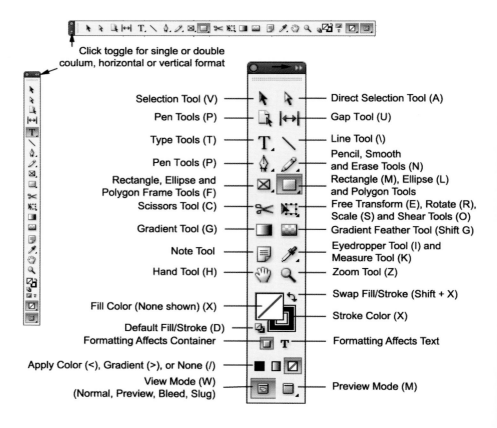

The InDesign CS5 Tools panel includes a variety of handy tools.

- The **Selection tool** allows you to select entire objects, and the **Direct Selection** tool is used when selecting points on a path or contents within a frame. You can use these tools when you want to resize, move, or select the item.

- The **Gap Tool**, new in InDesign CS5, provides a quick way to adjust the size of the gap between multiple items, or align several items at once.

- **Pen tools** create complex paths that require precision, and the **Pencil tool** provides free-form paths.

- The **Scissors tool**, **Erase tool,** and **Smooth tool** are used for editing paths.

- The **Scale tool**, **Free Transform tool**, and **Rotate tool** all change the size of an object or its point of origin, and the **Shear tool** changes an object's perspective.

- The **Type tools** create various shaped text boxes and type on selected paths.

- The **Rectangle Frame**, **Ellipse Frame**, and **Polygon Frame tools** create frames as containers to insert text and graphics. The **Line**, **Rectangle**, **Ellipse**, and **Polygon tools** are used to draw basic shapes.

- The **Eyedropper tool** samples color, and the **Gradient tool** and **Gradient Feather tool** blends one color into another.

- The **Measure tool** measures the distance between points along a path.

- The **Zoom tool** magnifies the document view, and the **Hand tool** is used to move the page document.

- The **Note tool** allows designers to leave messages to themselves and to one another when working on a team project to help with work flow.

CREATING FRAMES

With InDesign, as with any desktop publishing program, the designer creates a text box, picture box, or path before placing text or images in the document. InDesign uses frames as the containers for type and graphics (Figure 11-3). Some considerations when working with frames follow.

- You can select the Type tool (T) and diagonally drag a frame to start typing inside.

- Text and graphics can be put in either container, frame or shape. The Frame tools display a nonprinting X inside the shape. In the graphics industry, a box with an X has traditionally been used to show the location of an image or graphic.

- The empty frames created by the Rectangle, Ellipse, and Polygon shape tools are generally used for text inserts, although with InDesign, both containers can be used for type or graphics.

- Understanding where to place type (empty container) and graphics (container with an X) can help with your work flow by communicating specific elements to team members.

▷   FIGURE 11-3

**Creating various
frames that can be
used for type
and graphics.**

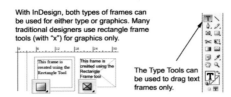

With InDesign, both types of frames can
be used for either type or graphics. Many
traditional designers use rectangle frame
tools (with "x") for graphics only.

This frame is
created using the
Reectangle Tool

This frame is
created using the
Rectangle
Frame tool

The Type Tools can
be used to drag text
frames only.

DISPLAYING PANELS AND THE WINDOW MENU

For the convenience of providing additional space on your desktop, InDesign displays its panels as tabs, which you can click to expand or make active from the
side as needed, then click again to contract when you are done, as has been done
with the rest of the CS5 suite of applications. Sometimes when you click on a
panel, it will be grouped with others for convenience. You can select a panel by its
title bar or tab and pull it onto your document work space. This process is called
undocking, and the panel becomes free-floating. When you have finished using
the free-floating panel, drag it back to the edge of the screen to *dock* it, or click
on the X button to close it (Figure 11-4). When you see two small arrows, as in the
Stroke panel, you can click the arrows to expand or contract the panel.

▷   FIGURE 11-4

**Displaying and
minimizing
(docking) panels
and using the
Window menu.**

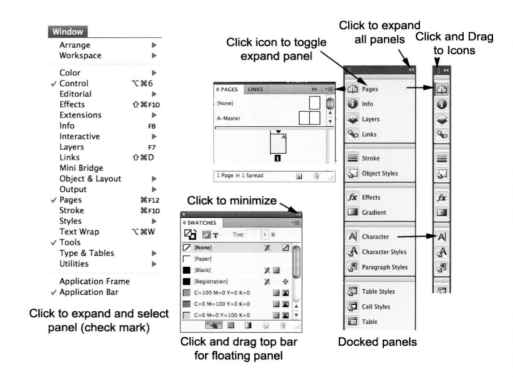

The Window menu also provides toggled check marks to expand or contract panels
to the side of the desktop screen. If a panel is not displayed or is contracted, then
the check mark is not displayed next to the panel name. Panels that are displayed

or are expanded show a check mark to indicate they are active. In InDesign, the Window menu allows you to save a specified work space, choose preset buttons for web pages, printed documents, or for creating interactive PDF's, and to display and hide documents. To create the work space, set up those panels you need, and save them for future use. As mentioned with other Adobe products, InDesign has an Application bar that provides a tabbed interface for displaying multiple images, and a Work spaces menu (Essentials default) for choosing preset work space settings, or you can select panels and save your own customized workspace. Function keys, which are usually the F function keys, can be used to display or hide the panels as well. For instance, the F5 key toggles to display or hide the Swatches panel.

THE CONTROL PANEL AND PAGES PANEL

The two panels you will use most often are the *Control panel* and the *Pages panel* (Figure 11-5). The **Control panel** is context sensitive, and it displays the most frequently used commands for a selected item or tool. With the selected frame box containing type, select the Type tool and highlight the type to be edited, and you will find frequent commands to format selected type. Click on the Rectangle tool and drag a diagonal box on the document, and you will find coordinates and formatting commands displayed. Functions that are displayed in the Control panel will vary, depending on the selected object or tool.

The **Pages panel** provides information about pages and allows you to control the layout of pages, spreads, and master pages. When you set up a document and the Facing Pages option is *not* checked, the Pages panel displays pages as individual pages and you can view thumbnail representations of your work on each page. When the Facing Pages option is checked when creating a new document, the pages are put together as left and right pages and is called a *spread.* The Facing Pages option is useful in projects such as books, in which you are creating spreads; otherwise, leave this option unchecked when you create a new document.

▷ FIGURE 11-5

InDesign Control panel and Pages panel.

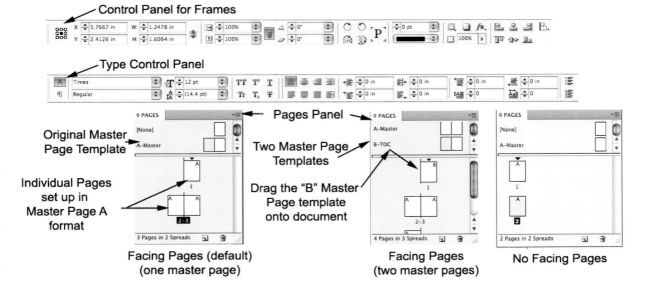

Master pages contain items that repeat from page to page, such as headers, footers, page numbers, and graphic elements. Master page elements appear in the same location on every page, creating layout consistency from page to page. For instance, the layout in this text has master pages set up for the table of contents, chapter introduction page, chapter body, glossary pages, and so forth. You will use the Pages panel more in the following chapter.

TYPOGRAPHY BASICS

When an intended reader receives an advertisement, magazine, or coupon, it only takes a split second for that person to decide to read it or put it in the trash. Choosing the right typeface to enhance the graphic elements can help with the success of that document. The terms *typeface* and *font* are used interchangeably; however, the term **type family** refers to a collection of all the related typefaces, such as Arial, Arial Black, and Arial Narrow. Type should create an appealing path that leads the reader in; it should also play a supporting role for graphic elements, and it helps determine the personality of a document.

What follows is a brief review of typography terms we discussed back in Chapter 2 (see also Figure 11-6).

▷ FIGURE 11-6

Typography basics and terminology.

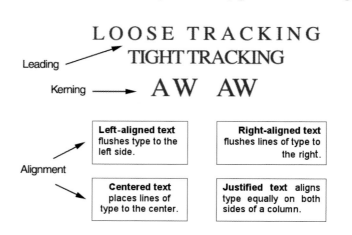

Arial Narrow, **Arial Rounded MT Bold,** Arial, and **Arial Black,** are all part of the same typeface or font family.

Times Roman is a serif type with extensions.
Arial is a sans-serif type without extensions.
Brush Script MT is a script type used in invitations.
Papyrus is used as a decorative type.
●ⓘ✻▶︎🚲✔ Symbol type (Webdings)

LOOSE TRACKING
Leading ➝ TIGHT TRACKING
Kerning ➝ AW AW

Alignment

| **Left-aligned text** flushes type to the left side. |
| **Centered text** places lines of type to the center. |

| **Right-aligned text** flushes lines of type to the right. |
| **Justified text** aligns type equally on both sides of a column. |

- A *family* is a group of fonts that share a basic character construction, like the Arial family, which comprises Arial Black, Arial Narrow, and Arial Alternative. This collection of characters is like having your family of uncles, aunts, cousins, and grandparents over for the holidays.

- A *font* or *typeface* is an individual member of a type family, such as Arial Black or Arial Narrow, both members of the Arial type family.

- Type falls into two main categories: *serif* and *sans serif.* Serif type displays footlike extensions at the top and bottom, like Times Roman or Minion; sans serif has no extensions, like Arial or Helvetica. Sans serif works nicely as a starting point for headlines and subheadlines, whereas serif type is easier to read in the body of a document.

- A font *size* is the measurement of type in points instead of inches (1 point = 1/72 inch). When you open an InDesign document, the default size is usually 12 points.

- Unlike other word processing and desktop publishing programs, InDesign does not allow you to create "fake" typefaces by clicking a bold or italic style button. When you specify a bold or italic typestyle, you are using an actual bold or italic font, not a stylized imitation.

- *Tracking* adjusts the spacing between characters and words. Adjusting the tracking of words too tightly in a paragraph can make it difficult to read, whereas adjusting too loosely can create "rivers" of white spacing in a paragraph. Justified alignment of type can also be the culprit, creating rivers of white.

- *Kerning* is a technique used for pairs of characters in titles or headlines that may need to be brought closer together for a more consistent look.

- *Leading* refers to the spacing between lines of text. Usually the default leading is 120 percent of the letter size for most documents. In long articles or newsletters, less space between lines of text tends to darken the document, whereas more space will lighten it up. The end result of what kind of message or mood you want to convey will determine how you will set up your text and what fonts you will need.

- The style or arrangement of setting type is called type *alignment.* Left aligned flushes type to the left and is easy to read, right aligned flushes type to the right side, as you might see in return addresses or columns of numbers to be added. Centered lines of type are used in some headlines or titles, and justified alignment places text equally on the left and right sides in a column.

TOOLKIT TIP To display text formatting controls in the Control Panel, a text frame needs to be selected in the document.

WELCOME AND HELP SCREENS

When you launch InDesign CS5, a Welcome Screen will display by default to provide choices to set up a new document, start one from a premade template to get your creative juices flowing, or open an existing document. You will also find links to tutorials in the basics of using InDesign CS5, Cool Extras for additional resources and features in InDesign CS5, and a What's New link to the Adobe website to gather more resources. Like the Help menu in version CS5 described in

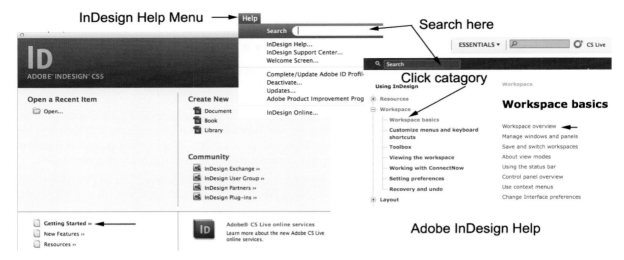

InDesign Help Menu

Search here

Click catagory

Workspace basics

Adobe InDesign Help

InDesign Welcome Screen

▷ FIGURE 11-7

InDesign Welcome screen and Help screens.

Illustrator and Photoshop, choosing Help in InDesign opens the Adobe Help and Support Center to search for tutorials, resources, and additional expert information and resources online, including documentation and community support from peers (Figure 11-7). There are also links to watch video how-to clips. You can select Help > InDesign Help and access various ways to get help, inlcuding an index, a search field, and various tutorial and web links.

Let us view a tutorial in using the Adobe Help Center for a quick review:

1. Launch InDesign. When the CS5 Welcome Screen comes up, select the *Getting Started link*, then browse around to get an overview of the many resources Adobe provides, including a link for a video tutorial in using the help services and about Adobe's Community Help Center. (To display the Welcome Screen, you can click on the Help menu in InDesign CS5 and choose Welcome Screen.)

2. Select Help > InDesign Help to bring up the Adobe Help Center.

3. From the list of categories select *Workspace > Workspace basics* and look at the first two links to get a feel for the InDesign desktop.

4. Get comfortable with this powerful feature, and feel free to browse around some of the other tutorials.

TOOLKIT TIP New in Adobe CS5 applications is the feature CS Review located on the Application bar, where a designer can sign in and have their work reviewed live by potential clients, fellow design team members, or their peers within the graphics community. It provides a simple way for creative professionals to be more productive by incorporating review feedback directly into their Creative Suite applications.

CLIENT ASSIGNMENT: Creating a Coupon Advertisement

Maria Dilorne wants to create a direct mail coupon for her pizzeria business. She contacts you and discusses the basic layout; it consists of an image of a pizza loaded with toppings surrounded by cheese and vegetables, the restaurant name, some text with the phone number underneath, and four coupons to entice customers to come visit the restaurant. The coupon will be included inside a direct mail envelope, which includes coupons from other businesses in the community. It will be mass mailed to the surrounding area, so Maria will not need to have the customer address on the back side. She also mentions that she would like a template made so that all she has to do is change the specials on the coupon and keep the original layout. You tell her you will have the ad completed by the end of the week for her to look over (Figure 11-8).

▷ FIGURE 11-8

Completed coupon advertisement.

ACTIONS ITEMS OVERVIEW

- You will need to create a custom size coupon measuring in inches.
- You will place and accurately position a graphic for the advertisement.
- Coupons will be created using dashed outlines from the Stroke panel for cutting edges.
- You will enter text and format using the Control panel's character formatting function.
- The text will need to be centered and justified using the Text Frame Options function.
- For displaying the "cents" as smaller type in the pricing, you will create superscripts for emphasis.
- You will learn to add and apply new swatches using Pantone Process colors.
- A graphic will be placed behind the entire coupon to become the new background and add a sense of warmth.
- A template will be created for future editing.

DESIGN TIP

When creating coupons or any advertisement for a client, it is important to understand the target market to make sure the ad reaches the intended audience for maximum success. How the ad will be distributed and the volume that will be generated also need to be considered.

SETTING UP THE COUPON ADVERTISEMENT

After discussion with the client and designing thumbnails and roughs, a designer should have a pretty good idea of what the final project will look like in the overall layout of the piece. Before laying out text and graphic items, preferences need to be set, and the final size and margins need to be set up.

CREATING AND ORGANIZING FOLDERS FOR OUTPUT

When you are going to be sending your materials to a commercial printer or web designer, you need to keep all documents, images, and fonts required in folders to be included with your InDesign document. This is crucial: without these elements, images may not print at full resolution and fonts may be substituted. It is also just as important to keep these folders with your InDesign document on your hard drive or on the same portable media, like a flash drive or final CD. All changes or saves to files will be made in these folders. Consider this as packing a suitcase to make sure you have everything you need for where you are going. Later on, you will be introduced to InDesign's ultility for packaging document files.

TOOLKIT TIP InDesign has a series of utilities for checking links and spelling and for packaging images, text, documents, and fonts; these are covered in the Advanced portion of this chapter, but it is still a good habit to make sure you are organized before you start your project. You will see how efficient InDesign can be when preparing documents for press.

Here you will create a folder to place your document and other folders in one area.

1. On your drive, locate the *Chapter 11* folder in your *Toolkit > InDesign* folder.

2. Create a new folder called *Coupon* (File > New Folder) that will become your main folder for your InDesign coupon project.

3. Create the folders *Images*, *Fonts*, and *Text* inside the *Coupon* folder. Now you have all the "suitcases" that you will need for your trip to the press.

4. Here is a look at your directory structure: *Toolkit > InDesign > Chapter 11 > Coupon > Images/Fonts/Text* (Figure 11-9). The InDesign coupon document project will also be saved inside the *Coupon* folder.

5. Drag the Pizza and Parchment image files that are inside the *Chapter 11* folder from the book CD to the desktop, then drag them to the new *Images* folder you just created inside the *Coupon* folder. Now you are organized.

▷ FIGURE 11-9

Creating images, fonts, and text folders inside the main *Coupon* folder for press.

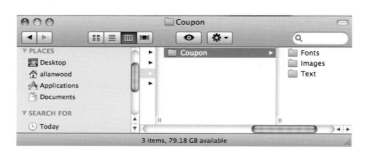

PREFERENCE SETTINGS

Setting preferences provides a convenient way to adjust settings and parameters in your work environment to work on your document productively. There are two types of preferences: **application-level preferences** affect work on all documents, and **document-level preferences** affect only the active document. When you change preferences with InDesign launched but no document open, you are changing the application preferences. When you change preferences with a document open, those changes apply only to that document. Preferences in InDesign should always be set up first before creating a new document. In Mac OS X, the InDesign Application menu is where you would set Preferences; in Windows, Preferences are set in the Edit menu. The settings in Preferences will still remain, even when you turn off the computer, until you go in to change them again.

Here you will set up the measurements preferences in your coupon ad (Figure 11-10).

1. Launch InDesign. If the Welcome Screen appears, select the Close button.

2. In Mac OS X, select InDesign > Preferences > Units & Increments; in Windows, use Edit > Preferences > Units and Increments.

3. Change the Ruler Units for Horizontal and Vertical document measurements to Inches.

4. Leave all other defaults as shown. Select OK.

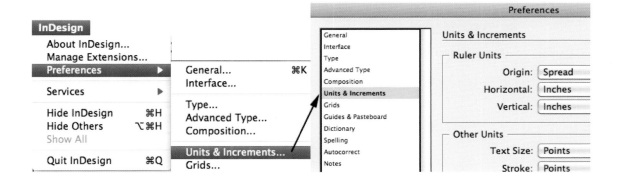

▷ FIGURE 11-10

Setting InDesign document preferences for Ruler Units to display in inches.

THE FILE MENU

The **File menu** is where you save, print, place text and graphics, and export to special files; it is also where you determine what kind of file you are going to create, such as documents, books, or libraries, which are used to store graphics. When you create a new document, you need to input information to describe the page layout. You will notice in the New Document window, choices display for margin and column sizes, gutter width, the layout name, and the document orientation, either portrait or landscape (Figure 11-11). There is also a convenient link icon that allows you to type one dimension for margins, for instance, and it will change all the other margins to the same measurement.

TOOLKIT TIP To set all margins at the same measurement, type in the measurement you want in the first box, then click on the link; the same dimensions will appear on the rest of the boxes. Margins and guidelines do not print out on your final document.

Next, you will set up margins and parameters for the Coupon assignment.

1. Select File > New > Document to open the New Document display box.

2. Select Landscape Orientation (right-side icon).

3. Type in an 8-inch Width and a 3.5-inch Height. (See Figure 11-11)

4. To set the Margin Guides as 0.25 inches all around, type in 0.25 in the first box, and click the link icon to make the margins all around 0.25 inches.

5. Uncheck the Facing Pages option and uncheck the Master Text Frame, because we are not creating a bound book or a magazine with long text articles. Keep all other default settings.

6. Click OK.

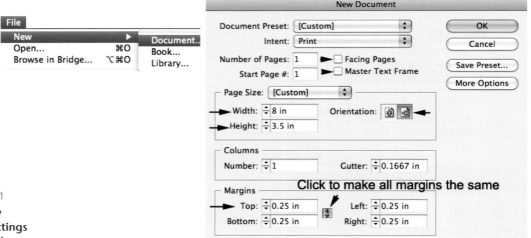

▷ FIGURE 11-11

InDesign new document settings for coupon ad.

TOOLKIT TIP The Facing Pages option sets up the document for printing books with left and right sides. The Master Textbox Frame option creates a page-size text box that includes the entire page for multiple page newsletters with long, continuous articles.

SAVING INDESIGN DOCUMENTS

There are many choices for how you can save your InDesign document besides the traditional Save and Save As commands. InDesign saves its documents within the File menu with an **INDD extension.** When you save the InDesign document, all nonprinting guides and margins are saved as well. A designer can also use the **Save a Copy** command, which creates a duplicate of the document under a different name, leaving the original document still active. An **InDesign template** can also be saved (Save As > InDesign CS5 Template) to use for future editing of a document without having to start all over from scratch. It saves the templates with an **INDT extension**. A template can contain settings, text, and graphics that you preset as a starting point for other documents. The **Revert** command will allow you to go back to the last time you saved your document to get you out of a possible jam. Feel free to use these features as you work on your assignment. If you need to save to the previous version of InDesign CS4, as long as the CS4 version is updated, you can export InDesign CS5 documents to the new InDesign Markup Language as **IDML** extension. This format replaces the earlier version CS3 and CS4 formats called InDesign Interchange (**INX**). This IDML format allows you to open the CS5 document in InDesign CS4 for direct editing.

TOOLKIT TIP If you are using the file management application Version Cue with the Creative Suite application, you can use the Save a Version command to save different versions, if you want to experiment while protecting the original document.

TOOLKIT TIP With InDesign, saving a document also updates the metadata, or file information, that is part of the InDesign document. This metadata includes a thumbnail preview, fonts used in the document, color swatches, and all metadata in the File Info dialog box, all of which enable efficient searching. For example, you might want to search for all documents that use a particular color. You can view this metadata in Adobe Bridge and in the Advanced panel of the File Info dialog box.

Now you will save the new document in your *InDesign > Coupon* folder.

1. Select File > Save As and locate the *Chapter 11* folder inside the *InDesign* folder you created on your hard drive, then save the document with the name *CouponAd* inside the *Coupon* folder; you can click on the right-side arrow by the Save As bar to expand the display box and locate the folder (Figure 11-12).

2. Select the InDesign document (not the template) and select Save using the Mac. It will automatically add the InDesign INDD extension to identify it as an InDesign document. For Windows users, Save As > InDesign CS5 Document.

▷ FIGURE 11-12

**Save as coupon ad
in coupon folder.**

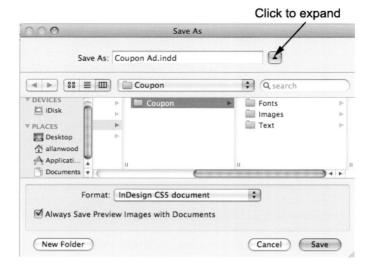

USING GUIDES AND THE VIEW MENU

Guides are used to accurately lay out various text and picture items. **Margin guides** use purple lines as a default for measurements set up in creating the initial document. In the View Menu, it is good practice to show the top and left-side rulers for precise measurement by selecting View > Show Rulers if they are not displayed. This allows you to drag layout guides for placing text and picture boxes. **Layout guides** are usually green in color and are guidelines dragged out from the top and left-side rulers. The cursor will display a double arrow to indicate a selected guideline. To move or remove a layout guide, click it with either the Selection or Direct Selection tool; when you observe a change in the cursor (double arrow with Selection tool, arrow point with Direction Selection tool), drag back into the ruler or select View > Hide Guides to hide all guides (Command/Ctrl R). Guides are nonprintable and can be set up in the View menu along with displaying rulers. You can also use the Control panel for exact placement by typing the location in the selected guide X- or Y-coordinate field (Figure 11-13). The View Menu provides all the various ways of displaying your document, rulers, and guides. Check marks indicate whether a command is active or a function is displayed. As with Photoshop and Illustrator, InDesign also has Smart Guides for precise alignment, resizing, and placement of multiple graphics and text (View > Guides and Grids > Smart Guides). With Smart Guides coordinates appear dynamically so you can easily snap an object's edge to other objects in your layout.

To help with converting inches to decimals, see the table on the next page to help jog your memory.

TOOLKIT TIP With InDesign CS3 and CS4, a document created in the version CS4 can be viewed and used by users who have the earlier version of InDesign CS, CS2, or CS3 by exporting the document to InDesign CS Interchange (INX) format. (File > Export > InDesign Interchange)

INCHES	DECIMAL	INCHES	DECIMAL
1	1.00	1/2	.50
7/8	.857	3/8	.375
3/4	.750	1/4	.250
5/8	.625	1/8	.125
		1/16	.0625

▷ FIGURE 11-13

Creating guides for placement of text and graphics.

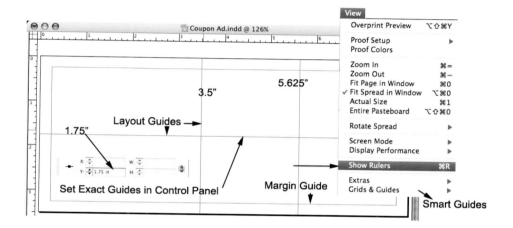

 TOOLKIT TIP For the most accurate placement of guides, use the Control panel by dragging out the guide and typing in the exact measurement in the X and Y coordinates. It provides you the flexibility of moving guides quickly to experiment with your layout.

Here you will create guides to align picture and text frames for the coupon ad.

1. To make sure the rulers are displayed, you should see left and topside rulers outside your document. If not, select View > Show Rulers; it will toggle to display the rulers.

2. To make sure that frame containers you drag to create easily snap to the guides, select View > Grids and Guides > Snap to Guides to make sure a check mark displays; if not, click it. To use the new Smart Guides, select View > Grids and Guides > Smart Guides.

3. To create the coupons to be cut out, drag vertical guides at the 3.5 (3-1/2) inch and 5.625 (5-5/8) inch marks to separate the two coupons. You can also use the Control panel and type in the coordinates as X coordinates for exact measurement (Figure 11-13).

DESIGN TIP
Maintain consistency when using frames with an X inside for graphics and those with an empty box for type, even though either box can handle text and graphics. It helps to keep your communications with the client and the service provider reliable and problem-free.

4. To split the amount of coupons offered to four, drag a horizontal guide to the 1.75 (1-3/4) inch mark. You can also use the Control panel and type in the coordinates as a Y coordinate for exact measurement.

5. Save the file. You are now ready to insert graphics and text.

CREATING GRAPHIC AND BOX FRAMES

When inserting graphics, typing in text, or importing text documents, you can create a frame box or container to put the contents in (Figure 11-14). With InDesign, designers may use the various shape or frame tools to place type or graphics or they may select the type tool and drag a rectangular box to place type only. It is generally accepted practice in the industry that if you have created a blank box where you intend to insert type, a box with an *X* in it created by one of the frame tools will usually be used for placing graphic elements. Graphics and type can also be placed without any container in InDesign. Clicking the mouse will drop the text or image on the document, with or without a box. This feature is one of the greatest efficiency features in InDesign—creating frames as you place. You can then make adjustments to the box and format the text or adjust the coordinates, stroke weight, and format a selected frame using the Control panel.

You will create frames to put text and graphics in for the coupon ad.

1. To create the frame for the graphic, select the Rectangle Frame tool (F) with a Stroke and Fill of None, and drag from the top left inside margin to the 3.5-inch ruler guide, then downward to the 1.75-inch guide. It should feel like it's "snapping" in place. You will notice the box will have an *X* inside.

 PROBLEM If an *X* does not appear and you have used the Frame tool, select **View > Extras > Show/Hide Frame edges.**

▷ FIGURE 11-14

Setting up text and graphic boxes. Creating dashed lines for coupons.

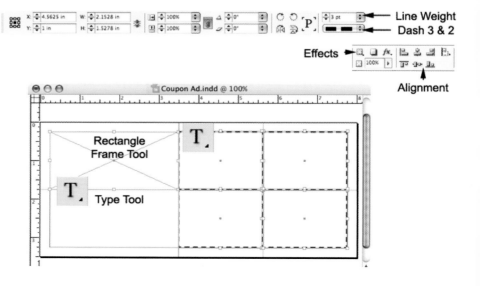

2. Select the Type tool (T) and drag a text box under the graphic frame from the left margin to the 3.5-inch guide for the restaurant information along the bottom margin guide (the Rectangle tool (M) can also be used instead, you just create the frame, select the box, then click inside the box with the Type tool).

3. Drag carefully to create the four boxes that will be used for the coupons on the right side. An arrow displays under the cursor when you start on a guide corner edge. The Snap to Guides option you selected in the previous exercise will help to align the boxes with precision. Smart Guides will display coordinates and its smart dimensions features will display arrows and center lines when the boxes are aligned.

TOOLKIT TIP You may notice light green dimension-like arrows displaying alongside the boxes to help you with proper alignment. This is the new Smart Dimensions feature. As you resize an object next to another object, Smart Dimensions creates a line segment with arrows at each end lets you snap the object to the same width or height as the adjacent object.

TOOLKIT TIP If using earlier versions, can drag one text box and then copy and paste the selected box to make an exact duplicate. You can then use the arrow keys on your keyboard to precisely align and place each box.

4. To create the coupon boxes with a dashed stroke, make sure the Control panel is displayed (Window > Control), zoom in to 200%, and then select each of the four boxes with the Selection Tool, clicking inside each text box frame or on the margins while holding down the Shift key.

5. In the Control panel, change the line thickness or weight to 3 points; change the line type to a Dashed (3 and 2).

6. Although Snap to Grid should have all four boxes aligned, if not, use the Selection tool and arrow keys to overlap the boxes if needed so the dotted lines appear as one. Make sure your alignment is accurate.

7. Save the file.

DESIGN TIP

Dashes in a coupon ad are universally accepted as proposed cutting lines to bring the coupon back to the vendor.

PLACING GRAPHICS IN AN INDESIGN DOCUMENT

You can create all kinds of picture-box shapes using these shape tools. As mentioned previously, an empty picture box should display an *X* inside the box after it is drawn for communicating that this will be used to insert graphics. Here are some other considerations when placing graphics files:

• Bring in or import images by selecting the Place command in the File menu. The Place command will provide the most accurate reproduction, although it can also copy and paste graphics or drag and drop from one document to another.

• The image that is Placed in the document will display as a low-resolution image. It is linked to the original, high-resolution image and may look pixeled on your computer screen. This makes it easier to move the image around in the document for placement on your monitor. (If you want to see a high-resolution version of the image, go to View > Display Performance > High Quality Display.)

• When the document is given the command to Print, InDesign replaces the linked, low-resolution image with the original, high-resolution image, located in the folder from whence you retrieved the file when you used the Place command.

• When a graphic is placed in a document, it is displayed in the Links panel. You can use the Links panel to identify, select, monitor, and update files that are linked to external files. Each object in the Links panel is represented with a thumbnail that provides more detailed information when clicked such as scale, rotation, and resolution, among other attributes. Click on the text or graphic link and find more info about that file.

• If an image covers the area up to the edges of a document, a designer may create a bleed that overflows the image outside the document's trim area to avoid a white line from trimming due to the shift of the paper sheets as they were transferred on the press.

• InDesign offers support for Illustrator's multiple artboards. You can place any selected artboard from Illustrator in its native format into your InDesign document.

• InDesign also provides an Edit With command (Edit > Edit With >) that allows a designer to choose the application to edit a placed item instead of relying on the operating system to default to a particular application.

DESIGN TIP

When importing images into a frame, the frame is only a "window" display. If the image is larger than the frame, then only the exposed portion of the image will display in the frame. If you cannot afford to crop portions of the image, resize your image in Photoshop to the picture box size before you bring it into InDesign.

TOOLKIT TIP When placing graphic images, InDesign will display on the computer as low resolution for easier maneuvering of the image in the document. If a designer needs to see what the final design will look like when printed, InDesign provides commands in the View menu to see various resolutions, such as Display Performance (High Quality Display). If you move the image from the location where you had originally used the Place command in the document, InDesign will be unable to locate the high-resolution image, because you have broken the link between the low-resolution copy and the high-resolution original image, and it will display a dialog box asking for the whereabouts of that image. Whenever you are changing the location of the image, you need to Place the same image again into the document for InDesign to locate that high-resolution image when it is ready to print.

InDesign uses the Links panel for keeping track of graphics, with their related info, that are used in a given InDesign document by providing direct links to those objects for easy access, and to be able to relink missing objects.

Let us insert the pizza graphic.

1. With the Selection tool, select the rectangle frame box with the *X* to place the graphic.

2. Select File > Place and locate the *Pizza* file in your *Chapter 11 (Coupon) Images* folder, where you are keeping your images for the printer.

3. You will notice that the larger image is placed under the frame window as shown in Figure 11-15. Use the Direct Selection tool with arrow keys to make adjustments to the frame.

4. You will also notice the Pizza image displayed looks like a layer in the Links panel (Window > Links). You can use this panel to monitor and update files linked to your document.

▷ FIGURE 11-15

Placing and positioning the graphic Links panel displays graphic thumbnails and related info.

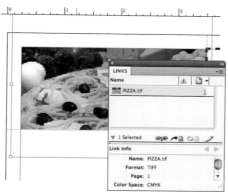
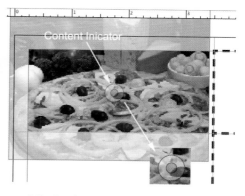

Image placed within graphic frame window. The pizza file is shown in the Links panel.

Adjusting image area with Content Indicator (doughnut) and Selection tool

REPOSITIONING SELECTED LARGER GRAPHICS

With InDesign CS5, graphic frames that contain content now display a transparent "doughnut" shape called a **Content Indicator** when you use the Selection Tool to select and reposition a graphic. This feature is effective when you have a larger graphic behind a frame window and need to view the entire image for repositioning. When you hover your mouse over the doughnut in the center of the image, the cursor turns into the familiar hand icon for moving around. You can use it to reposition content within its frame by simply clicking and dragging on the doughnut to move the graphic where you want it within the frame. When you let go, your content is repositioned. This new feature replaces the Position tool in earlier versions, which worked by the same principle. Clicking on the Content Indicator will select the content, but also keep the Selection tool active. This allows the designer to see the complete dimension of an image with a bounding box and to place the image within the frame with precision. You will notice the area outside the graphic frame will appear faint as you move it, much like the Crop tool in Photoshop, so you can place the image exactly as you would like relative to the graphic frame dimensions. A bounding box appears to show outer dimensions of the graphic.

With Figure 11-15 as a guide, use the Selection tool over the Content Indicator "doughnut" to move the graphic around.

1. Select the graphic using the Selection tool.

2. To see the full image to move around, when you hover your mouse over the center the cursor turns into a hand. Click and drag on the center position doughnut. You will see the area outside the graphic appear faint, but it can still act as guide to make an accurate placement of the image.

3. When you let go and select the image again, you may see a bounding box that surrounds the entire image area inside and out to get an idea of its size.

TOOLKIT TIP The Links panel is used to identify, select, monitor, and update files that are linked to external files. All files placed in a document are listed in the Links panel and they display as thumbnails for quick reference. The Links panel also provides more detailed information when clicked such as scale, rotation, and resolution, among other attributes. You can also click on the page number displayed to go directly to that file. Links can be files, text, graphics, or hyperlinks from local disks or from those managed on a server. However, files that are pasted from a website in Internet Explorer do not display in this panel.

TOOLKIT TIP InDesign also allows the designer to import many graphic file formats. For work that will be used for commercial press, as in this assignment, use images that have either TIF or EPS formats for the most accurate reproduction. TIF image formats are used extensively with photographs, and EPS formats work best using illustrations or when combining type, illustrations, and photographs. With increasing technology, many commercial printers will accept native format files from Adobe applications, especially where Adobe products work together within the CS suite. A placed PDF page displays at the best resolution possible for the given scale and screen resolution and is also acceptable to use in an InDesign document and for a service provider.

PLACEMENT AND FORMATTING OF TYPE

The Type commands on the Control panel have character formatting in the A button, and paragraph formatting commands, like alignment of blocks of type within text boxes, use the paragraph symbol button, which looks like a backwards *P*. The Type menu allows the designer to observe what the actual font looks like in a font sample display, instead of trial and error in choosing. The type frame must be selected and the copy highlighted before editing.

TOOLKIT TIP When creating a document for commercial press, a good designer needs to use fonts that have the style in their name, like Minion Pro Bold. Artificially applying a style such as bold by clicking the letter *B* may not duplicate exactly at the press, causing spacing problems. If an italicized font style is desired, look for font names with the word "italic" or "oblique" in them. Try to keep various font use to a minimum in any given project. Keep in mind—less is more!

TOOLKIT TIP Other options for an old style type for the restaurant title and contact information may be Script MT Bold (PC) or Book Antiqua Bold Italic. Try also Baskerville Old Face (Mac) or Baskerville (PC), Century Schoolbook Bold Italic (Mac), or Century Old Style Bold Italic (PC).

DESIGN TIP

The most important pieces of information that must appear in the ad are the company name, phone number, address, web address, e-mail, or other type of contact information, along with the and coupon displaying the sale amount for this type of ad. To emphasize the importance of these elements, increasing the type size and using color can go a long way toward grabbing the reader's attention.

DESIGN TIP

When working with italics, especially in traditional methods of design, they should only be used for emphasis. It's a good habit to keep a "less is more" attitude when applying this style.

Next, you will place all the text information first, then we will format it.

1. Use the Selection tool to activate the type frame under the graphic, then select the Type (T) tool and click inside the box. The Control panel will automatically select the character formatting button A.

2. Select a 24-point Minion Pro (or similar font) with a Bold and Italic Style and a black Fill. Type in "Mama Di's Pizzeria" (Figure 11-16). It will probably be left aligned as a default, which will be adjusted afterwards.

3. Press Return/Enter for the next line.

4. For the slogan, select a 14-point Minion Pro (or your own choice) font, Italic style, and type with quotes "Come Join the Family." Press Return/Enter twice to skip a line; a better method of adding space between parargraphs will be introduced later.

5. For the address, use the same size and style font and type "18 Main St., Anytowne," or put in your own info. Press Return/Enter.

6. For the phone line, increase the font size to either 18 or 24-point Minion Pro with a Bold Style and type "555-1234." If you observe a "red cross" being displayed or the line just disappears, it indicates the type is too big for the space. Decrease the font size until you can see your phone text line.

7. Highlight all the type you created, then click on the Character Formatting button (A) on the Control panel; choose to center align the type in the text frame if the monitor size permits; you may find both the paragraph and character formatting options are visible in the Control panel. You will further format the color and placement of the type in relation to the graphic later.

8. Save the file.

▷ FIGURE 11-16

Entering type using the Type tool. Character formatting using the Control panel.

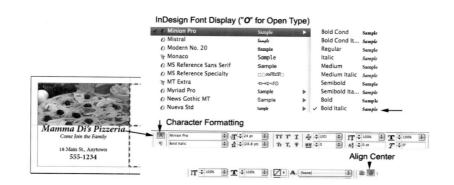

WORKING WITH TYPE WITHIN A FRAME

As a general rule, a designer would not want to have type placed directly next to the edges of the frame or against a graphic object. In this case, some space is needed between the pizza graphic and type for the title and where type is placed within the dashed frame of the coupons. In the Object menu, you can choose the **Text Frame Options command.** In this dialog box, you can specify an "inset" measurement that keeps copy away from the edge of the frame. After you specify the inset dimension, a guide will be visible inside the frame when it is selected with the Selection or Direct Selection tool. In the Vertical Justification > Align area of the Text Frame Options dialog box, you can align the copy to the top, bottom, or the center of the frame. You can also justify the copy, which spreads the lines of type from the top frame edge or inset to the bottom frame edge or inset. In CS5, you can also use this function on non-rectangular frames like rounded corners, which was not possible in earlier versions.

TOOLKIT TIP You can also use the key combo Command/Ctrl B to access the Text Frame Options dialog box or Control click for Mac (right-click for PC) to display the context menu to choose Text frame options.

Here you will use the Text Frame Options command to vertically center the type in the Restaurant information and to create spacing between type and the dashed outline within the coupons.

1. Select the type lines you created earlier under the pizza graphic.

2. Choose Object > Text Frame Options (or Cmnd/Ctrl + B) and select the General tab.

3. In the Vertical Justification area, select Align as Center, check Fixed Column Width to preserve the adjusted columns, and make sure the Preview button is checked. This will center the type within the type box (Figure 11-17). Click OK.

▷ FIGURE 11-17

**Using the Text
Frame Options box
to control verti-
cal center align-
ment and spacing
between type and
the frame.**

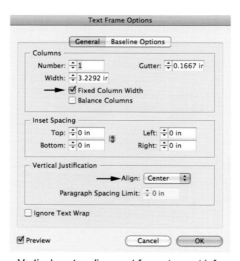

Vertical center alignment for restaurant info

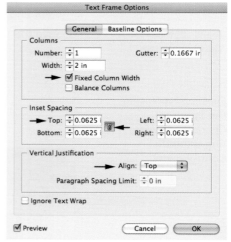

Text spacing for inside coupon frame boxes

4. Use the Selection tool and while holding down the Shift key, select all four coupon boxes.

5. To create breathing space between the type to be entered and the dashed line, choose the Text Frame Options dialog box again and enter in the Inset Spacing area ".0625," the equivalent of 1/16th of an inch, on all sides as shown in Figure 11-17. You can click on the center link icon to get this measurement. Click OK. Now you are ready to place type in the coupon boxes.

 PROBLEM If you find that the dashed lines are not overlapped as one, select inside the box with the Selection tool, then uncheck Fix Column Width in the Text Frame Options dialog box to make your adjustments.

6. Choosing Minion Pro Regular 12-point font, or a font that matches the restaurant info, type in the lines of type to indicate the specials inside the coupons as shown in Figure 11-18. Do not use decimal points for displaying cents in the dollar amounts. We will format them and the type in the next exercise.

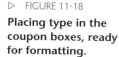

▷ FIGURE 11-18

Placing type in the coupon boxes, ready for formatting.

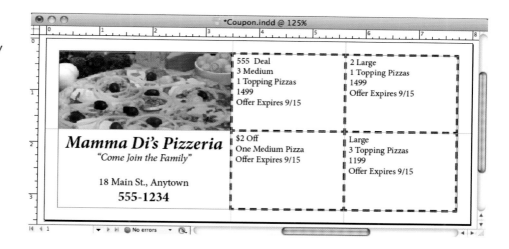

DESIGN TIP

It is good practice to create text margins within a frame before typing text, both for easier readability and to give the designer an idea of the allotment of space when using a particular font.

FORMATTING TYPE AND VERTICAL ALIGNMENT

To make the specials stand out, you can select a different font, change the font size, or select color, all of which you will do in the next exercise. This exercise will help you review how to use the Control panel to format and center align selected type using Character formatting, and use Text Frame Options to center the copy vertically inside the frame. For the coupons in this exercise we are going to use Bookman Old Style Bold font for easier reading, with Italic style added for pricing lines to make them stand out. To adjust the vertical spacing of the lines of type inside each coupon evenly from top to bottom, select Vertical Justification > Align > Justify in the Text Frame Options dialog box.

Next, you will format the type inside the coupons to make the specials display for easy reading.

DESIGN TIP

To make the specials stand out, look for a font that complements the restaurant info. A wide type font is also easier to read and will catch the viewer's attention.

1. First, to center align the type, select the Type tool (T), highlight all the lines of type *except* "Offer Expires 9/15," which we will keep as left aligned; click the Character formatting button on the Control panel.

2. Select the Align center button on the right side of the Control panel and perform the same operation for each coupon.

3. Select Character formatting button A and use the Type tool (T) to change all type lines *except* the expiration line and price lines to the Bookman Old Style Bold font, or stay with the same font you used under the pizza image changing to Bold style to make the coupons stand out.

4. Change the size in all coupons to 14 points, with the exception of the expiration lines.

5. Change the price in each coupon to a 24-point size, with a Bold Italic style. Make sure the style term is named with the font you are using. Because this is the most important attention getter. Change the line "555 Deal" to your selected font at 18-point size in the Bold Italic style. With the "$2 Off" line, change to a 24-point Bold Italic style of the same font.

6. Select the *Offer Expires 9/15* line in each coupon, and change it to 10- or 8-point size depending on the font used. This will stay left aligned for attention.

DESIGN TIP

When creating coupons, key words like *Free, Half (1/2) Off, $2 Off*, or high percentages, like *30% Off*, grab the viewer's attention because of the substantial savings they represent. When a coupon is made, the expiration date is extremely important; a good rule of thumb is to schedule the coupon to expire either at the end of the month or in the middle of the month.

7. To position the expiration lines near the bottom left of each coupon, click in front of each *Offer Expires 9/15* line and press Return/Enter once or twice if needed to separate it. If the line disappears you have put too much space and the line is outside the box.

8. To make sure the *Offer Expires 9/15* line is consistent along the bottom of each coupon, and to provide consistency in display of various lines of type in each coupon, you will use the Justify Alignment command in the Text Frame Options dialog box.

9. Highlight all lines in the first coupon and select Object > Text Frame Options to bring up the dialog box. Select Vertical Justification > Align > Justify. It should space all lines evenly along a vertical axis (Figure 11-19). Click OK.

10. Repeat the same procedure with the other three coupons. The expiration line should be consistent along the bottom of each coupon.

11. In some coupons, there is a significant gap between the expiration line and the offer. You may also notice that the top lines may also seem too close to the cutting edges or dashed lines. To adjust, select only the top line of each, except the "555 Deal", with the Type tool, then select Object > Text Frame Objects. Make sure alignment is still "Justified", and the Inset Spacing link is "broken" by clicking on it, than click on the Top inset up arrow a couple of times without losing the expiration lines. Click OK. Use Figure 11-19 as a guide.

▷ FIGURE 11-19

Formatting the type in each coupon, and justifying vertical alignment.

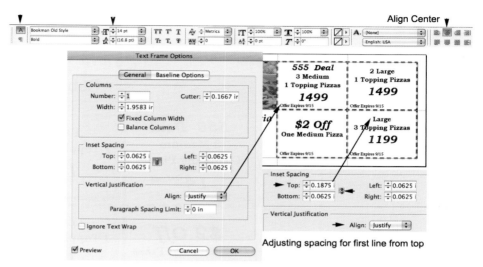

Using Justify for position of expiration line

TOOLKIT TIP When you have more copy than the frame is able to contain, a red plus sign may appear in the lower right corner of the frame, indicating that the text is overset. You can make the overset text fit by increasing the size of the frame or decreasing the size of the text. You can also use Command/Ctrl Z or the Edit menu to undo the action that caused the overset text to begin with.

APPLYING SUPERSCRIPTS

All type sits on an invisible line called a **baseline**. As you look at this line of type, you are reading along the baseline that the type sits on. A designer can use certain formatting techniques, like superscript and subscript, to shrink to a percentage of the font or to change how the font is positioned in alignment with the top of the font or on the baseline. To create the cents portion of the price, select the T1 (Superscript) button where the "1" is showing above the "T" on the Control panel. It will display the cents portion so that it aligns with the top portion of the font. A **superscript** is a percentage of the original font size and will display aligned with the top of the font. **Subscripts** are also percentages of a font that are displayed on or below the baseline of the font.

Here you will apply a superscript to shrink the cents portion of the prices to display aligned with the top portion of the font (Figure 11-20).

1. Highlight only the cents portion of each price with the Type tool and select the "Superscript" option to shrink the cents to align with the top of the font.

2. That is all there is to it. Save the file.

DESIGN TIP

In most cases the expiration date in any coupon should also include the year. For our purposes here, we removed the year in the coupon so as not to date the publishing of this book.

▷ FIGURE 11-20

Applying the super-
scripts option to for-
mat the cents in
each price.

CHOOSING AND APPLYING COLOR FROM SWATCH LIBRARIES

To apply color to type that is generally set without a stroke, select the Type Fill
color box in the Toolboox, choose a color from the Swatches panel, or double-
click the Type Fill color box in the Tools panel to bring up the Color Picker, where
you can choose a particular color. You can select from a random color or use the
Swatches panel to select from one of the color libraries. When sending a document to press, all colors need to be **CMYK process colors.** The swatch libraries
contain libraries or process colors specific to print media like Pantone and also for
RGB colors used for web media. Spot Colors used in print media are premixed,
much as you would get at the paint store, and they use a numbering system
to identify each specific color. You can then choose a color and save it in the
Swatches panel for future use for that document, however, it does not permanently remain in the Swatches panel for all documents.

TOOLKIT TIP You can select from a range of color libraries that are used for commercial press or for the web. Some of these may include the Pantone Process Color
System, Focoltone color system, the Trumatch color swatch system, and libraries
created especially for web use. Before using swatches from a color matching system,
consult with your prepress service providers to determine which ones they support.
A word of caution: professional designers need to be careful choosing colors for
commercial print using their monitors, although the technology in modern flat panel
monitors using calibration devices is widely acceptable. A designer can use an actual
print swatch book to be used in conjunction with the digital swatch libraries to be
extremely accurate. For our purposes in these exercises, we will use digital colors.

For the colors for type and dashes in the coupon ad, you will select from the Pantone-coated library colors.

1. Choose New Color Swatch in the Swatches panel menu (click the dashes in the upper-right corner to open the panel menu).

2. Make sure the Color Type is Process in the display; from the Color Mode list, choose Pantone Process Coated as the library to choose colors from.

3. For a deep red color, select Pantone DS 61-1 C as shown in Figure 11-21. You can also type "DS 61-1" in the Pantone dialog box. This will be used for the restaurant title, phone number, and coupon prices.

4. Select the Add button, and the color you chose will automatically be added to the Swatches panel. Do *not* click Done yet, so you can add another color if you want to by repeating Steps 1 and 2.

5. For a deep green color, add Pantone 261-1 C to the Swatches panel. This will be used for some of the type descriptions. Click Add.

6. With both colors selected, click the Done button on the dialog box to indicate that you have finished your choices.

7. To use the colors, highlight the *Mama Di's Pizzeria* title with the Type tool, and select the red Pantone DS 61-1 C in the Swatches panel. Make sure the type Fill color is displayed and the Stroke color is set to None in the Tools panel.

8. Repeat the same process with the phone number and prices in the coupons for consistency.

▷ FIGURE 11-21

Choosing Pantone process colors for selected type and dashed lines in the coupons and adding those colors to the Swatches panel.

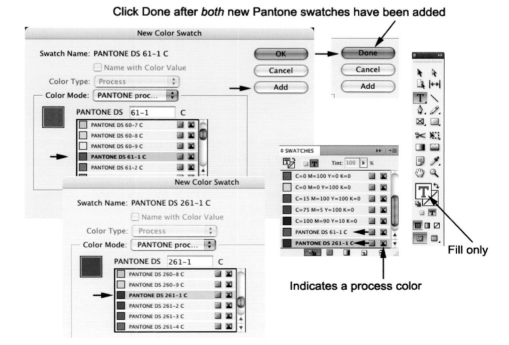

9. Highlight the line *555 Deal* and make it the green Pantone 261-1 C. You may want to color a few of the other lines, but less is usually better, and it keeps the attention to specific colors. The rest of the colors can remain the default black.

10. If you want to change the color of the dashes in the coupon boxes, leave the Fill color to None and select the Stroke color on the Tools panel.

11. Use the Selection tool to select the four coupon boxes while holding down the Shift key.

12. Select the Pantone green color you added in the Swatches panel to apply it. The dashes will turn green, then click outside the coupon with the Selection tool to deselect the coupons.

13. Save the file.

ARRANGING PLACEMENT OF GRAPHICS

The Object menu in InDesign, as well as in all Adobe products, allows you to place multiple graphics in front of or behind one another, much like you would rearrange the stacking order of sheets of paper. The command Send to Back and Send to Front arranges the graphic to appear directly on top of or underneath all the other graphics. The Send Backward and Send Forward commands move the graphic behind or in front of one graphic at a time. The coupon you have created is on a white background at this point and would look more appealing with a warmer tone background. You can place an image to act as the background behind the type and pizza image or have the ad printed on special colored paper. Here you will use a graphic to place behind the other elements to act as the background. If you have the Links panel open, you will also notice that the Links panel displays both the Pizza and Parchment graphic objects as thumbnails for future editing or modifying if needed.

 TOOLKIT TIP In InDesign, a bleed is usually added under Document Setup > More Options. Always add an eighth inch to each side that has a bleed.

In this exercise, to complete the ad and give it more color, you will place a graphic to cover the entire document and send it behind the type and graphic objects to act as the background.

1. Select the Rectangle Frame tool and draw a diagonal box over the entire document so that it extends or "bleeds" beyond the edges of the document about an eighth of an inch (0.125). This will prevent white lines created from trimming or paper shifting on the press. This will be covered more in depth later.

2. Select File > Place and choose the *Parchment* file located in your *Images* folder. Notice that the Links panel displays both the Pizza and Parchment graphic objects as thumbnails (Window > Links).

3. To move the graphic behind the other objects, use the Selection tool to make sure the graphic is selected, and then choose Object > Arrange > Send to Back. It will provide a warm tone background for those hot pizzas!

4. To see the completed work without guides, select View > Grids & Guides > Hide Guides. The margin guides will still show (Figure 11-22). Do not forget that guides do *not* print.

5. Look at the bottom of the window display of your ad you just created. If you see a green circle that reads "No errors" the automatic checker for graphics links assures you are ready to save and print a soft proof. Save the file when ready.

▷ FIGURE 11-22

Completed ad with parchment graphic placed behind all objects as the background.

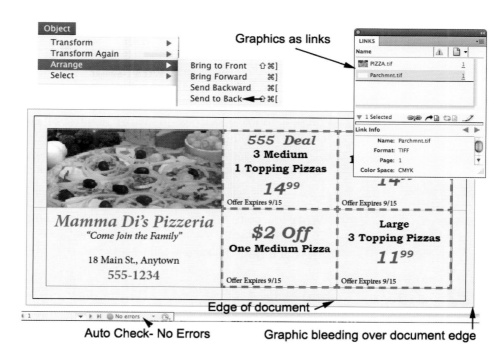

INDESIGN'S LAYERS PANEL

In InDesign CS5, there is a new Layers panel that behaves much the same way as the Layers panel in Illustrator. Each document layer now has a disclosure triangle that can be expanded to reveal the objects and their stacking order on that given layer. This allows you to click on a particular layer to display the objects or graphics created. Simply dragging the item name in the list, and dropping it where you want it within the panel can change the stacking order of objects. You can even drag and drop items into and out of groups, buttons, and multi-state objects. The Layers panel also provides you the ability to now toggle the visibility of individual page items, as well as the ability to lock and unlock them, providing choice as to what components can be edited or not. This behavior matches Illustrator in that a locked item cannot be edited, or even selected, without first unlocking it.

To see the locking features of the Layers panel, you'll lock the graphic objects.

1. In InDesign, open your saved *CouponAd.indd* file from your *Chapter 11* folder, then select the Layers panel (Window > Layers).

▷ FIGURE 11-23

InDesign's Layers panel for locking text and graphic objects.

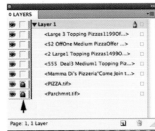

2. You can see on the Layers panel that Layer 1 is displayed. Click on the left side arrow next to the Layer 1 text to display sub layers of the individual graphics and text boxes under the initial layer.

3. Click to toggle a lock next to the two graphic sub layers, Pizza and Parchment as shown in Figure 11-23.

4. Try adjusting either graphic and you'll find you can't edit either graphic because it is locked. Leave these two graphics as locked as they will not need to be edited in future coupons.

5. Lock one of the text boxes, and then try to edit it. You should not be able to make any edits. You can see how useful this could be when you want to edit only some objects. We'll cover more on the Layers panel later.

6. Save and close the file when finished.

Need additional fun computer graphics tutorials and info, and an additional look at the projects you'll be creating in this book? Check out my Artist's Digital Toolkit website at: **http://www.digitoolkit.com**

CREATING A TEMPLATE FILE IN INDESIGN

If you are working on a design that may need to be used or duplicated later, saving your document as a template allows you to bring up what you have created as a new starting point that you can edit later without starting from scratch (Figure 11-24). InDesign saves the template file with an INDT extension so that it can be opened as a regular InDesign file ready to edit later. A template file can contain settings, text, and graphics that you preset as a starting point for other documents. Normally, if you are providing your file to someone who has an earlier version of InDesign, they will not be able to read your document successfully. Always keep this in mind when transferring files. Find out your client's version.

Next, you will save the final document as a template for future editing.

1. With the document active, select File > Save As > InDesign CS5 Template.

2. Save it in your *Coupon* folder in the *Chapter 11* folder.

You are all set at this time with the coupon ad. Time for a pizza break!

▷ FIGURE 11-24

Saving the document as a template file.

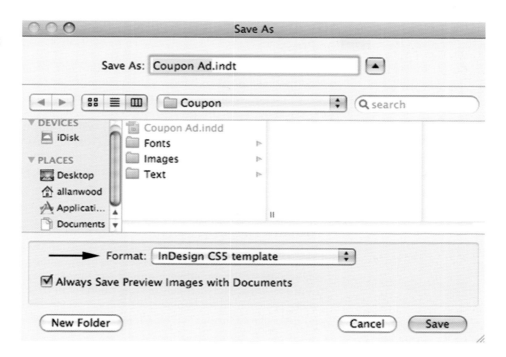

TOOLKIT TIP InDesign CS5 has a feature that allows you to save the document so that a designer or service provider who has an earlier InDesign CS4 version can read and edit the document. This can be done by using the Export command in the File menu and exporting the InDesign CS5 document to InDesign Markup Language, which will convert it to an IDML extension. This is covered in the Digital Toolkit Extra section.

ADVANCED USERS: Preflight, Packaging, and Preparing for Press

Suppose you are planning to give this assignment, or any other for that matter, to a commercial press to have a volume amount of copies professionally printed. InDesign comes with a few handy utilities and features to help you check your work, package it for the printer, and create soft proofs for the printer or client to use and approve as needed. Here you will go through the process involved with the coupon advertisement you just created. Taking a little extra time for a proactive approach to make sure your work is ready goes a long way in this profession. You will also have few if any surprises and a more confident client in your work as a professional.

TOOLKIT TIP Always talk to your service provider or printer first before sending anything. They may have specific requirements and suggestions that could help your project go more smoothly. Requirements for publishing on a commercial press will be different from publishing for a website. For both media, all required electronic files should be placed inside one titled *Folder* to keep them organized for the service provider. These include the InDesign project documents with images, text, and fonts placed inside their own folders.

DESIGN TIP

Images saved with a .JPG extension for the sake of compression need to be converted to .TIF files, because compressed files can create problems at the press and cause delays.

PRINT PUBLISHING GUIDELINES

When sending a job to be printed on a commercial press, care needs to taken to include a laser proof for accurate CMYK colors to show precise placement of all items, which should be larger than the trim size of the paper to show trim and registration marks. All electronic files need to be checked for up-to-date accuracy, and hard copy laser proofs should be provided with a job output report.

TOOLKIT TIP The actual page layout size should also be the trim size of the document.

As a general rule, when the job is ready to be handed over to the service provider for print publishing, it should contain the following components:

• Updated electronic files in organized folders.

• All items should be set in CMYK color mode for press inks. Native PSD and AI documents can also be used. Photographs, painted images, and detailed drawings can be saved as TIF images, while illustrations and images with text can be saved as EPS files. High resolution PDF files are also acceptable and keep formatting consistent.

• The most up-to-date laser proof needs to be included, labeled with name and date to provide hard copy confirmation of how the final layout should appear. It should also include trim and registration marks for the printer to follow.

• If you have a color laser PostScript printer, you can print separate color proofs as a guide for creating the color plates for the printing press. InDesign allows you to create these proofs, but we will not create them for this exercise.

• Folder and files, the document, and a report file generated by InDesign's Package utility provide all the files, fonts, and basic job information needed including the print specifications.

TOOLKIT TIP When sending projects to a commercial press, use fonts that have the style built into the name instead of selecting style buttons in your toolbar. This will ensure proper spacing of text in InDesign. When a bold or italic style is applied in InDesign, it is using the actual font. If the actual font is not available, the style will not be changed. For an italicized font, look for the word oblique or Italic in the font name.

CHECKING FOR SPELLING

Although this assignment should not contain any spelling errors, it is always a good habit to walk through the process to understand the importance of spell checking. InDesign has a spelling checking feature in the Edit menu that not only allows you to check for spelling errors, but also to autocorrect and add special words in the dictionary (Figure 11-25). When you check for spelling and a questionable word comes up, InDesign provides options or other words to take its place, or you can type in the correct word.

▷ FIGURE 11-25

Using the Check Spelling utility.

Here you will misspell a word and use the spell check to correct it.

1. Launch InDesign and open the *CouponAd* file you just created.
2. Add an extra *Z* in the word *pizza*.
3. Select Edit > Spelling > Check Spelling.
4. Choose the word *pizza* spelled correctly from the list of choices, and click on the Change button; or if it did not display, type in the word correctly, then select Change.
5. Select Done when you have finished and you are all set. You can see how this can be a great help when you are creating multipage documents or books with lots of text.
6. Save the file.

TOOLKIT TIP One of the biggest issues an amateur designer faces is forgetting to make sure that image and font files are stored in the same location as the document when bringing the document to a client or printer. If you are transporting your document to another computer on a portable storage device, make sure you have the images also on that device and that the same fonts are on the other computer you have chosen. Use InDesign's Preflight and Package operations to gather all the elements needed for production.

CHECKING GRAPHIC LINKS USING THE LINKS PANEL

Before sending any file or completed document, always check to see if your links are up to date. One way is to use the Links panel. Here is where the Links panel we so quietly mentioned in the coupon assignment comes to our aid. By double-clicking the file you are checking on the **Links panel**, you will find plenty of information, including file size and color mode, all kinds of descriptive attributes, and the file's location, so you can make your edits accordingly (Figure 11-26). Each object in the Links panel is represented with a thumbnail that provides more detailed additional information when clicked such as scale, rotation, and resolution, among other attributes. You can use the Links panel to find, sort, and manage all of your placed objects. For instance, if you are sending everything to commercial press, than you would want all your graphic files in CMYK color. If you found one in RGB mode, you could simply open it in its application, such as Photoshop or Illustrator, and change the mode to CMYK. Using the Links panel, you can also select the Relink icon to find where you put the file that is linked in the document. The Go To Link icon shows you the actual graphic's location in your document. The Update Link icon lets you update the link location.

TOOLKIT TIP When you open a document and a warning dialog box comes up regarding the need to update or looking for links to graphics, select to automatically fix the links. If this does not work, you probably moved the file away from its original position and it is trying to find the links to the graphics and fonts it was using. Find where the graphics and text are located and relink to the document. You can also do this by selecting the items manually from the Links panel. If you need to edit the graphic, select Edit > Edit With > and choose the application you want to use for editing.

▷ FIGURE 11-26

Using the Links panel to check file link and detailed information.

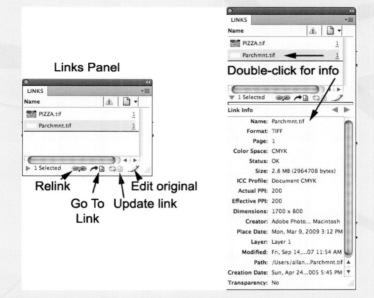

Let us check the links from the coupon ad you just created.

1. Make sure the Links panel is displayed (Window > Links).

2. Double-click on the *Pizza* graphic link layer to see information about it. If there is a yellow sign next to either graphic, the link has been broken and needs to be updated.

3. If both are linked correctly, you will see no warning signs or dialog boxes. If not, use the Links panel to locate and update the file.

PREFLIGHT

Before you send any work to a client or the **service provider**, which can be your commercial printer, web developer, or other professional who will provide a service for setting up your document for whatever output media you intend to use, you need to go through a process called **preflight** to check for any errors. With InDesign, the default preflight settings are to "Enable Preflight for All Documents" and "Preflight Document," which are located at the bottom of the window display. While you were creating the coupon ad InDesign was checking graphics and text from your work behind the scenes. InDesign also has a live Preflight panel to work along with the Links panel in identifying and correcting errors on the fly. With this new feature, a designer doesn't have to wait until the document is near completion before finding errors. There should be no problems displayed on the panel for your advertisement (Figure 11-26). The Preflight panel (Preflight utility in earlier versions) warns of problems, such as missing files, graphics, or fonts. This is especially helpful in working with long documents as you will be creating in the next chapter. You have just performed initial preflight operations in the previous assignments, so now you will check the document using the Preflight panel. You can always perform preflight during various stages of your project.

To check the coupon ad you just created do the following:

1. Launch InDesign and open up your *CouponAd* document, not the template, you just created. If you are using earlier versions you would choose File > Preflight.

2. Select the Preflight panel option at the bottom of the window display, you should not see any errors as shown in Figure 11-27. If you have any errors, it may be having to locate the graphic link. Use the Links panel to help find the graphic. In earlier versions, choose the Summary panel in the Preflight dialog box (File > Preflight) as a guide, you can select various menus to check fonts, links, graphics, and other information. A yellow sign alert icon indicates problem areas.

3. Although you can use the Preflight panel menu to generate a PDF report to give to a client, you'll be creating an in-depth report using the Package utility in the last exercise, so leave this alone for now and make sure all links are correct.

▷ FIGURE 11-27

Live preflighting to check files, fonts, and images.

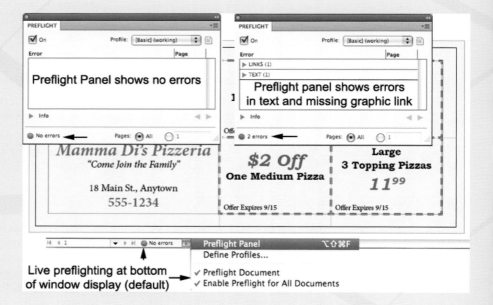

PREPARING THE PROJECT FOR PRINTING

With the project checked for spelling and appropriate fonts and images updated for accuracy and placement, it is time to get ready for press. Usually the commercial press you send your document and information to is called your *service provider* or *service bureau*.

THE POSTSCRIPT LANGUAGE

The commercial printing industry operates on a **page description language (PDL)**, created by your desktop publishing application and your computer, that defines precise position and composition of the images, text, and other elements in your document by mapping each pixel for the high-resolution output of your pages. The **PostScript language** is the most widely accepted and used PDL in the commercial printing industry. When you print your document to a disk file, a PostScript printer, or an output device, you are creating a PostScript language file that is processed by that device. PostScript functions as a computer programming language and a page description language (PDL). PostScript printers or image-setter devices also use a **raster image processor (RIP)** as an interpreter to convert the page information from the PostScript language into a bitmap image pattern for film or paper output.

TECHNICAL INFORMATION REGARDING POSTSCRIPT, TRUETYPE, AND OPENTYPE FONTS

Fonts fall into one of three types: *PostScript, TrueType,* and *OpenType*. OpenType is the standard most widely used in the commercial printing industry today. Most commercial printing service providers can handle fonts you supply or will find a suitable replacement. This is why it is important to include fonts as part of your packaging to the printer in case they need to install your fonts in their system. You can observe the type of font you are using when you look down the font list of any Adobe product. With technology in the printing industry today, you can usually use different types of fonts if needed. Always check with your service provider first.

PostScript fonts are bitmap-type fonts that contain two files: one for screen display and one for printer display. They are the most clear for printing and are preferred when sending to press. They also have set sizes, because they are bitmap files and cannot be resized without causing deterioration in quality. They were created initially by Adobe. Fonts that are PostScript are designated with a red *a*. PostScript fonts and files are divided into levels, with Level 1 being an older level. These levels help to specify compatibility with the interpreters in PostScript output devices. Level 2 will often improve the printing speed and output quality of graphics printed only on a PostScript Level 2 or greater output device. Level 3 provides the best speed and output quality, but requires a PostScript 3 device.

TrueType fonts, designated by an icon displaying two *T*s, are scalable and were initially created by Microsoft. When you open a Microsoft Word document and can quickly select the font size without any deterioration, usually that is a TrueType font. Although they are extremely popular, they can cause production problems with older RIP processors by slowing down production time. Most newer systems handle TrueType fonts without any problem.

OpenType fonts are the newest members and are also scalable and may include a number of additional features, such as swashes and discretionary ligatures found in many foreign languages, that are not available in current PostScript and TrueType fonts. They are designated with the letter *O* italicized. Looking in your Fonts directory, you will usually find these fonts and their designated icons next to them to identify their type. OpenType fonts are cross platform, eliminating the font issues that occur when moving documents between Mac and Windows operating systems.

PREPARING GRAPHICS

Before any graphics are sent to press, they may be saved as either an EPS for vector artwork or images with text or as a TIF file for photographic images or paintings. They can also be saved in their native formats, or as high quality PDF files. If an illustration is a composite of more than one graphic element, all the original files must be included in the delivery. Illustration and image files in TIF or EPS format are imported or placed so that the low-resolution preview appears on the page layout with a low-resolution link to the original high-resolution graphic. At print time, the low-resolution link locates the original high-resolution image and is immediately replaced to provide the high-resolution graphic data to the intended output. High resolution PDF files are used quite often for both text and graphics.

• Save graphics in uncompressed formats; no JPEGs. Use PDF files for communication, or if the service provider requests final proofs.

• Convert RGB images to CMYK. Make a duplicate RGB file first, then convert to CMYK to have two separate files.

• Do not change graphics file names unless you first relink them in InDesign.

PRINTING A FINAL PROOF

With the work completed, it is time to create a proof that can be used as a communication tool between you, your client, and the service provider you are working with. This exercise will provide insight about the printer settings or printer's marks for you to communicate the layout of the document, color accuracy, registration marks, and trim marks. The first thing is to make sure your "suitcase" of images is in the same place as your document and has not changed; otherwise you will only be able to print the low-resolution copy, because the link to the original image has been broken. You will need to set up the *CouponAd* document to be printed as centered on legal size paper in landscape orientation. This provides space for you or your client to write any information. **Printer's marks** include **registration marks**, which provide a place for pin registration of plates for the press (they look crosshairs in a rifle sight), and **color bars** to balance and check the color. **Crop marks** indicate where the cutting of the paper will be. If you are setting crop marks and want the artwork to contain a bleed or slug area, make sure that you extend the artwork past the crop marks to accommodate the bleed or slug. The **bleed area** is the part of text or objects that extend beyond the page boundaries after trimming, and the **slug area** is an area outside the page and bleed that contains printing instructions or job sign-off information. Also make sure that your media size is large enough to contain the page and any printer's marks, bleeds, or the slug area.

DESIGN TIP

If a graphic or color-filled box extends beyond the page margins, an eighth-inch bleed needs to be added to the outside of the document with the image or color bar extending to the bleed edge. Documents with images or elements that bleed to the edge of the document are printed on oversize paper and later cut down to finished size. Extending bleed images an eighth inch beyond the document trim compensates for any inaccuracies that may occur in the trimming process.

TOOLKIT TIP It is best to print to a sharp and clear color laser printer; for this exercise try to print from a color ink-jet printer if a color laser printer is unavailable. Print to a black-and-white laser printer if you need to look at layout only.

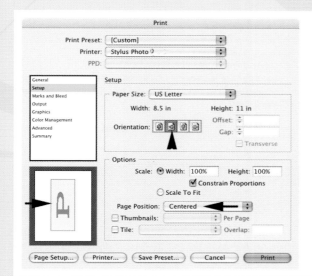

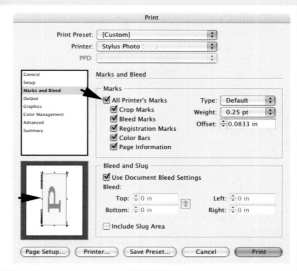

▷ FIGURE 11-28

Using the Packaging utility to place the job contents, files, images, and report in one folder.

For this exercise you will need to make sure you have your images in your folder linked to the *CouponAd* document. The same fonts you used to create your coupon ad should be on the computer you are going to print from or you may find either a dialog box to ask you for replacement fonts or it may substitute some evil font that will mess up your creation.

1. Since you have completed preflighting your document, your *CouponAd* file is ready to print. Select to Print the file (File > Print) and select the General tab from the menu.

2. Select the printer you wish to use. Consult with your instructor to choose the printer.

3. To set up the positioning of the document in relation to the page, select the Setup tab, set the Paper Size to Letter, choose Landscape Orientation, and a Page Position of Centered, as shown in Figure 11-28. Leave all other default settings. You will see the coupon page icon displayed in the window.

4. Finally, select the Marks and Bleed category, then check All Printer's Marks to observe special printer's marks (Figure 11-28).

5. To print the document with printer's marks, select the Print button at the bottom of the display and check your work. You should have a nice proof ready for approval by your client or to hand off to your service provider.

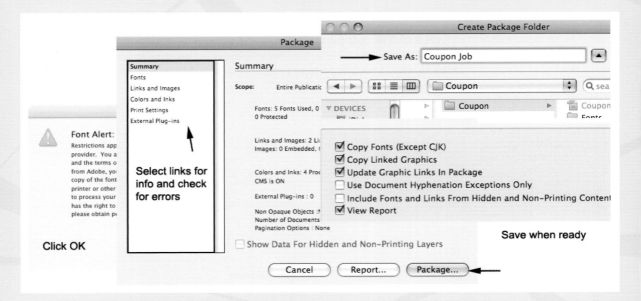

▷   FIGURE 11-29

Creating a proof with printer's marks.

PACKAGING YOUR DOCUMENT

One of the first good habits you made earlier in the chapter was to create folders to put your images, text, and fonts in for easy access and to maintain links to the document. If you are planning to transport all the information on a flash drive or other removable media, you will need to make sure you copy all the folders and files from your hard drive to the type of media you intend to bring to the service provider. You can do this manually, or InDesign has a handy utility called **Package** that will do it for you. When you package a file, you create a folder that contains the InDesign document, any necessary fonts, linked graphics, text files, and a customized report. This report, which is saved as a text file, includes the information in the Printing Instructions dialog box from the Preflight dialog box; a list of all used fonts, links, and inks required to print the document; and print settings. You should get in the habit of using InDesign's Preflight and Package utilities for all your documents to be organized and checked for accuracy. Usually, when you send a client a Fonts folder they would have to install the fonts onto their system manually if they didn't have the same font or same version. In CS5, when you choose to include the fonts used in a document or file when using the Package command, InDesign will now generate a folder named "Document Fonts." This way when you as the receiver, or your client, may need to open an INDD file, then InDesign will automatically install these fonts for you. Document installed fonts, however, are not the same as fonts available from the standard operating system font locations. They get installed for only that document when it is opened, and are subsequently uninstalled when the document is closed.

TOOLKIT TIP When you are packaging a document, InDesign automatically performs an up-to-date preflight check, making it unnecessary to perform a separate preflight check as described earlier. If problem areas are detected, a dialog box appears. However, it still helps to understand the process here.

TOOLKIT TIP Once a job is packaged, it creates a final copy of the document inside the packaged folder. When users still have the original document open and make changes, they do not realize that those changes will not be reflected in the document included in the package. Unless they do a Save As and replace the document in the package, they will actually be sending the printer an older version. That is why packaging should always be the last step.

In this exercise you will go through the process of packaging your folders, files, and document into another folder within your *Chapter 11* folder, or you can try to use this utility to transport to a removable media such as a flash drive.

1. Select File > Package, and using the Summary panel in the dialog box as a guide, you can select various menus to check fonts, links, graphics, and other information. There should be no errors before packaging.

2. With everything checked out OK, select Package, then select Save.

3. When the Printing Instructions dialog box comes up, put in all relevant information including contact information that will become part of the report, as if you were sending this document as a job to the service provider. Select Continue.

3. When the Create Package Folder dialog box comes up, save the publication in your *Coupon* folder as *Coupon Job,* or save it with all your other files on your removable drive media. Keep the first three boxes checked (default) in the dialog box (Figure 11-29), and click on the Package button.

4. When a Font Alert dialog box comes up reminding you of copyright issues, select OK for this exercise, unless your instructor advises against copying your fonts.

5. The Package utility will generate a folder that contains a copy of your document, related files or an *instructions.txt* file, fonts in a Document Fonts folder, and images in a Links folder, ready for press. You will also see a job report to provide instructions to the printer. Close that file when done.

6. That is all there is to it.

TOOLKIT TIP InDesign can also convert the files, graphics, and document for web use and also allows you to send a client a PDF version of your document.

EXPORTING INDESIGN CS5 DOCUMENTS FOR EVERYONE ELSE

Some clients may not have InDesign CS5 installed on their computers. Another way you can show a client a potential layout or bring an electronic proof of your work to a service provider or commercial press is to have a PDF created of your project that can be burned on CD or sent by e-mail to your client. Also, InDesign CS5 users have a feature that can export their document for earlier version InDesign CS4 users to read as an **InDesign Markup Language (IDML)** document. With both of these avenues available, most anyone should be able to view your creations. You'll be shown how to create an IDML document very soon.

CREATING A PDF DOCUMENT FOR ALL TO READ

Since some of your clients may not have InDesign CS5 installed, it normally would mean they could not read the document. With InDesign, if a universal proof is needed that embeds all fonts and graphics to provide to a printer, a designer can use the Export command to create a PDF document. This can be read by the free Acrobat Reader available on the Adobe site (Acrobat Reader was installed on your computer in an exercise in Chapter 1 of this text) and other graphic applications as well. InDesign also allows you to select the quality of the PDF file you wish to create. Press Quality is always the best for distributing to a commercial press, but if you want to send a document through e-mail for a preliminary proofing, you may want to choose Smallest File Size under the Adobe PDF Preset pulldown menu.

TOOLKIT TIP A PDF document cannot simply be opened in InDesign. It can only be placed in a document using the Place command.

Next, you will create a PDF file from the coupon ad you just made (Figure 11-30).

1. Open the coupon advertisement you just completed, and, with links checked and updated if needed, designate Press Quality by selecting File > Adobe PDF Presets > Press Quality.

2. Select Export for the PDF document to be saved in your *Coupon* folder. You can also just select File > Export > Adobe PDF.

3. This will bring up the dialog box to save the file. Save it in your *Coupon* folder.

4. When the Export Adobe PDF dialog box appears, select the Press Quality preset with a compatibility set for Adobe Acrobat 5 or 6 to cover most users since the coupon ad involved no specialized creations. Leave all other defaults.

5. To display all kinds of printer's marks for the press (which we will cover in more detail in the next chapter), select the Marks and Bleeds from the left side menu and select All Printer's Marks to display color calibration, trim marks, and registration marks on your document. Leave all other defaults.

6. Select Export to create the PDF version in your *Coupon* folder while the original InDesign file stays on the desktop.

7. You can double-click the new *CouponAd.pdf* file to open it in the free Acrobat Reader or in the Adobe Acrobat application which comes with the CS5 suite of applications, if it is installed on your computer; because Acrobat is the universal means to view any document, and the Reader is free, most computers have some version installed already.

8. You will notice the various printer's marks added to your document for the press to read for accuracy in color, registration of the plates, and trimming marks.

9. Print the PDF document and close it when you are done.

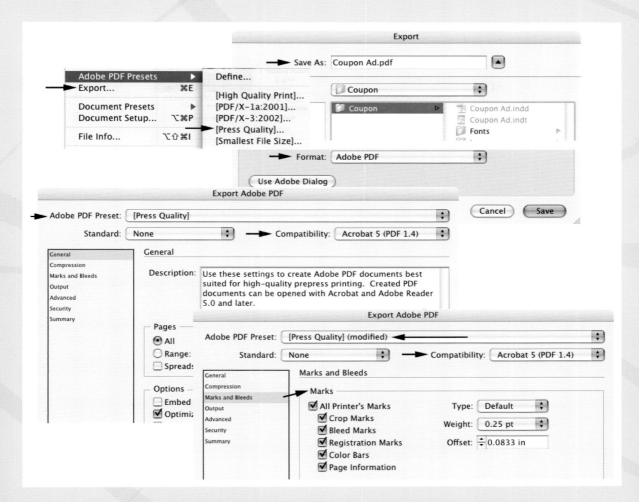

▷ FIGURE 11-30

Setting up to export an InDesign document as a press-quality PDF.

EXPORTING INDESIGN CS5 DOCUMENTS TO SAVE BACKWARDS

Normally, if you are providing your file to someone who has an earlier CS4 version of InDesign for further editing (unlike PDF files which are read only) in InDesign itself, they will not be able to read your document successfully. To open an InDesign CS5 document in InDesign CS4, you will need to do two things. First, in InDesign CS5, export the document to the new InDesign Markup Language as **IDML**. This format replaces the earlier version CS3 and CS4 formats called InDesign Interchange (**INX**). Second, the user can make sure that the computer running InDesign CS4 is updated with appropriate plug-ins so that it can be able to open the exported IDML file. To check, simply select Help > Updates to install any updates, or go to the Adobe web site and choose Support > Updates, then go to the InDesign Downloads page. Opening a document in a previous version of InDesign is also referred to as "saving down." It must also be noted that content using features that are specific to only the CS5 version may be modified or removed when you open the IDML document in InDesign CS4.

Next, you will save a CS5 document so that it can be opened by those using InDesign CS4.

1. Launch InDesign and open the InDesign document of the *CouponAd* file you just created if you had previously closed it.

2. Select File > Export then, from the File Type (Windows) or Format (Mac OS X) menu, select InDesign Markup (IDML).

3. Select to save the file in the *Coupon* folder. Choose Save when done.

4. The document will have an IDML extension to indicate that it can be read in version CS4. You can then open the *CouponAd.idml* file in InDesign CS4 to convert it to an untitled InDesign document for viewing and editing in InDesign CS4.

5. In your *Coupon* folder, you will find the *CouponAd* files in extensions INDD, INDT, IDML, and PDF.

TOOLKIT TIP For InDesign documents that need to be only read and have comments made between users without any editing of the document itself, save the document as a PDF file, which can be read regardless of what version of In-Design the document was created in. For strictly editing purposes of the actual document, this is where you would use and save backwards one version from CS5 to CS4. If the users has CS3, the document may still be read using InDesign CS4's INX interchange extension. To open the InDesign CS5 document in InDesign CS3, the user will need to open the exported IDML extension file in InDesign CS4, save it in CS4 as normal INDD file, export it again to InDesign CS3 Interchange (INX) extension, and then open the exported INX file in InDesign CS3. Again making sure that all versions have been updated. The CS3 document would then be saved in CS3 as normal INDD file.

DIGITAL TOOLKIT EXTRA: Creating a Photo Calendar with Tables

This assignment will demonstrate how to create a calendar template that can be used on your desk with your favorite image while displaying the current month using a table. A **table** consists of rows and columns of cells. A **cell** is like a text frame in which you can add text, inline graphics, or other tables. Tables provide a powerful tool for proper alignment and distribution of evenly spaced columns and rows or containers containing text and graphics. When you create a table, it fills the width of the container text frame that you create to place the table into. A table is inserted where you place the cursor insertion point. Tables can be created by using the Table menu to set up formatting and specifics. You can also create tables by using the Convert Text to Table command. In this extra assignment, you will create a calendar using both methods to see which you prefer (Figure 11-31). As always, with InDesign and most applications, there are many ways to create a project. Any selection of table cells or contents to be edited requires highlighting with the Type tool.

▷ FIGURE 11-31
Completed calendar.

SETTING UP THE DOCUMENT

First, you will set up the document as two columns in landscape letter-half mode to create a desk calendar (Figure 11-32). The left column will be used to place the month, and the right column will be used for the table to place the days. You will create a large gutter width of one inch in between the columns to act as guide for the margins. A **gutter** is the space between two columns. Gutters are used with layout guides, folding guides, and sometimes to help with margin guides.

It is time to set up the new document parameters.

1. Create a folder inside your Chapter 11 folder named *Calendar*. Move or copy the *Lighthse.tif* file that we'll use later into the folder. Launch InDesign, making sure the Units and Increments settings in preferences are set for Inches (InDesign > Preferences [Mac], or Edit > Preferences [Windows]).

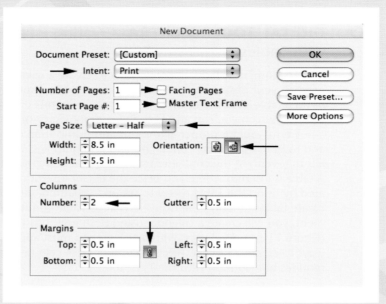

2. Select File > New > Document. When the display opens, make sure the Intent is set to Print, and the Facing Pages options and Master Text Frame options are *not* checked, because we are not creating a book or newsletter.

3. Set up the document in letter half size in landscape orientation, as 2 columns, with half-inch margins all around; you can click on the Link icon to make all measurements the same.

4. Create a half-inch gutter and leave all other defaults. Select OK.

5. Save the file in InDesign's native INDD format as *Calendar* in your *Calendar* folder within your *Chapter 11* folder.

SETTING UP THE LAYOUT GUIDES

Here you will set up some layout guides as preliminary guides to split the gutter visually to match the half-inch margin guides, and then you will set up guides for placement of the month, days of the week, and start of the table for the days of the month (Figure 11-33).

Next, we will set up the guidelines to make things easier.

1. Make sure rulers are displayed (View > Show Rulers). Also make sure Smart Guides is checked (View > Guides and Grids > Smart Guides).

2. Drag a vertical guideline from the left side ruler guide to the 4.25-inch (4-1/4) mark to split the gutter visually.

Layout guides for calendar.

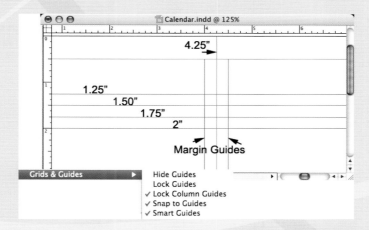

3. For the month title, year, days of the week, and start of the table for the days of the month, drag horizontal guides and use the Control panel (Y coordinate for horizontal lines) for precision by entering at 1.25 (1-1/4), 1.5 (1-1/2), 1.75 (1-3/4), and 2-inch marks.

4. You can resize your document window to display your document spread proportionately by selecting Fit Spread in Window in the View menu, then drag the bottom right corner of the window. Save the file.

FORMATTING AND COLORING TYPE

There are many different ways to enter type, whether in a table or in individual text frames. Sometimes having different text frames provides a little more flexibility when editing than having everything within a table. Here, you will put the title and year in their own text frame. Instead of creating a text frame with the shape or frame tools, you can also use the Type tool to create its own text frame.

TOOLKIT TIP To create individual text frames for headings, select the Type tool and create the text frame, type in the line, deselect by selecting the Selection tool or one of the tools on the Tools panel, then select the Type tool and draw another text frame. This way they can be edited individually.

Here, you will create frames using the Type tool and type in the month and year, center it horizontally and vertically, and color the text.

1. Select the Type tool and drag a diagonal box in the right-side column between the half-inch margin up top and the 1.25-inch horizontal guide. This will be for the month title.

2. Using the Type tool, make sure that you have a Stroke color of None and black Fill color in the Tools panel. You will select colors later.

3. Select from the Control panel a 36-point Copperplate Gothic Bold font, and type "January." You will center this later.

▷ FIGURE 11-34

Formatting type lines and setting up color to add to the Swatches panel.

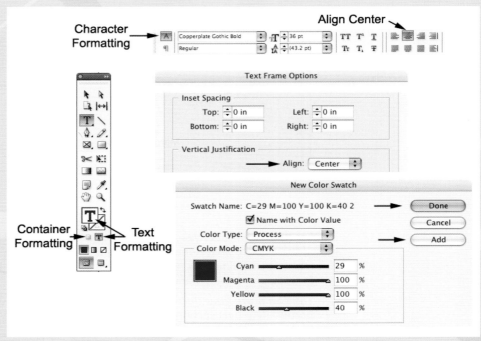

4. To start another text box, click on the Selection tool to reset, then Select the Type tool again and drag another text box this time diagonally up from the 1.5-inch horizontal line up to the 1.25-inch line. You may notice InDesign's Smart Dimensions displaying as dimension arrows when the two type boxes align together.

5. Select from the Control panel 24-point Copperplate Gothic Bold font, and type in the year 2012 as shown (Figure 11-35).

6. Highlight the text in the title with the Type tool and select the Character Formatting Controls button on the Control panel as shown in Figure 11-34. Select the icon to Align center the text. Repeat with the year text.

7. To vertically center the type line, highlight the title line, *January,* and select Object > Text Frame Options > Vertical Justification > Align Center. Repeat with the year text. There are also vertical adjustment buttons on the Control panel for quick access instead.

8. To select color for your type, choose either a deep blue, green, or red by double-clicking on the Type Fill color then selecting the color you want to use.

9. To add the color to the Swatches panel, select New Color Swatch from the Swatches panel menu and enter your color; we chose a deep red (CMYK) of C29, M100, Y100, and K40. Select Add to include the color in the swatch, then select Done to close the dialog box. You can also do this after you have set up the type in your type line.

10. Highlight the *January* text line, and tag the new color you chose in the Swatches panel (Figure 11-35). You can leave the year as black as shown, or choose another color.

TOOLKIT TIP When you want to color the cell itself or the text in the cell, under the Fill and Stroke colors are two icons, one is for coloring the cell (square) and one is for coloring the text (T). You can switch back and forth to choose what you want to color.

TOOLKIT TIP Use the Type tool to select rows and columns to place text into. You can use the Selection tool to double-click inside a cell to bring up Type tool options.

▷ FIGURE 11-35

Creating the month title and year.

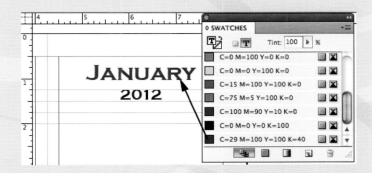

CREATING A TABLE

To place the weekdays and numbers in the month, you will create a table to distribute the information equally in the document. The easiest way to set up a text frame to place the table in is to use the Type tool again. You can then insert the table at the insertion point after creating the text frame. You will want to create the table on the right-side column of the document, because we will be putting an image on the left side later. To delete or move a table, use the Selection tool.

This is one method for creating the table.

1. Using the Type tool, draw a new text frame from the upper left corner on the right-side column from the horizontal guide at 1.75 (1-3/4), not 2 inch mark, and drag to the bottom right margin guide; make sure you drag to the bottom right margin guide and not just between the two horizontal guidelines. You will notice the blinking insertion point will display at the beginning of the text frame. Click on the Character formatting button to make it active, change the type size to 10 points as a minimum size with the same Copperplate Gothic Bold font.

2. Choose Table > Insert Table.

3. You need to specify the numbers of rows and columns. Enter 7 body rows and 7 columns. Leave all other defaults and select OK (Figure 11-36). Although most months would fit in six rows including the days of the week titles, there are a few rare times when seven rows are needed.

**Inserting a table
of seven rows and
seven columns.**

Insert Table

Table Dimensions
Body Rows: ⬍7
Columns: ⬍7
Header Rows: ⬍0
Footer Rows: ⬍0

OK
Cancel

Table Style: [Basic Table]

JANUARY
2012

TOOLKIT TIP If you are creating tables of various row or column widths and heights, you can always create a table for each type and use the arrow keys to position accurately. If your table spans more than one column or frame, specify the number of header or footer rows in which you want the information to be repeated.

RESIZING ROWS AND COLUMNS

Before editing any cells within a table, the cells need to be highlighted. For most editing, you can highlight cells with the Type tool and use the Control panel or Table menu to make an exact measurement. For almost any modifications, you need to use the I-beam from the Type tool. When you change the width of row and columns, the external dimensions of the table change. To resize rows or columns proportionally, hold down Shift while dragging the selected row or column. To resize rows or columns without changing the table width, hold down the Shift key while dragging an inside row or column edge (not the table boundary). One row or column gets bigger as the other gets smaller. Holding down Shift while dragging the right table edge will resize all the columns proportionally; holding down Shift while dragging the bottom table edge will resize all rows proportionally. To drag all rows or columns, select the right table border or bottom table edge.

Here you will use the Shift key to resize the cells for the days of the week, then drag the rows for the numbers to be distributed evenly to the bottom margin (Figure 11-37).

1. Select View > Grids and Guides and uncheck the Snap to Guides command here to freely drag the guidelines.

2. Make sure the Type tool is selected. Hold down the Shift key and click on the bottom horizontal line of the table you just drew when the cursor displays as a vertical double arrow, dragging the table straight downward very close to the bottom margin. If you drag to the margin, you may find one of the rows will disappear. We will adjust these in Step 4.

3. To create the cells for displaying the weekdays, hold down the Shift key again and click on the second horizontal line of the table drag up to the 2-inch guideline mark. You may notice that the second row for the first week's numerals is unequal to the rest. If the bottom row is moved away from the bottom margin, repeat Step 2.

4. To make all the cells that will display a number for the days of the week equal, highlight all the cells that will have the numbers with the Type tool (table rows 2-7) and select Table > Distribute Rows Evenly. You are ready to enter the numbers.

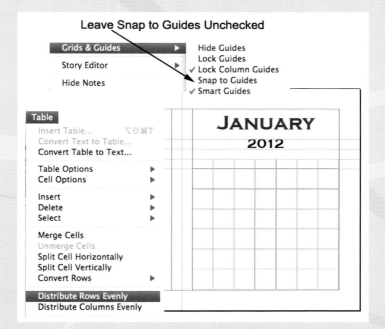

Creating and resizing the table cells.

PROBLEM If all your rows are different sizes, you can click and drag each row upwards to is original state, then Shift-drag all rows again or reinsert the table. Do not drag all the way to the bottom margin.

TOOLKIT TIP To select cells in the columns and rows you want to resize, you can also specify Column Width and Row Height settings in the Table panel or choose Table > Cell Options > Rows and Columns; specify Row Height and Column Width options, and then click OK. To move or copy a table, select the entire table, place the insertion point in the table, and choose Table > Select > Table. Choose Edit > Cut or Copy, then move the insertion point where you want the table to appear, and then choose Edit > Paste.

FORMATTING CONTENTS AND CELLS

To place the days of the week, you will highlight all the cells in the first row and set the type to Myriad Pro Bold font for easy readability. To go from one cell to another, it is best to use the Tab key once between each cell, or you can try and click in each cell with the mouse. You can then center align the type in each cell using either the Cell Options function in the Table menu, or simply highlight the type and cells you want to edit, and make the formatting changes using the Control panel (Figure 11-38).

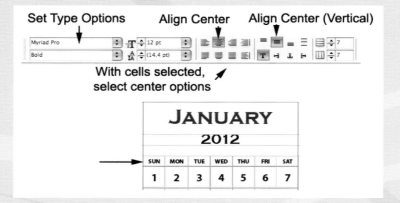

Next, you will use the Control panel to center-align the days of the week and the numbers in the calendar.

1. Select the Type tool, highlight the cells, and choose a 12-point Myriad Pro Bold font, or choose the same Copperplate Gothic Bold font, or some other fairly wide font.

2. Type in the three letters that signify the days of the week. Use the Tab key to move from one cell to the next. If you see only a red dot display in the cell, the type is too big for the cell. Reduce the size to 10 points.

3. For the numbers of the month, highlight all the remaining cells for numbers and use the same font as used for the days of the week, increasing the size to 18 points. Find the month of January in the particular year you want to create this calendar and start typing the number "1" in its correct place as shown here for the year 2012. Use the Tab key to go to the next cell to type in the next number. Tabbing will also bring you to the next row.

4. To center the days of the week and numbers within the cell, highlight the cells with the Type tool, which will change the Control panel display options; select the Align Center and vertical Align Center buttons on the Control panel. You can also use the individual Character panels on the right side of the desktop for more formatting functions.

5. Save the file.

 TOOLKIT TIP To find the calendar info for any year, you can connect to the Internet and open up Microsoft Word to search for the calendar. Microsoft will allow you to download free templates for specific years and types of calendars. You can also Google search for the calendar year you are looking for.

TOOLKIT TIP If you want the numbers to align right and at the top of each cell, highlight those cells with the Type tool, and select the Align Right for paragraph and vertical Align Top buttons on the Control panel. There are vertical justification buttons on the Control panel you can also use. In CS5, using the Text Frame Options inside the Object menu, you can now choose to have InDesign automatically balance across columns in a multiple column frame by turning on the Balance Columns option to evenly distribute the text across a number of columns.

APPLYING FILLS AND TEXT COLOR USING CELL OPTIONS

The **Cell Options command** gives you the flexibility to format text; rows and columns; strokes and fills, including tints; and diagonal lines. Under the color boxes on the Tools panel are two formatting icons: one indicates a Formatting Effects Container, which could be the cell or a frame, and the other looks like a *T*, which indicates Formatting Effects Text. These can be used with selected cells to edit the cell itself or the type within the selected cell. When placing graphic images, InDesign will display on the computer as low resolution for easier maneuvering of the image in the document. If a designer needs to see what the final design will look like when printed, InDesign provides various commands in the View menu to see various resolutions, such as Display Performance (High Quality Display).

TOOLKIT TIP To adjust a cell's color fill, click the Container formatting icon in the bottom Tools panel (Figure 11-39). To adjust a text color, click on the Text Formatting icon. You can easily go back and forth between the two types of formatting by clicking these icons.

DESIGN TIP

When coloring type in most cases, unless you are looking to outline a very light colored type, you would keep the stroke to None to maintain the exact shape of the font you are using.

Here you will add a little more color to your work using the Cell Options command, then you will add the final image.

1. To add a fill for the days of the week, highlight the row SUN through SAT with the Type tool. Select Table > Cell Options > Strokes and Fills.

2. Click on the Color button by the Cell Fill area, and select the deep red color you chose for the month of January as the Cell Fill; set up with 100% Tint and 1-point black stroke weight for the outline of the cell (Figure 11-39). This will be used to fill color into the cells for the days of the week. Select OK. We will change the color of the type next.

3. Highlight the days of the week cells again with the Type tool, and select the *T* formatting icon (Formatting Affects Text) located underneath the Fill color box.

4. If you kept a very deep color, click on the Swatches panel and select the standard yellow color with a 30% tint, as displayed in Figure 11-40, or select the white or "Paper" color to make the days of the week stand out. Try other combinations of fills for a good balance of color. Click on the Selection Tool to deselect the text.

▷ FIGURE 11-39

Formatting cells and contents using the Cell Options command.

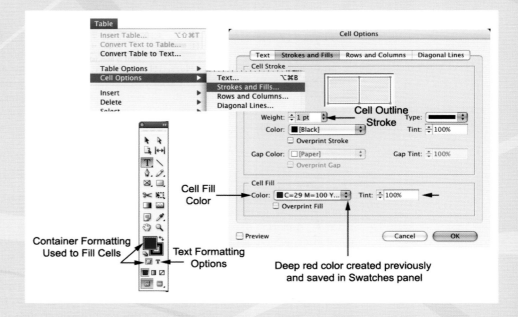

▷ FIGURE 11-40

Formatting type using Text formatting options on the Tools panel, and adjusting tint using the Swatches panel.

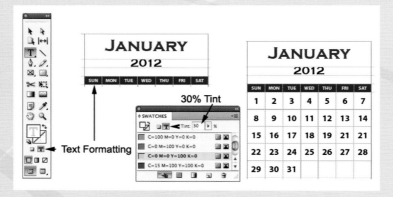

5. Be careful if you want to increase the stroke weight, because this will probably cause the bottom row of the table to disappear, and you will have to readjust the table.

6. If you want to change the color of the type in the days of the month, select the type, then select the *T* formatting icon (Formatting Affects Text) located underneath the Fill color box, then choose an appropriate color.

7. It is time to place the graphic for the month of January; you can also use your own graphic. To place a graphic on the left side to balance the calendar, draw a frame using the Rectangle Frame tool between the left side, top and bottom margin guides, and the 4-inch vertical guideline. It should display an *X* in the frame.

8. Select File > Place and place the *Lighthse.tif* file, which is a low-resolution image, for our purposes here, from either your *Chapter 11* folder or the *Calendar* folder you created earlier into the selected frame; you can also use your own graphic image. Use the arrow keys or the center doughnut (Content Indicator) on the image with the Selection tool to move the image around if needed. If you do not want the white page background, try to copy and insert the Parchment graphic used in the coupon ad and send to the back (Object > Arrange > Send to Back) or choose your own background image.

9. Optional: To apply a drop shadow effect on the image, select it with the Selection Tool. Choose Effects > Drop Shadow from the Object menu. Leave the default drop shadow effect or go ahead and experiment to add dimension to the image.

10. When you are set, select View > Grids and Guides > Hide Guides to view your work without the layout guides you used earlier. To remove all frame edges not previously drawn with stroke weight, select View > Extras > Hide Frame Edges. To view how the calendar will look at high resolution for print, select View > Display Performance > High Quality Display. Remember, for our purposes here, you are using a low resolution image.

11. Save the file as a regular InDesign document in your *Calendar* folder. It will have still have an INDD extension. Use the Links panel to check for links, and use the Preflight panel (near bottom of the window where there should be a green circle) to make sure there are no errors.

12. You can now create a monthly calendar template by choosing File > Save As > InDesign Template in your *Chapter 11* folder. It will have an INDT extension (Figure 11-41).

13. Save and Print the final file. Check with your instructor to choose whether to include crop marks and other printer's marks.

14. OPTIONAL: To create a package of all fonts and the lighthouse graphic to be copied into a folder, including other info mentioned in the Advanced section, select File > Package, then select Package. Put in any print instructions and select Continue. Name the new folder as *Calendar Job* and Save inside your Calendar folder. The graphic and fonts will be copied over for you. Nice and organized!

TOOLKIT TIP When ready to place a full-sized image into the frame window, unless you are fine with having a portion cropped, resize the image or graphic ahead of time in Photoshop before placing it in an InDesign document.

TOOLKIT TIP As a final note, in the next chapter you will be working with master pages. You can come back to the calendar document you just made and create the other eleven documents for each month from the master page; then simply place images or designs for each month and the appropriate numbering for each month. In CS5, you have a new Layers panel. Save the layer you just created as January. You can then duplicate and create 11 more layers, labeling each for each month. Then just edit for each month.

Placing the graphic, removing frame and guidelines, and saving as a template for future documents.

CONVERTING TEXT TO A TABLE (OPTIONAL)

Another method to create a table is either by importing text from a spreadsheet or by entering data using the Tab key to generate columns and then using the Return/Enter key to generate rows.

1. Set up preferences and the document layout as you did before.

2. Start typing in the numbers days of the week; hit the Tab key once after each word or number to create the columns, then use the Return/Enter key to make a paragraph return to create the rows.

3. To create the table, select Table > Convert Text to Table. The cells of rows and columns will be created around your type.

4. Size the rows and apply formatting as described in the earlier exercises. Have fun.

TABLE AND CELL STYLES

A more advanced function than what we will cover here allows a designer to create cell and table styles that serve as mini templates that contain all formatting, so you could create a cell style and then save that cell style to have the formatting copied to other cells. The same can be created using a table style, where you can also include cell styles within table styles. These styles are in their own Table Styles and Cell Styles panels, and you would use the panel menu to create new styles. Check in InDesign Help to view the tutorials for using these styles; we will look more at styles in the next chapter. You can also create inline notes in tables to other workers. You can store your notes linked to specific text in a table as well.

CHAPTER SUMMARY

You learned that in a desktop publishing program, you can create frames by using shape tools or the Type tool, or by clicking the mouse in the document for inserting text and graphics. You learned how to control the container contents using stroke and fill effects, and to use the Text Frame Options command and the Control panel to control formatting. In the advanced section, you were able to go through the process of preflight, packaging, and preparing a final proof of your document for either final client approval or for the service provider. Do not forget to check out the *Goodies* folder on the text CD for more projects and ideas.

REVIEW QUESTIONS

1. Explain the differences between word processing and desktop publishing.

2. Explain the differences between margin guides and layout guides.

3. Explain at least three different extensions InDesign can create and what purposes they serve.

4. What is the purpose of the Links panel?

5. Explain briefly the process of the preflighting and the Package utility.

6. Describe the following printer mark terms: *bleed, slug, crop, color bars,* and *registration marks.*

CHAPTER 11
Creating a direct
mail coupon ad
using InDesign.

CHAPTER 11 ADVANCED
Preflighting, packaging,
and preparing for press.

CHAPTER 11 EXTRA
Creating a desktop calendar
using tables in InDesign.

▷ FIGURE 11-42

Working with Multipage Documents

CHAPTER OBJECTIVES: To understand the importance of using InDesign to create effective multipage documents, in this chapter you will:

▷ Learn procedures to set up multipage InDesign documents for importing text and graphics.

▷ Set up a master page as a template for layout and design consistency.

▷ Navigate and edit the document using the Pages panel.

▷ Apply stroke and fill techniques for specific press-ready Pantone colors.

▷ Import text into multiple columns and multiple pages. Create jump lines into multiple pages.

▷ Create precise alignment columns using tabs.

▷ Apply special formatting techniques for headlines, body text, drop caps, rules, and pull quotes.

▷ ADVANCED USERS: Baseline alignment and automation with styles and object libraries.

▷ DIGITAL TOOLKIT EXTRA: Create an interactive PDF document.

One of the main uses that a desktop publishing program like InDesign provides is the ability to create multiple documents like newsletters, books, and other printed media with consistency in layout. Text documents created in another application can be easily imported into the project without having to retype the content. In this chapter you will create a four-page newsletter to learn the process of importing text and graphics and providing consistency in layout and design. You will learn how to automate repetitive tasks to save time and increase your productivity by using master pages as document templates, importing text into multiple columns and multiple pages, and applying styles for consistency in formatting of text.

Need additional fun computer graphics tutorials and info, and an additional look at the projects you'll be creating in this book? Check out my Artist's Digital Toolkit website at: **http://www.digitoolkit.com**

DESIGNING MULTIPAGE DOCUMENTS

Multipage documents include many types of documents, from booklets to newsletters. The key when working with multipage documents is consistency in layout, design, and character or paragraph formatting. The reader's eye can easily pick out a mistake or error if formatting is inconsistent. In creating newsletters or multipage documents, you may have various articles all vying for the reader's attention. Employing certain techniques discreetly helps to introduce or lead the reader to various articles within the multipage document, which heightens a reader's interest. Some of these techniques, such as filling a couple of text boxes with color, establishing visual hierarchy in headings, continuing an article to a later page to entice the reader to view other articles as they are turning to that page, and providing an index sheet all help to promote a positive reading experience. All pages created in InDesign can be accessed as thumbnail representations through Adobe Bridge or through the Mini Bridge application within InDesign.

NAMEPLATES AND CONTINUING BANNERS

Nameplates are the identifying sections located on the first or front page that usually consist of a company logo or identifiable graphic, the formatted title of the newsletter, and a color text box consisting of information such as the issue or volume number, edition description, and author or editor. Nameplates are also referred to as **mastheads**, although technically mastheads are found on the section of a newsletter that lists the name of the publisher and other pertinent data that may include staff names, contributors, subscription information, addresses, a logo, and so on. **Continuing banners** or **headers** are found in the top portion of the additional pages and have a continuing color scheme, text format for the title, and sometimes an identifiable company logo (Figure 12-1). The nameplate and continuing banners are used in each newsletter to identity them to the reader.

▷ FIGURE 12-1

Newsletter with nameplate and continuing banners.

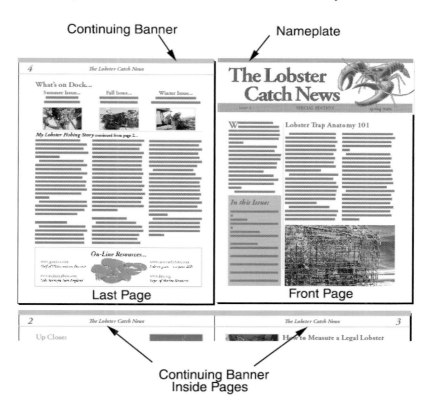

TYPE DESIGN FOR MULTIPAGE DOCUMENTS

When you are creating a document for printed media that contains articles or lots of paragraphs, in many cases choose a serif typeface for text in the body of the document; it helps to lead the reader's eyes from one line to the next.

• The default size for body text is usually 10 points, but it may be increased to 12 points depending on your target audience and the type of information you are printing.

• Using serif and sans serif headings and subheadings may depend on the body text being used. Selecting a font or style—such as bold, which widens the letter shape—to distinguish it from the body text, and should also complement the body text. Increasing the size or using color will also promote visual distinction.

DESIGN TIP

When using styles, like bold or italic, select fonts that contain the style name in them, like Garamond Bold. Using the Bold or Italic buttons may cause problems in spacing for documents being sent to the printer. In InDesign, you cannot use false bolds or italic; if it is not included in the font typeface, InDesign will not use it or display it.

- In a document that is going to be used electronically, such as on the web, for the body of the text, choose a sans serif option that is at least 2 to 4 points larger than you would use in the printed text body so that the text displayed electronically will read easier.

- When working with sentences, do not double space between sentences.

TOOLKIT TIP Nowadays, whether to use serif or sans serif text may also depend on what context it will be used in. For this book, as it is technology based, contains much terminology, and uses many exercises, sans serif text is more appropriate for users or readers that may need to go over steps or terms repeatedly to help in understanding processes or techniques.

CONVERTING INCHES TO DECIMALS OR PICAS AND POINTS

Although most designers create and align items in their documents in inches or fractions of inches, the designer who works at or for a commercial printing establishment may use points and picas as the standard of measurement for more precision. One inch is the equivalent of 72 points, whereas 12 points equals one **pica**. Six picas equal an inch. Points are used universally for measuring font sizes and spacing between text characters and text lines. In the printing industry, when measuring with picas and points, the designation "3" *before* the "p" indicates 3 picas, whereas "9" *after* the letter "p" indicates 9 points. The measurement "3p9" for instance, indicates 3 picas and 9 points, or the equivalent to 5/8 of an inch.

Here is a table to get you comfortable with this conversion.

INCHES	DECIMAL	POINTS	PICAS
1	1.00	72	6p
7/8	.875	63	5p3
3/4	.750	54	4p6
5/8	.625	45	3p9
1/2	.500	36	3p
3/8	.375	27	2p3
1/4	.250	18	1p6
1/8	.125	9	p9
1/16	.0625	4.5	p4.5

MASTER PAGES AND THE PAGES PANEL

There are two main sections in the **Pages panel**. The top section, or global level, contains icons for using **master pages**, which are used as guides or document templates with the same parameters and formatting for selected documents. They affect changes globally in the document. In a book for example, a designer might want to create separate master pages for a table of contents, a chapter introduction page, body text, glossary, and index. You can apply master pages by simply dragging the master page icons onto the document page icons below those documents that you would like to contain that master page format, or you can use the Panel menu display as in all Adobe panels. Because they are set as formatting guides or document templates, master pages can be edited or built upon previous master pages after they have been applied to a document. The bottom portion of the Pages panel, or local level, contains the document icons that represent the actual document pages being created and allow you to edit individual documents. This also helps you navigate through multiple pages, and these can be set up as individual documents, as was done in the previous chapter, or as facing pages for multiple documents. Multiple pages butted next to one another or viewed together, such as the two pages visible in a book or magazine, are referred to as a **spread**. In a master page spread, there is a left-hand and right-hand facing page with the first page of a spread on the right side (Figure 12-2). At the local level, as you create frames of graphics and text on your pages, you will see thumbnail graphic representations with master page letters displayed on each individual page for quick reference. In previous versions, if a user has a number of designs with different page sizes, they would have to create separate documents. In InDesign CS5, designers can use the Edit Pages function at the bottom of the Pages panel to define different page sizes for pages within a document. This works quite nicely for advertising campaigns where the user can create a number of different sized pieces (business cards, post cards, letterheads, envelopes, etc.) which would all share the same design elements and the designer could manage as one file.

▷ FIGURE 12-2

Pages panel contains master pages and documents individually and as spreads.

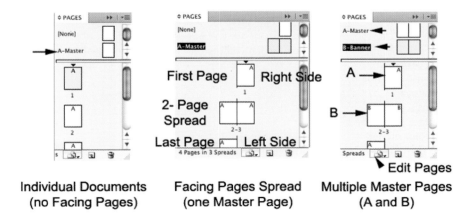

Individual Documents
(no Facing Pages)

Facing Pages Spread
(one Master Page)

Multiple Master Pages
(A and B)

CMYK PROCESS AND SPOT COLORS

Every color in the InDesign Swatches panel is defined as either a process color or a spot color. Commercial printers use inks that are percentages of a subtractive process of the colors cyan, magenta, yellow, and black (CMYK). The color black (K) is added last as a fourth color for purity in shadows and improved contrast and tones. These four colors are used in four separate plates during the printing process, hence the term CMYK **process colors**. Use process colors when a job requires so many colors that using individual spot inks would be expensive or impractical. This is the universally accepted and default method when designing with color for print. A **spot color** is a special premixed ink that is used instead of, or in addition to, CMYK process inks, and it requires its own printing plate on a printing press. Use spot colors when few colors are specified and color accuracy is critical. The Coca-Cola Company, for instance, uses a special spot color when printing its special red color used in its logo. Spot colors are easily converted into process color equivalents and are printed as CMYK plate separations rather than on a single plate (Figure 12-3).

TOOLKIT TIP Any RGB color graphic images that are to be printed on a press need to be converted to CMYK color mode before they are imported into the InDesign document. Before converting, create the CMYK as a separate file to retain the RGB color in the original file in case you may need to edit it in the future. If you must use a special spot color, like Coca-Cola would use a special spot color for the red in their cans, keep the number of spot colors you use to a minimum. Each spot color you create will generate an additional spot color printing plate for a printing press, which will increase your printing costs.

▷ FIGURE 12-3

CMYK process colors use percentages of cyan, magenta, yellow, and black inks with each color etched on its own plate for the press. Spot colors are premixed colors that use an additional plate during the printing process.

CMYK Process Colors

Spot Color

CLIENT ASSIGNMENT: Creating a Multipage Newsletter

Shelly Britton, a student editorial photographer at a local college, has been asked by the local newspaper to create a quarterly four-page newsletter insert that gives tourists to the area a glimpse into the life of lobstermen and fishermen. She has gone out on a few trips with a local lobsterman and has created the photographs and written a series of articles for this premier edition. Shelly has asked you to design the layout for her to give to the newspaper. You discuss that the layout will be set up in a three-column format with an index section, a story continuing on within the newsletter, line and fills applied to add color and dimension, and reference sections for special terms, websites, and upcoming issues. You lay out a rough idea of what the nameplate will look like to identify the newsletter and for future newsletters, which she approves. You tell Shelly you will have the layout completed by the end of the week for final approval (Figure 12-4).

ACTION ITEMS OVERVIEW

- Set Preferences to Pica measurement for more precision in your layout.
- Lay out the document with guides for text and graphics.
- Select specific four-color premixed Pantone colors to apply consistent color to text, continuing banners, and frames.
- Create a master page template that contains continuing banners with a continuing theme and automatic page numbering.
- Edit the front page document to include the nameplate to identify the newsletter.
- Place graphics into specific areas set by guides.
- Import text articles using the Place command into multiple columns and into multiple pages.
- Create jump lines to specify "Continued to" and "Continued from" between pages with the same article.
- Use the Tabs panel to align columns for index page and text frames.
- Create rules to separate articles and for use as pull quotes.
- ADVANCED USERS: Baseline alignment and automation with styles and object libraries.
- DIGITAL TOOLKIT EXTRA: Create an interactive PDF document.

LAYOUT USING FACING PAGES AND PICA MEASUREMENTS

To give you an idea of how to work with more precise measurements, you will need to set the preferences to picas for this assignment and then set up the document using facing pages. When you select the Facing Pages option in the File > Document Setup dialog box, document pages are arranged in spreads. Selecting

▷ FIGURE 12-4

**Completed
newsletter.**

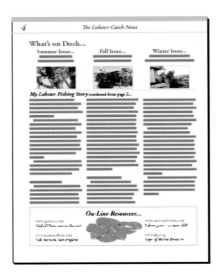

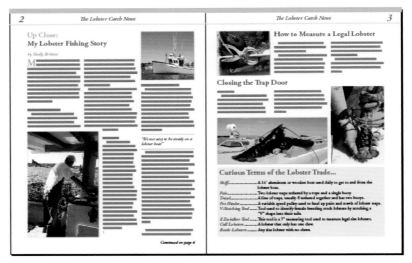

Completed Newsletter
(Page 1 starts on right side, Page 4 ends on left side)

the **Master Text Frame option** in the New Document dialog box flows large articles over a series of pages. For this assignment we will not need to have that option checked. Every InDesign spread includes its own **pasteboard**, which is an area outside a page where you can store objects that are not yet positioned within the active page. Each spread's pasteboard provides space to accommodate objects that bleed, or extend past the edge of a page, when the bleed setting is created under the document set up.

▷ FIGURE 12-5

Conversion table for inches, decimals, points, and picas.

Conversion Table			
12 Points = 1 pica	Example: 3p4 = 3 picas 4 points		
Inches	**Decimal**	**Points**	**Picas**
1	1.00	72	6
7/8	.875	63	5p3
3/4	.750	54	4p6
5/8	.625	45	3p9
1/2	.500	36	3
3/8	.375	27	2p3
1/4	.250	18	1p6
1/8	.125	9	p9

TOOLKIT TIP Six picas are equal to an inch, and 12 points equals 1 pica. When measuring with picas and points, the designation "4" in front of the letter "p" indicates 4 picas in measurement, whereas a "6" after the letter "p" indicates 6 points. The measurement "4p6," for instance, indicates 4 picas and 6 points, the equivalent of 0.75 (3/4) of an inch (Figure 12-5).

▷ FIGURE 12-6

Organizing folders and setting up the document for the newsletter with facing pages option and pica measurement.

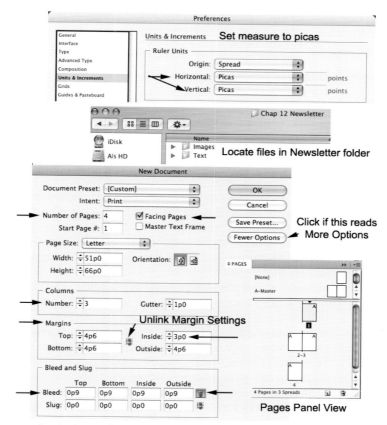

Create 4-page facing pages document

Next, you will set up the newsletter document.

1. To make sure you are using picas to measure margins and gutters, go into InDesign Preferences (InDesign > Preferences > Units & Increments [Mac] or Edit > Preferences > Units & Increments [PC]) and change the Horizontal Ruler Units and the Vertical Ruler Units to Picas for more precision in this assignment. Click OK.

2. On your drive, locate your *Chapter 12* folder inside your *Toolkit > InDesign* folder.

3. Locate the *Newsletter* folder inside your *Chapter 12* folder. Inside the *Newsletter* folder, you will find the folders *Images* and *Text*. You will copy fonts later.

4. Here is a look at your directory structure:

Toolkit > InDesign > Chapter 12 > Newsletter > Images/Text

The InDesign document project you will be working on here will also be saved as *Lobster* inside the *Newsletter* folder.

5. Select File > New > Document and enter the following information: Pages = 4, Facing Pages On, Page Size is letter with portrait orientation and Intent of Print, Columns = 3, Gutter = 1p0 (1 pica), Margins = picas. First, click the link icon to break it so you can put in these individual amounts: Top = 4p6 (equal to 0.75 inches), Bottom = 4p6, and Inside = 3p0 (equal to 0.5 inches), and Outside = 4p6. Click the More Options button and add a "0p9," or one-eighth inch, bleed along the outside edges. Use Figure 12-6 as a reference.

6. Save the file as *Lobster* inside your *Newsletter* folder. You can see the master page and document icons in the Pages panel.

7. At the bottom of the document window next to the green circle, click on the downward arrow and check that you have enabled Preflight options in the Preflight menu to have the document checked dynamically as you add text and graphics. Display the Preflight panel (Window > Output > Preflight).

DESIGN TIP

When working with spreads, the inside margins generally are smaller in width than the outside margins. Pica measurements work quite nicely when more precision is needed; this is the measurement that a designer might use when sending complex or multi-page documents to press.

SETTING UP THE MASTER PAGE TEMPLATE

Master pages allow the designer to set up guides, page numbers, color fills, and text formatting on a page that can be used as a formatting guide for documents and to build other master pages upon. Master pages provide one of the best ways to create consistency in layout when using multipage documents, and they save time in developing individual documents. In newsletters, the first page contains a nameplate to identify the set of documents. A continuing banner or header may be used in the following pages to continue with the theme of the newsletter. A continuing banner may contain the same colors or logo used, the newsletter title, and a formatted page number. By creating a master page, you can make changes to the template, such as creating the continuing banner for the following pages and removing it for the nameplate on the first page. You will first create the continuing banner master page template with components on the left side, then duplicate the same components to the right side for accurate placement. When working with facing pages, each master page spread has a left and right-hand page; elements such as page numbers that should appear on all pages should be placed on both the left and right master pages of a spread.

TOOLKIT TIP When you work with facing pages, you must make the same measurements and formatting to both the left and right side of the master page.

MEASURING LAYOUT GUIDES IN PICAS

Measuring layout guides in picas and points is much more accurate than using inches. You can also enter any decimal equivalent in the guide field. The smaller increments of the point measurement system are easier to visualize than inches as decimal equivalents. For instance, 24 points is easier to visualize for most people than .3472 inches. To create a continuing banner in the master page document to apply the template to all documents, use layout guides to position the newsletter title, page numbers, rule, and top color bar for a consistent look (Figure 12-7).

TOOLKIT TIP The top left black edge of the document is usually displayed as the zero point on the ruler guides (default). To create a zero point drag from the corner where the guides intersect to the black corner edge of the document. The red outline outside the document edge is the bleed area.

▷ FIGURE 12-7

Setting up horizontal layout guides for the master page continuing banner.

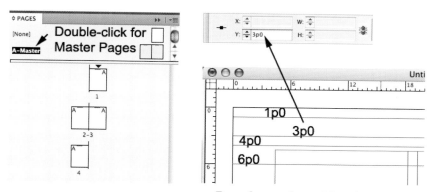

Drag from ruler guides downward
Document edges display as "0" on ruler guides

TOOLKIT TIP You can also change preferences in measurement to inches on the fly then back to points or picas by Control clicking (Mac) or right-clicking (Windows) on the rulers to toggle and select different units of measurement.

In this exercise, you will create the guides for the left and right side for the continuing banner on the master page.

1. Double-click the A-Master text on the global upper portion of the Pages panel. This will display both left and right master pages centered on your screen. If you select the icons, they will move to the selected side (Figure 12-7).

2. Zoom in to 100% or closer to see your work.

3. To set up guides for the continuing banner and the starting guide for the text frames, make sure Rulers display (if not, select View > Show Rulers), Snap to Guides is checked (View > Grids & Guides > Snap to Guides), Smart Guides and Lock Column Guides should also be checked in there as well. Choose the Selection tool, then, to make sure the guides span across both master page documents, hold down the Command (Mac)/Ctrl (PC) key while dragging horizontal guides at pica measurements of 1p0, 3p0, 4p0, and 6p0 from the ruler guides into the master pages. Use the Y Location box (horizontal axis) on the Control panel to help with exact measurements. For easier accuracy, you can start to drag out each guide, then type in the coordinates, pressing the Return/Enter key afterwards to put the guide in place.

4. With the document set at Facing pages, this will set up the continuing banner on all odd and even pages of your project.

DESIGN TIP

Some fonts to choose from are Garamond, Georgia, Times Roman, or Bookman Old Style. Whatever typeface you choose, be consistent with the text body and the overall look of the newsletter.

TOOLKIT TIP To move identical guides across two facing pages, using the Selection tool, hold down the Command (Mac)/Ctrl (PC) key and drag from the ruler guide. The guide line will span across both pages. To move guides to one page simply drag from the ruler guide using just the Selection tool.

TOOLKIT TIP To remove guides, select the guide with the Selection tool (a black square displays under the cursor) and press Delete. You can also drag them back into the ruler.

NEWSLETTER TITLE ON THE CONTINUING BANNER

The continuing banner continues the style, color, and theme of a multipage document thoughout the pages. You can continue the formatted name of the newsletter and page numbers to help the reader identify what they are reading. The newsletter title can be formatted for consistency on all pages with the same look (Figure 12-8).

▷ FIGURE 12-8

Creating the continuing banner title.

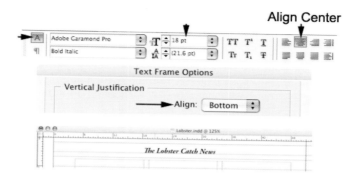

Here you will type and position the newsletter title, *The Lobster Catch News,* on the master page continuing banners.

1. To create the newsletter title for the continuing banner, zoom in at 100% or more and select the Type tool, dragging a text frame on the left-side master page document between the 1p0 and 3p0 pica measurements and the document edges (vertical black lines).

2. Select Adobe Garamond Pro Bold Italic font (Mac) or another serif font that specifies Bold and Italic in its name; select a size of 18 points, and type "The Lobster Catch News."

3. Select the Character formatting icon on the Control panel and Align center the text line.

4. With the cursor still in the text frame, select Object > Text Frame Options and change the Vertical Justification Alignment to Bottom. Now the text line should sit on the 3-pica guide.

5. Repeat the same process on the right-side master page, except drag the type frame box diagonally from the right side towards the left vertical line. The smart guides will display as arrows when you reach the left vertical line without overlapping onto the other text frame. To make sure you have just created this type line on Master Pages, click on the Pages panel and you should see a slight thumbnail representation of the type line on all four pages below in the local area.

CREATING AN AUTO PAGE NUMBER MARKER

InDesign provides the designer with lots of options in the Type menu to insert special characters. You can add a **page number marker** to your pages to specify where a page number sits on a page and how it is formatted. Because a page-number marker updates automatically, the page number it displays is always correct, even as you add, remove, or rearrange pages in the document. Page number markers can be formatted and styled as text. To create one, make sure you have the master page selected, then select the Type tool and drag the text frame until it is large enough to hold the largest number and any additional text you would like to include. Use the Insert Special Character > Markers > Current Page Number commands in the Type menu to display the master page prefix *A,* in this case on both the left and right sides. When you click on a document, it will automatically indicate the sequential page number you have created.

DESIGN TIP

Using the Auto Page or Markers functions allows you to move pages around without worrying about sequencing page numbers; it is done automatically. Text boxes by default can overlap one another without affecting each other. You can also choose to have them wrap around one another or around a graphic.

In this exercise, you will use the Insert Special Character command in the master pages to automatically format the page numbers (Figure 12-9).

1. To create the text frame for the page number, make sure the master page section is selected in the top portion of the Pages panel (A-Master). Select the Type tool and drag from the document edge at the 4p0 guide up to the 1p0 guide over to the 6 pica horizontal ruler mark (6p0) on the top left side of the left side document, the grey measurement cursor box should read W: 6.0 and H: 3.0 (Figure 12-9).

2. To create an automatic page number, change the size of the font you used for the newsletter title (The Lobster Catch News) to 30 points, and select Type > Insert Special Character > Markers > Current Page Number, or use Insert Special Character > Auto Page Number for earlier versions. An *A* will appear to show it is a master page number (A-Master displays in the Pages panel). If the text disappears and a red cross is displayed, the type is too big; decrease the size.

3. To center the Page number in the text frame, select Object > Text Frame Options and change the Vertical Justification Alignment to Center. Select to Align Center to center the text horizontally by clicking the icon in Character formatting on the Control panel.

4. Repeat the same process on the right-side master page, but have the page-number marker created on the right edge of the document. Draw the text frame box from the edge of the document up between the 4p0 and 1p0 pica guides to the horizontal ruler 96-pica mark. The grey measurement box guide should read W: 6.0 and H: 3.0.

5. To see the effect, double-click one of the documents in the lower document section of the Pages panel; you will notice the document number will display instead of the master page number, and the title line. Double-click the A-Master text, when you are done in the Pages panel, to continue working on the master page banner.

6. Save the file.

▷ FIGURE 12-9

Using the Type > Insert Special Character menus for creating auto pages in master page documents.

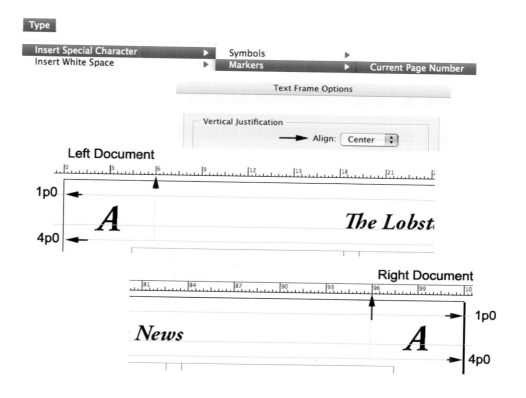

TOOLKIT TIP The Pages panel can display absolute numbering—labeling all pages with consecutive numbers, starting at the first page of the document—which is the default. It can also display section numbering to label pages by section, such as the preface, table of contents, text body, glossary, or index. Changing the numbering display affects how pages are indicated in the InDesign document and in the Pages panel and the page box you create. However, it does not change the appearance of page numbers on document pages. Click on the arrow above the document to see your numbering choices.

CREATING RULES AND COLOR BARS

Rules are lines that are used to help separate sections of articles in a pleasing way, and they can be created using the Line tool while holding down the Shift key. There are also paragraph rules that are used for pull quotes in long articles, which we will discuss later. Whenever working with graphics that involve a very wide stroke weight for color bars, you may find it easier to use one of the frame tools and create a graphic box to fill in the color. Color bars are technically not rules but may be used as a decorative touch. In CS5, you can use the Control panel to set stroke and fill settings with a pop up Swatches panel for quick access to color.

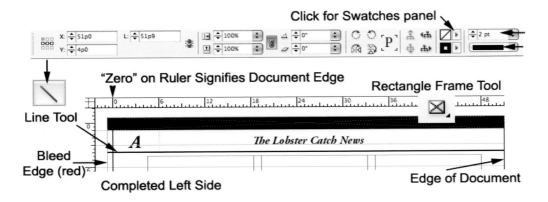

Click for Swatches panel

"Zero" on Ruler Signifies Document Edge

Rectangle Frame Tool

Line Tool

Bleed
Edge (red)

Completed Left Side

Edge of Document

The Lobster Catch News

▷ FIGURE 12-10

**Creating rules and
color bars for a
continuing banner.**

Here you will create a rule along the 4p0 layout guide to both edges of the document, then use the Rectangle Frame tool to create a color bar at the top of the document (Figure 12-10).

1. Make sure you are still working with a master page document (double-click A-Master) and Snap to Guides is checked (View > Grids & Guides > Snap to Guides).

2. Select the Line tool (\) in the Tools panel. In CS5, using the Control panel, choose a 2-point stroke weight. Make sure the Stroke is set to the default color, usually black, and the Fill color is set to None. Leave the default color; you will change it later. Make sure the entire document displays.

3. Hold down the Shift key and drag carefully on the left-side master page document along the 4p0 layout guide to create a perfectly straight line from the left side red bleed edge of the document to the right edge, making sure you don't overlap to the other document. You will notice when you are at the edge of the document that an arrow will display under the cross cursor. The grey measurement cursor box will also display L: 51.9. Release the mouse first, then release the Shift key.

DESIGN TIP

When sending a document with rules to the printer, avoid creating rules that are less than 1 point, sometimes referred to as *hairlines*, as they can cause problems and may not print clearly.

4. Create another rule the same way on the right side. Do not drag across both documents or overlap the graphics; this will not allow you to edit the rule on one document without affecting the other document when working with spreads. Select the Selection tool and click on the outer pasteboard to deselect the Line tool.

5. Optional: To delete the 4p0 guide, not the line, to see your work, move the Selection tool until it displays a black square underneath. Select the guideline and press the Delete key.

6. For the top color bar on the continuing banner, make sure the Fill color box is selected in front with the default black color and the Stroke color set to None.

7. Select the Rectangle Frame (F) tool and drag up the left-side bleed edge of the master page document from the 1p0 horizontal guide along the top bleed guideline (0p9 or 1/8 inch). Drag to the right edge of the document. Do not worry about the color; you will add that later. The dimensions should read W: 51p9 and H: 1p9.

8. Carefully repeat the same process on the right-side document to stay consistent. Do not overlap onto the left side color bar.

9. Use the Selection tool if needed to select and adjust the resizing handles of the selected box to extend the color over to the bleed edge.

10. Save the document.

SETTING UP PANTONE PROCESS COLORS

Just as you would select colors at a paint store, InDesign provides an almost limitless assortment of colors from various color-swatch manufacturers in what are called **color libraries**. Most of the commercial print industry in the United States uses color swatches by Pantone. You can install additional color libraries and load swatches from them in InDesign (Figure 12-11). Pantone Colors are one of the worldwide standards for color reproduction, and Pantone color guides and chip books are printed on coated, uncoated, and matte paper stocks to ensure accurate visualization of the printed result and better on-press control. You can print a solid Pantone color in CMYK. In InDesign, the settings you have in other Adobe applications can all be synchronized with InDesign for consistent color management. Before applying colors, it is best to select colors and add them to the Swatches panel for future use on your

▷ FIGURE 12-11

Selecting Pantone colors from the Color library to add to the Swatches panel.

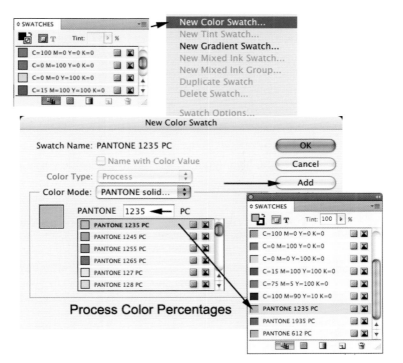

document. You will also notice that the box icon displaying the four CMYK colors to the right of each color will display the process CMYK color percentages when the cursor hovers over it. Remember that pros in the field do not rely solely on the monitor to display the correct color; they also may use print color swatches to check for color accuracy. As was discussed in using Illustrator colors, designers can access the Adobe Kuler color libraries to explore, create, and share various color themes, from this online community. Themes can be easily downloaded and moved into your Swatches panel. In CS5, you can use the Control panel to set stroke and fill settings with a pop up Swatches panel for quick access to color. As you add new colors to the Swatches panel, they are also added in the swatches pop up menu in the Control panel.

TOOLKIT TIP When you are looking for Pantone color reference numbers, they are sequential in terms of the first digits and in color tone. For instance, if you are looking for the number 1235, you need to be within numbers that start with 12; look past the first three digits, and you will find number 126 followed by colors in four digits, up to 1235.

Here you will select Pantone Solid to Process Coated inks for the banner color bars, rules, and to fill text boxes (Pantone 1235 PC, 1935 PC, 612 C).

1. To add premade Pantone process colors, it is easiest to create a new color swatch from the Swatches panel menu.

2. To access the Swatches panel, choose Window > Color > Swatches. Choose New Color Swatch in the Swatches panel menu.

3. When the New Color Swatch dialog box opens, from the Color Mode list, choose the library file *Pantone Solid to Process.*

4. Type in 1235, then click Add, *NOT OK,* then type in, 1935, click Add, and 612, click OK for the color, color PC swatches respectively from the Pantone Solid to Process library: click Add, *NOT OK,* after selecting each color (Figure 12-11).

5. When you have selected the colors, select Done on the dialog box.

6. You will notice the new swatches you have selected will display on the Swatches panel to use for your newsletter.

7. Save the file in your *Newsletter* folder inside your *Chapter 12* folder.

TOOLKIT TIP In InDesign and other Adobe applications you can share most of the solid swatches you create in one Adobe application with any other Adobe application by saving a swatch library for exchange. The colors appear exactly the same across applications as long as your color settings are synchronized. In the Swatches panel, create the process and spot-color swatches you want to share, and remove any swatches you do not want to share. Select Save Swatches from the Swatches panel menu, name the swatches, and save in an easily accessible location. The Load Swatches command retrieves swatches used in other InDesign documents.

TOOLKIT TIP When you set up color management using Adobe Bridge or Mini Bridge within the application, color settings are automatically synchronized across applications. This synchronization ensures that colors look the same in all **Adobe Creative Suite** applications. If color settings are not synchronized, a warning message appears at the top of the Color Settings dialog box in every Creative Suite application. To synchronize color settings through the suite of applications, click the Go to Bridge icon on the Control panel, then choose Edit > Creative Suite Color Settings. Select a color setting from the list and click Apply.

APPLYING COLORS USING THE SWATCHES PANEL

The Swatches panel is the most productive way to apply accurate color. You only need to select the frame, text, or object to apply the color, or tag the color in the Swatches panel to apply it. When this is done within a master page, the color is universally applied with any formatting to all pages that are based on that master page. When applying color to fill a frame, use the Fill color in the Tools panel or in CS5, in the Control panel with the selected graphic or text; when applying color to a rule, make sure the Stroke Color box is selected and that the fill color is set to None (Figure 12-12). The Stroke and Fill operations are duplicated in the upper left corner of the Swatches panel. Using the Swatches panel to apply stroke and fill is usually faster than returning to the Tools panel.

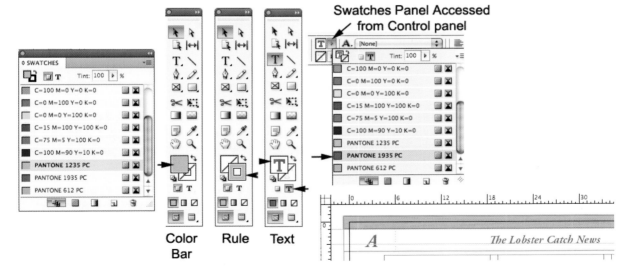

▷ FIGURE 12-12

Using stroke and fill settings to apply colors for the continuing banner.

Next, you will apply color to the continuing banner and text to complete the master page.

1. With the Master Page A document active, select the top color bar on the left-side document with the Selection tool. Check the Tools panel color boxes or boxes displayed on the Control panel, and make sure that the Stroke is set to None and the Fill color is in front.

2. Use the Selection tool to select the left-side color bar. Select the golden Pantone 1235 PC color in the Swatches panel. The color bar will become that selected color without a stroke border.

3. Repeat the same process with the right-side color bar.

4. Apply Pantone 1235 PC to the bottom rule at the 4p0 guide mark. Select the rule, and make sure the Fill color is set to None and the Stroke color is active in the Tools panel. Apply Pantone 1235 PC.

5. To apply the red Pantone 1935 PC color to the text, highlight the Auto Page "A" on the left master page with the Type tool. The type fill icon on the Tools panel should be on top, or active, and the stroke icon underneath should display a red diagonal line through the icon. Apply Pantone 1935 PC to the auto page number on the right-hand master page, as well as The Lobster Catch News header on both pages. Feel free with CS5 to try using the Control panel instead of the Tools panel.

6. Congratulations: you now have your master page set up. Feel free to double-click your page documents on the lower portion of the Pages panel; click the tab to display the panel to see the continuing banner applied with text formatted and the appropriate page numbers displayed.

7. Save the file in InDesign's INDD format.

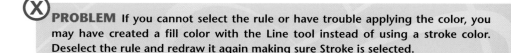

ⓧ PROBLEM If you cannot select the rule or have trouble applying the color, you may have created a fill color with the Line tool instead of using a stroke color. Deselect the rule and redraw it again making sure Stroke is selected.

ⓧ PROBLEM If you notice, when you click on the page 1 or page 4 thumbnail, that the color bar or rule extends the length of an additional document, it is because the graphics are overlapping. Readjust in Master Pages view, then recheck the pages.

EDITING THE MASTER PAGE ITEMS AND PLACING THE NAMEPLATE OR MASTHEAD

What happens if you want to only use a portion of the master page layout for the front page of the newsletter? In that case, you would need to remove the continuing banners and replace them with the newsletter nameplate. You can do this by a process called *overriding the master objects*. The **master page items** are the individual components you created that together make the continuing banner. If a master page contains most of the elements you want, but you need to customize the appearance of a page or a few pages, you can override master page objects on that page or those pages instead of removing the master. On the document level, master page items are displayed with a dotted guideline. To override a single master page item on the document level and not the master page itself, press Command Shift (Mac)/Ctrl Shift (PC) as you click the master page item. Change or delete the object as desired.

The Place command in the File menu is best used to bring in graphics. In CS5, you can carefully reposition a larger graphic within the frame window using the Selection tool and, as you hover your mouse over the image center, a non-printable guide that looks like a shaded doughnut graphic called the **Content Indicator**. If you are using an earlier version of InDesign, you have a **Position Tool** on the tools panel that looks like a hand for repositioning your larger graphic. When adjusting the graphic, use the Selection tool with the shaded doughnut shaped graphic in the center to view the graphic behind the frame window, then, when the graphic is in position, adjust the resizing handles to align with the edges of the graphic.

ABOUT THE FRONT PAGE

The first page of a newsletter is the initial eye-catcher that entices the reader to take a look at various articles. A newsletter has a nameplate that identifies the newsletter and what the reader may expect. It may also include relevant information like the author or editor, issue number, and additional information the reader might need. It usually contains a graphic or logo with a formatted title to make it stand out. The *nameplate,* sometimes called the *masthead,* identifies the newsletter and carries important information like the issue number and the formatted logo. Technically, the **masthead** is on one of the other pages that list the publisher, subscription rates, and so on. A small index box may be included to help the reader navigate through various articles. A **drop cap** is a larger letter that drops down to extend over more than one line of text to start off an article. This technique is used frequently in the front page's first article.

TOOLKIT TIP To override all master page items, target a spread and then choose Override All Master Page Items in the Pages panel menu. You can now select and modify any and all master page items as you wish. To remove a master from document pages, apply the None master from the masters section of the Pages panel. When you remove a master from a page, however, its layout no longer applies to the page. To delete a master from a document, drag a selected master page or spread icon to the Delete icon at the bottom of the Pages panel.

▷ FIGURE 12-13

Removing master page objects to Place the nameplate graphic.

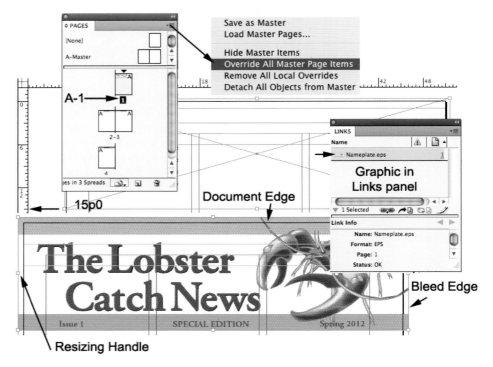

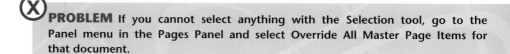

TOOLKIT TIP References to pages such as page 1, or document A-1, technically refer to the document as Master Page 1, based on Master Page A. Please keep this in mind when working on various pages.

To prepare for the nameplate, you will remove the continuing banner master page objects from the first page document. You will then import the *Nameplate* file using the Place command, then use the Content Indicator doughnut with the Selection tool to move it into place.

1. In the Pages panel, double-click on the A-1 page in the local formatting level on the bottom of the Pages panel, where the A designates the master page "A" applied (default) and the "1" indicates the first page in the document. This will open up the first page of the newsletter indicated by the page number 1 on the right side.

2. Zoom in about 150% and with the Selection tool, press Command/Ctrl + Shift as you select the rule, color bar, and text on the continuing banner master page objects. Also select the bottom of the "1" auto page number.

Ⓧ **PROBLEM** If you cannot select anything with the Selection tool, go to the Panel menu in the Pages Panel and select Override All Master Page Items for that document.

3. Press the Delete key to remove the objects. That's it! It only affects the first page you were working on.

4. Using the Selection tool, drag a horizontal guide to the 15-pica mark.

5. Before placing the *Nameplate* file on a spread, first select the Rectangle Frame tool (F) and drag from the 15-pica mark on the vertical ruler guide from the left bleed edge (not margin) over to the right bleed edge of the document up and over the document bleed edge.

6. Select File > Place and locate the *Nameplate* file in the *Images* folder within your *Chapter 12* folder on your drive. Select Open to place the graphic in the document.

7. Use the Selection tool to move the graphic into place by clicking on the Content Indicator that looks like a central doughnut. You will notice the lobster antennae will stick out above the document; position so the bottom line of text displays with spacing and the color bars meet at the bleed edges (Figure 12-13).

8. If needed, with the Selection tool (V, Escape), drag the top middle resizing handle above the document and adjust the graphic to fit in the window as shown in Figure 12-13. Do not worry about the margins; they will not print.

9. Align the top color bar to the bleed edge of the document. You will notice that the graphic may appear pixeled, because it is displaying as a low-resolution image for easier maneuvering. When it is ready to print, it will link to the high-resolution file for accurate sharp printing.

10. If adjustment is still needed, when the graphic is positioned, use the Selection tool and select the horizontal sizing handles to adjust the graphic frame to align with the bleed edges ouside the document, eliminating the extra lobster antennae. Remember that whatever displays through the graphic "window" will print. Whatever is outside the document edge and not in a bleed dimension will not print. You should have artwork sized beforehand to extend out to the specified bleed dimension. Deselect the graphic when you are done.

11. Save the file. You will notice the *Nameplate* file and related info is also displayed in the Links panel.

 PROBLEM If the image only displays as a gray box, especially if you are using Windows, open the file in your Illustrator program and resave the image onto your drive (not CD) as an Illustrator EPS file as the original. Place the file again in your frame and the image should be displayed.

GUIDES, GRAPHIC FRAMES, AND PLACING GRAPHICS

If you have laid out your design in a rough draft for positioning of text and graphics, and you have received client approval, you will need to size your graphics to approximate the specifications you set up in your design. Before placing text, try to place your graphics to get a feel for the layout. Here the graphics have already been sized for the newsletter. Dragging layout guides helps in positioning

DESIGN TIP

The title "The Lobster Catch News" contains red text overlaid on top of black text which is offset slightly to provide a slight shadow-like appearance for depth. This technique is used quite often for titles in magazines and newsletters of graphics. The Rectangle Frame tool (F) sets up the window for the graphics to display, but the Place command is still the best way to import graphic images. You can use the Selection tool to further adjust the size of the graphic window to accommodate the text flowing around it later. In CS5, you can carefully reposition a larger graphic within the frame window using the Selection tool and the shaded "doughnut graphic." If you are using an earlier version of InDesign, use the Position Tool on the tools panel that looks like a hand for repositioning your larger graphic.

PLACING GRAPHICS IN PAGES 1 AND 2

In page 1 you will place a graphic that continues across two columns. On the second page you are going to place a graphic that extends half way over to the second column. This will be used to accent a very long article and to wrap text around the outside of the graphic. Using graphics that face in toward the document lead the reader into articles they may want to read. In CS5, there is a Layers panel that works much like the one in Illustrator. You can create individual layers of your document to match your pages and lock the graphics or text frames so they cannot be adjusted by mistake. You can also right-click on the layer item to select it on the document, which helps when you have lots of items on a page. Each layer here will represent one page. For that layer to be active and to observe its contents, you will need to select the page in the Pages panel first.

DESIGN TIP

When placing graphics, outlining the graphic in a thin 1-point weight helps to balance the image. To continue the color theme on the banners and the color bar on the nameplate, a 1-point stroke Pantone 1235 PC is applied to the frame edge of each graphic. Select a black color if you prefer.

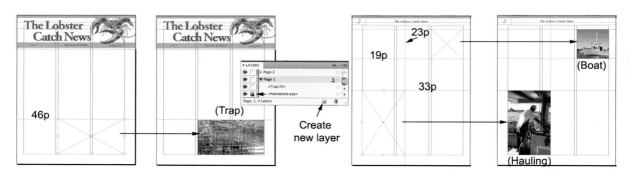

Page 1   Page 2

▷ FIGURE 12-14

Layout of guides, using Rectangle Frame tool for graphic frames, and placement of graphics for pages 1 and 2.

TOOLKIT TIP If precision is needed when dragging guides, hold down the Shift key and drag slowly to move the guide in 1-point increments. You can also select the guide with the Selection tool and type the number you wish to move to the Y box of the Control panel. To remove these guides, click on them using the Selection tool, then press the delete key.

Here you will drag layout guides and create graphic frames using the Rectangle frame tool for placement of graphics on pages 1 and 2 of the newsletter. You will then use the Place command to import each graphic. You will then use the Layers panel to lock in the *Nameplate* graphic on the *Page 1* layer.

DESIGN TIP

In traditionally designed documents, it is good practice to have some stroke color outline around a placed rectangular graphic, especially a photo image. It makes the document more professional in appearance.

1. For the front page, document A-1 (page 1), drag (or type 46p0 in the Y axis box) a horizontal guide to the 46-pica mark. Using the Rectangle Frame tool (F), drag a graphic frame—with a Fill of None and a 1-point Stroke of Pantone 1235 PC from the Swatches panel—from the second column at the 46-pica mark to the bottom corner margin of the third column as shown in Figure 12-14; you can also use the Rectangle tool (M) which has a 1-point stroke as a default, then only the stroke color needs to be changed.

2. Select the frame and place the file *Trap* in the frame (File > Place). Page 1 is now done. In CS5, open the Layers panel (Window > Layers) and rename the *Layer 1* layer as *Page 1*. When you click on the downward arrow next to that layer you'll notice both graphics. Click to lock just the *Nameplate* graphic, then create a new layer naming it Page 2 for the next step.

3. For the A-2 document (page 2), double-click the A-2 document icon in the Pages panel to bring up the second page. Zoom in at 100% or larger making sure page 1 is not displayed. Check to make sure *Page 2* in the Layers panel is highlighted.

4. Using the Selection tool, drag horizontal guides to the 19- and 33-pica marks. Drag a vertical guideline to the 23-pica mark to place the graphic overlapping into the second column or type in 23p0 in the X axis box on the Control panel.

5. Using the Rectangle Frame tool (F), create a graphic frame in the third column with a Fill of None and a 1-point Stroke of Pantone 1235 PC between the 6- and 19-pica marks to the right margin guide.

DESIGN TIP

The boat image with the front area (the bow) facing into the document helps to lead the reader's eye back to the document.

6. Create a second frame in the first column with same color stroke from the 33-pica mark down to the bottom margin and over to the 23-pica mark halfway into the second column, as shown in Figure 12-14.

7. Select the frame and place the *Boat* file in the upper third column, then use the Selection tool and center "doughnut" to position the larger graphic within the frame so that boat displays. Place the *Hauling* file in the bottom left corner as shown (Figure 12-14). Page 2 is now all set. Use the Selection tool to delete the guidelines used for placing the graphics to avoid confusion.

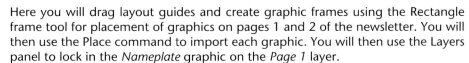

TOOLKIT TIP Made a mistake with your guidelines or just want to remove them? The easiest way is to select guides with the Selection tool and when you observe a black square under the cursor, press Delete to remove the guide. Another method is to click on the guidelines with the Selection tool and drag the guides back to the ruler area.

TOOLKIT TIP The Layers panel will show both images when you open the Page 2 layer. If you want to access the layer corresponding to a particular page, select the page document using the Pages panel first. References to pages such as page 1, or document A-1, technically refer to the document as Master Page 1, based on Master Page A. Please keep this in mind when working on various pages.

PLACING GRAPHICS IN PAGE 3

In page 3, you will use graphics to accent two very short articles to also help to frame the text. You will also create a *Page 3* layer in the Layers panel.

Here you will drag layout guides and create graphic frames to place graphics on page 3 of the newsletter.

1. For the A-3 document (page 3), double-click the A-3 document icon in the Pages panel to bring up the third page. In the Layers panel, create two more empty layers and rename them as *Page 3* and *Page 4* respectively as you had done with the first two pages. Make sure *Page 3* layer is highlighted.

2. Drag and type in horizontal guides to the 18, 21, 30, and 42-pica marks.

3. Create the following rectangle graphic frames with the Fill of None and a 1-point Stroke color, Pantone 1235 PC, from the Swatches panel. First, in the first column between the 6- and 18-pica marks; second, from the 30- and 42-pica marks across the first and second column; and last, in the third column, between the 21- and 42-pica marks (Figure 12-15).

▷ FIGURE 12-15

Placement of graphic frames and importing graphics into page 3.

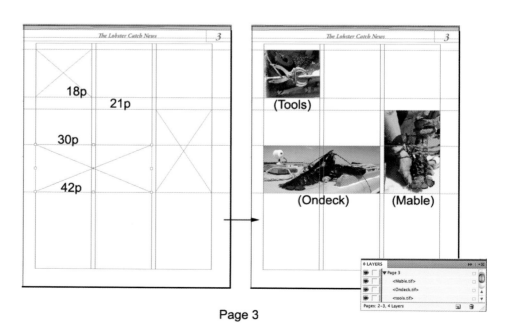

Page 3

4. Select the frame and place the *Tools* file in the upper rectangle frame in the first column. Select and place the *Ondeck* file in the frame that stretches across the first two columns. Select and place the *Mable* file in the third column frame. Adjust the images with the doughnut of the Content Indicator and Selection tool as needed, and delete guidelines used for graphics.

5 Open the Page 3 layer in the Layers panel to observe the graphics. Page 3 is all set.

PAGE 4: USING SMART GUIDES AND SMART SPACING WITH GRAPHICS

With Smart Guides turned on, you can not only have x and y coordinates appear dynamically, you can easily find the central points of multiple objects or shapes by aligning their center lines. To align items to match, Smart Spacing and Smart Dimensions (which are features turned on when you select Smart Guides) arrow indicators appear as you move your selection. Smart spacing evenly spaces multiple items by snapping objects into position. When the arrows display and center lines appear you have perfect alignment with other objects. When you stop, the guides disappear, so your layout remains uncluttered. If you need to move your objects in relation to the others you want to match, Smart Dimensions will highlight when the dimensions match the others. With these new tools you get immediate feedback with precise positioning. You can also use the Align panel if you are using earlier versions with the same accuracy, and CS4 and CS5 use align icons for selected tools in their tool's option bar.

For page 4, you'll have the opportunity to duplicate the same size frame for consistency in declaring what will be appearing in forthcoming issues. You'll then align the graphic using smart guides for precision. You will then lock the three images using the Layers panel to keep them from being moved in future editions. You will also place an illustrative graphic near the bottom of the page for balance of the text that will be imported to the middle of the document.

1. Make sure Smart Guides is checked on (View > Grids & Guides > Smart Guides). Double-click the A-4 document icon in the Pages panel to bring up the fourth page, making sure it is only displaying. Make sure the *Page 4* layer is highlighted in the Layers panel.

2. Drag or type in horizontal guides to the 13, 19, 21, and 51-pica marks.

3. First, you are going to create three rectangle graphic frames of equal size in each of the three columns. In the first column, select the Rectangle Frame tool as before, but instead of dragging to create a frame, click on the document to bring up the Rectangle Frame dialog box (Figure 12-16).

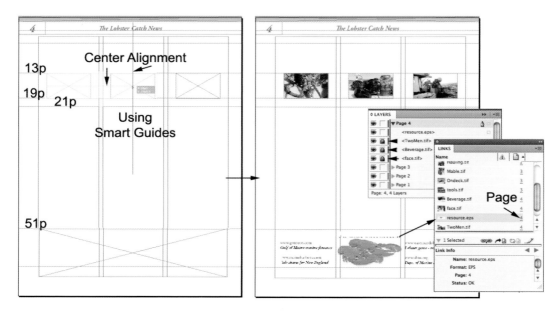

Page 4

▷ FIGURE 12-16

Placement of graphic frames and importing graphics into page 4.

4. Enter a Width of 10p2 (10 picas, 2 points) and a Height of 6p (6 picas). Click OK. Create a 1-point Stroke color of Pantone 1235 PC and a Fill of None.

5. Position the graphic frame with the Selection tool so it is centered in the first column between the 6p and 16p6 marks on top and between the 13 and 19 horizontal pica guides you just made (Figure 12-16). With Smart Guides turned on, you will find a vertical center line display when the box is in between the guidelines.

6. Use the Edit menu, or Option/ALT to copy the graphic box size two more times so that each frame lines up within the same horizontal guidelines in the second and third columns. Using smart guides, when you drag the second box into position, you will find the green horizontal center line intersecting with a blue vertical center line, indicating you have perfect alignment (Figure 12-16).

7. When you select and move the third frame into position, not only will you see the horizontal center line displayed, but when the frame is equidistant from the other two objects, you'll find arrows displayed (Smart Dimensions) under the other two frames for precise alignment.

8. Place the file *Face* in the first column frame, the file *Beverage* in the second column, and the file *TwoMen* in the third column graphic frame. Adjust with the Selection tool as needed.

TOOLKIT TIP In Indesign CS5, the Gap tool (U) on the Tools panel provides a quick way to adjust the size of a gap or resize between multiple items that have commonly aligned edges all at once, while keeping the gaps between them fixed. Just hover your mouse over the gap area you want to adjust, then click and drag to resize the items aligned to the gap. Also, when distributing multiple selected objects, and you want to resize the space between the selected items instead of resizing the actual items, use the Selection tool to drag the bounding box resizing handle while holding down the space bar on your keyboard.

9. For the Resources graphic box, which contains an illustration and text, drag a rectangle graphic frame across the three columns between the 51-pica horizontal guide and the bottom margin.

10. Place the *Resource* graphic file in this graphic frame; adjust with the Selection tool to align the baseline of the e-mail addresses on the 59-pica line; you can also click on the images to toggle between the Selection and Direct Selection tools to make adjustments. Change the Pantone 1235 PC Stroke color to a 2-point weight. Deselect the graphic and lock the three graphics aligned at the top in the *Page 4* layer of the Layers panel. Page 4 is all set for graphics.

11. If you look at the Links panel, you will notice all graphics are placed there for future reference, including the associated page numbers for updated linking, and editing of graphics if needed. The graphics on the Links panel are all set as thumbnails for quick reference. Click on the graphic for more related information.

12. Save the file. Make sure you do not change where these graphics are kept, or you will break the link to the original files. What you will see on your document at this point are the low-resolution copies of the originals so they will look blotchy.

TOOLKIT TIP You will also notice that when you lock a graphic in the Layers panel, that it is outlined with a padlock icon on it on the document page. This way it can't be edited until you unlock it. To view one of the pages and toggle the locked graphics, you must select the page in the Pages panel first, then you can access the components of that layer. Using the Layers panel you can also right-click on the item and choose to select it, which comes in quite handy when you have lots of items in a page. Note: These images are medium resolution at 150 dpi for these exercises. When using actual images for a document that will go to press, maintain a high resolution of 300 dpi.

TOOLKIT TIP When placing graphics and text in InDesign, you can place PSD and PDF layered graphics in a document. You can selectively display and output layers and layer comps from Photoshop (PSD) and layers from PDF files, and you can modify layer visibility in placed graphics. Graphics appear in the Links panel after they have been imported. You can reuse InDesign layouts by creating and placing *snippets,* which are portions of a document, or by placing the entire InDesign document into another InDesign document. All the links remain intact, and InDesign lets you know if any changes are made.

INDESIGN'S EFFECTS

InDesign provides the designer to create Photoshop like effects, such as drop shadows, bevels, and embossing. It also provides other great effects using InDesign's Effects panel. You can use the Effects panel (Window > Effects) to specify the opacity and blending mode of objects and groups, isolate blending to a particular group, knock out objects inside a group, or apply a transparency effect. These effects can also be accessed from most of the tools as part of the appropriate tool's menu bar or in the Control panel bar. If you want, try creating drop shadow effects on the three images you placed in page 4 to see if the effect may accent the final newsletter, or try applying this effect afterwards when all text is placed in the newsletter. InDesign provides corner effects on the fly if you want to create accented corner effects. In CS5, to view these live, you will see a yellow square which, when you click on it will display yellow diamond shapes on each corner. If you click and drag on a corner box you can create a rounded radius effect on all corners. Hold down the Option/ALT key while clicking on the diamond to view other special effects. Although we will not be using this technique in the exercises, go ahead and unlock the graphics in the Layers panel and play if you want.

TYPING AND IMPORTING TEXT

Text and graphic components need to complement one another. Text provides the description or identifies what the images are trying to convey to the reader. The images provide the visual representation of what the text message defines to the reader. In this section, you will not only type in text elements and apply basic formatting; you will learn to import text articles using the Place command to flow into multiple columns and into multiple pages. Although the Control panel handles many of the most widely used character and paragraph commands for text, the Type menu provides all the essential commands and features you will need, such as inserting special characters, displaying specific panels—like Tab, Character, and Paragraph formatting—including style panels for consistency in formatting. The Type menu provides a central location to apply any formatting needed to text. Sometimes when you place type into a frame container, there is no type that appears, only a red plus sign. This is called an **overset** symbol. It is a text "overflow" symbol indicating too much text is in the frame container.

TOOLKIT TIP All text for articles in this newsletter have been created in plain text format. If you have a pretty good idea the kind of font you wish to create, you can open each document in Microsoft Word if it is available, highlight the text and format to your chosen font and font size (try 10 or 11 point size), then save the document before placing the text in your InDesign document. It is important when doing this that you are using the same operating system, and InDesign has the same font as your chosen Word font.

TYPING IN TEXT INFORMATION

As you were doing in the previous chapter, you can type in text and apply formatting when small amounts of type are called for in a given section; afterward, you will also see how easy it is to import text from a document created in another application. This will serve as a brief review of using the character formatting buttons on the Control panel when the Type tool is used. To create a true ellipsis (which indicates "and so forth") which are three evenly spaced dots, select the Option/ALT key and then press the semicolon key.

▷ FIGURE 12-17

Typing and formatting text components.

What's On Dock...

Summer Issue...	Fall Issue...	Winter Issue...
Favorite Lobster Dishes	Growth Cycle of the Lobster	Make Your Own Lobster Trap
Local Lobster Eating Tips	Where do Lobsters Winter?	Off-Shore Lobstering 60 Miles Out

Because this is a quarterly newsletter, you will type in brief information in the upcoming quarters and format it using the Control panel.

1. Notice the Pages panel displays thumbnail views of the placed graphics for a quick visual reference. Double-click on the A-4 document to bring up the fourth page in the document if it is not already open. Zoom in to around 150% and scroll to the top. Make sure the *Page 4* layer is highlighted in the Layers panel.

2. Using the Selection tool, drag horizontal guides to the 8-pica and 12-pica marks.

3. To create the headline, use the Type tool to drag a text frame across the columns between the 6- and 8-pica marks, then type in "What's on Dock..." with the font you have chosen (we are using Adobe Garamond Pro) using the bold style. Use the Option/Alt key followed by a semicolon to enter a "true" ellipsis. Or, you may open the Glyphs panel and double-click; an ellipsis will appear at the insertion point of the text cursor.

DESIGN TIP

To help with workflow, if you have the three type lines formatted in the first type box, you can copy those lines into the other two text boxes, then simply type over the changes. The formatting will remain the same.

4. Change the Fill color to Pantone 1935 PC in the Swatches panel, and resize to 24-points.

5. Select the Type tool and create three separate text frames above each photo between the 8- and 12-pica marks and the column margin edges.

6. In the First column frame, type "Summer Issue…" making sure to create a "true ellipsis," as described above. Change the Fill color to Pantone 1935 PC in the Swatches panel, and format type to 16- or 18-point Bold style in the font you have chosen. We used the Adobe Garamond Pro font here.

7. Click at the end of the ellipse dots to display the blinking cursor. Press Return/ Enter to create another line; change the size to 11- or 12-point size, depending on the font you are using, with a black Fill and Italic style and type "Favorite Lobster Dishes"; press, Return/Enter, then type "Local Lobster Eating Tips" on the next line.

8. To center the text in the frame, select all three lines of text and choose the Character Formatting icon on the Control panel. Select the Align Center button (Figure 12-17).

9. If the type disappears, or the red plus overset text sign appears, adjust the text size to display the new formatted text lines.

10. To place the lines of text along the bottom guideline of the text frame, with the text highlighted, select Object > Text frame Options. Select the Vertical Justification of Align Bottom.

11. Repeat the same process with the Fall and Winter issues, as shown Figure 12-17.

12. Notice on the Layers panel (Page 4) the text also displays in addition to the image files. Save the file when done.

TOOLKIT TIP If the guides are making your work appear to cluttered, you can remove the guides created earlier for placing images by using the keyboard shortcut Command + Option + G + Delete using a Mac, or, Control + ALT + G + Delete using Windows. This will remove the guides placed on the document level but not the guides on the master page level. You can also click on the line with the Selection tool and when it shows a black square under the cursor, drag it back to the ruler guide bar.

IMPORTING TEXT INTO TEXT FRAMES

One of the great features of any desktop publishing program like InDesign is the ability to import text from other documents into individual text frames and to connect multiple text frames together, flowing text into multiple columns (Figure 12-18). When importing text, the Place command is again the most appropriate command to use. To use the Place command, you can use the key combination Command D/Ctrl D or select File > Place. When placing text, a space needs to be created between the bottom of the text line within the text frame and sometimes above the top line, to allow for breathing space so that text does not sit on the edges of the text frame. In the Object > Text Frame Options command, you can adjust the inset spacing within each text frame. Creating an **inset** provides space for the text so that type is not placed next to a graphic frame or one that may have a stroke weight or is filled with color. Inset settings apply to all text in a text frame. The space between columns is called the **gutter**.

 FIGURE 12-18

Importing text into selected frame, providing inset spacing at the bottom.

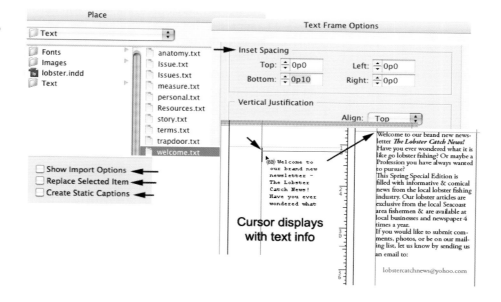

DESIGN TIP

When working with body text in various articles, use the same size and font throughout; remember that serif fonts work best. Keep the point size at a minimum of 10 points or a maximum of 12 points for easy reading, depending on the placement of the articles. Here we used an 11-point Adobe Pro Garamond (serif) font for easier reading throughout.

 TOOLKIT TIP Any frame can be converted to a text frame by clicking inside the frame with the Type tool. When the Place dialog box opens, select Replace Selected Items to replace the contents in the text frame with the placed text. A good production habit is to deselect the previous frame before placing the next image or text file. Selecting Show Import Options controls how different versions of a text document are to be handled. Keep these options unchecked in these exercises.

DESIGN TIP

When inserting paragraphs of type, keep the same font and size consistent for easier readability between columns and multiple documents. A font size of 10 points is a standard size used in most documents.

Here, you will import a small text file into a single text frame on the front cover.

1. Make sure the document A-1 (first page) is selected, not the top master page. Make sure *Page 1* in the Layers panel is selected.

2. Drag a horizontal guideline to the 17-pica and 38-pica marks.

3. Select the Type tool and drag diagonally to create a text frame—do not just click in the first column—from the vertical 17-pica mark about half way down to the 38-pica mark between the left margin and first gutter.

4. Select File > Place or Command/Ctrl D and locate the *Welcome* text file in your *Text* folder. Leave Replace Selected Item, Create Static Captions, and Show Import Options Select unchecked here. Select Open to import the text.

5. The cursor may display a thumbnail view of the text first lines. Click in the top left corner of the text box and the text will flow into the column. If you see a red plus sign (overset symbol) at the bottom or end of the article, more text needs to be displayed. Choose the Selection tool, select inside the frame, and drag the bottom resizing handle down to display all text.

6. Select all the text and change to the font you have chosen in its Regular style to an 11-point size for easier reading. We have chosen Adobe Garamond Pro Regular to continue with this document. You may decide with your chosen font to use the standard 10 point size.

7. Select the text *The Lobster Catch News!* in the first sentence and change it to an Italic Bold style to identify the title of the newsletter.

8. Select the e-mail address and change the color to the red Pantone 1935 PC, then Align center the e-mail line using the Control panel. Click in front of the e-mail line, and press the Return/Enter key to create a line space as shown in Figure 12-18.

9. To create a space for the bottom of the text frame, with the text frame first selected using the Selection tool, select Object > Text Frame Options and enter Inset Spacing Bottom of 10-points (0p10) with Top, Left, and Right Insets set at 0. Use Vertical Justification to Align Top. Make sure the frame meets the guides you created, again, use the resizing handles with the Selection tool if necessary.

10. Save the file.

MANUALLY THREADING TEXT FRAMES

To import text into multiple columns manually, you do not need to create text frames. You can create a text frame before placing text, or you can manually flow text between columns and adjust the frame dimensions using the Selection tool; the text flow will adjust automatically. The space between columns is called the **gutter**. The process of creating linked text frames is **threading text**. After threading has been completed, the frames are linked. You can flow text between linked columns in different pages and in adjacent multi-column text frames. When placing imported text into a text frame, a loaded text cursor displays—which will look like lines of type inside a dotted page outline—indicating that text is ready to be dropped into a frame. Click on the text frame to dump the text that needs to be displayed. If a red plus sign displays, this is called the **overset symbol**, which indicates that there is more text. Click in the next column to continue flowing the text, and adjust the frame using the Selection tool to cause the text flow to adjust automatically, giving you room to experiment with formatting and placing graphics; this perceptual technique may be used instead of creating inset spacing, although it may look inconsistent in the document.

Although headings are included in the original text document for identification, you can cut and paste them on a separate text frame that spans across the columns, connected to the text body frames. When using text, sometimes it makes better sense to create separate text frames for the headings of an article, especially if the heading is to expand across multiple columns. This allows you to format the headings or lines of type without adversely affecting the text body in the article.

In this exercise, you will manually import and place text files in multiple columns in page 1. You will place the headings into separate text frames for formatting later.

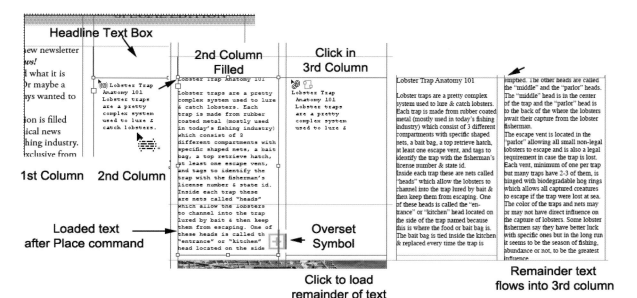

▷ FIGURE 12-19

Threading text manually across multiple columns.

TOOLKIT TIP References to pages, such as page 1, or document A-1, refer to the document as Master Page 1, based on Master Page A. Please keep this in mind when working on various pages.

1. For a headline text box, with Document A-1 (page 1 based on Master Page A) displayed, select the Type tool, and drag a box from the 17-pica mark in the second column over to the right-side margin (third column) and down to the 20-pica mark. Zoom in close if needed.

2. Use the Type tool to create another frame only in the center second column extending from the 20-pica mark to the 45-pica mark above the *Trap* graphic.

3. In this second frame, select the Place command and place the *Anatomy* file from your *Text* folder.

4. Observe the overset text symbol at the bottom of the text column which appears as a red plus sign; in the next step, you will now flow the copy into the next text frame.

5. Using the Type tool, drag another text frame in the third column, again from the 20-pica mark to the 45-pica mark as done in the second column. Click on the overset symbol in the text frame in the middle column with the Selection tool. This process creates a *loaded text cursor.*

6. Click the loaded cursor on the upper left corner of the third column at the 20-pica mark, below the text box for the headline (don't click inside the headline text box) which may display a link icon, click and flow the remaining text into that column. Don't worry if the text is not all displayed with your chosen font, you will remove the title to make room in the next exercise. Click the Selection tool to reset.

7. Select the Type tool and highlight the "Lobster Trap Anatomy 101" headline, then cut (Edit > Cut) the headline out of the first column, then click and Paste the heading into the headline text box, in the second column; you will format it later. Click inside the top second column underneath and delete the line space until the paragraph rests at the top of the text body frame. This should allow enough room to observe the remainder of the text. Use the frame handles to shorten or lengthen the depth of the text frames to balance out the columns (Figure 12-19).

DESIGN TIP

In most cases, in traditional design, you will want to have a space between the paragraphs or type lines, and the graphic nearby.

8. Select the text and format to the same font you chose in the "welcome" column. In our example we are using an 11-point size Adobe Garamond Pro font throughout. Choose a point size of 10, 11, or 12 that fills both text columns depending on the font, and keep the same size throughout. Don't forget the headline as well.

9. With each text frame selected, select Object > Text Frame Options and enter Inset Bottom settings of 10 points (0p10) with top, left, and right insets set at 0 and a Vertical Justification of Align Top. This provides space between graphic and text.

10. Adjust the text in the columns until they appear balanced. Use the frame resizing handles to shorten or lengthen the depth of the text frames to balance out the columns (Figure 12-19). You can also select the resizing handle of the trap graphic below and include a little more of the image if too much negative space displays. Check the Layers panel and you can see that the individual text frames are displayed. Leave as is.

11. Save the file.

UNTHREAD TEXT FRAMES

If you make a mistake threading text frames, you can unthread the frame to start again. When you unthread a text frame, you break the connection between the frame and all subsequent frames in the thread. Any text that previously appeared in the frames becomes overset text with all subsequent frames left empty; no text is deleted. To unthread a frame using the Selection tool, double-click on the out-port arrow at the bottom of the text frame that indicates a thread to another frame, or click the in-port arrow on the top left of the second or additional frame. You can also position the loaded text icon over the previous or next text frame to display the unthread icon, which looks like a broken link; then click in the frame.

FLOWING SHORT ARTICLES ACROSS COLUMNS

On the third page, you will repeat the process you used for the first page. Make sure that the text is balanced across columns and that there is sufficient space between the images and the text. You can also view the text threads between columns by selecting Show Text Threads in the View menu.

Now you will manually import and place text files to thread between multiple columns in document A-3 (page 3), then place the headings into separate text frames for formatting later.

1. For document A-3, double-click the document A-3 on the local section of the Pages panel to bring up the third page of the document. You will notice a "3" will appear in place of the automatic page number created from the master page. Make sure Page 3 is highlighted in the Layers panel.

2. Drag horizontal guidelines at the 6 (if it isn't already there) 9, 19, and 22-pica marks for the headlines and the articles.

3. Use the Type tool to create a frame that stretches across the second and third columns between the 6- and 9-pica horizontal guides. Type in the headline, "How to Measure a Legal Lobster."

4. For the body text, start by drawing a text frame between the 9- and 18-pica guides in the second column. Use the Selection tool if needed to drag sizing handles.

5. For the body of the article to flow into the top second and third columns, select the Place command and locate the *Measure* text file. Select Open.

▷ FIGURE 12-20

Manually importing and threading text into multiple text frames.

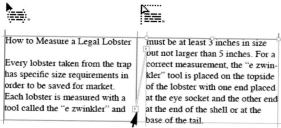

Text shown threaded

Article threaded

6. With the Type tool, click on the upper corner of the second column of the page under the headline text frame around the 9-pica mark. The text will flow into that column.

7. With both of the text frames selected, select Object > Text Frame Options and enter Inset Bottom settings of 10 points (0p10) with top, left, and right insets set at 0 and a Vertical Justification of Align Top.

8. To see the threaded text display, select View > Extras > Show Text Threads and click in the second column text frame with the Selection tool.

9. Click the red overset plus symbol, then click the loaded text cursor in the third column, creating a thread over the third column. You will see the connection made showing the threads between the two columns of text.

10. Cut out the "How to Measure a Legal Lobster" headline, and Paste it into the headline text frame above the body text you just imported.

11. Delete the excess space in the body text frame below. Change the font and font size to match the rest of the document, and adjust the resizing handles to even out both columns of text if possible, as shown in Figure 12-20.

12. For the next article, "Trap Door," create the headline text frame first across the first and second columns from the 19- and 22-pica guides (Figure 12-21).

▷ FIGURE 12-21

Threading text for the "Trap Door" article.

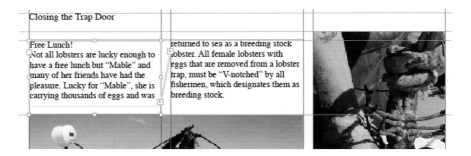

13. Drag the text frame for the body text between the 22- and 30-pica marks in the first column.

14. Locate and Place the *Trapdoor* text file starting at the 22-pica mark under the headline text frame and in the first column to the 30-pica mark, click on the overset symbol with the Selection tool, then click in the second column to fill in the remainder of the text. Format the text lines and title line to your chosen document format and type size.

15. For inset spacing, select Object > Text Frame Options and enter Inset Bottom settings of 10 points (0p10) with top, left, and right insets set at 0 and a Vertical Justification of Align Top.

16. This time cut and paste the headline "Closing the Trap Door" above the body text. Even out the lines of text by adjusting with the Selection tool until they are both even, as shown in Figure 12-21. As you can see you can also cut and paste parts of text lines into selected frames.

17. Save the file.

TOOLKIT TIP With the headline included in the article, another method would be to use the Enter key to push the copy from one frame or column to the next. This function can also be found under Type > Insert Break Character or by holding the Control key (Mac) or right-click (Windows) to access the Context menu.

FLOWING TEXT INTO MULTIPLE PAGES

▷ FIGURE 12-22

Using the semi-auto flow method to flow text between columns and pages.

There are various methods that can be used to flow text into multiple documents. You can use the Manual method shown previously, in which text is added one frame at a time, but you will need to reload the Selection cursor each time. The manual loaded text cursor looks like a page with lines. There is also the Autoflow method for large articles, which adds pages automatically and frames into multiple documents until all the text is flowed into your project; this is done by holding down the Shift key and clicking into the area of the document to start. The loaded text cursor is a solid, sideways "S" curve. The semi-autoflow method, which you will perform in the next exercise, provides control and allows you to place the text in adjacent or nonadjacent columns (Figure 12-22). What is nice about this technique is that the cursor is automatically loaded each time a frame is covered with text, until all text is flowed into the project. The loaded text cursor here looks like a sideways "S" curve half solid and half dotted. With the Selection tool still active, hold down the Option/Alt key to set up for semi-autoflow.

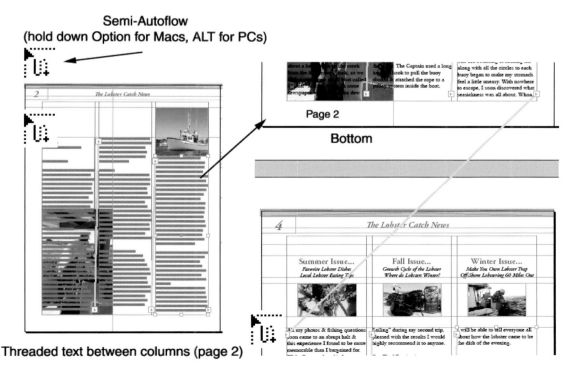

Semi-Autoflow
(hold down Option for Macs, ALT for PCs)

Page 2

Bottom

Threaded text between columns (page 2)

Threaded text between columns and pages

Here you will place a large article to semi-autoflow between document A-2 and document A-4.

1. Double-click on document A-2 (page 2) of the newsletter on the Pages panel, then click once on the *Page 2* layer on the Layers panel.

2. Drag a horizontal guide to the 14-pica mark, then drag a text frame in the first column from the 14-pica mark to the top edge of the graphic underneath.

3. Choosing the Selection tool, choose File > Place and locate the *Story* file in the *Text* folder. Select Open to bring in the file.

4. With the Selection tool still active, hold down the Option/Alt key to see the loaded text cursor show the sideways, half-solid, half-dotted "S" to indicate it is in semi-autoflow mode.

5. Click in the first column of document A-2 under the 14-pica guideline.

6. Hold down the Option/Alt key and click the loaded text cursor into the second column, and then do the same in the third under the boat graphic. If the loaded text cursor does not display, click the overset icon in the first column with the Selection tool, and hold down the Option/Alt key again. Do not worry if the text flows over the graphic; you will fix that soon.

7. You will notice that the overset red cross symbol displays at the text bottom of each column to indicate that the text cursor is loaded each time.

8. Select the A-4 document (page 4) of the newsletter by double-clicking on A-4 document in the Pages panel or by scrolling to the A-4 document. Click on the *Page 4* layer in the Layers panel.

9. Choose the Selection tool again and hold down the Option/Alt key, then click the loaded text cursor into the first, second, and third columns under the graphic frame at the 21-pica mark. If the semi-autoflow does not show, click the overset icon back in page 2 to load the cursor.

10. The text is now threaded across multiple pages. If you have trouble with semi-autoflow, you can always employ the manual method you used earlier. Use the Selection tool to resize frames if needed. Notice with the "show text frames" option you set earlier you can get a good visual of the flow you just created. These red lines will never print but act as guides.

11. Double-click the A-2 document in the Pages panel, and click Page two in the Layers panel. For the "My Story" headline, select the Type tool and drag a text frame across the first and second columns between the 6- and 14-pica marks. Click the Selection tool to highlight the frame and using the Control panel, create a 1-point stroke with a fill of None.

12. Cut (Edit > Cut) the "Up Close: My Lobster Fishing Story by Shelly Britton" out of the first column, then Paste the heading into the text frame above the body text; you will format it later.

13. Highlight all the text (click inside the story text frame and press Cmd + A for Mac, or Ctrl + A for PC, it will highlight text frames flowing between both documents) and change the font (Adobe Pro Garamond for this example) and font size (11 point) to match the rest of the document body text. Use the

Selection tool to resize text frames as needed around the graphics. We'll take care of the "lobsterman" graphic that is half way into the second column of Page 2 next.

14. Save the file.

TOOLKIT TIP After clicking on the overset symbol with the Selection tool, you can also hold down the Shift key to thread text automatically over columns and create new pages. A threaded set of frames is called a **story**. In CS4, although advanced for this text, InDesign has incorporated a Smart Text Reflow function to also automatically add pages at the end of a story, selection of text, or document. This feature works along with another new feature called Conditional text that allows a designer to deliver multiple versions of a document for print and for electronic uses. There is also a new Cross-references feature to help simplify production as content can be dynamically updated as it is changed or moved within a document.

DESIGN TIP
When a graphic is used to split a column of text, be careful to make sure that at least three words minimum display on each line to not distract the viewer from reading. Also, avoid limited spacing that may result in hyphenating too many words. Sometimes changing to a different font (for the entire document) may correct the problem.

TEXT WRAP AROUND GRAPHICS

When importing graphics into a document, a designer needs to decide how to place text to support the graphic or object. He or she may need to apply a certain amount of space between the graphic object and the text or overlap the two. You learned to create an inset space for text within a text frame; there is another method, called **text wrap,** in which a space is created between the graphic and the text that surrounds it or overlaps the two frames or objects. To wrap text around graphics, InDesign has a Text Wrap panel in the Window menu that you can select to wrap text around the outside of a graphic using its shape or bounding box as guides, place it within transparent areas, or overlay the graphic itself (Figure 12-23). Here you will use the bounding-box method. Because the text frames have overlapped the graphics when performing a semi-autoflow, you can use the Selection tool and drag the text frame to the edge of the graphic to expose it.

▷ FIGURE 12-23

Setting text wrap options to allow space between graphics and text.

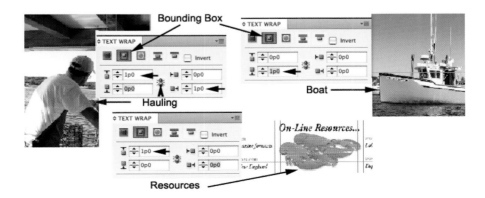

DESIGN TIP

Spacing of at least a pica between paragraphs and graphics provides breathing room for each to compliment one another.

In this exercise, using the bounding-box method on the selected graphic, you will provide a 1-pica space along some edges in documents A-2 and A-4.

1. Double-click on the A-2 document in the Pages panel and select Page 2 in the Layers panel.

2. Select the bottom of the text frame created in the first column and drag up to expose the bottom left graphic, *Hauling* which is a picture of a lobsterman. The text will flow into the other columns.

3. Choose Window > Text Wrap to display the Text Wrap panel; select the photo.

4. To wrap text to the rectangle formed by the graphic's height and width, choose the Wrap around bounding box icon.

5. Make sure the link icon is broken so you can specify individual settings. Set the Top Offset and Right Offset spacing to 1 pica (1p0). You will notice the text will space away from the graphic.

6. Select the lobster boat image in document A-2 (page 2) and enter a Bottom Offset of 1 pica, or 1p0.

7. In document A-4 (page 4), and Page 4 of the Layers panel, drag up the text boxes to expose the *Resources* graphic.

8. Create a 1-pica Top Offset space between it and the remaining text. Adjust the graphic or spacing if needed to accommodate the text font you have chosen. You may have to decrease the offset space here instead.

9. Feel free to apply text wrap to any other graphic if needed, depending on the font choice. To remove the thread display, select View > Extras > Hide Text Threads.

10. Save the file.

AUTOMATING AND APPLYING SPECIAL FORMATTING TECHNIQUES

Desktop publishing programs like InDesign have many special formatting techniques that allow the designer to automate repetitive tasks, so that when changes are made, the position or the formatting adjusts to the change. There are also special techniques that can be used to format text, break up articles, and insert special characters to grab the viewer's attention, including the ability to precisely align columns of information with the use of tabbing. Here you will use a sample of some of these powerful features.

ADDING JUMP LINES

Because the story on page 2 continues on to page 4 of the newsletter, you can let readers know where to locate the rest of the article. To do this you create a **jump line** that says "Continued on page 4." Use a jump-line page number to automatically update the number of the page containing a story's next or previously threaded text frame when you move or reflow the story's text frames. The jump line always needs to be in a separate text frame that is touching the linked frame it refers to. That way, the jump-line page number remains in position even if the story's text reflows. The page number automatically updates to reflect the current location of the next or previous frame of the story (Figure 12-24).

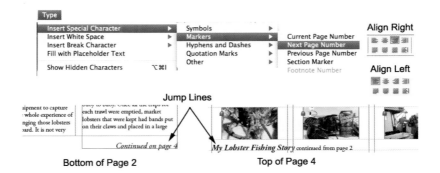

▷ FIGURE 12-24

Inserting automatic jump lines for continuing articles to other pages.

TOOLKIT TIP The text frame containing the jump line must touch the frame-linked text for the automatic page number to work properly. For books and many page documents, if you insert an Auto Page Number character in the Find/Change dialog box, jump-line page numbers can also be found and changed.

Next, you will create a jump line to and from the designated pages in the newsletter article you just threaded.

1. Double-click the A-2 document (page 2) in the Pages panel. Zoom in to 200% and navigate to the bottom right third column.

2. Select the Type tool and drag a text frame with a Stroke of None and a Fill color of black *under* the bottom margin in the third column where you want the jump line to appear.

3. With the Selection tool, position the new text frame so that it touches or overlaps the text frame containing the story in the third column.

4. To add an automatic jump-line page number, select the Type tool and click an insertion point in the new text frame.

5. Select Object Text Frame options and set a Top Inset space of 1 pica (1p0) to allow spacing between the bottom of the text body baseline and the jump line. Click OK.

6. Type "Continued on page " and make sure to leave a space after the last word; then choose Type > Insert Special Character > Markers > Next Page Number (in earlier versions, Type > Insert Special Character > Next Page Number). This inserts the number of the page containing the story's next frame; in this case, page 4.

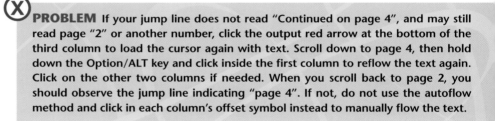

PROBLEM If your jump line does not read "Continued on page 4", and may still read page "2" or another number, click the output red arrow at the bottom of the third column to load the cursor again with text. Scroll down to page 4, then hold down the Option/ALT key and click inside the first column to reflow the text again. Click on the other two columns if needed. When you scroll back to page 2, you should observe the jump line indicating "page 4". If not, do not use the autoflow method and click in each column's offset symbol instead to manually flow the text.

7. Select the jump line text with the Type tool, then on the Control panel, select Align right formatting to place the text on the right edge of the text frame (Figure 12-24).

8. Change the font to the body text font you are using and include an Italic style while increasing the font size to 14 points to make it noticeable to the reader.

9. To create an automatic page number to display as "continued from" on page 4, double-click the A-4 document from the Pages panel to display page 4.

10. Select the Type tool and drag a text frame with a Stroke of None and a Fill color of black from the left margin between the 19- and 21-pica marks across *both* columns to the right side of the second column, where you want the jump line to appear.

11. With the Selection tool, position the new text frame so that it touches or overlaps the text frame containing the story in the first column.

12. To add an automatic jump-line page number, select the Type tool again and click an insertion point in the new text frame.

13. Type "My Lobster Fishing Story continued from page "; make sure to leave a space after the last word. Then choose Type > Insert Special Character > Markers > Previous Page Number. This inserts the number of the page containing the story's previous frame, which is in page 2.

14. Select Align left on the Control panel to place the text on the left side of the text box.

15. The page number 2 automatically displays to reflect the current location of the previous frame of the story.

16. Change the font to the body text font you are using, increasing the font size to 18 points (or less depending on the font you are using). Change the "My Lobster Fishing Story" phrase to Bold Italic, while keeping the "continued from page 42" line as a italic style 14-point size.

17. To have the type sit on the bottom of the text frame, select Object > Text Frame Options > Vertical Justification > Align Bottom.

18. To create some spacing between the "continued from" jump line and the body text, you can choose to create a guide line at the 22-pica mark and drag the text frames in the three columns to the 22-pica mark or, you can create a Top Inset space of 1 pica in each of the three text frame columns. You'll notice the text will easily reflow as you make adjustments.

19. Save the file.

TOOLKIT TIP To prevent the story from being moved without its jump line, Shift-select the frames with the Selection tool, then choose **Object > Group**.

CREATING DROP CAPS

Drop caps are used to lead the viewer into an introductory article or into an article that may span multiple pages or columns. You can add drop caps to one or more paragraphs at a time. The drop cap's baseline sits one or more lines below the baseline of the first line of a paragraph. Drop caps should be used sparingly and not in every article or paragraph in a document to maintain a more professional look. To create a drop cap, you simply highlight the character or characters to edit in the paragraph where you want the drop cap to appear. In the Paragraph panel or Control panel, type a number for Drop Cap Number of Lines to indicate the number of lines you want the drop cap to occupy. In the next field to the right, select the number of characters to be dropped.

DESIGN TIP

As a quick reference, any text formatting that involves individual characters, type lines or titling, use Character formatting. Formatting that involves individual paragraphs, or sometimes paragraph components, like drop caps, use Paragraph formatting on the Control panel.

TOOLKIT TIP You may have to remove the line space between the e-mail address line at the bottom and the "e-mail to:" line, so it is directly underneath to accommodate the change. As a designer you may need to reconfigure and rearrange text and graphics components to achieve the overall best layout for the project.

▷   FIGURE 12-25

Creating a 2-line drop cap to introduce the newsletter.

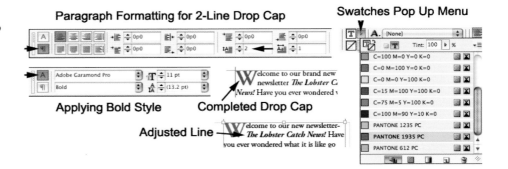

Here you will create a single character drop cap for the initial "Welcome" article on the front page.

1. Select document A-1 (page 1) in the Pages panel to make it active. Zoom in to the first article on the top left side. Select *Page 1* in the Layers panel.

2. Select the Type tool, highlight the first letter "W," then select the Paragraph Formatting button on the Control panel.

3. Enter the number "2" in the Drop Cap Number of Lines box, then click on the Character Formatting Controls button on the Control panel, and select a Bold style for the font to make the character stand out (Figure 12-25).

4. With the letter still highlighted, select the Pantone 1935 PC color from the pop up Swatches panel on the Control panel in CS5, or use the Swatches panel. Remove the word "brand" from the first sentence so that the newsletter title "The Lobster Catch News!" will stand out as its own line (as a designer, you may have to ask permission to do this from the author in some cases).

5. If the e-mail address disappears and a red plus sign displays indicating too much text and space in the text frame, you will need to adjust the spacing to bring it visibly back. Save the file.

USING RULES FOR ARTICLE SEPARATION

Rules are thin lines, usually 1 point or slightly wider in weight, that can be used to provide a separation between specific articles. To create rules, the Line tool works nicely. To create perfectly straight lines vertically, horizontally, and at 45 degree angles, hold the Shift key while you drag with your mouse.

TOOLKIT TIP To see colored rules instead of the guidelines they are drawn over, select View > Grids & Guides > Hide Guides to observe your work. Toggle to Show Guides when you are ready to continue.

Vertical rule applied between articles

Horizontal rule applied to separate issues and continued story

▷ FIGURE 12-26

Applying vertical and horizontal rules to separate articles.

DESIGN TIP

Use pull quotes sparingly within a multipage document. Too many can become a distraction to the reader. Usually you will find only one pull quote used in a long article.

DESIGN TIP

When creating pull quotes from paragraph rules, provide enough space to avoid text line bleeds. The text inside should also be larger than the body text and is usually italicized to grab the reader's attention.

You will create a vertical rule to separate articles on page 1, then you will create a horizontal rule to separate the continued article onto page 4.

1. Double-click on the A-1 document on the Pages panel if needed.

2. Zoom in 200% and drag a vertical guide using the Selection tool to be placed in the middle of the gutter that separates the first and second columns to around the 17p4 mark for starters, or type it into the X-coordinate field in the Control panel. With smart guides you will see the arrow indicators split to two arrows to display the center of the gutter space.

3. Select the Line tool and hold down the Shift key to create a straight vertical line from roughly the 17-pica mark to the 58-pica mark. You have now separated the "Welcome" article (Figure 12-26).

4. With the rule still selected or active, apply a Pantone 1235 PC Stroke color from the pop up Swatches panel (Fill color None) and a 1-point weight in the Control panel.

5. To create a rule to isolate the continuing article on page 4 from the Coming Issues section above, double-click document A-4 in the Pages panel or scroll to display Page 4.

6. With the Selection tool, drag a horizontal guide at the 19p6 mark or type in the Y coordinate in the Control panel.

7. Using the Line tool while pressing the Shift key down, drag a horizontal line across the three columns along the guide.

8. With the rule still selected or active, apply a Pantone 1235 PC Stroke color from the Pop up Swatches panel (Fill color None) and a 1-point weight in the Control panel.

9. Save the file.

CREATING PARAGRAPH RULES AS PULL QUOTES

The width of a paragraph rule is determined by the width of the column. Rules are used in the creation of pull quotes. **Pull quotes** are used in long articles to "pull" a line or comment out of an article that helps to identify that article to the reader. Pull quotes are inserted in between two paragraphs with enough offset spacing to make them stand out. The **Paragraph panel** provides most of the formatting essentials to type lines, including paragraph rules you will need, and it is selected in the Type menu (Type > Paragraph), or in the Window menu (Window > Type & Tables > Paragraph). The Control paragraph panel also contains these features. You can use the Control paragraph panel or Paragraph panel to control the amount of space between paragraphs. If a paragraph begins at the top of a column or frame, InDesign does not insert extra space before the paragraph. In such a case, you can increase the leading of the first line of the paragraph or increase the top inset of the text frame in InDesign by adjusting the appropriate values using the Space Before and Space After options in the Paragraph panel or the Control panel.

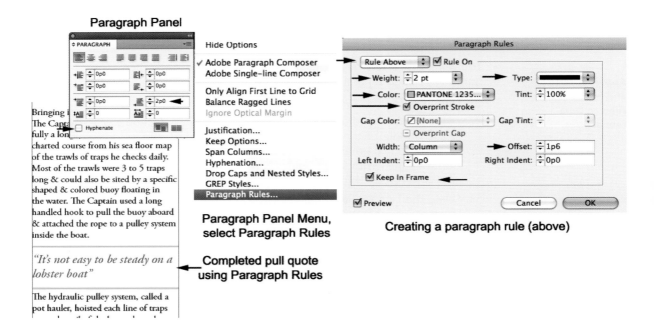

To create a pull quote from the multipage "My Lobster Fishing Story" to identify the article, here is what you need to do.

▷　FIGURE 12-27

Creating pull quotes using Paragraph Rules.

1. Double-click on page 2 in the Pages panel and zoom back out to 100%. Make sure the Paragraph panel is displayed (Type > Paragraph).

2. In the third column, there is a subheadline that reads "Bringing in the Lobsters." In the Paragraph panel (Figure 12-27) or the Conrol panel, select the last line of text that includes the words "inside the boat"; use the Space After function to enter 2p0 to increase the leading. Click at the end of the "boat" sentence of the last line, hold down the Shift key and press the Return/Enter key to create a line space. Then, using the Type tool, type in the line *with* quotes "It's not easy to be steady on a lobster boat."

3. Change the Space After to 1p0, hold the Shift key and press the Return/Enter key to create a line space below the line.

4. Highlight the text and change the font to Adobe Garamond Pro Bold Italic or a similar style to match the font you are using, and then increase the font size to 14 points with the Fill color of Pantone 1935 PC to apply the lobster color theme.

5. To create the rule above the text line, choose Paragraph Rules in the Paragraph panel menu or Control menu on the far right of the Control panel. At the top of the Paragraph Rule dialog box, select Rule Above then select Rule On. Type in an Offset of 1p6.

6. For Weight, choose 2 points, then select the Pantone 1235 PC color in the Swatches panel for Color.

7. Select Preview to see what the rule will look like. Select Overprint Stroke to make sure that the stroke does not knock out underlying inks on a printing press, and check Keep in Frame, to avoid overlapping. Select OK to accept the rule (Figure 12-27).

8. For the bottom rule, choose the Paragraph Rules in the Paragraph panel menu again, select Rule Below, then select Rule On. Repeat the same procedure, but type in an Offset of 1p0. Click OK.

9. Save the file.

 PROBLEM If the display box is grayed out, make sure the Rule On box is checked.

 TOOLKIT TIP In CS5, you have the ability, when in a multi-column text frame, to use the Span Column feature in deciding whether a paragraph should span all columns or a maximum number of columns using either the Paragraph panel menu (Figure 12-27), or using the Paragraph formatting function in the Control panel and clicking on that right side panel menu to observe your options. This new feature also helps in balancing text between frames.

USING TABS TO CREATE THE INDEX BOX

The index box lets the reader know what articles are in the newsletter and where they are located. The page numbers are aligned properly using tabs. **Tabs** are important for creating accurate columns of data. Here are some considerations when working with tabs:

DESIGN TIP

When working with text in frames filled with color or using an outline edge, make sure there is an inset spacing set to provide space between the text and the edge of the frame for a more professional look. About 6 points is a good starting point for creating an inset space here.

• When you are planning to tab data, do the typing first, making sure you press the Tab key once between columns of data. It may not look correct, but that will be adjusted afterwards when you set what are called *tab stops*.

• In the Tabs panel you will notice various methods of setting tabs using the tab arrows to align flush left, right, centered, or on special characters, such as decimal points, or the "=" sign of an equation.

• For multiple lines of tabbing, and to help keep the data focused, you can create leading characters, such as periods, in the Leader box that lead the viewer to the tabbed information, like you would see leading up to page numbers in a table of contents. To create indents without any lead characters, make sure the Leader field is blank.

• The Tabs panel also contains a Magnet icon to align the tab ruler with the selected text. This provides a visual for the designer to properly align the tabbing arrows with precision. The Tabs panel is displayed using the Type menu (Type > Tabs).

• It is a good habit to only tab once between columns of information that need to be tabbed.

• You can observe if you have tabbed correctly by showing **hidden characters**. These are nonprinting characters that display spaces, tabs, ends of paragraphs, index markers, and ends of stories. These special characters are visible only in a document window on the screen and can be toggled on or off in the Type menu.

• When setting tabs, an inset space can be used to provide space for the text so that type is not placed next to a graphic frame that may have a stroke weight color or be filled with color. Inset settings apply to all text in a text frame.

DESIGN TIP

Adding dot-leader fills to tabbed copy assists readers in tracking across columns of type.

TOOLKIT TIP If you do not get the Tab locations correct the first time, you can select the Tab Stop icon in the ruler and drag to the location you desire, or select the icon and type the location in the X-value box. To remove a tab, click on the tab and drag it up and out. To change alignment you can Option/Alt click on tab stops.

Here you will set up the Index box with appropriate tabbing to align articles corresponding to the pages they start on using the Tabs panel in the Type menu. You will also format the text frame.

1. Display the front page document by clicking on the A-1 document in the Pages panel and zoom in to around 125%. Select *Page 1* in the Layers panel.

2. Choose Type > Show Hidden Characters to display nonprintable hidden characters; they can also be toggled off by selecting Type > Hide Hidden Characters. Tabs will display as double arrows, paragraphs will display as a backwards *P*, and so on.

3. Select the Rectangular Frame tool with a Stroke of None and a Fill of Pantone 612 PC selected from the Swatches panel or pop up Swatches panel in the Control panel. Drag from the 37-pica mark to the bottom margin. Adjust the Tint in the Swatches panel to 75%.

4. Select the Type tool and click in the top corner of the frame.

5. Select Object > Text Frame Options and click the link icon to make all settings the same link; enter an inset setting of 6 points (0p6) for all edges. Under Vertical Justification, select Align Center (Figure 12-28).

▷   FIGURE 12-28

Setting tabs for alignment of page numbers and second line indents.

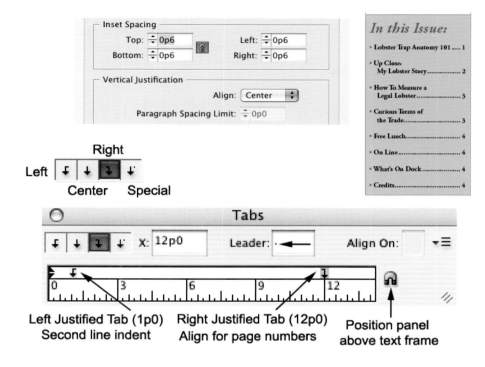

Right

Left

Center   Special

Left Justified Tab (1p0)
Second line indent

Right Justified Tab (12p0)
Align for page numbers

Position panel
above text frame

6. Use the Place command to locate the *Index* file in your *Text* folder. Select Open to insert the text. The text has already been tabbed once in each category for the page numbers, although you may need to make further adjustments. You can also type and tab the list on your own instead to get a feel for the layout.

7. Format the text to the font you are using in body of the document with a Bold style, choosing the same size you are using for the document, and then highlight all lines of text except the first line, "In This Issue."

8. To open the Tabs panel, select Type > Tabs and you will see the Tabs panel above the selected type.

9. On the right side of the Tabs panel, click the Magnet icon to align the tab ruler with the selected text (Figure 12-28). If the magnet is grayed out, it is already aligned. The magnet does not work when the view is magnified if the frame edges extend beyond the viewable area.

10. To make the tabbed page numbers right aligned, click on the Right-Justified Tab icon.

11. Click inside the blank white box *above* the ruler number 12 to display the right justified arrow and to set the distance for the page numbers as shown in Figure 12-28. Make sure you select inside the blank white box. You can then move the right align tab stop arrow to place it accurately, or you can type in a 12p0 coordinate in the X-coordinate box, then press Return/Enter.

DESIGN TIP

Dot leaders are frequently used for quick reference to page numbers and other info when indexing, providing definitions, etc. They help the viewer to focus attention by leading their eye to the intended information.

12. The tabs leading to the page numbers will be created with dotted lines called **dot leaders**. To create a dot leader to the pages numbers, type a period and a space in the Leader field and press Enter or Return. Make sure all page numbers are aligned accurately.

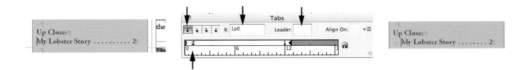

▷ FIGURE 12-29

Creating the second line indent at 1 pica.

13. To create a second line indent, click in front of the word you want to use to start the second line (click on front of the M in "My Lobster Story") and press Return/Enter (Figure 12-29). In the Tabs panel select the Left justified tab arrow, then type 1p0 in the X coordinate box, remove the dot in the Leader box, and press Return/Enter. Make sure you use the Left justified tab or it will not work.

14. Click in front of the second line and press the Tab key once to tab over 1 pica. The second line should align under the second character of the first line. Repeat this same procedure with the other two lines as shown in Figure 12-28.

15. If a line space is not already displayed between the text lines, click after each page with the cursor and press the Return/Enter key to make space between the lines or article names as shown in Figure 12-28.

16. Select the headline "In This Issue" and change the type to a 24-point Bold Italic style font with a Pantone color of 1935 PC at 100% tint.

17. Select the headlines of text and apply a bold style. Keep the size to 11 points.

18. To make bullets for emphasis, click in front of the first line of type, select Type > Insert Special Character > Symbols > Bullet Character (or press Option + 8 on the Mac). Press the space bar once after the bullet to create a space between it and the first word. To make the bullets stand out, highlight each and select the Pantone 1935 color (Figure 12-28).

19. To hide the hidden character display to view your work, select Type > Hide Hidden Characters. Toggle to display when finished.

20. Save the file.

DESIGN TIP

Creating color bullets to match the title color helps to provide consistency within the index box.

TOOLKIT TIP If you need regular circle bullets or universal special characters such as copyright symbols, trademark symbols, and so on, you can find these in the Type menu (Type > Insert Special Character > Symbol). Another option is the Glyphs panel. A **glyph** is a specific form of a character. For example, in certain fonts the capital letter A is available in several forms, such as swash and small cap. You can use the Glyphs panel to locate any glyph in a font. Choose Type > Glyphs or Window> Type and Tables > Glyphs. You can also use the Glyphs panel to view and insert OpenType attributes such as ornaments, swashes, fractions, and ligatures.

SETTING TABS FOR TERMS AND DEFINITIONS

This is basically the same process as creating the index, except this time you are aligning to two columns; the term on the left and its definition on the right use leading dotted lines again. When placing text across multiple columns in a page, or to ignore wrapping around a graphic, you can place a check mark in the **Ignore Text Wrap** box in the Text Frame Options display box. This will ensure the text will flow across columns in the length or width determined by the text frame drawn. You will also see how to remove the leader characters between lines for tabbing multiline definitions. You will also adjust the background fill color in the Swatches panel to a 30 percent tint to lighten up the background.

TOOLKIT TIP This exercise poses another solution to a problem. If, as in the case here, you want to use a dot leaders to align the term with the definition, the Tabs panel will also do this if you have more than one line for a definition, making the layout look sloppy with too many tabbed periods. To be able to have a tab align in the second definition line without the dot leaders you created for the initial line, you need to insert an Indent to Here nonprinting character using the Type tool; click the insertion point where you would like to indent (Choose Type > Insert Special Character > Other > Indent To Here), and the text line will be properly aligned under where you placed the Indent to Here insertion point. The Indent to Here, also called a *hanging indent,* should be used to indent the second line of the definitions.

In this exercise, you will create a light-toned background, place the lobster terms, and align the columns using the Tabs panel. Then you will apply formatting.

1. Double-click page 3 in the Pages panel, select Page 3 in the Layers panel, then drag horizontal guides to the 43- and 46-pica marks for two text frames for the headline and terms with definitions.

2. If hidden characters are not displayed, choose Type > Show Hidden Characters if you want to check your work.

3. Select the Rectangular Frame tool with a Stroke of None and a Fill of Pantone 612 PC selected from the Swatches panel, and drag from the 43-pica guide across the three columns and to the right side and bottom margins; depending on the placement of your lobster graphic, allow about 1 pica of space.

4. Using the Swatches panel to change the Fill color to a 30% tint, select the arrow next to the Tint box and drag the slider to 30% as shown in Figure 12-30.

5. Select the Type tool and drag a text frame across the three columns between the 43- and 46-pica marks for the headline.

6. Select Object > Text Frame Options and enter Left Inset and Top Inset settings of 6 points (0p6) with the rest at 0 points. Click to break the link icon. Set a Vertical Justification of Align Top. To make sure the text runs across the columns, click in a check mark in the Ignore Text Wrap box. Select OK.

7. With the Type tool, drag a second text frame from the 46-pica mark to the margins across the three columns for placement of the terms and definitions. Use the Selection tool if needed to adjust resizing handles so both boxes touch.

▷ FIGURE 12-30

Settings for placing terms and definitions across columns.

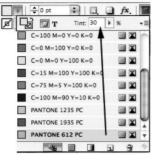

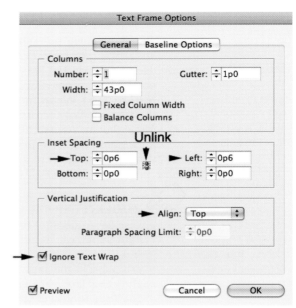

Ⓧ **PROBLEM** After you Place the text in the box, if it appears empty with only the overset icon (red cross) displayed, go back to step 8 and make sure you have the Ignore Text Wrap box checked.

8. Select Object > Text Frame Options and enter inset settings for a space of 6 points (0p6) all around by clicking the link icon to make all settings the same, with a Vertical Justification of Align Center. To make sure the text runs across the columns, click to put a check mark in the Ignore Text Wrap box. Select OK.

9. Select the Type tool and choose File > Place to open the file *Terms* in the text frame.

10. Highlight the headline "Curious Terms of the Lobster Trade" and select Edit > Cut; click inside the headline text frame you created, and select Edit > Paste to place the headline in its own frame; to create a true ellipsis, select the three periods, then hold down Option/Alt and press the semicolon key.

11. Click inside the second text frame below the headline, and delete the top space to bring the text lines near the top of the frame, then delete the extra line space between each line of text to display all terms within the text box.

12. Highlight the text terms and definitions and select Type > Tabs for the Tabs panel to display above the selected type. Click the Magnet icon to align the ruler with the selected text.

13. To apply tabs, click on the Left justified tab stop and click in the blank white box above the ruler number 10, or type 10p0 in the X-coordinate box to set the distance for the definitions, or drag over to the 10-pica mark the stop created earlier. Press Return/Enter. Understand that this example is one of the few times a left tab stop is used with a leader.

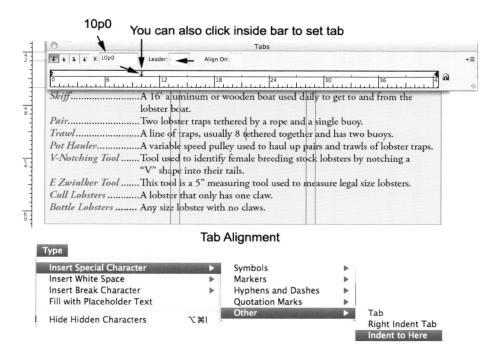

▷ FIGURE 12-31

Tab settings for terms and definitions and applying formatting.

14. To create a dot leader to the definitions, type a period and a space in the Leader field and press Enter or Return. Remove the dash after each term, then click in front of the definition and press tab. The definitions should align to the 10 pica (10p0) mark you just created with dots leading to each definition. Use Figure 12-31 as a starting guide.

15. Change the font size to 14 points to stand out. If the box is empty, you can either adjust the text frame height to include all the text, or change the size to 12 points, depending on the font you chose.

16. To create an indented second line without lead dots, click in front of the first word "A" across from the Skiff term; then choose Type > Insert Special Character > Other > Indent To Here to align the words "lobster boat" underneath (Figure 12-31).

17. Repeat the same for the "V-notching tool" term.

18. To format the headline, highlight the "Curious Terms of the Lobster Trade" headline, and change the font to a bold style, increasing the size to 24 points with a Pantone color of 1935 PC at 100% tint.

19. To format the terms with the same red, select each term and change the font style to Bold Italic, then choose Pantone 1935 PC to make the terms stand out with the lobster color theme, as shown in Figure 12-31.

20. To remove the hidden characters, select Type > Hide Hidden Characters. Save the file.

DESIGN TIP

Using special techniques for headlines, like increasing font size, applying a style, and adding a universal color that is utilized in the theme of the newsletter, helps to grab the reader's attention. Make sure you are using a consistent font throughout the project. Leave subheads left aligned to stand out over indented paragraphs.

FINAL FORMATTING AND LAYOUT ADJUSTMENTS

It is time to format headlines that stand out to grab the reader's attention by increasing the size, adding a style, such as Bold, and adding color. **Subheads** or subheadlines are used to break components of a large article into smaller parts to keep the viewer focused. In the Advanced section, you will learn about setting up paragraph and character styles to apply the same formatting easily to any characters or paragraphs in the document. You will also create a drop cap to start off the feature article. As a design feature, you can also end each article with a symbol or character to let the reader know they have finished the article. This works nicely when there are many articles to read. Selecting a symbol in the Wingdings font is a starting point. Paragraphs should also be indented for easier reading. This can be done using the First Line Indent field in the Paragraph formatting controls. When finishing final formatting techniques, you may need to readjust text frames and graphics to provide consistent spacing and accommodate all text. Selecting text frames and making adjustments in the Text Frame Options box can help, along with using the Selection tool and to adjust graphics. Be careful not to leave widows or orphans when splitting paragraphs between columns or pages. A **widow** is a single or partial line of a paragraph that falls at the bottom of a column or page. An **orphan** is one line of a paragraph that falls at the top of a column in a page, although it should be noted that these two terms are constantly defined interchangeably. Adjust frames or use the Control panel to make sure widows or orphans do not occur in the final document.

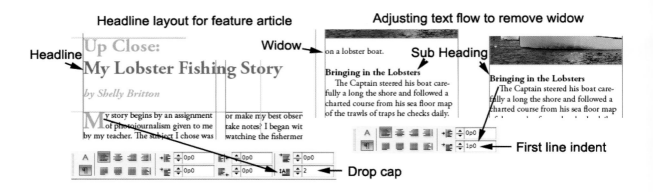

▷ FIGURE 12-32

Applying formatting for headlines and sub headings. Reflowing text to remove widows.

First, you will apply the same formatting to the headlines in the newsletter, then format the subheads with consistency (Figure 12-32).

1. Display page 1, select the Type tool with a Stroke color of None and a Fill color of Pantone 1935 PC, and highlight the "Lobster Trap Anatomy 101" headline.

2. Select the Character Formatting icon in the Control panel, and select the font you have been using in a Bold style; increase the size to around 24 points, depending on the font. If the text disappears, or if the overset icon appears, the text size is too big in the frame; decrease the font size.

3. To align the text to the top of the frame, if it is not top aligned already, select Object > Text Frame Options > Vertical Justification > Align Top.

4. Repeat the same process for the lines on page 2, "My Lobster Fishing Story," and page 3, "How to Measure a Legal Lobster," and "Closing the Trap Door."

5. On page 2, select the headline "Up Close:" and increase the point size to 24 or 28; use the Pantone 612 PC color to indicate it as the feature article.

6. For the author line "by Shelly Britton," create a line space if needed, and increase the size to 14 point in the font you are using with a Bold Italic style with a Pantone color of 612 PC to make it stand out.

7. In the story below, create a two-line drop cap using the Paragraph Formatting button in the Control panel of the first letter "M" to start the story. Use a Bold style with a Pantone color of 612 PC.

8. To create the subheadings in page 2 and page 4, highlight the following subheading lines and add a Bold style to make them stand out: *Sunrise on the Dock, Out to Sea, Bringing In the Lobsters, My Second Trip Out,* and *Our Final Destination.* If you increase the subhead size to 12 points, you may need to decrease the leading space between the subhead and the first line for consistency.

9. On page 2 of the "My Lobster Fishing Story" article, you may notice a single line with "lobster boat" in the third column under the boat picture. This is a widow that needs to be adjusted. Drag a horizontal guideline to the 13p6 mark, and adjust the first and second column text frames up to reflow the text. If this still does not work, adjust the headline frame and decrease the text line "Up Close:" to reflow the text. This may take a few adjustments to flow the text so that the "Bringing in the Lobsters" subhead appears below the lobster boat graphic (Figure 12-32).

10. On page 4, you may notice the overset symbol displayed in the third column, indicating more text to be displayed; select each text frame and drag up to the 50-pica mark above the Resources graphic. Choose Object > Text Frame Options. Place a check in Ignore Text Wrap and change the Vertical Justification to Align Bottom.

11. To indent the paragraphs (except those with a drop cap), using the Type tool, click in front of the line to indent, select the Paragraph Formatting button in the Control panel, and type in a 1p0 seting in the First Line Left Indent box (Figure 12-32). Press the Return/Enter key. Repeat for all paragraphs (you will learn to create a paragraph style for convenience in the Advanced section).

12. Optional: Feel free to type a subtle symbol, like an anchor or something, to go with the theme at the end of each article to signify the ending. The F key on the keyboard created an anchor using the Wingdings font.

13. To view your work without guidelines, you can click on the Preview icon on the bottom right of the Tools panel; pressing *W* will hide your guides and gray out the pasteboard, or you can select View > Grids & Guides > Hide Guides Also select View > Hide Frame Edges to remove nonprinting frame guides.This also allows you to check to see if there are any stray frame stroke weights that were colored instead of set as transparent.

14. Make final adjustments for consistency of spacing and layout between text frames and graphics, and you are all set. Feel free to check your sub layers in the Layers panel, right-click to select text frames. Use the Links panel to make sure all you graphics are still correctly linked.

15. Save the file as an InDesign document (INDD) and as an InDesign Template (INDT) to use as a guide for future documents. If you wish to further complete the project in the Advanced section, skip the next steps in preparation and printing until you have completed the Advanced section; otherwise, continue on.

> **TOOLKIT TIP** You can choose Edit > Spelling > Dynamic Spelling to check for misspellings on the fly. There is a new all language user dictionary (Edit > Spelling > Dictionary) feature that allows you to add a custom word or name to a user dictionary and all languages will treat the term as correctly spelled. Use the Links and Preflight panel features to check for graphic and text links and related info. You can also apply special page transitions using the Page Transitions panel for special presentation effects that you can then output to PDF pages (Window > Interactive > Page Transitions). The Package command will create a folder and copy all documents and graphics files, and the document copy with a report for the service provider.

 Need additional fun computer graphics tutorials and info, and an additional look at the projects you'll be creating in this book? Check out my Artist's Digital Toolkit website at: **http://www.digitoolkit.com**

16. To prepare for the printer, as described in the previous chapter, Edit > Spelling > Check Spelling to make sure spelling is correct, although there will be lots of terms and words you will simply choose to skip or ignore. Select the Preflight menu panel at the bottom of the document window (File > Preflight in earlier versions) to check to make sure graphics are still linked, correct fonts are displayed, and images are set to CMYK colors for press.

17. Choose File > Print and use all the printer's marks to create proofs of the four pages. This is the soft proof you would look at and have your client check for any problems before setting up to package all files and documents.

18. After checking for any problems, you can package for press; select File > Package and create a folder within the *Newsletter* folder or on a portable media to transport the image and text files, and name the new folder *Chapter 12 Newsletter*.

19. You can create a final PDF soft proof for press: choose File > Export > keep most defaults with Press quality, and place the PDF in the *Newsletter* folder. To create special transitional effects for your pages, try playing with the Page Transition panel (Window > Interactive > Page Transitions). Then create another PDF as the smallest file size for electronic presentation.

20. Congratulations! You have just completed a complicated and universally accepted project with many of InDesign's special features and with terminology that is used in the desktop publishing industry (Figure 12-33).

▷ FIGURE 12-33

Completed newsletter with formatting.

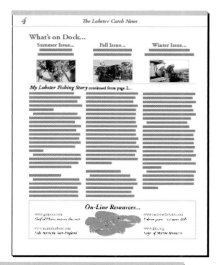

Completed newsletter with formatting

ADVANCED USERS: Baseline Alignment and Automation with Styles and Object Libraries

When working with multicolumn and multipage documents, a professional look can be acquired when the text lines align evenly across the columns in each document. This can be done by displaying baseline grids to align adjacent text frames. When multiple tasks or procedures are needed, InDesign provides various ways to save these repetitive tasks to apply in one step as opposed to recreating them through a multitude of steps. A designer can use character styles and paragraph styles to handle repetitive formatting and create object libraries to hold graphic and text objects for future use.

TEXT ALIGNMENT USING BASELINE GRIDS

To help with final alignment of text lines in adjacent columns, you can select to display **baseline grids**, which align the baseline of the text from a starting point across the document for the designer to view how text aligns crosswise along columns to ensure a consistent look (Figure 12-34). Using a baseline grid ensures consistency in the location of text elements on a page. This is useful if you want the baselines of text in multiple columns or adjacent text frames to align. In the Paragraph panel or Control panel, click Align to Baseline Grid . You can view baseline grids by selecting View > Grids & Guides > Show Baseline Grid. To make incremental adjustments for consistency across columns, select the Text Frame Options display. Using the Text Frame Options display, you can experiment and enter values for your baseline grid in points to match text size and leading on selected paragraphs. With pull quotes, the Only Align First Line to Grid option is used from the Paragraph menu or Control panel menu. To ensure that the leading of your text does not change, set the baseline grid leading to the same leading value as your text.

▷ FIGURE 12-34

Adjusting to baseline grids to flow text lines evenly across columns.

My story begins by an assignment of photojournalism given to me by my teacher. The subject I chose was to learn all about the lobster fishing industry. Why not? How and where do these bulging-eyed shellfish come to be such a delight as a popular East coast dish anyhow? My experience spending time on a lobster boat was far beyond a boat ride around the sea, picking up dozen's of lobsters.

Sunrise On the Dock

Just before sunrise, I was at the dock excited & anxious. I was thinking, should I begin shooting right away or make my best observation and just take notes? I began with observation watching the fishermen prepare for their day at sea. They suited up in full-length bibs, and put on waterproof boots. I dressed warm, slipped on my boots and brought an extra set of clothes just in case.

The lobster boat was moored about a half a mile up the creek from the fisherman's dock, so we all jumped into a small boat called a "skiff" and sat down on some newspaper we brought, the dew being heavy that morning. As we motored along up the creek, I took out my camera and took some pictures of the brightly colored morning sunrise as it reflected into the boats wake.

Out to Sea

Once on the fishing vessel, noticing that there was no rear tailgate on this 40-foot boat, I scoped out all the rails

Bringing in the Lobsters

The Captain steered his boat carefully a long the shore and followed a charted course from his sea floor map of the trawls of traps he checks daily. Most of the trawls were 3 to 5 traps long & could also be sited by a specific shaped & colored buoy floating in the water. The Captain used a long handled hook to pull the buoy aboard & attached the rope to a pulley system inside the boat.

"It's not easy to be steady on a lobster boat"

The hydraulic pulley system, called

You can view baseline grids and adjust the text frames for consistency in lines of text across columns in the document. Your baseline grid should begin with the same increment as the leading value.

1. To display nonprinting baseline grids, select View > Grids & Guides > Show Baseline Grid. Observe whether the text line flows across fairly evenly.

2. Select text frames and make adjustments in the Text Frame Options display box using the General tab for the purposes of this exercise. If you want to venture into the Baseline Options tab to make adjustments, save the file first at this point and play, then choose File > Revert if you have experimented too far to return to the previous Save.

3. If you increased the subhead size to 12 points, you may need to decrease the leading between the subhead and the first line for consistency. Your baseline grid should begin with the same increment as the leading value.

4. For the pull quotes, use the Type tool to highlight the second text line of the pull quote you created and the first line of the next paragraph that talks about the hydraulic pulley system; then choose Only Align First Line to Grid from the Paragraph menu or Control panel menu.

5. For paragraphs, select the paragraphs you want to align; then, in the Control panel menu or paragraph menu, you can click the Align to Baseline Grid icon to check for accuracy.

6. Try to use methods to have text align as evenly as possible across all columns; this can be a little time consuming to be precise, but the overall look will be very appealing to the reader and to your client.

7. Toggle to hide the baseline grids when you are finished.

8. Save the file and print the document using the last steps (steps 16-19) in the last newsletter exercise.

FORMATTING USING CHARACTER AND PARAGRAPH STYLES

As you learned with other Adobe applications, to make work flow more productive, you can create character and paragraph styles for consistency in formatting. A **character style** is a collection of formatting attributes that can be applied to text that already has a paragraph style assigned. A **paragraph style** includes both character and paragraph formatting attributes, and can be applied to a selected paragraph or range of paragraphs. A paragraph style can be used for headlines as well. When you change the formatting of a style, all text to which the style has been applied will be updated with the new format. Paragraph styles can also include rules, tabs, spacing, and many other attributes. By default, each new document contains a basic Paragraph or Character default style that is applied to text you type. You can edit this style, but you cannot rename or delete it. After you create a custom paragraph or character style, you simply highlight the text, select the style you want, and the style is automatically applied. You can then add additional formatting to your style, which will automatically be updated in all text to which the style has been applied. You can base a style on an existing style to save time and for consistency. You can find the Styles panels in the Type menu and the Window menu (Window > Type and Tables), or you can use the F11 key for Paragraph styles and Shift F11 for Character styles.

CHARACTER STYLES FROM FORMATTED TEXT

A designer can create a specialized format for a text line or characters by high-lighting the formatted text and creating a paragraph or character style from it to apply to future documents. A new style is created by choosing New Character Style from the Paragraph or Character Styles panel menu. Character styles work within Paragraph styles to format selected copy or individual characters.

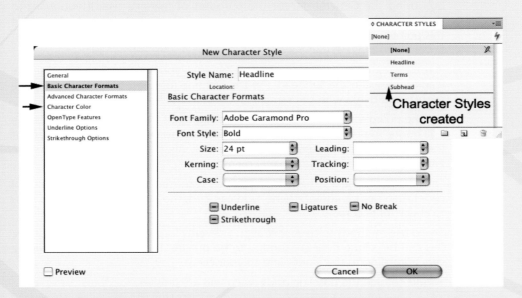

▷ FIGURE 12-35

Creating a character style from high-lighted headline text. Completed character styles are displayed in the Character styles panel.

In this exercise, you will highlight the formatting you already created for head-lines, subheads, drop caps, and terms to create individual character styles for future editing (Figure 12-35).

1. With the front page displayed, highlight the Lobster headline.

2. To display the Character Styles panel, select Type > Character Styles.

3. From the Character Styles panel, click the panel menu, select New Character Style. Another method is to hold the Option/Alt key and click the new style button in the lower right corner. This automatically opens the dialog box.

4. In the Basic Character Formats tab, you will notice that all the attributes of the highlighted headline are already displayed (the color of the formatted style is in the Character Color tab). Name the Style Name *Headline* then select OK. The new style will display in the Character Styles panel.

5. Repeat the same procedure above for character styles for subheads, (red) drop caps, and the terms labeling each. If some of the information is missing in the Basic Character Formats tab, type it in and select OK when done.

6. Feel free to create additional character styles that you think might be a nice addition to your arsenal of formatted styles. Experiment!

7. To apply any style, just highlight the text you want to format and click on the style in the Character Styles panel to apply the formatting. That's it!

8. Save when done.

CREATING PARAGRAPH STYLES

Tired of indenting all the paragraphs in the newsletter project? Creating a paragraph style allows you to tag each paragraph to automatically apply the formatting. Applying a paragraph style will not remove any existing character formatting or character style applied to part of a paragraph, although you can remove existing formatting after you have applied the style. You have the option to apply the same style as the copy from which it is being created. A plus sign appears next to the current paragraph style in the Paragraph Style panel if the selected text uses a character or paragraph style and also uses additional formatting that is not part of the applied style. This additional formatting is called an **override**. Paragraph styles can also include formatted tabs, rules, and many other attributes.

▷ FIGURE 12-36

Creating a paragraph style for Garamond body text with a left indent.

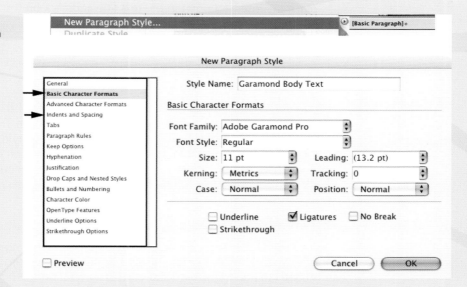

Here you will create the body text style of the font you have chosen with an indented first line based on the default style that you will apply to headings in the newsletter (Figure 12-36).

1. Double-click on page 1 in the Pages panel.

2. To display the Paragraph Styles panel, select Type > Paragraph Styles, press F11 or Command F11 (Mac) on your keyboard, or press the tab if it displays on the right side of your desktop.

3. To base a new paragraph style on the formatting of existing text, highlight the first few lines of the sample paragraph with an indented first line in the body text that contains the font and font size you plan to use. We used 11-point Adobe Garamond Pro for our example.

4. Choose New Paragraph Style from the Paragraph Styles panel menu, and select the Basic Character Formats tab. For the Style Name, type "Garamond Body Text," or whatever font you have chosen to use, for your new style. Make sure the font information is displayed or type it in. In the general tab, choose Based On None. When you base styles on another style, any changes to the style it is based on will affect the paragraph style. Leave the display open.

5. In the Indents and Spacing tab, make sure the First Line Indent is set for 1p0 spacing. Leave all other default settings and select OK. Your paragraph style will display in the Paragraph Styles panel.

6. You can also create another paragraph style with another serif font to see what the newsletter will look like with that font.

7. To apply the style, you do not need to highlight the entire paragraph, just place the insertion point in the text line and click on the new style.

8. Try to see if you can create a style based on one of the tabs you created earlier.

9. Save the file when done.

TABLE AND CELL STYLES

InDesign allows a designer to create cell and table styles that contain all formatting, so you can create a cell style and save it to have the formatting copied to other cells. The same can be created using a table style, where you can also include cell styles within table styles. These styles are in their own new Table Styles and Cell Styles panels, where you would use the Panel menu to create new styles. Check in InDesign > Help to view the tutorials in using these styles.

QUICK APPLY

You can use Quick Apply to locate a style quickly by typing part of its name. You can also use Quick Apply to find and apply menu commands and most other commands that use keyboard shortcuts. You will find the quick apply icon, a little lightning bolt on the Control panel right side, and the style panels to search for and apply formatting.

Here is a quick summary of how to use it.

1. Create a new document and use the Frame tool to make a frame.

2. With the Selection tool, select the text or frame to which you want to apply the style or menu command.

3. Choose Edit > Quick Apply or press Command Return (Mac) or Ctrl Enter (Windows).

4. Start typing the name of the item you want to apply. The name you type does not need to be an exact match. Try typing "color" and you will find a bunch of choices.

5. Select the Tools > Apply color option and the frame will be colored with the colors you have on your Color Picker on the Tools panel.

6. Close without saving. Go ahead and play.

OBJECT STYLES

Just as you use paragraph and character styles to quickly format text, you can use **object styles** to quickly format graphics and frames. Object styles include settings for stroke, color, transparency, drop shadows, paragraph styles, text wrap, and more; you can also assign different transparency effects for the object, fill, stroke, and text. You control which settings the style affects by including or excluding a category of settings in the definition. You can find the object style panel in the Window menu (Window > Object Styles). When creating styles, you can base one object style on another. When you change the base style, any shared attributes that appear in the "parent" style change in the "child" style as well. With any style, you select the object or item first, locate the style you want to apply, and select the style in the panel. Go ahead check out InDesign > Help to learn how to use this.

CREATING OBJECT LIBRARIES

Object libraries help you organize the graphics, text, and pages you use most often. You can also add ruler guides, grids, drawn shapes, and grouped images to a library. You can create as many libraries as you need: for example, you can create different object libraries for varied projects or clients. If an object library includes text files, make sure that the file's fonts are available and active on all systems that will access the library. When you add a page element, such as a graphic, to an object library, InDesign preserves all attributes that were imported or applied. For example, if you add a graphic from an InDesign document to a library, the library copy will duplicate the original, including the original's link information, so that you can update the graphic when the file on disk changes. If you delete the object from the InDesign document, the object's thumbnail will still appear in the Library panel, and all of the link information will remain intact. If you move or delete the original object, a missing link icon will appear next to the object's name in the Links panel the next time you place it in your document from the Library panel. When adding an item to an object library, InDesign saves all page, text, and image attributes automatically. Elements grouped in an InDesign document when dragged to the Library panel stay grouped when dragged out of the Library panel. Object libraries have an **INDL extension**. InDesign also provides support for new 3D Photoshop artwork.

Next, you will create object libraries of some newsletter objects and the front page of the newsletter for future use (Figure 12-37).

1. Select File > New > Library and leave the default Library name, placing the file in the *Newsletter* folder. The Library panel will display.

2. To save the entire front page document as a guide for future issues, drag across the entire document with the Selection tool. Drag the combined selection into the Library panel or select Add Items on Page 1 from the Library panel menu.

3. To rename the library object, double-click on the Untitled label in the object thumbnail to bring up the display box, and rename it *Front Page*. Select Object type as Page, then select OK.

4. To add individual components, select the Nameplate in the front page and drag it into the Library panel. It will contain the name of the file Nameplate in the thumbnail, which can also be edited. Instead of dragging, you could also select Add Item or Add Items on Page in the Library Panel menu display.

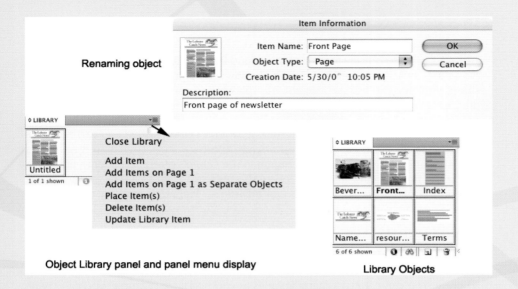

Object Library panel and panel menu display

Library Objects

▷ FIGURE 12-37

**Creating an Object
library for frequently
used objects and a
front page for
future use.**

5. Go ahead and create separate objects for the Resources graphic, any images you want to use for later, the Index box, and the Curious Terms box, so you will not have to tab over again. This is one cool feature!

6. To add any of these objects, including the entire front page, to a document, create the document and simply drag the object from the Object Library panel into the document window. The object is copied into the document. Go ahead and give it a try.

7. To open the Object Library in the future, select File > Open and locate the name of the Library file (INDL). It will then display the Library panel again with object thumbnails.

8. If you have not already done so, to prepare the document for press as described in *Chapter 11*, select Edit > Spelling > Check Spelling to make sure spelling is correct, although there will be lots of terms and words you will simply choose to skip or ignore.

9. Use the Preflight panel menu at the bottom of the document window (or File > Preflight for earlier versions) to check to make sure graphics are still linked, correct fonts are displayed, and images are set to CMYK colors for press. Check the Links panel as well.

10. Choose File > Print and use all printer's marks to create proofs of the four pages you could show to a client for final approval.

11. To package for press, select File > Package and create a folder with the *Newsletter* folder, or save it on a portable medium to transport the files and name the new folder *Chap 12 Newsletter*.

12. To create a PDF soft proof for press, choose File > Export > and keep most defaults with Press quality; place the PDF in the *Newsletter* folder.

13. You now have a newsletter project with plenty of styles, libraries, and features for future issues without having to start over in layout or formatting from scratch.

DIGITAL TOOLKIT EXTRA: Create an Interactive PDF Document

InDesign has the capability of creating interactive PDF documents that you can use to locate other documents, hyperlink to websites, and play movies and sounds. This is a valuable feature when you want to send a potential client available information, resources, movies, or sound clips in a universal PDF format. Here you will also learn to use the Button panel to create interactive buttons. As was discussed in previous exercises in creating documents with images and text, all components, including the InDesign document, should be in the same folder to keep everything together and linked as needed. For images in this project, you can use the kayak image you completed in Chapter 5 and the Map illustration you created in Chapter 8. Note: You can access this tutorial for earlier versions like CS3, in the Goodies Chapter 12 folder, as many changes have been made recently.

▷ FIGURE 12-38

Completed interactive PDF document.

Here you will create a folder for all components, then set up the document with the *Kayak Ad* file you worked on in Chapter 5 without the sale items, then lay out guides for the buttons.

1. Change the workspace setting on your Application bar from Essentials to Interactivity to set up the appropriate panels. Set Preferences to Inches, and create a new letter size document in landscape orientation with one column; set default margins at a half inch all around. Leave Facing Pages and Master Text Frame unchecked, because this will be a single document. Select OK. Make sure Smart Guides is selected.

2. Name the file *PDF Ad* and place it in the folder called *Chap 12 Extra* in the *Chapter 12* folder. Make sure at the bottom of the document window next to the green circle, that you have enabled Preflight options to have the document checked dynamically as you add text and graphics.

3. Drag Horizontal guidelines at the 5.5, 6, and 6.5-inch marks. Drag vertical guidelines at the 2- and 9-inch marks to center the image and at 2.25, 3.5, 4, 5.25, 5.75, 7, 7.5, and 8.75 inch marks to place in the buttons afterwards (Figure 12-37).

4. Using the Rectangle Frame tool, drag a rectangular frame in between the 2- and 9-inch guides to the 5.5-inch horizontal guide to place the image.

5. Optional: You can choose to launch Photoshop and open the *KayakAd* image you worked on in Chapter 5, creating a duplicate copy and removing the sale text lines, leaving the title and subtitle to identify the ad. Choose File > Place to place the image in the rectangular frame centered horizontally. If you want, you can select the title lines and italicize them as show in Figure 12-39.

6. The adjusted *Kayak Ad* file is located in the *Chap 12 Extra* folder within the *Chapter 12* folder if you do not wish to perform step 4. Choose File > Place to place the image in the rectangular frame centered horizontally inside the frame (Figure 12-39).

7. Save the file.

▷ FIGURE 12-39

Layout guides for image and buttons. Placing an image centered in the document.

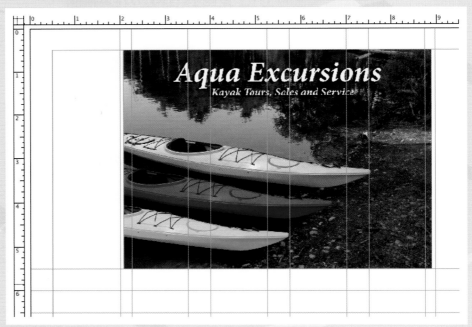

CREATING INTERACTIVE BUTTONS

The **Buttons panel** (Window > Interactive > Buttons) allows you to create interactive buttons for your document. After creating a button, you make it interactive by selecting various **Appearances** or **States** to see what chosen Events need to occur with the mouse when it is either over the graphic (Rollover), away from the graphic (Normal), or clicking the graphic (Click). **Rollovers** are a change state that occurs when your mouse hovers over the button or graphic (Figure 12-40).

You can change how text displays and other states when the mouse is over, clicking the button, and so on. Earlier versions used a Button tool and a States panel to perform the same operations that we will discuss here. Although the button names display when creating these graphics, they are only guides and will not appear. There are a couple of ways to create buttons; creating your own shapes or by using the panel menu's Sample Buttons panel which includes a number of pre-created buttons that you drag into your document, access these through the Button panel menu. To put in text headings, you need to create a text frame, type in the button name, then use the Character Formatting icon on the Control panel and the Text Frame Options command in the Object menu to center the text.

▷ FIGURE 12-40

Creating rollover states for interactive buttons when the mouse is over the button graphic.

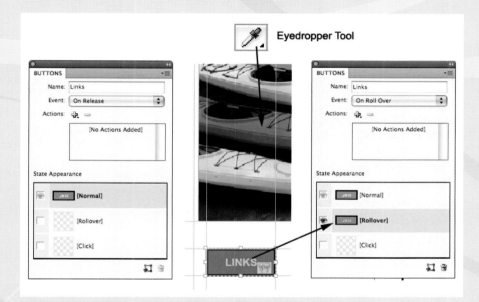

When creating your own interactive shape buttons, you will sample the green kayak color with the Eyedropper tool, then create rollover states that change the color of text for each button (Figure 12-40).

1. With the *PDF Ad* document open, select the Rectangle tool and drag between the 6- and 6.5-inch horizontal guides in between the 2.25- and 3.5-inch vertical guides.

2. Select the Stroke color box on the Tools panel, then using the Stoke panel apply a black, 3-point stroke; click to put the Fill color in front in the Tools panel.

3. Select the Eyedropper tool and sample the green kayak color to fill in the button.

4. Option/ALT copy the graphic to position the other three buttons equidistant from one another using the Smart Guides, Smart Spacing, and Smart Dimension features.

5. Select Window > Interactive > Buttons (or labeled States in earlier versions) to bring up the Buttons (States) panel.

6. Select the first graphic button with the Selection tool, and click in the frame with the Type tool. Using Arial Bold as the font, or another wide sans serif font, type "Links" in a 14-point size, choosing a white or light color to stand out over the green button color.

7. Center the text by choosing Center Align in the Character Formatting icon on the Control panel, then center vertically using the Text Frame Option command from the Object menu.

8. You will notice the Buttons panel will display the light text in the Appearance "Normal" state, as shown in Figure 12-40. If it does not, click outside the button with the Selection tool, then click the button again to bring up the Buttons panel. Name the button *Links* and make sure the Event is set at On Release.

9. In the Buttons panel menu, select the Rollover state for Appearance and select On Roll Over as the Event in the Buttons panel. With that Appearance highlighted, select the *Links* text line on the button and change the color to yellow or choose your own color as the Rollover state. Select the button with the Selection tool, then select the two states in the Buttons panel to see how the button text changes.

10. Change the second Button name to *Choices*, third Button change to *Cape Map*, and fourth Button to *Why Wait* (Figure 12-38)? Repeat the same process in steps 6 through 9 with the other three buttons, creating rollover states. We'll create Actions (Behaviors) for each button in the next exercise.

11. Save the file.

SETTING BUTTON ACTIONS

Actions in InDesign (earlier versions referred as behaviors) identify what a button will do when it is selected with the mouse (open a document, locate a URL, play a movie, etc.). After creating a button, it makes good sense to determine the behavior of the button using the Actions display in the Buttons panel. This is what makes the document interactive. When you are locating documents or files that are *not* saved as PDFs, you will need to make sure you select Enable: All Documents to make all documents eligible for inclusion in the document when you locate these files. Files that are saved as PDFs will appear as Bookmarks as part of multiple PDF documents. InDesign allows you to Export multiple documents as PDFs, creating a Bookmark for each page.

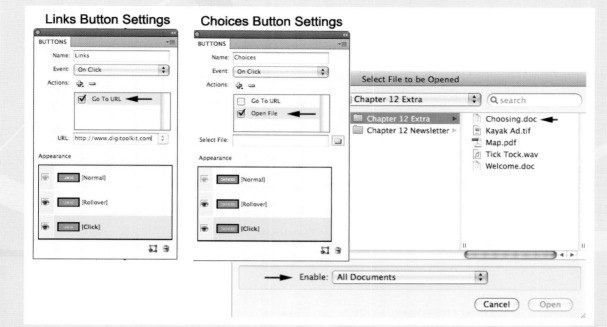

Links Button Settings   **Choices Button Settings**

▷ FIGURE 12-41

Creating an action for Links and Choices buttons to locate URL and a document when clicked.

Now you will link to a website, locate a document and the map illustration, and set up to play a sound file.

1. For the first button, you will link to a website or kayak resources. Select the *Links* button graphic with the Selection tool, then choose On Click, in the Event drop down list. In the Name box, type in the name "Links" if it is not already indicated in the Appearance box on the Buttons panel, select the Click layer, and make sure the text of the selected Links panel is the same color as when it is a Rollover state, in our case we chose yellow. The Click state is set.

2. To set the action when the Links button is clicked, click on the "plus sign" in the Actions display on the Actions tab to locate the file. In the Actions drop-down list, select Go to URL and type in *http://www.kayakonline.com* or another local sporting site you may be familiar with. You've created an action to locate the website upon clicking on the Links button (Figure 12-41).

TOOLKIT TIP I created a website at www.digitoolkit.com that contains more tutorials and resources using Photoshop, Illustrator, or InDesign to continue learning these cool applications. Feel free to use this link instead for your Links button, or just check it out.

3. To create the action that locates the File *Choosing*, which contains information in choosing a kayak, when the button Choices is clicked, repeat the same process again from step 2, selecting the Choices button graphic to bring up the Buttons panel. In the Name box, change the name to *Choices* if it is not already indicated.

4. In the Actions drop-down list, select Open File, then click the folder in the Select File box to locate the *Choosing* file in your *Chap 12 Extra* folder. Select Enable: All Documents, to make all documents eligible, then select Open to set up the link (Figure 12-41).

5. In the Control panel, when most any drawing or selection tool is active you can add special effects like drop shadows to your selected buttons (See Figure 12-42).

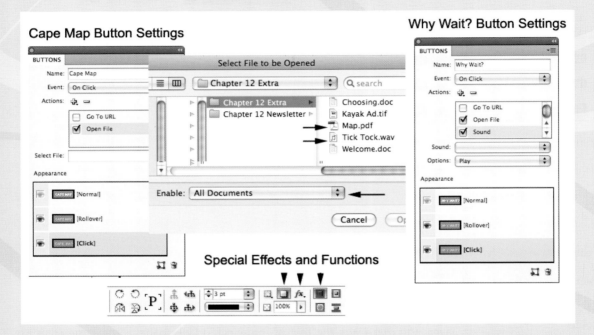

▷ FIGURE 12-42

Creating actions for buttons Cape Map and Why Wait?

TOOLKIT TIP To deactivate actions (or behaviors), make sure the check box is deselected next to the action. You can change the order by dragging and dropping actions just as is done with layers.

6. For the Cape Map button, you can open the map illustration you created in Chapter 8 and save it as a PDF file in the *Chap 12 Extra* folder, or you can open a PDF file already placed in the *Chap 12 Extra* folder.

7. To locate a PDF document map, repeat the same process as step 2 again, selecting the *Cape Map* button graphic to bring up the Buttons panel. In the Name display, change the name to *Cape Map* if it is not already indicated.

8. Locate the map in the *Chap 12 Extra* folder, and follow the same procedures as done with the Choosing button to add the action of locating the file when clicked to the button. Select Enable: All Documents to make all documents eligible (Figure 12-42). The file will open as a Bookmark to the original document when clicked.

9. The fourth button will play a sound. Name the button *Why Wait?.* Now you will need to select to open the file as done previously and locate the *Tick Tock.wav* file in the *Chap 12 Extra* folder. Make sure you have selected Enable: All Documents to make all documents eligible.

10. To make the next action to play the file, select Sound as the next action and select Play as the Option. You will notice the two actions listed on the left side (Figure 12-42).

11. Save the file; it is time to check your efforts.

EXPORTING THE DOCUMENT AS AN INTERACTIVE PDF

Now that the buttons have been created with rollover states and events are set up, it is time to use the Export command to set the document to be created as an interactive PDF. It is important again to make sure all files are located in the same place as the document at this point. In order to play the sound file or a movie file, you must make sure when exporting the document that the Buttons and Media: Include All is checked, you can save as a distinct Interactive PDF, with older versions when you export, make sure the Interactive Elements options is checked. Function is checked. For compatibility specify the appropriate PDF version and then click the Export command in the File menu. Then all you have to do is open the document using the free Acrobat Reader that you can download off the Adobe website, click on the buttons, and step into the future of electronic documents!

TOOLKIT TIP To play movies and sound clips, the computer in use must have QuickTime 6 or later installed. Use the Help menu and feel free to try creating a movie button from a movie file.

It is time to export your document to create an interactive PDF.

1. With the buttons created, select File > Export, Adobe PDF (Interactive) Save As *PDF Ad* in your *Chap 12 Extra* folder with Format set as Adobe PDF Interactive format (Figure 12-43). Select Save.

2. In CS5, when the Export to Interactive PDF dialog box opens, make sure you check Buttons and Media, Include All, and do not check Open in Full Screen Mode. Click OK. For earlier versions, when the Export Adobe PDF dialog box displays, select Smallest File Size for the Adobe PDF Preset, as if the document would be sent over e-mail or the Internet with Compatibility of Acrobat 6.0.

3. If you are using an earlier version than CS5, when the Export Adobe PDF dialog box displays, select Smallest File Size for the Adobe PDF Preset, with Compatibility of Acrobat 6.0. In the Include section, click check marks next to Hyperlinks, Bookmarks, and Interactive Elements. Click Export.

4. To check your work, launch Acrobat Reader, and click on the buttons. You will notice that as you move the mouse over the button, the text will rollover to the new color you selected in the Buttons panel earlier. One word of caution: Open the *Cape Map* last, because it is a PDF and replaces the interactive document you have just opened.

5. Have fun and try to create or change links for the buttons. All you have to do is make the changes and save the document to replace the existing PDF.

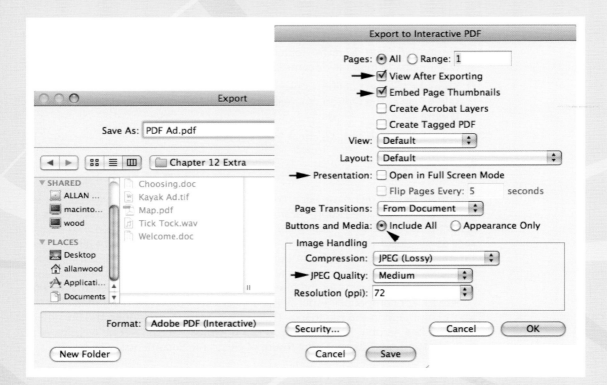

▷ FIGURE 12-43

Using the Export command to convert the document to an interactive PDF document.

INDESIGN'S GAP TOOL

The Gap tool (U) provides a quick way to adjust the size of a gap or resize between multiple items that have commonly aligned edges all at once, while keeping the gaps between them fixed. The Gap tool ignores Master Page items and locked items so you can work freely to adjust multiple items around your white space area, instead of having to individually select page items and resize them. You use the Gap tool by hovering your mouse over the gap area you want to adjust, then click and drag to resize the items aligned to the gap. The gap is highlighted with transparent gray shading.

Although it is not necessary for this project, to give you an idea of the power of this new tool, try to adjust the gap between the buttons and the image. You can use the Gap tool to drag between the action buttons you just created and the image dimensions to a set amount. You can also click between the buttons to resize between each button universally. Feel free to use the same *PDF AD.indd* file you just created, go ahead and play with this tool, close when finished, and *do not save* the file unless you save as a different name. Create a series of aligned squares and try this tool. Go ahead and play!

CHAPTER SUMMARY

You have just completed the most intensive chapter in the book. Not only did you work with creating master pages, layout graphics, and text components, along with formatting automated features like jump lines and automatic page numbering, but you also worked in the pica and points measurement format as opposed to the inches measurement you are probably more accustomed to. You learned an abundance of terminology used extensively in the desktop publishing and printing industries, you created rules and pull quotes, tabbed precisely for alignment of data and definitions, and threaded text between multiple columns and multiple pages. In the Advanced section, you learned to align text lines to a baseline grid for consistency across columns, automated formatting tasks using character and paragraph styles, and created object libraries for graphics, text, and the front page of the newsletter to be used in future documents.

REVIEW QUESTIONS

1. Explain the difference between spot and process colors.
2. What is the purpose of creating master pages?
3. Explain three uses of the Pages panel.
4. Explain the process of semi-autoflow of text into multiple text frames.
5. What is the overset symbol used for?
6. What is the difference between a widow and an orphan in desktop publishing?
7. What are jump lines?

CHAPTER 12
Creating a 4-page Newsletter Spread using InDesign.

▷ FIGURE 12-44

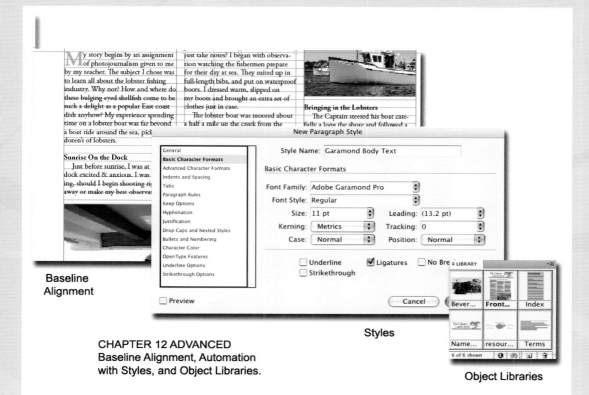

My story begins by an assignment of photojournalism given to me by my teacher. The subject I chose was to learn all about the lobster fishing industry. Why not? How and where do these bulging-eyed shellfish come to be such a delight as a popular East coast dish anyhow? My experience spending time on a lobster boat was far beyond a boat ride around the sea, pic[...] dozen's of lobsters.

Sunrise On the Dock

Just before sunrise, I was at dock excited & anxious. I was [...]ing, should I begin shooting ri[...] away or make my best observa[...]

just take notes? I began with observation watching the fishermen prepare for their day at sea. They suited up in full-length bibs, and put on waterproof boots. I dressed warm, slipped on my boots and brought an extra set of clothes just in case.

The lobster boat was moored about a half a mile up the creek from the

Bringing in the Lobsters

The Captain steered his boat carefully along the shore and followed a

New Paragraph Style

General
Basic Character Formats
Advanced Character Formats
Indents and Spacing
Tabs
Paragraph Rules
Keep Options
Hyphenation
Justification
Drop Caps and Nested Styles
Bullets and Numbering
Character Color
OpenType Features
Underline Options
Strikethrough Options

Style Name: Garamond Body Text

Basic Character Formats

Font Family: Adobe Garamond Pro
Font Style: Regular
Size: 11 pt   Leading: (13.2 pt)
Kerning: Metrics   Tracking: 0
Case: Normal   Position: Normal

☐ Underline   ☑ Ligatures   ☐ No Bre[...]
☐ Strikethrough

☐ Preview   Cancel

Baseline Alignment

LIBRARY

Bever...   Front...   Index
Name...   resour...   Terms
6 of 6 shown

Styles

Object Libraries

CHAPTER 12 ADVANCED
Baseline Alignment, Automation with Styles, and Object Libraries.

Aqua Excursions
Kayak Tours, Sales and Service

Links   Choices   Cape Map   Why Wait?

CHAPTER 12 EXTRA
Creating an interactive PDF document using InDesign.

▷ FIGURE 12-45

4

Digital Publishing: InDesign CS5

One of the more popular assignments you will receive as a designer is creating brochures for clients. Here you will see how to set up and position guides, images, and text for a three-way folding brochure, or tri-fold. You will also use the map you completed in Illustrator in Chapter 8 and the images of the kayaks you completed in Photoshop in Chapter 5 to understand how using all the applications you have been working with interrelates in the creation and placement of imagery and text for specific purposes.

CLIENT ASSIGNMENT: Creating a Tri-fold Brochure

Alyce Powell, for whom you have previously created a direct mail ad piece for her business, Aqua Excursions, wants to create a tri-fold brochure to promote the business's kayak tours and kayak sales and service. She discusses using the brochure for display at various retail stores, restaurant establishments, and other places that promote local tourism. In discussing the layout of the brochure, she mentions that she wants the sections divided into the front section for the basic business information, the back section to display the directions and special tours, and the other sections to provide a business summary, information on various tours, special events, FAQs, and pricing for rentals. The brochure will contain various images for different types of kayak enthusiasts and will be printed commercially on glossy coated paper using four-color CMYK processing. Two fonts will be used, Myriad Pro Bold for the headlines and subheadlines, and Adobe Garamond Pro Regular for the body text. After getting her approval on a final rough you created, Alyce looks forward to the finished proof (Figure UR4-1).

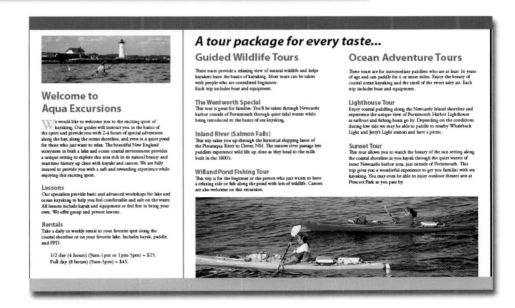

▷ FIGURE UR4-1

Completed tri-fold brochure.

ACTION ITEMS OVERVIEW

Here is a breakdown of what needs to be done to complete the tri-fold brochure.

• Create a folding dummy to show the layout and placement of graphics and text.

• For the master page, create green color bar for the top and a gold color bar for the bottom for framing using Pantone color selections to add in the Swatches panel.

 Need additional fun computer graphics tutorials and info, and an additional look at the projects you'll be creating in this book? Check out my Artist's Digital Toolkit website at: **http://www.digitoolkit.com**

• Import graphics onto both pages and adjust them according to guides. (You can also use two images from previous projects you created in earlier chapters or use alternative images in the review folder.)

• Import and format text and create character and paragraph styles to apply formatting easily for a more productive work flow.

• Save the file as an InDesign document and as a template for future use and prepare the document for press.

SETTING UP THE BROCHURE PROJECT

After discussion with the client and designing thumbnails and roughs, a designer should have a pretty good idea of what the final project will look like in the overall layout of the piece. Before laying out text and graphic items, preferences need to be set, and the final size and margins need to be set up.

CREATING AND ORGANIZING FOLDERS FOR PRESS

When you will be sending your materials to a commercial printer or web designer, you need to keep all documents, images, and fonts in folders to be included with your InDesign document in one main folder. Any font you use in a document should also be copied into a *Fonts* folder along with text and image folders. This is crucial, otherwise images may not print at full resolution or fonts may be substituted. It is also just as important to keep these folders with your InDesign document on your hard drive or on the same portable medium, like a flash drive or CD. All changes or saves to files will be made in these folders. InDesign provides preflight operations and the Package utility to take care of this for you.

Here you will locate the *Review* folder to place your document with the *Images* and *Text* folders in one area.

1. On your drive, locate your *Unit 4 Review* folder inside your Toolkit > InDesign folder. This folder already contains the *Images* and *Text* folders with content for the brochure assignment.

2. Here is a look at your directory structure:

   Toolkit > Unit 4 Review > Images/Text. The InDesign brochure project will also be saved inside the *Unit 4 Review* folder. Now you have all your "suitcases" that you will need to transport your work to the service provider.

CREATING A FOLDING DUMMY

To serve as a helpful guide for placement of items, a folding guide, or **folding dummy**, is made to provide a visual reference. This is where you would sketch in headlines and graphic elements, along with the type of fold you will use. This also helps to explain the layout to a client. The brochure that you are creating is based on what is called a *tri-fold design*. A **tri-fold** is simply a document divided into three sections folded toward the center, like a book. The individual sections of the document that are folded are called the **panels**. When designers create a folding document, they need to take into consideration the placement of items and text for easy reading and to keep the attention of the reader. The blank space between the columns is called the *gutter width.* For the brochure project, it also serves as the folding area. As shown in Figure UR4-2, you will notice that in the outside document, the front title piece is located on the far right panel, and the back piece is located in the center column.

▷ FIGURE UR4-2

Creating a folding dummy to observe layout, folds, and placement of graphics and text headlines.

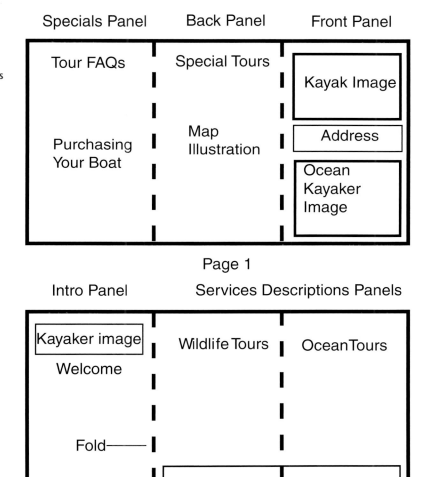

Specials Panel	Back Panel	Front Panel
Tour FAQs	Special Tours	Kayak Image
Purchasing Your Boat	Map Illustration	Address
		Ocean Kayaker Image

Page 1

Intro Panel	Services Descriptions Panels	
Kayaker image	Wildlife Tours	Ocean Tours
Welcome		
Fold———		
	Touring Kayakers Image	

Page 2 (inside panels)

Here is how to make a folding dummy as a guide.

1. Place two pieces of 8.5 × 14-inch paper (legal size) and position length-wise (landscape).

2. Divide evenly and fold the left and right pieces into the center.

3. Sketch the headings as shown in Figure UR4-2 on both pages. Here is your guide.

INCH PREFERENCES AND NEW DOCUMENT SETTINGS

Setting preferences provides a convenient way to adjust settings and parameters in your work environment to work on your document productively. Because there is not much call for precise measurement here, we will use inches as the preferred measurement. If you would like to use picas, feel free to make the conversions. Preferences can be changed anytime while working on the document. Units of measure can be changed on the fly by holding down the Option/Alt key and clicking on the rulers. In Mac OS X, the InDesign Application menu is where you would set Preferences; in Windows, Preferences are set in the Edit menu. For the brochure project document settings, you will be creating two, nonfacing pages in landscape orientation with three columns. The two pages will constitute the inside portion of the brochure and the outside portion, and the pages will be set in legal size, 8.5 x 14 inch paper, to provide room for the graphics and text content to make the brochure stand out (Figure UR4-3).

Here you will set up the measurements preferences to inches for your brochure.

1. Launch InDesign. In Mac OS X, select InDesign > Preferences > Units & Increments, and in Windows use Edit > Preferences > Units & Increments.

2. Change the Ruler Units for Horizontal and Vertical document measurements to Inches.

3. Leave all other defaults as shown. Select OK. Change the workspace on your Application bar to Essentials to bring up the panels that will be mostly used for this project.

4. Select File > New > Document to open the New Document display box.

5. Select Intent of Print. Select Page Size: Legal with Landscape Orientation (right side icon). The size will display as 8.5 x 14 inch paper. Enter one page for now.

6. To set the Margin Guides as 0.375 (3/8) inches all around, type in 0.375 in the first box, and click the link icon. Enter "3" for the number of columns.

7. Set the Gutter width at 0.75 inches. Uncheck the Facing Pages option and uncheck the Master Text Frame, because we are not creating a bound book or magazine with long text articles. Maintain a 0.125 inch Bleed on all sides of the document.

8. Click on OK. Make sure Smart Guides is checked. At the bottom of the window of your document, choose to have Preflight Document checked from the Preflight menu. Display the Preflight panel (Window > Output > Preflight).

9. Save the document in your *Unit 4 Review* folder as *Brochure*.

▷ FIGURE UR4-3

New document settings for tri-fold brochure.

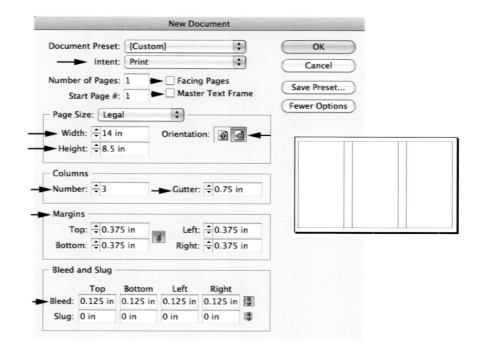

▷ FIGURE UR4-3

New document settings for tri-fold brochure.

CREATING COLOR BARS FOR THE TOP AND BOTTOM

Color bars help frame a document with a particular color theme, like we did in the newsletter project last chapter. To match the outdoor theme, you will create a green color bar across the top margin and a gold color bar across the bottom margin. This green color theme will also be used for text headings and sub-headings, with the gold for an initial drop cap. Because these will be considered graphics, you will use the Rectangle Frame tool. You will also select the colors from the Pantone Swatch library. You will create the color bars in the master page section to be used for the second page as well. With CS5, as you add new colors to the Swatches panel, they are also added in the swatches pop up menu in the Control panel for quick access.

Now you will create the top and bottom color bars for the master page template. You will need to select the appropriate colors from the Swatch panel library first.

1. With the A-Master displayed to create the color bars on a master template, select the Swatches panel. Choose New Color Swatch in the Swatches panel menu.

2. In the display make sure the Color Type is Process, and then from the Color Mode list, choose Pantone process coated as the library from which to choose.

3. For a green color select Pantone DS 284-2 C, as shown in Figure UR4-4. Select the Add button and the color you choose will automatically be added to the Swatches panel.

4. For a gold color, add Pantone DS 6-2 C to the Swatches panel. With both colors added, click on the Done button in the dialog box to indicate you have finished your choices.

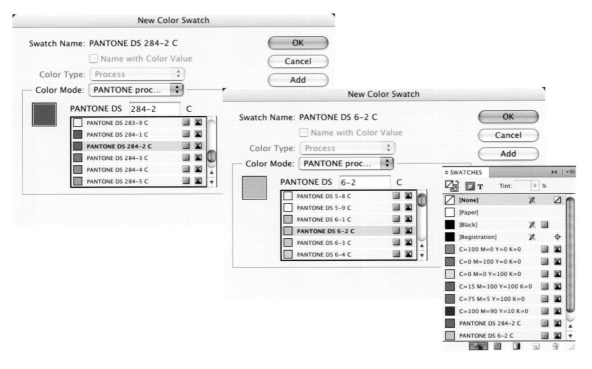

▷ FIGURE UR4-4

Selecting Pantone colors for color bars and headings.

5. Select the Rectangle Frame tool, and choose the green Pantone 284-2 C as the Fill color with a Stroke of None.

6. Drag across the top of the document from the margin to extend the frame to the bleed dimension an eighth inch away from the document's left, right, and top edges. Drag downward to the .375-inch margin line.

7. For the bottom color bar, choose Pantone DS 6-2 C as the Fill color from the Swatches panel with a Stroke of None, and drag from the bottom margin to bleed out beyond the edge of the document.

8. Select the Layers panel, and rename the *Layer 1* default layer to *Page 1* to keep track of graphics and text frames. Save the file.

ADDING A PAGE TO YOUR DOCUMENT

You can add another page to your document by selecting the A-Master page and dragging it to the document level underneath page 1. Or click the Create New Page icon in the lower right corner of the Pages panel.

1. To add another page based on the A-master, select the A-Master in the upper panel of the Pages panel and drag below the page 1, and release the mouse (Figure UR4-5). Page 2 will appear with an "A" at the top of the page, indicating that this new page is formatted with the A-Master. With the Pages panel selecting page 2, create a new layer in the Layers panel and name it *Page 2*.

2. Double-click page 1 to continue with the next exercises.

▷ FIGURE UR4-5

Creating a new page based on the master page by clicking and dragging under the document.

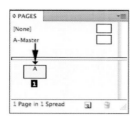

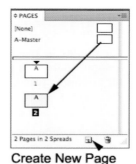

SETTING LAYOUT GUIDES AND ADJUSTING THE ZERO POINT

Designers use guides consistently to lay out various text and picture items with precision. Margin guides use purple lines as a default and are what you created previously in the initial set up. Layout guides are green in color and are guide-lines dragged out from the top and left side rulers. To start your document with the margin edges set at a **zero point** for easier measuring, you can drag from the upper left-hand corner where the rulers intersect, then release the mouse where the margins themselves intersect (Figure UR4-6). You can also use the zero point to set the measurements from where the margins intersect.

▷ FIGURE UR4-6

Setting zero-point guides to measure from the margins instead of the edge of the first document.

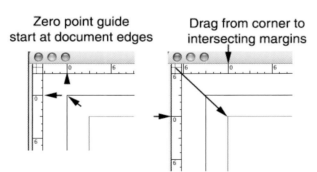

Here you will set up the zero point guides inside the margins as a point of reference for measurement and create guides to align picture and text boxes for the front and back of the first page.

1. Double-click document A-1 (page 1) in the Pages panel. Select Page 1 in the Layers panel.

2. To make sure the rulers are displayed, you should see left and topside rulers outside your document. If you do not, select View > Show Rulers; it will toggle to display the rulers.

3. To make sure that boxes easily snap to the guides, select View > Grids & Guides > Snap to Guides to make sure a check mark displays; if one does not, click it.

4. To create the zero point, click the box in the upper left corner where the two rulers intersect (dotted lines crossed) and drag to the intersection of the two margin guides. The zero point will remain in that position for document A-2 (page 2).

5. For guides to place upper and lower color bars, and for placement of the images on the first page for the front and back of the brochure, drag horizontal guides to place the logo image, select document A-1 in the Pages panel, click on the top ruler bar, and drag the horizontal guideline down to the 3.25, 3.75, 4.125, and 6-inch marks, or type in the Y coordinates for precision.

6. Draw one vertical guide in the center of the gutter between the first and second columns for a vertical rule later, or type "4.3" in the X-coordinate box.

7. Draw a second vertical line in the center of the gutter between the second and third columns to use as a guide for bleeding the images. Type "8.95" in the X-coordinate box. Both vertical guides serve as folding marks.

8. Save the file.

DESIGNING THE FRONT, BACK, AND SPECIAL PANELS (PAGE 1)

Use the paper folding guide you created earlier as a guide. The outside document, which is set up as Page 1 or document A-1 in InDesign, includes the brochure front, back, and specialty information panels. In designing this document, keep in mind that the "front page" panel of this tri-fold will be on the right side, and the "back" will be in the center of this tri-fold. The front panel identifies what the document is about; it is the attention-getter that sparks the reader's curiosity to continue reading the rest of the information. In a tri-fold, the back panel located in the center provides information that summarizes or complements the front page, and the specialty page located on the left side may include specialty information to entice the reader to look inside for what the brochure is about. You can also use the image of the kayaks completed in Photoshop (Chapter 5), and the map illustration you completed in Illustrator (Chapter 8) to see how these applications interrelate with one another for their intended purpose.

TOOLKIT TIP InDesign allows you to place layered graphics and edit them using the Links panel. With the application open, say Photoshop with the kayaks, you can make edits such as changing colors, and the changes are also made to the linked graphic in InDesign through the Links panel.

CREATING THE FRONT PANEL

The front panel will contain two images that contrast the type of kayaking offered with the Aqua Excursion logo on the top image. The images will be placed so they overlap into the gutter and bleed off the edge of the document. Here you can use the image of the kayaks you completed in Chapter 5, removing the sale lines, or a similar image from the *Images* folder within the *Unit 4 Review* folder if you prefer. If you are going to use the image of the kayaks, you will need to decrease the size using Photoshop to fit in the window, as a designer would have to do. You will also create a separating color bar between the two images that will display the address and phone number of the business in white text. When adding text in the color bar, you can insert a circle bullet as a special character between the address and phone (Figure UR4-7).

TOOLKIT TIP The images being used are low resolution for educational purposes here and may not appear clear when printed. They will, however, provide a guide as to what to expect in a layout. Normally, when sending images to the press, use a resolution of 300 dpi. Resize images ahead of time before placing them in the graphic frame window.

DESIGN TIP

Usually in most cases of traditional tri-fold brochure design, the front page is located on the rightmost side of the document.

TOOLKIT TIP If you would like to use the *KayakAD* image you created in Photoshop in Chapter 5, open the image in Photoshop, duplicate the image to make a copy, remove the sale lines, choose whether to italicize the title lines or leave in their original regular version, then resize the image to roughly 5 inches (width) by 4 inches and save the image in the Review/Images folders where your document is. It is also a good habit to flatten the completed file beforehand, although InDesign will allow layered files.

Right Side Panel

Kayak Ad image from Chapter 5

Address Line

Waves Image

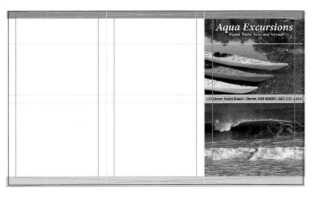

▷ FIGURE UR4-7
Completed front panel.

Next, you will create graphic frames and place the graphics in the front panel. Then you will create the color bar to put in the business info.

1. Document A-1 (Page 1) should still be selected, but if it is not, display the Pages panel and double-click Document A-1, and then scroll to the right side of the page to create the front panel. Make sure you have Page 1 selected in the Layers panel as well.

2. Using the Rectangle Frame tool, drag three graphic frames with a Stroke and Fill color of None: one from the gutter center vertical guide to the edge of the document to the 3.75 guide (providing you still have your zero point set on the margins and not at the edge of the document), a second between the 3.75 and 4.125 guides for the color bar, and a third between the 4.125 guide and the bottom margin. Elements that bleed should be extended to the .125 bleed guide outside the document's trim edges.

3. Select the top frame with the Selection tool and choose File > Place to locate the *Kayaks* file in the *Images* folder inside the *Unit 4 Review* folder. The image has been resized to about 5.5 inches wide by 4 inches. Try using your own kayak image completed from Chapter 5, removing the sale lines from the ad, and resizing it to fit in the window, extending the outer edge of the image to the bleed guide.

4. Use the Direction Selection tool to adjust the image so that the title is centered between the column margins.

5. Select the bottom frame and Place the file *Waves* in the frame, adjusting as mentioned in step 4.

6. To create a bleed for trimming, drag the frames of both images to about the one-eighth inch bleed line beyond the right document edge.

7. Select the middle frame and fill the color with Pantone DS 6-2 C.

8. Using the Type tool, drag a text frame inside the bar, choose a 12- or 14-point Myriad Pro Bold or similar font, and type with a black Fill and no Stroke, "123 Dover Pt Rd "; Leave a space after "Rd" as shown.

9. To place a bullet for the next line, select Type > Insert Special Character > Symbols > Bullet Character, and a bullet will be placed (CS2 and earlier versions use Type > Insert Special Character > Bullet Character).

10. After another space, type "Dover NH 03820 "; leave a space after the zip, and insert another bullet and another space, then type "603-555-1234"; center the text horizontally and vertically.

11. Your front panel is all set. Save the file.

CREATING THE BACK PANEL

The back panel describes the business, sometimes offers directions or relevant information, and usually provides a special promotion to attract the reader's attention. Here on the back panel, you can use the *Map* image you created in Chapter 8 in Illustrator to promote its annual lighthouse tour. You will also import a text frame into the panel using the Place command; resize it and save it in an EPS format, or use the image in the *Unit 4 Review* folder. An alternative image is also provided in the *Unit 4 Review* folder.

DESIGN TIP

The back panel of a traditional tri-fold brochure describes the business, sometimes offers directions or relevant information, and usually provides a special promotion to attract the reader's attention.

TOOLKIT TIP When you are unsure of what kind of word processor your client is using, save the text documents as plain documents using either a TXT or RTF extension, which can be opened universally by any word processing application on any computer system (although most people are using Microsoft Word).

TOOLKIT TIP To use the Map image you completed in Illustrator (Chapter 8), resize the image to about 3.5 inches wide by 3 inches proportionally, holding down the Shift key. Save it as an EPS file if you are going to use this image for placement into the InDesign document, or you can leave it in its native AI extension. Commercial printers usually accept native files.

▷ FIGURE UR4-8

Completing the back panel using the map illustration.

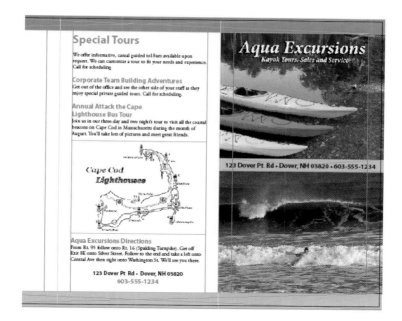

Back Panel   Front Panel

First you will place the map graphic, then place two text documents for the back panel, leaving a top and bottom inset space of .125 inches. You will then format the headings. Click OK if a font warning appears when you place the text Files (Figure UR4-8).

1. Using the Rectangle Frame tool, drag a graphic frame between the 3.25- and the 6- inch horizontal guides and the column margins in the center column; an alternative method would be to click and drag a frame that extends to the guides while placing the image.

2. Select File > Place and import either the map illustration you created in Chapter 8 (see Toolkit Tip) or the alternative *Map* file in the *Unit 4 Review > Images* folder.

3. Use the Direct Selection tool to center the map in the frame and make slight adjustments to the graphic frame if needed.

4. To import text above the graphic, drag a text frame with the Type tool and select File > Place. Locate the *Special* file in the *Text* folder within the *Unit 4 Review* folder and import the text into the frame. Use the Space After function icon in the Control Panel to create some breathing room between the heading *Special Tours* and the text.

5. Select Object >Text Frame Options and set the Bottom and Top inset spacing to .125 (1/8) inchs with the right and left at 0. Set the Vertical Justification to Top and select OK.

6. To create a vertical rule between the Special Tours panel and the Tour FAQs panel you will create next, select the Line tool with a Pantone DS 284-2 C green color Stroke of 2 points. Using the Shift key, drag along the vertical guide in the center of the gutter at the 4.3 inch mark from the upper green color until it touches the gold color bar.

7. Drag a text frame using the Type tool from the 6-inch horizontal guide to the bottom margin.

8. Select File > Place, locate the *Directions* file in the *Text* folder, and import it into the frame. Repeat the inset spacing settings in step 6 for consistency. If you get the overset symbol don't worry, we'll format the text next.

9. Format the text for both frames to 12-point Adobe Garamond Pro Regular or choose alternative fonts, like Times New Roman or Georgia. Keep the same font throughout for body text.

10. To format the heading *Special Tours*, select the line of text with the Type tool; change the font to 20- or 24-Point Myriad Pro Bold, or try Charcoal, Arial Rounded MT Bold, or Minion Pro Bold as alternatives, with the green Pantone DS 284-2 C color as the Fill color with a Stroke of None.

11. Create two lines of text from the one-line heading from the *Annual Attack the Cape Lighthouse Bus Tour* subheading, between the words "Cape" and "Lighthouse."

12. To format the subheadings (*Annual Attack...*, *Corporate Team...*, and *Directions*), highlight each subheading with the Type tool and change the size to 14-point with the same font, style, and color you used in the "Special Tours" heading, using the Eyedropper tool for an accurate match. Select and format the phone number as well to make it stand out.

13. Horizontally center the address above the phone number, and apply 12-point Myriad Pro Bold with black color.

14. Select Type > Insert Special Character > Symbols > Bullet character to insert a bullet between the spacing from the street address and town.

15. Adjust the frames if needed, then drag off some of the guides with the Selection tool. Save the file when done.

DESIGN TIP

The left side panel of the outside page of a traditional tri-fold brochure, known at times as the special info panel, is used to help answer questions, and as its name implies, provides most relevant information to encourage a viewer to want to look at the rest of the brochure.

CREATING THE SPECIAL INFO PANEL

This panel is important in that it is the inner folder panel that the reader will observe on the right side when opening up the brochure. This panel is located on the left side of the document page. This is a good place to have special information that may answer some potential questions that a reader might have and encourage them to read further. This panel also serves as a point of reference for acquiring needed information. In this brochure it provides answers to most frequently asked questions, or what is known as an *FAQ sheet.* It also provides information about choosing a boat, and it informs the reader what supplies the store carries. This is also known as a *soft sell panel,* because it is presented as a resource for the customer and does not attempt to jump out and convince the reader to buy merchandise (Figure UR4-9).

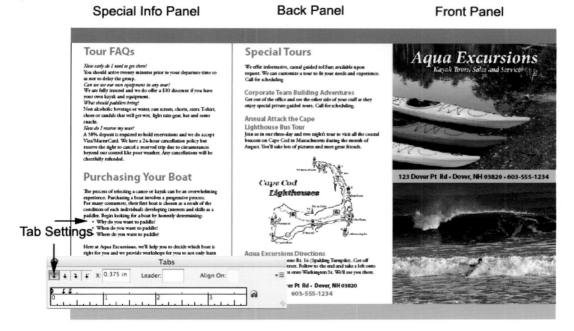

▷ FIGURE UR4-9

Completed page 1 InDesign document with front, back, and special information panels.

Here you will import the FAQ panel and perform a little tabbing and formatting.

1. Using the Type tool, drag a text frame inside the entire first panel column.

2. Select File > Place and locate the *FAQs* document importing it into the panel. If a font warning appears, click OK.

3. Use the same body text font and size as used in the back panel. In our example we used 11-point Adobe Garamond Pro.

DESIGN TIP

Remember: the more you have set up the text info ahead of time, the less time you need for adjustments when placing text in the InDesign document.

4. Format the headlines "Tour FAQs" and "Purchasing Your First Boat" lines using the same font and formatting as you used for the "Special Tours" headline for consistency.

5. Under the "Tour FAQs" headline, highlight each question and apply an italic style using the same font you chose to make the questions stand out.

6. To create a special character bullet for the why, when, and where questions about paddling, under the "Purchasing Your Boat" headline, click before the first word, "Why," and then select Type > Insert Special Character > Symbols > Bullet Character. Repeat for the other two lines.

7. To create a tab for the bullet and a tab for the starting word, select the three lines, then select Type > Tabs to bring up the Tabs panel. Click on the Left Align arrow first, and set the type in the white box above the rules using a .25 inch tab that you type in the X-coordinate box. Press Return/ Enter after entering the amount.

8. Click on the .375 measurement on the white box above the ruler display, or type it in again in the X-coordinate box. Make sure the Leader box contains no periods or characters.

9. For each line, click in front of the bullet and tab for the first measurement, then click in front of the "W" and tab for the second measurement. Repeat for all three lines; you can also create a left indent under the first line to achieve this.

10. In the paragraph underneath, apply a bold style to the business name, Aqua Excursions.

11. Adjust and edit any frames and text lines as needed to make everything fit within the panel. Save the file when completed. You now have page 1 completed.

CREATING CHARACTER AND PARAGRAPH STYLES

Here is where you have the opportunity to create styles from what you have made in the first page to apply in the next page to increase your production flow. You can apply character styles to selected lines of text or individual characters, while creating a paragraph style that may include character styles if desired; this allows you to tag each paragraph to automatically apply the formatting. You can also create a style based on the tabs you set in the last exercise. Remember, character styles are subordinate styles used within paragraph styles. The easiest way to set formatting is to simply highlight what is already formatted and name it as a style. To apply any style, just highlight the text you want to format and click on the style in the or Paragraph Style panel to apply the formatting. That's it!

▷   FIGURE UR4-10

Completed character styles and paragraph styles to use in brochure.

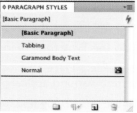

In this exercise, you will highlight the formatting you already created for headlines, subheads, italicized questions, and bold style for the business name to create individual character styles for future editing. You will then create a paragraph style for tabs and for the body text.

1. Highlight the "Special Tours" headline.

2. To display the Character Styles panel, select Type > Character Styles.

3. From the Character Styles panel, open the panel menu, select New Character Style, or click the New Character Style icon in the lower right side of the panel.

4. In the Basic Character Formats tab, you will notice that all the attributes of the highlighted headline are already displayed, and the color of the formatted style is in the Character Color tab. Name the style *Headline*, then exit out of the Character Styles panel.

5. Highlight the "Corporate Team Building" subheadline and repeat the same procedure above for character styles, naming it *Subhead.* Create a character style for the list of questions naming it *Questions,* and then create a character style highlighting the bold style applied to the Aqua Excursions business name, naming it *Business.* You are all set to apply these styles, or any additional styles you may wish to create and try out, to any selected text lines or characters. Highlight the copy first, then apply the style you want.

6. To display the Paragraph Styles panel, select Type > Paragraph Styles.

7. To create a new paragraph style on the formatting of existing text, highlight the first few lines of any sample paragraph in the body text that contains the font and size you plan to use.

8. Choose New Paragraph Style from the Paragraph Styles panel menu or click the New Paragraph Style icon in the lower right corner of the panel. Select the Basic Character Formats tab, then for the Style Name, type "Garamond Body Text," or whatever font you have chosen to use, for your new style. Make sure the font information is displayed or type it in. In the General tab, choose Based On: No Paragraph Style. Then select OK. Your paragraph style will display in the Paragraph Styles panel.

9. Optional: If you wish to use indents, in the Indents and Spacing tab, make sure the First Line Indent is set for .25-inch spacing. Leave all other default settings and select OK.

10. To create a paragraph style based on the tabs you created for the bulleted questions, highlight the three questions you created tabs for under the "Purchasing Your Boat" headline. Choose New Paragraph Style from the Paragraph Styles panel menu, select the Tabs section, then for the Style Name, type "Tabs." Select OK to place the style in your Paragraph Style panel. (Note: This is an exercise to get you comfortable playing with styles. If you wanted to keep the tabbed section as part of the main paragraph style, you could also have highlighted more of the copy before making the style).

11. Save the file. Your styles are ready to be applied in the next document page (Figure UR4-10).

DESIGNING THE INSIDE PAGE FOR INTRODUCTION AND TOUR INFO

Turning to the inside page document A-2 (page 2) is like opening a book to start reading the chapters. The reader wants to know what the brochure is about and what benefits he or she might find, so the content here is designed to encourage the reader to check out the business. The first panel on the left side is the introduction or welcome page that identifies the business with specific pertinent information. The following panels describe services and products being offered. In designing this inside portion, you will place the graphics then import the text. Using the character and paragraph styles you created in the last exercise, you can apply simple formatting to text lines and paragraphs to provide consistency throughout the brochure.

PLACING THE GRAPHIC IMAGES

Placing graphic images first helps to set up the text content that describes what the graphics are about. Again, both text and graphics need to complement one another. Using a touch of yellow color for the yellow kayak in the introduction panel is a great attention getter. Red is also used sparingly but grabs the viewer's attention. The bottom image spans across two columns, because the information is similar in both columns. It promotes a sense of continuity for the information being presented. You will note that these images are low resolution for our purposes here; for a job going to the press, you would need images at 300 dpi resolution, but these images will provide what you need for graphic layout and placement. A vertical rule will also be created to separate the introduction section and the section promoting the various tours.

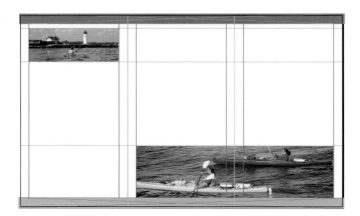

Now you will drag guidelines and place the graphics for the inside of this page.

1. Go to document A-2 (page 2) in the Pages panel, and double-click to make the second page active. Select *Page 2* in the Layers panel.

2. Make sure the zero point is dragged to start where the upper left margins intersect, then drag vertical guides to the 4.3- and 8.95-inch marks to mark center lines for the gutters.

DESIGN TIP

The inside area of a tri-fold brochure gives the reader additional information as to what the business is all about.

DESIGN TIP

Placing the graphics so they face into the document helps to focus the viewer's attention on the content at hand. Notice how the touring kayakers image will face the first "Welcome" introduction panel (Figure UR4-11).

▷ FIGURE UR4-11

Placement of graphics in page 2 (inside panels).

3. For guidelines for placement of the graphics, drag horizontal guides to the .25, 1.75, and 5.5-inch marks.

4. In the left panel (introduction panel) using the Rectangle Frame tool, drag between the column guides and the .25- and 1.75-inch guides. Use a Stroke and Fill of None.

5. Select File > Place and import the *Light* file into the Frame. Use the Position or Direct Selection tool to adjust the size and position of the image so that the lighthouse and the kayaker fit in the frame window.

6. To place an image across two columns, drag a graphic frame using the Rectangle Frame tool between the second and third columns and between the 5.5-inch horizontal guide and the bottom margin.

7. Select File > Place and locate the *Touring* image. Import the image into the frame and adjust to display the two kayakers.

8. To create a vertical rule to separate between what will be the Welcome panel and the Tour Package panels, select the Line tool with Pantone DS 284-2 C green color Stroke of 2 points. Using the Shift key, drag along the vertical guide in the center of the gutter at the 4.3 inch mark from the upper color bar until it touches the gold color bar.

9. Save the file.

COMPLETING THE WELCOME PANEL

The introduction or welcome panel identifies and summarizes the business, and in this case, it supplies brief information regarding offering lessons and rentals. With the graphics in place, it is time to bring in the text. You can also apply formatting using the character and paragraph styles you created earlier, once the text is set up. You will apply styles to the subheads and pricing and create an initial drop cap (Figure UR4-12).

▷ FIGURE UR4-12

Completed introduction panel with applied formatting.

TOOLKIT TIP When designing brochures, be careful not to give too much information: the purpose is for the customer or client to contact the business. Be also wary of providing too many prices, especially if they are prone to frequent or seasonal changes.

You will place text and format character and paragraph styles, and you will create an initial drop cap.

1. With document A-2 or page 2 active, scroll to the left panel as displayed. This will be the welcome or introduction panel.

2. With the zero point at the intersection of the two upper margins, drag horizontal guidelines to the 2-inch and 2.75-inch margins to create a separate text frame for the main headline.

3. Using the Type tool, drag a text frame between the column guides and the 2-inch and 2.75-inch guides.

4. Type in "Welcome to"; then press the Return/Enter key to create another line, and type "Aqua Excursions."

5. To apply the character style *Headline,* select Type > Character Styles to display the Character Styles panel. Highlight the two lines, and click on the *Headline* style. The color and formatting will be applied.

6. Select Object > Text Frame Options and make sure Vertical Justification is set to Align Top with no inset spacing needed. Click OK.

7. For the body text, drag a text frame with the Rectangle Frame tool from the 2.75-guide to the bottom margin. Select the Type tool and click in the frame.

8. Select File > Place and locate the *Welcome* file. When the text displays in the frame, remove the title line "Welcome to Aqua Excursions," and delete the space until the first line is at the top of the frame. Click OK if the font warning appears.

9. Select Object > Text Frame Options and make sure Vertical Justification is set to Align Top with Top and Bottom Inset Spacing at .125 inches. Right and left need no inset spacing. Click OK.

10. Highlight the text and apply the body style text of the font you are using in the Paragraph Styles panel. Adjust until the overset symbol is gone. We used Adobe Garamond Pro in an 11-point size.

11. To create an initial drop cap, set your cursor in the first line of the paragraph, and specify a drop cap using the Paragraph Formatting button in the Control panel; create a two-line drop cap with a bold style and the gold Pantone DS 6-2 C color.

12. Highlight the subheads "Lessons" and "Rentals," and apply the *Subheadline* character style.

13. Highlight the two rental pricing lines near the bottom, and select the *Tabs* Paragraph style. Click in the front of both lines, and press the tab key once to indent each line according to the style. Increase the size of each line to 12 points to make them stand out slightly.

14. Make any adjustments as needed, and save the file. The welcome panel is complete.

COMPLETING THE TOUR PACKAGES PANELS

The two inner panels are used to encourage the reader to check out special services and products, so they may call to get more information. Here is where you let the reader see what the business is mostly about. With the graphic displayed across the last two columns, you can create a major headline that also carries across both columns to tie the services in (Figure UR4-13).

▷ FIGURE UR4-13

Completed tour services panels.

Here you will create a headline across columns, then import and format the text.

1. For the main headline, drag a horizontal guideline to the .375-inch mark with the zero point marked at the intersecting margins.

2. Using the Type tool, drag a text frame from the .125 guide used for the image under the green color bar margin to the .375 mark across the second and third columns.

3. Type "A tour package for every taste…," (to create a true ellipse, which are three evenly spaced dots, select the Option/ALT key and then press the semi-colon key) then apply Headline formatting with the Character Style panel (Type > Character Styles) as a starting point. Increase the size of the font to 24 points or so and use a Bold Italic style font.

DESIGN TIP

The two other inner panels of a tri-fold brochure, located in the center and on the right side, are used to encourage the reader to check out special services and products, so they may call to get more information.

4. Select Object > Text Frame Options, and make sure Vertical Justification is set to Align Top with no inset spacing needed.

5. For the text about wildlife tours, drag a text frame using the rectangle frame tool from the .375 mark to the bottom of the margin in the second column.

6. Select the Type tool and click in the frame, then select File > Place and locate the *Wildlife* file. Apply the body text formatting style in the Paragraph Styles panel. Click OK if the font warning appears.

7. Repeat the same process as in step 5 in the third column, and locate the *Ocean* file to place.

8. For the "Guided Wildlife" and "Ocean" headlines, apply the *Headline* style; use the Space After command in the Command menu panel to provide spacing after each line. Press Enter after each line.

9. Apply the *Subheadline* style to all the tour titles.

10. Select Object > Text Frame Options, and make sure Vertical Justification is set to Align Top with top inset spacing of .125 if needed.

11. Adjust the graphic of the kayakers to avoid too much empty white space.

12. To view your work free of guides and frames, select View > Grids & Guides > Hide Guides, and select View > Hide Frame Edges.

13. Look in your Layers panel, and see when you lock some of the frames or graphics that they cannot be edited until you unlock them. You can also right-click on the sub layers of your text frames or graphics to quickly select them. Very helpful when controlling your editing.

14. Check your links in the Links panel to make sure your graphics show current locations. You can also click on the link graphic, then select the Edit original button at the bottom of the Links panel to open the graphic in the default image editing program you have on your computer. Go ahead and play.

15. Save the file as a document and additionally as a template for future use in your Unit 4 review folder (Figure UR4-14).

TOOLKIT TIP If a body copy style is selected in the character mode of the control panel when copy is placed, that copy will be assigned a character style, and the paragraph style will not override it unless the user does it manually. It is important that the word "None" is in the Character Style field of the control panel when placing text.

TOOLKIT TIP If you would prefer not to have a white background, try using the *Parchment* image file you used in the coupon ad in *Chapter 11,* and send the file behind the graphics and the text. Feel free to experiment.

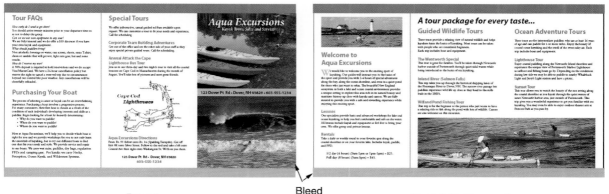

Page 1   Bleed   Page 2 (inside page)

▷ FIGURE UR4-14

Completed brochure pages for tri-fold format.

Need additional fun computer graphics tutorials and info, and an additional look at the projects you'll be creating in this book? Check out my Artist's Digital Toolkit website at: **http://www.digitoolkit.com**

READY FOR PRESS

In the final exercise here, you will again prepare the documents for press. Take note that the images used in this exercise are low resolution (75 to 100 dpi) for our educational purposes here; you would need 300 dpi for use on a commercial press. When getting ready for press, always check for spelling errors, then perform Preflight, print soft proofs for visual reference, and then Package all files. Your final proof will then be exactly what needs to be sent to the printer.

1. Save the file as an InDesign document (INDD) and as an InDesign Template (INDT) to use as a guide for future documents.

2. To prepare your material for the printer as described in *Chapter 11*, select Edit > Spelling > Check Spelling to make sure spelling is correct.

3. Use the Links panel and the Preflight panel to check to make sure graphics are still linked, correct fonts are displayed, and images are set to CMYK colors for press.

4. Choose File > Print and use all printer's marks, creating proofs of the two pages.

5. To package for press, select File > Package and create a folder within the *Unit 4 Review* folder, or click "New Folder" and let InDesign create a separate folder located in a portable place that you specify to transport the files; name the new folder *InDesign Review*.

6. To create a PDF final soft proof for press, choose File > Export and keep most defaults with Press quality; place the PDF in your *InDesign Review* folder.

7. Congratulations, you have created a tri-fold brochure. Time to get outdoors!

Tour FAQs

How early do I need to get there?
You should arrive twenty minutes prior to your departure time so as not to delay the group.

Can we use our own equipments in any tour?
We are fully insured and we do offer a $10 discount if you have your own kayak and equipment.

What should paddlers bring?
Non alcoholic beverage or water, sun screen, shorts, extra T-shirt, shoes or sandals that will get wet, light rain gear, hat and some snacks.

How do I reserve my tour?
A 50% deposit is required to hold reservations and we do accept Visa/MasterCard. We have a 24-hour cancellation policy but reserve the right to cancel a reserved trip due to circumstances beyond our control like poor weather. Any cancellations will be cheerfully refunded.

Purchasing Your Boat

The process of selecting a canoe or kayak can be an overwhelming experience. Purchasing a boat involves a progressive process. For many consumers, their first boat is chosen as a result of the condition of each individual's developing interests and skills as a paddler. Begin looking for a boat by honestly determining:

- Why do you want to paddle?
- When do you want to paddle?
- Where do you want to paddle?

Here at **Aqua Excursions**, we'll help you to decide which boat is right for you and we provide workshops for you to not only learn the essentials of kayaking, but to try out different boats to find one that fits your needs and style. We provide service and repair to our boats. We carry wet suits, paddles, dry bags, regulation PFDs and camping gear. For kayaks we carry Necky, Perception, Ocean Kayak, and Wilderness Systems.

Special Tours

We offer informative, casual guided to18urs available upon request. We can customize a tour to fit your needs and experience. Call for scheduling

Corporate Team Building Adventures

Get out of the office and see the other side of your staff as they enjoy special private guided tours. Call for scheduling.

Annual Attack the Cape Lighthouse Bus Tour

Join us in our three-day and two night's tour to visit all the coastal beacons on Cape Cod in Massachusetts during the month of August. You'll take lots of pictures and meet great friends.

Aqua Excursions Directions

From Rt. 95 follow onto Rt. 16 (Spalding Turnpike). Get off Exit 8E onto Silver Street. Follow to the end and take a left onto Central Ave then right onto Washington St. We'll see you there.

123 Dover Pt Rd • Dover, NH 03820
603-555-1234

Aqua Excursions
Kayak Tours, Sales and Service

123 Dover Pt Rd • Dover, NH 03820 • 603-555-1234

Welcome to Aqua Excursions

We would like to welcome you to the exciting sport of kayaking. Our guides will instruct you in the basics of the sport and provide you with 2-4 hours of special adventures along the bay, along the ocean shoreline, and even in a quiet pond for those who just want to relax. The beautiful New England ecosystem in both a lake and ocean coastal environment provides a unique setting to explore this area rich in its natural beauty and maritime history up close with kayaks and canoes. We are fully insured to provide you with a safe and rewarding experience while enjoying this exciting sport.

Lessons

Our specialists provide basic and advanced workshops for lake and ocean kayaking to help you feel comfortable and safe on the water. All lessons include kayak and equipment or feel free to bring your own. We offer group and private lessons.

Rentals

Take a daily or weekly rental to your favorite spot along the coastal shoreline or on your favorite lake. Includes kayak, paddle, and PFD.

1/2 day (4 hours) (9am-1pm or 1pm-5pm) = $25.
Full day (8 hours) (9am-5pm) = $45.

A tour package for every taste...

Guided Wildlife Tours

These tours provide a relaxing view of natural wildlife and helps kayakers learn the basics of kayaking. Most tours can be taken with people who are considered beginners. Each trip includes boat and equipment.

The Wentworth Special

This tour is great for families. You'll be taken through Newcastle harbor outside of Portsmouth through quiet tidal waters while being introduced to the basics of sea kayaking.

Inland River (Salmon Falls)

This trip takes you up through the historical shipping lanes of the Piscataqua River to Dover, NH. The narrow river passage lets paddlers experience wild life up close as they head to the mills built in the 1800's.

Willand Pond Fishing Tour

This trip is for the beginner or the person who just wants to have a relaxing ride or fish along the pond with lots of wildlife. Canoes are also welcome on this excursion.

Ocean Adventure Tours

These tours are for intermediate paddlers who are at least 16 years of age and can paddle for 6 or more miles. Enjoy the beauty of coastal ocean kayaking and the smell of the sweet salty air. Each trip includes boat and equipment.

Lighthouse Tour

Enjoy coastal paddling along the Newcastle Island shoreline and experience the unique view of Portsmouth Harbor Lighthouse as sailboat and fishing boats go by. Depending on the conditions during low tide we may be able to paddle to nearby Whaleback Light and Jerry's Light station and have a picnic.

Sunset Tour

This tour allows you to watch the beauty of the sun setting along the coastal shoreline as you kayak through the quiet waters of inner Newcastle harbor area, just outside of Portsmouth. This trip gives you a wonderful experience to get you familiar with sea kayaking. You may even be able to enjoy outdoor theater arts at Prescott Park as you pass by.

UNIT REVIEW IV
Creating a tri-fold brochure using InDesign

▷   FIGURE UR4-15

Completed Projects and Tutorials

CHAPTER 1: WELCOME TO THE LAND OF OS

▷ FIGURE A-1

Macintosh OS X Leopard Desktop

Windows 7 Desktop

CHAPTER 1
Learning to navigate around usng Macintosh OS X and Windows 7 operating systems, while having some desktop fun.

▷ FIGURE A-2

Mac OS X Quick Look

Mac OS X Preview

Slide Show Tab Link

Windows Media Player

Windows 7 Pictures Library Toolbar

Windows 7 Media Center

Windows 7 Photo Viewer

CHAPTER 1 ADVANCED
Applications included in
Mac OS X and Windows 7
used in creating electronic
slide shows.

▷ FIGURE A-3

CHAPTER 1 EXTRA
Creating musc playlists in libraries to burn music CDs using iTunes (top)
and Windows Media Player (bottom)

CHAPTER 2: DESIGNING FOR THE CLIENT

▷ FIGURE A-4

CHAPTER 2
Excerpts: Design Elements and Principles, Design Process, Typography, Imagery, and Color.
Chapter project involves using design components to lay out contrary color images to match
descriptions to be used in a color (or black-and-white) spread.

Design Elements:
Line, Shape, Value, Texture, Contrast, Depth Perception,
Perspective, Motion, Color, and Format

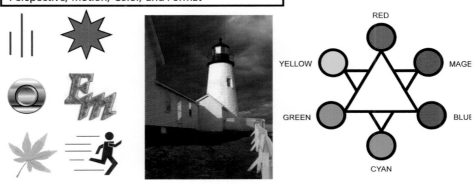

Design Principles:
Balance, Space, Emphasis, Rythym, and Unity

Color and Typography

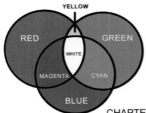

Book Antiqua (serif type)
Arial **Bold** (sans-serif type**)**
Papyrus (decorative type)
Brush Script Italic (script type)
vfbts((symbol type)

CHAPTER 2 ADVANCED: Identify Design Elements and Principles in Various Ads
CHAPTER 2 EXTRA: Internet Resources

CHAPTER 3: ADJUSTING IMAGES IN PHOTOSHOP

▷ FIGURE A-5

Originals

Convertng colors for accuate
black and white tones

Adjust contrast,
shadow, and highlights

Auto Color Adjustment

CHAPTER 3
Corrected images using special commands
in Photoshop's Image menu.

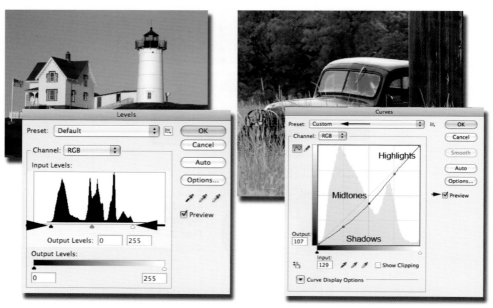

CHAPTER 3 ADVANCED
Using Histograms, Levels, and Curves adjustments in Photoshop to adjust
shadows, midtones, and highlights for quality images.

Adobe Bridge interface to retrieve, observe, and manage all types of graphic files.

Using Adobe Bridge to create an instant slideshow of your photos or artwork.

Path Bar

Search

Mini Bridge, in CS5, provides the power of the parent Adobe Bridge locally within the Photoshop application for searching, filtering, and displaying files.

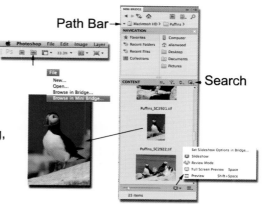

CHAPTER 3 EXTRA

Adobe Bridge, and the new Mini Bridge, which is inside each Adobe application like Photoshop, allows you to import, retrieve, observe, manage, and edit files, and they can play slide shows.

▷ FIGURE A-6

CHAPTER 4: WORKING WITH SELECTIONS AND CHANNELS

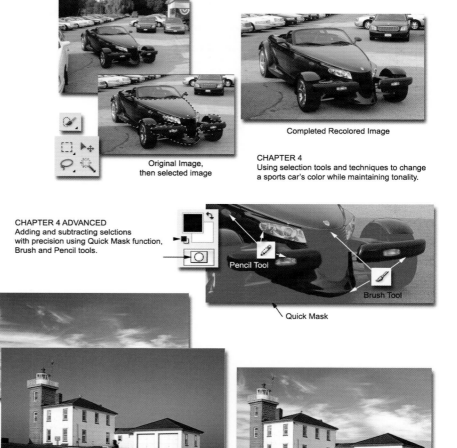

Completed Recolored Image

Original Image,
then selected image

CHAPTER 4
Using selection tools and techniques to change
a sports car's color while maintaining tonality.

CHAPTER 4 ADVANCED
Adding and subtracting selctions
with precision using Quick Mask function,
Brush and Pencil tools.

Pencil Tool

Brush Tool

Quick Mask

CHAPTER 4 EXTRA Combining images for dramatic effects, using either the Paste Into Command, or selecting
by Color Range and using the Masks panel for more detail work.

▷   FIGURE A-7

CHAPTER 5: USING LAYERS

◁ FIGURE A-8

CHAPTER 5
Multicolor product advertisement created
using selections developed for kayak
color change and for the entire kayak,
with use of various types of layers.

CHAPTER 5 ADVANCED
Taking a flat raw file captured in a digital
camera and making precise adjustments
using the Camera RAW function in
Photoshop. The new digital darkroom.

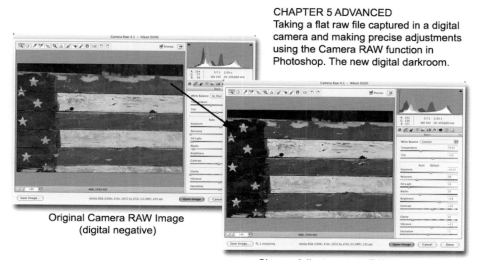

Original Camera RAW Image
(digital negative)

Chosen Adjustments to RAW Image

▷ FIGURE A-9

CHAPTER 5 EXTRA
Using the Content-Aware Fill and Spot Healing Brush to remove unwanted distractions in an image (top).

Using Content-Aware Scale to resize unimportant image elements with accuracy.

Creating Photo Business cards using Photoshop's Picture Package plug-in (bottom).

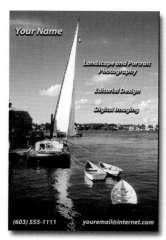

Completed Photo Business Card

Completed Sheet of Business Cards

CHAPTER 6: RESTORING AND COLORING A BLACK AND WHITE PHOTOGRAPH

▷ FIGURE A-10

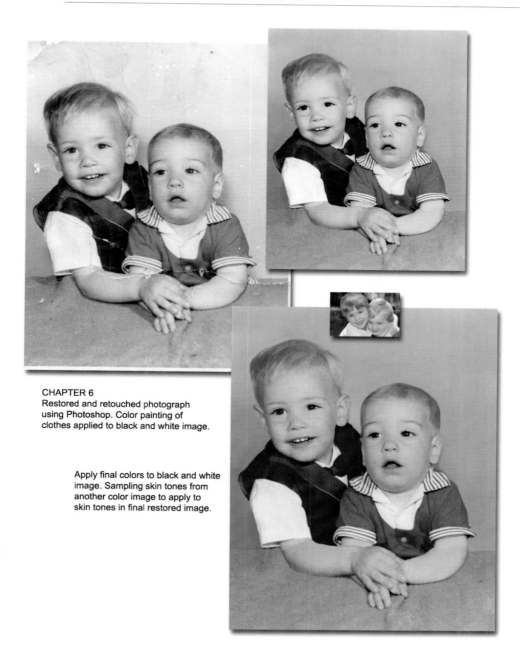

CHAPTER 6
Restored and retouched photograph using Photoshop. Color painting of clothes applied to black and white image.

Apply final colors to black and white image. Sampling skin tones from another color image to apply to skin tones in final restored image.

Original Color Cast Image

Corrected Image

Before

After

CHAPTER 6 ADVANCED
Neutralizing shadow and highlights to correct color cast images.
Neutralizing digital white balance color casts.

CHAPTER 6 EXTRA
Using adjustment layers and masks
to create special compositions.

UNIT REVIEW 2: DIGITAL IMAGE EDITING: ADOBE PHOTOSHOP CS5

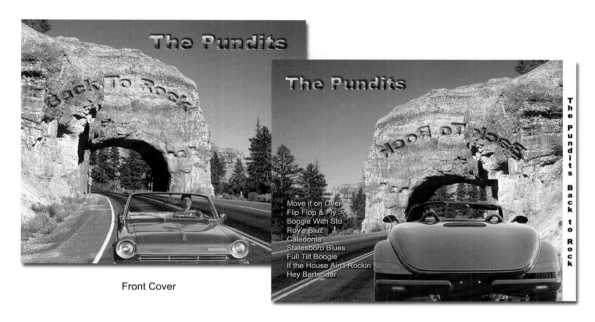

Front Cover

Back Cover

Images used for CD covers

UNIT II REVIEW
Creating the CD covers (front and back)
from multiple images using Photoshop.

▷ FIGURE A-12

CHAPTER 7: CREATING SHAPES WITH ILLUSTRATOR

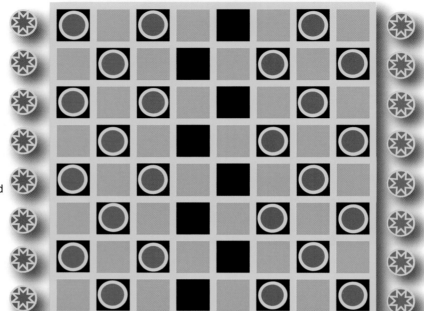

CHAPTER 7
Electronic checkerboard
created in Illustrator
using shapes.

CHAPTER 7 ADVANCED
Building a lighthouse
by creating and combining
complex shapes in Illustrator.

CHAPTER 7 EXTRA
Creating playing cards using custom shapes,
Shape Builder tool, and Object menu.

▷ FIGURE A-13

CHAPTER 8: WORKING WITH BRUSHES, SYMBOLS, AND LAYERS

▷ FIGURE A-14

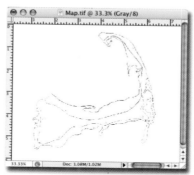

Sketch of Map
of Cape Cod, Massachusettes

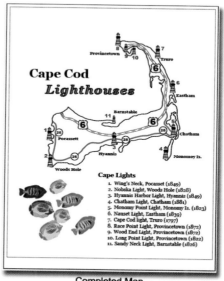

Completed Map

CHAPTER 8
Creating a scaleable tourist map from a drawing sketch in Illustrator. Using symbols for visual enhancement.

CHAPTER 8 ADVANCED
Freestyle shapes with the Blob Brush.
Placing logo on multiple artboards.

CHAPTER 8 EXTRA
3-D bottle shape with label created and mapped onto bottle.

CHAPTER 9: PRECISION WITH THE PEN TOOL

CHAPTER 9
Logo created using the Pen
tool and type paths in Illustrator.

Original logo as business card

Alternative option

CHAPTER 9 ADVANCED
Laying out business cards with graphic logo
and type. Creating alternative options.

Alternative option used
for sheet of cards

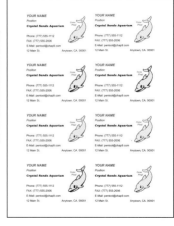

CHAPTER 9 EXTRA
Clock face created in Illustrator
using guideleines and the
Gradient tool.

▷   FIGURE A-15

CHAPTER 10: INTEGRATING PHOTOSHOP AND ILLUSTRATOR FILES FOR WEB USE

CHAPTER 10
Web banners created by integrating
elements from Photoshop and Illustrator.

CHAPTER 10 ADVANCED
Understanding PDF and EPS files

Original scanned image

Live Trace to create paths

Live Paint Bucket to apply new colors

CHAPTER 10 EXTRA
Using Live Trace and Live Paint in Illustrator
to generate editable paths from various types
of images and apply color.

▷ FIGURE A-16

UNIT REVIEW 3: DIGITAL ILLUSTRATION: ADOBE ILLUSTRATOR CS5

UNIT 3 REVIEW
Create guitar graphic from sketch.
Set up logo for mug.
Create 3-D version of promotional mug with shading and lighting applied.
Edit artowrk on multiple artboards for various uses.

▷   FIGURE A-17

CHAPTER 11: INDESIGN FUNDAMENTALS

▷ FIGURE A-18

CHAPTER 11
Creating a direct
mail coupon ad
using InDesign.

CHAPTER 11 ADVANCED
Preflighting, packaging,
and preparing for press.

CHAPTER 11 EXTRA
Creating a desktop calendar
using tables in InDesign.

CHAPTER 12: WORKING WITH MULTIPAGE DOCUMENTS

▷ FIGURE A-19

CHAPTER 12
Creating a 4-page Newsletter using InDesign.

CHAPTER 12 ADVANCED
Baseline Alignment, Automation with Styles, and Object Libraries.

Object Libraries

CHAPTER 12 EXTRA
Creating an interactive PDF document.

UNIT REVIEW 4: DIGITAL PUBLISHING: INDESIGN CS5

UNIT REVIEW IV
Creating a tri-fold brochure using InDesgn.

Tour FAQs

How early do I need to get there?
You should arrive twenty minutes prior to your departure time so as not to delay the group.

Can we use our own equipment in any tour?
We are fully insured and we do offer a $10 discount if you have your own kayak and equipment.

What should paddlers bring?
Non alcoholic beverage or water, sun screen, shorts, extra T-shirt, shoes or sandals that will get wet, light rain gear, hat and some snacks.

How do I reserve my tour?
A 50% deposit is required to hold reservations and we do accept Visa/MasterCard. We have a 24-hour cancellation policy but reserve the right to cancel a reserved trip due to circumstances beyond our control like poor weather. Any cancellations will be cheerfully refunded.

Purchasing Your Boat

The process of selecting a canoe or kayak can be an overwhelming experience. Purchasing a boat involves a progressive process. For many consumers, their first boat is chosen as a result of the condition of each individual's developing interests and skills as a paddler. Begin looking for a boat by honestly determining:

- Why do you want to paddle?
- When do you want to paddle?
- Where do you want to paddle?

Here at **Aqua Excursions**, we'll help you to decide which boat is right for you and we provide workshops for you to not only learn the essentials of kayaking, but to try out different boats to find one that fits your needs and style. We provide service and repair to our boats. We carry wet suits, paddles, dry bags, regulation PFDs and camping gear. For kayaks we carry Necky, Perception, Ocean Kayak, and Wilderness Systems.

Special Tours

We offer informative, casual guided to18urs available upon request. We can customize a tour to fit your needs and experience. Call for scheduling.

Corporate Team Building Adventures
Get out of the office and see the other side of your staff as they enjoy special private guided tours. Call for scheduling.

Annual Attack the Cape
Lighthouse Bus Tour
Join us in our three-day and two night's tour to visit all the coastal beacons on Cape Cod in Massachusetts during the month of August. You'll take lots of pictures and meet great friends.

Cape Cod
Lighthouses

Aqua Excursions Directions
From Rt. 95 follow onto Rt. 16 (Spalding Turnpike). Get off Exit 8E onto Silver Street. Follow to the end and take a left onto Central Ave then right onto Washington St. We'll see you there.

123 Dover Pt Rd · Dover, NH 03820
603-555-1234

Aqua Excursions
Kayak Tours, Sales and Service

123 Dover Pt Rd · Dover, NH 03820 · 603-555-1234

Welcome to
Aqua Excursions

We would like to welcome you to the exciting sport of kayaking. Our guides will instruct you in the basics of the sport and provide you with 2-4 hours of special adventures along the bay, along the ocean shoreline, and even in a quiet pond for those who just want to relax. The beautiful New England ecosystem in both a lake and ocean coastal environment provides a unique setting to explore this area rich in its natural beauty and maritime history up close with kayaks and canoes. We are fully insured to provide you with a safe and rewarding experience while enjoying this exciting sport.

Lessons
Our specialists provide basic and advanced workshops for lake and ocean kayaking to help you feel comfortable and safe on the water. All lessons include kayak and equipment or feel free to bring your own. We offer group and private lessons.

Rentals
Take a daily or weekly rental to your favorite spot along the coastal shoreline or on your favorite lake. Includes kayak, paddle, and PFD.

1/2 day (4 hours) (9am-1pm or 1pm-5pm) = $25.
Full day (8 hours) (9am-5pm) = $45.

A tour package for every taste...
Guided Wildlife Tours

These tours provide a relaxing view of natural wildlife and helps kayakers learn the basics of kayaking. Most tours can be taken with people who are considered beginners. Each trip includes boat and equipment.

The Wentworth Special
This tour is great for families. You'll be taken through Newcastle harbor outside of Portsmouth through quiet tidal waters while being introduced to the basics of sea kayaking.

Inland River (Salmon Falls)
This trip takes you up through the historical shipping lanes of the Piscataqua River to Dover, NH. The narrow river passage lets paddlers experience wild life up close as they head to the mills built in the 1800's.

Willand Pond Fishing Tour
This trip is for the beginner or the person who just wants to have a relaxing ride or fish along the pond with lots of wildlife. Canoes are also welcome on this excursion.

Ocean Adventure Tours

These tours are for intermediate paddlers who are at least 16 years of age and can paddle for 6 or more miles. Enjoy the beauty of coastal ocean kayaking and the smell of the sweet salty air. Each trip includes boat and equipment.

Lighthouse Tour
Enjoy coastal paddling along the Newcastle Island shoreline and experience the unique view of Portsmouth Harbor Lighthouse as sailboat and fishing boats go by. Depending on the conditions during low tide we may be able to paddle to nearby Whaleback Light and Jerry's Light station and have a picnic.

Sunset Tour
This tour allows you to watch the beauty of the sun setting along the coastal shoreline as you kayak through the quiet waters of inner Newcastle harbor area, just outside of Portsmouth. This trip gives you a wonderful experience to get you familiar with sea kayaking. You may even be able to enjoy outdoor theater arts at Prescott Park as you pass by.

▷ FIGURE A-20

Glossary

A

Absolute numbering involves labeling all pages with consecutive numbers, starting with the first page of the document.

Actions in InDesign (referred to as behaviors in earlier versions) are interactive macros or mini programs that identify what the button will do when it is selected with the mouse (open a document, locate a URL, play a movie, play sound, etc.).

Adjustments command in the Photoshop Image menu, allows you the flexibility to select quite a variety of color adjustments for an image.

Adjustment layers within an image allow a designer to create a series of layered effects over the original image that are non-destructable, so that the pixels in the original image are not manipulated. Each adjustment layer is on its own individual layer, and can easily be edited.

Adobe Bridge is the hub for retrieving and editing files and their information to help with file management and automation between files and those applications within the Adobe Creative Suite.

Adobe Creative Suite consists of Adobe products for all media (Photoshop, Illustrator, InDesign, Dreamweaver, Acrobat, with other special applications) and all work together in working with various types of files.

Adobe Help Center displays tasks, index help, and bookmarks of previously visited help areas. Topics can be searched by using keywords, an alphabetized index, or by selecting underlined text links. The Adobe Help Center also lets you seek help with other Adobe applications in a web-like format, and provides additional links to resources and expert product support.

Aerial perspective is used to add drama to an image by using visual perspective from higher angles than a viewer's normal eye level.

AI extension is Illustrator's native format extension.

AIT (Adobe Illustrator Template) **extension** is the extension used for Illustrator templates.

Alias is a link or shortcut for Macintosh computers to drives, most frequently used applications, files, and folders that you can create on your desktop.

Align panel in Illustrator is used to align multiple selected items along a horizontal or vertical axis and along their centers. The Align panel can also be used to evenly space the distance between multiple objects.

Alpha channels in Photoshop are channels used to save and store selections of an image area permanently so they can be used and edited in the future.

Anchor links are links within a web page.

Anchor points are nonprinting marks that define where line segments begin and end on paths or objects.

Anti-alias keeps square pixel edges from looking jagged by softening the transition between colors.

Appearance panel in Illustrator is used to edit and display properties of selected 3-D objects.

Apple menu in Macintosh OS X allows you to find information about your Mac system and files, which includes a listing of the most recently opened applications and files.

Application menu in Mac OS X contains commands for information about the application, changing settings, preferences, and quitting the application.

Application-level preferences affect work on all documents.

Applications are software programs for a particular use, such as Photoshop is an application used for digital image editing.

Applications command in the Macintosh Go menu displays all programs in the Applications folder.

Art brushes in Illustrator stretch evenly along a path and are used for various types of art strokes, like the charcoal brush.

Artboard in an Illustrator document is the area inside the document where a designer creates and modifies illustrations.

Artboard tool (Shift + O) in Illustrator controls how you move, resize, and edit artboards, with one artboard selected at a time.

Artboards panel in Illustrator allows the designer to create new artboards, reorder artboards, rearrange artboards, and create duplicate artboards.

Artwork is a term for an illustration or illustrations created in Illustrator using shapes, tools, paths, and panels.

ASCII type is an American type standard; it is not formatted and can be read universally by any application or computer.

Auto Color command in Photoshop looks for color casts in an image and adjusts any imbalanced colors for correct color.

Auto Contrast command in Photoshop works well with images that need lightening and darkening of highlights and shadows.

Auto Levels command in Photoshop adjusts the tonal balance of colors by rearranging an image's tones slightly to show detail in highlights and shadows.

Average command in the Illustrator Object menu connects path end points that need to be drawn in to make one smooth, flowing path.

B

Background layer is the initial layer of a Photoshop image that contains the original image. The Background remains locked at the bottom of the Layers panel until you double-click the "Background" text and rename it. It then behaves as a normal layer and can be moved around between other layers.

Baseline in typography is an invisible line that the type sits on.

Baseline grids align the baseline of the text from a starting point across the document for the designer to view how text aligns crosswise along columns for a consistent look.

Bézier curves are created by setting anchor points with the Pen tool and dragging the mouse to define the shape of the curve.

Bi-fold is simply a document folded once, usually with the fold on the left side, like a booklet. This is used for mailers, brochures, menus, and other informational material.

Bitmap or raster images are photographs, paintings, or complex designs that use millions of colors to record subtle gradations of tone in the image and are nonscalable.

Bleeds extend solid color boxes of graphics beyond the trim edge of a document to ensure good color coverage at the edges of printed material so no white lines are generated from the graphic edge.

Blending modes in Photoshop allow the designer to determine how pixels in one layer blend with the underlying pixels in the image. Different blending modes produce different results between layers and allow a designer to create a variety of special effects.

Blob Brush tool in Illustrator is used to paint filled shapes that you can intersect and merge with other shapes of the same color.

Blur tool used to smooth out pixels or imperfections of an image.

Bounding box in Illustrator is made when selecting objects to move or resize. It has resizing handles in its corners and can be used to reshape, copy, or rotate an object.

Bristle Brush in Illustrator allows a designer to create brush strokes with the appearance of a natural brush with bristles.

Brush libraries contain a variety of organized preset brushes, which appear in a new panel and are added by selecting the brush and dragging it to the Brushes panel.

Brush tools are used for painting on an image.

Brushes in Illustrator allow you to apply various freehand strokes of artwork in various ways to existing paths or objects. Brushes can be applied to existing selected paths or used to create a path.

Brushes panel allows you to create your own brush artwork or to use predefined brushes in four different categories: Calligraphic, Scatter, Art, and Pattern.

Burn is a term meaning to write documents, images, video, and music onto recordable CDs using a CD recorder drive.

Button tool in InDesign is used to create buttons that can be used for navigation and interactivity to saved PDF files.

C

Calligraphic brushes give the appearance of hand-drawn strokes with an angled pen tip.

Camera raw file contains unprocessed picture data from a digital camera's image sensor. It lets photographers interpret the image data rather than letting the camera make the adjustments and conversions.

Cell options command in InDesign is used to format text; rows and columns; strokes and fills, including tints and diagonal lines.

Cells are the individual "boxes" inside a table.

Channels in Photoshop are saved with the document and can be reopened and edited at any time. Channels store an image's color mode information in separate color channels, like RGB would store red, green, and blue channels.

Channels panel is used to store selections permanently and color mode information in separate channels in Photoshop.

Character styles panel in Illustrator and InDesign contains many formatting commands for setting text options and is used for applying character formatting techniques to selected characters or lines of text.

Clipboard is a temporary place in memory to store text and graphics that have been cut or copied before pasting them into another document or another location.

Clipping mask in Illustrator allows any shape, type, or path placed on top of a graphic to cut out that image below in the shape of the path above it, much like a cookie cutter.

Clone Stamp tool in Photoshop allows you to sample a group of pixels from a source area and transfer or clone those pixels to a target area. Hold down the Option/Alt key and click a clean area to sample from.

CMYK mode reflects the computer's secondary colors, which are cyan, magenta, and yellow, with "K" standing for the black used to increase contrast. Mix red and blue and you get magenta, for instance.

CMYK process colors comprise cyan, magenta, yellow, and black (CMYK). These four colors are used in four separate plates during the printing process.

Color bars on a proof sheet show accuracy of colors to be used.

Color Guide panel in Illustrator CS3 provides quick access to color groups and to colors that complement one another, so designers can experiment with colors in their artwork, and then create custom groupings of colors.

Color libraries in InDesign are an assortment of colors from various color swatch manufacturers like Pantone.

Color modes in the Illustrator Toolbox below the Fill and Stroke boxes determine how color is applied to either the fill or stroke of an object or path. They are the Color (default), Gradient, and None (red line) modes.

Color panel allows the designer to select or sample any colors to use as either background or foreground colors in Photoshop or as stroke and fill colors in Illustrator.

Color Picker is displayed when the color boxes, background, and foreground in Photoshop or the Stroke and Fill boxes (located beneath the tool buttons) in Illustrator and InDesign are double-clicked. The Color Picker lets you select an object's color by choosing from a color spectrum, defining colors numerically, or clicking a swatch.

Color Range command in Photoshop is used for selecting same areas of color and color tones.

Color Replacement tool in Photoshop replaces the color of a selected area with whatever the foreground color is.

Color Sampler tool used to sample any color in an image and provide color information.

Color stops in Photoshop's Gradient Editor are used to adjust, add, and remove gradient combinations of colors.

Color tools in Photoshop, like the Eyedropper and Color Sampler tools, are used to sample any color on any image to make a new foreground color by default and provide color information.

Complementary colors are opposite colors on the color wheel.

Composite proofs (using the same page description language) allow the designer to create a single sheet that is an exact replica of the intended output.

Comps show exactly what the final design will look like when printed.

Constrain Proportions in Photoshop allows you to increase or reduce the image size proportionately to avoid distortion.

Content Aware Fill in Photoshop has the ability to remove an image element and replace it with details that blend in closely to match the lighting, tone, and noise of the surrounding area.

Content-Aware Scale function in Photoshop allows you to resize an image without changing the important elements like people, buildings, animals, etc., by affecting pixels in areas that aren't visually important.

Content Indicator in InDesign displays a transparent "doughnut" shape to adjust graphic frames that contain content larger than the frame window. It is used with the Selection Tool to select and reposition a graphic.

Continuing banners are found in the top portion of the additional pages within a newsletter and have a continuing color scheme, text format for the title, and sometimes an identifiable company logo.

Continuous-tone images are usually photographs or paintings that have a high color bit depth (millions of colors), which display subtle gradations of shades of color, and generate large file sizes.

Control panel in Illustrator provides options and information based on selected artwork, including information regarding object dimensions and location, fill and stroke colors, opacity, and selecting the Bridge application.

Control panel in Windows allows you to make modifications within your computer, like adding hardware, adding and removing programs, updating applications, and modifying system functions and monitor display.

Convert Anchor Point tool is used to convert a smooth curve anchor point to a corner point and vice versa.

Crop marks indicate where the cutting of the paper will be when sending a document to press.

Crop tool allows you to draw rectangular selections inside the image area and crop the area outside the selection to trim the image.

Cross-platform files and applications can be read by different operating systems, like Vista and Mac OS X.

Curves adjustment which allows the designer or photographer more precision in adjusting for toning in highlights, midtones, and shadow details using a system of plotting points in those areas that need adjustments.

D

Dashboard is a feature of Mac OS X that contains small programs called **widgets** that have a wide variety of uses for everyday tasks such as checking stock prices, finding local or global weather information, and some widgets are linked with larger applications, etc.

Decorative type is used sometimes in headlines to create a specific meaning.

Desktop is the screen displayed on your computer monitor. It displays your drives, and most frequently used applications, files, and folders.

Desktop publishing programs allow designers to bring in text and graphic items or elements from other applications and assemble and lay out these items accurately inside text and picture boxes in an organized manner.

Device Central enables Photoshop users to preview how Photoshop files will look on a variety of mobile devices.

Dialog box window appears and provides more commands or functions when you select a command or function.

Digital imaging involves scanning or importing images into the computer, which converts them into digital images.

Direct Select Lasso tool in Illustrator is great for quickly making a freehand selection in a small area between end points of paths to be joined.

Direct Selection tool allows you to select and move individual anchor points or path segments. It works in conjunction with the Pen tool to adjust with precision the shape of a path the Pen tool creates by adjusting its anchor points and direction lines.

Direction lines are nonprinting lines that extend from anchor points that can be dragged to modify a curve or any path with precision. Dragging two anchor points in the same direction creates an "S" curve while dragging two anchor points in the opposite direction creates a "C" curve. Anchor points and direction lines do not print with the artwork.

Directory structure is an organized method used to save files within folders, like having file cabinets with drawers to organize them.

Dithering is a process in which colors are substituted to simulate the missing color in the web panel, which can sometimes result in a spotty looking appearance.

DOCX is the extension used to identify Microsoft Word documents.

Dock is used to display active applications, files, and folders on the Mac OS X operating system.

Document-level preferences in InDesign affect only the active document.

Dot Leaders in desktop publishing create a series of dotted periods or dots that lead the reader to info like page numbers.

Downloading files involves sending the files from the web host server to your hard drive for possible editing.

DPI (dots per inch) refers to measuring an image's resolution for print purposes.

Draw Behind mode in Illustrator allows you to draw behind all artwork on a selected layer if no artwork is selected. If an artwork is selected, the new object is drawn directly beneath the selected object.

Draw Inside mode in Illustrator allows you to draw inside the selected object. The Draw Inside mode eliminates the need for multiple steps to perform tasks such as drawing and altering stacking order or drawing, selecting, and creating a clipping mask.

Drawing Modes in Illustrator, located near the bottom of the Tools panel, provide options to draw inside and behind artwork, eliminating multiple tasks.

Draw Normal mode is the default drawing mode in Illustrator.

Drop cap is a larger letter or group of letters that extend over lines of text to start off an article.

Duplicate command in Photoshop creates an exact image copy.

Dust and Scratches filter in the Photoshop Filter menu can help to smooth out and blend in pixels and remove small dust spots.

E

Edges referred in Illustrator's Live Paint command are the stroke or outlined areas of the path.

Edit menu allows you to work with text and graphics, including selecting all components in a document. It allows you to undo actions; copy, cut, and paste items; and see what is on the Clipboard.

Editing and retouching tools in Photoshop help to improve or enhance an image. They are the Color Replacement tool, Healing and Path Brush tools, Eraser, Gradient, Paint Bucket, Blur, Smudge, Sharpen, Burn, Dodge, Sponge, Clone and Pattern Stamp tools.

Electronic Media proof is used for website designers or multimedia designers. It shows indications for pixel dimensions, software used, resolution requirements, text and image locations, and information needed for publishing for the web, along with any special requirements.

Ellipse (which means "and so on") are three evenly spaced dots, created by selecting the Option/ALT key followed by a semicolon.

Ellipse Frame tool in InDesign creates frames as containers to insert text and graphics.

Embedded files are added permanently to a file, which increases the file size, and any changes made to the image in one document will not be updated in any other documents.

Emphasis provides direction to various elements in a given design, promoting the concept that some things are more important than others.

EPS (Encapsulated PostScript) extensions are used in page layout programs for press. EPS files work quite nicely with text and graphic elements and are used predominantly in the commercial press industry, especially when vector graphics are needed to maintain sharpness and clarity.

Eraser tool in Illustrator removes anchor points and path segments. In Photoshop it removes the background color.

Expand command in Illustrator Auto Trace function is used to convert the tracing outline to a series of connected paths.

Exposé is another mini application on the Mac that helps you move or copy items between different windows in an application and from one application to another, it is used quite frequently in combination with the Spaces.

Extract command in Photoshop works with very minute details searching for edge pixels, like a person's hair against the background. The Extract command provides a nice transition when placing various images together by removing distracting backgrounds.

Extrude command in Illustrator is used to take a two-dimensional object like a circle and convert it into a 3-D object like a cylinder.

Eye icon displayed on the Photoshop Layers panel indicates that the layer is visible. You can hide or show a layer by clicking the eye icon.

Eyedropper tool in Photoshop is used to sample and place a color in the Color Picker. It can sample color from a current image or another image. From the sample you can read the color mode information in the Color panel if you need to record it.

F

Faces in Illustrator's Live Paint are the inside areas of a closed path or shape.

Fade command, in Photoshop's Edit menu, used to adjust the amount of effect being applied.

File menu allows you to create new folders, search for and get info about folders and files, duplicate items, and create links or shortcuts to files and folders.

Fill is the inside color of an object in Illustrator.

Fill box in Illustrator is used to fill color inside an object.

Filter Gallery in Photoshop's Filter menu allows the designer to preview and apply various specialized filter effects on an image.

Finder menu lets you organize how icons are displayed, much like a librarian organizes books. It can create, manage, and locate files and folders and navigate around the computer.

Flattening the image involves merging all the layers in a document into a single layer.

Focal point determines a component's size, shape, color, texture, or position in the layout as the most important feature.

Folding dummy is made to provide a visual reference for a brochure and is where you would sketch in headlines and graphic elements along with the type of fold you will use.

Font is the immediate family of characters with the same shape construction and style, such as Arial or Times New Roman.

Font size is measurement of type in points instead of inches.

Font style is applying a change to a character, such as bold, underline, or italics.

Formal balance places elements with equal distribution to convey trustworthiness and integrity, a technique financial institutions or insurance companies might use.

Frames in InDesign are boxes or containers that allow designers to bring in text and graphic objects or elements from other applications and assemble and lay out these items accurately in an organized manner.

Framing techniques are employed in which another subject surrounds the main subject for emphasis. Using tree branches in the foreground, for instance, provides emphasis to a distant subject.

Free transform tool changes the size of an object or its point of origin.

FTP (File Transfer Protocol) is the process of uploading your files to a web host server.

FXG extension format in Illustrator is useful when the need involves preserving maximum appearance and availability for accurate editing, and for animation purposes using Flash Catalyst.

G

Gadgets are mini programs in Windows which offer information at a glance and provide easy access to frequently used tools.

Gap tool in InDesign provides a quick way to adjust and resize the gap between multiple selected items that commonly align edges.

Gaussian Blur filter is used to soften a matte surface or a portrait image.

GIF extension files do not use more than 256 colors and artwork can contain no applied gradients, but it allows transparency within the artwork and creates a small file size compared to a JPEG format.

Glyph is a specific form of a character. For example, in certain fonts the capital letter A is available in several forms, such as swash and small cap.

Go menu in Mac OS X lets you view your favorite places and folders and connect to a server to share information with other computers. You can jump to any location on your computer, the Internet, or on your network.

Gradient is a transition or blend of one color into another.

Gradient Editor in Photoshop displays to select various preset gradient combinations, which can also be customized and applied by the user.

Gradient Feather tool blends one color into another.

Gradient panel in Illustrator is the control center for creating gradients. You can select colors from the Swatches or Color panels and drag these into the gradient bar to create color.

Gradient Sliders that can be adjusted to blend in special colors. You can even select a gradient color mode to work in on the Toolbox.

Gradient tool applies selected gradient colors in a linear or radial direction.

Graphic style libraries are collections of present graphic styles.

Graphic Styles panel (Window > Graphic Styles) is used to create, name, and apply effects to graphic objects or text in conjunction with the Appearance panel.

Grids comprise a network of intersecting horizontal and vertical lines that allow the designer to unify a series of designs to relate to one another. They provide a consistent framework for placing type and graphics.

Group Selection tool in Illustrator selects paths in a group.

Guidelines are nonprinting lines used as a guide for laying out individual images or groups of images for composites.

Gutter is the space between two columns. Gutters are used with layout guides, folding guides, and sometimes to help with margin guides.

Gutter width is the blank space between the columns of text in a document.

H

Hand tool in Photoshop is like moving a document with your own hands and is great for quick positioning.

Headers are found in the top portion of the additional pages and have a continuing color scheme, text format for the title, and sometimes an identifiable company logo.

Healing Brush tool works the same way as the Clone Stamp tool by selecting a reference area while holding down the Option/Alt key; it then works like the Patch tool and analyzes the texture, lighting, and color and blends that into the defective area.

Help and Support in Windows Vista in the Start menu is where you will also find all kinds of tutorials, troubleshooting, and maintenance information to help keep your computer performing optimally and to customize your settings; a box area also allows you to search for information.

Hidden characters are nonprinting characters that display spaces, tabs, ends of paragraphs, index markers, and ends of stories.

Histogram in Photoshop is a graph that shows the highlight, shadow, and middle tone properties of an image in the Levels dialog box. By adjusting the histogram you can control the amount of detail in the highlights and shadows by redistributing pixels to generate the full range of tones.

Histograms panel in Photoshop displays the before (gray) and after (black) histograms to show the changes made in an image.

History Brush tool in Photoshop is used to paint back to a previous state in the History panel by erasing pixels back to a previous state.

History panel in Photoshop records previous actions in what are called **states**, so you can go backwards in a series of steps as if going through multiple undo commands. You can click on a previous state or drag the most recent states into the Trash.

Hue is the name of the color (red, green, blue, etc.).

Hue/Saturation command lets you adjust the hue, saturation, and lightness of an image or selected areas of an image. The Hue slider is used to select new colors, and the Saturation and Lightness sliders adjust color purity and intensity.

I

ICC profile is a color identity profile that defines colors and embeds the color information with the file.

Icons are small picture representations of drives and most frequently used applications, files, and folders.

Ignore Text Wrap box in the Text Frame Options display box in InDesign ensures the text will flow across columns in the length or width determined by the text frame drawn.

Image menu in Photoshop contains commands for all kinds of image enhancements and modifications.

Image Size command within the Photoshop Image menu provides changing "Pixel Dimensions" for electronic media or "Document Size" for print output.

Import involves transporting text, artwork, or images into a document.

INDD extension identifies an InDesign native document.

InDesign Interchange (INX) allows you to save the document so that a designer or service provider who has the earlier InDesign version can read the document. Using the Export command initiates this.

InDesign Markup Language (IDML) is InDesign's file extension in CS5 for saving documents that need to be read by users who have the earlier CS4 version of InDesign.

InDesign template can be saved to use for future editing of a document without having to start all over from scratch. It saves the templates with an INDT extension.

INDL extension identifies an InDesign object library.

INDT extension identifies an InDesign template document.

Informal balance uses elements that counterbalance one another to create a harmonious composition. This type of balance gives the appearance of being casual, energetic, modern, and trendy.

Inset setting in InDesign provides space for the text so that type is not placed too close to a graphic frame that may have a stroke weight or be filled with color. Inset settings apply to all text in a text frame.

Interpolation adds pixels in between the actual pixels and deteriorates the image sharpness and quality. Scanning an image larger than its optical resolution causes interpolation.

Isolation mode in the Layers panel in Illustrator allows a designer to edit a symbol or graphic while greying out the surrounding area to focus on the graphic.

J

Job package needed by the service provider or printer contains all the necessary elements for outputting and verifying information about the project.

Join command in Illustrator makes sure that end points are joined together as one path.

JPEG format files generate smaller compressed files and are used primarily for the web or when smaller file sizes are needed. They are a universal format and can be read by most any graphic application.

Jump line is a line that indicates an article continues to or continues from another page.

Jump lists in Windows 7 allows you to navigate around recent files, images, or tasks.

Justified alignment places text equally on left and right sides in a column.

K

Kerning is a technique used for pairs of characters in titles or headlines that may need to be brought closer together for a more consistent look.

Kuler panel allows a designer to explore online and download various color group themes that can be saved in the Swatches panel.

L

Landscape orientation displays a document in a horizontal format, where the width is greater than the height.

Lasso tools work well with selections that are needed as either freeform or complex selections.

Layer Comps panel in Photoshop allows the designer to capture various stages or states of development of a document by recording layers with existing settings for visibility or opacity of layers and their effects on the previous layers, their position in the document, and various blending options.

Layer Groups are a number of layers grouped into one folder for ease of use.

Layer masks provide a window for various (adjustment) layer effects as they trickle down through the layers giving total control to the user.

Layer menu is used to display, modify, edit, copy, group, or delete layers and includes other various commands and options for layers and layer effects.

Layer Style effects allow you to create shadows, embossing and bevels, overlays, glow, and stroke effects on selected portions of an image and on text.

Layers in Photoshop are like stacks of transparent sheets with parts of an image laid one on top of another. Layers are used to modify selected portions of an image and to combine different images or selected areas together. Special effects can also be added to each layer.

Layers panel is used to display, modify, edit, copy, group or delete layers; includes various other commands and options for layers and layer effects. The Layers panel allows you to view thumbnails of the parts of the image displayed in each layer and to move layers for specific effects.

Layout guides are sometimes green in color and are guidelines dragged out from the top and left side rulers. They are used for exact placement of specified text and graphics boxes.

Leading refers to the spacing between lines of text.

Leading lines is a design technique used to create the effect of depth perception.

Levels command in the Photoshop Image menu provides more subtlety and precision to images by making adjustments to display details in the highlights and shadows of an image.

Libraries in Illustrator provide a vast selection of preset images a designer can base complex images on or add to an existing image. Some libraries contain symbols, brushes, swatches, and the new graphic style libraries used to apply special effects to selected objects.

Libraries in Windows 7 can be used to gather content for special folders from various locations to be placed in certain categories of files.

Line art can be any drawing or sketch created by traditional drawing utensils, like pencil, pen, charcoal, and so on.

Line Segment tool in Illustrator is used to create straight lines at any angle.

Line tool can be used to create perfect straight lines when used in combination with the Shift key.

Linear gradients are applied in a straight line at a given angle.

Linear perspective is where a horizon line is placed to approximate the eye level of the artist. Invisible lines or edges from within the image disappear into what are called **vanishing points** that lead the eye into the image.

Lines can be straight, angular, or curved as different line types drawn in horizontal, vertical, or diagonal directions. A line's visual quality determines how a line is drawn, whether thick or thin, broken or smooth.

Linked files will automatically update when the original file is edited. This keeps the file size small.

Links panel in InDesign provides information including file size, color mode, and whether the document is linked correctly to files and graphics, so you can update links if needed.

Live Color in Illustrator is used by designers to find colors that complement one another or to experiment with colors in their artwork and then create custom groupings of colors.

Live corner feature in InDesign allows a designer to apply different corner effects or corner radii on the fly.

Live Paint in Illustrator detects and corrects gaps to create closed paths for fills and strokes for painting. It treats all paths as being on the same canvas without any layering.

Live Paint Bucket tool in Illustrator is used to create Live Paint Groups and to fill in the faces or color the edges.

Live Paint Group in Illustrator makes closed paths fully editable where filled-in colors can be adjusted as individual paths are adjusted.

Live Paint Selection tool in Illustrator lets you select and then delete faces and edges of a Live Paint group. When paths are deleted with the Live Paint Selection tool, the color of the surrounding paths fills in the deleted path.

Live Trace in Illustrator is a complex tracing function that follows the contours and outlines of drawings and bitmap images to create vector drawings. You can set a variety of parameters for various types of images, sketches, and drawings to trace.

Log In is used to set up your personal settings on the computer.

Lossless compression is the process of compressing continuous-tone images without losing any detail, though this may create a larger file size.

Lossy compression images are compressed, usually in JPEG format, where details are thrown out every time the image is edited and saved. The file size is smaller than with lossless compression.

M

Mac Help in Mac OS X provides answers to questions, instructions on how to perform various functions by clicking underlined links, and a list of topics to look for information.

Macintosh OS X is the most recent operating system used on Macintosh computers.

Magic Eraser tool in Photoshop erases a single color background on the image to make it transparent.

Magic Wand panel in Illustrator is used to select the amount of similar colors based on a tolerance setting.

Magic Wand tool selects parts of an image based on similar tints or shadings of colors. This tool is used for areas with difficult outlines or soft edges that cannot be traced with the lasso tools.

Mapping artwork in Illustrator is done in the 3-D Options dialog box to precisely match the artwork to the 3-D surface. It involves wrapping the artwork around an object's projected surface to match what it would look like on the actual product.

Margin guides use purple lines as a default and are created in the initial set up. They are used to create outer margins and for spacing between text and graphic boxes for folding and alignment.

Marquee tools in Photoshop select rectangular boxes, elliptical areas, and single pixel row or column selections.

Mask Edge command in the Masks panel in Photoshop is used to define the masks edges.

Masks in Photoshop are used to protect parts of an image from being changed the same way an auto body shop masks off parts of an auto not to be painted. Using a mask covers areas outside the selected area with a colored overlay. All exposed areas (unmasked or not red) display the image and are part of the selection made for making changes.

Masks panel in Photoshop selects by color range or inverts a selection, and defines the selection edges using the Mask Edge function. It creates a layer mask that sits next to the thumbnail effect or image in the Layers panel.

Master page items in InDesign are the individual components you created that together make the continuing banner.

Master pages are document templates that a designer can modify to provide a consistency in placed items, page formats, formatting, and guidelines for multiple documents.

Master Text Frame option is used in creating booklets.

Mastheads are found on the section of a newsletter that lists the name of the publisher and other pertinent data, which may include staff names, contributors, subscription information, addresses, logo, etc.

Measure tool measures the distance between points along a path.

Media Eject key is located on the upper right corner of the Macintosh keyboard and looks like an arrow with a line underneath. It is used to eject CDs.

Media Library in Windows stores selected audio tracks to be burned onto a recordable CD.

Median filter in Photoshop is used to get rid of dust and scratches or clean up solid color areas, like the blue sky in an image.

Menu bar contains commands from various menus that are specific to the desktop interface or for a particular application, like Photoshop.

Merge Visible command in Photoshop merges only those layers that display the eye icon.

Merging layers still maintains the image quality and allows you to group any combination of layers together.

Mini Bridge is an extension within an Adobe application, like Photoshop. It allows you to search for, sort, display thumbnails, batch process for multiple tasks, and also create slideshows from Mini Bridge's panel when you launch the application.

Mode Command in Photoshop's Image menu, assigns different color modes and profiles for various output media.

Move tool moves a selection onto another image or portion of the same image. It is used to drag selection areas within the image to create additional layers, or to drag selections created from other images onto the Layers panel of the image you are working on.

Multiple artboards in Illustrator are useful for creating a variety of things such as multiple page PDFs, printed pages with different sizes or different elements, independent elements for websites, etc.

N

Nameplates are the identifying section located on the first, or front, page that usually consists of a company logo or identifiable graphic, the formatted title of the newsletter, and a color text box containing information such as the issue or volume number, edition description, and author or editor.

Native file is a file created by an application that is saved with that application's exclusive extension to identify it.

Navigation in an image in Photoshop can be done with the Zoom tool or Hand tool.

Navigator panel in Photoshop helps the designer to see portions of an image.

Negative space, or space that is absent of visual elements, is a visual element that may promote luxury or elegance and sometimes a sense of mystery.

Nested styles in InDesign are multiple styles that can be applied to a line of text or paragraph with different styles of formatting, such as applying one character style to the beginning of a paragraph, then determining where that character style stops and where the next character style begins.

Note tool allows designers to leave messages to themselves and to one another when working on a team project to help with workflow.

Notes and Annotation tools in Photoshop allow you to leave electronic or audio notes to yourself or other members of your team who are working on the same project.

O

Object libraries in InDesign help you organize the graphics, text, and pages you use most often. You can also add ruler guides, grids, drawn shapes, and grouped images to a library.

Object menu in Illustrator is used for editing, combining, and transforming objects to any specified option needed.

Object styles are used to quickly format graphics and frames. Object styles include settings for stroke, color, transparency, drop shadows, paragraph styles, text wrap, and more; you can also assign different transparency effects for the object, fill, stroke, and text

Objects in Illustrator are vector images that have starting and ending points and determine the shape of an image. Objects can be closed, like circles, or open, like lines.

One-point perspective involves using converging lines to lead the eye to a subject or point along a horizontal line to provide depth in perspective within the image.

Opacity Stops in Photoshop's Gradient Editor vary the amount of blended colors.

OpenType fonts are designated with the letter *O*, are scalable, and may include swashes and discretionary ligatures found in many foreign languages that are not available in current PostScript and TrueType fonts. OpenType fonts are cross platform, eliminating the font issues that occur when moving documents between Mac and Windows operating systems.

Operating system, sometimes referred to as an "OS," makes sure hardware and software are working together nicely.

Optical resolution, which is set by the manufacturer, is what the scanner actually sees (i.e., 4000 dpi) or the original size of the image.

Orphans are one line of a paragraph that fall at the bottom of a column or page.

Outline view in Illustrator displays just the outlines of shapes for accurate placement.

Override is created as a plus sign (+) that appears next to the current paragraph style in the Paragraph Style panel if the selected text uses a character or paragraph style and also uses additional formatting that is not part of the applied style.

Overset symbol in InDesign indicates that there is more text that needs to be displayed. It displays as a red cross.

P

Package utility in InDesign creates a folder that contains the InDesign document, any necessary fonts, linked graphics, text files, and a customized report.

Page description language (PDL) used by the commercial printing industry is created by your desktop publishing application and your computer and defines precise position and composition of images, text, and other elements in documents by mapping each pixel for high-resolution output.

Page number marker in InDesign automatically adjusts page numbers as you move around documents. It specifies where a page number sits on a page and how it is formatted.

Pages panel in InDesign contains Master Page icons that affect changes globally in the document. The bottom portion or local level contains the document icons that represent the actual document pages being created and allows you to edit individual documents.

Paint Bucket tool used to fill an area with the foreground color for various background effects.

Painting and drawing tools in Photoshop allow you to apply brush or shape effects. They are the Shape, Brush, Pencil, History, and Art Brushes and the Pen, Path, and Direct Select tools.

Panel Menu button in Photoshop displays commands used for each particular panel.

Panels display many options, and help modify and control information about your project. Some panels or panels provide thumbnail representations of the project to help with your editing.

Paragraph panel in InDesign provides most of the formatting essentials to type lines, including paragraph rules.

Paragraph Styles panel (in Illustrator) **and panel** (in Photoshop) apply special paragraph formatting commands to selected paragraphs.

Paste Into command in Photoshop allows the designer to paste an image behind another image's selection "window."

Pasteboard is an area outside a page where you can store objects that are not yet positioned within the page.

Patch tool in Photoshop samples patterns and textures of an image; it analyzes the texture and lighting and matches the source pixels to blend in with a destination area.

Path Type tools allow the designer to place type on any path created. One allows the type to be placed horizontally and the other vertically along the path.

Pathfinder panel in Illustrator allows the designer to combine various shapes by adding, subtracting, excluding, and intersecting overlapping shapes to create one composite shape.

Paths in Illustrator have starting and ending points and determine the shape of an image. Paths can be closed, like circles, or open, like lines.

Pattern brushes in Illustrator paint in tiled sections along the middle, end, or corner of a path.

PCs are computers that use the Windows operating system.

Peek function located as a small rectangle at the edge of the taskbar in Windows, gives you the opportunity to watch open windows instantly turn transparent to display only the Windows desktop.

Pen tool is where the designer can create perfect straight lines between anchor points by clicking from one point to the next and create complex shapes from special Bézier curves of path segments.

Pencil tool in Illustrator allows the designer to draw freely or trace from a template any drawing or image. As a line is drawn, a path is automatically created with anchor points when the mouse is released.

Peripherals are outside hardware, like scanners, printers, digital cameras, and so forth that connect to your computer.

Photoshop Toolbox provides the tools to select, edit, manage, and manipulate image pixels and to draw or add type to images.

Pica is a measurement used by a printer where 12 points equals one pica. One inch is the equivalent of 72 points.

Picture Package command in Photoshop allows you to combine images onto one sheet that can be printed out. The images are automatically created on separate image and text layers and can then be flattened into one layer.

Pinning in Windows 7 allows you to pin your favorite programs or files to the taskbar.

Pixels are individual colored square dots and are the smallest picture elements on your computer screen.

Place command for text imports the copy into its own text block so it can easily be moved around into position and edited. When an image is placed, it can be rotated and resized before the Return/Enter key is pressed.

Place command in an Illustrator template allows any sketch or drawing to be made into a template, when the Template option is checked, so it can be traced manually by either the Pencil or Pen tool.

Placing symbols is done by dragging the symbol onto the artboard or by using the Symbols panel option Place Symbol Instance. The placed symbols, called **symbol instances**, can be resized visually using the bounding box, or they can be modified with Symbolism tools.

PNG format supports varying levels of transparency and also preserves gradients. It is effective at compressing continuous-tone images without losing detail, called lossless compression, but it may create a larger file size than JPEG compressed images.

Points are the measurement method for type and small graphics; one point is equal to 1/72 of an inch.

Polygon Frame tool in InDesign creates frames as containers to insert text and graphics.

Polygon tool in Illustrator allows the designer to create any number of equidistant sides to a shape outlining a particular radius.

Portable Document Format (PDF) is used for electronic publishing and can be read by Adobe Acrobat Reader or Adobe applications.

Portrait orientation is the vertical display of a document.

Position tool in InDesign works in conjunction with the Selection tool to help control the placement of content within a frame, as well as to change the size of the frame.

Positive space uses content to fill up space to identity or explain something in a particular page.

PostScript fonts are bitmap-type fonts that contain two files: one for screen display and one for printer display. They are the most clear for printing and are preferred when sending to press. They also have set sizes, because they are bitmap files and cannot be resized without causing deterioration in quality.

PostScript language is the most widely accepted and used PDL in the commercial printing industry. When you print your document to a disk file, a PostScript printer, or a PostScript output device, you are creating a PostScript language file that is processed by that device.

PPI (pixels per inch) refers to images measured at the screen resolution that you see on your computer monitor. All web pages are measured in pixels per inch, with 72 pixels per inch as the standard computer screen measurement.

Preflight utility in InDesign warns of problems, such as missing files, graphics, or fonts. It also provides helpful information about your document or book, such as the inks it uses, the first page a font appears on, and print settings.

Preview application in Mac OS X is used not only for slideshows, but you can also perform basic editing operations and you can view all kinds of documents, as well as images.

Preview view in Illustrator displays artwork with all colors, as it will look when printed.

Print proof is used to show indications for folding, cutting, bleeding, trapping, registration, or any special requirements.

Printer's marks are made on a proof sheet and include registration marks, trim marks, color bars, bleeds, and other color information a pressman might need.

Process colors use inks that are percentages of a subtractive process of the colors cyan, magenta, yellow, and black (CMYK). These four colors are used in four separate plates during the printing process.

Profiles determine what color will display most accurately based on which media the final image will be exported to.

Proof sheet shows the service provider how the final layout should look by providing color information, accurate layout of elements, and printer's marks.

PSD extension is Photoshop's extension when saving an image. In the case of Photoshop, the extension would be as a native file. It can be read by other Adobe products or other Photoshop users and edited with ease without losing quality, but since it is generally not an extension that can be read by all graphic applications universally, some may not be able to read it.

Pull quotes are used in long articles to pull a line or comment out of the article that helps to identify that article to the reader.

Q

Quick Look function in Mac OS X looks like an eye icon to create quick slide shows.

Quick Mask is used in creating complex selections by painting the mask to include and exclude areas within a selection. The red overlay mask acts much like taping those parts not to be painted in an auto body shop. Those areas not covered represent the selected areas to be edited.

Quick Selection tool (W) selects similar colors, tints, or shadings of colors and allows you to "paint" a selection of a predefined brush width you set in the Tool options bar, then looks for similar adjacent colors.

R

Radial balance arranges elements around a central point and is used to promote unity or separate-but-equal relationships. Teams of professionals may use these techniques.

Radial gradients spread out from an inner position to the outer edges of an object.

Raster effects in Illustrator are effects that generate pixels on bitmap images, rather than vector images. Raster effects include all of the effects in the bottom section of the Effect menu, and the Drop Shadow, Inner Glow, Outer Glow, and Feather commands in the Effect > Stylize submenu.

Raster image processing (RIP) is used by PostScript printers or image setter devices on a commercial press. It also acts as an interpreter to convert the page information from the PostScript language into a bitmap image pattern for film or paper output.

Raster images see *bitmap image*

Rectangular Frame tool in InDesign creates frames as containers to insert text and graphics into.

Recycle bin stores and restores deleted files in Windows, much like the Macintosh Trash icon.

Refine Edge in Photoshop provides methods for handling the edges of selections. A designer can choose options, such as various masks, to view the effects or softening and sharpening selection edges.

Registration marks on a proof sheet allow for precise placement of individual color plates. They are used by the printer as guides for exact placement of plates so that colors are overlaid exactly on top of one another.

Removable media are flash drives, Zip disks, iPods, floppy disks, CDs, or portable external hard drives that can be transported to other computers.

Rendering is the process of having the computer figure out and apply a 3-D surface effect to an outline.

Resample image increases or decreases its resolution either for print or for the web.

Resolution in an image determines the amount of detail in an image: the higher the resolution, the more detail in shading, highlights, and tonality; and the larger the file size.

Resolution Independent Effects (RIE) capability in Illustrator in the effect dialog box makes it possible to make changes in the effect so that there is minimal or no change in the appearance of the effect. This will only work with embedded files, not linked graphics.

Revert command in InDesign allows the designer to go back to the last Save on the document to get out of trouble spots while working on a project.

Revolve command in Illustrator allows the designer to revolve an object around the axis of a 2-D outline, along an open or closed path, to create a 3-D object.

RGB mode colors are created by mixing the electronic primary colors red, green, and blue. Computers use an additive process to create color from the primary colors.

Rhythm is a visual pattern that creates a sense of movement between repeating elements. Variation in rhythm can be adjusted by changing the shape, size, color, spacing, and position of elements in a design.

Ripping involves copying audio tracks from a music CD to convert audio music to a format that can be used on the computer.

Rollovers are a change state that occurs when your mouse hovers over a button or graphic.

Rotate Canvas command in the Photoshop Image menu allows the designer to flip or rotate a document 90 or 180 degrees.

Rotate tool is used to change the size of an object, or rotate it from its point of origin.

Roughs are created as result of combining specific elements from each thumbnail, or they may be the result of one good thumbnail.

RTF or Rich Text Format files are universal text files with this extension that contain most formatting commands.

Rule of thirds is a technique used by artists to visibly divide an image into thirds for placement of elements within the composition.

Rules are lines that are used to help separate sections of articles in a pleasing way.

S

Sans serif describes type characters without (*sans*) extensions or strokes at the top and bottom; these fonts are more legible for labeling illustrations, headlines, and titles.

Saturation describes the intensity of a color (bright red or dull red).

Save a Copy command creates a duplicate of the document under a different name, leaving the original document still active.

Save a Version command in InDesign is used to save different versions if you want to experiment while protecting the original document.

Save As command saves files with different extensions for various purposes, saves to different locations, and creates different file names of the same file.

Save as template option allows designers to save documents as templates in Illustrator for future projects.

Save command saves the file as the same name with the same extension and to the same location.

Save for Web and Devices command converts artwork for exclusive web or electronic use.

Scalable Vector Graphic (SVG) is a vector format that describes images as shapes, paths, text, and filter effects. The resulting files are compact and provide high-quality graphics that are used in the development of web pages.

Scale Styles box in Photoshop, if effects are applied, scales these effects proportionately without distortion when you are resizing.

Scale tool changes the size of an object or its point of origin.

Scatter brushes in Illustrator spread objects randomly over a path.

Scissors tool in Illustrator is used to cut paths and shape lines.

Scratch area in an Illustrator document is the area outside the artboard area. This is a nonprinting area where you can store artwork components.

Script fonts are used in announcements or invitations and they have the appearance of being created with a pen or brush.

Secondary colors are orange, green, and violet, which can be further mixed for many color variations.

Section numbering involves labeling pages by section, such as the preface, table of contents, text body, glossary, or index.

Segments are curved or straight lines between various anchor points.

Select menu in Photoshop contains commands to edit selections on an image.

Selection mask in Photoshop displays areas that are exposed or selected (white) and areas that are hidden (not selected) are displayed in black.

Selection tool in Illustrator creates a bounding box around selected paths.

Selection tools in Photoshop select and isolate image areas. They are the Marquee, Magic Wand, Lasso, and Crop tools.

Serif type characters have what look like extensions or strokes on the top and bottom and are used to convey a conservative look; serif fonts are easier to read with long articles or bodies of text.

Service provider is an agency that will help set up and publish documents on a commercial press or as a web page document.

Shadow/Highlight command in Photoshop corrects overexposed or underexposed areas in photographic images.

Shake function in Windows works by clicking the window pane you want to focus on and give your mouse a shake. All other open windows will disappear except for your chosen window.

Shape Builder Tool in Illustrator allows a designer to create one complex shape out of a group of selected shapes.

Shapes are usually considered to be closed forms or an outline of something. How a shape is drawn gives it a specific quality, like a curved shape or an angular shape.

Shear tool in InDesign changes an object's perspective

Slug area in printing a proof for the service provider is an area outside the page and bleed that contains printer instructions or job sign-off information.

Smart Dimensions feature. As you resize an object next to another object, a line segment with arrows at each end lets you snap the object to the same width or height as the adjacent object.

Smart Guides are temporary snap to guides that appear when you create or manipulate objects or artboards. They help you align, edit, and transform objects or artboards relative to one another by snap-aligning and displaying X, Y location and delta values.

Smart objects in Photoshop allow a designer to scale, rotate, and warp Illustrator vector images within the layer without fear of pixeling or degrading the artwork. They allow the designer to make edits within Illustrator, which will be automatically updated in the Photoshop document.

Smart Sharpen filter in Photoshop provides additional sharpening controls over the Unsharp Mask filter. You can also control the amount of sharpening that occurs in shadow and highlight areas.

Smart Spacing in InDesign evenly spaces multiple items on your page by snapping objects into position working with Smart Dimensions and center line intersections.

Smooth tool in Illustrator moves and deletes anchor points to help smooth out crooked freehand path segments.

Snap feature in Windows 7, allows you to resize open windows, simply by dragging them to the edges of your screen.

Snapshot is a saved state in the Photoshop History panel for later editing as long as the document remains open. It is removed when the file is closed.

Spaces used on a Mac allows you to organize your work in groups according to projects, applications used, or whatever by dragging the documents, or images between windows.

Spatial recession is a technique in which varying the size of similar shape objects and blending tonal values to match the background gives the illusion of depth, as if objects were receding into the background.

Spot colors are special color libraries of premixed inks that will produce a certain color with one ink layer. Spot colors usually are designated by a title description and a number and are printed as a single ink plate rather than a combination of CMYK inks.

Spot Healing Brush tool in Photoshop allows the user to simply click on smaller areas that need to be replaced without having to use the Option/Alt key to set the resampled area; it makes the change automatically.

Spreads are multiple documents viewed together, such as the two pages visible whenever you open a book or magazine.

Stacks in Mac OSX springs documents and folders from the Dock to display the contents when any folder placed on the Dock's right side.

Star tool in Illustrator is used to created various pointed shapes.

Start menu or icon is the control center for Windows. It can select from the most recently used applications, documents, stored images, and music and launch any programs on your computer, connect to the Internet, access e-mail, use the Search command to locate files and folders, and look for help.

States are sequential recorded actions displayed in the Photoshop History panel, so you can go backwards in a series of steps, as if going through multiple undo commands.

States indicate in InDesign what changes if any occur with the mouse when it is either over the graphic, away from the graphic, or clicking the graphic. Up first, then Rollover, and then Down state.

States panel in InDesign is used to indicate how a button will react with the mouse (rollover, change type etc.).

Stop action involves the illusion of motion freezing something or awaiting anticipation in a given time and space.

Story is a threaded set of text frames

Stroke defines the outline or edge of an object.

Stroke box in Illustrator is used to fill the outline of an object.

Stroke panel in Illustrator determines the stroke thickness based on an entered value; it is also used to determine how stroke lines are joined, capped, or changed to dashed strokes.

Stroke weight determines the thickness measured in points of the outline or stroke of an object.

Styles apply automatic formatting commands to selected characters or paragraphs.

Subheads or subheadlines are used to break components of a large article into smaller parts to keep the viewer focused.

Subscripts are percentages of a font that are displayed on or below the baseline of the font.

Subtractive process comprises percentages of inks in the colors cyan, magenta, yellow, and black (CMYK) for commercial printers.

Superscript is a percentage of the original font size and will display aligned with the top of the font.

Swatch Libraries in Illustrator are used for specific color combinations. You can select colors to be placed in the main Swatches panel for future use.

Swatches panel is a selection of predefined colors from which you can choose. Custom colors can also be created and saved in the Swatches panel.

SWF extension allows a document or graphic to be used as an animated web graphic to be read by computers that use Macromedia Flash.

Symbol instances in Illustrator are repeating symbol designs of a particular symbol within a document.

Symbol libraries in Illustrator are organized collections of preset symbols with a wide variety of symbols in each. When you open a symbol library or any library it displays in a new panel.

Symbol Sizer tool in Illustrator is used to adjust the size of a graphic.

Symbol Spinner tool in Illustrator is used to vary the direction of the selected symbol instance.

Symbol Stainer tool in Illustrator changes the color of symbol instances.

Symbol type is a collection of related symbols used as bullets, map symbols, logos, and so forth.

Symbolism tools in Illustrator allow the designer to modify the size, color, and distribution of symbol instances.

Symbols are art objects that you can create from combinations of paths, text, images, or groups of objects and save for later use in the Symbols panel in your document. Symbols can also include brush strokes, special effects, blending of colors, and so forth.

Symbols panel in Illustrator is used to place, store, and create symbols.

Symmetrical balance places elements equally on both sides of the frame.

System Preferences program on the Mac within the Apple menu allows you to make modifications within your computer, like adding hardware, adding and removing programs, updating applications, and modifying system functions and monitor displays

T

Table menu in InDesign creates specified tables. It creates a spreadsheetlike table that automatically divides into a specific number of rows and columns as entered.

Tabs provide consistency in the alignment of numbers and text in columns. You can set tabs aligning flush left, right, or centered on special characters or by either decimal points or commas.

Tactile texture involves the actual feeling of a surface texture like a sculpture.

Taskbar in Windows is used to display minimized active files and applications, like the Dock on the Mac.

Template is a premade document or artwork that can be used as a starting point for other documents.

Template layer in Illustrator is a nonprinting, faded version of the original image that acts as a tracing guide for drawing tools. Illustrator also has customized template designs that can be edited to suit your needs.

Tertiary colors are created by mixing one primary color and one secondary color, like mixing blue and green to get blue green.

Text Frame Options command in InDesign allows the user to specify an "inset" measurement or spacing that keeps text copy away from the edge of the frame.

Text wrap is a process of creating space between the graphic and the text that surrounds it or to overlap two frames or objects.

Texture describes a surface quality, like rust, velvet, or sandpaper.

Threading text involves connecting text between selected frames in InDesign.

Threshold command in Photoshop works in conjunction with the Color Sampler tool. You use the Threshold command to find the darkest blacks and whitest whites in an image.

Thumbnails are sketched variations of an idea. In software applications, they are small representations of documents, images, or image components in specific panel.

TIF format files can be edited repeatedly and still be as accurate as the original image. They can be edited in any graphic application without losing quality because, they can be read by any graphic application. Graphic files saved with a TIF extension are preferred in the commercial printing industry. They also generate the largest file sizes.

Title bar contains the file or function name and the icon boxes to close, minimize, maximize, and restore the window size.

Tolerance setting on the Tool Options bar for the Magic Wand tool is important, because it determines the amount of similar colors selected; the lower the tolerance, the less similar colors are selected.

Tonal value involves the lightness and darkness of an image by varying its tone or value to the surrounding background.

Tones are low intensity versions of a color.

Tool Options bar in Photoshop displays options for each selected tool.

Toolbar displays special commands and functions from each application.

Tools panel in Illustrator contains all the tools to select, create, and manipulate objects.

Tracking adjusts the spacing between characters and words.

Traditional primary colors are red, yellow, and blue. These colors are the main colors that create all others, such as orange is created by combining red and yellow.

Transform command inside the Photoshop Edit menu, and the Illustrator Object menu allows you to move, rotate, reflect, scale or shear an object to a specified size.

Transparency panel in Illustrator adjusts the opacity of a particular color.

Trash is a special function icon used for removing and restoring files and ejecting Zip disks and CDs. The Trash icon is located on the right side or bottom of the Dock on the Macintosh OS X computer. Within applications, it is used to remove unwanted images or layers and for burning data onto a CD.

Tri-fold is a document divided into three sections folded towards the center to open like a book.

Trim marks on a proof sheet show the edges of the document to be cut or trimmed.

TrueType fonts designated by an icon displaying two Ts, are scalable and were initially created by Microsoft.

Two-point perspective involves a more natural approach, similar to how we view the world around us, at an angle with two edge points along the horizon line. In this view, vanishing points recede at either end of a horizontal line.

TXT is the extension for plain text files.

Type alignment is the style or arrangement of setting type.

Type family is a group of fonts that share a basic character construction, like the Arial family comprises Arial Black, Arial Narrow, Arial Alternative, and so on.

Type tool in Photoshop creates its own text layer specifically for the text. Wherever you click, you can start to type on a path line.

Type tools bring text into your images with various type orientations and type masks.

Typeface or sometimes referred as a type family, is a group of fonts that share a basic character construction, like the Arial family, which includes Arial Black, Arial Narrow, Arial Alternative, and so on.

Typography is the study and use of text styles in a document.

U

Unity is the organization of elements in a design so they appear to belong together. Unity establishes continuity with a variety of elements and promotes consistency.

Unsharp Mask is a filter that provides precision sharpening of an image or selected portions of an image.

URL is the address of a website or web page.

Use Global light option in Photoshop, when checked, is used to cast all the shadows at the same angle so that all shadows in future layers will look like they have the same light source for visual accuracy.

V

Value is the shading, tonality, and tint of a color (light blue and dark blue). It determines depth and dimension of an element by its range of lightness or darkness.

Value contrast determines the relationship between different elements, producing both visual and emotional effects.

Vector images are illustrations, logos, drawings, or clip art that have a limited number of colors but can be enlarged to any size without affecting the quality of the original image.

Vibrance command in Photoshop controls the intensity of saturated colors. It adjusts the saturation so that clipping is minimized as colors approach full saturation.

View menu displays files and folders on various drives and disks. It lets you customize the toolbar and to change the way files look and are arranged on your system. Check marks and Hide displays indicate whether a command is active or if a function is displayed on the screen.

Visual texture is creating the illusion of texture using varying line qualities, patterns, or by adjusting the value and colors of an element.

W

Welcome window provide links to tutorials, opening existing or starting new documents, and provides help.

White Balance, used in digital cameras, sets the color balance for various lighting conditions.

Widows are one line of a paragraph that fall at the top of a column in a page.

Window menu on the Macintosh desktop allows you to minimize any active window on the desktop into the Dock or maximize an active window to fill the screen.

Window toolbar displays special commands and functions of each application. It provides Back and Forward buttons to navigate to previously opened windows.

Windows 7 is the most recent operating system for PC computers.

Windows Media Player is an application in Windows that burns CDs from audio tracks, video files, and photos.

Word processing programs create documents of formatted text for reports, short articles, or single-page brochures with fixed inserted graphics. This is usually not suitable for printing on a commercial press, but it works well for home or office use.

Z

Zero point is used to set intersecting lines at "0" for easier measuring. You can drag from the upper left-hand corner where the rulers intersect, then release the mouse where you want to start the measurement at zero.

Zoom tool allows you to get in close and then zoom out to observe the whole image.

Index